T0190499

Communications
in Computer and Information Science   2066

Rationale

The CCIS series is devoted to the publication of proceedings of computer science conferences. Its aim is to efficiently disseminate original research results in informatics in printed and electronic form. While the focus is on publication of peer-reviewed full papers presenting mature work, inclusion of reviewed short papers reporting on work in progress is welcome, too. Besides globally relevant meetings with internationally representative program committees guaranteeing a strict peer-reviewing and paper selection process, conferences run by societies or of high regional or national relevance are also considered for publication.

Topics

The topical scope of CCIS spans the entire spectrum of informatics ranging from foundational topics in the theory of computing to information and communications science and technology and a broad variety of interdisciplinary application fields.

Information for Volume Editors and Authors

Publication in CCIS is free of charge. No royalties are paid, however, we offer registered conference participants temporary free access to the online version of the conference proceedings on SpringerLink (http://link.springer.com) by means of an http referrer from the conference website and/or a number of complimentary printed copies, as specified in the official acceptance email of the event.

CCIS proceedings can be published in time for distribution at conferences or as post-proceedings, and delivered in the form of printed books and/or electronically as USBs and/or e-content licenses for accessing proceedings at SpringerLink. Furthermore, CCIS proceedings are included in the CCIS electronic book series hosted in the SpringerLink digital library at http://link.springer.com/bookseries/7899. Conferences publishing in CCIS are allowed to use Online Conference Service (OCS) for managing the whole proceedings lifecycle (from submission and reviewing to preparing for publication) free of charge.

Publication process

The language of publication is exclusively English. Authors publishing in CCIS have to sign the Springer CCIS copyright transfer form, however, they are free to use their material published in CCIS for substantially changed, more elaborate subsequent publications elsewhere. For the preparation of the camera-ready papers/files, authors have to strictly adhere to the Springer CCIS Authors' Instructions and are strongly encouraged to use the CCIS LaTeX style files or templates.

Abstracting/Indexing

CCIS is abstracted/indexed in DBLP, Google Scholar, EI-Compendex, Mathematical Reviews, SCImago, Scopus. CCIS volumes are also submitted for the inclusion in ISI Proceedings.

How to start

To start the evaluation of your proposal for inclusion in the CCIS series, please send an e-mail to ccis@springer.com.

Guangtao Zhai · Jun Zhou · Long Ye · Hua Yang ·
Ping An · Xiaokang Yang
Editors

Digital Multimedia Communications

20th International Forum on Digital TV and
Wireless Multimedia Communications, IFTC 2023
Beijing, China, December 21–22, 2023
Revised Selected Papers, Part I

 Springer

Editors
Guangtao Zhai 🆔
Shanghai Jiao Tong University
Shanghai, China

Jun Zhou 🆔
Shanghai Jiao Tong University
Shanghai, China

Long Ye
Communication University of China
Beijing, China

Hua Yang 🆔
Shanghai Jiao Tong University
Shanghai, China

Ping An
Shanghai University
Shanghai, China

Xiaokang Yang
Shanghai Jiao Tong University
Shanghai, China

ISSN 1865-0929   ISSN 1865-0937 (electronic)
Communications in Computer and Information Science
ISBN 978-981-97-3622-5   ISBN 978-981-97-3623-2 (eBook)
https://doi.org/10.1007/978-981-97-3623-2

This Springer imprint is published by the registered company Springer Nature Singapore Pte Ltd.
The registered company address is: 152 Beach Road, #21-01/04 Gateway East, Singapore 189721, Singapore

If disposing of this product, please recycle the paper.

Preface

This volume contains the selected papers presented at IFTC 2023: 20th International Forum of Digital Multimedia Communication, held in Beijing, China, on December 21–22, 2023.

IFTC is a summit forum in the field of digital media communication. The 20th IFTC served as an international bridge for extensively exchanging the latest research advances in digital media communication around the world. The forum also aimed to promote technology, equipment, and applications in the field of digital media by comparing the characteristics, frameworks, and significant techniques and their maturity, analyzing the performance of various applications in terms of scalability, manageability, and portability, and discussing the interfaces among varieties of networks and platforms.

The conference program included invited talks focusing on Artificial Intelligence for Multimedia Communication by four distinguished speakers from University of Rochester (USA), Communication University of China (China), Tsinghua University (China), and Baidu (China), as well as an oral session of eleven papers, and a poster session of forty-six papers. The topics of these papers ranged from audio/image/video processing to artification intelligence as well as multimedia communication. This book contains the 57 papers selected for IFTC 2023.

The proceeding editors wish to thank the authors for contributing their novel ideas and visions that are recorded in this book, and all reviewers for their contributions. We also thank Springer for their trust and for publishing the proceedings of IFTC 2023.

IFTC 2023 was hosted by the Shanghai Image and Graphics Association (SIGA). It was organized by the State Key Laboratory of Media Convergence and Communication, the School of Data Science and Media Intelligence of Communication University of China, and was co-organized by Key Laboratory of Media Audio & Video of Ministry of Education (Communication University of China), and Guangdong South New Media Inc.. The Forum was co-sponsored by Shanghai Jiao Tong University (SJTU), the Shanghai Institute for Advanced Communication and Data Science, Shanghai Telecom Company, Shanghai Key Laboratory of Digital Media Processing and Communication, and Shanghai Qing Assistant Technology Company Ltd.

January 2024

Guangtao Zhai
Jun Zhou
Long Ye
Hua Yang
Ping An
Xiaokang Yang

Organization

General Chairs

Xiaokang Yang	Shanghai Jiao Tong University, China
Ping An	Shanghai University, China
Long Ye	Communication University of China, China
Guangtao Zhai	Shanghai Jiao Tong University, China

Program Chairs

Yue Lu	East China Normal University, China
Jun Zhou	Shanghai Jiao Tong University, China
Yuan Zhang	Communication University of China, China
Haonan Cheng	Communication University of China, China
Hua Yang	Shanghai Jiao Tong University, China

Tutorial Chairs

Xiangyang Xue	Fudan University, China
Yuming Fang	Jiangxi University of Finance and Economics, China
Jiantao Zhou	University of Macau, China

International Liaisons

Weisi Lin	Nanyang Technological University, Singapore
Patrick Le Callet	Nantes Université, France
Lu Zhang	INSA Rennes, France

Finance Chairs

Yi Xu	Shanghai Jiao Tong University, China
Hao Liu	Donghua University, China

Beibei Li   Shanghai Polytechnic University, China
Xuefei Song   Shanghai Ninth People's Hospital, China

Publications Chairs

Hong Lu   Fudan University, China
Feiniu Yuan   Shanghai Normal University, China
Menghan Hu   East China Normal University, China
Liquan Shen   Shanghai University, China

Award Chairs

Zhijun Fang   Donghua University, China
George Wang   Guangdong South New Media Inc., China
Xiaolin Huang   Shanghai Jiao Tong University, China
Hanli Wang   Tongji University, China
Yu Zhu   East China University of Science and Technology,
                               China

Publicity Chairs

Bo Yan   Fudan University, China
Wei Zhong   Communication University of China, China
Juanjuan Cai   Communication University of China, China
Gang Hou   Central Research Institute of INESA, China

Industrial Program Chairs

Yiyi Lu   China Telecom Shanghai Company, China
Zhiye Chen   Guangdong South New Media Inc., China
Guozhong Wang   Shanghai University of Engineering Science,
                               China
Chen Yao   Third Research Institute of the Ministry of Public
                               Security, China
Yan Zhou   Renji Hospital, China

Arrangements Chairs

Cheng Zhi   Shanghai Image and Graphics Association, China
Jia Wang   Shanghai Jiao Tong University, China

Program Committee

Xiaokang Yang   Shanghai Jiao Tong University, China
Ping An   Shanghai University, China
Guangtao Zhai   Shanghai Jiao Tong University, China
Jun Zhou   Shanghai Jiao Tong University, China
Long Ye   Communication University of China, China
Haonan Cheng   Communication University of China, China
Wei Zhong   Communication University of China, China
Cong Bai   Zhejiang University of Technology, China
Juanjuan Cai   Communication University of China, China
Patrick Le Callet   Nantes University, France
Xun Cao   Nanjing University, China
Zhenzhong Chen   Huazhong University of Science and Technology,
                             China
Zhiye Chen   Guangdong South New Media, China
Chenwei Deng   Beijing Institute of Technology, China
Lianghui Ding   Shanghai Jiao Tong University, China
Weisheng Dong   Xidian University, China
Xiaopeng Fan   Harbin Institute of Technology, China
Xin Fan   Dalian University of Technology, China
Li Fang   Communication University of China, China
Lu Fang   University of Science and Technology of China,
                             China
Zhijun Fang   Donghua University, China
Yuming Fang   Jiangxi University of Finance and Economy,
                             China
Hanlong Guo   China Telecom Shanghai Company, China
Junwei Han   Northwestern Polytechnical University, China
Menghan Hu   East China Normal University, China
Fei Hu   Communication University of China, China
Ruimin Hu   Wuhan University, China
Xiaolin Huang   Shanghai Jiao Tong University, China
Yongmin Huang   Southeast University, China
Huiyu Duan   Shanghai Jiao Tong University, China
Rongrong Ji   Xiamen University, China

Xiangyang Ji	Tsinghua University, China
Tingting Jiang	Peking University, China
Ke Gu	Beijing University of Technology, China
Jianhuang Lai	Sun Yat-sen University, China
Beibei Li	Shanghai Polytechnic University, China
Dapeng Li	Nanjing University of Posts and Telecommunications, China
Fanchang Li	Soochow University, China
Hongliang Li	University of Electronic Science and Technology, China
Dingxiang Lin	Shanghai Oriental Pearl (Group) Co. Ltd., China
Weisi Lin	Nanyang Technological University, Singapore
Dong Liu	University of Science and Technology of China, China
Hao Liu	Donghua University, China
Jing Liu	Tianjin University, China
Jiaying Liu	Peking University, China
Ju Liu	Shan Dong University, China
Tangyou Liu	Donghua University, China
Xianming Liu	Harbin Institute of Technology, China
Yebin Liu	Tsinghua University, China
Yingying Liu	Yinrui Information Technology Co. Ltd., China
Yue Liu	Beijing Institute of Technology, China
Zhi Liu	Shandong University, China
Fuxiang Lu	Lanzhou University, China
Guo Lu	Shanghai Jiao Tong University, China
Hong Lu	Fudan University, China
Ke Lu	University of Chinese Academy of Sciences, China
Yiyi Lu	China Telecom Shanghai Company, China
Yue Lu	East China Normal University, China
Lizhuang Ma	Shanghai Jiao Tong University, China
Siwei Ma	Peking University, China
Lin Mei	Third Institute of The Ministry of Public Security, China
Xiongkuo Min	Shanghai Jiao Tong University, China
Bingbing Ni	Shanghai Jiao Tong University, China
Yi Niu	Xidian University, China
Feng Shao	Ningbo University, China
Liquan Shen	Shanghai University, China
Xiaofeng Shen	East China Normal University, China
Zhenwei Shi	Beihang University, China

Li Song	Shanghai Jiao Tong University, China
Xuefei Song	Shanghai Ninth People's Hospital, China
Qiudong Sun	Shanghai Polytechnic University, China
Shiliang Sun	East China Normal University, China
Wei Sun	Shanghai Jiao Tong University, China
Xinmei Tian	University of Science and Technology of China, China
Yonghong Tian	Peking University, China
Hanli Wang	Tongji University, China
Jicheng Wang	Tongji University, China
Meng Wang	Hefei University of Technology, China
Pei Wang	Shanghai Normal University, China
Shigang Wang	Jilin University, China
George Wang	Guangdong South New Media, China
Guozhong Wang	Shanghai University of Engineering Science, China
Zhou Wang	Waterloo University, Canada
Fei Wu	Zhejiang University, China
Jinjian Wu	Xidian University, China
Shiming Xiang	Institute of Automation of Chinese Academy of Sciences, China
Jian Xiong	Shanghai Jiao Tong University, China
Ruiqin Xiong	Peking University, China
Xiangmin Xu	South China University of Technology, China
Yi Xu	Shanghai Jiao Tong University, China
Xiangyang Xue	Fudan University, China
Junchi Yan	Shanghai Jiao Tong University, China
Jie Yang	Shanghai Jiao Tong University, China
Chao Yang	Shanghai University, China
Hua Yang	Shanghai Jiao Tong University, China
Jingyu Yang	Tianjing University, China
Xinyan Yang	Communication University of China, China
You Yang	Huazhong University of Science and Technology, China
Haibing Yin	Hangzhou Dianzi University, China
Li Yu	Huazhong University of Science and Technology, China
Jun Yu	Hangzhou Dianzi University, China
Bin Zeng	University of Electronic Science and Technology, China
Chongyang Zhang	Shanghai Jiao Tong University, China
Lu Zhang	INSA de Rennes, France

Wenjun Zhang	Shanghai Jiao Tong University, China
Wenqian Zhang	Shanghai Maritime University, China
Ya Zhang	Shanghai University, China
Yuan Zhang	Communication University of China, China
Zhao Zhang	Zhejiang Normal University, China
Cheng Zhi	Shanghai Image and Graphic Association, China
Yao Zhao	Beijing Jiaotong University, China
Chengxu Zhou	Beijing University of Technology, China
Jiantao Zhou	University of Macau, China
Yuchen Zhu	Shanghai Jiao Tong University, China
Yu Zhu	East China University of Science and Technology, China
Li Zhuo	Beijing University of Technology, China

Contents – Part I

Media Computing

Metaverse and Virtual Reality

Multimedia Communication

Contents – Part II

Application of AI

Image Processing

AquaSAM: Underwater Image Foreground Segmentation

Muduo Xu[1,2], Jianhao Su[3], and Yutao Liu[1(✉)]

[1] Faculty of Information Science and Engineering, Ocean University of China,
Qingdao, China
liuyutao@ouc.edu.cn
[2] Heriot-Watt University, Edinburgh, UK
mx2003@hw.ac.uk
[3] University of Dundee, Dundee, UK
2441423@dundee.ac.uk

Abstract. The Segment Anything Model (SAM) has revolutionized natural image segmentation, nevertheless, its performance on underwater images is still restricted. This work presents AquaSAM, the first attempt to extend the success of SAM on underwater images with the purpose of creating a versatile method for the segmentation of various underwater targets. To achieve this, we begin by classifying and extracting various labels automatically in SUIM dataset. Subsequently, we develop a straightforward fine-tuning method to adapt SAM to general foreground underwater image segmentation. Through extensive experiments involving eight segmentation tasks like human divers, we demonstrate that AquaSAM outperforms the default SAM model especially at hard tasks like coral reefs. AquaSAM achieves an average Dice Similarity Coefficient (DSC) of 7.13 (%) improvement and an average of 8.27 (%) on mIoU improvement in underwater segmentation tasks.

Keywords: Underwater Image Segmentation · Underwater Image · Segment Anything · SAM

1 Introduction

Semantic segmentation is a notable problem in the domains of computer vision [1–3] for its usefulness in estimating scene geometry, inferring interactions and spatial relationships among objects, salient object identification, and more. Underwater image segmentation is a fundamental task in underwater imaging analysis which involves identifying and delineating regions of interest (ROI) in various underwater images. Accurate segmentation is indispensable for many applications, including underwater image detection, classification and underwater image enhancement (UIE).

Recently, there have been significant advancements in the field of natural image segmentation with the support of segmentation foundation models [4–6].

G. Zhai et al. (Eds.): IFTC 2023, CCIS 2066, pp. 3–14, 2024.
https://doi.org/10.1007/978-981-97-3623-2_1

These models enable accurate and efficient segmentation of objects in a fully automatic or interactive manner. Typically based on transformer architectures, these models leverage pre-trained weights to achieve state-of-the-art performance and demonstrate an unprecedented ability to generalize across a wide range of natural images.

The first and most notable segmentation foundation model is the Segment Anything Model (SAM) [7]. SAM is trained on over 1 billion masks and possesses strong capabilities for generating accurate object masks based on prompts such as bounding boxes, points, or texts, as well as in a fully automatic manner. However, the applicability of these models to underwater image segmentation remains limited due to significant discrepancies between natural images and target-oriented underwater images. Several studies have demonstrated that SAM may struggle with typical underwater image segmentation tasks [4,8–13], as well as other challenging scenarios [10,14–16,31–33], particularly when the targets have weak boundaries. This outcome is unsurprising since SAM's training set primarily comprises natural and high-quality image datasets where objects typically possess strong edge information.

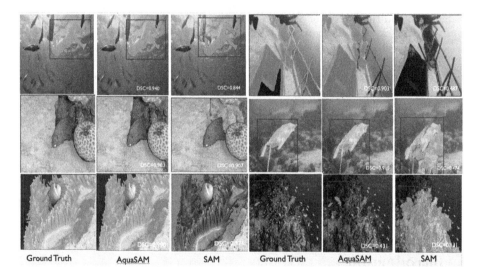

Fig. 1. Visualized Samples of the AquaSAM model and pre-trained SAM model segmentation results. AquaSAM significantly improves the segmentation performance across various modalities, depth and segmentation tasks.

In this study, we present AquaSAM, the first attempt to adapt the Segment Anything Model (SAM) to the underwater domain for universal image segmentation. Drawing inspiration from SAM's robust capacity, primarily achieved through large-scale supervised training, we begin by classifying and extracting various labels automatically in SUIM dataset. We analyze the network architecture components of SAM and evaluate their potential usefulness in image segmentation tasks. Lastly, we propose a fine-tuning approach to adapt SAM specifically for underwater image segmentation. Our experiments, encompassing 8 image segmentation tasks, demonstrate significant performance improvements achieved by our method in the realm of underwater image segmentation when compared to SAM alone.

2 Related Work

2.1 Underwater Image Segmentation

Underwater image segmentation has gained significant attention in recent years due to its wide range of applications in underwater robotics, marine biology, and underwater archaeology. Various machine learning methods have been proposed to tackle the challenges associated with underwater imagery, such as low visibility, color distortion, and texture degradation. In this section, we present a comprehensive review of the state-of-the-art (SOTA) techniques and their achievements in underwater image segmentation. Early approaches to underwater image segmentation primarily relied on traditional computer vision techniques, such as thresholding, region-based methods, and clustering algorithms. These methods often struggled to handle the unique characteristics of underwater images, resulting in limited segmentation accuracy. As a result, researchers turned their attention towards machine learning methods, which demonstrated better performance in capturing the complex relationships within underwater image data.

One popular approach in underwater image segmentation is based on deep learning techniques. Deep learning has shown remarkable success in various computer vision tasks and have been adapted to handle the challenges of underwater imagery. For instance, Drews-Jr, P. et al. (2021) proposed the first work to use a CNN approach to underwater image segmentation in the wild given the real underwater images in the wild and their respective ground truths [17]. Similarly, Arain. et al. introduced combining feature-based stereo matching with learning-based segmentation to produce a more robust obstacle map [18] which considers direct binary learning of the presence or absence of underwater obstacles.

To address the distorted color issue in underwater images, several works have focused on color correction techniques. Zhang et al. proposed a color balance strategy which balances the color differences between channel a and channel b in the CIELAB color space [19], effectively improving the performance of underwater image segmentation. In a similar vein, Li et al. [20] introduced an underwater color image segmentation method via RGB color channel fusion to obtain the grayscale image with high foreground-background contrast and improves color space accuracy.

Furthermore, researchers have explored the integration of multi-modal information, such as depth maps and polarization images, to enhance and access underwater image segmentation performance. Islam et al. [21] presented a deep residual model which balances the trade-off between performance and computational efficiency, providing competitive performance while ensuring fast inference.

2.2 Segment Anything Model (SAM)

The Segment Anything Model (SAM) incorporates a transformer-based architecture [22], known for its effectiveness in natural language processing [23] and image recognition tasks [24]. SAM utilizes a vision transformer-based image encoder to extract image features and prompt encoders to incorporate user interactions. It further employs a mask decoder to generate segmentation results and confidence scores based on the image embedding, prompt embedding, and output token.

To handle high-resolution images (i.e., 1024×1024), the vision transformer in the image encoder is pre-trained using masked auto-encoder modeling [25]. The resulting image embedding is then downscaled by a factor of 16 (64×64). SAM supports four different prompts: points, boxes, texts, and masks. Each point is encoded using Fourier positional encoding [26] and two learnable tokens to specify foreground and background. The bounding box is encoded by using the point encoding of its top-left and bottom-right corners. Free-form text is encoded using the pre-trained text-encoder in CLIP [27]. The mask prompt maintains the same spatial resolution as the input image and is encoded using convolutional feature maps.

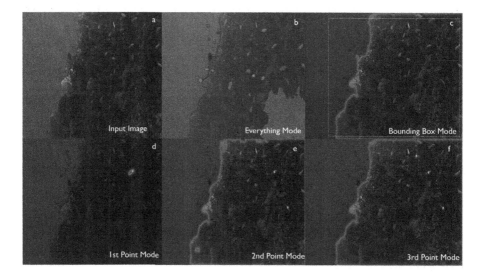

Fig. 2. Segmentation Results on Underwater Images when applied SAM in different modes

The mask decoder in SAM follows a lightweight design, comprising two transformer layers with a dynamic mask prediction head and an Intersection-over-Union (IoU) score regression head. The mask prediction head generates three $4\times$ downscaled masks, representing the whole object, a part of the object, and a subpart of the object, respectively.

By leveraging the strengths of transformer-based architectures and incorporating various prompt encoders, SAM aims to achieve accurate and versatile segmentation of diverse objects in images. The pretrained image encoder, tailored prompt encoders, and lightweight mask decoder collectively contribute to the effectiveness and efficiency of the Segment-Anything Model.

3 Method

3.1 Mode Selection in SAM

Three main segmentation modes including everything mode, bounding box mode and point mode are provided by SAM. Figure 2 shows the three segmentation results of underwater images with different modes. Several regions including fish and grass are divided in the segment-anything mode. However, these segmentation results have limited utility for two primary reasons. Firstly, the obtained result (Fig. 2b) lacks the accuracy of segmentation, a number of fish inside it cannot be segmented, which restricts its interpretability and practical application. Secondly, granted that Segment Anything Model promises that even if it is not trained on underwater datasets, it can perform well in underwater domains, the lack of depth in underwater environments can cause problems. In underwater scenarios, researchers are primarily interested in identifying and analyzing specific regions of interest (ROIs) that hold optical significance, such as the human divers, ruins and coral reefs. Compared with the segment-anything mode, the bounding box mode (Fig. 2c) can perform better in the segmentation of the task-oriented background by just giving the upper-left and bottom-right points. What's more, the point segmentation mode tries to segment the deep fish one by one in the foreground. Although the first-point result (Fig. 2d) looks satisfying, the second-point and the third-point result (Fig. 2e) (Fig. 2f) is not guaranteed.

In a nutshell, when employing SAM for underwater image segmentation, the "segment-everything" mode tends to generate partitions that are not useful and ceases to reach high accuracy of segmentation, while the "point-based" mode introduces ambiguity and necessitates multiple iterations for prediction-correction. In contrast, the "bounding box-based" mode enables clear specification of the ROI and produces reasonable segmentation results without the need for repeated trial and error even if the target where hidden in depth can sometimes be unsegmented. Hence, we contend that the bounding box-based segmentation mode holds greater practical value in underwater image segmentation tasks with SAM, compared to the segment-everything and point-based modes.

3.2   AquaSAM: Specialized Foundation Models for Underwater Image Segmentation

To adapt SAM for underwater image segmentation, the selection of a suitable user prompt and network component for fine-tuning is crucial. After careful analysis, it is determined that the bounding box prompt is an appropriate choice for precisely specifying the segmentation target. SAM's network architecture comprises three primary components: image encoder, prompt encoder, and mask decoder. Different combinations of these components can be fine-tuned based on specific requirements. Notably, the image encoder, which is built on a vision transformer, incurs the highest computational overhead within SAM. In order to minimize computation costs, we opt to keep the image encoder frozen and focus on fine-tuning the remaining components.

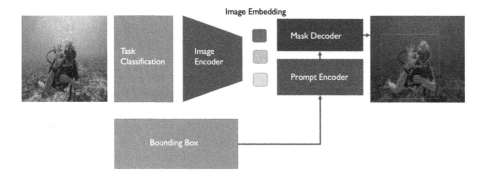

Fig. 3. AquaSAM: fine-tuning SAM for underwater image segmentation

The images and the corresponding ground truths are classified first and trained separately which can help guarantee the efficiency of each foreground segmentation task. Given the limited number of underwater images, we begin by curating various tasks to reach higher accuracy. The positional information of the bounding box is encoded by the prompt encoder, which can be reused from the pre-trained bounding-box encoder in SAM. Consequently, we also freeze this component during fine-tuning. Figure 3 illustrates that the remaining component requiring fine-tuning is the mask decoder. To enhance training efficiency, we can compute the image embedding for all training images beforehand, as the image encoder can be applied prior to prompting the model. This eliminates the need for repetitive computation of the image embedding per prompt. By pre-computing the image embedding, significant improvements in training efficiency can be achieved. Furthermore, due to the clarity provided by the bounding box prompt in most scenarios, the mask decoder only needs to generate a single mask rather than three masks when focusing on the foreground specifically in the underwater domains. This is because the bounding box prompt effectively specifies the intended segmentation target.

4   Experiments and Results

4.1   Data Preprocessing

We select SUIM dataset with 8 segmentation tasks to commit further experiments. It includes Background, Human divers, Aquatic plants and sea-grass, Wrecks and ruins, Robots, Reefs and invertebrates, Fish and vertebrates and Sea-floor and rocks. We believe that these foreground and background segmentation task are indispensable for later researches. We handle the preprocessing of underwater images for a specific label (anatomy) using the provided ground truth, underwater images, image size, and the encoder SAM model. Moreover, we apply resizing, thresholding, and other transformations to the input images and masks. By virtue of the salient capacity of SAM encoding model, it generates image embeddings using the model which will return the preprocessed images, masks, and embeddings. Here we focus on performing data preprocessing pipeline for underwater images with various foreground targets, generating labeled data for a specific anatomy using a specified model type and checkpoint. It demonstrates the steps involved in reading, preprocessing, and saving the data for further analysis or model training.

4.2   Training Protocol

Each dataset was randomly divided into 80 for training and 20 for testing. Segmentation targets with fewer than 100 pixels were excluded from the analysis. We employed a pre-trained ViT-Base model as the image encoder and computed image embeddings offline by inputting normalized images into the image encoder. The image encoder re-scaled the images to a size of $3 \times 1024 \times 1024$. During training, the bounding box prompt was generated from the ground-truth mask with a random perturbation of 0–20 pixels. As this work focusing on providing a fundamental segmentation model for underwater image enhancement and the foreground segmentation is indispensable here, the loss function used was the unweighted sum of the Dice loss and cross-entropy loss, which has demonstrated robustness in various segmentation tasks [28,29]. The network was optimized using the Adam optimizer [30] with an initial learning rate of 1e-5.

4.3   Results on Eight Underwater Segmentation Tasks

We utilized the Dice Similarity Coefficient (DSC) and mean Intersection over Union (mIoU) as evaluation metrics to assess the region overlap ratio and boundary consensus between the ground truth and segmentation results, which are commonly employed in segmentation tasks [31]. Various comparisons between the pretrained SAM (ViT-B) model and our AquaSAM on 8 foreground and background underwater image segmentation tasks are presented in Table 1. AquaSAM shows significant improvements across all 8 segmentation tasks, achieving an average improvement of 7.13(%) on DSC and an average improvement of 8.27(%) on mIoU. The results of improvements can be further improved greatly when the corresponding dataset is enormous enough.

While the pretrained SAM model exhibited good performance in single target-oriented segmentation tasks, such as Robots (RO) (Fig. 4e) and Aquatic plants and Sea-grass (PF) (Fig. 4h), it yielded unsatisfactory results for multiple target-oriented foreground segmentation tasks, such as Wrecks and ruins (WR) (Fig. 4c) and Fish and vertebrates (FV) (Fig. 4g). This can be attributed to the fact that the pre-trained SAM model can not adapt the underwater environments especially deep information is needed in certain images. Moreover, the accuracy of segmentation is far from the expected. In contrast, our AquaSAM model outperforms the pretrained SAM model by a significant margin in both DSC and mIoU scores across almost all tasks.

Table 1. Segmentation performance comparison of SAM and AquaSAM on SUIM dataset

Task	Mean Dice Score (%)			Mean IoU Score (%)		
	AquaSAM	SAM	Improve (%)	AquaSAM	SAM	Improve (%)
BW	87.83	83.04	5.80	82.34	76.50	7.61
HD	86.32	78.35	10.14	77.82	69.63	11.76
WR	87.01	70.07	24.37	78.85	59.50	32.57
SR	77.88	74.04	5.16	68.08	64.52	5.53
RO	90.02	85.63	5.39	84.08	78.85	6.65
RI	82.61	77.13	7.05	75.82	68.08	11.31
FV	77.88	52.41	32.19	68.15	45.58	49.79
PF	54.87	63.06	−12.95	42.92	51.43	−16.48

Additional segmentation examples are presented in Fig. 4. The pretrained SAM model is particularly prone to producing over-segmentation results, making it challenging to accurately segment targets with weak boundaries. For instance, the pretrained SAM failed to provide accurate segmentation results for Wrecks and ruins (WR) (Fig. 4c) and Fish and vertebrates (FV) (Fig. 4g), even with a relatively tight bounding box prompt. Moreover, when the content inside the bounding box is heterogeneous, the model may struggle to identify the correct segmentation target. Additionally, when segmenting targets with clear boundaries, SAM may generate outliers when the surrounding objects also exhibit good contrasts, as observed in Fish and Vertebrates (FV) segmentations.

AquaSAM has significantly enhanced the model's ability to identify challenging segmentation targets. Specifically, AquaSAM has demonstrated two major improvements over the pretrained SAM. Firstly, it has improved the model's capability to accurately identify small objects, even in the presence of multiple segmentation targets within the bounding box prompt. Secondly, the model has shown increased robustness towards depth-required underwater image segmentation.

Ground Truth   AquaSAM   SAM   Ground Truth   AquaSAM   SAM

Fig. 4. More examples of AquaSAM and SAM on various underwater image segmentation tasks

4.4   Discussion

We have demonstrated that specifying the oriented tasks and fine-tuning the mask encoder can result in substantial enhancements across different foreground segmentation tasks and image modalities. Nonetheless, the performance of our approach still falls short compared to specialized models designed specifically for underwater image segmentation. Additionally, there is significant potential for improvement in Aquatic plants. Although the results of certain segmentation tasks may not appear satisfying as the ground truth, Fig. 5. shows that AquaSAM performs better than SAM when applied to multiple segmentation. Moreover, if multiple similar instances surround the segmentation target, a large bounding box can lead to incorrect segmentation results.

To address the limitations of AquaSAM, we believe that leveraging larger models and increasing the dataset size would be beneficial given that now there is no such a large dataset for underwater image segmentation. In our study, we utilized the smallest image encoder (ViT-base) and did not fine-tune the image encoder to reduce computational burden. By employing larger backbone models and fine-tuning the image encoder, the model's capacity can be further enhanced to learn more features from underwater images. We plan to expand our training set to this scale in the future to further enhance AquaSAM's performance.

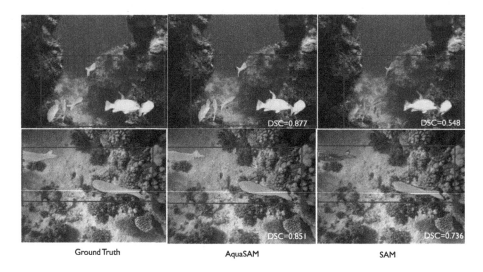

Fig. 5. The Performance of AquaSAM and SAM when applied to multiple segmentation

5   Conclusion

In a nutshell, the success of SAM in natural image segmentation demonstrates the feasibility of building segmentation foundation models. This work makes the first attempt to adapt SAM to underwater image segmentation by fine-tuning the pre-trained model on underwater image datasets. We have achieved remarkable performance improvements across various tasks and image modalities. We hope that this work will inspire further studies to develop segmentation foundation models in the underwater image domain, and we anticipate significant advancements in the near future. Our code and trained model are publicly available, accompanied by a step-by-step tutorial on fine-tuning SAM on custom datasets.

Acknowledgement. This work was supported by the National Science Foundation of China under grant 62201538 and Natural Science Foundation of Shandong Province under grant ZR2022QF006.

References

1. Barik, D., Mondal, M.: Object identification for computer vision using image segmentation. In: 2010 2nd International Conference on Education Technology and Computer, vol. 2 IEEE (2010)
2. Illarionova, S., et al.: Object-based augmentation for building semantic segmentation: Ventura and Santa Rosa case study. In: Proceedings of the IEEE/CVF International Conference on Computer Vision, (2021)
3. Suri, J.S.: Computer vision, pattern recognition and image processing in left ventricle segmentation: the last 50 years. Pattern Analy. Appli. **3**(3), 209–242 (2000)
4. Jing, Y., Wang, X., Tao, D.: Segment anything in non-euclidean domains: challenges and opportunities. arXiv preprint arXiv:2304.11595 (2023)

5. Deng, R., et al.: Segment anything model (SAM) for digital pathology: Assess zero-shot segmentation on whole slide imaging. arXiv preprint arXiv:2304.04155 (2023)
6. Ma, J., Wang, B.: Segment anything in medical images. arXiv preprint arXiv:2304.12306 (2023)
7. Kirillov, A., et al.: Segment anything. arXiv preprint arXiv:2304.02643 (2023)
8. Li, X., et al.: MapReduce-based fast fuzzy c-means algorithm for large-scale underwater image segmentation. Futur. Gener. Comput. Syst. **65**, 90–101 (2016)
9. Ma, W., Feng, X.: Underwater image segmentation based on computer vision and research on recognition algorithm. Arab. J. Geosci. **14**, 1–11 (2021)
10. Yan, Z., Zhang, J., Tang, J.: Modified water wave optimization algorithm for underwater multilevel thresholding image segmentation. Multimedia Tools Appli. **79**, 32415–32448 (2020)
11. Zhang, T., et al.: A method of underwater image segmentation based on discrete fractional brownian random field. In: 2008 3rd IEEE Conference on Industrial Electronics and Applications. IEEE (2008)
12. Lee, E., et al.: Data augmentation using image translation for underwater sonar image segmentation. PLoS ONE **17**(8), e0272602 (2022)
13. Chen, Z., et al.: Underwater sonar image segmentation combining pixel-level and region-level information. Comput. Electr. Eng. **100**, 107853 (2022)
14. Bai, J., et al.: Underwater image segmentation method based on MCA and fuzzy clustering with variational level set. In: OCEANS 2016 MTS/IEEE Monterey. IEEE (2016)
15. O'Byrne, M., et al.: Semantic segmentation of underwater imagery using deep networks trained on synthetic imagery. J. Marine Sci. Eng. **6**(3), 93 (2018)
16. Zhang, H., et al.: Novel approaches to enhance coral reefs monitoring with underwater image segmentation. Inter. Archives Photogrammetry, Remote Sens Spatial Inform. Sci. **46**, 271–277 (2022)
17. Drews-Jr, P., et al.: Underwater image segmentation in the wild using deep learning. J. Braz. Comput. Soc. **27**, 1–14 (2021)
18. Arain, B., et al.: Improving underwater obstacle detection using semantic image segmentation. In: 2019 International Conference on Robotics and Automation (ICRA). IEEE (2019)
19. Zhang, W., et al.: Underwater image enhancement via minimal color loss and locally adaptive contrast enhancement. IEEE Trans. Image Process. **31**, 3997–4010 (2022)
20. Li, X., Mingjun, Z.: Underwater color image segmentation method via RGB channel fusion. Opt. Eng. **56**(2), 023101 (2017)
21. Islam, M. J., et al.: Semantic segmentation of underwater imagery: Dataset and benchmark. In: 2020 IEEE/RSJ International Conference on Intelligent Robots and Systems (IROS). IEEE (2020)
22. Vaswani, A., et al.: Attention is all you need. In: Advances in Neural Information Processing Systems 30 (2017)
23. Brown, T. B., et al.: Language models are few-shot learners. arXiv preprint arXiv:2005.14165 (2020)
24. Dosovitskiy, A., et al.: An image is worth 16x16 words: Transformers for image recognition at scale. In: International Conference on Learning Representations (2020)
25. He, K., Chen, X., Xie, S., Li, Y., Dollár, P., Girshick, R.: Masked autoencoders are scalable vision learners. In: Proceedings of the IEEE/CVF Conference on Computer Vision and Pattern Recognition, pp. 16000–16009 (2022)

26. Tancik, Met al.: Fourier features let networks learn high frequency functions in low dimensional domains. In: Advances in Neural Information Processing Systems 33, pp. 7537–7547 (2020)
27. Radford, A., et al.: Learning transferable visual models from natural language supervision. In: International Conference on Machine Learning, pp. x8748–8763 (2021)
28. Dice, L.R.: Measures of the amount of ecologic association between species. Ecology **26**, 297–302 (1945)
29. Sørensen, T.: A method of establishing groups of equal amplitude in plant sociology based on similarity of species and its application to analyses of the vegetation on Danish commons. Biologiske Skrifter **5**, 1–34 (1948)
30. Kingma, D.P., Ba, J.: Adam: a method for stochastic optimization. In: International Conference on Learning Representations (2015)
31. Liu, Y., et al.: Unsupervised blind image quality evaluation via statistical measurements of structure, naturalness, and perception. IEEE Trans. Circuits Syst. Video Technol. **30**(4), 929–943 (2020)
32. Liu, Y., Zhai, G., Gu, K., Liu, X., Zhao, D., Gao, W.: Reduced-reference image quality assessment in free-energy principle and sparse representation. IEEE Trans. Multimedia **20**(2), 379–391 (2018)
33. Liu, Y., Gu, K., Wang, S., Zhao, D., Gao, W.: Blind quality assessment of camera images based on low-level and high-level statistical features. IEEE Trans. Multimedia **21**(1), 135–146 (2019)

RAUNE-Net: A Residual and Attention-Driven Underwater Image Enhancement Method

Wangzhen Peng[1]ⓘ, Chenghao Zhou[2], Runze Hu[3], Jingchao Cao[1], and Yutao Liu[1(✉)]

[1] Department of Computer Science and Technology, Ocean University of China, Qingdao, China
wangzhenpeng@stu.ouc.edu.cn, {caojingchao,liuyutao}@ouc.edu.cn
[2] School of Management Engineering, Qingdao University of Technology, Qingdao, China
[3] School of Information and Electronics, Beijing Institute of Technology, Beijing 100080, China

Abstract. Underwater image enhancement (UIE) poses challenges due to distinctive properties of the underwater environment, including low contrast, high turbidity, visual blurriness, and color distortion. In recent years, the application of deep learning has quietly revolutionized various areas of scientific research, including UIE. However, existing deep learning-based UIE methods generally suffer from issues of weak robustness and limited adaptability. In this paper, inspired by residual and attention mechanisms, we propose a more reliable and reasonable UIE network called *RAUNE-Net* by employing residual learning of high-level features at the network's bottle-neck and two aspects of attention manipulations in the down-sampling procedure. Furthermore, we collect and create two datasets specifically designed for evaluating UIE methods, which contains different types of underwater distortions and degradations. The experimental validation demonstrates that our method obtains promising objective performance and consistent visual results across various real-world underwater images compared to other eight UIE methods. Our example code and datasets are publicly available at https://github.com/fansuregrin/RAUNE-Net.

Keywords: Underwater image enhancement · Deep learning · Image processing · Deep Neural Network · Attention · Residual

1 Introduction

Underwater image enhancement (UIE), a challenging yet promising research direction, has garnered growing interest among researchers in recent years. Nowadays, a wide array of methods have been put forward for enhancing underwater images [13]. These UIE techniques can be broadly categorized into four

G. Zhai et al. (Eds.): IFTC 2023, CCIS 2066, pp. 15–27, 2024.
https://doi.org/10.1007/978-981-97-3623-2_2

types [8]: supplementary information-based, non-physical model-based, physical model-based, and data-driven methods. With the rise of deep learning and the utilization of large-scale datasets, data-driven methods have revolutionized UIE. However, it is worth noting that data-driven UIE methods still have several limitations. We have evaluated these previously proposed deep learning-based methods on multiple real-world underwater image datasets. As illustrated in Fig. 1, these five methods tend to produce visually poor results when dealing with images that they are not proficient at enhancing. Therefore, further research and development are necessary to overcome these challenges and create more reliable and adaptable UIE techniques.

| WaterNet | UWCNN | SGUIE-Net | SyreaNet | CycleGAN |

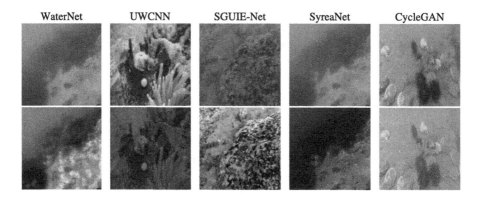

Fig. 1. Poor results of five UIE methods with weak robustness

Based on above analysis, we propose a **R**esidual and **A**ttention-driven **UN**derwater image **E**nhancement **Net**work called *RAUNE-Net* to process a wide variety of underwater images. Our main contributions can be summarized as follows:

- We incorporate residual and attention mechanisms into UIE to construct an effective and efficient network called RAUNE-Net, which is capable of handling a wide range of underwater scenes comprehensively.
- Our method achieves remarkable objective performance and consistent subjective results on both referenced and non-referenced real-world underwater image test sets.

2   Related Work

2.1   Convolutional Neural Network-Based UIE Methods

In the early stages, Wang et al. [27] first presented an end-to-end framework (i.e., UIE-Net) based on Convolutional Neural Network (CNN) for enhancing visual quality of underwater images. In [7], an underwater image dataset was synthesized firstly through an underwater image formulation algorithm based on underwater scene priors, which includes two types of water environments and five levels of distortions. Subsequently, they devised a lightweight CNN network (i.e., UWCNN) to enhance images from different underwater scenes. In contrast to aforementioned methods that used synthetic datasets for model training, Li et al. [8] created a real-world underwater image dataset (i.e., UIEB). Then, they trained an enhancement network called Water-Net on this dataset. In detail, they generated three input images by applying white balance, histogram equalization, and gamma correction algorithms to the original underwater image. These inputs were then transformed into refined inputs using the Feature Transformation Units. Subsequently, Water-Net utilized a gated fusion network to learn three confidence maps, which were used to combine three refined inputs and produce an enhanced result. These methods either rely on synthesized images for model training or require preprocessing on raw underwater images, which still have much room for improvement.

2.2 Generative Adversarial Network-Based UIE Methods

Li et al. [11] introduced an approach called WaterGAN, which adopted a GAN [4] to learn realistic representations of water column properties. Then, they used these generated underwater images along with their corresponding depth maps to train a color restoration network capable of real-time compensation for water column effects at a specific location. Unlike the previous method, where GAN was used solely for generating training samples, in [3], a GAN-based network (i.e., UGAN), which utilizes the Wasserstein GAN [1] with gradient penalty, was employed to directly enhance distorted underwater images. Subsequently, Islam et al. [6] proposed a network called FUnIE-GAN. In order to supervise the adversarial training process, they designed several loss functions based on global content, color, local texture, and style information. In [9], a weakly supervised network based on CycleGAN was applied to the UIE task. It maps color and style of underwater images to those of above-water natural images, thereby correcting the color cast in underwater images.

2.3 Other Deep Learning-Based UIE Methods

Differing from CNN, which adopts local receptive kernels to extract features from images, Vision Transformer (ViT) [2] treats an image as a sequence composed of multiple patches and uses self-attention computation to capture global information of the image. Inspired by this, Peng et al. [21] introduced Transformer into UIE for the first time. They proposed a U-shape Transformer network consisting of a channel-wise multi-scale feature fusion transformer module and a spatial-wise global feature modeling transformer. In addition, some UIE methods have reexamined physical models and combined deep neural networks with them. SyreaNet [29] integrated both synthetic and real-world data under the guidance of a revised underwater image formation model to fulfill the enhancement aim. Furthermore, apart from using physical models to guide the UIE models, there are also methods aiming to leverage high-level information to guide learning process of the network. In [22], they managed to use information from semantic segmentation to force network to learn region-wise enhancement features from underwater images and their paired high-quality reference images.

3 Methodology

3.1 RAUNE-Net

We have observed significant improvements in objective metrics for some deep neural networks that utilized residual [5] and attention [30] mechanisms. Consequently, we combine residual modules and attention blocks to design the RAUNE-Net. As demonstrated in Fig. 2, our network follows an end-to-end manner. Given a raw underwater image, by feeding it through the network, we can obtain an enhanced result. Mathematically, this enhancement process can be written as:

$$Y_e = \Phi(X_i), \tag{1}$$

where X_i are input underwater images, Φ is RAUNE-Net, and Y_e are enhanced outputs.

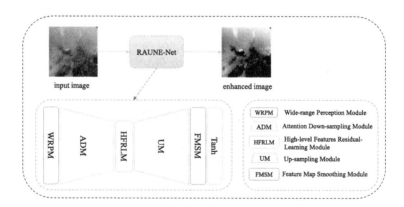

Fig. 2. The data-flow and architecture of RAUNE-Net

Overall, the RAUNE-Net consists of a wide-range perception module (WRPM), an attention down-sampling module (ADM), a high-level features residual-learning module (HFRLM), an up-sampling module (UM), and a feature map smoothing module (FMSM) followed by a Tanh activation layer. The detail structure of our network is illustrated in Fig. 3.

In detail, the WRPM contains a reflection padding layer, a convolutional layer, a normalization layer, and a non-linear activation layer. Specifically, this convolutional layer has a large kernel size of 7×7, which can cover a larger receptive field, enabling the network to capture more extensive contextual information, identify the overall structure and important features in the image. We set the default number of convolutional kernels to 64, use Instance Normalization [26] as the default normalization layer, and employ ReLU as the activation function.

ADM consists of multiple blocks, each block containing a 4×4 kernel size convolutional layer with a stride of 2 and a padding size of 1, followed by a normalization layer, a LeakyReLU [20] activation layer, an optional dropout [25] layer, and an attention module. Specifically, the attention module in ADM combines channel attention calculation and spatial attention calculation in a sequential manner [30]. After down-sampling, HFRLM consists of several residual blocks, where each residual block contains two convolutional layers with padding layers placed before them and normalization layers assigned after them. A ReLU activation layer and an optional dropout layers are inserted between the two convolutional layers to prevent overfitting and improve the network's robustness.

Similar to down-sampling stage, the UM is composed of multiple up-sampling blocks. Each up-sampling block includes a convolutional transpose layer with a kernel size of 4×4, stride of 2, and padding size of 1, followed by a normalization layer, a non-linear activation layer, and an optional dropout layer. After up-sampling, we do not directly output the result. Instead, we add a module called FMSM, which consists of a reflection padding layer and a convolutional layer with a kernel size of 7×7. We adopt this module because we have observed that the enhanced images often exhibit varying degrees of checkerboard artifacts. By performing a convolution operation with a large kernel, we can smooth the feature maps and reduce the occurrence of jagged edges and noise. This makes the up-sampled images more natural, thereby improving the visual quality [14,19] of the output. Lastly, we incorporate a Tanh non-linear activation layer to map the pixel values of the image to the range of -1 to 1, enhancing its contrast and color variation range.

3.2 Loss Function

To train our model, we use a weighted combination of three types of loss functions as the overall loss, i.e., the pixel content loss $\mathcal{L}_{pcont}$, the structural similarity loss $\mathcal{L}_{ssim}$, and the semantic content loss $\mathcal{L}_{scont}$:

$$\mathcal{L} = \lambda_{pcont} \cdot \mathcal{L}_{pcont} + \lambda_{ssim} \cdot \mathcal{L}_{ssim} + \lambda_{scont} \cdot \mathcal{L}_{scont}. \qquad (2)$$

Pixel Content Loss. The pixel content loss is designed to measure the discrepancy in pixel values between the output image Y_e generated by the model and the reference image Y_{ref} across the red, green, and blue color channels. Here, to reduce computational cost, we utilize the absolute distance between pixel values to represent the difference between the two images. The mathematical formula is defined as:

$$\mathcal{L}_{pcont} = \mathbb{E}\left[\|Y_e - Y_{ref}\|_1\right]. \qquad (3)$$

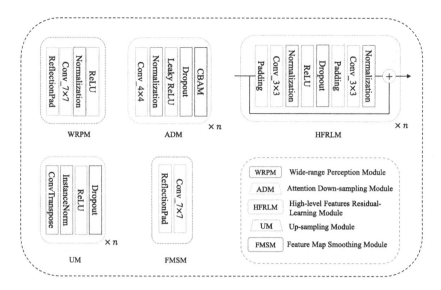

Fig. 3. The detail structure of RAUNE-Net

Structural Similarity Loss. Structural Similarity Index Measure (SSIM) [18, 28] is a metric that quantifies the structural similarity between two images based on luminance, contrast, and structural information. The main purpose of incorporating this metric into the loss function is to encourage the network to generate enhanced images that are closer to the ground truth in these three aspects. Specifically, the value of SSIM ranges from 0 to 1, and a value closer to 1 indicates a higher similarity to the reference image. However, typically in optimization, the value of objective function is minimized. Therefore, during the training process, the expression for SSIM Loss is:

$$\mathcal{L}_{ssim} = \mathbb{E}\left[\frac{1 - SSIM\left(Y_e, Y_{ref}\right)}{2}\right], \tag{4}$$

where Y_e are enhanced images, Y_{ref} are reference images, and the $SSIM\left(*, *\right)$ [28] represents structural similarity index map between two images. Additionally, the index map is calculated as:

$$SSIM(x, y) = \frac{\left(2\mu_x\mu_y + c_1\right)\left(2\sigma_{xy} + c_2\right)}{\left(\mu_x^2 + \mu_y^2 + c_1\right)\left(\sigma_x^2 + \sigma_y^2 + c_2\right)}, \tag{5}$$

where the μ_x and μ_y represent the pixel sample mean of image x and image y, the σ_y^2, σ_y^2 and σ_{xy} stand for variances and covariance of x and y, and c_1 and c_2 are two variables to stabilize the division with weak denominator, respectively.

Semantic Content Loss. In networks used for image classification, the features obtained from deeper convolutional layers to some extent represent the semantic content of the input image. Therefore, we consider extracting high-level features obtained from last several layers of a classification network to evaluate the semantic discrepancy between the enhanced image and the reference image. Specifically, we utilize the pre-trained VGG19_BN [24] model trained on the ImageNet-1k_v1 [23] dataset. As shown in Fig. 4, we extract feature maps obtained from the last five convolutional layers for both the enhanced image and the reference image. Finally, we calculate the weighted sum of the L1 distances between each pair of feature maps, which serves as the semantic content loss. Mathematically, this loss can be written as:

$$\mathcal{L}_{scont} = \sum_{i=1}^{5} k_i \cdot MAE(\Omega_i(Y_e), \Omega_i(Y_{ref})), \tag{6}$$

where k_i is the i-th weight for summing, $MAE(*,*)$ is the Mean Absolute Error (i.e., L1 loss), and the $\Omega_i(*)$ is the last i-th convolutional layer in VGG19_BN.

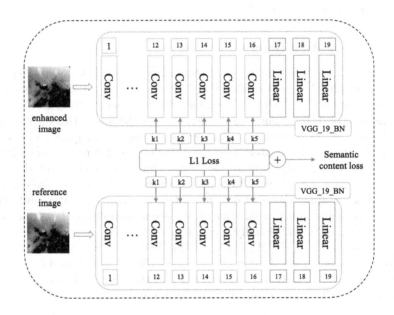

Fig. 4. Diagram of the semantic content loss

4 Experiments

4.1 Datasets

Firstly, we select the LSUI3879 dataset for training, which consists of 3879 real-world underwater images and their corresponding reference images randomly partitioned from the LSUI [21] dataset. For testing, we use four different datasets, namely LSUI400 (the remaining 400 pairs of images from LSUI), UIEB100 (100 pairs of images randomly selected from UIEB [7]), OceanEx, and EUVP_Test515 (515 pairs of test samples from EUVP [6]). In particular, OceanEx is a test set collected and constructed by ourselves. We gather 40 high-quality underwater images from NOAA Ocean Exploration. Then, we apply CycleGAN [31] to add underwater distortions and degradation styles to these images, making them the samples to be enhanced, while keeping the original high-quality images as reference images. These four datasets are used for objective evaluation of networks' performance, with the evaluation metrics being peak signal-to-noise ratio (PSNR) and structural similarity (SSIM). In addition to that, we also employ three datasets for subjective evaluation. They are U45 [10], RUIE_Color90 (90 images randomly selected from the UCCS subset of RUIE [12] dataset), and UPoor200. Among them, UPoor200 is a dataset we collected and curated from the internet, which consists of 200 real-world underwater images with poor visual quality. It includes distortions [17] such as blue-green color cast, low lighting, blurriness [16], noise, and haze.

4.2   Implementation Details

Before training, the input images are first resized to a resolution of 256×256 and then normalized. The normalization is performed by setting the mean and standard deviation to 0.5. During training, the optimizer we used is Adam with a learning rate of 0.0001. The two coefficients (i.e., betas) of this optimizer are set to 0.9 and 0.999 respectively. The weights assigned to pixel content loss, SSIM loss, and semantic content loss are 1.0, 1.0, and 1.0 respectively. During each training process, the network is trained for 100 epochs, and the trainable parameters are saved every five epochs. Every 500 iterations, the enhanced results of four sampled images from the testset are displayed. We conducted a series of experiments on the number of attention modules and residual modules in RAUNE-Net. Additionally, we compared RAUNE-Net with eight other UIE methods (i.e., UT-UIE [21], SyreaNet [29], WaterNet [8], UGAN [3], FUnIE-GAN [6], UWCNN [7], SGUIE-Net [22], Cycle-GAN [9]). To ensure a fair comparison, we retrained some networks mentationed in these methods (i.e., WaterNet, UGAN, and FUnIE-GAN) using the LSUI3879 dataset.

4.3   Objective Evaluations

The results of objective evaluation [15] of nine UIE methods, including RAUNE-Net and other eight UIE methods compared to it, are demonstrated in Tabel 1. From the table, our RAUNE-Net achieves highest PSNR values and SSIM values, which are marked as red color, on LSUI400, EUVP_Test515 and UIEB100 testsets. On OceanEx, RAUNE-Net achieves the highest PSNR value and the second highest SSIM value, but the SSIM value is already very close to the highest value obtained by WaterNet. It is worth noting that WaterNet achieves slightly lower performance values (except for SSIM value on OceanEx), which are indicated with blue color, than RAUNE-Net on the four test sets. The reason for the improved performance after retraining is the use of SSIM loss and the larger training dataset (i.e., LSUI), which contains more diverse underwater scenes. The UWCNN consistently achieves the lowest objective values on all four datasets. This is mainly due to its training on synthesized images using a physical model, which results in weak generalization and poor adaptability.

Table 1. Objective evaluation results of different UIE methods

Methods	LSUI400		EUVP_Test515		UIEB100		OceanEx	
	PSNR	SSIM	PSNR	SSIM	PSNR	SSIM	PSNR	SSIM
UT-UIE [21]	24.351	0.829	25.214	0.813	20.916	0.764	21.270	0.822
SyreaNet [29]	18.050	0.766	<u>17.721</u>	0.743	16.501	0.836	20.243	0.865
WaterNet [8]	26.688	0.874	25.285	0.833	22.279	0.868	22.132	0.887
UGAN [3]	25.117	0.846	23.636	0.805	21.368	0.825	22.436	0.822
FUnIE-GAN [6]	23.272	0.818	24.077	0.794	19.614	0.813	20.448	0.855
UWCNN [7]	<u>17.366</u>	<u>0.725</u>	17.725	<u>0.704</u>	<u>14.155</u>	<u>0.686</u>	<u>15.960</u>	<u>0.724</u>
SGUIE-Net [22]	19.910	0.819	19.187	0.760	21.178	0.872	18.677	0.834
Cycle-GAN [9]	18.320	0.749	17.963	0.709	17.714	0.758	21.007	0.828
RAUNE-Net	26.812	0.876	26.331	0.845	22.751	0.879	22.728	0.876

4.4 Subjective Evaluations

As can be observed from Fig. 5, RAUNE-Net is capable of enhancing bluish, greenish and hazy underwater images, while the other methods have exhibited improper or insufficient handling of these images. Specifically, UT-UIE and FUnIE-GAN incompletely remove the green color tone when processing the second and third images, resulting in noticeable green color residue in the results. Although SyreaNet effectively eliminates the blue-greenish color tone and foggy effect, it reduces the clarity and brightness of the source images. From the first four images, we can clearly see that WaterNet only partially removes the blue-green bias, as there are still blue or green artifacts preserved at the edges of objects in the images. UGAN, while not showing unpleasant artifacts, fails to effectively remove the blue and green color bias. For example, in the second result image, a large area of green color is retained, and in the fourth result image, the blue color style is still prominent.

Unfortunately, UWCNN completely fails to enhance the original image and instead makes the input image appear more turbid and with reduced visibility. This is particularly evident in the last two result images. Similarly, SGUIE-Net's ability to handle color shifts is not as impressive as that of RAUNE-Net. CycleGAN also failed to properly handle the green color shift and introduced

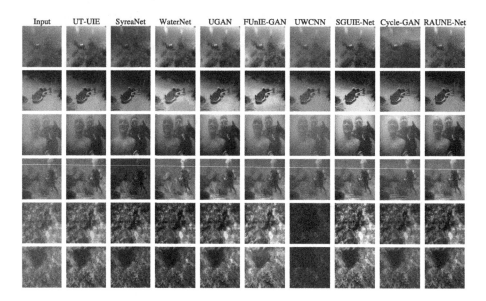

Fig. 5. Subjective evaluation results of different methods on U45

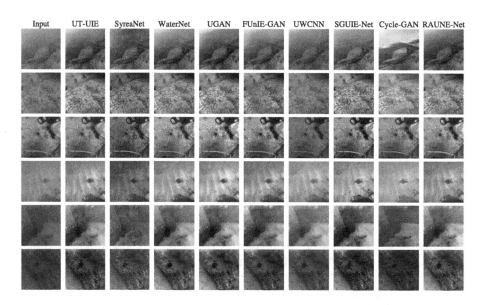

Fig. 6. Subjective evaluation results of different methods on RUIE_Color90

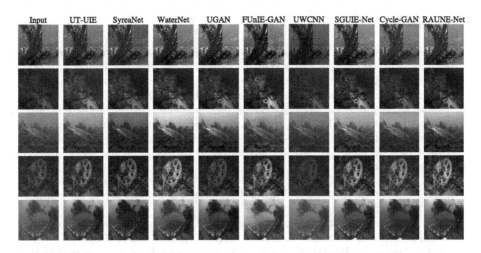

Fig. 7. Subjective evaluation results of different methods on UPoor200

strange textures that altered the original image content. Furthermore, as shown in Figs. 6 and 7, we can observe consistent results from subjective evaluations on other two testsets. All in all, compared to other eight enhancement methods, RAUNE-Net coherently achieves remarkable visual effects.

5   Conclusion

In this paper, we devised a novel underwater image enhancement structure named *RAUNE-Net* driven by residual learning, channel attention and spatial attention. We found that the residual learning on high-level features can help the network to learn more detail information to enhance input images and the channel attention and spatial attention blocks connected sequentially can assist the enhancing system to notice important areas to be enhanced and how to enhance them. By employing objective and subjective evaluations on seven test sets, we discovered that our network obtain an outstanding and reliable enhancing capability on various underwater attenuation types, such as bluish or greenish color shift, hazy or foggy distortion, and low-light condition. To contrive a fair and generalized assessment for different UIE methods' performances, we also constructed two datasets (a set with reference images called OceanEX and the other set with no ground-truth images named UPoor200), which contains diverse kinds of real-world underwater images. Furthermore, we found using PSNR and SSIM as indicators of the objective performance of enhanced images is still inaccurate, a non-reference quality assessment of these enhanced images is a focal point of our future research.

Acknowledgements. This work was supported by the National Science Foundation of China under grants 62201538 and 62301041, and the Natural Science Foundation of Shandong Province under grant ZR2022QF006.

References

1. Arjovsky, M., Chintala, S., Bottou, L.: Wasserstein generative adversarial networks. In: International Conference on Machine Learning, pp. 214–223. PMLR (2017)
2. Dosovitskiy, A., et al.: An image is worth 16x16 words: Transformers for image recognition at scale. arXiv preprint arXiv:2010.11929 (2020)
3. Fabbri, C., Islam, M.J., Sattar, J.: Enhancing underwater imagery using generative adversarial networks. In: 2018 IEEE International Conference on Robotics and Automation (ICRA), pp. 7159–7165. IEEE (2018)
4. Goodfellow, I., et al.: Generative adversarial networks. Commun. ACM **63**(11), 139–144 (2020)
5. He, K., Zhang, X., Ren, S., Sun, J.: Deep residual learning for image recognition. In: Proceedings of the IEEE Conference on Computer Vision and Pattern Recognition, pp. 770–778 (2016)
6. Islam, M.J., Xia, Y., Sattar, J.: Fast underwater image enhancement for improved visual perception. IEEE Robot. Autom. Lett. **5**(2), 3227–3234 (2020)
7. Li, C., Anwar, S., Porikli, F.: Underwater scene prior inspired deep underwater image and video enhancement. Pattern Recogn. **98**, 107038 (2020)
8. Li, C., et al.: An underwater image enhancement benchmark dataset and beyond. IEEE Trans. Image Process. **29**, 4376–4389 (2019)
9. Li, C., Guo, J., Guo, C.: Emerging from water: Underwater image color correction based on weakly supervised color transfer. IEEE Signal Process. Lett. **25**(3), 323–327 (2018)
10. Li, H., Li, J., Wang, W.: A fusion adversarial underwater image enhancement network with a public test dataset. arXiv preprint arXiv:1906.06819 (2019)
11. Li, J., Skinner, K.A., Eustice, R.M., Johnson-Roberson, M.: Watergan: unsupervised generative network to enable real-time color correction of monocular underwater images. IEEE Robot. Autom. Lett. **3**(1), 387–394 (2017)
12. Liu, R., Fan, X., Zhu, M., Hou, M., Luo, Z.: Real-world underwater enhancement: challenges, benchmarks, and solutions under natural light. IEEE Trans. Circuits Syst. Video Technol. **30**(12), 4861–4875 (2020)
13. Liu, Y., et al.: Uiqi: a comprehensive quality evaluation index for underwater images. IEEE Trans. Multimedia (2023)
14. Liu, Y., Gu, K., Li, X., Zhang, Y.: Blind image quality assessment by natural scene statistics and perceptual characteristics. ACM Trans. Multimedia Comput. Commun. Appli. (TOMM) **16**(3), 1–91 (2020)
15. Liu, Y., Gu, K., Wang, S., Zhao, D., Gao, W.: Blind quality assessment of camera images based on low-level and high-level statistical features. IEEE Trans. Multimedia **21**(1), 135–146 (2018)
16. Liu, Y., Gu, K., Zhai, G., Liu, X., Zhao, D., Gao, W.: Quality assessment for real out-of-focus blurred images. J. Vis. Commun. Image Represent. **46**, 70–80 (2017)
17. Liu, Y., Gu, K., Zhang, Y., Li, X., Zhai, G., Zhao, D., Gao, W.: Unsupervised blind image quality evaluation via statistical measurements of structure, naturalness, and perception. IEEE Trans. Circuits Syst. Video Technol. **30**(4), 929–943 (2019)
18. Liu, Y., Zhai, G., Gu, K., Liu, X., Zhao, D., Gao, W.: Reduced-reference image quality assessment in free-energy principle and sparse representation. IEEE Trans. Multimedia **20**(2), 379–391 (2017)
19. Liu, Y., Zhai, G., Zhao, D., Liu, X.: Frame rate and perceptual quality for HD video. In: Ho, Y.-S., Sang, J., Ro, Y.M., Kim, J., Wu, F. (eds.) PCM 2015. LNCS, vol. 9315, pp. 497–505. Springer, Cham (2015). https://doi.org/10.1007/978-3-319-24078-7_50

20. Maas, A.L., Hannun, A.Y., Ng, A.Y., et al.: Rectifier nonlinearities improve neural network acoustic models. In: Proc. ICML, Atlanta, Georgia, USA, vol. 30, p. 3 (2013)
21. Peng, L., Zhu, C., Bian, L.: U-shape transformer for underwater image enhancement. IEEE Trans. Image Process. (2023)
22. Qi, Q., Li, K., Zheng, H., Gao, X., Hou, G., Sun, K.: Sguie-net: semantic attention guided underwater image enhancement with multi-scale perception. IEEE Trans. Image Process. **31**, 6816–6830 (2022)
23. Russakovsky, O., et al.: ImageNet large scale visual recognition challenge. Inter. J. Comput. Vis. (IJCV) **115**(3), 211–252 (2015). https://doi.org/10.1007/s11263-015-0816-y
24. Simonyan, K., Zisserman, A.: Very deep convolutional networks for large-scale image recognition. arXiv preprint arXiv:1409.1556 (2014)
25. Srivastava, N., Hinton, G., Krizhevsky, A., Sutskever, I., Salakhutdinov, R.: Dropout: a simple way to prevent neural networks from overfitting. J. Mach. Learn. Res. **15**(1), 1929–1958 (2014)
26. Ulyanov, D., Vedaldi, A., Lempitsky, V.: Instance normalization: the missing ingredient for fast stylization. arXiv preprint arXiv:1607.08022 (2016)
27. Wang, Y., Zhang, J., Cao, Y., Wang, Z.: A deep cnn method for underwater image enhancement. In: 2017 IEEE international conference on image processing (ICIP), pp. 1382–1386. IEEE (2017). https://doi.org/10.1109/ICIP.2017.8296508
28. Wang, Z., Bovik, A.C., Sheikh, H.R., Simoncelli, E.P.: Image quality assessment: from error visibility to structural similarity. IEEE Trans. Image Process. **13**(4), 600–612 (2004)
29. Wen, J., et al.: Syreanet: a physically guided underwater image enhancement framework integrating synthetic and real images. arXiv preprint arXiv:2302.08269 (2023)
30. Woo, S., Park, J., Lee, J.-Y., Kweon, I.S.: CBAM: convolutional block attention module. In: Ferrari, V., Hebert, M., Sminchisescu, C., Weiss, Y. (eds.) ECCV 2018. LNCS, vol. 11211, pp. 3–19. Springer, Cham (2018). https://doi.org/10.1007/978-3-030-01234-2_1
31. Zhu, J.Y., Park, T., Isola, P., Efros, A.A.: Unpaired image-to-image translation using cycle-consistent adversarial networks. In: Proceedings of the IEEE International Conference on Computer Vision (ICCV) (Oct 2017)

Depth Map Super-Resolution via Asymmetrically Guided Feature Selection and Spatial Affine Transformation

Jintao Fan[ID] and Yi Xu[✉][ID]

Shanghai Key Laboratory of Digital Media Processing and Transmission,
Shanghai Jiao Tong University, Shanghai 200240, China
{fjt0324,xuyi}@sjtu.edu.cn

Abstract. Guided depth image super-resolution (GDSR) is a fundamental task that involves reconstructing a low-resolution (LR) depth image to a high-resolution (HR) version using an aligned HR color image as guidance. The effective utilization of the HR color image to guide the depth image super-resolution process is a critical consideration in algorithm design. In this paper, we propose a novel asymmetric channel-spatial fusion (ACSF) module to address this concern. Specifically, the depth feature is iteratively refined by corresponding color feature in both channel and space dimensions with ACSF during feature extraction. For channel dimension, we utilize asymmetric channel attention to achieve the goal of feature selection, and affine transformation is applied in the space dimension to modulate the depth feature with the guidance color feature. The resulting deep depth map features, which comprehensively integrate the information from RGB modal, are then employed to reconstruct high-resolution depth maps. In other words, The asymmetry is reflected in the fact that we only explicitly update the depth features. The effectiveness of our approach is demonstrated through quantitative and qualitative experiments. The visualization results indicate that the ACSF module enables the network to focus more on areas with larger errors in the super-resolution results, typically corresponding to object edges with sharp changes in the depth map. In terms of quantitative evaluation, our proposed method achieves new state-of-the-art (SOTA) on three widely used benchmarks under different scales.

Keywords: Guided Depth Super-Resolution · Channel Attention · Affine Transformation

1 Introduction

The depth map plays a crucial role in various computer vision tasks such as 3D reconstruction, semantic segmentation, and autonomous driving. However, depth maps obtained from commonly used sensors often suffer from low resolution, thereby limiting their widespread applicability. Consequently, research

G. Zhai et al. (Eds.): IFTC 2023, CCIS 2066, pp. 28–42, 2024.
https://doi.org/10.1007/978-981-97-3623-2_3

on depth map super-resolution holds considerable practical significance. Single-image depth map super-resolution is a challenging problem due to its ill-posed nature. Currently, the predominant research approach involves leveraging high-resolution RGB guidance images to facilitate the super-resolution reconstruction of the depth map, commonly referred to as "guided depth map super-resolution" (GDSR).

Many methods have been proposed to solve GDSR. Traditional methods include filtering-based and optimization-based. Based on the difference in filter kernel construction process, filtering-based methods can be further divided into bilateral filter [20] and its variants, non-local means filter [1] and its variants, guided filter [6] and its variants, and dynamic filters. The dynamic means that some factors in the filter are dynamic, such as dynamic guidance [5], dynamic neighbors [23], etc.

Optimization-based methods for guided depth map super-resolution (GDSR) employ an optimization framework to tackle the inherent ill-posed nature of the problem and incorporate diverse priors. Although specific technical details may vary, most methods within this category follow a similar framework. The primary objective is to minimize the discrepancy between the observed low-resolution (LR) depth map and the degraded reconstruction output while incorporating a regularization term. This term aims to promote smoothness in the reconstruction result and ensure its structural consistency with the guidance image. Various optimization-based approaches [2,14,27] differ primarily in the formulation of their respective regularization terms.

Learning-based methods for guided depth map super-resolution encompass dictionary learning methods and deep learning methods. Dictionary learning methods aim to discover a set of basis atoms (dictionary) that allow the input signal to be expressed as a sparse combination of these atoms. In contrast, deep learning methods directly learn the nonlinear mapping from the two inputs, namely the guidance image and the low-resolution depth map, to the ground truth depth map using deep neural networks. An important consideration in the design of deep learning-based methods is the fusion of depth features and color features. Previous works have explored various fusion methods. For instance, JIIF [19] employed two backbone networks to separately extract guidance and depth features, followed by a simple concatenation of the output features to predict a specific pixel given its coordinates. GeoDSR [21] attempted to fuse the guidance and depth features using an "AND" operation, which essentially involved element-wise multiplication of the two features. AHMF [26] utilized channel attention to selectively attend to these two features and combined the results by addition, with attention weights calculated based on the concatenated result of the input guidance and depth features. These methods employed different techniques such as concatenation, multiplication, and attention mechanisms. The common characteristic among these methods is their symmetrical treatment of input features and output features of both modalities, i.e., from the perspective of input, swapping the two inputs does not affect the fusion result, and the fusion results are also symmetrically generated based on the fact they either produce a single fused feature or update the features of two modalities at the same time. In addition, there are methods that employ asymmetric fusion approaches. For example, DCTNet [25] utilizes edge information derived from color image features through discrete cosine transform (DCT) transformation to guide the upsampling of depth map features. Li et al. [12] propose a correlation-controlled color guidance block (CCGB) to improve the accuracy of the guidance image and avoid texture-transfer and depth-bleeding artifacts. The CCGB is made up of three major parts: correlation computing, weight learning, and guidance channel re-weighting. These methods explore alternative strategies that deviate from the symmetrical treatment of two modalities.

In this paper, we focus on a more efficient fusion of depth and RGB modal features. While the symmetric feature fusion is simple, it overlooks the fact that depth maps and color images inherently contain different amounts of useful information for super-resolution reconstruction. For example, color features encompass richer information compared to depth features but also contain redundant information unrelated to depth. These methods treat the two modals equally and rely heavily on the network's powerful fitting capacity to learn an adaptive fusion method for different types of information. However, the design of the network architecture itself does not take into account the asymmetry in information representation between these two modalities. Our work shares a similar motivation with asymmetric feature fusion methods, aiming to design a more efficient feature fusion module that explicitly considers the different contributions of the two features to the super-resolution results. Specifically, we propose the ACSF (Asymmetric Channel-Spatial Fusion) module, which utilizes both channel attention and spatial affine transformation to refine depth features with the guidance color features in an asymmetric manner. For channel attention, we generate channel attention weights by combining depth features and color features, which are then used to scale the depth features thus obtaining the updated features, i.e., we select the critical depth feature with the guidance of color feature along with the depth feature itself. For spatial fusion, we generate scale and shift coefficients based on the color features as well as the depth features. These coefficients are utilized to perform affine transformations on the depth features, effectively refining the depth features in the space dimension. The aforementioned channel attention and spatial affine transformation modules are cascaded to form the ACSF module. ACSF modules are repeatedly placed between the two feature extraction networks that extract color and depth features respectively to iteratively refine the depth feature during the feature extraction.

In summary, the main contributions of this work are as follows:

- We propose a novel approach to address Guided Depth Map Super-Resolution (GDSR). In our model, two backbone networks continuously engage in feature interaction during the feature extraction stage with the feature fusion module, ultimately yielding depth features that comprehensively integrate the information from RGB modal.
- We propose the ACSF(Asymmetric Channel-Spatial Fusion) module, which leverages both channel attention and spatial affine transformation to refine depth features with the guidance of color features in an asymmetric way.

During the feature extraction, ACSF iteratively refines the depth features, resulting in a comprehensive fusion of information from both modalities in the final depth features.
- We conduct extensive experiments to validate the effectiveness of our proposed model. Our method achieves a new state-of-the-art (SOTA) performance in most experimental settings. Visualizations and ablation experiments further confirm the effectiveness of our proposed ACSF module in feature fusion.

The rest structure of this paper is organized as follows. In Sect. 2, we introduce our proposed model in detail. Section 3 shows the experimental results including the quantitative and qualitative ones. In Sect. 4 we conclude this paper and give some discussions on this work.

2 Methodology

In this section, we introduce our proposed method to solve the guided depth map super-resolution task. First, we describe the overall architecture of our model and then the main contributions of our work, i.e., ACSF module are introduced in detail.

2.1 Overall Architecture

As a usual setting, our model takes a high-resolution guidance image $X_g \in \mathbb{R}^{H \times W \times 3}$ and a low-resolution depth map $X_d \in \mathbb{R}^{h \times w \times 1}$ as inputs and output of the model is super-resolved depth image $Y_d \in \mathbb{R}^{H \times W \times 1}$. As shown in Fig. 1, in our model, X_d is first up-sampled to the size of target resolution using simple bicubic interpolation, the result of which we denote as $\hat{X}_d$. Then $\hat{X}_d$ and X_g are separately fed into different backbones with the same architecture to extract depth and guidance features. During the feature extraction, features from the depth branch are continuously refined by the features from the color branch. At the end of the feature extraction, the output feature of the depth branch is fed into a convolution layer to get the final depth image super-resolution result along with a global residual connection. We only employ depth features for the final reconstruction prediction because, due to the presence of our proposed ACSF module, color features continuously update the depth features during the feature extraction. As a result, the final extracted depth features comprehensively integrate all the crucial information for depth reconstruction from the color features.

2.2 Backbone

As shown in Fig. 1, the backbone network is composed of convolutional groups with global residual connections. A convolutional group is made up of convolutional blocks by cascading them together and residual connection is also included within a group, where convolutional block is the basic unit in our backbone design and it basically consists of two convolutional layers.

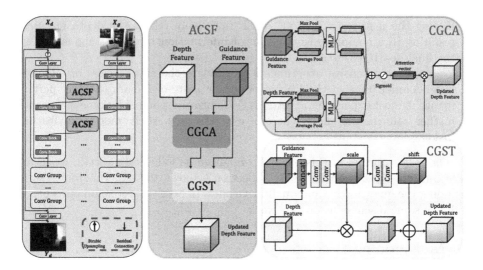

Fig. 1. Illustration of our proposed model. The left part is the overall structure. During the feature extraction stage, ACSF module is repeatedly applied between the two branches to iteratively refine the depth feature with the guidance of color feature. The middle column is the pipeline of ACSF and ACSF consists of two sub-modules: CGCA and CGST which perform color-guided channel attention and color-guided spatial transformation respectively and the third column shows the detail of them.

2.3 ACSF Module

To achieve better feature fusion between the guidance feature and depth feature, we introduce the Asymmetric Channel-Spatial Fusion (ACSF) module. The ACSF module serves as an asymmetric fusion block that takes both the color and depth features as inputs and produces the refined depth feature with the guidance of color feature. Consequently, the output of the ACSF module yields a color-guided depth feature, which subsequently serves as the input depth feature for the subsequent convolutional block in depth branch.

In order to enhance the utilization of information in guidance feature for refining depth features, we have incorporated both channel guidance and spatial guidance which are essentially asymmetric channel attention and spatial affine transformation respectively. To this end, ACSF module consists of two sub-modules, namely the Color-Guided Channel Attention (CGCA) module and the Color-Guided Spatial Transformation (CGST) module.

Color-Guided Channel Attention. The commonly used channel attention mechanism [9] follows a "squeeze and excitation" structure. Initially, the input feature is spatially average pooled, reducing its spatial dimensions. This process is known as "squeeze" because the information of a certain channel is denoted by a single value after pooling. Subsequently, the pooled feature is passed through a multi-layer perceptron (MLP) to fuse information across different channels, resulting in an attention vector that represents the attention weights assigned to each channel. The attention weights are then employed to scale the corresponding channels of the original input feature, generating the output feature, referred to as "excitation".

In the Color-Guided Channel Attention (CGCA) module, our objective is to obtain attention weights for scaling the depth feature. While traditional channel attention derives attention weights solely from the input feature itself, our aim is to generate attention weights that incorporate both the depth feature and the color feature information, i.e., our goal is to emphasize crucial ones of the depth feature with the guidance of color feature along with depth feature itself. To achieve this, our color-guided channel attention module is designed as follows.

"Squeeze and excitation" ructure is also adopted in CGCA. As shown in the top right part of Fig. 1, input color and depth features are max-pooled and average-pooled to obtain four feature vectors. Then the feature vectors of guidance and depth are separately fed into two distinct MLPs to get output vectors. Finally, four output vectors are summed, and applying the sigmoid activation to the summation result gives us the attention weights, which are then utilized to scale the depth feature. Formally, the aforementioned process can be represented by the following:

$$v_d^{mean} = MLP_1(AvgPool(f_d^{in})) \tag{1}$$

$$v_d^{max} = MLP_1(MaxPool(f_d^{in})) \tag{2}$$

$$v_c^{mean} = MLP_2(AvgPool(f_c^{in})) \tag{3}$$

$$v_c^{max} = MLP_2(MaxPool(f_c^{in})) \tag{4}$$

$$w = Sigmoid(v_d^{mean} + v_d^{max} + v_c^{mean} + v_c^{max}) \tag{5}$$

$$f_d^{out} = w \cdot f_d^{in} \tag{6}$$

where f_d^{in} and f_c^{in} are input depth and color features and f_d^{out} is the output depth feature of CGCA, which can be presented in a summary way:

$$f_d^{out} = CGCA(f_c^{in}, f_d^{in}) \tag{7}$$

Color-Guided Spatial Transformation. For color-guided spatial Transformation(CGST), the underlying intention behind our design is to find and emphasize the crucial areas in the space dimension of depth features with the guidance of color features which encompass richer information compared to depth features but also contain redundant information unrelated to depth.

To accomplish the previously mentioned objective, the Color-Guided Spatial Transformation (CGST) module is designed as follows. We leverage the guidance features along with the depth feature itself to generate per-pixel scaling and shifting coefficients for the depth features, allowing for the refinement of the depth features through scaling and shifting operations. This process essentially applies an affine transformation to the depth features, where the transformation coefficients are derived from the color features and depth features. Specifically, as depicted in the bottom right of Fig. 1, the scaling and shifting coefficients are obtained by passing concatenation of the depth feature and guidance feature through dedicated convolutional blocks. Furthermore, the CGST module incorporates residual connections to facilitate information flow. Note that previous work [22] also utilizes a similar module to introduce a semantic segmentation map as guidance to facilitate the super-resolution of natural images. The scale and shift for the image feature are obtained with only the segmentation map. In the context of natural image super-resolution, the edges in the segmentation image correspond one-to-one with the edges in the natural image. However, in GDSR, the aligned color image used as guidance could contain redundant details for the same object surface, meaning that the edges in the color image may not necessarily correspond to the edges (depth variations) in the depth image. This is the reason why we jointly generate scale and shift using color features and guidance features. The CGST module can be mathematically described as follows:

$$scale = Conv^1_{scale}(\sigma(Conv^0_{scale}(concat(f^{in}_c, f^{in}_d)))) \tag{8}$$

$$shift = Conv^1_{shift}(\sigma(Conv^0_{shift}(concat(f^{in}_c, f^{in}_d)))) \tag{9}$$

$$f^{out}_d = f^{in}_d + (scale \cdot f^{in}_d + shift) \tag{10}$$

where f^{in}_d, f^{in}_c and f^{out}_d have the same meaning as described in 2.3. $\sigma(\cdot)$ denotes the activation function and it is leaky-ReLu here. The whole procedure is:

$$f^{out}_d = CGST(f^{in}_c, f^{in}_d) \tag{11}$$

Asymmetric Channel-Spatial Fusion. As shown in the middle of Fig. 1, with the presence of both CGCA and CGST, the cascading of these two modules forms the module ACSF, i.e.

$$f^{out}_d = CGST(f^{in}_c, CGCA(f^{in}_c, f^{in}_d)) \tag{12}$$

The pipeline of the ACSF module has been elucidated thus far. It is incorporated between the two backbone networks repeatedly to iteratively refine the depth feature during the feature extraction process. More specifically, after each convolutional block, the ACSF module is applied once. This entails refining the output depth feature of a particular convolutional block by utilizing the ACSF module with the corresponding color feature at the same stage. The refined depth feature is then fed into the subsequent convolutional block, thus ensuring progressive refinement throughout the whole feature extraction stage.

3   Experiments

3.1   Implementation Details

Dataset. We select three widely used benchmark RGB-D datasets for the guided depth super-resolution task:(1) NYU v2 dataset [18]. This dataset provides 1449 RGB-D image pairs acquired by Microsoft Kinect [24]. Following previous works, we use the first 1000 samples for training and the rest 449 samples for testing.

(2) Lu dataset [15]. This dataset consists of 6 RGB-D pairs captured by ASUS Xtion Pro camera and we use it only for testing. (3) Middlebury dataset [8,17]. This dataset contains 30 RGB-D pairs and it's also only used for evaluation.

We test our model under three scales (×4, ×8, ×16). The LR depth input is obtained by applying bicubic downsampling on HR(GT) depth image.

Model and Training Details. As illustrated in 2.2, our backbone network is composed of cascading several convolutional groups, where a convolutional group consists of several cascaded convolutional blocks. In all our models, the number of convolutional groups and the number of convolutional blocks in a convolutional group are both set to 8. Channel dimension is set as 64 during feature extraction. Our training setting is almost following previous works and the detail is as follows: we train our model for 200 epochs with the batch size of 1 and the learning rate is set to $1e-4$ at the beginning of the training and reduced by 0.2 times every 60 epochs. We use Adam [11] as the optimizer and the parameters are set as the default values in Pytorch [16]. We use a GeForce RTX 3090ti GPU to train our model. We apply data augmentation by randomly flipping the image pairs vertically or horizontally in training. We train different models for different scales.

Evaluation Metrics. For the quantitative result comparison, we use the average RMSE of the depth value for the evaluation metric, which is defined as:

$$RMSE = \sqrt{\frac{1}{N} \sum_{i=1}^{N} (gt_i - pred_i)^2}, \tag{13}$$

where N is the number of pixels, gt_i and $pred_i$ are ground-truth value and predicted value for pixel ij.

3.2 Quantitative Results

We compare the proposed method with the state-of-the-art models, including recent learning-based JIIF [19], AHMF [26], and GeoDSR [21] etc., the simple bicubic interpolation is also compared. We test on three benchmarks under three scales including ×4, ×8 and ×16. Following previous works, the average RMSE is measured in centimeters for the NYU v2 dataset. The depth values are scaled to [0, 255] to calculate RMSE because the source data is provided in grayscale.

The detailed result is shown in Table 1 and the RMSE value is reported. Among the total of 9 experimental results, 6 of them have achieved a new SOTA. Our model obtains better results on a smaller scale, for example, under ×4 scale our model achieves SOTA on all three datasets and improves by a great margin(0.2) on NYU v2. For ×16, an improvement compared to previous methods is not as obvious as ×4. Note that the Lu dataset only contains 6 images, so the results of the other two datasets are relatively more reliable for testing a model.

Table 1. Quantitative comparison with the state-of-the-art methods in terms of RMSE. The best result for each setting is shown in **bold** and the second best result is underlined.

Dateset	NYU v2			Middlebury			Lu		
Scale	x4	x8	x16	x4	x8	x16	x4	x8	x16
Bicubic	4.28	7.14	11.58	2.28	3.98	6.37	2.42	4.54	7.38
DG [4]	3.68	5.78	10.08	1.97	4.16	5.27	2.06	4.19	6.90
DJF [13]	3.54	5.20	10.21	2.14	3.77	6.12	2.54	4.71	7.66
CUNet [3]	1.92	3.70	6.78	1.10	2.17	4.33	0.91	2.23	4.99
FDKN [10]	1.86	3.55	6.96	1.09	2.17	4.51	0.82	2.09	5.03
DKN [10]	1.62	3.26	6.51	1.23	2.12	4.24	0.96	2.16	5.11
FDSR [7]	1.61	3.18	5.86	1.13	2.08	4.39	1.29	2.19	5.00
JIIF [19]	1.37	2.76	5.27	1.09	1.82	3.31	0.85	1.73	4.16
AHMF [26]	<u>1.40</u>	2.89	5.64	1.07	<u>1.63</u>	3.14	0.88	1.66	**3.71**
GeoDSR [21]	1.42	<u>2.62</u>	**4.86**	<u>1.04</u>	1.68	<u>3.10</u>	**0.81**	<u>1.59</u>	<u>3.92</u>
Ours	**1.23**	**2.57**	<u>5.05</u>	**1.03**	**1.61**	**3.05**	<u>0.84</u>	**1.53**	4.02

3.3 Quanlitative Results

Reconstruction Results. Besides the quantitative result, we also compare the visual quality of different methods, and the result is shown in Fig. 2 where the scale ×8 is considered. The reconstruction result and corresponding absolute error are both compared. In an error map, a brighter area means a more significant error. Samples are selected from NYU v2 test dataset. From the visual result, we can find that our proposed model obviously achieves a more precise and accurate reconstruction result, especially on the sharp edge areas.

Effect of ACSF. To better illustrate the effect of ACSF, we conduct an experiment where we compare the difference between the input and output of an ACSF module. Three samples are selected from the Lu [15] dataset and we test under the scale ×4. We select 3 ACSF modules located in different stages of the backbone into consideration. Detailed results are shown in Fig. 3, where 3(b), 3(c) and 3(d) are the result of the 8th ACSF module of 2, 4 and 7 convolutional groups respectively, which are located in the start, middle and the end stage of the backbone network. From Fig. 3, we can observe that during the process of feature extraction, the ACSF tends to remove redundant noise or texture in the areas that are not related to depth change but reserves the edges areas in the corresponding depth map where significant depth variations actually occur.

3.4 Ablation Study

ACSF. First, we focus on the design of ACSF. For the two sub-modules of ACSF, i.e., CGCA and CGST, we replace ACSF with either CGCA or CGST

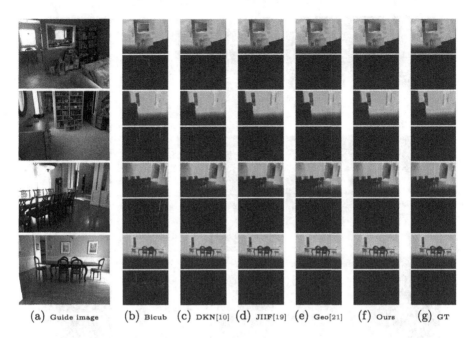

(a) Guide image   (b) Bicub   (c) DKN[10]   (d) JIIF[19]   (e) Geo[21]   (f) Ours   (g) GT

Fig. 2. Visual result comparison of upsampled depth images ($\times 8$). For each sample, the first row is the upsampling result and the second row is the corresponding error map, the value of which is the absolute difference between the upsampling result and the ground truth. The brighter area in the error map means a more significant error. "Bicub" and "Geo" are short for "Bicubic" and "GeoDSR" respectively. Best viewed after zooming in.

individually. Additionally, we also consider the scenario where neither of them is used. In this case, the two backbones don't interact during feature extraction, instead, the features extracted separately by the color and depth backbones are concatenated and directly input into convolutional layers for reconstruction. We test on the NYU v2 test dataset under scale $\times 4$. The result is shown in Table 2, it can be observed that compared to the scenario where neither CGCA nor CGST is used, the individual usage of either sub-module leads to performance improvement compared to simple concatenation. Furthermore, the combined usage of both sub-modules (ACSF) yields the best performance.

Table 2. Ablation study result of ACSF tested on NYU v2 test dataset under scale $\times 4$

	Concat	CGCA only	CGST only	ACSF
RMSE	1.42 (+0.19)	1.37 (+0.14)	1.29 (+0.06)	1.23

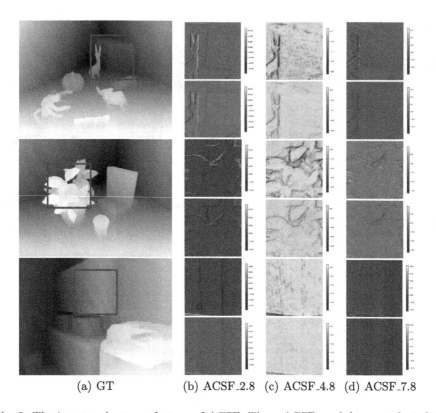

(a) GT   (b) ACSF_2.8   (c) ACSF_4.8   (d) ACSF_7.8

Fig. 3. The input and output feature of ACSF. Three ACSF modules are selected to present the result. The first column is the ground-truth depth map and the three right columns are the results of features of three different ACSF modules. In each column of the feature result, for a certain sample, the upper row is the input feature and the bottom row is the output feature. "ACSF_2.8" means the result of the 8th ACSF module in block 2. All features are averaged along the channel dimension.

As already illustrated, our model only utilizes the depth feature to make the final reconstructed prediction based on the intuition that the ACSF module has already integrated the critical information of the color feature into the depth feature during the feature extraction stage. We design experiments to numerically validate this hypothesis. In the control experiment, besides the utilization of ACSF, we concatenate the color features and depth features obtained from the backbone and pass them through convolutional layers to generate the reconstruction results. As shown in Table 3, the quantitative results of these two methods are comparable and this confirms our hypothesis and validates the effectiveness of ACSF in feature fusion.

CGCA. In our design of CGCA, we use two MLPs to handle the pooling results of depth and color features respectively, another option is applying a shared MLP for the pooled features. The quantitative comparison between these two

Table 3. Ablation study result on the utilization of color features tested under scale ×4

	NYU v2	Middlebury	Lu
depth only	**1.23**	**1.03**	0.84
depth+color	1.24	**1.03**	**0.83**

methods is shown in Table 4 and we can find that the separated MLPs produce a better quantitative result than a shared MLP. Visual differences of the output features between these two methods are also given in Fig. 4, and the outputs of the whole ACSF with different MLP settings in CGCA are compared. Note that the parameter count of the two models differs by only 0.3%. It's apparent that applying distinct MLPs in CGCA for features from two modalities generates features with clearer edges.

Table 4. Ablation study result on the MLP in CGCA tested under scale ×4

	NYU v2	Middlebury	Lu
Shared MLP	1.25	1.06	0.86
CGCA (Separated MLP)	**1.23**	**1.03**	**0.84**

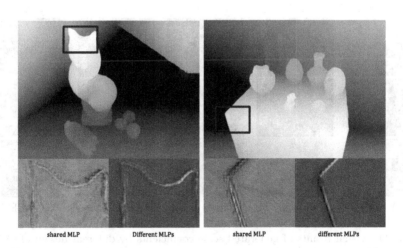

shared MLP   Different MLPs   shared MLP   different MLPs

Fig. 4. The output features of ACSF under different MLP settings in CGCA. The output feature of different MLPs produces sharper (narrower) boundaries.

CGST. For the design of CGST, we utilize the input depth feature and color feature to jointly generate the scale and shift coefficients which are used to apply spatial transformation for the depth feature. We compare this pipeline with the one that only utilizes color features.

Besides, another potential design for CGST is that the shape of the generated scale can be set to $H \times W \times 1$, and the potential rationale behind this design is based on the consideration that in low-level tasks, although feature maps may not have distinct meanings across channels, they still correspond to specific details and therefore, scale coefficients can potentially be shared among channels.

We compare our proposed CGST with the aforementioned two different designs. Quantitative results are shown in Table 5 and it shows that our CGST gives a better result. Visual results of generated scale coefficients are shown in Fig. 5. We can observe that the scale generated with only color feature has many redundant details that are not related to depth change in depth map. For the shape of scale coefficients, we can find that a scale of $H \times W \times C$ produces clearer edges compared to the scale of $H \times W \times 1$.

Table 5. Ablation study result on design of CGST under scale ×4

	NYU v2	Middlebury	Lu
w/o depth	1.27	1.06	**0.83**
$H \times W \times 1$	1.24	1.05	0.85
CGST	**1.23**	**1.03**	0.84

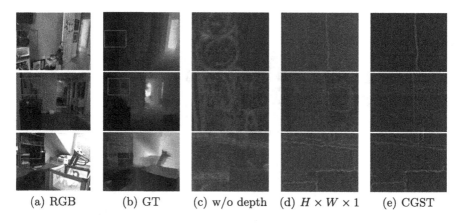

   (a) RGB   (b) GT   (c) w/o depth (d) $H \times W \times 1$ (e) CGST

Fig. 5. The visual results of generated scale coefficients by different design of CGST. "w/o depth" means using color feature only to generate the scale and "$H \times W \times 1$" means the generated scale is in the shape of $H \times W \times 1$. Our CGST generates the scale with both depth and color features and the generated scale is in the shape of $H \times W \times C$. The scales of CGST and CGST w/o depth are averaged along the channel dimension for displaying.

4 Conclusion

In this paper, we present a novel approach to address Guided Depth Map Super-Resolution (GDSR) by introducing the Asymmetric Channel-Spatial Fusion (ACSF) module. The ACSF module serves as a feature fusion module that facilitates a more efficient fusion of color and depth features, resulting in improved reconstruction outcomes. Specifically, ACSF employs an asymmetric approach to leverage color features for refining depth features, employing both channel attention and spatial affine transformation. By integrating essential information from both modalities, ACSF enhances the quality of the extracted depth features. Extensive experimental evaluations demonstrate the effectiveness of our proposed method, as it achieves state-of-the-art (SOTA) performance across various experimental settings. Building upon this work, there are two potential directions for further improvement. Firstly, exploring the integration of a more powerful backbone architecture, such as transformer, which has been relatively unexplored in the context of GDSR. Secondly, refining the design of the feature fusion module to further optimize performance by investigating more advanced fusion strategies.

References

1. Buades, A., Coll, B., Morel, J.M.: A non-local algorithm for image denoising. In: 2005 IEEE computer society conference on computer vision and pattern recognition (CVPR'05). vol. 2, pp. 60–65. Ieee (2005)
2. De Lutio, R., Becker, A., D'Aronco, S., Russo, S., Wegner, J.D., Schindler, K.: Learning graph regularisation for guided super-resolution. In: Proceedings of the IEEE/CVF Conference on Computer Vision and Pattern Recognition, pp. 1979–1988 (2022)
3. Deng, X., Dragotti, P.L.: Deep convolutional neural network for multi-modal image restoration and fusion. IEEE Trans. Pattern Anal. Mach. Intell. **43**(10), 3333–3348 (2020)
4. Gu, S., Zuo, W., Guo, S., Chen, Y., Chen, C., Zhang, L.: Learning dynamic guidance for depth image enhancement. In: Proceedings of the IEEE Conference on Computer Vision and Pattern Recognition, pp. 3769–3778 (2017)
5. Ham, B., Cho, M., Ponce, J.: Robust guided image filtering using nonconvex potentials. IEEE Trans. Pattern Anal. Mach. Intell. **40**(1), 192–207 (2017)
6. He, K., Sun, J., Tang, X.: Guided image filtering. IEEE Trans. Pattern Anal. Mach. Intell. **35**(6), 1397–1409 (2012)
7. He, L., et al.: Towards fast and accurate real-world depth super-resolution: Benchmark dataset and baseline. In: Proceedings of the IEEE/CVF Conference on Computer Vision and Pattern Recognition, pp. 9229–9238 (2021)
8. Hirschmuller, H., Scharstein, D.: Evaluation of cost functions for stereo matching. In: 2007 IEEE Conference on Computer Vision and Pattern Recognition, pp. 1–8. IEEE (2007)
9. Hu, J., Shen, L., Sun, G.: Squeeze-and-excitation networks. In: Proceedings of the IEEE Conference on Computer Vision and Pattern Recognition, pp. 7132–7141 (2018)

10. Kim, B., Ponce, J., Ham, B.: Deformable kernel networks for joint image filtering. Int. J. Comput. Vision **129**(2), 579–600 (2021)
11. Kingma, D.P., Ba, J.: Adam: A method for stochastic optimization. arXiv preprint arXiv:1412.6980 (2014)
12. Li, T., Lin, H., Dong, X., Zhang, X.: Depth image super-resolution using correlation-controlled color guidance and multi-scale symmetric network. Pattern Recogn. **107**, 107513 (2020)
13. Li, Y., Huang, J.-B., Ahuja, N., Yang, M.-H.: Deep joint image filtering. In: Leibe, B., Matas, J., Sebe, N., Welling, M. (eds.) ECCV 2016. LNCS, vol. 9908, pp. 154–169. Springer, Cham (2016). https://doi.org/10.1007/978-3-319-46493-0_10
14. Liu, W., Zhang, P., Lei, Y., Huang, X., Yang, J., Ng, M.: A generalized framework for edge-preserving and structure-preserving image smoothing. IEEE Trans. Pattern Anal. Mach. Intell. **44**(10), 6631–6648 (2021)
15. Lu, S., Ren, X., Liu, F.: Depth enhancement via low-rank matrix completion. In: Proceedings of the IEEE Conference on Computer Vision and Pattern Recognition, pp. 3390–3397 (2014)
16. Paszke, A., et al.: Pytorch: an imperative style, high-performance deep learning library. Adv. Neural Inform. Process. Syst. **32** (2019)
17. Scharstein, D., Pal, C.: Learning conditional random fields for stereo. In: 2007 IEEE Conference on Computer Vision and Pattern Recognition, pp. 1–8. IEEE (2007)
18. Silberman, N., Hoiem, D., Kohli, P., Fergus, R.: Indoor segmentation and support inference from RGBD images. In: Fitzgibbon, A., Lazebnik, S., Perona, P., Sato, Y., Schmid, C. (eds.) ECCV 2012. LNCS, vol. 7576, pp. 746–760. Springer, Heidelberg (2012). https://doi.org/10.1007/978-3-642-33715-4_54
19. Tang, J., Chen, X., Zeng, G.: Joint implicit image function for guided depth super-resolution. In: Proceedings of the 29th ACM International Conference on Multimedia, pp. 4390–4399 (2021)
20. Tomasi, C., Manduchi, R.: Bilateral filtering for gray and color images. In: Sixth international conference on computer vision (IEEE Cat. No. 98CH36271), pp. 839–846. IEEE (1998)
21. Wang, X., Chen, X., Ni, B., Tong, Z., Wang, H.: Learning continuous depth representation via geometric spatial aggregator. In: Proceedings of the AAAI Conference on Artificial Intelligence, vol. 37, pp. 2698–2706 (2023)
22. Wang, X., Yu, K., Dong, C., Loy, C.C.: Recovering realistic texture in image super-resolution by deep spatial feature transform. In: Proceedings of the IEEE Conference on Computer Vision and Pattern Recognition, pp. 606–615 (2018)
23. Yin, H., Gong, Y., Qiu, G.: Side window filtering. In: Proceedings of the IEEE/CVF Conference on Computer Vision and Pattern Recognition, pp. 8758–8766 (2019)
24. Zhang, Z.: Microsoft kinect sensor and its effect. IEEE Multimedia **19**(2), 4–10 (2012)
25. Zhao, Z., Zhang, J., Xu, S., Lin, Z., Pfister, H.: Discrete cosine transform network for guided depth map super-resolution. In: Proceedings of the IEEE/CVF Conference on Computer Vision and Pattern Recognition, pp. 5697–5707 (2022)
26. Zhong, Z., Liu, X., Jiang, J., Zhao, D., Chen, Z., Ji, X.: High-resolution depth maps imaging via attention-based hierarchical multi-modal fusion. IEEE Trans. Image Process. **31**, 648–663 (2021)
27. Zuo, Y., Wu, Q., Zhang, J., An, P.: Explicit edge inconsistency evaluation model for color-guided depth map enhancement. IEEE Trans. Circuits Syst. Video Technol. **28**(2), 439–453 (2016)

Welding Defect Detection Using X-Ray Images Based on Deep Segmentation Network

Yawen Fan[1(✉)], Zhengkai Hu[1], Xuefeng Fang[2], Junge Sun[3], and Qinxin Li[1]

[1] National Engineering Research Center of Communications and Networking,
Nanjing University of Posts and Telecommunications, Nanjing, China
ywfan@njupt.edu.cn
[2] Nanjing Boiler and Pressure Vessel Inspection and Research Institute, Nanjing,
China
[3] Shanghai Electro-Mechanical Engineering Institute, Shanghai, China

Abstract. Automated detection of welding defects in X-ray images is critical for ensuring the quality of welded structures. However, accurately locating welding defects remains challenging because of various complex factors, including low contrast, weak texture, and the limitation of small-scale datasets. In this research, we developed a framework that combines deep convolutional neural network and data augmentation techniques for semantic segmentation of welding defects with high accuracy. Specifically, we develop a modified U-Net network that can effectively and efficiently identify defects in X-ray images of weld seams. The proposed network is trained using a small-scale dataset that is augmented online to improve its robustness and generalization ability. Experiments on the public dataset GDXray demonstrate that the proposed method performs better than other models, with an F1-score of 0.85 and a mIoU of 0.75. Additionally, the proposed model's simple structure allows for faster referencing and hardware space savings, making it suitable for practical industrial applications.

Keywords: Welding Defects · Semantic Segmentation · X-ray · Data Augmentation · Small-scale Dataset

1 Introduction

In modern manufacturing industries, welding defect detection using X-ray images plays a crucial role. Welding is a common method for joining metal components; however, defects within welds can lead to reduced structural strength, fracture, or failure, thereby adversely affecting product quality and safety. Therefore, timely and accurate detection of welding defects is essential for ensuring product quality and improving manufacturing efficiency. X-ray inspection techniques offer advantages of non-invasiveness, high sensitivity, and rapid detection, making them widely applied in the field of weld defect detection.

With the rapid development of AI technology, there is a growing number of works in X-ray welding defect detection that utilize deep learning techniques [1].

G. Zhai et al. (Eds.): IFTC 2023, CCIS 2066, pp. 43–54, 2024.
https://doi.org/10.1007/978-981-97-3623-2_4

Theses researches can be broadly categorized into three groups: defect classification (see Fig. 1(b)), defect detection (see Fig. 1(c)), and defect segmentation (see Fig. 1(d)). One commonly used approach is CNN-based image classification, where convolutional neural networks are trained to identify and categorize weld defects. Researchers such as Hou et al. [2], Jiang et al. [3], and Kumaresan et al. [4] have developed different deep learning models, achieving accurate classification of different defect categories. To accurately locate the defects in X-ray images, target detection methods like Faster R-CNN and YOLO are utilized. For example, Yang et al. [5] and Gong et al. [6] both introduced feature pyramid networks (FPN) into Faster R-CNN for improved detection of small defects. Based on YOLO v3-tiny, Yang et al. [7] developed a specialized model named YOLO-Xweld for welding defects detecting in pipeline applications. Furthermore, a lightweight YOLO model was proposed by Liu et al. [8], which aims to achieve accurate and efficient defect detection while minimizing computational resources. The methods mentioned above utilize classification and target detection techniques to obtain better detection performance of welding defects. But, these techniques typically rely on a substantial amount of training data and may only provide coarse information regarding the defects. Precise localization of weld defects, specifically achieving pixel-level semantic segmentation,

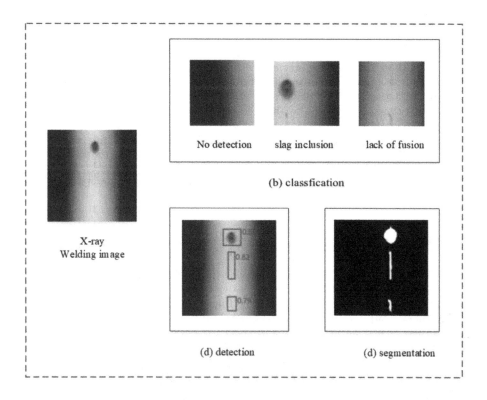

Fig. 1. Examples of welding defect detection tasks

is a crucial research area in industrial non-destructive testing. Researchers have explored various deep learning approaches for weld defect segmentation. For example, Tokime et al. [9] employed SegNet to detect porosity defects in real welding parts. In their work, Chang et al. [10] first proposed a preprocessing method to improve the visibility of defect areas in an image, and then used an enhanced SegNet network for the detection of welding gap defects. Xu et al. [11] designed a semantic segmentation network based on FPN-ResNet-34 for the RIWD dataset, which consists of radiographic images of welding defects. However, the availability of publicly accessible datasets for for research purposes in this field is currently limited, making the GDXray dataset [13] a valuable resource for researchers.

This dataset consists of 10 valid welding X-ray images with pixel-level annotations, enabling researchers to develop and evaluate different techniques and algorithms for accurately identifying and segmenting welding defects. For example, Kothari et al. [12] trained a simplified U-Net network based on this dataset. Yang et al. [13, 15, 16] proposed three enhanced U-Net network models to address issues such as complex background and low-contrast. These models incorporated modifications such as skip connection layers, sequential BiConvLSTM, and attention modules combining Squeeze and Excitation (SE). Experimental results on the GDXray dataset showed that these models achieved promising detection performance.

While the aforementioned approaches have shown promising results in detecting segmentation, one potential limitation is that they can increase the complexity of the model. In contrast to above research, this paper addresses the challenge of learning from small-scale weld dataset by focusing on simplifying the model structure. Based on the hypothesis, it is suggested that a simplified and efficient deep learning model could potentially achieve comparable or superior performance using a smaller dataset, when compared to a complex model trained on a larger dataset without domain knowledge. This hypothesis proposes that simplicity and efficiency in the model's architecture could lead to improved generalization and reduced overfitting.

Based on the analysis and discussion above, this paper introduces a pruning-based U-Net framework for defects segmentation in X-ray images of welds, which takes advantage of the skip connection structure of the U-Net model and the feature extraction capabilities of convolutional neural networks to accurately segment defects in welds. To address overfitting issues caused by excessive skip connections and limited dataset size, a skip connection pruning strategy is applied to simplify the model architecture and improve its generalization performance. This paper primarily focuses on three main aspects as follow:

1. Introducing an end-to-end deep segmentation network for automatic welding defect detection at pixel-level.

2. Implementing a skip connection pruning strategy to address overfitting caused by excessive skip connections and limited dataset size. This strategy simplifies the model architecture and improves its overall performance.
3. Performing sufficient online random data augmentation to tackle the problem of an extremely small dataset size and ensure that the model could fully learn the features of welds.

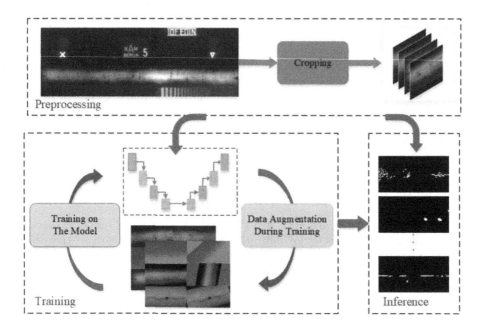

Fig. 2. Proposed welding defect segmentation framework

This paper is organized as follows. The algorithm framework and network structure is described in Sect. 2. The data preprocessing methods and experimental results analysis are discussed in Sect. 3. Finally, the conclusions and prospect are described in Sect. 4.

2 The Proposed Segmentation Framework

2.1 Overview of the Framework

To achieve welding defect detection with a small-scale training dataset, we propose a deep segmentation framework as depicted in Fig. 2. This framework includes 3 processes: preprocessing, training, and inference. Firstly, the dataset is constructed by cropping the original X-ray images into small patches and divided into training set and testing set. Then, a model is built to perform supervised training using the online augmented data. Finally, using the trained model, defect detection is performed on X-ray weld seam images, which can provide more information for further quality assessment. The core of the entire framework is a modified U-Net network that is both effective and efficient.

2.2 Backbone Architecture

The U-Net network was originally designed for medical image segmentation and has demonstrated impressive performance in that field [17]. Taking into account the characteristics of the welding defect images, we propose a modified version of the U-Net named UNet-weld, designed specifically for small-scale dataset. The network structure of UNet-weld is depicted in Fig. 3.

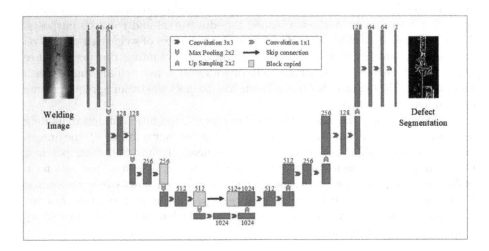

Fig. 3. Proposed network

The main difference between UNet-weld and the original U-Net is that we used fewer skip connections to avoid overfitting and make the training and inference faster. This is necessary because the training sample is limited and the background of X-ray weld images is relatively simple. By reducing the number of skip connections, we can effectively prevent the model from memorizing the training data and improve its generalization ability

2.3 Loss Function

The loss function chosen to measure the discrepancy between the ground truth mask and the predicted segmentation mask is binary cross-entropy (BCE). During the training process, the network parameters are iteratively updated by minimizing this loss function, with the objective of reducing the differences between

the predicted and ground truth maps. The mathematical definition of the BCE
loss function is as follows:

$$L_{BCE} = -\sum_i^N [y_i \cdot plog(\widehat{y}_i) + (1 - y_i) \cdot plog(1 - \widehat{y}_i)] \tag{1}$$

where y_i represents the real label and $\widehat{y}_i$ represents the prediction value within
a prediction map that have a total number of N pixels.

3   Experiments and Analysis

3.1   Dataset and Preprocessing

For this experiment, the GDXray dataset [13] is adopted, which is a publicly
accessible X-ray image dataset intended for educational and research purposes.
The subset called "welds" is a collection of X-ray images of weld with pixel-level
annotations, which can be used for training and evaluating the performance
of the model. However, this subset only provides 10 X-ray welding images with
annotations. The quantity is far from sufficient to meet the training requirements
of deep learning models.

Considering that the raw welding images have a resolution of approximately
4K, and the welded area only covers center region (as shown in Fig. 4), the images
and the corresponding masks are cropped sequentially into 366×722 patches.
Cropping provides benefits in two ways. Firstly, it can be considered as a form
of data augmentation. Secondly, the utilization of a fixed small size is well-suited
for a segmentation network, enabling efficient processing and analysis. Finally,
the data is randomly partitioned into two subsets with a ratio of 5:1, to facilitate
model training and testing.

3.2   Online Data Augmentation

To further increase the amount of training samples, an effective train-time data
augmentation is employed to expand the data set. During the training process,
data augmentation techniques were utilized to introduce variations in the data
fed into the model at different epochs. This approach can not only enhances the
model's generalization ability but also improves the overall performance.

In this work, two common augmentations are adopted. Firstly, images are
flipped horizontally or vertically. Secondly, random rotations within the range
of 0 to 90° are applied to the images. This introduces additional diversity by
simulating different angles at which X-ray images may be captured. In cases
where the final image size is smaller than the desired 366×722 pixels, padding
is used to increase the dimensions, which ensures that all images have consistent
sizes.

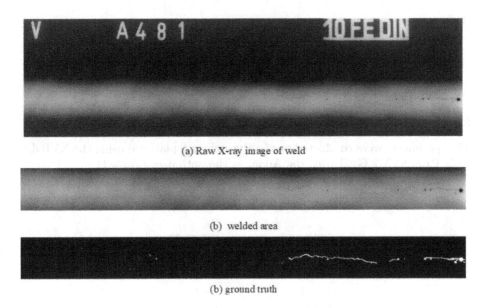

(a) Raw X-ray image of weld

(b) welded area

(b) ground truth

Fig. 4. Samples from the GDXray dataset

3.3   Evaluation Indicators

We comprehensively evaluate the proposed network using several evaluation metrics, which include Precision (Pr), Recall (Re), Accuracy (Acc), Intersection over Union (IoU) and F1-score.

(1) Precision (Pr): It indicates the accuracy of correctly predicting positive pixels, as Eq. (2).

$$Pr = \frac{TP}{TP + FP} \qquad (2)$$

(2) Recall (Re): It reflects the sensitivity of the model, as Eq. (3).

$$Re = \frac{TP}{TP + FN} \qquad (3)$$

(3) Accuracy (Acc): It indicates the model's overall performance in accurately identifying both positive and negative pixels, as Eq. (4)

$$Acc = \frac{TP + TN}{TP + TN + FP + FN} \qquad (4)$$

(4) Intersection over Union (IoU): the spatial overlap between the predicted and ground truth masks is quantified, as Eq. (5).

$$IoU = \frac{TP}{TP + FP + FN} \qquad (5)$$

where TP, FP, and FN refer to the true positive, false positive, and false negative, respectively.

(5) The $F1$-score and Dice coefficient are calculated in the same way for segmentation tasks, as Eq. (6).

$$F1 = \frac{2 \times Pr \times Re}{Pr + Re} \qquad (6)$$

3.4 Network Parameter Setting

All experiments were conducted on the Pytorch 1.10 platform using the NVIDIA Tesla P100 SXM2 GPU with the Adam as the optimizer (Table 1).

Table 1. Parameter Setting

Index	Parameter
Memory	16 GB
Initial learning rate	1e–5
Epoch	1000
batch size	16
Dropout rate	0.5

3.5 Ablation Experiments

In this subsection, an ablation study was performed to evaluate the effectiveness of the proposed defect segmentation network.

Table 2. Comparison experiments of skip connection skipping

Methods	Pr	Re	Acc	mIoU	F1
None	**0.9395**	0.6064	0.9929	0.5782	0.7184
L4	0.8415	**0.8672**	**0.9952**	**0.7464**	**0.8517**
L3	0.8989	0.7167	0.9941	0.6645	0.7944
L2	0.8798	0.7122	0.9938	0.6475	0.7843
L1	0.7098	0.8156	0.9919	0.6103	0.7551
L4, L3	0.9148	0.7411	0.9947	0.6938	0.8154
L4, L2	0.9143	0.6970	0.9941	0.6536	0.7864
L4, L1	0.9025	0.6932	0.9937	0.6443	0.7757
L3, L2	0.9174	0.6859	0.9939	0.6454	0.7810
L3, L1	0.9170	0.6995	0.9942	0.6576	0.7904
L2, L1	0.9269	0.7040	0.9944	0.6666	0.7972
L4, L3, L2	0.9343	0.6776	0.9940	0.6461	0.7802
L4, L3, L1	0.8986	0.7381	0.9944	0.6819	0.8072
L4, L2, L1	0.9040	0.7165	0.9942	0.6656	0.7952
L3, L2, L1	0.9103	0.7098	0.9942	0.6632	0.7937
L4, L3, L2, L1	0.9095	0.7529	0.9949	0.7012	0.8214

It aimed to assess the impact of different levels of skip connection skipping on the network's performance.

As indicated in Table 2, the notation Ln represents a connection between the n-th level encoder and its corresponding decoder. $L1$ denotes the lowest level, whereas $L4$ corresponds to the highest semantic level. The symbol "None" represents there is no skip connection. It can be observed that utilizing only the highest-level skip connection slightly sacrifices precision, but other metrics are optimized. The underlying reason may be attributed to the relatively simple background of the weld seam compared to medical image segmentation tasks. When dealing with limited training sample size, introducing excessive low-level detailed features may lead to overfitting issues.

3.6 Performance Comparison

We select the classic algorithms of the U-Net series including original U-Net [17], UNNet++ [18], and Attention U-Net [19] algorithm for comparison. U-Net was initially designed to tackle the challenge of limited training samples in medical image segmentation tasks. UNet++ incorporates more skip connections in both the encoder and decoder. While Attention U-Net incorporates attention mechanisms to guide the model to pay more attention to significant features during the segmentation process. Table 3 presents the experimental results of each model. Obviously, our model exhibits superior performance compared to other models, except for the precision metric. It is widely known that the recall rate, also referred to as the sensitivity indicator, is more important for quality monitoring. And clearly, our model surpasses other models significantly in terms of this metric. Moreover, in comparison to the original U-Net, the precision of our method has only slightly decreased, but the recall rate has increased by 11.43%.

Table 3. Comparison experiments of different models on X-ray welding images

Models	Pr	Re	Acc	mIoU	F1
U-Net	**0.9095**	0.7529	0.9949	0.7012	0.8214
UNet++	0.5027	0.8107	0.9877	0.4083	0.7317
Attention U-Net	0.8518	0.7465	0.9939	0.6487	0.7853
Proposed	0.8415	**0.8672**	**0.9952**	**0.7464**	**0.8517**

To provide a more intuitive comparison of the semantic segmentation results, Fig. 5 displays the outcomes of different models on five sample X-ray weld images. Overall, our model is capable of detecting more complete defects with clearer edges Among them, it was obviously that the UNet++ had limited capability in extracting defect details. It tended to fail in extracting complete crack defects and misjudged circular defects in their surrounding areas. In the case of sample

(1), all modes missed the defection labeled by the red box. For the defect labeled by the green box in sample (4), it was not marked in the ground truth even by experts as it was very subtle. However, all models except for U-Net detected it. It demonstrates improved performance in capturing fine defect details while maintaining a robust ability to identify subtle anomalies that may be overlooked by human experts.

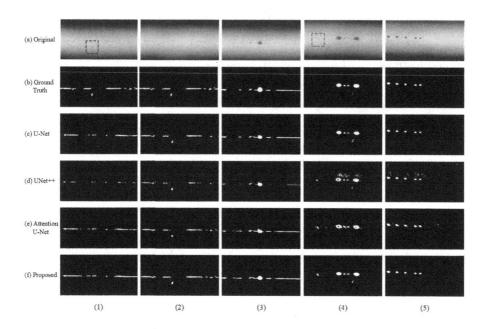

Fig. 5. Segmentation results of sample images in Welds set

3.7   Time Analysis

In defect detection, both segmentation accuracy and computational efficiency are crucial factors. Therefore, we evaluated the efficiency of our method by measuring the processing time for each X-ray welding image. As shown in Table 4,

Table 4. Parameter Setting

Index	Parameter	Time(s)
1	U-Net	0.4352
2	UNet++	1.5641
3	Attention U-Net	0.5380
4	Proposed	0.4248

our model' processing speed is significantly faster than UNet++and Attention U-Net. Additionally, compared to the U-Net model, our approach maintains comparable inference efficiency, with no notable advantage in speed. But, the simplicity of our model's structure enables hardware space savings, which makes it well-suited for practical industrial applications.

4 Conclusion

This paper introduces a framework for segmenting welding defects in X-ray images based on UNet-weld network. The experiments on a small-scale dataset demonstrate that the proposed method achieves higher detection accuracy and faster processing speed compared to other methods. These findings indicate that the proposed framework is well-suited for practical industrial deployment. However, to further improve the performance of the model, it is essential to gather more annotated datasets. In future research, we aim to extract additional defect parameters, such as defect category, size, and length, to provide more comprehensive information for quality assessment.

Acknowledgements. This work is partially Sponsored by NUPTSF (NY220001).

References

1. Naddaf-Sh, M.M., Naddaf-Sh, S., Zargaradeh, H., et al.: Next-generation of weld quality assessment using deep learning and digital radiography. In: Artificial Intelligence in Manufacturing, AAAI Spring Symposium Series (2020)
2. Hou, W.H., We, Y., Jin, Y., et al.: Deep features based on a DCNN model for classifying imbalanced weld flaw types. Measurement **131**, 482–489 (2018)
3. Jiang, H., Hu, Q., Zhi, Z., et al.: Convolution neural network model with improved pooling strategy and feature selection for weld defect recognition. Weld. World Le Soudage Dans Le Monde **65**(1), 731–744 (2020)
4. Kumaresan, S., Aultrin, K.S.J., Kumar, S.S., et al.: Deep learning-based weld defect classification using VGG16 transfer learning adaptive fine-tuning. Int. J. Interact. Des. Manuf. **17**, 2999–3010 (2023)
5. Yang, D., Cui, Y., Yu, Z., et al.: Deep learning based steel pipe weld defect detection. Appl. Artif. Intell. **35**(15), 1237–1249 (2021)
6. Gong, Y., Luo, J., Shao, H., et al.: A transfer learning object detection model for defects detection in X-ray images of spacecraft composite structures. Compos. Struct. **284**, 115136 (2022)
7. Yang, J., Fu, B., Zeng, J., et al.: YOLO-Xweld: efficiently detecting pipeline welding defects in X-ray images for constrained environments. In: 2022 International Joint Conference on Neural Networks (IJCNN), Padua, Italy, pp. 1–7 (2022)
8. Liu, M., Chen, Y., He, L., et al.: LF-YOLO: a lighter and faster YOLO for weld defect detection of X-ray image. IEEE Sens. J. **23**(7), 7430–7439 (2023)
9. Tokime, R.B., Maldague, X. Automatic defect detection for X-ray inspection: identifying defects with deep convolutional network. In: Conference: Canadian Institute for Non-destructive Evaluation (CINDE), Edmonton, Canada (2019)

10. Chang, Y., Wang, W.: A deep learning-based weld defect classification method using radiographic images with a cylindrical projection. IEEE Trans. Instrum. Meas. **70**, 1–11 (2021)
11. Xu, H., Yan, Z.H., Ji, B.W., et al.: Defect detection in welding radiographic images based on semantic segmentation methods. Measurement **188**, 110569 (2022)
12. Kothari, J.D.: Detecting welding defects in steel plates using machine learning and computer vision algorithms. Int. J. Innov. Res. Comput. Commun. Eng. **7**(9), 3682–3686 (2018)
13. Mery, D., Riffo, V., Zscherpel, U., et al.: GDXray: the database of X-ray images for nondestructive testing. J. Nondestruct. Eval. **34**, 42 (2015)
14. Yang, L., Song, S., Fan, J., et al.: An automatic deep segmentation network for pixel-level welding defect detection. IEEE Trans. Instrum. Meas. **71**, 1–10 (2022)
15. Yang, L., Fan, J., Huo, B., et al.: A nondestructive automatic defect detection method with pixel wise segmentation. Knowl.-Based Syst. **242**, 108338 (2022)
16. Yang, L., Xu, S., Fan, J., et al.: A pixel-level deep segmentation network for automatic defect detection. Expert Syst. Appl. **215**, 119388 (2023)
17. Ronneberger, O., Fischer, P., Brox, T.: U-Net: convolutional networks for biomedical image segmentation. In: Navab, N., Hornegger, J., Wells, W.M., Frangi, A.F. (eds.) MICCAI 2015. LNCS, vol. 9351, pp. 234–241. Springer, Cham (2015). https://doi.org/10.1007/978-3-319-24574-4_28
18. Zhou, Z., Rahman Siddiquee, M.M., Tajbakhsh, N., Liang, J.: UNet++: a nested U-net architecture for medical image segmentation. In: Stoyanov, D., et al. (eds.) DLMIA/ML-CDS -2018. LNCS, vol. 11045, pp. 3–11. Springer, Cham (2018). https://doi.org/10.1007/978-3-030-00889-5_1
19. Oktay, O., Schlemper, J., Folgoc, L.L., et al.: Attention U-Net: learning where to look for the pancreas (2018). https://doi.org/10.48550/arXiv.1804.03999

Wide Activation Fourier Channel Attention Network for Super-Resolution

Xuan Wu, Ming Tan, Liang Chen$^{(\boxtimes)}$, and Yi Wu

Fujian Provincial Key Laboratory of Photonics Technology, Fujian Normal University,
Fuzhou, China
cl_0827@126.com, wuyi@fjnu.edu.cn

Abstract. Attention mechanisms, especially channel attention, have been widely used in a wide range of tasks in computer vision. More recently, researchers have begun to apply channel attention mechanisms to tasks involving single image super-resolution (SISR). However, these mechanisms, borrowed from other computer vision tasks, may not be well-suited for SISR, which primarily focuses on re-covering high-frequency information. Consequently, existing approaches may not adequately reconstruct high-frequency details. To address this limitation, we propose a novel channel attention block, i.e., the Fourier channel attention block (FCA). This block leverages the Fourier transform to extract high-frequency information and subsequently compresses the spatial information, thereby emphasizing the high-frequency components within the image. To further enhance the performance, we propose a wide activation Fourier channel attention super-resolution network (WFCASR) to enhance the residual block by incorporating the wide activation mechanism and FCA. Results in the development of. By integrating the FCA block and the wide activation mechanism into our network, the high-frequency information can be effectively reconstructed and thus the accuracy and effectiveness of SISR can be effectively improved. Experimental results demonstrated that Our FCA channel attention mechanism has better performance.

Keywords: Single image super-resolution · Channel attention · Fourier transform

1 Introduction

SISR [1, 2] has been a major research topic in the field of computer vision, with the aim of recovering high-resolution (HR) images from low-resolution (LR) images. With the development of deep-learning neural network (DNN), Dong et al. [3] propose a deep convolutional neural network for SR, which is the first time using convolutional neural network (CNN) for image reconstruction. Since then, many SISR methods based on DNN have been proposed. Kim et al. first use residual learning in their very deep CNN (VDSR) [3] and deeply-recursive convolutional network for image super-resolution (DRCN) [4], which improve performance by increasing the network depth. After this, many researchers continue to increase the network depth to improve network performance.

© The Author(s), under exclusive license to Springer Nature Singapore Pte Ltd. 2024
G. Zhai et al. (Eds.): IFTC 2023, CCIS 2066, pp. 55–68, 2024.
https://doi.org/10.1007/978-981-97-3623-2_5

Ledig et al. [5] propose a super-resolution residual network (SRResNet) that is deeper than VDSR networks. Lim et al. [6] modify SRResNet by removing redundant batch normalization layers of the residual network (ResNet) [7] and propose a deeper network. Zhang et al. [9] propose a residual dense network (RDN), which adds dense connections into residual blocks. This helps to solve the phenomenon of gradient disappearance caused by the increase of network depth and thus increases network depth.

Although deeper networks improve network performance, network depth cannot be increased without limits. Most CNN-based methods process all information equally internally, making it difficult to effectively utilize the more important high-frequency information in images. This results in the reconstructed SR image lacking sufficiently sharp edges.

Since Squeeze and Excite Network (SENet) is proposed by Hu et al. [10], this type of differential treatment of different features has received significant attention in the field of SR. The "squeeze and excitation block" (SE) in SENet compresses the channel weight of spatial information through pooling. Then adaptively adjusts this weight through learning, which can be said to be the selective use of information from the network. Zhang et al. [12] directly apply the SE mechanism to SR and achieved promising results. Woo et al. [11] propose a convolutional block attention model (CBAM). In addition to average pooling, the "channel attention block" (CA) of CBAM also adds max pooling to obtain more information in the information compression stage. Recently, many SR methods [13–16] also add CA to the model. However, SE and CA are designed for other computer vision tasks, which do not pay enough attention to high-frequency information. Therefore, the SR model using them still cannot obtain images with sharp edges.

Recently, Liang et al. [17] propose an image reconstruction network using Swin Transformer [18], which greatly improved the model performance. Thereafter, many scholars have used Transformer [19] for SR tasks. Many of them used channel attention to improve the performance of transformer models [20, 21]. Channel attention is also applicable to transformer-based SR models.

In this paper, we propose a "Fourier Channel Attention Block" (FCA) to address the issue of other channel attention blocks paying insufficient attention to high-frequency information, let the network focus more on high-frequency information in images. Yu et al. [22] demonstrate that under the same parameters and computational budget, an SR model with wider features before ReLU activation has better performance. This is the "wide activation mechanism".

A summary of our main contributions can be found in the following:

- We propose an FCA block that focuses on high-frequency information. Our FCA has good adaptability and can be easily added to various SR models.
- We improve the residual block using the wide activation mechanism and FCA. We call it the "Wide Activation Fourier channel attention block" (WFCA).
- To validate the effectiveness of our proposed approach, we perform extensive experiments and comparisons with advanced SR methods.
- Our proposed method achieves significant improvements in image reconstruction for SR tasks, demonstrating the potential of leveraging high-frequency information for better SR results.

2 Related Works

In this section, we will describe the squeeze and excitation (SE) block, the channel attention (CA) block, and the residual block with wider activation and linear low-rank convolution (WDSR-B) in detail.

2.1 SE

The SE block, proposed by Hu et al. [10], is a mechanism that selectively emphasizes informative features in a network. It consists of two main operations: squeezing and exciting. In the squeezing operation, the SE block compresses the channel-wise feature maps by global average pooling, reducing the spatial dimensions to 1×1. This operation captures the channel-wise statistics of the feature maps. In the exciting operation, the compressed feature maps are passed through two fully connected layers, followed by a sigmoid activation function. This process generates a channel-wise attention map that scales the original feature maps. By adaptively recalibrating the feature maps, the SE block enables the network to focus on more informative channels and suppress less useful ones. Proceed as follows:

$$M = \sigma(FC_2(\delta(FC_1(P_a(z))))), \tag{1}$$

where FC_1 and FC_2 represent two different fully connected layers. The final generated channel attention map is M and the input for the block is z. σ and δ are the sigmoid function and the relu function respectively. P_a is average pooling.

2.2 CA

The CA block, proposed by Woo et al. [11], is another mechanism that aims to enhance the representation power of CNNs by selectively attending to informative channels. It consists of two operations: average pooling and max pooling. In the pooling stage, the CA block applies average pooling and max pooling operations to the input feature maps separately. This allows the block to capture both the global average and the maximum values of each channel. The pooled representations are then concatenated and passed through a shared fully connected layer, followed by a sigmoid activation function. This generates a channel-wise attention map that scales the original feature maps. Similar to the SE block, the CA block enables the network to selectively attend to informative channels and suppress less useful ones. The process is as follows:

$$M = \sigma(FC_2(\delta(FC_1(P_a(z)))) + FC_2(\delta(FC_1(P_m(z))))), \tag{2}$$

where P_a and P_m represent average pooling and max pooling, respectively.

2.3 WDSR-B

The WDSR-B block, as introduced by Yu et al. [22], is a crucial component designed to enhance the performance of super-resolution (SR) models by leveraging broader features before the activation function. It comprises three main operations: a 1×1 convolution to increase the number of channels, an activation function, and a subsequent 3×3 convolution. In the initial step, the input feature maps pass through a 1×1 convolution layer, which effectively widens the feature maps by increasing the number of channels. This operation is essential for capturing channel-wise dependencies. Following the 1×1 convolution, an activation function is applied to introduce non-linearity, thereby enhancing the model's expressive capabilities. After the activation function, another 1×1 convolution layer is employed to reduce the number of channels. This step helps compress the information and subsequently reduces the computational complexity of subsequent operations. Finally, a 3×3 convolution is applied to the feature maps. This operation extracts spatial information and enhances the representation of local features. By combining channel expansion, activation function application, channel reduction, and spatial convolution, the WDSR-B block aims to improve the performance of SR models by effectively utilizing broader features before the activation function. This approach enables the model to capture more intricate and informative representations, ultimately leading to superior super-resolution results. The entire process is as follows:

$$y = x + Co_{3\times3}(Co_{down}(\delta(Co_{up}(x)))) \tag{3}$$

where x and y are the input and output of WDSR-B, Co_{down}, and Co_{up} are a 1×1 convolution that reduces the number of channels and a 1×1 convolution that expands the number of channels, respectively. $Co_{3\times3}$ is a 3×3 convolution.

3 Method

In our proposed WFCASR (Wide Activation Fourier Channel Attention Network for Super-Resolution) approach, we have improved the performance of the residual block by incorporating the Fourier Channel Attention (FCA) block and wide activation mechanism. The FCA block plays a crucial role in enhancing the recovery of high-frequency information in the super-resolution task. By utilizing Fourier analysis, it focuses on the Fourier domain representation of the input images. This enables the FCA block to effectively analyze and manipulate the frequency components of the image. By selectively enhancing the high-frequency information, the FCA block ensures that important details, such as fine textures, edges, and patterns, are captured and reconstructed accurately in the output image.

Additionally, our approach incorporates a wide activation mechanism, which further enhances the performance of the residual block. The wide activation mechanism allows for a more expressive and powerful representation of the feature. It enables the network to capture and preserve more intricate details during the super-resolution process.

3.1 Network Architecture

Figure 1 illustrates the architecture of our WFCASR (Wide Activation Fourier Channel Attention Network for Super-Resolution) model, which encompasses two primary segments:

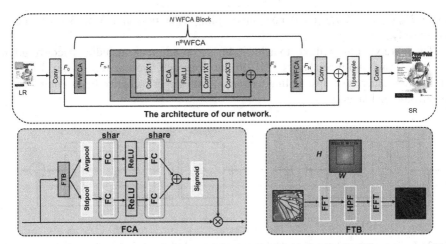

Fig. 1. The overall architecture of our proposed network and the details of each component. The two fully connected layers within the red box in the FCA share parameters.

Feature Extraction Part: The feature extraction module, serving as the initial stage, begins with the LR (Low-Resolution) input, denoted as I^{LR}. Following the principles outlined in prior research, particularly [6, 7], we initiate the process with a 3×3 convolutional layer, which effectively generates shallow features denoted as F_0. These shallow features serve as the foundation for subsequent processing. Additionally, within this part of the model, we incorporate multiple WFCA (Wide activation Fourier Channel Attention) blocks to extract deeper information from the input, further enhancing the feature extraction process.

The comprehensive details and workings of these components will be discussed in more detail in the sections that follow, offering a thorough understanding of our WFCASR model. F_0 is generated through the following process:

$$F_0 = H_{F0}(I^{LR}), \tag{4}$$

F_0 is generated through the application of a 3x3 convolutional layer denoted as $H_{F0}(\cdot)$. Subsequently, the resulting feature map F_0 is fed into the WFCA block to further extract deep features, leading to the following:

$$F_e = F_0 + H_{F1}(H_W^N(H_W^{N-1}(\cdots H_W^1(F_0)\cdots))), \tag{5}$$

where $H_W^N(\cdot)$ stands for the N-th WFCA block, and N is set to 16 in our network. $H_{F1}(\cdot)$ is a 3×3 convolutional layer.

After obtaining the deep features F_e from the WFCA block, they are subsequently input into the image reconstruction part of the WFCASR model. Image Reconstruction Part: Leveraging the deeper features obtained through the WFCA blocks, our model transitions to the image reconstruction module. Here, the objective is to produce the high-resolution counterpart, I^{SR} (Super-Resolution Image).

The key steps in this process can be summarized as follows:

$$I^{SR} = H_{F2}(H_{up}(F_e)), \tag{6}$$

where $H_{up}(\cdot)$ and $H_{F2}(\cdot)$ denote upsampling operation and 3×3 convolution respectively.

There are various methods to achieve image upsampling, including deconvolution layers [23] and sub-pixel layers [24]. In our approach, we opt for sub-pixel layers, which offer a learnable upsampling technique with larger receptive fields compared to deconvolutional layers.

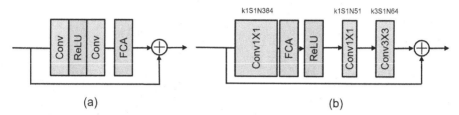

Fig. 2. (a) is a commonly used method to improve residual blocks using channel attention and (b) is our wide activation Fourier channel attention block.

3.2 Wide Activation Fourier Channel Attention Block (WFCA)

This notes Fig. 2(b) illustrates the structure of the WFCA (Wide Activation Fourier Channel Attention) model. In this model, we utilize the notation K1S1N384, where K represents the convolution kernel size, S signifies the step size, and N denotes the number of convolution kernels. This notation succinctly describes a convolution layer with a 1 $\times$ 1 kernel size, a step size of 1, and 384 convolution kernels.

To enhance the performance of the WDSR-B block, we have introduced a novel FCA (Fourier Channel Attention) block that places a heightened focus on high-frequency details. Unlike conventional approaches that apply channel attention after the final convolutional layer, our WFCA model incorporates channel attention immediately following the first convolutional layer. This design choice aligns with the fact that WDSR-B expands the number of channels right after the initial convolutional layer, enabling our WFCA model to capture a more comprehensive range of channel-dependent information.

Let F_{N-1} and F_N represent the input and output of the N-th WFCA block, respectively, where FCA signifies the Fourier Channel Attention block itself. The formulation for F_N r is as follows:

$$F_N = F_{N-1} + Co_{3\times3}(Co_{1\times1a}(\delta(FCA(Co_{1\times1b}(F_{N-1}))))), \tag{7}$$

where $Co_{1\times1a}(\cdot)$ and $Co_{1\times1b}(\cdot)$ represent two different 1×1 convolutional layers, $Co_{3\times3}(\cdot)$ is a 3×3 convolutional layer.

The FCA block is a component that applies channel attention to the input feature map F_{N-1} after the first convolutional layer. This channel attention mechanism helps to enhance the high-frequency details in the feature map. After applying channel attention, the feature map goes through an activation function and two additional convolutional layers. These layers further process the feature map and extract more meaningful information. Finally, the output of the WFCA block is added to the input feature map F_{N-1} to obtain the output feature map F_N.

3.3 Fourier Channel Attention Block (FCA)

The Fourier Channel Attention (FCA) block is a component that aims to enhance the representation of high-frequency information in a feature map. Figure 1 shows how the FCA Block is structured.

First, the FCA block includes a Fourier Transform Block (FTB) that extracts high-frequency information from the input feature map. The FTB consists of three sequential operations: a Fourier transform, a high-pass filter, and an inverse Fourier transform. The high-pass filter is crafted to permit the passage of solely high-frequency elements, effectively eliminating low-frequency components. As shown in Fig. 1, the FTB uses a box filter with edge length $Min(H, W)//\alpha$, α is a learnable parameter, allowing the network to adaptively adjust it for optimal performance. The initial value of α is set to 5. Next, the extracted high-frequency information is used in the squeeze operation to aggregate information. In this stage, the spatial information is compressed using both standard deviation pooling and average pooling. The goal of the squeeze stage is to obtain channel statistics that represent the richness of high-frequency information in each channel. Finally, the sigmoid function is applied to generate channel weights. These weights indicate the richness of high-frequency information within each channel. It is noteworthy to mention that during the squeeze stage, standard deviation pooling is used instead of max pooling. This choice is made to obtain more accurate channel statistics without introducing unnecessary interference that may be caused by max pooling.

Overall, the FCA block aims to enhance the representation of high-frequency details in the input feature map by extracting and aggregating high-frequency information using Fourier transform, high-pass filtering, and channel weight generation through squeeze operations. The process is as follows:

$$W = \sigma(FC(P_a(FT(F_i))) + FC(P_s(FT(F_i)))), \tag{8}$$

where W is the channel weight, P_a and P_s are average pooling and standard deviation pooling, respectively. F_u and F_i represent the output and input of FCA. FC represents the learning part consisting of two fully connected layers and relu. FT is FTB (Fourier Transform Block). The output of the FCA block is as follows:

$$F_u = F_i \times W. \tag{9}$$

4 Experiments

4.1 Datasets

Our experiments used the DIV2K [33] dataset for training. This dataset consists of 800 RGB HR training images together with their corresponding LR training images for three downscaling factors (x2, x3 and x4). Four commonly used datasets were used for evaluation purposes: Set5 [34], Set14 [35], BSD100 [36], and Urban100 [37]. Set5, Set14 and BSD100 consist of natural images, while Urban100 contains images focusing on building structures with complex features. We computed two metrics, the peak signal-to-noise ratio (PSNR) and the structural similarity index (SSIM), to assess the performance of our super-resolution (SR) model. After converting the images to YCbCr channels, these metrics were calculated on the Y channel.

4.2 Implementation Details

During the training process, we employ various settings to enhance the performance of our model. Firstly, for each batch input, we randomly crop 16 48 × 48 LR image patches. Additionally, to further enhance the data set, we apply random horizontal flipping and 90-degree rotation.

To optimize the training process, we set the initial learning rate to 2×10^{-4} and decrease it by half every 200 epochs. This learning rate schedule helps to converge the model gradually. We utilize the ADAM optimizer with $\beta 1 = 0.9$, $\beta 2 = 0.999$, and $\varepsilon = 10^{-8}$. These values are commonly used and have been proven effective in optimizing deep learning models. To balance the trade-off between sharpness and accuracy, we choose to use the L1 loss function instead of the L2 loss. The L1 loss tends to produce sharper images compared to the L2 loss. In terms of implementation details, in the WFCASR model, we set the number of WFCA modules to 16. The other convolutional layers in the network are set to a size of 3 × 3, except for the convolutional layers within the WFCA modules. Specifically, we set the number of convolution kernels to 384, 51, and 64 for the two 1 × 1 convolutional layers and one 3 × 3 convolutional layer in the WFCA modules, respectively. This configuration helps to capture and enhance the important features in the image. Lastly, following the approach of most previous methods, we utilize the sub-pixel layers to upscale the last coarse features to fine features. This technique is frequently employed in super-resolution tasks to enhance the resolution of the output images. The suggested network was implemented using the PyTorch 1.10 framework and underwent training on an NVIDIA 2060 Super GPU.

4.3 Model Analysis

Comparison with Other Channel Attention Blocks. To ensure a fair comparison, we created four WDSR networks using WDSR-B, each comprised of 16 WDSR-B blocks. We introduced an attention block after the final convolutional layer of WDSR-B. For x2 super-resolution (SR), our primary objective was to minimize the impact of the number of convolution kernels on the channel attention modules. These networks maintain identical numbers of filters and WDSR-B blocks.

As illustrated in Table 1, the performance of the CA block was subpar in the shallow network we devised, particularly on Urban100, a dataset known for its intricate edge details, where we observed a substantial drop in performance. Given that the main distinction between CA and SE is the additional max-pooling introduced by CA, we hypothesize that the information introduced by max-pooling could interfere with The super-resolution model learning process. In the last column of Table 1, we excluded FTB from FCA. In contrast to CA, this attention module replaces max pooling with standard deviation pooling. Empirical results further substantiate our viewpoint regarding the adverse effect of max pooling in CA on super-resolution tasks. In contrast, SE displayed commendable performance in SR tasks, aligning with previous methods that employed SE to enhance SR networks [25, 26]. Our FCA demonstrated superior performance in the SR task. This is attributed to FCA incorporating FTB before pooling, allowing our FTB to extract high-frequency information from the image and subsequently utilize average pooling and standard deviation pooling to compress spatial information. In comparison to maximum pooling, standard deviation pooling can more accurately extract high-frequency information from the image. In summary, our FCA enhances the network and effectively harnesses high-frequency information.

In Fig. 3, we visualize the input of the final attention block from the network in Table 1 and extract the corresponding channel weights. We opted for a subset of these channels. In comparison to the standard SE, our FCA assigns higher weights to channels with sharp image contours and lower weights to channels with blurred image contours. This discrepancy arises because FCA extracts high-frequency information prior to compressing spatial information, enabling the channel statistics obtained after pooling to represent the richness of high-frequency information more accurately within the channels. CA assigns a weight close to 1 (>0.99) to 76.56% of the channels and a weight close to 0 (0.01<) to 9.38% of the channels. CA falls short in effectively selecting channel information, indicating its inability to provide appropriate channel weights to the network. This excessive weight distribution may even hinder the network's information processing capabilities and potentially lead to information loss (assigning weights of zero to certain channels). In contrast, our FCA allocates weights more judiciously, empowering the network to efficiently leverage high-frequency information.

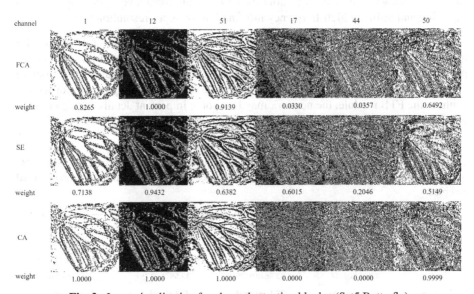

Fig. 3. Input visualization for channel attention blocks. (Set5 Butterfly)

Ablation Experiments. To compare the effects of adding our WFCA block at different positions in the WDSR-B network, we conducted two experiments. In the first experiment, we added our WFCA block after the first convolutional layer of WDSR-B, resulting in a network called WFCASR. In the second experiment, we added the FCA block after the last convolutional layer of WDSR-B, resulting in a network called WDSR-E. In both experiments, we used the same configuration for the FCA block, which includes the FTB module before pooling and the average pooling and standard deviation

Table 1. The performance of ×2 SR by our proposed FCA and the existing method. w/o FTB means remove FTB from FCA, other settings are the same as WDSR+FCA. The best and second-best performances are shown in red and blue.

Dataset	WDSR PSNR/SSIM	WDSR+SE PSNR/SSIM	WDSR+CA PSNR/SSIM	WDSR+FCA PSNR/SSIM	w/o FTB PSNR/SSIM
Set5	38.00/0.9607	38.01/0.9609	38.01/0.9608	38.04/0.9609	38.00/0.9608
Set14	33.54/0.9174	33.52/0.9174	33.49/0.9163	33.56/0.9175	33.52/0.9171
BSD100	32.16/0.8890	32.17/0.8894	32.15/0.8896	32.18/0.8894	32.16/0.8894
Urban100	32.45/0.9303	32.45/0.9308	32.20/0.9292	32.48/0.9321	32.46/0.9313

pooling operations. The experimental results showed that both WFCASR and WDSR-E achieved improved performance compared to the baseline WDSR-B network. However, WFCASR outperformed WDSR-E in terms of PSNR and SSIM on all datasets. This indicates that adding our WFCA block after the first convolutional layer is more effective in capturing and utilizing high-frequency information for super-resolution tasks.

We assess the effectiveness of FTB by removing FTB in FCA. The role of the FTB module in the FCA block is to extract the high frequency information from the image prior to the pooling process. This helps to preserve important details during the pooling process and allows the network to make better use of the high-frequency information. Without the FTB module, the network may lose some important details during pooling, which can result in a degradation of performance (Table 2).

Table 2. ×2 SR performance for ablation experiment. w/o FTB means remove FTB from FCA, other settings are the same as WFCA. The best and second-best performances are shown in red and blue.

Dataset	WDSR PSNR/SSIM	WDSR-E PSNR/SSIM	w/o FTB PSNR/SSIM	WFCASR PSNR/SSIM
Set5	38.00/0.9607	38.04/0.9609	38.02/0.9608	38.06/0.9611
Set14	33.54/0.9174	33.56/0.9175	33.55/0.9175	33.58/0.9176
BSD100	32.16/0.8890	32.18/0.8894	32.16/0.8894	32.19/0.8897
Urban100	32.45/0.9303	32.48/0.9321	32.49/0.9322	32.50/0.9324

Table 3. Comparison of our WFCASR with other SR models. The best and second-best performances are shown in red and blue.

Scale	Method	Params	Set5 PSNR / SSIM	Set14 PSNR / SSIM	BSD100 PSNR / SSIM	Urban100 PSNR / SSIM
x2	MemNet	677K	37.78/0.9597	33.23/0.9142	32.08/0.8978	31.31/0.9195
	SRMDNF	1513K	37.79/0.9600	33.32/0.9150	32.05/0.8980	31.33/0.9200
	CARN	1592K	37.76/0.9590	33.52/0.9166	32.09/0.8978	31.92/0.9256
	SRRAM	942K	37.82/0.9592	33.48/0.9171	32.12/0.8983	32.05/0.9264
	IMDN	694K	38.00/0.9605	33.63/0.9177	32.19/0.8996	32.17/0.9283
	RFDN-L	626K	38.08/0.9606	33.67/0.9190	32.18/0.8996	32.24/0.9290
	A²F-L	1363K	38.09/0.9607	33.78/0.9192	32.23/0.9002	32.46/0.9313
	WFCASR	1299K	38.06/0.9611	33.58/0.9176	32.19/0.8897	32.50/0.9324
x3	MemNet	677K	34.09/0.9248	30.00/0.8350	28.96/0.8001	27.56/0.8376
	SRMDNF	1530K	34.30/0.9256	30.32/0.8417	29.07/0.8039	28.12/0.8507
	CARN	1592K	34.29/0.9255	30.29/0.8407	29.06/0.8034	28.06/0.8493
	SRRAM	1127K	34.30/0.9256	30.32/0.8417	29.07/0.8039	28.12/0.8507
	IMDN	703K	34.36/0.9270	30.32/0.8407	29.09/0.8050	28.17/0.8519
	RFDN-L	633K	34.47/0.9280	30.35/0.8421	29.11/0.8053	28.32/0.8547
	A²F-L	1367K	34.54/0.9283	30.41/0.8436	29.14/0.8062	28.42/0.8580
	WFCASR	1304K	34.55/0.9286	30.25/0.8430	29.15/0.8063	28.45/0.8589
x4	MemNet	677K	31.74/0.8893	28.26/0.7723	27.40/0.7281	25.50/0.7630
	SRMDNF	1555K	32.13/0.8932	28.54/0.7800	27.56/0.7350	26.05/0.7834
	CARN	1592K	32.13/0.8937	28.60/0.7806	27.58/0.7349	26.07/0.7837
	SRRAM	1090K	32.13/0.8932	28.54/0.7800	27.56/0.7350	26.05/0.7834
	IMDN	715K	32.21/0.8948	28.58/0.7811	27.56/0.7353	26.04/0.7838
	RFDN-L	643K	32.28/0.8957	28.61/0.7818	27.58/0.7363	26.20/0.7883
	A²F-L	1374K	32.32/0.8964	28.67/0.7839	27.62/0.7379	26.32/0.7931
	WFCASR	1310K	32.33/0.8971	28.53/0.7836	27.65/0.7382	26.29/0.7909

4.4 Comparison with Other Methods

We compared the WFCASR method with several classical super-resolution methods, including SRMDNF [27], IMDN [28], MemNet [29], RFDN-L [25], A^2F-L [30], CARN [31], and SRRAM [32]. In comparison to these existing methods, we wanted to evaluate the effectiveness of our WFCASR method.

Table 3 shows the performance comparison results for different upscaling factors (x2, x3, and x4). It is observed that our WFCASR method may not achieve outstanding performance in x2 super-resolution compared to A^2F-L. This could be attributed to the fact that we trained our x2SR model directly without utilizing pre-training parameters. However, our WFCASR method performs better in x3 and x4 super-resolution tasks while having fewer parameters than A^2F-L. These results suggest that our WFCASR method has the potential to excel in higher upscaling factors, such as x3 and x4, and can achieve competitive performance while maintaining a relatively compact model size.

In our visualization comparison experiments, we evaluated the performance of several models, including CARN [31], SRRAM [32], RFDN-L [25], A^2F-L [30], and IMDN

[28]. The results from these experiments revealed that our WFCASR model exhibited superior edge recovery capabilities compared to the other models. This highlights the effectiveness of our WFCA (Weighted Feature Channel Attention) mechanism in enabling the network to leverage high-frequency information more efficiently, ultimately enhancing the overall model performance (Figs. 4 and 5).

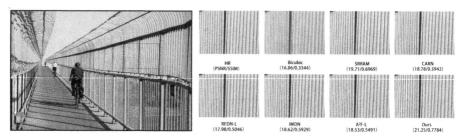

Fig. 4. Comparison of × 4 SR results on Urban100 (img_024).

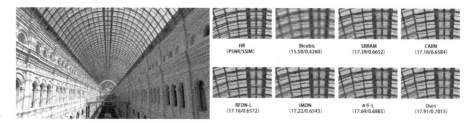

Fig. 5. Comparison of × 4 SR results on Urban100 (img_008).

5   Conclusion

We introduce a novel FCA (Fourier Channel Attention) block, which is designed to extract high-frequency information through Fourier transform. This block subsequently employs pooling to compress spatial information, prioritizing the high-frequency components within the image. Besides, to further enhance the effectiveness of the residual block, we integrate both a wide activation mechanism and an FCA block. This specialized block forms the foundation of our WFCASR (Wide Feature Channel Attention Super-Resolution) network.

Experimental results show this proposed enhanced attention mechanism to be effective. Consequently, the WFCASR model exhibits improved SR performance. We are committed to integrating our FCA technique into other SR models in our future work.

References

1. Freeman, W.T., Pasztor, E.C., Carmichael, O.T.: Learning low-level vision. Int. J. Comput. Vis. **40**, 25–47 (2000)
2. Clerk Maxwell, J.: A Treatise on Electricity and Magnetism, 3rd edn., vol. 2, pp. 68–73. Clarendon, Oxford (1892)
3. Dong, C., Loy, C.C., He, K., Tang, X.: Learning a deep convolutional network for image super-resolution. In: Fleet, D., Pajdla, T., Schiele, B., Tuytelaars, T. (eds.) ECCV 2014. LNCS, Part IV, vol. 8692, pp. 184–199. Springer, Cham (2014). https://doi.org/10.1007/978-3-319-10593-2_13
4. Kim, J., Lee, J.K., Lee, K.M.: Accurate image super-resolution using very deep convolutional networks. In: CVPR 2016, pp. 1646–1654 (2016)
5. Kim, J., Lee, J.K., Lee, K.M.: Deeply-recursive convolutional network for image super-resolution. In: Proceedings of the IEEE Conference on Computer Vision and Pattern Recognition, pp. 1637–1645 (2016)
6. Ledig, C., et al.: Photo-realistic single image super-resolution using a generative adversarial network. In: CVPR 2017, pp. 4681–4690 (2017)
7. Lim, B., Son, S., Kim, H., Nah, S., Mu Lee, K.: Enhanced deep residual networks for single image super-resolution. In: CVPR 2017 Workshops, pp. 136–144 (2017)
8. He, K., Zhang, X., Ren, S., Sun, J.: Deep residual learning for image recognition. In: CVPR 2016, pp. 770–778 (2016)
9. Zhang, Y., Tian, Y., Kong, Y., Zhong, B., Fu, Y.: Residual dense network for image super-resolution. In: CVPR 2018, pp. 2472–2481 (2018)
10. Hu, J., Shen, L., Sun, G.: Squeeze-and-excitation networks. In: Proceedings of the CVPR 2018, pp. 7132–7141 (2018)
11. Woo, S., Park, J., Lee, J.Y., Kweon, I.S.: CBAM: convolutional block attention module. In: Ferrari, V., Hebert, M., Sminchisescu, C., Weiss, Y. (eds.) ECCV 2018. LNCS, vol. 11211, pp. 3–19. Springer, Cham (2018). https://doi.org/10.1007/978-3-030-01234-2_1
12. Zhang, Y., Li, K., Li, K., Wang, L., Zhong, B., Fu, Y.: Image super-resolution using very deep residual channel attention networks. In: Ferrari, V., Hebert, M., Sminchisescu, C., Weiss, Y. (eds.) ECCV 2018. LNCS, vol. 11211, pp. 294–310. Springer, Cham (2018). https://doi.org/10.1007/978-3-030-01234-2_18
13. Li, Y., et al.: Single-image super-resolution for remote sensing images using a deep generative adversarial network with local and global attention mechanisms. IEEE Trans. Geosci. Remote Sens. **60**, 1–24 (2021)
14. Pan, B., Qu, Q., Xu, X., Shi, Z.: Structure–color preserving network for hyperspectral image super-resolution. IEEE Trans. Geosci. Remote Sens. **60**, 1–12 (2021)
15. Yang, Y., Wang, X., Gao, X., Hui, Z.: Lightweight image super-resolution with local attention enhancement. In: Peng, Y., et al. (eds.) PRCV 2020. LNCS, Part I, vol. 12305, pp. 219–231. Springer, Cham (2020). https://doi.org/10.1007/978-3-030-60633-6_18
16. Xin, J., Jiang, X., Wang, N., Li, J., Gao, X.: Image super-resolution via deep feature recalibration network. In: Peng, Y., et al. (eds.) PRCV 2020. LNCS, Part I, vol. 12305, pp. 256–267. Springer, Cham (2020). https://doi.org/10.1007/978-3-030-60633-6_21
17. Liang, J., Cao, J., Sun, G., Zhang, K., Van Gool, L., Timofte, R.: SwinIR: image restoration using SWIN transformer. In: CVPR 2021, pp. 1833–1844 (2021)
18. Liu, Z., et al.: Swin transformer: hierarchical vision transformer using shifted windows. In: CVPR 2021, pp. 10012–10022 (2021)
19. Vaswani, A., et al.: Attention is all you need. In: Advances in Neural Information Processing Systems, 30 (2017)

20. Chen, X., Wang, X., Zhou, J., Qiao, Y., Dong, C.: Activating more pixels in image super-resolution transformer. In: CVPR2023, pp. 22367–22377 (2023)
21. Wang, H., Chen, X., Ni, B., Liu, Y., Liu, J.: Omni aggregation networks for lightweight image super-resolution. In: CVPR 2023, pp. 22378–22387 (2023)
22. Yu, J., et al.: Wide activation for efficient and accurate image super-resolution. arXiv preprint arXiv:1808.08718 (2018)
23. Dong, C., Loy, C.C., Tang, X.: Accelerating the super-resolution convolutional neural network. In: Leibe, B., Matas, J., Sebe, N., Welling, M. (eds.) ECCV 2016. LNCS, Part II, vol. 9906, pp. 391–407. Springer, Cham (2016). https://doi.org/10.1007/978-3-319-46475-6_25
24. Shi, W., et al.: Real-time single image and video super-resolution using an efficient sub-pixel convolutional neural network. In: CVPR 2016, pp. 1874–1883 (2016)
25. Liu, J., Tang, J., Wu, G.: Residual feature distillation network for lightweight image super-resolution. In: Bartoli, A., Fusiello, A. (eds.) ECCV 2020. LNCS, vol. 12537, Part III, pp. 41–55. Springer, Cham (2020). https://doi.org/10.1007/978-3-030-67070-2_2
26. Hu, Y., Li, J., Huang, Y., Gao, X.: Channel-wise and spatial feature modulation network for single image super-resolution. IEEE Trans. Circuits Syst. Video Technol. **30**(11), 3911–3927 (2019)
27. Zhang, K., Zuo, W., Zhang, L.: Learning a single convolutional super-resolution network for multiple degradations. In: CVPR 2018, pp. 3262–3271 (2018)
28. Hui, Z., Gao, X., Yang, Y., Wang, X.: Lightweight image super-resolution with information multi-distillation network. In: ACM MM, pp. 2024–2032 (2019)
29. Tai, Y., Yang, J., Liu, X., Xu, C.: MemNet: a persistent memory network for image restoration. In: CVPR 2017, pp. 4539–4547 (2017)
30. Wang, X., et al.: Lightweight single-image super-resolution network with attentive auxiliary feature learning. In: Proceedings of the Asian conference on computer vision (2020)
31. Ahn, N., Kang, B., Sohn, K.A.: Fast, accurate, and lightweight super-resolution with cascading residual network. In: Ferrari, V., Hebert, M., Sminchisescu, C., Weiss, Y. (eds.) ECCV 2018. LNCS, vol. 11214, pp. 256–272. Springer, Cham (2018). https://doi.org/10.1007/978-3-030-01249-6_16
32. Kim, J.H., Choi, J.H., Cheon, M., Lee, J.S.: Ram: residual attention module for single image super-resolution, vol. 2, no. 1, 2. arXiv preprint arXiv:1811.12043 (2018)
33. Timofte, R., et al.: NTIRE 2017 challenge on single image super-resolution: methods and results. In: CVPR Workshops 2017, pp. 1110–1121 (2017)
34. Bevilacqua, M., Roumy, A., Guillemot, C., Alberi-Morel, M.: Low-complexity single-image super-resolution based on nonnegative neighbor embedding. In: BMVC, pp. 1–10. BMVA Press (2012)
35. Zeyde, R., Elad, M., Protter, M.: On single image scale-up using sparse-representations. In: Boissonnat, J.D., et al. (eds.) Curves and Surfaces. Curves and Surfaces 2010. LNCS, vol. 6920, pp. 711–730. Springer, Heidelberg (2012). https://doi.org/10.1007/978-3-642-27413-8_47
36. Martin, D.R., Fowlkes, C.C., Tal, D., Malik, J.: A database of human segmented natural images and its application to evaluating segmentation algorithms and measuring ecological statistics. In: ICCV 2001, pp. 416–425 (2001)
37. Huang, J., Singh, A., Ahuja, N.: Single image super-resolution from transformed self-exemplars. In: CVPR 2015, pp. 5197–5206. IEEE Computer Society (2015)

LightNet+: Boosted Light-Weighted Network for Smoke Semantic Segmentation

Kang Li[1], Chunmei Wang[2], Chunli Meng[2], and Feiniu Yuan[2(✉)]

[1] Mathematics and Science College, Shanghai Normal University, Shanghai 200234, China
[2] College of Information, Mechanical and Electrical Engineering, Shanghai Normal University, Shanghai 201418, China
yfn@ustc.edu

Abstract. Smoke is a crucial indicator of early fires and gas leaks. By segmentation of smoke in the image, the detailed information such as smoke direction of spread, and source location can be obtained. Considering the popularity of video surveillance systems, smoke segmentation is of great significance. This paper uses an efficient boosted light-weighted network for smoke semantic segmentation with only 0.53M network parameters. Firstly, we propose a novel Smoke Feature Extractor (SFE) to improve the capability of smoke feature representation in encoders. The SFE achieves scale invariance by repeatedly stacking Multiscale Foreground Enhancement Module (MSFEM) at different coding stages. The MSFEM increases the field of view of features by down-sampling the feature maps, and fusing information from different scale spaces into weights to enhance smoke foreground information. Secondly, we propose a novel Attention-guided Coupled Feature Fusion Module (ACFFM) that introduces Self-Refinement Coefficients (SRCs) generated from cross-layer fusion to weight the original layer images. This two-stage fusion approach effectively utilizes information from different scales to alleviate the impact of scale changes and performs hierarchical decoding. ACFFM serves as a step-by-step recovery model that guides cross-level feature mapping. It retains the original feature size to capture local information, while effectively preventing small objects from being ignored. Finally, we propose a Smoke Feature Decoder (SFD) and utilize a Global Coefficient Path to further aggregate feature expression capabilities. The smoke feature decoder fuses the outputs from different levels of ACFFM and weights them with deep global semantic attention coefficients. Experimental results on synthetic and forest smoke datasets show the effectiveness and superiority of our proposed method.

Keywords: Smoke segmentation · cross-level fusion · lightweight network · foreground enhancement

1 Introduction

Disaster management is a crucial field of study that has received significant attention from scholars in recent years. Because it has a direct bearing on human well-being and life-saving measures [1, 2]. Such as floods and fires pose particular challenges.

G. Zhai et al. (Eds.): IFTC 2023, CCIS 2066, pp. 69–84, 2024.
https://doi.org/10.1007/978-981-97-3623-2_6

Because they require effective implementation of monitoring and early warning systems to enable timely response measures [3]. In these types of disasters, the threat of fire to human life and property is enormous. Therefore, it is essential to achieve accurate early fire detection to minimize the potential for humans, the environment and property damage [4]. Detecting smoke as the primary indicator of a fire is an effective means of averting the damage that can result from a fire [5]. Preventing damage caused by fires has led to the development of fire and smoke detection methods based on traditional and visual sensors [6, 7]. Among these methods, visual-based smoke detection systems have received a great deal of attention from researchers.

In contrast to traditional smoke detection methods, the deep learning-based approach uses learned features to identify and segment smoke. These methods are optimized with convolution, pooling and a fully connected layer for learning visual concepts. Such as W-Net [5] and [8], These employ different models for smoke detection and segmentation, unfortunately, these network models occupy a large space and have high computational complexity. Therefore, their application in real-time IoT scenarios is limited [4].

To solve these problems effectively, we propose a new research method for smoke detection and segmentation using efficient Convolutional Neural Networks (CNNs). And this method is also effective in real-world IoT environments. Specifically, we propose a boosted light-weighted networks for smoke semantic segmentation, termed the network LightNet+. In this paper, we focus on the semantic segmentation of small, semi-transparent, or invisible smoke, and the recognition of haze and clouds. The semi-transparency of smoke is a major challenge in the segmentation task. Because it is often confused with the sky, the ground and other backgrounds, which greatly reduces the accuracy of smoke segmentation. The modeling of smoke foreground is particularly important. Thus, we propose a Multi-scale Foreground Enhancement Module (MSFEM), structured in a simple way into an encoder, to capture the nuanced features to represent smaller or translucent smoke. In addition, we introduce an Attention-guided Coupled Feature Fusion Module (ACFFM). Distinguishing smoke from clouds is a challenge due to their strikingly similar visual appearance. We extract the inter-channel interdependence information by Self-Refinement Coefficients (SRCs). Finally, we use a Global Coefficient Path (GCP) to generate an attention coefficient map containing extensive global and contextual information, and then fuse with the output of the ACFFM at different stages of the stepped cascade to obtain the final segmentation maps. Numerous experimental results consistently confirm that LightNet+ exhibits superior performance in dealing with both synthetic and real smoke images. The primary innovations and contributions of our research method can be summarized as follows:

- We propose a novel Smoke Feature Extractor (SFE) to improve the capability of smoke feature representation in encoder. The MSFEM increases the field of view of features by down-sampling the feature maps and fuses information from different scale spaces into weights to enhance smoke foreground information. To achieve scale invariance, MSFEM iteratively stacks at various encoding stages of SFE.
- We propose an ACFFM. The ACFFM introduces SRCs generated by cross-layer fusion to weight the original layer images. This secondary fusion approach utilizes information from different scales to alleviate scale changes and performs hierarchical decoding. ACFFM is a step-by-step restoration model that guides feature maps across

layers. It not only retains the original feature size to obtain local context, but also avoids small objects being ignored.

- We propose a Smoke Feature Decoder (SFD), and utilize a GCP to further aggregate feature expression ability. The SFD fuses the outputs from different levels of ACFFM, and weights them with deep global semantic attention coefficients.

2 Related Works

2.1 Traditional Smoke Detection

In the past research, Nguyen [9] uses the diffusion characteristics of smoke, approximate median background subtraction is used to detect the moving area in the video frame. Dimitropoulos et al. [10] introduced high order linear dynamic system descriptor to analyze dynamic texture, and proposed a method combining multidimensional dynamic texture analysis based on particle swarm optimization and space-time modeling of smoke. Zhao [11] used Kalman filter to update the video background and eliminate the interference of static smoke objects (such as clouds), and proposed a candidate smoke region segmentation method based on rough set theory. Zhang et al. [12] proposed a smoke image segmentation algorithm by combining rough sets and region growth methods. Tung [13] adopted four-stage smoke detection techniques including the approximate median method, fuzzy c-means, parameter extraction, and classification via support vector machines. Most of these methods are based on diffusion and color low-level features for smoke recognition and detection.

In addition, Filonenko et al. [14] employed shape and color features, etc., and adopted CUDA for accelerated calculation. Yuan [15] proposed to combine the cumulative motion model of integral images with chroma detection to eliminate the interference of artificial light sources and smokeless moving objects. Tian et al. [16] proposed dual dictionaries to address the sparse representation issue of smoke and background components, and introduced a method based on the concept of image matting to separate the actual smoke from background elements within smoke detection results. The primary disadvantage of these smoke detection techniques is their restricted accuracy in identifying smoke that is either small in size or located at a considerable distance.

In order to solve the above problems, some researchers proposed several intelligent smoke detection methods. Yuan et al. [17] proposed a dual-threshold AdaBoost algorithm combined with staircase search technique was proposed to classify smoke features. Smoke is also considered to be a kind of optical flow. Appana et al. [18] detected smoke through the spatial-temporal features extracted from optical smoke flow patterns and spatial-temporal energy analysis. In addition, Alamgir et al. [19] combined the local binary patterns with the cooccurrence of texture features in color space to characterize various manifestations of smoke and extract smoke features.

2.2 Deep Learning-Based Smoke Segmentation

In recent years, deep learning-based technologies have become the standard in the fire or smoke detection and segmentation. For example: Yuan et al. [20] and Frizzi et al. [21] introduced different smoke segmentation algorithms based on VGG16 [22]. Wang et al. [23] proposed an innovative fire and smoke recognition method. This method optimizes the deficiencies of the DeepLabV3+ [24] network in smoke segmentation. Kundu et al. [25] proposed a novel double-layer framework that combines smoke generation and transformer networks to enhance the dataset. Cao et al. [26] proposed a feature foreground module to facilitate the learning of smoke temporal representation. Tao and colleagues [27] proposed a pixel-level supervision neural network aimed at learning discriminative feature representations for the detection of forest smoke. Yuan et al. [28] effectively enhanced the accuracy of smoke segmentation by utilizing tri-directional convolutions technology and the ratio of smoke to non-smoke pixels. Xia et al. [29] proposed a texture-aware network that captures changes in transparency within smoke, allowing for a precise pixel-wise estimation of smoke density.

Nevertheless, most of the smoke segmentation techniques mentioned above rely on powerful and complex backbone networks, such as VGG16 [22] and ResNet [30] et al. While these networks have achieved outstanding results in the field of smoke detection, they have also brought a significant increase in computational complexity and a substantial rise in the number of parameters. As a result, such large models are not suitable for deployment in resource-limited environments or on mobile devices. When UAVs are used as lightweight mobile platforms, such constraints can be problematic [31]. To address this issue, Hossain et al. [32] proposed a novel up-sample method based on transposed convolution, which makes segmentation CNNs much lighter. Xia et al. [33] proposed a lightweight, high-precision and rapid outdoor smoke detection algorithm based on Yolo-attention. Yuan et al. [34] successfully carried out similar work, proposing a lightweight encoder-decoder network for smoke segmentation based on the ResNet-Style architecture, which has achieved good results. Next, our focus will be on further innovation and optimization of the network [34] to achieve even better performance.

3   Methodology

In order to more effective timely detection of smoke. We have made a groundbreaking improvement to [34], and Fig. 1 shows the overall network structure after the improvement. The new encoder is constructed bySmoke Feature Extractor (SFE). As shown in Fig. 2 (a), we stack several Multi-scale Foreground Enhancement Module (MSFEM) in different stages of our SFE. The decoder network mainly consists of two key modules: an Attention-guided Coupled Feature Fusion Module (ACFFM) with a Self-Refinement Coefficients (SRCs) and a Smoke Feature Decoder (SFD). Among them, the Global Coefficient Path (GCP) in SFD is exactly the same as that in [34]. Finally, we add three segmentation heads for training.

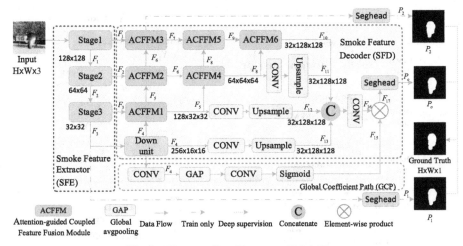

Fig. 1. The overall architecture of LightNet+.

3.1 Encoding Stages

3.1.1 Multi-scale Foreground Enhancement Module

As shown in Fig. 2 (a), In the transition between adjacent stages, we use the same Down unit as the ENet [35] network. To extract multi-scale features effectively, we designed a Multi-scale Foreground Enhancement Module (MSFEM), which is depicted in Fig. 2 (b). This module is repeatedly applied at different encoder stages. "s" denotes the scale factor.

Our MSFEM is a light weighted and efficient feature extraction module. Although, our MSFEM follows the overall style of CSSAM [34], its core unit has undergone a revolutionary change. To effectively decrease the number of parameters, accelerate computation speed, enhance the model's ability to capture smoke foreground information, and obtain rich multi-scale information. We implemented a dual-path structure after channel split which first utilizes max-pooling and adaptive pooling methods, followed by 3×3 group convolution (G-Conv) [36].

Secondly, X_2 undergoes adaptive pooling, group convolution, and upsample. At the same time, it performs element-wise addition with the spatial features of the original scale space potential to obtain output X_2'. Meanwhile, the scale space coefficients X_2'' are generated through sigmoid function to guide the feature extraction of smoke main response. The formal formula is as follows:

$$X_2' = Up(F_{G-Conv}(Down(X_2))) \oplus X_2 \tag{1}$$

$$X_2'' = \sigma(X_2') \tag{2}$$

where $Down$, $\oplus$, F_{G-Conv}, Up and σ represent the adaptive pooling, element-wise sum, 3×3 group convolution, bilinear interpolation and sigmoid function.

Thirdly, X_1 undergoes 3×3 max-pooling to enhance the main response of smoke features (i.e., the foreground information), and is then concatenated with X_2' through

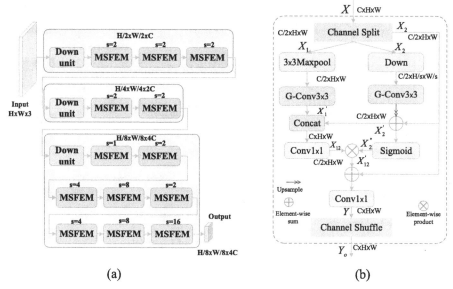

Fig. 2. (a) Smoke feature extractor (SFE). "s" denotes the scale factor. (b) Multi-scale foreground enhancement module (MSFEM).

group convolution. Then, a 1×1 convolution is applied to reduce the dimension to obtain feature map X_{12}. The scale space coefficients X_2'' are multiplied element-wise with X_{12}, and the channel features to the smoke foreground are weighted to obtain feature maps X_{12}'. The formal formula is as follows:

$$X_1' = F_{G-Conv}(P_{Max}(X_1)) \tag{3}$$

$$X_{12} = F_{1 \times 1}(Concat(X_1', X_2')) \tag{4}$$

$$X_{12}' = X_{12} \otimes X_2' \tag{5}$$

where P_{Max}, F_{G-Conv}, $Concat$, $F_{1 \times 1}$ and $\otimes$ represent the max-pooling, 3×3 group convolution, concatenate, 1×1 convolution operation and element-wise product.

Finally, the smoke feature X_{12}' enhanced by fusion and added element-wise to the original size feature X_2 can help alleviate the gradient vanishing or explosion phenomenon of the model. After a 1x1 convolution operation and channel shuffle, the output of MSFEM denoted as Y_o.

3.1.2 Smoke Feature Extractor

The shape, size, and proportion of smoke targets are typically variable due to distances and different environments. It is extremely difficult to effectively extract smoke features that vary on different scales. Consequently, we applied MSFEM iteratively across three scales of feature maps, as depicted in Fig. 2 (a). In the initial stage, we stacked three

MSFEMs to capture contextual information. Two MSFEMs were introduced into second stage. During the third stage, we meticulously employed eight MSFEMs with distinct scale factors to deeply extract both global and local features. The optimal results were achieved by numerous experiments on the scale factor sequence {1, 2, 4, 8, 2, 4, 8, 16}. Thus, multi-scale features were obtained.

3.2 Decoding Stages

3.2.1 Self-refinement Coefficients

In the ACFFM module, we achieve feature complementarity by combining features from different levels of fusion and obtaining a comprehensive feature expression coefficient. Therefore, we designed a self-refinement coefficient (a mechanism for refining and enhancing feature mapping) to further improve the effectiveness of feature mapping. The overall structure of SRCs is shown in Fig. 3.

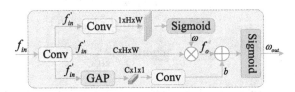

Fig. 3. Self-refinement coefficient (SRCs).

Specifically, we first preserve useful information through a 1×1 convolution layer and output it as f'. Then, we send the feature f' into a 1×1 convolution layer with output channels of only 1, generate a mask ω through sigmoid, multiply the original feature f' by ω, and output the result as f_o. In another branch, f' is adaptively pooled into $C \times 1 \times 1$, undergoes 1×1 convolution and expansion to form a bias b, and is added to f_o for output. Finally, sigmoid is applied to form a self-refinement coefficient. The main process can be described as:

$$\omega = \sigma(Conv_1(f'_{in})) \tag{6}$$

$$f_o = \omega \times f'_{in} \tag{7}$$

$$b = Conv_2(GAP(f'_{in})) \tag{8}$$

$$f_{out} = \sigma(f_o + b) \tag{9}$$

where $Conv_1(\cdot), GAP(\cdot), Conv_2(\cdot)$ and σ represent the 1×1 convolution (output channel of only one), global average pooling, 1×1 convolution and sigmoid function.

3.2.2 Attention-Guided Coupled Feature Fusion Module

Semantic segmentation is a pixel-level fine-grained classification task, where the form, size and proportion of smoke targets are typically variable, and inter-class interference can be enormous, such as with clouds or fog. To address these challenges, we propose an Attention-guided Coupled Feature Fusion Module (ACFFM) that weights the raw layer images through the introduction of Self-Refinement Coefficients (SRCs) resulting from cross-layer fusion, performs secondary fusion to utilize information from different scales to alleviate scale changes, and performs layer-wise decoding. The ACFFM has strong adaptability to targets of different scales and its structure is shown in Fig. 4. ACFFM is a cross-layer guidance feature map that gradually restores the model, which not only maintains the original feature size to obtain local context but also avoids small objects from being ignored.

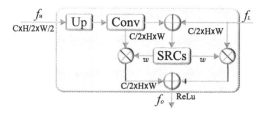

Fig. 4. Attention-guided Coupled Feature Fusion Module (ACFFM).

Specifically, we take f_H as the high-level feature, f_L as the low-level feature. The cross-level fusion process can be described as:

$$f_H' = Conv(Up(f_H)) \tag{10}$$

$$\omega = SRCs(f_H' + f_L) \tag{11}$$

$$f = ReLu(\omega \times (f_H' + f_L)) \tag{12}$$

where $Conv(\cdot)$ and represent the 1×1 convolution and upsample.

3.2.3 Smoke Feature Decoder

As depicted in Fig. 1, our smoke feature decoder works as a pixel-wise classifier. Firstly, the output from stage 3 of the smoke feature extractor is further deepened by passing it through a down-sampling unit, with the output denoted as F_4. Then, F_4 and F_3 are input into ACFFM1 to output F_5, and the remaining 5 ACFFMs are processed similarly. From top to bottom, the final outputs of each ACFFM layer are denoted as F_{10}, F_8, and F_5. At the same time, we concatenate F_4, F_5 and F_8 from three different scales of features after the convolution layer and up-sample to the same scale as F_{10}, and pass them through a convolution layer to reduce the dimension and output F_{16}. Additionally, the deep feature F_4 undergoes convolution layer, global average pooling, convolution layer and sigmoid (this process is called GCP) to form the global attention coefficient F_{15}, which is used to re-weight the fused output F_{16} to obtain a feature map with rich spatial details and semantic fusion information. Finally, the output is refined through a segmentation head [34].

3.3 Multiple Loss Function

Smoke segmentation is a pixel-level binary classification problem, the binary cross-entropy (BCE) loss is the most widely used loss in binary classification and segmentation. F^3Net [37] improved the losses to weighted BCE loss (ℓ_{BCE}^{ω}) and IoU loss (ℓ_{IoU}^{ω}). By calculating the difference between the center pixel and its surrounding environment, different weights are assigned to each pixel, allowing hard pixels to receive more attention.

To achieve a good convergence speed, we have employed multiple loss functions to improve the performance of our network. We use the weighted BCE loss and IoU loss for supervision. Our multiple loss function is formulated as:

$$L(P,G) = \ell_{BCE}^{\omega}(P,G) + \ell_{IoU}^{\omega}(P,G) \tag{13}$$

where P and G represent the prediction result and ground truth, and they have the same size.

Therefore, the total loss L_{total} for our method can be formulated as:

$$L_{total} = L(P_o, G) + \lambda_1 L(P_1, G) + \lambda_2 L(P_2, G) \tag{14}$$

where P_o is final outputs, P_1, P_2 are the two auxiliary supervision outputs and λ_1, λ_2 are the weight for different auxiliary supervision path. We set λ_1 and λ_2 to 0.4 and 0.6.

4 Experiments

4.1 Datasets

Considering the pressing need for authentic smoke segmentation datasets, we have launched a project to construct a batch of forest smoke segmentation datasets, namely the FSD dataset. We collected smoke images through tower-line cameras and manually annotated smoke segmentation masks. During the data cleaning process, we prioritize challenging smoke images, such as those with small or low-contrast smoke areas. The FSD dataset was constructed with 1719 forest smoke images of 480×480 size. We used 1375 images as the training set and 344 images as the test set.

Our method was compared with other models on the two datasets, the FSD dataset constructed in this paper and the SSS dataset proposed in DSS [20]. The SSS dataset contains 70,632 RGB-channel smoke images of 256×256 size.

4.2 Implementation Details

We implemented the method on a single RTX 2080Ti GPU by PyTorch. To obtain a better model initialization, we employed Stochastic Gradient Descent with a momentum of 0.9, and set the weight decay to 1e−5 within the optimizer. We set the batch size to 16 and the initial learning rate to 1e−2. Finally, we could obtain the best performance by training our LightNet+ for 100 epochs in our experiments.

We employed three widely used metrics to evaluate the accuracy performance of our method, including Dice coefficient (Dice), mean Intersection over Union (mIoU) and Accuracy (Acc). Furthermore, we also calculated the frames per second (FPS) to evaluate efficiency of our methods.

4.3 Ablation Studies

4.3.1 Ablation Study for Modules

To evaluate the performance of our individual modules, we conducted a series of ablation experiments, such as progressively removing or adding certain modules. Therefore, we designed eight variants of the method as shown in Table 1. Based on the experimental results, we drew several important conclusions.

Table 1. Smoke segmentation results on the DS01 test set for different configurations of our model.

Variants	SFE	ACFFM1	ACFFM2	ACFFM3	ACFFM4	ACFFM5	ACFFM6	GCP	DS01	
									Acc (%)	mIoU (%)
Model 1	√								90.1	70.3
Model 2	√	√							90.7	71.9
Model 3	√	√	√						90.5	71.6
Model 4	√	√	√	√					90.7	72.8
Model 5	√	√	√		√				91.7	73.7
Model 6	√	√	√	√	√	√			92.0	74.8
Model 7	√	√	√	√	√	√	√		92.2	75.9
Model 8	√	√	√	√	√	√	√	√	92.7	76.8

Firstly, conducting segmentation experiments using only the smoke feature extractor achieved a precision of 90.1% and the mIoU score of 70.3% on the DS01 test set. The primary reason is that MSFEM provides a wealth of multi-scale and foreground information about smoke, effectively extracting smoke features. Secondly, the iterative output of ACFFM during the decoding stage also achieved excellent results. Finally, the optimal state was achieved by fusing the deep global information generated by GCP. It can be seen that the mIoU of model 8 is 76.8%, which outperforms the baseline Model 1 by 6.5%.

4.4 Comparisons with Other Methods

We evaluated our LightNet+ on SSS and FSD datasets. Subsequently, we benchmarked our results against those produced by several outstanding semantic segmentation networks. These comparison networks include some lightweight semantic segmentation networks, including ERFNet [38], LEDNet [39], DFANet [40], CGNet [41], ESPNet [42], and dedicated networks for smoke segmentation, such as DSS [20], Frizzi [21], W-Net [5], HANUN [43], TANet [29] and LightNet [34].

Table 2. Smoke segmentation results of different methods on SSS datasets.

Methods	mIoU (%)			Parameters (M)	FPS
	DS01	DS02	DS03		
ERFNet [38]	69.9	67.9	68.7	2.06	60.5
LEDNet [39]	69.0	67.8	68.5	0.91	58.9
DFANet [40]	63.2	59.4	61.8	2.18	32.4
CGNet [41]	68.6	65.5	67.2	0.49	53.0
ESPNet [42]	61.9	61.9	62.8	0.4	-
DSS [20]	71.0	70.0	69.8	29.9	32.5
Frizzi [21]	70.4	70.0	70.7	57	60.4
W-Net [5]	73.1	74.0	73.4	31.1	–
HANUN [43]	76.0	75.6	75.3	300	–
TANet [29]	76.8	75.8	75.0	16	–
LightNet [34]	74.2	72.5	72.8	0.88	68.8
LightNet+ (Ours)	76.8	76.7	76.6	0.53	62.5

Table 2 presents the quantitative segmentation results of eleven comparison methods on the SSS datasets. Our LightNet+ achieves the best performance. Although ESPNet has an advantage in parameters, it is not enough to make up for the difference in mIoU. In the comparison of FPS, our method also has some advantages. Our method has a comparable mIoU score with TANet on the DS01 test set, it outperforms TANet by 0.9% on the DS02 test set and even by 1.6% on the DS03 test set, but our method parameters are only 0.53M. Additionally, our LightNet+ significantly outperforms LightNet [34] of the same level, especially on the DS02 test set, the mIoU of LightNet+ is 76.7%, which performs better than LightNet by over 4.2%.

Figure 5 displays the visualization of segmentation results from various methods on synthetic smoke images. To highlight the excellence of our method more effectively, we have chosen a selection of exemplary segmentation results for detailed analysis. The results indicate that our optimized lightweight smoke segmentation network has significantly better segmentation results on all samples compared to other comparison methods.

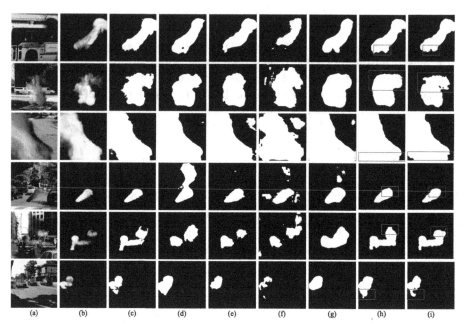

Fig. 5. Results on synthetic smoke images. (a) Synthetic smoke images. (b) Density maps. (c) Ground truths. Segmented results by (d) LEDNet, (e) CGNet, (f) DFANet, (g) ERFNet, (h) Light-Net and (i) our methods. Some segmentation details are highlighted by using red boxes. (Color figure online)

We highlighted the differences with red bounding boxes, visually highlighting the excellent performance of the optimized model. Our network achieves more precise locations and notably clearer edge details of the smoke region, especially on inconspicuous smoke images.

Table 3. Smoke segmentation results of different methods on forest smoke datasets.

Method	ERFNet	LEDNet	DFANet	CGNet	LightNet	Our method
mIoU (%)	45.63	44.55	39.19	39.59	47.47	52.32
Dice (%)	58.50	57.88	51.24	52.04	60.49	64.91
Acc (%)	98.12	98.14	98.08	98.09	98.18	98.20

To improve the effectiveness of our network on real images, we employed some excellent lightweight networks and our LightNet+ to train and test on the FSD dataset. As shown in Table 3, among the five comparison methods, our network achieved the highest mIoU, Dice, and Acc scores for real smoke images, reaching 52.32%, 64.91%, and 98.20% respectively.

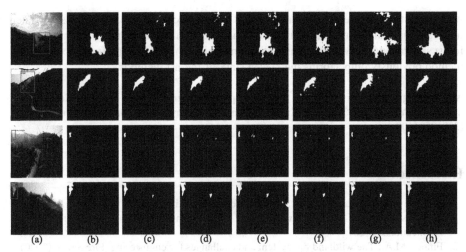

Fig. 6. Visualised experiments on FSD dataset. (a) Forest smoke images, (b) Ground truths. Visualised results by (c) ERFNet, (d) LEDNet, (e) DFANet, (f) CGNet, (g) LightNet, (h) our method. Some smoke details are highlighted by using red boxes. (Color figure online)

Figure 6 shows the visual segmentation results achieved by the comparative methods on our created FSD dataset. This method has the characteristics of good segmentation effect and low background interference. For images of invisible smoke or smoke-like objects, our LightNet+ also achieves higher segmentation results than others, as shown in the third row of Fig. 6. Other five methods all made some mistakes in segmenting, misclassifying smoke-like clouds as smoke. However, our method can accurately locate and segment small smoke. Our method also performs well for image segmentation tasks of larger targets and outperforms these comparative methods.

5   Conclusion

In this paper, we focused on the smoke segmentation of invisible, semi-transparent, or tiny smoke. The semi-transparency of smoke is a major difficulty in segmentation tasks, it is often confused with the background such as sky and ground, greatly reducing the segmentation accuracy. It is particularly important to model the smoke foreground. Therefore, we proposed a Multi-scale Foreground Enhancement Module (MSFEM), which increases the receptive field of features by down-sampling feature maps, fuses information from different spatial scales into weights, and enhances the smoke foreground information. Then, by stacking MSFEM repeatedly in different encoding stages, a Smoke Feature Extractor was constructed to capture features representing subtle, or semi-transparent smoke. In addition, we also introduced an Attention-guided Coupled Feature Fusion Module (ACFFM). It is difficult to distinguish between smoke and clouds because they have visually similar appearances. We extracted the inter-channel dependencies using Self-Refinement Coefficients generated by cross-level fusion and weighted the original layer images. Finally, the global coefficient path generates some attention coefficient maps containing more global and contextual information, we fused them with the outputs of the ACFFM at different stages of cascading in a stepwise manner to obtain the final segmentation map. Extensive experimental results on synthetic and forest smoke datasets validate that all these modules can improve performance, and our method obviously outperforms the eleven state-of-the-art methods.

Acknowledgments. This work was partially supported by the National Natural Science Foundation of China (61862029), and Capacity Construction Project of Shanghai Local Colleges (23010504100).

References

1. Muhammad, K., Khan, S., Baik, S.W.: Efficient convolutional neural networks for fire detection in surveillance applications. In: Deep Learning in Computer Vision: Principles and Applications (2020)
2. Finney, M.A.: The wildland fire system and challenges for engineering. Fire Saf. J. (2020)
3. Muhammad, K., Hussain, T., Tanveer, M., Sannino, G., de Albuquerque, V.: Cost-effective video summarization using deep CNN with hierarchical weighted fusion for IoT surveillance networks. IEEE Internet Things J. **7**(5), 4455–4463 (2020)
4. Cui, F.: Deployment and integration of smart sensors with IoT devices detecting fire disasters in huge forest environment. Comput. Commun. **150**, 818–827 (2020)
5. Yuan, F., Zhang, L., Xia, X., Huang, Q., Li, X.: A wave-shaped deep neural network for smoke density estimation. IEEE Trans. Image Process. **29**, 2301–2313 (2020)
6. ByoungChul, K., JunOh, P., Jae-Yeal, N.: Spatiotemporal bag-of-features for early wildfire smoke detection. Image Vis. Comput. **31**(10), 786–795 (2013)
7. Muhammad, K., Ahmad, J., Lv, Z., Bellavista, P., Yang, P., Baik, S.W.: Efficient deep CNN-based fire detection and localization in video surveillance applications. IEEE Trans. Syst. Man Cybern. Syst. **99**, 1–16 (2018)
8. Jing, T., Meng, Q., Hou, H.: SmokeSeger: a transformer-CNN coupled model for urban scene smoke segmentation. IEEE Trans. Ind. Inform. (2023)
9. Nguyen, T.K.T., Kim, J.M.: Multistage optical smoke detection approach for smoke alarm systems. Opt. Eng. **52**(5) (2013)
10. Dimitropoulos, K., Barmpoutis, P., Grammalidis, N.: Higher order linear dynamical systems for smoke detection in video surveillance applications. IEEE Trans. Circuits Syst. Video Technol. **27**(5), 1143–1154 (2017)
11. Zhao, Y.: Candidate smoke region segmentation of fire video based on rough set theory. J. Electr. Comput. Eng. (2015)
12. Wang, H., Chen, Y.A.: Smoke image segmentation algorithm based on rough set and region growing. J. Forest Sci. **65**(8) (2019)
13. Tung, T., Kim, J.: An effective four-stage smoke-detection algorithm using video images for early fire-alarm systems. Fire Saf. J. **46**(5), 276–282 (2011)
14. Filonenko, A., Hernandez, D.C., Jo, K.-H.: Fast smoke detection for video surveillance using CUDA. IEEE Trans. Ind. Inf. **14**(2), 725–733 (2018)
15. Yuan, F.: A fast accumulative motion orientation model based on integral image for video smoke detection. Pattern Recognit. Lett. **29**(7), 925–932 (2008)
16. Tian, H., Li, W., Ogunbona, P.O., Wang, L.: Detection and separation of smoke from single image frames. IEEE Trans. Image Process. **27**(3), 1164–1177 (2018)
17. Yuan, F., Fang, Z., Wu, S., Yang, Y., Fang, Y.: Real-time image smoke detection using staircase searching-based dual threshold AdaBoost and dynamic analysis. IET Image Process. **9**(10), 849–856 (2015)

18. Appana, D.K., Islam, M.R., Khan, S.A., Kim, J.: A video-based smoke detection using smoke flow pattern and spatial-temporal energy analyses for alarm systems. Inf. Sci. **418**, 91–101 (2017)
19. Alamgir, N., Nguyen, K., Chandran, V., Boles, W.: Combining multi-channel color space with local binary co-occurrence feature descriptors for accurate smoke detection from surveillance videos. Fire Saf. J. **102**, 1–10 (2018)
20. Yuan, F., Zhang, L., Xia, X., Wan, B., Huang, Q., Li, X.: Deep smoke segmentation. Neurocomputing **357**(10), 248–260 (2019)
21. Frizzi, S., Bouchouicha, M., Ginoux, J.-M., Moreau, E., Sayadi, M.: Convolutional neural network for smoke and fire semantic segmentation. IET Image Process. **15**(6), 634–647 (2021)
22. Simonyan, K., Zisserman, A.: Very deep convolutional networks for large-scale image recognition. In: Proceedings of the International Conference on Learning Representation (2014)
23. Wang, Y., Luo, Z., Chen, D., Li, Y.: Semantic segmentation of fire and smoke images based on dual attention mechanism. In: 2022 4th International Conference on Frontiers Technology of Information and Computer (ICFTIC), pp. 185–190 (2022)
24. Chen, L.C., Zhu, Y., Papandreou, G., Schroff, F., Adam, H.: Encoder-decoder with atrous separable convolution for semantic image segmentation. In: Ferrari, V., Hebert, M., Sminchisescu, C., Weiss, Y. (eds.) ECCV 2018. LNCS, vol. 11211, pp. 833–851. Springer, Cham (2018). https://doi.org/10.1007/978-3-030-01234-2_49
25. Kundu, S., Maulik, U., Sheshanarayana, R., Ghosh, S.: Vehicle smoke synthesis and attention-based deep approach for vehicle smoke detection. IEEE Trans. Ind. Appl. **59**(2), 2581–2589 (2023)
26. Cao, Y., Tang, Q., Wu, X., Lu, X.: EFFNet: Enhanced feature foreground network for video smoke source prediction and detection. IEEE Trans. Circuits Syst. Video Technol. **32**(4), 1820–1833 (2022)
27. Tao, H., Duan, Q., Lu, M., Hu, Z.: Learning discriminative feature representation with pixel-level supervision for forest smoke recognition. Pattern Recognit. **143** (2023)
28. Yuan, F., Dong, Z., Zhang, L., Xia, X., Shi, J.: Cubic-cross convolutional attention and count prior embedding for smoke segmentation. Pattern Recognit. **131** (2022)
29. Xia, X., Zhan, K., Peng, Y., Fang, Y.: Texture-aware network for smoke density estimation. In: IEEE International Conference on Visual Communications and Image Processing, pp. 1–5 (2022)
30. He, K., Zhang, X., Ren, S., Sun, J.: Deep residual learning for image recognition. In: Proceedings of the Conference on Computer Vision and Pattern Recognition (CVPR), pp. 770–778 (2016)
31. Carrio, A., Sampedro, C., Rodriguez-Ramos, A., Campoy, P.: A review of deep learning methods and applications for unmanned aerial vehicles. J. Sens. (2017)
32. Anim Hossain, F.M., Zhang, Y.: MsFireD-Net: a lightweight and efficient convolutional neural network for flame and smoke segmentation. J. Autom. Intell. **2**(3), 130–138 (2023)
33. Xia, W., Yu, F., Wang, H., Hong, R.: A high-precision lightweight smoke detection model based on SE attention mechanism. In: 2022 2nd International Conference on Consumer Electronics and Computer Engineering (ICCECE), pp. 941–944 (2022)
34. Yuan, F., Li, K., Wang, C., Fang, Z.: A lightweight network for smoke semantic segmentation. Pattern Recognit. (2023)
35. Paszke, A., Chaurasia, A., Kim, S., Culurciello, E.: ENET: a deep neural network architecture for real-time semantic segmentation. arXiv preprint arXiv:1606.02147 (2016)
36. Krizhevsky, A., Sutskever, I., Hinton, G.E.: ImageNet classification with deep convolutional neural networks. In: Advances in Neural Information Processing Systems, pp. 1097–1105 (2012)

37. Wei, J., Wang, S.H., Huang, Q.M.: F^{3}Net: fusion, feedback and focus for salient object detection. In: AAAI (2020)

38. Romera, E., Álvarez, J.M., Bergasa, L.M., Arroyo, R.: ERFNet: efficient residual factorized ConvNet for real-time semantic segmentation. IEEE Trans. Intell. Transp. Syst. **19**(1), 263–272 (2018)

39. Wang, Y., Zhou, Q., Liu, J., Xiong, J., Latecki. L.J.: LEDNet: a lightweight encoder-decoder network for real-time semantic segmentation. In: Proceedings of the IEEE International Conference on Image Processing, pp. 1860–1864 (2019)

40. Li, H., Xiong, P., Fan, H., Sun, J.: DFANet: deep feature aggregation for real-time semantic segmentation. In: Proceedings of the IEEE/CVF Conference on Computer Vision and Pattern Recognition (CVPR), pp. 9514–9523 (2019)

41. Wu, T., Tang, S., Zhang, R., Cao, J., Zhang, Y.: CGNet: a light-weight context guided network for semantic segmentation. IEEE Trans. Image Process. **30**, 1169–1179 (2021)

42. Mehta, S., Rastegari, M., Caspi, A., Shapiro, L., Hajishirzi, H.: ESPNet: efficient spatial pyramid of dilated convolutions for semantic segmentation. In: Ferrari, V., Hebert, M., Sminchisescu, C., Weiss, Y. (eds.) ECCV 2018. LNCS, vol. 11214, pp. 561–580. Springer, Cham (2018). https://doi.org/10.1007/978-3-030-01249-6_34

43. Guo, W., Xiao, X., Hui, Y., Yang, W., Sadovnik, A.: Heterogeneous attention nested u-shaped network for blur detection. IEEE Signal Process. Lett. **29**, 140–144 (2022)

Local Dynamic Filter Network
for Low-Light Enhancement
and Deblurring

Nanxin Huang⬛, Yirui Wang⬛, Lifang Yang(✉), Xianglin Huang,
and Nenghuan Zhang

Communication University of China, Dingfuzhuang East Street, Chaoyang District,
Beijing, China
{hnancy,yanglifang}@cuc.edu.cn

Abstract. Under specific conditions, capturing clear images that meet
human vision requirements is challenging due to limitations in electronic
devices and scene capture. Traditional low-light enhancement methods primarily focus on brightness enhancement, neglecting issues like
image blurring. This paper presents the Local Dynamic Filter Network
(LDFN), an encoder-decoder framework that effectively restores texture
information in low-light images. The encoder extracts multi-scale features, serving as input for the filter generation network, which produces
local dynamic filters for the decoder. These filters restore texture details
and reduce blur in the decoder. Additionally, pixel shuffle is utilized as
an upsampling module. Experimental results on real-world and synthesized datasets demonstrate the method's advantages and robustness. By
addressing texture restoration and blur removal, LDFN offers a promising approach for enhancing low-light image quality.

Keywords: Image Processing · Low-light enhancement · Deblurring

1 Introduction

Compared to normal-light images, low-light images often exhibit uneven brightness and unclear edges and textures. They present two major issues. Firstly,
the overall illumination of the image is typically low due to inadequate lighting.
Secondly, the light intensity can be non-uniform in dark environments, resulting
in variations in light absorption and reflection by objects and leading to local
highlights or dark areas in the image. To address these challenges, the task of
low-light enhancement (LLE) aims not only to improve brightness but also to
restore details and reduce blurring and noise. Traditionally, low-light enhancement and image deblurring have been treated as separate tasks by researchers,
with independent assumptions made in each specific problem.

Traditional low-light enhancement methods aim to enhance the brightness
and gain the enhanced image, such as retinex-based approaches [1–3]. These
methods decompose images into reflection maps and illumination maps. They
are relatively simple and easy, but they tend to amplify noise and cause blurry

G. Zhai et al. (Eds.): IFTC 2023, CCIS 2066, pp. 85–97, 2024.
https://doi.org/10.1007/978-981-97-3623-2_7

edges. Recently, deep low-light enhancement algorithms based on supervised learning [3,4] and unsupervised learning [5,6,31] are proposed and achieve great results. However, the output images of these methods still have problems such as lack of detail, color deviation, and residual noise.

In light of the limitations of combining traditional image enhancement and deblurring methods sequentially, this paper proposes a novel approach to address the issues of edge and texture blurring in low-light images. Specifically, we introduce a low-light image enhancement and deblurring network that leverages a dynamic local filter to perform convolutional filtering operations on local texture information. This filter is designed to enhance the structural texture information in low-light images, thereby improving the overall image quality. In addition, we incorporate an edge loss function into our network to further enhance the structure and texture information in low-light blurred images. The edge loss function is inspired by edge detection algorithms [9] and is designed to extract object boundaries and textures from the image. We then use L1 constraints to retain the extracted information, which helps to improve the enhancement effect of low-light images.

The main contributions of this paper can be summarized as follows:

1) We design an end-to-end network that can handle joint tasks, including low-light enhancement and image deblurring.
2) We design local dynamic filters for low-light enhancement and deblurring. The local dynamic filers can restore the texture details, thus enhancing the low-light images.

2   Related Work

2.1   Image Low-Light Enhancement

Land [8] first proposed the Retinex theory, which suggests that the world is colorless, and the colors we see are the result of the interaction between light and matter, known as color constancy. This is achieved by the retina and cerebral cortex working together, collectively known as Retinex. The Retinex theory decomposes an image into reflection and incident components. The reflection component represents the essential attribute obtained as the enhancement result through prior or regularization decomposition. The incident component represents different lighting conditions. The basic idea of the Retinex theory is to remove or reduce the influence of the incident component while retaining the reflection component that reflects the essence as much as possible. Inspired by the Retinex theory, some LLE networks have been proposed [2,10–12,32,33]. These networks commonly split the input low-light images into reflectance and illumination maps, and then adjust the illumination map to enhance the intensity. For example, the RetinexNet [27] is composed of Decom-Net and Enhance-Net, the first one is used for image split low-light input, the second part is used to adjust the illumination map. In this literature, a large-scale dataset, called LOL, is proposed, which provides a universal dataset for subsequent LLE research. However, the joint task of LLE and deblurring has not yet been investigated in the literature.

Some unsupervised methods have been proposed to improve the generalization capability of models.Zero-DCE [13] and Zero-DCE++ [14]formulate light enhancement as a task of image-specific curve estimation. Their training adopts several manually defined loss functions to supervise exposure or color, without the limitation of paired or unpaired training data. As a result, Zero-DCE can be easily extended to generic lighting adjustments.

Adversarial-based methods, such as EnlightenGAN [15], are the first unsupervised learning algorithms for low-light image enhancement that do not require paired data. By incorporating a dual discriminator structure and a self-regularizing structure, these techniques successfully enhance low-light images in an efficient manner. This approach greatly enhances the ability to generalize the improvements to real-world scenarios. Additionally, fusion-based methods have proven to be highly successful in preserving intricate image details and generating visually realistic outcomes. For instance, LLNet [16] utilizes an encoder-decoder architecture with skip connections and a fusion module. The fusion module is designed to combine information from multiple scales, including global and local features, to produce high-quality results.

2.2   Image Deblurring

A lot of Deep networks have been proposed for dynamic scene deblurring [17–19]. One line of research has focused on the design of network architectures. For example, Tao [17] proposed the Multi-scale Deep Network (MDN), which uses a multi-scale feature extraction and fusion strategy to handle blur at different scales. Kupyn [18] proposed the Recurrent Inference Machine (RIM), which adopts a recurrent network to iteratively refine the deblurred image. Another line of research focuses on handling complex blur patterns. For instance, Ren et al. propose a novel method for deblurring dynamic scenes using spatially varying recurrent neural networks (SVRNN) [19]. This approach involves training an SVRNN on a sequence of blurred images to estimate the spatially varying blur kernel that caused the blur. Once the blur kernel is estimated, it can be used to deblur the image and recover the sharp underlying scene (Fig. 1).

3   Method

This section first introduces the overall framework of the low-light enhancement network. Then introduces the specific implementation of the improved upsample method the Local Dynamic Filter(LDF) algorithm and the loss function-specific design. The encoder for low-light enhancement (LE-Encoder) and the decoder for deblurring (De-Decoder). The encoder part is composed of three scale blocks: every scale block contains one residual block, one residual downsample block [20] a Pyramid Pooling Module(PPM) [21] and a Curve Non-linear Unit(CurveNLU)

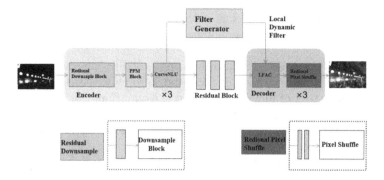

Fig. 1. The framework of the LDFN. It is mainly composed of two parts, the low-light enhancement encoder and deblurring Decoder

[22]. The decoder includes multi-scale local dynamic filters [24], two residual blocks and pixel shuffle module [25]. The following will provide a specific introduction to the encoder and the decoder.

3.1 Low-Light Enhancement Encoder

Given an input image x, the optical enhancement network inputs the image into the LE-Encoder. After initialization, it first goes through the encoder block for downsampling convolution to obtain 128×128 feature maps of 64 channels. Then input the obtained feature maps into the PPM, which can increase the receptive field of the network without downsampling, and obtain multi-scale features. After the PPM, the picture is input into a CurveNLU, which can utilize the estimated curve parameters for feature transformation. Expressed with an iterative function as follows:

$$C_n(p) = \begin{cases} A_1 F(p)(1 - F(p)) + F(p), n = 1 \\ A_{n-1} C_{n-1}(p)(1 - C_{n-1}(p)) + C_{n-1}(p), n > 1 \end{cases} \quad (1)$$

Where p represents the position coordinates of the feature, and A_{n-1} is the n-th pixel level curve parameter of the estimated curve. To promote intermediate supervision, the obtained feature map is re-input into an encoder block, spatial convolution PPM with the same structure, and the operation is repeated again and finally respectively. Get feature maps with 64 channels size of 128×128, 128 channels size of 64×64, and 128 channels size of 32×32.

3.2 Deblurring Decoder

The De-Decoder focuses on deblurring, it contains three convolution blocks and inserts a dynamic filter in the De-Decoder. Subsequently, the three feature maps obtained by the LE-Encoder are respectively input into the De-Decoder. Due to the enhanced function of the LE-Encoder, the De-Decoder can be more focused on deblurring, which contains three convolution blocks, each convolution block has two residual blocks, an upsampling block, and a dynamic filter, the dynamic filter used for bridge the LE-Encoder and De-Decoder. The three feature maps are respectively input into the dynamic filter with the smallest ratio, and the filter performs dynamic filtering on each pixel, and then inputs the obtained feature map into the decoding block for upsample convolution, and finally obtains 32 channel 256×256 size enhanced result graph α.

In our proposed framework, the LE-Encoder is responsible for the low light enhancement portion, while the De-Decoder has a deblurring function. Specifically, each Decoder block consists of three parts, namely, two residual connection blocks, a residual pixel shuffle block which responsible for upsampling, and an FAC block that connects the LE-Encoder and De-Decoder. Next, we will introduce the FAC block in detail.

Local Dynamic Filter. Among the numerous solutions to blur problems in motion, the Filter Adaptive Convolutional layer [23] proposes that for feature maps of different sizes obtained by encoders, each element in the feature map will use a convolutional filter once. Zhou [22] designed a filter adaptive skip connection (FASC). This skip connection utilizes the enhanced information fused from the LE-Encoder and adds it to the filter network to solve the deblurring problem. The filters learned in traditional convolutional layers are usually fixed after training, so Dynamic Filter Network [24] proposes to dynamically generate corresponding dynamic filters based on input. A dynamic filter module consists of a filter generation network and a dynamic filtering layer. The former generates different filters based on feature maps of different input sizes, while the latter generates filters for corresponding patches of inputs.

Based on the dynamic filtering layer, a corresponding extension has also been proposed: the Dynamic Local Filtering Layer (As shown in Fig. 2.). The filtering operation in the dynamic filtering layer is carried out by translation, but unlike it, the inspiration for the dynamic local filtering layer comes from the traditional local connection layer. At different positions $I_b(i,j)$ of the input, there will be a specific dynamic local filter $F_\theta(i,j)$ that performs convolutional filtering operations on the position centered region $I_B(i,j)$.

The local dynamic filtering layer is not only specific to the sample but also to different positions in the feature map. The schematic diagram of the dynamic filtering layer is shown in Fig. 2. The dynamic filtering layer is shared on the spatial dimension of the feature map, and the dynamic local filtering layer replaces each input I_B element with an element selected from its surrounding local neighborhood. Provides a natural method for modeling local spatial deformation for another input I_A.

The dynamic local filtering layer can not only perform a single transformation like the dynamic convolution layer but also perform specific positional transformations like local deformations.

Before or after applying dynamic local filtering operations, we can add dynamic pixel level deviations to each input I_B element to solve the deblurring problem from a texture perspective(Expressed by the formula: $G(i,j) = F_\theta(i,j)(I_B(i,j))$). Similarly, this dynamic bias can be generated by the same filter-generating network that generates the local filter.

We propose the LFAC layer based on the previous work. In our proposed LDF layer, for enhanced feature maps$E \in R^{H*W*C}$ of different sizes obtained from the LE-Encoder, the filter generation network used consists of three 1×1 convolutional layers and one 3×3 convolutional layer (AS shown in Fig. 3), The size of the filter generated after generating the network through the filter is $F \in R^{H*W*Cd^2}$, which can effectively expand the feature dimension. Then, in the LFAC layer, filter and transform the feature maps $D \in R^{H*W*C}$ decoded in each level of the De-Decoder. For each element of feature map D, LFAC will use the corresponding convolution operator, using the corresponding size $d*d$ in filter K. The kernel of d further refines the decoded feature map. We set the kernel size d to 5 on three scales, which is consistent with the setting in [22].

Pixel Shuffle. In our decoder, the process of upsampling is a very important part. In normal circumstances, convolution operations will reduce the height and width of the feature map. When $stride = \frac{1}{r} < 1$, we can increase the height and width of the convolutional feature map. In pixel shuffle [25], we first obtain one feature map of r^2 channel (the size of the feature map is consistent with the input low-resolution image), and then use periodic filtering to obtain this high-resolution image, where r is the upsampling factor, which is the magnification of the image. Specifically, the proposed approach involves partitioning the initial low-resolution pixel into smaller grids of size $r \times r$ and subsequently populating these grid cells with the values extracted from the corresponding positions of the $r \times r$ feature maps according to certain rules. Following the same rules, the reorganization process is completed by filling the small grids divided by each low-resolution pixel. In this process, the model can adjust the weights of $r \times r$ shuffle channels to continuously optimize the generated results.

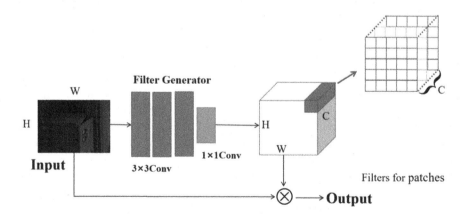

Fig. 2. The framework of filter generators and Local Dynamic Filter. The multi-scale feature maps generated by the LE-Encoder are inputs of this network. And then the generated Local Dynamic Filters are parts of the DE-Decoder.

Loss Function. The loss function usually guides the direction of model training. In order to further refine the edge and reduce blur, this chapter introduces an edge enhancement loss L_{edge} during training to restore the model to a clear edge close to the real image, and better guarantee the accuracy of recovering the edges of objects in the image is improved. L_{edge} is introduced to additionally measure the difference between the predicted edge and the ground truth. The Sobel filter is a differentiable edge extraction filter. L_{edge} uses the Sobel operator to obtain the approximate value of the derivative of the image color intensity in the horizontal and vertical directions on the ab channel of the CIE Lab of the image, thereby extracting the edge of the image. The resulting edge gradient is written in the form:

$$S\left(I_{ab}\right) = \sqrt{\left(G_x * I_{ab}\right)^2 + \left(G_y * I_{ab}\right)^2} \tag{2}$$

$$G_x = \begin{bmatrix} 1 & 0 & -1 \\ 2 & 0 & -2 \\ 1 & 0 & -1 \end{bmatrix}$$

$$G_y = \begin{bmatrix} 1 & 2 & 1 \\ 0 & 0 & 0 \\ -1 & -2 & -1 \end{bmatrix}$$

G_x and G_y are the horizontal and vertical Sobel filters convolved with the image respectively, S returns the gradient size, and I_{ab} represents the a and b channel images. The edge loss Ledge is formally written as:

$$L_{edge} = \left\| S\left(I_{ab}\right) - S\left(I_{ab}^{gt}\right) \right\|_2^2 I_{ab}^{gt} \tag{3}$$

Among them, I_{ab}^{gt} represents the a and b channel maps of the ground truth. The enhancement loss L_{en} mainly supervises the exposure of the intermediate output, which adopts the L_1 loss function and the perceptual loss function under the $\times 8$ downsampling ratio. The enhancement loss L_{en} can be written as the following formula:

$$L_{en} = \|\hat{y} - y\|_1 + \lambda \|\Phi\left(\hat{y} - y\right)\|_1 \tag{4}$$

where $\phi\left(\cdot\right)$ represents the pre-trained VGG19 network. In the work in this chapter, L_1 loss and perceptual loss are used as the deblur loss L_{deb}, which is defined as follows:

$$L_{deb} = \|\hat{y} - y\|_1 + \lambda \|\phi\left(\hat{y}\right) - \phi\left(y\right)\|_1 \tag{5}$$

The overall loss function of the network can be shown as:

$$L_{total} = \alpha L_{en} + \beta L_{deb} + \gamma L_{edge} \tag{6}$$

L_{en} and L_{deb} represent enhancement loss and deblurring loss respectively, and α, β, γ are used to balance the loss weight between the three loss functions of Len, L_{deb} and L_{edge}. In the work of this chapter, α, β, γ are respectively set to 0.01, 0.8, 0.01, and λ is set to 1.

Table 1. Quantitative evaluation on the LOL-Blur dataset

Model	LOL-Blur				LSRW			
	PSNR↑	SSIM↑	LPIPS↓	NIQE↓	PSNR↑	SSIM↑	LPIPS↓	NIQE↓
RetinexNet	17.03	0.640	0.384	4.84	15.48	0.391	0.432	4.15
EnlightenGAN	19.84	0.749	0.230	4.83	17.08	0.503	0.327	**3.46**
Zero-DCE	18.33	0.589	0.476	5.07	15.86	0.477	0.317	3.72
Kind++	21.26	0.753	0.359	4.88	15.86	0.419	0.354	3.43
SCI	18.57	0.606	0.325	4.76	15.02	**0.675**	**0.211**	3.66
LEDNet	25.74	0.850	0.224	4.76	16.83	0.528	0.423	4.85
IAT	23.38	0.809	0.318	4,69	16.33	0.513	0.385	4.11
Ours	**26.59**	**0.864**	**0.181**	**4.17**	**17.15**	0.558	0.411	3.96

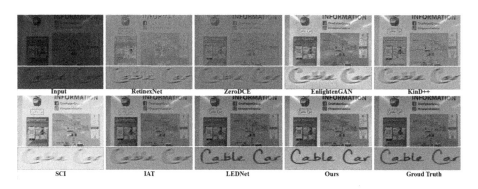

Fig. 3. A comprehensive visual evaluation was conducted on the LOL-Blur dataset to compare the performance of various state-of-the-art low-light image enhancement methods. The framed region in the figures shows that our results are superior to other model results in terms of low-light enhancement and texture restoration.

4   Experiment

The method proposed in this chapter is to cut the image into blocks with a length and width of 256 for training, set the Batch size to 8, use the Adam optimizer to train the network, and adopt unified parameter settings, $\beta_1 = 0.9$, $\beta_2 = 0.99$, a total of 240000 iterations were performed, the initial learning rate was set to 10^{-4}, and the cosine annealing strategy was used to update.

4.1   Datasets

We use the training set of the LOL-Blur [22] dataset to train our network and other baselines. LOL-Blur is the first large-scale dataset that can be used to describe the coexistence of low light and blur and can be used to combine low light enhancement and deblurring. It is formed through a new data synthesis

Fig. 4. Visual comparison on the LSRW dataset among state-of-the-art low-light image enhancement approaches. Our results are superior to other model results. The results of model(f) are lighter than our results, but these results are too exposed and do not conform to the subjective visual perception in terms of low light enhancement and texture restoration.

pipeline that models real-world low-light blur degradation., It contains 12000 low-degree blur/normal definition pairs with different darkness and motion blur, with a resolution of 1120×640. In the experiment, we used 160 sequences (9600 pairs) for training and 10 sequences (600 pairs) for validation.

In the test, we randomly select 30 sequences from the LOL-Blur dataset, namely 1800 pairs of images. Besides the LOL-Blur dataset, we also select 15 low-light images from the LSRW dataset [26], a total of 2 datasets as the test set. The LSRW dataset is a dataset of real scenes, we select the part that is shot by a Huawei mobile phone and professional Nikon camera. It mainly focuses on outdoor scenes, with a resolution of 960×640, the LOL dataset is also a dataset for real scenes, consisting of low light and normal light image pairs, with a resolution of 1120×640. We use two GPUs Nvidia Geforce RTX3090 during the training and test process.

4.2 Evaluation on Datasets

Evaluation Metrics. We employ the PSNR and SSIM metrics for evaluation on the synthetic LOL-Blur dataset. We also report the perceptual metric LPIPS for references to evaluate the perceptual quality of restored images.

To fully evaluate the effectiveness and progressiveness of our method proposed in this chapter, the method proposed in this chapter is compared with other more advanced end-to-end low light image enhancement methods. Including Zero-DCE [13], RetinexNet [27], Kind++ [28], EnlightenGAN [15], SCI [7], IAT [29] and LEDNet [22] (Fig. 5).

Quantitative Evaluations. This indicator can effectively evaluate feature differences and is similar to human evaluation. As shown in Table 1, the proposed method achieves the highest PSNR and SSIM score, indicating that our results are the most structurally similar to ground truth in terms of structural similarity.

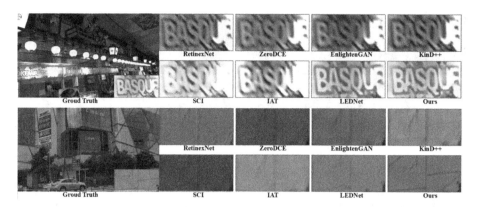

Fig. 5. Visual comparisons outdoor scene. The proposed method achieved better results in texture detail restoration

Our network also obtains the best LPIPS and NIQE scores, the first indicator can effectively evaluate feature differences and is similar to human evaluation and the second one shows our results have the best image qualities that are well in line with human perception.

Qualitative Evaluations. Other end-to-end baseline networks trained on the LOL-Blur dataset (As shown in Fig. 2 and Fig. 4) are also less effective given the real-world inputs, as their architecture just can handle low-light enhancement. Overall, the proposed network shows the best visual quality, with fewer artifacts and blurs. The better performance is attributed to the LFAC and edge loss, which enable our method to perform spatially varying feature transformations for both intensity enhancement and blur removal.

Table 2. Quantitative evaluation on LOL-Blur dataset. PSNR/SSIM↑: the higher, the better; LPIPS↓: the lower, the better

Model	PSNR	SSIM	LPIPS
w/DF	25.34	0.838	0.219
w/LDF	25.56	0.847	0.225
w/o pixel shuffle	25.34	0.838	0.219
w/pixel shuffle	25.61	0.845	0.221
w/edge loss	26.26	0.852	0.219

4.3   Ablation Study

In this subsection, we present an ablation study to demonstrate the effectiveness of the main modules in our Network.

Effectiveness of Pixel Shuffle. The pixel shuffle module can make our model achieve better learning ability. Compared to low-pixel feature maps, convolution after upsampling to obtain high-pixel feature maps has a better representation learning ability. Table 2 shows the pixel shuffle improved upsampling performance in our model.

Effectiveness of LFAC. Comparing variant with Dynamic Filter(w/DF) and with Local Dynamic Filter(w/LDF) in Table 2, the one with an LDF connection achieves better performance compared to the DF. This is because the saturated and unsaturated areas in the night scenes follow different blur models. The local dynamic filter can better filter different regions.

Effectiveness of Edge Loss. The edge loss L_{edge} is necessary for our method. Removing it from training harms the performance as shown in Table 2. It is because this loss helps restore clear edges of the model that are close to the real image and better ensures the accuracy of object edges in the restored image.

5 Conclusion

In this paper, we successfully design an end-to-end yet effective framework. The encoder of the network is responsible for low-light enhancement. In the decoder, we use multi-scale local dynamic filters to retain the texture information of the feature image in the encoder and choose pixel shuffle as our upsample module. We designed an edge loss function to better control the training of the decoder. In addition, we perform extensive experiments to indicate our effectiveness and superiority in low-light image enhancement.

References

1. Jobson, D.J., Rahman, Z.-U., Woodell, G.A.: Properties and performance of a center/surround retinex. IEEE Trans. Image Process. **6**(3), 451–462 (1997)
2. Rahman, Z.-U., Jobson, D.J., Woodell, G.A.: Multi-scale retinex for color image enhancement. In: Proceedings of 3rd IEEE International Conference on Image Processing, vol. 3, pp. 1003–1006 (1996)
3. Wu, W.-B., Weng, J., Zhang, P., Wang, X., Yang, W., Jiang, J.: URetinex-Net: retinex-based deep unfolding network for low-light image enhancement. In: 2022 IEEE/CVF Conference on Computer Vision and Pattern Recognition (CVPR), pp. 5891–5900 (2022)
4. Jiang, K., et al.:Degrade is upgrade: learning degradation for low-light image enhancement. ArXiv arxiv:2103.10621 (2021)
5. Lu, K., Zhang, L.: TBEFN: a two-branch exposure-fusion network for low-light image enhancement. IEEE Trans. Multimedia **23**, 4093–4105 (2021)
6. Tang, L., Ma, J., Zhang, H., Guo, X.: DRLIE: flexible low-light image enhancement via disentangled representations. IEEE Trans. Neural Netw. Learn. Syst. **35**, 2694–2707 (2022)

7. Ma, L., Ma, T., Liu, R., Fan, X., Luo, Z.: Toward fast, flexible, and robust low-light image enhancement. In: 2022 IEEE/CVF Conference on Computer Vision and Pattern Recognition (CVPR), pp. 5627–5636 (2022)
8. Land, E.H.: The retinex theory of color vision. Sci. Am. **237**(6), 108–128 (1977)
9. Kim, E., Lee, S., Park, J., Choi, S., Seo, C., Choo, J.: Deep edge-aware interactive colorization against color-bleeding effects. In: 2021 IEEE/CVF International Conference on Computer Vision (ICCV), pp. 14647–14656 (2021)
10. Fu, X., Zeng, D., Huang, Y., Liao, Y., Ding, X., Paisley, J.W.: A fusion-based enhancing method for weakly illuminated images. Signal Process. **129**, 82–96 (2016)
11. Guo, X., Li, Y., Ling, H.: LIME: low-light image enhancement via illumination map estimation. IEEE Trans. Image Process. **26**, 982–993 (2017)
12. Ren, X., Yang, W., Cheng, W.-H., Liu, J.: LR3M: robust low-light enhancement via low-rank regularized retinex model. IEEE Trans. Image Process. **29**, 5862–5876 (2020)
13. Guo, C., et al.: Zero-reference deep curve estimation for low-light image enhancement. In: 2020 IEEE/CVF Conference on Computer Vision and Pattern Recognition (CVPR), pp. 1777–1786 (2020)
14. Li, C., Guo, C., Loy, C.C.: Learning to enhance low-light image via zero-reference deep curve estimation. IEEE Trans. Pattern Anal. Mach. Intell. **44**, 4225–4238 (2021)
15. Jiang, Y., et al.: EnlightenGAN: deep light enhancement without paired supervision. IEEE Trans. Image Process. **30**, 2340–2349 (2019)
16. Lore, K. G., Akintayo, A., Sarkar, S.: LLNet: a deep autoencoder approach to natural low-light image enhancement. ArXiv arxiv:1511.03995 (2015)
17. Tao, X., Gao, H., Wang, Y., Shen, X., Wang, J., Jia, J.: Scale-recurrent network for deep image deblurring. In: 2018 IEEE/CVF Conference on Computer Vision and Pattern Recognition, pp. 8174–8182 (2018)
18. Kupyn, O., Martyniuk, T., Wu, J., Wang, Z.: DeblurGAN-v2: deblurring (orders-of-magnitude) faster and better. In: 2019 IEEE/CVF International Conference on Computer Vision (ICCV), pp. 8877–8886 (2019)
19. Ren, W., et al.: Deblurring dynamic scenes via spatially varying recurrent neural networks. IEEE Trans. Pattern Anal. Mach. Intell. **44**, 3974–3987 (2021)
20. Zamir, S.W., et al.: Learning enriched features for fast image restoration and enhancement. IEEE Trans. Pattern Anal. Mach. Intell. **45**, 1934–1948 (2020)
21. Zhao, H., Shi, J., Qi, X., Wang, X., Jia, J.: Pyramid scene parsing network. In: 2016 IEEE Conference on Computer Vision and Pattern Recognition (CVPR), pp. 6230–6239 (2016)
22. Zhou, S., Li, C., Loy, C.C.: LEDNet: joint low-light enhancement and deblurring in the dark. In: Avidan, S., Brostow, G., Cisse, M., Farinella, G.M., Hassner, T. (eds.) ECCV 2022. LNCS, vol. 13666, pp. 573–589. Springer, Heidelberg (2022). https://doi.org/10.1007/978-3-031-20068-7_33
23. Zhou, S., Zhang, J., Pan, J.-S., Xie, H., Zuo, W., Ren, J.S.J.: Spatio-temporal filter adaptive network for video deblurring. In: 2019 IEEE/CVF International Conference on Computer Vision (ICCV), pp. 2482–2491 (2019)
24. Jia, X., Brabandere, B. D., Tuytelaars, T., Van Gool, L.: Dynamic filter networks. ArXiv arxiv:1605.09673 (2016)
25. Shi, W., et al.: Real-time single image and video super-resolution using an efficient sub-pixel convolutional neural network. In: 2016 IEEE Conference on Computer Vision and Pattern Recognition (CVPR), pp. 1874–1883 (2016)

26. Hai, J., et al.: R2RNet: low-light image enhancement via real-low to real-normal network. J. Vis. Commun. Image Represent. **90**, 103712 (2021)
27. Wei, C., Wang, W., Yang, W., Liu, J.: Deep retinex decomposition for low-light enhancement. ArXiv arxiv:1808.04560 (2018)
28. Zhang, Y., Guo, X., Ma, J., Liu, W., Zhang, J.: Beyond brightening low-light images. Int. J. Comput. Vision 1–25 (2021)
29. Cui, Z., et al.: You only need 90K parameters to adapt light: a light weight transformer for image enhancement and exposure correction. In: British Machine Vision Conference (2022)
30. He, K., Zhang, X., Ren, S., Sun, J.: Deep residual learning for image recognition. In: 2016 IEEE Conference on Computer Vision and Pattern Recognition (CVPR), pp. 770–778 (2015)
31. Zhao, M., Cao, G., Huang, X., Yang, L.: Hybrid transformer-CNN for real image denoising. IEEE Signal Process. Lett. **29**, 1252–1256 (2022)
32. Song, G., Tao, Z., Huang, X., Cao, G., Liu, W., Yang, L.: Hybrid attention-based prototypical network for unfamiliar restaurant food image few-shot recognition. IEEE Access **8**, 14893–14900 (2020)
33. Zhao, Q., Cao, G., Zhou, A., Huang, X., Yang, L.: Image tampering detection via semantic segmentation network. In: 2020 15th IEEE International Conference On Signal Processing (ICSP), vol. 1, pp. 165–169 (2020)

Spatial-Angular Decoupling Interaction Networks for Light Field Angular Super-Resolution

Baoshuai Wang, Yilei Chen, Xinpeng Huang, and Ping An[⊠]

Key laboratory of Specialty Fiber Optics and Optical Access Networks, School of Communication and Information Engineering, Shanghai University, Shanghai 200444, China
anping@shu.edu.cn

Abstract. The light field image simultaneously captures both the intensity and directional information of light rays, making it a valuable tool for acquiring four-dimensional spatial data. However, the restriction of sensor resolution results in a trade-off between angular and spatial resolution, which hinders our ability to simultaneously acquire light field with high spatial and angular resolution. In this paper, we focus on the sparse light field reconstruction task, which aims to construct densely-sampled light fields for higher angular resolution. To achieve this goal, we propose a spatial-angular decoupling interaction network. The method is based on the light field decoupling mechanism, which interactively fuses and updates spatial and angular features to achieve global spatial and angular features. Moreover, four directions epipolar plane features are extracted to obtain more disparity information. Finally, the global spatial and angular features are interacted with the fused epipolar plane features, and the dense views light field is reconstructed by the fused features. Experimental results indicate that the spatial-angular decoupling interaction network outperforms other state-of-the-art methods in angular domain reconstruction, and achieves more refined texture details in the reconstructed views.

Keywords: Light Field · Angular Super-Resolution · Spatial-Angular Decoupling Interaction

1 Introduction

Different from traditional two-dimensional images, light field images inherently possess abundant simultaneous spatial and angular information, breaking the bottleneck that traditional images can only record the spatial position information of light rays. As a result, light field images have vast potential for development in digital refocusing [1,2], depth estimation [3–5], 3D scene reconstruction [6,7], and virtual reality [8]. Due to sensor resolution limitations, a compromise arises between angular and spatial resolution. Consequently, the captured light

© The Author(s), under exclusive license to Springer Nature Singapore Pte Ltd. 2024
G. Zhai et al. (Eds.): IFTC 2023, CCIS 2066, pp. 98–108, 2024.
https://doi.org/10.1007/978-981-97-3623-2_8

field cannot achieve both high spatial and high angular resolution simultaneously. To tackle this challenge, researchers have introduced methods for light field angular super-resolution and spatial super-resolution. In this paper, our emphasis is on light field angular super-resolution, aiming to reconstruct a densely-sampled light field from a sparsely-sampled one.

Recently, the widespread adoption of deep learning in light field angular super-resolution has gained prominence. Kalantari et al. [9] pioneered the use of convolutional neural networks for reconstructing densely sampled light fields. They divided the reconstruction process into disparity estimation and color estimation and modeled the densely sampled light field separately by two convolutional neural networks. Shi et al. [10] introduced a light field reconstruction network that operates pixel-wise and feature-wise. The approach involves obtaining the depth map for each view using a lightweight optical flow estimation network. Reconstruction is performed in both the pixel and feature domains. A learned soft mask is then applied to combine the results of pixel-wise and feature-based reconstructions. Jin et al. [11] introduced a geometry-aware network designed for large baseline, sparsely-sampled light field angular domain reconstruction. The approach incorporates a depth estimation module to explicitly model scene geometry. Subsequently, the network synthesizes new views using physical warping and incorporates a light field blending module for overall light field reconstruction. However, the effectiveness of the reconstruction is contingent on the accuracy of the estimated depth information, which may be constrained in scenarios involving occlusions and non-Lambertian surfaces.

Wu et al. [12] employed neural networks to 2D EPIs (Epipolar Plane Images) and introduced a "blurring-recovering-deblurring" network framework for light field super-resolution. In addition, they [13] proposed a framework that integrates multiple sets of shear EPIs to achieve large disparity light field super-resolution. Wang et al. [14] suggested an end-to-end light-field super-resolution network utilizing stacked Epipolar Plane Images (EPIs). The approach incorporates 2D strided convolutions and two 3D convolutions to form the Pseudo 4D convolution. This pseudo-4D convolution is then utilized to recover high-frequency detail in the angular domain. However, the performance of those methods is also limited because it relies only on EPI information. Yeung et al. [15] uses spatial-angular alternating convolution to obtain high-dimensional spatial and angular clues to reconstruct the light field. But it ignores the disparity information between different views of the light field.

To efficiently process 4D light field data for light field super-resolution, Wang et al. [16] introduced a domain-specific convolution to decouple the light field images from three dimensions: spatial, angular, and EPI. However, the proposed method only exploits the EPI features in two directions, which does not adequately utilize the disparity information of the light field views. In addition, given the restricted receptive field of Convolutional Neural Networks (CNN), the above method only learns the local information between SAIs, but ignores the non-local spatial and angular features in the light field views.

Therefore, to attain comprehensive extraction of both spatial and angular features, we present the Spatial-Angular Decoupling Interaction Network for light field angular super-resolution, built upon the light field decoupling mechanism [16], and use it to interactively fuse and update the spatial and angular features. Moreover, two sloping directions are added in the EPI feature extraction process to obtain more disparity information. Finally, the global spatial and angular features are combined with four epipolar plane features to accomplish the light field reconstruction of the angular domain. The experiment demonstrates that the spatial angular decoupling interaction module can extract the light field information globally. Furthermore, the reconstruction model introduced in this paper exhibits better reconstruction performance on quantitative metrics and also has a finer texture structure.

In the second section of this paper, the proposed spatial-angular interaction model based on the decoupling mechanism [16] and its advantages are explained in detail. In the third section, this model is compared with the current state-of-the-art angular domain super-resolution model to demonstrate the superiority of our model. Finally, in the fourth section, a summary of the entire study is provided.

2   Proposed Method

The quality of light field reconstruction hinges on the extent to which the available light field information is effectively leveraged. The global features of light field images have been increasingly emphasized in light field super-resolution [17,18] in recent years. Inspired by the DistgASR model [16], this paper introduces a light field angular super-resolution network incorporating spatial-angular interaction. The presented method effectively utilizes both spatial and angular disparity information of the light field. Additionally, it extracts global information to overcome the restricted receptive field of the CNN. As a result, it surpasses the performance of current state-of-the-art reconstruction methods. Figure 1 illustrates the overall framework.

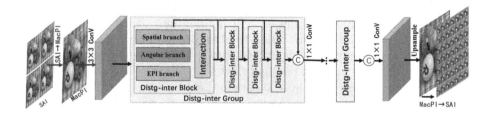

Fig. 1. An overview of the spatial-angular decoupling interaction network.

2.1   Overview of Network Architecture

Derived from the two-plane light field (LF) model [19], an LF image can be expressed as a 4D function $\mathcal{L}(u,v,s,t) \in \mathbb{R}^{U \times V \times H \times W}$, where U and V denote the angular resolution, and H and W represent the spatial resolution. In this paper, we use the square of SAIs array where the dimensions are $A=U=V$. Given the sparsely-sampled SAIs array $\mathcal{L}_{SAI}^{LR} \in \mathbb{R}^{A \times A \times H \times W}$ as input, this network outputs a densely-sampled SAIs array $\mathcal{L}_{SAI}^{HR} \in \mathbb{R}^{\alpha A \times \alpha A \times H \times W}$, where α is the angular upsampling factor.

Our network first converts the input SAIs array $\mathcal{L}_{SAI}^{LR} \in \mathbb{R}^{A \times A \times H \times W}$ into a low-resolution Macro-pixel image (MacPI) $\mathcal{L}_{MacPI}^{LR} \in \mathbb{R}^{AH \times AW}$, which allows more evenly mixing of spatial and angular features and enables more effective extraction of detailed structural information from the LF. Afterward, we use four decoupling interaction groups to perform feature decoupling interactions on $\mathcal{L}_{MacPI}^{LR}$, and each decoupling interaction group contains four decoupling interaction blocks. Each interaction block is made up of three feature extraction branches (i.e., Spatial feature extraction branch, Angular feature extraction branch, EPI feature extraction branch) and a Spatial-Angular Interaction module. × To maximize the use of LF features extracted at each stage, the network cascades the features extracted from various decoupling interaction blocks and feeds them into a 1×1 convolution for feature fusion in each decoupling interaction group. The fused feature $\mathcal{F}_{fuse}^{temp} \in \mathbb{R}^{AH \times AW \times C}$ is utilized as input for the next decoupling interaction group, and cascaded fusion is executed at the end. After four groups of interactive decoupling, we upsample the angle of the final fused features $\mathcal{F}_{fuse} \in \mathbb{R}^{AH \times AW \times C}$ to obtain the final MacPI feature $\mathcal{F}_{MacPI}^{out} \in \mathbb{R}^{\alpha AH \times \alpha AW \times C}$, where α represents the upsampling factor. Finally, we downsample the MacPI channels and convert them to the SAIs array to obtain the densely sampled LF.

2.2 Decoupling Interaction Block

Due to the limitation of the CNN receptive field, the global features of LF cannot be fully explored, which makes LF super-resolution always ineffective in large disparity scenes. To address this, We use LF-InterNet [20] to further explore the global features of LF. The block structure is shown in Fig. 2. Each decoupling interaction block comprises a spatial branch, an angular branch, an EPI branch, and a spatial-angular interaction module.

In the spatial branch, a convolutional layer with a 3×3 kernel size and a dilation of A is utilized. This layer extracts spatial information from the input MacPI feature $\mathcal{L}_{MacPI}^{LR} \in \mathbb{R}^{AH \times AW}$ to acquire the initial spatial feature $\mathcal{F}_{spa}^{0} \in \mathbb{R}^{AW \times AH \times C}$.

In the angular branch, we use a convolutional layer with a kernel size of A × A and a stride of A. This layer extracts the angular information from the input MacPI feature $\mathcal{L}_{MacPI}^{LR} \in \mathbb{R}^{AH \times AW}$ to obtain the initial angular features $\mathcal{F}_{ang}^{0} \in \mathbb{R}^{H \times W \times C}$.

The limitations of the CNN receptive field make us impossible to learn this global information. Therefore, We use LF-InterNet [20] to further explore the global features of LF. Specially, we input the initial spatial feature $\mathcal{F}_{spa}^{0} \in \mathbb{R}^{AH \times AW \times C}$ and the initial angular feature $\mathcal{F}_{ang}^{0} \in \mathbb{R}^{H \times W \times C}$. Through the

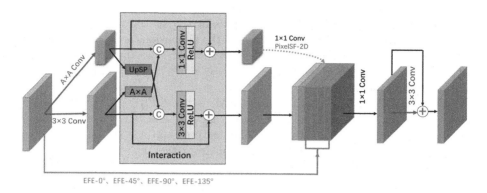

Fig. 2. An overview of the spatial-angular decoupling interaction network.

interactive operation, we obtain the ultimate output spatial feature $\mathcal{F}_{spa}^{out} \in \mathbb{R}^{AH \times AW \times C}$ and output angular feature $\mathcal{F}_{ang}^{out} \in \mathbb{R}^{AH \times AW \times C}$. This process can be formulated as

$$\mathcal{F}_{spa}^{out} = H_{3 \times 3} \left(\left[\mathcal{F}_{spa}^{0}, \left(\mathcal{F}_{ang}^{0} \right) \uparrow \right] \right) + \mathcal{F}_{spa}^{0} \tag{1}$$

$$\mathcal{F}_{ang}^{out} = H_{1 \times 1} \left(\left[\mathcal{F}_{ang}^{0}, H_A \left(\mathcal{F}_{spa}^{0} \right) \right] \right) + \mathcal{F}_{ang}^{0} \tag{2}$$

where $\uparrow$ represents the upsampling operation, $H_{3 \times 3}$ and $H_{1 \times 1}$ represent a 3×3 convolution and a 1×1 convolution, H_A represents a convolutional layer with a kernel size of A $\times$ A and a stride of A.

Different from LF-InterNet, we apply it to the LF angular domain super-resolution. LF spatial super-resolution needs to emphasize the extraction of local detailed texture information of the image, while angular super-resolution is more centered on capturing information about the entire scene and the global consistency among multiple views. We discovered that LF-InterNet can effectively extract global spatial features from the initial features. As shown in Fig. 3(a,b), we output the spatial feature maps before and after the addition of LF-InterNet. We can observe that when the interaction module is added, the new spatial feature maps pay more attention to the global spatial information such as global illumination, color, object outlines, etc. The results demonstrate that LF-InterNet extracts global features of LF to substantially enhance the performance of LF angular super-resolution.

There is an issue that the post-interaction spatial features have a small response to the whole scene, disregarding local details and texture information. Therefore, we adopt the post-interaction angular features to capture the local details and texture information of the LF, as shown in Fig. 3(c). Following this, we merge the interacted spatial features and angular features, enabling us to capture both global and local features.

In addition, LF-InterNet only considers the spatial and angular information of the LF, which ignores the rich disparity information of the LF. To exploit the disparity information of the LF and to ensure the geometric consistency of the reconstructed LF, we introduce an EPI branch for four directions ($0°$, $45°$, $90°$, $135°$) to realize more d disparity information extraction. We utilize a shared convolutional layer with a 3×3 kernel size, which extracts EPI information from EPI in each of the four directions to obtain four EPI features $\mathcal{F}_{epi}^0, \mathcal{F}_{epi}^{45}, \mathcal{F}_{epi}^{90}, \mathcal{F}_{epi}^{135}$. Then we cascade the EPI features in all four directions to acquire the intermediate EPI feature $\mathcal{F}_{epi}^{temp} \in \mathbb{R}^{H \times W \times 4C}$, and a combination of a 1×1 convolutional layer and a 2D pixel shuffling layer is employed to upsample the intermediate EPI feature, resulting in the final output EPI feature. $\mathcal{F}_{epi}^{out} \in \mathbb{R}^{AH \times AW \times C}$.

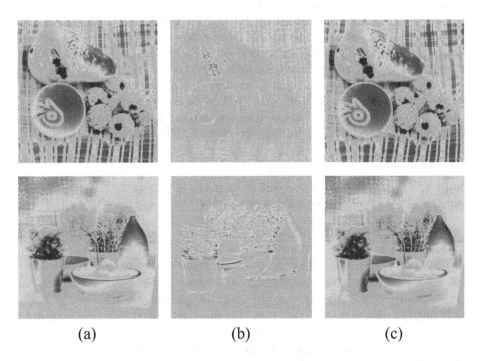

(a)   (b)   (c)

Fig. 3. Column a displays the pre-interaction spatial features, column b shows the post-interaction spatial features and column c represents the post-interaction angular features. It is evident that the spatial features after interaction emphasize global features, while the angular features after interaction emphasize local features.

Finally, we cascade the spatial feature $\mathcal{F}_{spa}^{out}$, the angular feature $\mathcal{F}_{ang}^{out}$ and the EPI feature $\mathcal{F}_{epi}^{out}$, and employ a 1×1 convolutional layer with a stride of 1 for the initial feature fusion. Then we use two 3×3 convolutions to realize the deep integration of spatial information and connect the initial spatial features with it in a local residual learning manner to obtain the output of the spatial angular decoupling interaction block, i.e., the fused features $\mathcal{F}_{fuse} \in \mathbb{R}^{AW \times AH \times C}$.

3   Experiments

3.1   Datasets and Implementation Details

To follow the latest advancements [16, 21, 22] in LF angular super-resolution, we incorporated a combination of synthetic LF datasets (HCInew [23] and HCIold [24]) as well as real-world LF datasets (Kalantari et al. [9] and STFlytro dataset [25]) for training and testing purposes. Specifically, our training set consisted of 20 synthetic scenes and 100 real-world scenes. For evaluation, we utilized 4 scenes from HCInew dataset [23], 5 scenes from HCIold dataset [24], 30 scenes from Kalantari et al. dataset [9], along with 25 Occlusion category scenes and 15 Reflective category scenes from STFlytro dataset [25].

The model is implemented on an NVidia RTX3090 GPU using PyTorch, with a fixed batch size of 4. The initial learning rate is $2 \times e^{-4}$, halving every 15 epochs, and the training runs for a total of 70 epochs. L1 loss is employed for training and the Adam optimizer [26] with $\beta_1 = 0.9$ and $\beta_2 = 0.999$ is used.

For data augmentation, random horizontal flipping, vertical flipping, and 90-degree rotation are applied to all SAIs. RGB color is transformed to the YCbCr color space, and PSNR and SSIM metrics are used for quantitative evaluation on the Y channel of the images. Average scores for PSNR and SSIM are computed for each test dataset.

Table 1. PSNR/SSIM scores for various methods in 2×2 to 7×7 angular super-resolution. The best results are highlighted in **bold**

Method	HCInew	HCIold	30scenes	Occlusion	Reflective
ShearedEPI [13]	31.84/0.898	37.61/0.942	39.17/0.975	34.41/0.955	36.38/0.944
P4DCNN [14]	29.61/0.819	35.73/0.898	38.22/0.970	35.42/0.962	35.96/0.942
Kanlantari [9]	32.85/0.909	38.58/0.944	41.40/0.982	37.25/0.972	38.09/0.953
LFASR-geo [11]	34.60/0.937	40.84/0.960	42.53/0.985	38.36/0.977	38.20/0.955
FS-GAF [21]	**37.14**/0.966	41.80/0.974	42.75/0.986	38.51/0.979	38.35/0.957
DistgASR [16]	34.70/0.974	42.18/0.978	43.67/0.995	39.46/0.991	39.11/0.978
Ours	34.96/**0.976**	**42.48/0.982**	**44.19/0.996**	**40.11/0.992**	**39.37/0.979**

3.2   Experimental Results

Our model was compared to six state-of-the-art methods, which include ShearedEPI [13], P4DCNN [14], Kalantari's proposed method [9], LFASR-geo [11], FS-GAF [21] and DistgASR [16]. To ensure fairness in the method comparison, we applied all of the above LF angular super-resolution methods to the same dataset for training and testing.

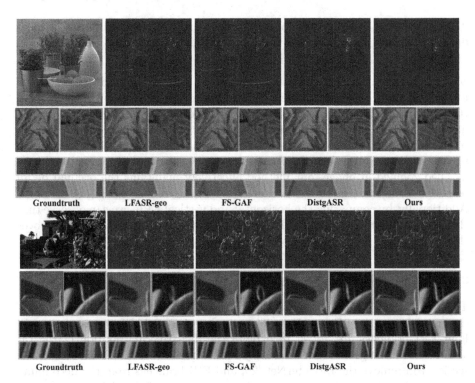

Fig. 4. Visual outcomes of diverse methods on scenes *herb* [24] and *IMG 1555* [9] in the tasks of 2×2 to 7×7 angular super-resolution. The top to bottom sequence includes the central viewpoint error map, zoomed-in regions and EPIs.

Quantitative Results: Table 1 displays the quality outcomes of seven methods for LF angular super-resolution ranging from 2×2 to 7×7. Among the methods, the quality of Sheared EPI [13], P4DCNN [14] is much inferior to the other methods, which is due to the fact that they only extract LF information from EPI and severely underutilize the LF information. While in LFASR-geo [11], FS-GAF [21], and Kalantari's methods [9], they synthesize new views by disparity estimation and obtain good performance metrics. However, the performance is affected by the quality of the estimated disparity maps, which is not good in scenes with occlusions and reflections. The DistgASR [16] model extracts LF information from three branches: spatial, angular, and EPI, and also obtains a good performance score. However, it neglects the problem of CNN receptive field localization, and it uses only horizontal and vertical EPI information, ignoring the disparity information of EPI in other directions.

Our model proposes to use the LF decoupling interaction module to compensate for the localization of the CNN, and to use the 4-direction EPI to obtain more disparity information for the angular super-resolution. Owing to these advancements, Our proposed model attains the highest SSIM values across all datasets (a total of 5 datasets) and the highest PSNR values on 4 out of the 5 datasets (slightly lower than FS-GAF on the HCInew dataset).

Visual Results: To better evaluate our results, we compared the four methods for reconstructing the central view of the LF and the ground truth. We present their differences in the form of error maps and detailed zoom maps. As shown in Fig. 4, we can observe that the reconstructed LF view of our model is closer to the ground truth view, with smaller error values. And it has more detailed textures, e.g., the edge part of the grass in the scene herb is well preserved. In the detailed zoomed-in image, our method effectively maintains the original detail textures, while other methods all show different degrees of blurring or artifacts. Additionally, by comparing the horizontal and vertical EPIs, we can observe that the EPIs of our reconstructed LF are closer to the ground truth, which proves that our method can achieve better geometric consistency.

3.3   Ablation Studies

To address the CNN receptive field limitation problem, the decoupling interaction model uses the LF-InterNet [20] to explore the global features of the LF. Four EPI branches are added to explore the disparity information of the LF and to ensure the geometric consistency of the reconstructed LF. Therefore, the section will remove the LF-InterNet [20] and EPI branches from the decoupling interaction block selectively to verify the effectiveness of the above modules.

Table 2. Comparison of PSNR/SSIM in 2×2 to 7×7 tasks of the ablation experiment model

	InterNet	EPI	30 scenes	Occlusion	Reflective
model_1	×	×	43.67/0.995	39.46/0.991	39.11/0.978
model_2	✓	×	44.12/0.996	39.95/0.992	39.26/0.978
Our	✓	✓	**44.19/0.996**	**40.11/0.992**	**39.37/0.979**

After removing the two EPI branches, we renamed it as model 2. The model2 retains the LF-InterNet module to explore the global features of LF without using the EPI branches to explore the disparity information. As shown in Table 2, we can notice that the PSNR is correspondingly reduced on all three real scene datasets compared to the original model. Average PSNR reduced by 0.11db. This indicates that EPI branches favor LF angular super-resolution performance.

After removing the EPI branches and LF-InterNet module, the model was renamed model1. This new model only incorporates the original feature decoupling module and doesn't include the LF-InterNet module to explore the global features of the LF, nor does it include the EPI branches to explore the disparity information. According to Table 2, the PSNR on all three real scene datasets has decreased compared to the model2. Average PSNR reduced by 0.36db. This showcases the efficacy of the LF-InterNet module in the LF angular super-resolution task.

4   Conclusions

In this paper, we propose a decoupling interaction model for LF angular super-resolution. By using the spatial-angular feature interaction module, our method overcomes the problem of the localization of the receptive field of the CNN. Additionally, we extract the EPI information from four directions to capture more LF disparity information. Through comprehensive experimental results, the Spatial Angular Decoupling Interaction model can extract global features from LFs and our method achieves state-of-the-art performance in $2\times2 \rightarrow 7\times7$ task. The performance improvement of our method is remarkable in comparison with existing methods. In the future, we plan to conduct additional investigations into the method and extend its application to other LF image-processing tasks utilizing CNNs. Moreover, we intend to optimize the model parameters further to achieve a more lightweight configuration.

References

1. Van Duong, V., Canh, T.N., Huu, T.N., Jeon, B.: Focal stack based light field coding for refocusing applications. In: 2019 IEEE International Symposium on Broadband Multimedia Systems and Broadcasting (BMSB), pp. 1–4. IEEE (2019)
2. Wang, Y., Yang, J., Guo, Y., Xiao, C., An, W.: Selective light field refocusing for camera arrays using bokeh rendering and superresolution. IEEE Signal Process. Lett. **26**(1), 204–208 (2018)
3. Jin, J., Hou, J.: Occlusion-aware unsupervised learning of depth from 4-D light fields. IEEE Trans. Image Process. **31**, 2216–2228 (2022)
4. Khan, N., Kim, M.H., Tompkin, J.: Differentiable diffusion for dense depth estimation from multi-view images. In: Proceedings of the IEEE/CVF Conference on Computer Vision and Pattern Recognition, pp. 8912–8921 (2021)
5. Leistner, T., Mackowiak, R., Ardizzone, L., Köthe, U., Rother, C.: Towards multimodal depth estimation from light fields. In: Proceedings of the IEEE/CVF Conference on Computer Vision and Pattern Recognition, pp. 12953–12961 (2022)
6. Cai, Z., Liu, X., Peng, X., Gao, B.Z.: Ray calibration and phase mapping for structured-light-field 3D reconstruction. Opt. Express **26**(6), 7598–7613 (2018)
7. Zhang, J., Yao, Y., Quan, L.: Learning signed distance field for multi-view surface reconstruction. In: Proceedings of the IEEE/CVF International Conference on Computer Vision, pp. 6525–6534 (2021)
8. Overbeck, R.S., Erickson, D., Evangelakos, D., Pharr, M., Debevec, P.: A system for acquiring, processing, and rendering panoramic light field stills for virtual reality. ACM Trans. Graph. (TOG) **37**(6), 1–15 (2018)
9. Kalantari, N.K., Wang, T.C., Ramamoorthi, R.: Learning-based view synthesis for light field cameras. ACM Trans. Graph. (TOG) **35**(6), 1–10 (2016)
10. Shi, J., Jiang, X., Guillemot, C.: Learning fused pixel and feature-based view reconstructions for light fields. In: Proceedings of the IEEE/CVF Conference on Computer Vision and Pattern Recognition, pp. 2555–2564 (2020)

11. Jin, J., Hou, J., Yuan, H., Kwong, S.: Learning light field angular super-resolution via a geometry-aware network. In: Proceedings of the AAAI Conference on Artificial Intelligence, vol. 34, pp. 11141–11148 (2020)

12. Wu, G., Liu, Y., Fang, L., Dai, Q., Chai, T.: Light field reconstruction using convolutional network on EPI and extended applications. IEEE Trans. Pattern Anal. Mach. Intell. **41**(7), 1681–1694 (2018)

13. Wu, G., Liu, Y., Dai, Q., Chai, T.: Learning sheared EPI structure for light field reconstruction. IEEE Trans. Image Process. **28**(7), 3261–3273 (2019)

14. Wang, Y., Liu, F., Wang, Z., Hou, G., Sun, Z., Tan, T.: End-to-end view synthesis for light field imaging with pseudo 4DCNN. In: Proceedings of the European Conference on Computer Vision (ECCV), pp. 333–348 (2018)

15. Yeung, H.W.F., Hou, J., Chen, J., Chung, Y.Y., Chen, X.: Fast light field reconstruction with deep coarse-to-fine modeling of spatial-angular clues. In: Proceedings of the European Conference on Computer Vision (ECCV), pp. 137–152 (2018)

16. Wang, Y., et al.: Disentangling light fields for super-resolution and disparity estimation. IEEE Trans. Pattern Anal. Mach. Intell. **45**(1), 425–443 (2022)

17. Jin, K., Yang, A., Wei, Z., Guo, S., Gao, M., Zhou, X.: Distgepit: enhanced disparity learning for light field image super-resolution. In: Proceedings of the IEEE/CVF Conference on Computer Vision and Pattern Recognition, pp. 1373–1383 (2023)

18. Liang, Z., Wang, Y., Wang, L., Yang, J., Zhou, S., Guo, Y.: Learning non-local spatial-angular correlation for light field image super-resolution. arXiv preprint arXiv:2302.08058 (2023)

19. Levoy, M., Hanrahan, P.: Light field rendering. In: Proceedings of the 23rd Annual Conference on Computer Graphics and Interactive Techniques, pp. 31–42 (1996). https://doi.org/10.1145/237170.237199

20. Wang, Yingqian, Wang, Longguang, Yang, Jungang, An, Wei, Yu, Jingyi, Guo, Yulan: Spatial-angular interaction for light field image super-resolution. In: Vedaldi, Andrea, Bischof, Horst, Brox, Thomas, Frahm, Jan-Michael. (eds.) ECCV 2020. LNCS, vol. 12368, pp. 290–308. Springer, Cham (2020). https://doi.org/10.1007/978-3-030-58592-1_18

21. Jin, J., Hou, J., Chen, J., Zeng, H., Kwong, S., Yu, J.: Deep coarse-to-fine dense light field reconstruction with flexible sampling and geometry-aware fusion. IEEE Trans. Pattern Anal. Mach. Intell. **44**(4), 1819–1836 (2020)

22. Duong, V.V., Huu, T.N., Yim, J., Jeon, B.: Light field image super-resolution network via joint spatial-angular and epipolar information. IEEE Trans. Comput. Imaging **9**, 350–366 (2023). https://doi.org/10.1109/TCI.2023.3261501

23. Honauer, Katrin, Johannsen, Ole, Kondermann, Daniel, Goldluecke, Bastian: A dataset and evaluation methodology for depth estimation on 4D light fields. In: Lai, Shang-Hong., Lepetit, Vincent, Nishino, Ko., Sato, Yoichi (eds.) ACCV 2016. LNCS, vol. 10113, pp. 19–34. Springer, Cham (2017). https://doi.org/10.1007/978-3-319-54187-7_2

24. Wanner, S., Meister, S., Goldluecke, B.: Datasets and benchmarks for densely sampled 4D light fields. In: VMV. vol. 13, pp. 225–226 (2013)

25. A. S. Raj, M. Lowney, R.S., Wetzstein, G.: "stanford Lytro light field archive" (2016)

26. Kingma, D.P., Ba, J.: Adam: A method for stochastic optimization. arXiv preprint arXiv:1412.6980 (2014)

Coding Prior-Driven JPEG Image Artifact Removal

Dongliang Cui[1], Youwei Pan[1], Wuzhen Shi[1(✉)], Yang Wen[1], Zicheng Liu[2], and Yutao Liu[3]

[1] Guangdong Province Engineering Laboratory for Digital Creative Technology, College of Electronics and Information Engineering, Shenzhen University, Shenzhen, China
{wzhshi,wen_yang}@szu.edu.cn

[2] College of Ulsan Ship and Ocean, Ludong University, Yantai, China

[3] School of Computer Science and Technology, Ocean University of China, Qingdao, China

Abstract. Image priors play an important role in JPEG image artifact removal. However, most existing methods ignore the use of coding priors. This paper proposes a Coding Prior-driven JPEG Image Artifact Removal (dubbed CPIAR) method to improve the performance of JPEG image artifact removal. In the JPEG compression algorithm, because the algorithm divides the image into 8×8 blocks and then performs quantization operations, this will cause serious blocking artifacts at the block boundaries. In order to make use of this information, we introduce a mask to represent the boundaries of image blocks. The introduction of this mask makes up for the lack of information about the JPEG compression process in the current deep blind method. We fuse this mask with image features, which can guide the model to focus the boundaries of image blocks, thereby better eliminating the blocking artifacts in JPEG images. In addition, we introduce the Degradation-Aware Dynamic Adjustment Block(DADA Block), which has better nonlinear expression capabilities and can dynamically adjusts the model based on estimated quality factors. Through this improvement we further enhancing its performance in handling JPEG images with varying quality factors.

Keywords: JPEG Compression · Quality Factor · Artifact Removal · Coding Prior · Dynamic Perception Network

1 Introduction

JPEG is a widely adopted image compression algorithm and format [24] favored for its simplicity and fast encoding/decoding speeds. The process involves an initial conversion of the original RGB image into a YCrCb image. Subsequently, the image is divided into 8×8 data blocks to facilitate discrete cosine transform. Next, the discrete cosine transform produces the corresponding sparse matrix. The final step consists of quantizing and encoding the coefficient matrix using a quantization table, resulting in a JPEG image. The quantization table is usually expressed as a quality factor (QF), which is an integer ranging from 0 to 100. A lower quality factor means less storage space, but at the cost of increased information loss. Motivated by the achievements of deep neural networks (DNN) in image classification, researchers turned to DNNs to solve the task of mitigating JPEG artifacts and achieved significant progress.

With the emergence and rapid development of deep learning, deep learning has been successfully applied to many image restoration tasks [6,8], including compressed image artifact removal tasks. Dong et al. [4] first proposed using deep learning methods to remove compression artifacts. Their network contains 4 convolutional layers, demonstrating the great potential of end-to-end trained convolutional neural networks in effectively removing various compression artifacts. Galteric et al. [9] adopted a generative adversarial network. Compared with other methods, this method uses generative adversarial training to improve the removal of artifacts in compressed images, resulting in better visual restoration effects than other methods. However, this type of method may introduce false details into the processed image, making it difficult to apply to scenes that require high image authenticity.

Existing deep learning-based artifact removal methods also make use of transform domains, such as wavelet domain and DCT domain. Chen et al. [3] proposed a method based on discrete wavelet transform. Guo et al. [10] developed a DNN that jointly removes artifacts in the DCT domain and pixel domain. Zhang et al. [29] proposed a fast post-processing method for JPEG images based on dual-domain learning. First, feature extraction is performed on the compressed image in the DCT domain, and then IDCT is used to map the restored DCT coefficients back to the pixel domain. The output is used as part of the input of the pixel domain network, and finally compression artifacts are removed through the pixel domain network. The distortion caused by JPEG compression is because each 8×8 pixel block is quantized after the discrete cosine transform. Therefore, the decompression artifact method based on the DCT domain design can better utilize the compressed prior information. Such networks can often Achieve better artifact removal performance.

Furthermore, most deep learning-based methods require training multiple networks on compressed images with different quality factors to cope with varying degrees of compression artifacts. However, there is bound to be a large parameter redundancy between multiple models of this type of method, which not only consumes a lot of time to train the model, but also takes up a large storage space. To solve this problem, Jiang et al. [14] and others proposed the FBCNN network, which predicts the quality factor of the image and uses this important parameter to guide the artifact removal process. However, current deep learning methods often do not fully utilize the prior information of image segmentation in the JPEG compression process when dealing with JPEG compression artifacts. This lack makes it possible that current models fail to fully understand and exploit the underlying structure of compression when dealing with artifacts. Therefore, in order to more fully understand and solve the problem of JPEG compression artifacts. This paper further explores based on existing research, paying special attention to the full utilization of prior information of JPEG image block. At the same time we proposed a Degradation-aware Dynamic Adjustment Block(DADA Block), using modulation parameter γ embedding the given quality factor to perform dynamic feature fusion. Specifically, we propose a learnable quality factor embedder which generates a modulation parameter γ. Then our DADA block predicts a convolutional kernels and channel-wise modulation coefficients based on the modulation parameter representation γ to o perform feature adaption.

To sum up, this article has the following three contributions: First, we introduce a boundary mask that effectively marks the boundaries of 8×8 pixel blocks in JPEG images to enhance the model's understanding of the JPEG compression process and thus handle artifacts more accurately. Second, we introduce a Degradation-aware Dynamic Adjustment Block(DADA Block), it can flexibly utilize quality factor embedding parameter γ to achieve dynamic perception and adjust feature maps. Due to the depth-wise convolution and channel-wise modulation coefficient in the DADA Block which enhance the nonlinear expression of the network, thereby achieving better image reconstruction. Third, we demonstrate the effectiveness of the method on JPEG images.

2   Related Work

Deep learning is an important research field in machine learning. Because it can automatically extract image features and use back propagation algorithms to update model parameters, it greatly improves the feature expression ability of data-driven methods and is now widely used in the field of computer vision. Convolutional neural networks are often used in image compression artifact removal methods, using local receptive fields, weight sharing and spatial aggregation to achieve feature expression invariant to displacement, scale and shape, and then through TensorFlow [18] , Pytorch [13], etc. The deep learning framework implements network training. Deep learning technology, with its powerful feature fitting ability and generalization ability, far surpasses the performance of traditional artifact removal methods. This section will discuss in detail various deep learning research methods in the field of JPEG image compression artifact removal.

ARCNN [4] first proposed a design scheme using deep learning methods to remove compression artifacts. Its network consists of four convolutional layers. It uses the feature extraction capabilities of the convolutional neural network to train a mapping function from compressed images to reconstructed images, demonstrating the great potential of end-to-end trained CNNs on artifact removal tasks. Based on the fact that human thinking is persistent, Tai et al. [21] proposed a deep persistent memory network, using recursive units and threshold units to form a memory module. The final network achieved good results on multiple image restoration tasks. Zheng et al. [32] uses an autoencoder supplemented by a deep residual network module to first extract features from the input image, and then restore the potential mapping from the feature domain to the original size. The automatic encoding and decoding structure can effectively reduce the amount of network parameters. Galteric et al. [9] uses Generative Adversarial Networks (GAN) and proposes to use structural similarity loss instead of mean square error loss to generate more realistic image details. Using the method of Generative Adversarial Networks, the reconstructed image can be obtained Better visual sensory effects. Xie et al. [26] proposes a weakly connected dense generative adversarial network to remove compression artifacts in high compression ratio images. It uses hybrid convolution, weakly dense connected blocks, hybrid attention mechanisms, etc. to effectively remove compression artifacts and generate Clearer edge texture details. However, this type of method will cause pseudo-details to appear in the processed image. The appearance of pseudo-details makes it difficult to apply to certain scenes that require high image authenticity. Jin et al. [15] proposes to use a dual-stream recursive network to process specific artifacts in high-frequency components and low-frequency components respectively, and reduce the overall parameter amount of the network through a parameter sharing mechanism. Zhang et at. [31] designs a general network that is suitable for a variety of image restoration tasks, using the global attention mechanism to capture the correlation between pixels to enhance the network feature expression ability. This type of method mainly takes advantage of the powerful generalization ability of convolutional neural networks and can adapt to different image restoration tasks by simply providing corresponding training sets. Fu et al. [7] increases the interpretability of the artifact removal network by separately extracting pixel-level features and semantic-level features, and modeling and solving pixel-level priors and semantic-level priors, so that the network can obtain better artifact removal performance. Lee et al. [16] designs a network for image compression artifacts and motion blur, and uses the channel attention mechanism and JPEG automatic encoding loss function to reconstruct compressed images.

With the progress in research on mitigating JPEG compression artifacts, researchers have increasingly focused on transforming images into the frequency domain for processing. Chen et al. [3] proposed a method based on discrete wavelet transform (DWT), which maps the compressed image from the pixel domain to the DWT domain, and then decomposes the image into four sub-images of different frequencies, using soft decoding without introducing Improve image quality with additional coding bits, and finally implement an end-to-end artifact removal method through feature learning. Guo et al. [10] designed a convolutional neural network that jointly learns the prior knowledge of JPEG images in the DCT domain and pixel domain, making full use of the prior knowledge in the DCT domain to achieve an effective artifact removal network. Zhang et al. [29] proposes a fast post-processing method for JPEG images based on dual domains. First, the features of the compressed image are extracted in the DCT domain, and then the extracted features are extracted using the Inverse Discrete Cosine Transform (IDCT). The feature matrix is remapped into the pixel domain, and compression artifacts are removed through the pixel domain network. Sun et al. [20] directly designs an artifact removal network in the DCT domain, and achieves the removal of compression artifacts by reconstructing DCT coefficients. Zhang et al. [30] proposed a generalized JPEG compression artifact removal framework, using a correction network and a quality factor estimator to predict the quality factor, and then using a multi-domain learning cascaded residual encoder network to adaptively restore the compressed image. The distortion caused by the JPEG compression algorithm is due to each pixel block being quantized after DCT transformation. Therefore, the compression artifact removal method based on the DCT domain design can better utilize the prior information of compression and solve the artifacts from the essence of compression artifacts.

Most current deep learning-based methods require training multiple networks for compressed images with different quality factors to cope with different degrees of compression. There is bound to be a large redundancy between such multiple models, which not only consumes a lot of time to train the model but also takes up a large storage space. To solve this problem, Guo et al. [11] estimates the perceptual quality of the reconstructed image through high-level feature perceptual loss, and uses a discriminant network to measure the naturalness of the reconstructed image, and then uses the offset averaging strategy to eliminate the blocking effect, and proposes Blind artifact removal network. Amaranageswarao et al. [2] proposed a network based on densely connected parallel convolution to remove compression artifacts. Parallel convolution can save computing resources, and dense skip connections can alleviate the gradient disappearance problem, ultimately achieving blind artifact removal. QGCN [17] creatively uses the quantization table in JPEG compression, which can remove artifacts from compressed images under multiple quality factors through a single network parameter. However, QGCN's use of the quantization table is relatively rough and does not fully utilize the prior information of the quantization table. Jiang et al. [14] proposes to solve the problem of JPEG non-aligned secondary compression in real scenes, and proposes a blind compression artifact removal scheme that supports interaction. This is the first attempt in the field to solve the problem of JPEG non-aligned secondary compression.

3   Proposed Method

In this section, we introduce an innovative method that aims to fully exploit a prior information in JPEG image compression, specifically focusing on the structure of image blocks. We conducted an in-depth analysis of the shortcomings of existing deep learning methods in handling JPEG compression artifacts and found that current methods generally fail to fully consider the key information of image blocking, which may limit the model's ability to perform artifact removal tasks performance. In view of this, we propose a novel and effective method that introduces a mask that represents the boundaries of image patches, and fuse it into image features. This strategy aims to better guide the model to learn the artifacts caused by JPEG compression and improve the accuracy and effect of artifact removal. Additionally, we propose DADA Block, which uses depthwise convolution and channel-wise modulation coefficients, further enhances the model's capacity for nonlinear feature expression. This innovative addition aims to overcome the limitations associated with existing attention modules and boost the overall performance of the artifact removal process. Below we introduce our proposed method and its key components in detail to demonstrate its superiority in handling JPEG image artifacts.

3.1 Overall Structure

Figure 1 illustrates the overall architecture of our proposed method. Our method is an end-to-end model that takes JPEG images as input and directly generates output images. Specifically, Our method consists of four parts: Encoder, QF Estimator, Learnable Quality Factor Embedder and Decoder, each component is designed to achieve a specific task.

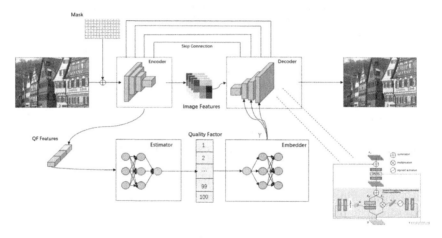

Fig. 1. An architecture of our method to remove JPEG artifacts. It consists of four parts, encoder, quality factor estimator, Learnable Quality Factor Embedder and decoder. The encoder extracts deep features from the input corrupted JPEG images and then splits them into image features and QF features, which are subsequently fed to the decoder and quality factor estimator respectively. Get the estimated QF from the estimator and then generate the QF embedding. The Degradation-Aware Dynamic Adjustment Block enables the embedder to make the decoder produce different results according to different QF embeddings.

3.2 Encoder

The encoder is designed with the goal of extracting deep features from the input image and decoupling underlying quality factors. The structure consists of four scales, each with identity skip connections to the decoder. Each scale consists of 4 residual blocks, and each residual block contains two 3×3 convolutional layers with a ReLU activation function in between. To reduce the scale, we use a 2×2 stride convolution. The number of output channels from the first layer to the fourth layer is set to 64, 128, 256, and 512 respectively. The image features generated by the encoder are passed to the decoder. At the same time, these features are also shared by a quality factor estimation module. In order to introduce prior information about JPEG image blocking, we concatenate the mask used to represent the image blocking information with the input image before passing it to the encoder module, and then input it to the encoder. This strategy aims to better guide the model to learn the boundaries of image patches and thus better eliminate the blocking effect in JPEG images.

3.3   Quality Factor Estimator

QF estimator consisting of three layers of MLP, whose input is the 512-dimensional QF feature and the output is the QF prediction value of the compressed image (QF_{est}). In order to improve the prediction effect, we set the number of nodes in each hidden layer to 512. During the training process, due to the small size of image patches, which may only contain limited information and may correspond to multiple QFs, it may be difficult to accurately predict QFs, leading to instability in training. To solve this problem, we choose to use the L1 loss function to avoid imposing excessive penalties on outliers in training. Assuming N is the batch size during training, the loss of QF estimation in each batch can be expressed in the following form:

$$L_{QF} = \frac{1}{N} \sum_{i=1}^{N} \|QF_{est}^i - QF_{gt}^i\| \tag{1}$$

3.4   Learnable Quality Factor Embedder

The Learnable Quality Factor Embedder is composed of 4 layers MLP and use the quality factor which represents the degree of loss in image compression as input. The goal of the embedder is to take the provided quality factor embedding and integrate it into the decoder to achieve multi-faceted tuning. Motivated by recent research on spatial feature transformation [19, 28], the embedder generates a mapping function that produces a modulation parameter γ that embeds a given quality factor as output. Specifically, the first three layers of the MLP generate a shared intermediate state, which is then divided into three parts corresponding to the three scales in the decoder. In the last layer of the MLP, we learn different parameters at different scales, and the shared γ is passed into the degradation-aware dynamic adjustment block within the same scale.

3.5   Decoder

The image decoder is composed of three scales and receives image features from embedder and QF embedding parameters γ to produce the reconstructed image.

Our DADA block plays an important role in image reconstruction process. The number of DADA blocks in each scale is set to 4. The learned parameter γ which embeds of the quality factor adaptively influences the outputs. Given N training samples in a batch, the goal of the image decoder is to minimize the following L1 loss function between the reconstructed image I_{rec} and the original ground truth image I_{gt}:

$$L_{rec} = \frac{1}{N} \sum_{i=1}^{N} \|I_{rec}^i - I_{gt}^i\|_1 \tag{2}$$

Overall, the complete training loss function can be written as:

$$L_{total} = L_{rec} + \lambda \cdot L_{QF} \tag{3}$$

where λ controls the balance between image reconstruction and QF estimation.

3.6 Degradation-Aware Dynamic Adjustment Block

Inspired by recent research in Degradation-Aware SR Network [25], a Degradation-Aware Dynamic Adjustment Block is proposed to process a modulation parameter γ which embeds the given quality factor. Modulation parameter γ is the output which comes from a mapping function learned by the Learnable Quality Factor Embedder. Our method differs from theirs in that our γ. It is a parameter embedded with a quality factor, and in their method, a parameter is used to represent the degradation representation of the image. Figure 2 illustrates the architecture of our Degradation-Aware Dynamic Adjustment Block. In our DADA Block, two Dynamic Perception Degradation Information Fusion layers are used for feature fusion based on the modulation parameter γ embedding the given quality factor, as shown in Fig. 2. Inspired by the statement that Convolutional kernels of models trained for different restoration levels exhibit similar patterns, but their statistics differ [12], our Dynamic Perception Degradation Information Fusion layer learns to reshape modulation parameter γ into a convolutional kernel $w \in R^{C \times 1 \times 3 \times 3}$ after passing through two full-connected(FC) layers. Meanwhile, γ is sent to another two FC layers and a sigmoid activation layer to generate channel-wise modulation coefficients v. Specifically, the image features are convolved with a 3×3 kernel from w, subsequently passing through a 1×1 convolution to produce F_w. Then, the channel-wise modulation coefficients v modulates the different channel components of the feature map F, resulting in F_v. Finally, F_w is summed up with F_v and passed to the next Dynamic Perception Degradation Information Fusion layers to produce the output feature F_o.

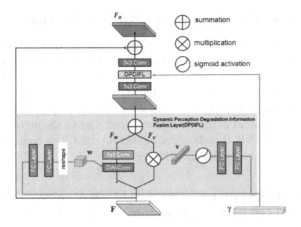

Fig. 2. Degradation-Aware Dynamic Adjustment Block (DADA Block) contains two dynamic-aware degradation information fusion layers. First, the embedded quality factor representation γ is adjusted to the convolution kernel w through learning. Then, the generated channel-level modulation coefficients v are applied to convolution operations respectively to modulate and fuse the features. Finally, the adjusted features are output to more effectively adapt to image processing with different quality factors and improve the removal effect of JPEG artifacts.

4   Experiments

In order to verify the effect of our method, we conducted multiple sets of experiments, involving models that only added masks, models that only introduced new attention mechanism modules, and models that introduced both masks and new attention mechanism modules. To ensure a fair comparison, we use JPEG images generated by the MATLAB JPEG encoder for training and evaluation. When doing color image comparisons, we use RGB channels. As training data, we selected DIV2K [1] and Flickr2K [22], which is consistent with the previous study on [5]. During training, we randomly extracted image patch pairs of size 128×128 with quality factors randomly sampled from 10 to 95. We set the hyperparameter λ to 0.1. To optimize the parameters of the model, we used the Adam solver [23] with a batch size of 256. The learning rate starts from 1×10^{-4}, is halved every 4×10^4 iterations, and is finally set to 1.25×10^{-5}. We trained the model on NVIDIA A100 Tensor Core GPU via PyTorch.

4.1   Comparison Method

The method in this article is mainly compared with the current representative methods based on deep learning: FBCNN [14], QGAC [17]. It should be noted that ARCNN trains a single network for each specific quality factor, while QGAC, FBCNN and our method cover the full range of quality factors. This article compares with other methods on three indicators, namely PSNR, SSIM and PSNR-B [27].

4.2   Performance Comparison with Existing Methods

The quantitative analysis results under single image compression are shown in Table 1. It can be seen from the experimental results in the table that in the case of single image compression, the method in this paper has reached an advanced level in the PSNR index. It is better than QAGC and FBCNN in both SSIM index and PSNR-B index. This means that our methods proposed in this article can achieve effective blind artifact removal. And due to the significant improvement in SSIM and PSNR-B indicators of this method, the reconstructed image can obtain better subjective visual effects.

Table 1. PSNR|SSIM|PSNRB results of different methods on color JPEG images. The best and the second best results are highlighted in red and blue colors, respectively.

Dataset	QF	JPEG	QAGC	FBCNN	Our Method
LIVE1	10	25.69|0.743|24.20	27.62|0.804|27.43	27.77|0.803|27.51	27.91|0.805|27.66
	20	28.06|0.826|26.49	29.88|0.868|29.56	30.11|0.868|29.70	30.24|0.872|29.91
	30	29.37|0.861|27.84	31.17|0.896|30.77	31.43|0.897|30.92	31.58|0.901|31.10
	40	30.28|0.882|28.84	32.05|0.912|31.61	32.34|0.913|31.80	32.49|0.915|31.97
BSDS500	10	25.84|0.741|24.13	27.74|0.802|27.47	27.85|0.799|27.52	27.94|0.801|27.62
	20	28.21|0.827|26.37	30.01|0.869|29.53	30.14|0.867|29.56	30.25|0.871|29.66
	30	29.57|0.865|27.72	31.33|0.898|30.70	31.45|0.897|30.72	31.58|0.900|30.85
	40	30.52|0.887|28.69	32.25|0.915|31.50	32.36|0.913|31.52	32.20|0.916|31.66
ICB	10	29.44|0.757|28.53	32.06|0.816|32.04	32.18|0.815|32.15	33.17|0.857|33.13
	20	32.01|0.806|31.11	34.13|0.843|34.10	34.38|0.844|34.34	35.59|0.887|35.53
	30	33.20|0.831|32.35	35.07|0.857|35.02	35.41|0.857|35.35	36.76|0.900|36.69
	40	33.95|0.840|33.14	32.25|0.915|31.50	36.02|0.866|35.95	37.41|0.902|37.33

4.3   Visual Presentation

We selected two distinct images from the LIVE1_COLOR datasets, subjecting them to JPEG compression with quality factors of 10 and 20. Subsequently, we applied the FBCNN and our proposed method to remove artifacts. The results of artifact removal are illustrated in Fig. 3 and Fig. 4.

4.4   Ablation Experiment

In order to verify the effectiveness of each module of this method, Table 2 shows a series of ablation experimental results to verify the contribution of the mask and DADA Block to the network. Since the method in this chapter has stable performance under various quality factors, and for the convenience of analysis, only the test results of networks with quality factors of 10, 20, 30 and 40 in the LIVE1 data set are listed in the ablation experiment. When the experimental settings are consistent with the method in this article, the ablation experiment is shown in Table 2. In the ablation experiment, Model 1 removed the mask mechanism and only retained the new attention mechanism module. In Model 2, the new attention mechanism module is removed, and only the mask mechanism is retained. Our method retains both the mask mechanism and the new attention mechanism module. It can be seen from the ablation experimental results that the mask mechanism and the new attention mechanism module proposed in this chapter have a great contribution to the artifact removal performance of this method.

Table 2. PSNR|SSIM|PSNRB results of ablation experiments on color JPEG images

Dataset	QF	Model 1(Mask)	Model 2(DADA Block)	Ours
LIVE1	10	27.83|0.804|27.58	27.81|0.803|27.56	27.91|0.805|27.66
	20	30.16|0.870|29.74	30.14|0.869|29.73	30.24|0.872|29.91
	30	31.49|0.898|30.99	31.47|0.897|30.97	31.58|0.901|31.10
	40	32.39|0.914|31.85	32.37|0.913|31.82	32.49|0.915|31.97
BSDS500	10	27.90|0.800|27.58	27.89|0.799|27.57	27.94|0.801|27.62
	20	30.20|0.869|29.60	30.18|0.868|29.61	30.25|0.871|29.66
	30	31.53|0.898|30.78	31.51|0.898|30.76	31.58|0.900|30.85
	40	32.45|0.915|31.58	32.43|0.914|31.55	32.20|0.916|31.66
ICB	10	33.06|0.857|33.01	33.05|0.856|33.02	33.17|0.857|33.13
	20	35.48|0.887|35.41	35.47|0.885|35.44	35.59|0.887|35.53
	30	36.65|0.899|36.56	36.66|0.899|36.60	36.76|0.900|36.69
	40	37.30|0.901|37.20	37.30|0.900|37.23	37.41|0.902|37.33

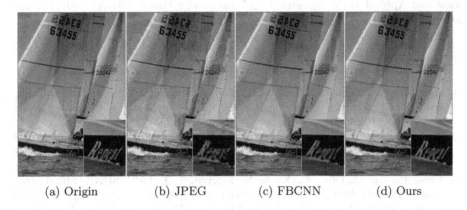

(a) Origin   (b) JPEG   (c) FBCNN   (d) Ours

Fig. 3. Visual comparisons of different methods on a single JPEG image 'LIVE1: sailing3' with QF = 10.

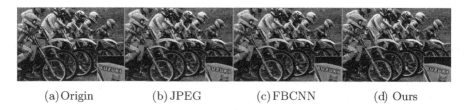

(a) Origin   (b) JPEG   (c) FBCNN   (d) Ours

Fig. 4. Visual comparisons of different methods on a single JPEG image 'LIVE1: bikes' with QF = 20.

5   Conculusion

This article presents an innovative approach to solving the problem of artifact removal from JPEG images. By introducing boundary masks and DADA Blocks, we make substantial improvements over existing depth-blind methods. In the JPEG image compression process, the 8×8 pixel block is the basic processing unit, but existing depth-blind methods often ignore this key information. By adding boundary masks, the model is able to more accurately capture image patch information of JPEG images, resulting in better performance in artifact removal tasks. We also propose a Degradation-Aware Dynamic Adjustment Block (DADA block) to perform dynamic feature fusion using modulation parameters γ embedded with a given figure of merit. Experimental results demonstrate the flexibility, effectiveness, and versatility of our proposed method in recovering different types of degraded JPEG images.

Acknowledgments. This work was supported in part by the National Science Foundation of China under Grants 62101346 and 62301330, and in part by the Guangdong Basic and Applied Basic Research Foundation under Grants 2021A1515011702 and 2022A1515110101.

References

1. Agustsson, E., Timofte, R.: Ntire 2017 challenge on single image super-resolution: dataset and study. In: Proceedings of the IEEE Conference on Computer Vision and Pattern Recognition Workshops, pp. 126–135 (2017)
2. Amaranageswarao, G., Deivalakshmi, S., Ko, S.B.: Blind compression artifact reduction using dense parallel convolutional neural network. Signal Process. Image Commun. **89**, 116009 (2020)
3. Chen, H., He, X., Qing, L., Xiong, S., Nguyen, T.Q.: DPW-SDNET: dual pixel-wavelet domain deep CNNs for soft decoding of jpeg-compressed images. In: Proceedings of the IEEE Conference on Computer Vision and Pattern Recognition Workshops, pp. 711–720 (2018)
4. Dong, C., Deng, Y., Loy, C.C., Tang, X.: Compression artifacts reduction by a deep convolutional network. In: Proceedings of the IEEE International Conference on Computer Vision, pp. 576–584 (2015)

5. Ehrlich, M., Davis, L., Lim, S.-N., Shrivastava, A.: Quantization guided JPEG artifact correction. In: Vedaldi, A., Bischof, H., Brox, T., Frahm, J.-M. (eds.) ECCV 2020. LNCS, vol. 12353, pp. 293–309. Springer, Cham (2020). https://doi.org/10.1007/978-3-030-58598-3_18

6. Fu, D., Shi, Y.Q., Su, W.: A generalized Benford's law for jpeg coefficients and its applications in image forensics. In: Security, Steganography, and Watermarking of Multimedia Contents IX, vol. 6505, pp. 574–584. SPIE (2007)

7. Fu, X., Wang, X., Liu, A., Han, J., Zha, Z.J.: Learning dual priors for JPEG compression artifacts removal. In: Proceedings of the IEEE/CVF International Conference on Computer Vision, pp. 4086–4095 (2021)

8. Fu, X., Zha, Z.J., Wu, F., Ding, X., Paisley, J.: JPEG artifacts reduction via deep convolutional sparse coding. In: Proceedings of the IEEE/CVF International Conference on Computer Vision, pp. 2501–2510 (2019)

9. Galteri, L., Seidenari, L., Bertini, M., Del Bimbo, A.: Deep generative adversarial compression artifact removal. In: Proceedings of the IEEE International Conference on Computer Vision, pp. 4826–4835 (2017)

10. Guo, J., Chao, H.: Building dual-domain representations for compression artifacts reduction. In: Leibe, B., Matas, J., Sebe, N., Welling, M. (eds.) ECCV 2016. LNCS, vol. 9905, pp. 628–644. Springer, Cham (2016). https://doi.org/10.1007/978-3-319-46448-0_38

11. Guo, J., Chao, H.: One-to-many network for visually pleasing compression artifacts reduction. In: Proceedings of the IEEE Conference on Computer Vision and Pattern Recognition, pp. 3038–3047 (2017)

12. He, J., Dong, C., Qiao, Y.: Modulating image restoration with continual levels via adaptive feature modification layers. In: Proceedings of the IEEE/CVF Conference on Computer Vision and Pattern Recognition, pp. 11056–11064 (2019)

13. Imambi, S., Prakash, K.B., Kanagachidambaresan, G.: Pytorch. Programming with TensorFlow: solution for edge computing applications, pp. 87–104 (2021)

14. Jiang, J., Zhang, K., Timofte, R.: Towards flexible blind JPEG artifacts removal. In: Proceedings of the IEEE/CVF International Conference on Computer Vision, pp. 4997–5006 (2021)

15. Jin, Z., Iqbal, M.Z., Zou, W., Li, X., Steinbach, E.: Dual-stream multi-path recursive residual network for JPEG image compression artifacts reduction. IEEE Trans. Circuits Syst. Video Technol. **31**(2), 467–479 (2020)

16. Lee, D., Lee, C., Kim, T.: Wide receptive field and channel attention network for jpeg compressed image deblurring. In: Proceedings of the IEEE/CVF Conference on Computer Vision and Pattern Recognition, pp. 304–313 (2021)

17. Li, J., Wang, Y., Xie, H., Ma, K.K.: Learning a single model with a wide range of quality factors for JPEG image artifacts removal. IEEE Trans. Image Process. **29**, 8842–8854 (2020)

18. Pang, B., Nijkamp, E., Wu, Y.N.: Deep learning with tensorflow: a review. J. Educ. Behav. Stat. **45**(2), 227–248 (2020)

19. Qiu, Y., Wang, R., Tao, D., Cheng, J.: Embedded block residual network: a recursive restoration model for single-image super-resolution. In: Proceedings of the IEEE/CVF International Conference on Computer Vision, pp. 4180–4189 (2019)

20. Sun, M., He, X., Xiong, S., Ren, C., Li, X.: Reduction of JPEG compression artifacts based on DCT coefficients prediction. Neurocomputing **384**, 335–345 (2020)

21. Tai, Y., Yang, J., Liu, X., Xu, C.: Memnet: a persistent memory network for image restoration. In: Proceedings of the IEEE International Conference on Computer Vision, pp. 4539–4547 (2017)

22. Timofte, R., Agustsson, E., Van Gool, L., Yang, M.H., Zhang, L.: Ntire 2017 challenge on single image super-resolution: methods and results. In: Proceedings of the IEEE Conference on Computer Vision and Pattern Recognition Workshops, pp. 114–125 (2017)
23. Tutunov, R., Li, M., Cowen-Rivers, A.I., Wang, J., Bou-Ammar, H.: Compositional ADAM: an adaptive compositional solver. arXiv preprint arXiv:2002.03755 (2020)
24. Wallace, G.: The JPEG still picture compression standard. IEEE Trans. Consum. Electron. **38**(1), xviii–xxxiv (1992). https://doi.org/10.1109/30.125072
25. Wang, L., et al.: Unsupervised degradation representation learning for blind super-resolution. In: Proceedings of the IEEE/CVF Conference on Computer Vision and Pattern Recognition, pp. 10581–10590 (2021)
26. Xie, B., Zhang, H., Jung, C.: WCDGAN: weakly connected dense generative adversarial network for artifact removal of highly compressed images. IEEE Access **10**, 1637–1649 (2021)
27. Yim, C., Bovik, A.C.: Quality assessment of deblocked images. IEEE Trans. Image Process. **20**(1), 88–98 (2010)
28. Zhang, K., Zuo, W., Zhang, L.: Learning a single convolutional super-resolution network for multiple degradations. In: Proceedings of the IEEE Conference on Computer Vision and Pattern Recognition, pp. 3262–3271 (2018)
29. Zhang, X., Yang, W., Hu, Y., Liu, J.: DMCNN: dual-domain multi-scale convolutional neural network for compression artifacts removal. In: 2018 25th IEEE International Conference on Image Processing (ICIP), pp. 390–394. IEEE (2018)
30. Zhang, Y., Chandler, D.M., Mou, X.: Multi-domain residual encoder-decoder networks for generalized compression artifact reduction. J. Vis. Commun. Image Represent. **83**, 103425 (2022)
31. Zhang, Y., Li, K., Li, K., Zhong, B., Fu, Y.: Residual non-local attention networks for image restoration. arXiv preprint arXiv:1903.10082 (2019)
32. Zheng, B., Sun, R., Tian, X., Chen, Y.: S-Net: a scalable convolutional neural network for JPEG compression artifact reduction. J. Electron. Imaging **27**(4), 043037–043037 (2018)

Media Computing

Where to Forget: A New Attention Stability Metric for Continual Learning Evaluation

Haojie Wang, Qingbo Wu[✉], Hongliang Li, and Fanman Meng

University of Electronic Science and Technology of China, Chengdu, China
wanghaojie@std.uestc.edu.cn, {qbwu,hlli,fmmeng}@uestc.edu.cn

Abstract. Continual learning aims to accumulate knowledge from data streams of multiple tasks, which may suffer catastrophic forgetting due to the data incompleteness in each separate training task. To date, the average accuracy and forgetting rate are the two most popular metrics for continual learning evaluation. However, these two metrics only care about the overall increment of mistaken samples when a model updated by the new task is applied to the old tasks, which fails to *localize* the trajectory of forgetting through multiple training stages. In this paper, we propose a new Attention Stability Metric (ASM) to explicitly illustrate and quantify the forgetting degree of a continual learning model by jointly considering the Changes in Regions of Interest (CRoI) and classification accuracy, which measures the performance of continual learning model in terms of a two-dimensional distance and prefer the models producing consistent changes in terms of RoI and classification accuracy. Experiments show that our evaluation metric offers new insight for analyzing the forgetting characteristics of different continual learning algorithms.

Keywords: Continual Learning · Evaluation Metric · Attention Stability · Two-dimensional Measurement

1 Introduction

Currently, Deep Neural Networks (DNNs) have achieved impressive progress in many image processing tasks such as image classification, detection and segmentation, which is usually based on a model being trained and tested on a complete data with static distributions [4, 8, 12]. However, data flow is often not static in reality. After the first training completed, DNNs needs to be trained and tested on new data that springs up from time to time [3]. The training

This work was supported in part by the National Key R&D Program of China (2021ZD0112001), the National Natural Science Foundation of China (No.61971095), and the Independent Research Project of Civil Aviation Flight Technology and Flight Safety Key Laboratory (FZ2022ZZ06).

G. Zhai et al. (Eds.): IFTC 2023, CCIS 2066, pp. 125–137, 2024.
https://doi.org/10.1007/978-981-97-3623-2_10

data continues to increase, but the data of old tasks is no longer available due to storage limitation or privacy protection. At this time, the catastrophic forgetting of DNNs will lead to poor performance of test accuracy especially on old tasks [1,10]. In other words, DNNs cannot adapt to dynamically changing data distributions over time. Specific to Class Incremental Learning (CIL) in continual learning, the model needs to face an increasing number of tasks and each task contains new classes that need to be recognized. During the inference, task identity is unknown and the model must give discriminant result among all learned classes [14]. Catastrophic forgetting makes the model lose ability to recognize old classes, trapping it in recognizing only a limited number of classes in a static environment.

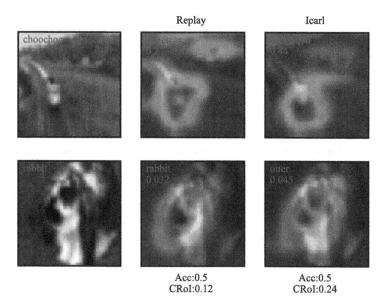

Fig. 1. Although these two CIL algorithms Icarl and Replay have the same average classification accuracy when predicting the two test images choochoo and rabbit of CIFAR100, the average Changes in Regions of Interest (CRoI) are different. In this figure, the first line in the upper left corner of each heat map is the classification result predicted by the CIL algorithm model, and the second line is the CRoI score, respectively.

To solve catastrophic forgetting problem of DNNs when facing dynamic data flow, improvement algorithms have been proposed based on model regularization [5], sample replay [11] and dynamic network expansion [15–17]. The evaluation of improvement of these algorithms in CIL is often given by classification accuracy of the model [9,21]. The main evaluation metrics include Incremental Accuracy (IA), Average Accuracy (AA), Forgetting Rate (FR) and Average Forgetting (AF). IA is the classification accuracy of the model on test data of all classes that it has learned. AA is the average of IA after every task trained. FR refers to the degree to which the model's classification accuracy drops on test data of each old task it has learned before. The AF refers to the average FR generated by each learned task. Although these metrics based on classification accuracy can reflect the final performance of CIL model, they are not specific to the catastrophic forgetting of DNNs. The reasons behind it lack intuitive explanation due to single measurement dimension. Therefore, it is necessary to add metrics based on different dimensions to better understand why DNNs forget. Although sometimes the prediction accuracy is the same, the network's attention of different algorithms to the image has changed differently, as shown in Fig. 1. Through experiments, we found that despite some CIL algorithms have improved accuracy, the stability of regions of interest is not very high. Furthermore, the accuracy of some algorithms with relatively stable regions of interest has dropped sharply, which is shown in Fig. 2.

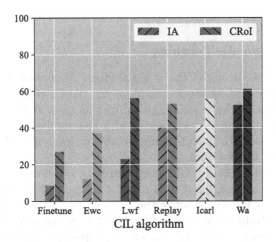

Fig. 2. Incremental Accuracy (IA) and Changes in Regions of Interest (CRoI) of different CIL algorithms on CIFAR100 after 10 tasks learning.

In order to provide an intuitive explanation and quantifiable evaluation of the catastrophic forgetting of DNNs in more dimensions, we proposed to use Class Activation Mapping (CAM) [19] that explains the degree of model's attention to different areas of an input image to measure the forgetting of model. In addition to this, the overall process performance of a CIL algorithm is evaluated combined with classification accuracy. Due to its uninterpretable characteristics, DNNs often use CAM to visualize model's basis for prediction making. The basic idea is to take output feature map of the last convolution layer and apply weight parameters to obtain a CAM. Combining CAM with the input image to form a heat map can clearly show different levels of importance for the model of different areas of input image. In image classification task, it is reflected in whether the classification target to the corresponding label in the image is accurately found. We proposed to apply Gradient-weighted Class Activation Mapping (Grad-CAM) [13] to the evaluation, and designed quantifiable metrics to measure the stability on image regions of interest. What's more, an evaluation metric combined with IA is constructed to measure the entire continual learning process. Specifically, the contributions of this article are as follows:

*We used Grad-CAM to design a quantifiable evaluation metric to re-measure the forgetting of DNNs in CIL from new perspective of model attention.

*We designed new comprehensive evaluation metric combined with classification accuracy and model attention changes, and quantitatively and visually compared the specific performance of different CIL algorithms.

*Through experimental analysis of multiple CIL algorithms and evaluation using the metrics we designed, the quantifiable comparison performance of different algorithms are demonstrated.

2   Preliminary

2.1   Class Incremental Learning

Class Incremental Learning (CIL) is a paradigm of continual learning, which means training and testing models on dynamic data streams, with the model accessing only part of the training data during a task. A CIL model builds a universal classifier among all seen classes with the number of classes increasing task by task. A good CIL model should be able to learn new classes knowledge without forgetting the old ones.

Let t represent the ID of a CIL task, and let $t = 0$ be the first task learned by the model. By analogy, input data of the t-th task is labeled $D_t = \{x_t, y_t\} \cup \{\tilde{x}_t, \tilde{y}_t\}$, where x_t is the image set of the t-th task, y_t is the corresponding label set. $\{x_t, y_t\}$ is the training data and $\{\tilde{x}_t, \tilde{y}_t\}$ is the test data. And let C_t represent the number of classes of the t-th task, and N_t represent the number of samples of test data of the t-th task. T is the total number of tasks. For CIL, different tasks have different classes to learn and there is no class overlap, which means $y_i \cap y_j = \emptyset, i \neq j$. The model must identify a test image from all learned classes because the ID of task which the test image belongs to is not given at inference.

2.2   Grad-CAM

Class Activation Mapping (CAM) is a neural network visualization tool that can be used to explore the interpretability of the model. For a test image, we can generate it's CAM by scoring the pixels at every position on the image, with the highest being 1 and the lowest being 0. We can get a saliency map which can be viewed as contribution distribution to the model's prediction. The higher the score, the higher the response and the greater the contribution of the corresponding area to the model's prediction, and vice versa. Gradient-weighted Class Activation Mapping (Grad-CAM) [13] can obtain CAM using only the trained model without additional training. Specifically, Grad-CAM uses the trained model weights to back-transmit to the parameter layer that needs to visualize such as a convolution layer, and obtains a gradient map whose size as same as the output feature map of the parameter layer. Then global average pooling of spatial dimensions is performed on the gradient map to obtain a weight vector. The weight vector that has equal length to number of the feature's channel is used to weight each channel of the feature layer. CAM map is finally obtained by adding all weighted channels. Grad-CAM does not need to modify structure and retrain the original model, but only use the trained weights to extract the gradient of back propagation.

Let $z \in R^{m \times n}$ represent a CAM with width m and height n for class c. First, we calculate the gradient of the last fully connected layer class logit y_c of the classification network to a certain convolutional layer output feature map F_k (k is the number of channels). The shape of the gradient of G_k is the same as the feature map F_k. Then we can get the weight θ_k^c of the k-th channel by Eq. 1 through global average pooling.

$$\theta_k^c = \frac{1}{m * n} \sum_i \sum_j G_{ij}^k \tag{1}$$

Applying θ_k^c to weight the feature map F_k, CAM z of the test image corresponding to class c on the interesting convolutional layer is obtained:

$$z = \mathrm{ReLu}\left(\sum_k \theta_k^c F^k \right) \tag{2}$$

3   Proposed Methods

In this section, the specific design and calculation methods of metrics proposed in this paper will be explained. The core idea is that DNNs' forgetting of old knowledge can be manifested as Changes in Regions of Interest (CRoI) in the same test image. Measuring this regional change of attention to the target area can reflect the extent to which the deep neural network forgets knowledge. Therefore, we proposes to use Grad-CAMs at different CIL task stages to measure effectiveness of CIL algorithms in curbing catastrophic forgetting and gives the quantitative metric CRoI. Further, two more intermediate metrics Deviation (DV) and Relevance (RL) are formed based on the both CRoI and classification accuracy. Finally, DV and RL are combined as Attention Stability Metric (ASM) to measure overall performance of CIL algorithms (Fig. 3).

3.1   CRoI

For each task t of CIL, when the model M completes the training of data $\{x_t, y_t\}$, class activation map (CAM) z_t^i of the i-th image x_t^i of test data $\{\tilde{x}_t, \tilde{y}_t\}$ on its true label $\tilde{y}_t^i$ is saved and set to the standard CAM of i-th image. And let z_t

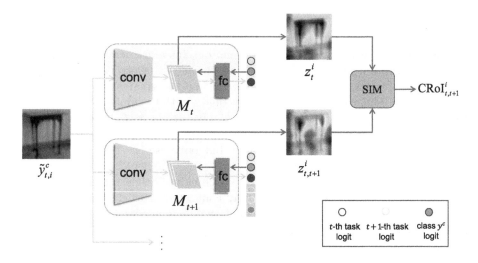

Fig. 3. Illustration of calculational progress of Changes in Regions of Interest (CRoI). M_t infers to model of t-th task and M_{t+1} infers to model of $t + 1$-th task. Light blue arrows shows flow of inference and deep blue arrows shows flow of CRoI generation.

be the representation of all z_t^i. Incremental Accuracy (IA) of test datas of all learned tasks is calculated after task t training based on Eq. 3 where $\hat{y}$ is the model prediction label and I denotes an indicator function.

$$IA_t = \frac{\sum\limits_{0 \leq m \leq t} \sum\limits_{0 \leq i \leq N_m} I\left(\hat{y}_m^i = \tilde{y}_m^i\right)}{\sum\limits_{0 \leq m \leq t} N_m} \tag{3}$$

Then CAM $z_{m,t}$ of test data $\{\tilde{x}_m, \tilde{y}_m\}(m < t)$ belongs to old task m on the model M_t after completing the current task t training is calculated, which is used to generate CRoI. For test data of current task t, there is $z_{t,t} = z_t$. For $t = 0$, there is no old task test data. CAM $z_{m,t}$ of old task test data and its standard CAM z_m generated by its first training model are subjected to probability normalization preprocessing in order to measure the Changes in Regions of Interest. To amplify the degree of representation of regional differences of interest, the probability distribution is normalized using a exponential function. For a CAM z, the processing process is shown by Eq. 4.

$$z'(p,q) = \text{softmax}(\frac{z(p,q)}{\rho}) = \frac{\exp(\frac{z(p,q)}{\rho})}{\sum_m \sum_n \frac{z(m,n)}{\rho}} \tag{4}$$

z' represents the CAM that has completed probability normalization, and (p,q) represents the point on CAM whose abscissa and ordinate are respectively p and q. ρ is the nonlinear mapping amplification parameter. Here, $\rho = 0.1$ is taken to amplify the class activation map from a numerical distribution range of 0–1 to 0–10 to fully reflect the difference in Changes in Regions of Interest.

Afterwards, we perform matrix similarity (SIM) measurement on $z'_{m,t}$ and z'_m. SIM takes smaller value comparing the corresponding position elements of two matrices and then sums them as showed on Eq. 5. If the two matrices' distributions are completely same, the SIM score is 1. If the two distributions have no intersection at all, the SIM score is 0.

$$\text{SIM}(z'_{m,t}, z'_m) = \sum_p \sum_q \text{MIN}(z'_{m,t}(p,q), z'_m(p,q)) \tag{5}$$

In each task t, CAMs of old tasks are compared with the standard CAM to obtain the similarity score. Average value of all of them is taken as the score CRoI_t for current task t based on Eq. 6.

$$\text{CRoI}_t = \frac{\displaystyle\sum_{0 \leq m \leq t}\sum_{0 \leq i \leq N_t} SIM\left(\text{softmax}\left(\frac{z^i_{m,t}}{\rho}\right), \text{softmax}\left(\frac{z^i_m}{\rho}\right)\right)}{\displaystyle\sum_{0 \leq m \leq t} N_t} \tag{6}$$

When $0 \leq m < t$ and $t \geq 1$, CRoI of test data from past tasks is defined as $\text{CRoI}_t -$past. In the same way, past tasks classification accuracy $\text{FA}_t -$past when $0 \leq m < t$ and $t \geq 1$ can be obtained.

3.2   DV, RL and ASM

In order to measure overall attention stability and classification accuracy performance in CIL, Deviation (DV) and Relevant (RL) were constructed combined with Incremental Accuracy (IA). The specific method is to take CRoI_t as the abscissa, IA_t as the ordinate, and the coordinate $(\text{CRoI}_0, \text{IA}_0)$ of the first task as the standard point. The Euclidean distance between the subsequent task t point $(\text{CRoI}_t, \text{IA}_t)$ and the standard point is defined as DV_t. In addition, a straight line with a slope of 1 passing through the standard point is set as the standard line. The distance from the subsequent task t point to the standard line is defined as RL_t.

$$\text{DV}_t = \frac{\displaystyle\sum_{1 \leq m < T} \sqrt{(\text{CRoI}_t - \text{CRI}_0)^2 + (\text{IA}_t - \text{IA}_0)^2}}{T - 1} \tag{7}$$

$$\text{RL}_t = \frac{\displaystyle\sum_{1 \leq m < T} |\text{CRoI}_t - \text{IA}_t - \text{CRoI}_0 + \text{IA}_0|}{\sqrt{2}\,(T - 1)} \tag{8}$$

DV represents integrated Changes of Incremental Accuracy and Regions of Interest after the first training of model. Ideally, DV should be consistent with the initial performance and equal to 0. RL shows whether the model shows consistency in the degree of decline in regional attention stability and classification accuracy in subsequent tasks. The larger the value of RL, the lower the correlation between the model's classification accuracy and the stability of regional attention in subsequent tasks of CIL, and the more serious the model's loss of ability of mapping relationship between target's area and classification accuracy in learned tasks.

To merge DV and RL, we use an S-shaped curve to normalize and multiply the two metrics respectively to measure overall performance. Finally, the difference between 1 and their product forms Attention Stability Metric (ASM) as shown on Eq. 9, which measures both RoI and classification accuracy of overall CIL process. A good CIL algorithm's ASM should be close to 1, while some with poor performance will approach 0.

$$\text{ASM} = 1 - \frac{DV}{DV + \alpha_1} \cdot \frac{RL}{RL + \alpha_2} \tag{9}$$

α_1 and α_2 in Eq. 9 are the S-curve normalization parameters of DV and RL respectively. Since the ratio of the possible maximum values of DV and RL is $\text{MAX}(DV)/\text{MAX}(RL) = 2$, there is $\alpha_1 = 2\alpha_2$ to keep the normalized dynamic range consistent when the two values are merged. In the following experiment, α_2 is set to 0.1 and α_1 is set to 0.2.

4   Experimental Results

4.1   Implementation Details

We use CIFAR100 [6] as experiment dataset, which contains a total of 100 classes. Each class has 500 training images and 100 testing images respectively, for a total of 60,000 images. The size of each image is 32×32. In CIFAR100, 100 classes are divided into 10 tasks, each task has 10 classes to learn to perform CIL.

The deep neural network structure used in the experiment is ResNet32 [4], and the Grad-CAM is used to generate class activation mapping (CAM). Experiments performed on a single RTX3090ti based on codesets PYCIL [20] and pytorch-grad-cam [2]. In order to display the experimental results more clearly and accurately, values of all metrics on tables and figures are enlarged from 0–1 to 0–100.

4.2   Selected Algorithms

(1) Finetune: Does not use any additional actions to prevent catastrophic forgetting and directly finetunes the model on different tasks' data.
(2) Ewc [5]: Uses a parameter matrix to estimate the importance of model parameters. When the model learns new tasks, it hinders changes in parameters that are important to old tasks.
(3) Lwf [7]: Copys and freezes the model on old tasks, and uses distillation strategy to approximate the response of training copied model to the freezed old model's while training on new task data.
(4) Replay: Retains a small portion of samples from old task data and trains the model together with new task data.

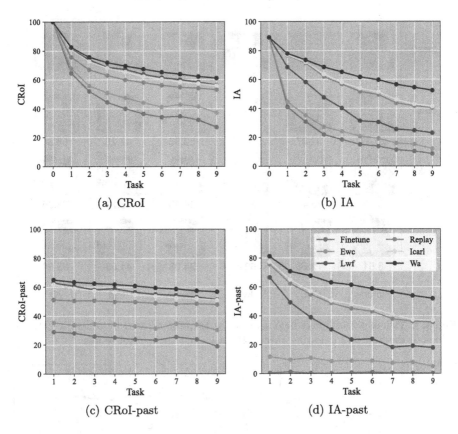

Fig. 4. CRoI, IA, CRoI-past and IA-past of different CIL algorithms on CIFAR100.

(5) Icarl [11]: Retains old task data through targeted filtering and combines the distillation loss of the old model responses to train CIL model.
(6) Wa [18]: Reduces the imbalance between old classes and new classes by aligning average value of the weight vectors of the last fully connected layer.

4.3 Results

By observing Fig. 4(a) and Fig. 4(b), we can see that CRoI curves reflect the scores of different algorithms on Changes in Regions of Interest. The performance of different algorithms on CRoI is basically consistent with the performance of their IA curves. However, although some algorithms such as Lwf have higher CRoI scores, their IA scores are very low. This is also reflected in the CRoI-past and IA-past curves on Fig. 4(c) and Figure (d).

Figure 5 shows that CAMs and their CRoI scores on the same test image belongs to class **table**. The quantitative scores of Changes in Regions of Interest are basically consistent with subjective observation of the degree of shift of CAMs in different tasks. The CRoI-past of each algorithm are decomposed into correctly

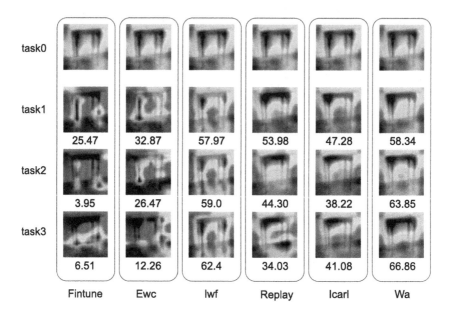

Fig. 5. CAMs of a test image belongs to class **table** generated by different CIL algorithms in the first and following three CIL tasks and their CRoI scores.

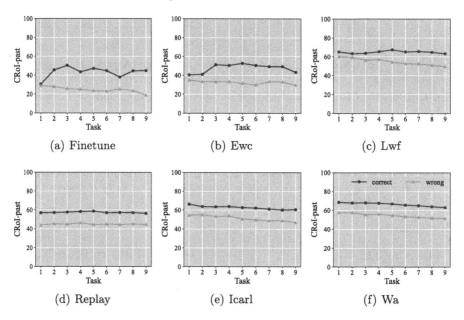

Fig. 6. CRoI-past corresponding to correct classification and wrong classification respectively of different CIL algorithms on CIFAR100

classified samples and wrongly classified samples, as shown in Fig. 6. The average CRoI-past score of correctly classified test samples is higher than that of wrongly classified samples in different CIL tasks, which shows that the stability of regions of interest is a basis for good classification accuracy performance.

Table 1. DV, RL and ASM of different CIL algorithms after 10 tasks learning.

Algorithms	Finetune	Ewc	Lwf	Replay	Icarl	Wa
DV(Normalized)	82.13	80.73	75.32	72.55	70.81	67.01
RL(Normalized)	43.25	47.94	53.0	30.87	23.82	27.56
ASM	64.48	61.3	60.08	77.6	83.13	81.53

The CRoI-IA curves of different CIL algorithms in each task of CIL are drawn in Fig. 7. DV, RL and ASM are calculated as shown in Table 1. Algorithms that do not use sample replay, such as Ewc and Lwf, have better DV than the baseline. But their ASM is lower than the baseline due to poor correlation performance,

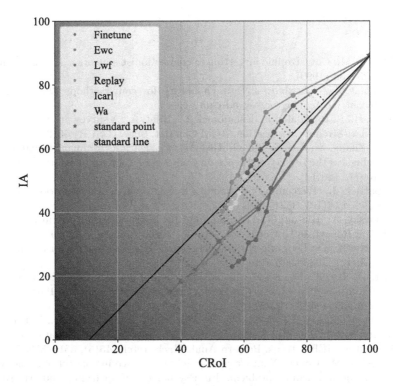

Fig. 7. Illustration of DV and RL on a CRoI-IA plot. Star point represents the standard point and black line is the standard line. The distance between task t point $(CRoI_t, IA_t)$ and the standard point $(CRoI_0, IA_0)$ is demonstrated with circle around standard point by gradation of color, which represents DV. Dotted lines shows the distance from different tasks' points to the standard line, which represents RL

indicating that although these algorithms maintain high classification accuracy, mapping relationship between regional attention and final classification accuracy has changed significantly. ASM scores of CIL algorithms that use the old task sample replay are significantly improved compared to the baseline, indicating that the stability of the regions of interest and mapping relationship between the regions of interest and classification accuracy are both well maintained.

5 Conclusion

In this article, we designed novel metrics for evaluating performance of Class Incremental Learning algorithms beyond traditional ones that are based on single classification accuracy. It describes effectiveness of CIL algorithms from a different dimension, which is the degree to the model maintains regions of interest of a test image and achieves quantitative comparison. Moreover, a comprehensive evaluation metric was introduced combined with classification accuracy. Finally, the evaluation results of our metrics on different CIL algorithms were demonstrated in specific experiments and show these algorithms' performance from a new perspective.

References

1. French, R.M.: Catastrophic forgetting in connectionist networks. Trends Cogn. Sci. **3**(4), 128–135 (1999)
2. Gildenblat, J., Contributors: Pytorch library for cam methods (2021). https://github.com/jacobgil/pytorch-grad-cam
3. Gomes, H.M., Barddal, J.P., Enembreck, F., Bifet, A.: A survey on ensemble learning for data stream classification. ACM Comput. Surv. (CSUR) **50**(2), 1–36 (2017)
4. He, K., Zhang, X., Ren, S., Sun, J.: Deep residual learning for image recognition. In: Proceedings of the IEEE Conference on Computer Vision and Pattern Recognition, pp. 770–778 (2016)
5. Kirkpatrick, J.: Overcoming catastrophic forgetting in neural networks. Proc. Natl. Acad. Sci. **114**(13), 3521–3526 (2017)
6. Krizhevsky, A., Hinton, G.: Learning multiple layers of features from tiny images. Technical Report. 0, University of Toronto, Toronto, Ontario (2009)
7. Li, Z., Hoiem, D.: Learning without forgetting. IEEE Trans. Pattern Anal. Mach. Intell. **40**(12), 2935–2947 (2017)
8. Liang, M., Hu, X.: Recurrent convolutional neural network for object recognition. In: Proceedings of the IEEE Conference on Computer Vision and Pattern Recognition, pp. 3367–3375 (2015)
9. Masana, M., Liu, X., Twardowski, B., Menta, M., Bagdanov, A.D., Van De Weijer, J.: Class-incremental learning: survey and performance evaluation on image classification. IEEE Trans. Pattern Anal. Mach. Intell. **45**(5), 5513–5533 (2022)
10. McCloskey, M., Cohen, N.J.: Catastrophic interference in connectionist networks: the sequential learning problem. In: Psychology of Learning and Motivation, vol. 24, pp. 109–165. Elsevier (1989)
11. Rebuffi, S.A., Kolesnikov, A., Sperl, G., Lampert, C.H.: ICARL: incremental classifier and representation learning. In: Proceedings of the IEEE Conference on Computer Vision and Pattern Recognition, pp. 2001–2010 (2017)

12. Ronneberger, O., Fischer, P., Brox, T.: U-Net: convolutional networks for biomedical image segmentation. In: Navab, N., Hornegger, J., Wells, W.M., Frangi, A.F. (eds.) MICCAI 2015. LNCS, vol. 9351, pp. 234–241. Springer, Cham (2015). https://doi.org/10.1007/978-3-319-24574-4_28
13. Selvaraju, R.R., Cogswell, M., Das, A., Vedantam, R., Parikh, D., Batra, D.: Gradcam: visual explanations from deep networks via gradient-based localization. In: Proceedings of the IEEE International Conference on Computer Vision, pp. 618–626 (2017)
14. Van de Ven, G.M., Tolias, A.S.: Three scenarios for continual learning. arXiv preprint arXiv:1904.07734 (2019)
15. Wang, F.Y., Zhou, D.W., Ye, H.J., Zhan, D.C.: Foster: feature boosting and compression for class-incremental learning. In: European Conference on Computer Vision, pp. 398–414. Springer, Heidelberg (2022). https://doi.org/10.1007/978-3-031-19806-9_23
16. Yan, S., Xie, J., He, X.: Der: dynamically expandable representation for class incremental learning. In: Proceedings of the IEEE/CVF Conference on Computer Vision and Pattern Recognition, pp. 3014–3023 (2021)
17. Yoon, J., Yang, E., Lee, J., Hwang, S.J.: Lifelong learning with dynamically expandable networks. In: 6th International Conference on Learning Representations, ICLR 2018. International Conference on Learning Representations, ICLR (2018)
18. Zhao, B., Xiao, X., Gan, G., Zhang, B., Xia, S.T.: Maintaining discrimination and fairness in class incremental learning. In: Proceedings of the IEEE/CVF Conference on Computer Vision and Pattern Recognition, pp. 13208–13217 (2020)
19. Zhou, B., Khosla, A., Lapedriza, A., Oliva, A., Torralba, A.: Learning deep features for discriminative localization. In: Proceedings of the IEEE Conference on Computer Vision and Pattern Recognition, pp. 2921–2929 (2016)
20. Zhou, D.W., Wang, F.Y., Ye, H.J., Zhan, D.C.: Pycil: a python toolbox for class-incremental learning. arXiv preprint arXiv:2112.12533 (2021)
21. Zhou, D.W., Wang, Q.W., Qi, Z.H., Ye, H.J., Zhan, D.C., Liu, Z.: Deep class-incremental learning: a survey. arXiv preprint arXiv:2302.03648 (2023)

Unbiased Image Caption Generation Based on Dynamic Counterfactual Inference

Jinfei Zhou[1]([✉])(iD), Cheng Yang[1](iD), Yaping Zhu[2], and Yana Zhang[1](iD)

[1] State Key Laboratory of Media Convergence and Communication, Communication University of China, Beijing, China
{zhoujinfei,chy,zynjenny}@cuc.edu.cn
[2] Queensland University of Technology Online, Brisbane, Australia
yaping.zhu@qut.edu.au

Abstract. Recent research has focused on exploring causality in image description generation. Some studies have proposed using backdoor criteria to eliminate visual confounding factors and language confounding factors in images and annotations of datasets, by computing co-occurrence probabilities between objects and between words. These methods can effectively deconfound the visual and language confounders simultaneously. However, the impact of language priors on generating descriptions still needs to be explored during sequence generation. Language priors can be classified into two types: good and bad. Good language priors make word generation more fluent, while bad language priors can lead to spurious associations between generated objects. Therefore, in this paper, we first investigate how image caption generation models introduce bad language priors during the word generation process. Inspired by the causal effect, we propose a framework based on dynamic counterfactual inference to eliminate the generation of false objects. This framework utilizes noisy features and input words to capture the direct language effect during word generation, and reduces the influence of bad language bias by dynamically subtracting the direct language effect. Experimental results demonstrate that our proposed counterfactual inference framework achieves competitive performance on the MSCOCO dataset for image caption generation tasks, and effectively reduces the incidence of false objects in the description.

Keywords: image captioning · cause effect · counterfactual inference

1 Introduction

Image captioning algorithms aim to generate sentences that describe an image by understanding the semantic information and relationships between the main objects in the image. Image captioning plays a critical role in aiding visually impaired individuals in perceiving the real world and in human-robot interaction

G. Zhai et al. (Eds.): IFTC 2023, CCIS 2066, pp. 138–152, 2024.
https://doi.org/10.1007/978-981-97-3623-2_11

research for intelligent robots. Recent research has focused on causal generation in image captioning algorithms, specifically studying the impact of visual and language confounders in datasets. These confounders often lead to the emergence of spurious associations during sentence generation. For example, in datasets, the words "plate" and "table" often co-occur, leading the model to develop the misconception that "table is a part of a plate" during training. Even in cases where there is no table in the image, the model might generate descriptions like "the plate is on the table". Such harmful associations have a negative impact on the accuracy and consistency of image captioning.

Regarding the causality issue in image description generation, researchers Yang et al. [23] pointed out that image features are influenced by large scale pre-trained models, which can inherit inherent features from the pre-training dataset into downstream tasks. Therefore, they employed a structured causal graph approach to analyze causal relationships in image captioning and proposed the DIC framework. Although the DIC framework effectively mitigates confounders from pre-training datasets, it overlooks the influence of language confounders during the description generation process. To tackle visual and language confounders in image captioning, Liu et al. [8] introduced the CIIC framework. The framework intervenes in the object detector and Transformer decoder modules using a back-door criterion to alleviate confounders in both visual and language domains. The language and visual confounders arise from the co-occurrence of certain objects and words in the dataset, which leads the model to learn spurious associations between them during training. The back-door criterion mitigates the impact of these co-occurrence objects and words by statistically analyzing the occurrence probabilities of objects in the images and words in the sentences.

The CIIC framework effectively resolves the issue of the co-occurrence of visual objects in image features and words in text features from a causal perspective, and achieves excellent results. However, the impact of language priors on generating descriptions still needs to be explored during sequence generation. Image caption generation is a process that converts visual features into text, where each generated word is influenced by both visual information and previously generated words. Visual information is crucial for ensuring the accuracy of the generated sentence content, while the previous words utilize language priors in the dataset to ensure the fluency of sentence generation. We believe that the main reason for generating spurious associations lies in the influence of language priors in the dataset, such as language bias for words like "plate" and "table". However, not all language priors are harmful. In fact, there are useful common collocations in language priors, such as "live in", "sit on", and so on. Our research goal is to enable the image captioning model to learn useful language priors during the training process while simultaneously avoiding the generation of harmful object associations.

Based on the considerations mentioned above, and inspired by the counterfactual framework of causal inference, we propose the Dynamic Counterfactual Inference Framework (DCF-IC) to eliminate harmful language priors by using the total indirect effect in the counterfactual framework. In addition, we believe

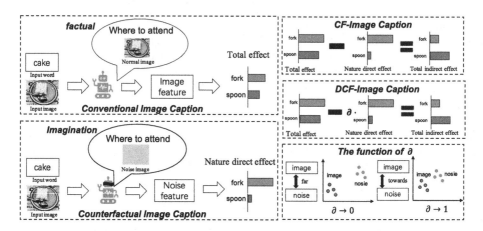

Fig. 1. Our cause-effect look at language bias in image caption. Conventional Image captioning depicts the fact where machine hears the previously generated word and the observed image content. Counterfactual image caption depicts the scenario where machine hears the previously generated word but the image is blocked. We subtract the pure language effect from the total effect for debiased inference.

that language priors can be divided into two types: good language priors and bad language priors. In the case of good visual feature representation, language priors play an important role in generating sentences. For example, after generating the word "sitting", language priors make it easier to generate accurate and common collocations such as "at" or "on". Meanwhile, when the visual feature representation is weak, bad language priors can lead to the generation of words that tend to follow common sentence patterns, such as generating the sentence "sitting on the beach" even if the object "bench" has not appeared in the image. Therefore, our proposed DCF-IC framework has two key functions: (1) to eliminate the influence of language priors, and (2) to dynamically eliminate harmful language priors. As shown in the Fig. 1, we introduce two scenarios, namely the conventional image captioning and the counterfactual image captioning. These can be defined in the following ways:

(1) **Conventional image captioning:** *What is the next word to generate? The model makes a choice based on the previously generated word and the observed image content.*

(2) **Counterfactual image captioning:** *What is the next word to generate? The model makes a choice based on the previously generated word and the observed noisy image.*

The conventional image captioning generates descriptions corresponding to input words by selecting appropriate image features. This process can be seen as a mapping from text to vision and back to text, which we call the total effect. In the counterfactual image captioning, we interrupt the input of visual information and transform it into a process from text to mediation (generally it's noise data with no information) and back to text. Since the model cannot access any visual information in the counterfactual generation process, it is forced to rely on the language priors learned during training to generate the next word. Therefore, the counterfactual image captioning is able to capture language biases generated by the dataset, which we refer to as the direct indirect(language) effect. Based on the causal inference theory, we can obtain unbiased generation results by subtracting the direct language effect from the total effect.

In previous discussions, we mentioned that language priors are not always harmful. When the visual information is relatively ambiguous, the model tends to overly rely on bad language priors to generate the next word, resulting in "false" objects that do not align with the image content. Conversely, when the visual information is clearly expressed, the model effectively utilizes both visual features and previous words to generate the next word based on good language priors. Based on these considerations, we introduce a dynamic adjustment mechanism to counterfactual inference framework. This mechanism allows us to dynamically decide at each time step of sequence generation whether to subtract the direct language effect from the total effect. Specifically, when the visual features have strong representation, we reduce the weight of subtracting the direct language effect. On the other hand, when the visual features do not have strong representation, we increase the weight of subtracting the direct language effect. To evaluate the representation score of visual features, we calculate the similarity of the output features obtained by inputting image features and noise features into the decoder. When the distance between the image output features and the noise output features is close, it means that the current visual features do not have strong representation. Conversely, if their distance is far, it indicates that the current visual features have strong representation.

The main contributions of this paper are as follows:

(1) To the best of our knowledge, we are the first to employ a counterfactual inference framework to investigate how language bias in image caption generation tasks affects word generation and conduct causal analysis on the generation process of objects detached from image content.
(2) We propose a method called DCF-IC to address the issue of language bias in the word generation process. The algorithm leverages total effects and dynamically eliminates the influence of language bias based on the representation of image features.
(3) We implement the DCF-IC method and extensively evaluate it on the MSCOCO benchmark dataset. The results demonstrate that the DCF-IC method achieves competitive performance.

2   Related Work

2.1   Image Captioning

Mainstream image captioning typically follow an encoder-decoder paradigm [2,10,20,22]. In this paradigm, the encoder (usually based on CNN) is used to encode the image into a feature vector, while the decoder (usually based on LSTM units) utilizes the image feature vector to generate the corresponding descriptive sentences. Specifically, each word generated at each time step is jointly determined by the image feature and the words from previous time steps. In early image description methods [20], image features were only used for initializing the parameters of the LSTM, resulting in descriptions primarily depending on previous words, leading to an inability to cover detailed content in the images and being greatly influenced by language priors. With the application of the attention mechanism [3] to image captioning [2,22], image features are fully utilized in the word generation process. At each time step, the attention mechanism weights the image feature regions, then inputs them into the decoder to generate the next word. Descriptions generated using this method have been able to encompass many details of objects in the image and reduce the influence of language priors. Recently, the Transformer framework [18] based on self-attention mechanism has achieved considerable success in image captioning tasks. The cross-attention mechanism in the Transformer utilizes the relationship between the current input word and the image features to select the currently more relevant image feature to generate the word at the next time step. Transformer-based image description methods [5] have achieved a better mapping from visual to textual information, relying more on the content of the images during the generation process, further reducing the impact of language priors. Despite the significant progress made by Transformer-based image description methods, they are still affected by language biases in sentence generation. Therefore, this paper will explore this problem from the perspective of counterfactual inference and causal theory.

2.2   Causal Inference

In the training phrase of deep learning models, it is typically necessary to utilize large-scale datasets to train model parameters, thereby learning the statistical correlations between the data. In order to transition model training from statistical correlation to causality, some researchers have started incorporating causal inference into deep learning models in the field of computer vision. These efforts have endowed deep neural networks (DNNs) with the ability to learn causal relationships, significantly improving the performance of many computer vision and natural language processing models, including tasks such as image classification [9], visual feature representation [21], visual dialogue [15], and image caption generation [23]. For example, Wang et al. proposed VC R-CNN [21], a convolutional neural network based on visual commonsense regions, to enhance the learning performance of visual feature representation. They utilized causal interventions instead of traditional probabilities to predict contextual objects in regions. Additionally, Yang et al. developed the Deconfounded Image Captioning (DIC) framework and causal attention mechanisms to handle confounding factors. Furthermore, Liu et al. proposed the CIIC framework targeting confounders in the visual and language domains, where they introduced deconfounding modules into the encoder and decoder to eliminate confounders in the visual and language domains Although these methods have achieved promising results in terms of performance, the current research on causal analysis during the caption generation process is still insufficient. Therefore, this paper analyzes the generation of confounding factors from the perspective of word generation and proposes an approach based on dynamic counterfactual inference framework to eliminate harmful language priors generated during the word generation process.

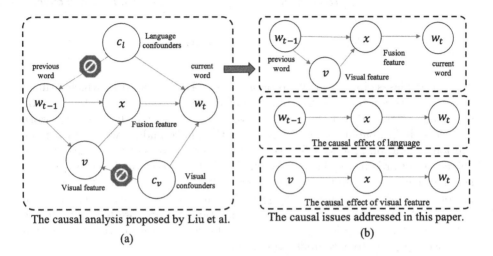

The causal analysis proposed by Liu et al.

(a)

The causal issues addressed in this paper.

(b)

Fig. 2. The causal analysis of image captioning.

3   Methods

3.1   Cause-Effect Look

Image caption generation is the process of generating sentences based on the visual content of an image. Specifically, at each time step of word generation, the image feature v is fused with the previous word w_{t-1} to obtain the attention-fused feature x. This process can be represented as a structured causal graph $w_{t-1} \rightarrow x \leftarrow v$, as shown in Fig. 2(a). The word generated at current time step is determined by the fused feature x, represented as $x \rightarrow w_t$. Due to biases in the training dataset, caption generation is susceptible to the influence of language confounders and visual confounders, leading to the generation of "false" words. For example, if the co-occurrence of "cake" and "fork" is frequent in the dataset, the model may mistakenly believe that "cake" and "fork" are a single entity, resulting in the generation of the word "cake" followed by the addition of the description "with fork". Biases exist in both the image and text components of the dataset. For visual confounders, they affect the visual feature v and the generated word w_t, represented in the structured causal graph as $v \leftarrow c_v \rightarrow w_t$. For language confounders, they affect the previously generated word and the currently generated word $w_{t-1} \leftarrow c_l \rightarrow w_t$. To mitigate the problem

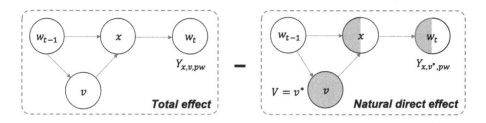

Fig. 3. The illustration of TIE computation.

of dataset biases, Liu et al. [8] proposed the CIIC framework, which utilizes backdoor criterion to block the influence of visual and language confounders on the image feature v and the previous word w_{t-1}. Specifically, the framework considers the probabilities of all objects in the image and all words during the caption generation process, effectively eliminating the bias of "co-occurrence" of objects and words in the dataset. While the CIIC method eliminates visual and language confounders in the dataset, there still exists a causal effect of language priors $(w_{t-1} \rightarrow x(w_t))$ on $v \rightarrow x(w_t)$ in the link $w_{t-1} \rightarrow x(w_t) \leftarrow v$, as shown in Fig. 2(b). To further achieve causal generation, we propose to eliminate the influence of language priors $(w_{t-1} \rightarrow x(w_t))$ from $v \rightarrow x(w_t)$ during the caption generation process to accomplish this goal.

According to the counterfactual notation [13], we can define that the next time step generated word w_t is determined by the visual feature v and the previous time step word w_{t-1}:

$$Y_{v,w_{t-1}}(w_t) = Y(w_t, v, w_{t-1}) \tag{1}$$

As shown in the structured causal graph in Fig. 2(b), both w_{t-1} and v first point to x, and then x points to w_t. We can rewrite Eq. (1) as:

$$Y_{v,w_{t-1}}(w_t) = Z_{v,x,w_{t-1}} = Z(X = x, V = v, W_{t-1} = w_{t-1}) \tag{2}$$

The total effect of image caption generation is represented as the outcome under the treatment of "$V = v$". We define the total effect (TE) as:

$$TE = Z_{v,w_{t-1}} - Z_{v^*,w_{t-1}^*} \tag{3}$$

where, v^* and w_{t-1}^* represent setting the input image feature and input word to void. In the previous discussion, due to the influence of language prior $(w_{t-1} \rightarrow x(w_t))$ on the causal generation of $v \rightarrow x(w_t)$, we need to understand the impact of language prior on the generated word outcome, and we refer to this process as the natural direct effect (NDE) of language, defined by the following equation:

$$NDE = Z_{v^*,w_{t-1}} - Z_{v^*,w_{t-1}^*} \tag{4}$$

The NDE represents the estimation of the natural language effect by computing the difference between the input word being "$W = w_{t-1}$" (treatment group) and "$W = w_{t-1}^*$" (control group) when the image feature is controlled to be void. As the effect of visual features is blocked (e.g., $V = v^*$), NDE directly captures the language bias. According to the counterfactual inference framework, we can eliminate language bias by subtracting the natural direct effect of the language bias from the total effect. The specific calculation process is shown in Fig. 3, and the detailed calculation method is given by formula 5.

$$TIE = TE - NDE = Z_{v,w_{t-1}} - Z_{v^*,w_{t-1}} \tag{5}$$

By using formula 5, we can calculate the result of the total indirect effect (TIE) at each word generation moment to obtain the word generation results that eliminate the language bias.

3.2 Implementation

Model. To further eliminate language confounders, we will implement the dynamic counterfactual framework proposed in this paper on the CIIC model. Formula 2 is divided into three modules, namely visual encoder $multiHead_v$, the sequence encoder $multiHead_{w_{t-1}}$, and the cross-modal fusion function. The specific calculations are as shown in formulas (6), (7), (8), and (9).

$$Z_v = multiHead_v(v) \tag{6}$$

$$Z_{w_{t-1}} = multiHead_{w_{t-1}}(w_{t-1}) \tag{7}$$

$$Z_x = Z_{v,w_{t-1}} = cross\_attention(v, w_{t-1}) \tag{8}$$

$$Z_{v,w_{t-1},x} = h(Z_v, Z_{w_{t-1}}, Z_x) \tag{9}$$

where, $multiHead_v$ represents the visual branch, $multiHead_{w_{t-1}}$ represents the language branch, and $cross\_atention$ represents the visual-language branch. The final score for generating a word is calculated through the function h, which computes the fused features to obtain the score $Z_{v,w_{t-1},x}$. As mentioned in Sect. 3.1, the "no treatment" condition is defined as blocking signals from either visual or language inputs. We use $V = v^* = \emptyset$ to represent the "no treatment" condition. Since neural networks cannot have empty sets as input variables for the "no treatment" condition, we assume the model acquires "noise" variables with no meaningful information under the "no treatment" condition. Here, Z_v can be expressed as (Fig. 4):

$$Z_v = \begin{cases} multiHead_{w_{t-1}}(v), & V = v \\ z_v^* = c, & V = \emptyset \end{cases} \tag{10}$$

where, c is a learnable parameter. Similar to Niu et al. [11], we use a uniform distribution with the same dimension as v. This uniform distribution does not contain any visual information and can make the training more stable.

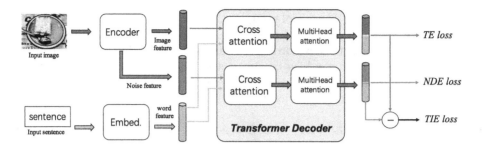

Fig. 4. The pipeline of our proposed DCF-IC model.

Dynamic Counterfactual Inference Image captioning(DCI-IC): In Sect. 1, we discussed language priors can be divided into "good" and "bad" ones during sequence generation. The "good" language priors make sentence generation fluent by learning contextual relationships in the dataset, while the "bad" language priors capture false associations in the dataset, such as the simultaneous appearance of "plate" and "table". Therefore, we propose a dynamic counterfactual inference framework to eliminate the "bad" language priors while preserving the "good" language priors. To achieve this goal, we introduce a controlling parameter α in the TIE formula to adjust the weight of NDE.

$$TIE = TE - \alpha \cdot NDE = Z_{v,w_{t-1},x} - \alpha \cdot Z_{v^*,w_{t-1},x} \qquad (11)$$

NDE describes the effect of language bias when controlling visual features. For "good" language priors, TE can effectively utilize contextual information to predict the next word to be generated without subtracting the influence of language bias. In this case, the value of α tends towards 0. Conversely, for "bad" language priors, TE is influenced by spurious language associations, and it is necessary to eliminate the impact of language bias. In this case, the value of α tends towards 1. The role of α reflects whether language bias needs to be eliminated. When the visual features have strong representation, there is a strong correlation between visual and language, making it easier to generate text that describes the image content accurately. Conversely, when the representation of visual features is insufficient, the correlation between visual and language weakens, leading to the generated words being influenced by "bad" language bias. Therefore, we evaluate the scores of visual feature representation by measuring the distance between input image features and noise features. The formula for calculating α is as follows.

$$\alpha = \max(w(\|z_x - z_x^*\|) + b, 0) \qquad (12)$$

where w and b are learnable parameters, z_x represents the fused feature output of the decoder given the input visual features, and z_x^* represents the fused feature output of the decoder given the input features as noise in the "untreated" condition. This means that α measures the influence of visual features on the fused feature. When there is a large difference between z_x and z_x^*, it indicates a strong representation of the visual features. Conversely, when the difference between z_x and z_x^* is small, it indicates weak representation of the visual features.

Training. We adopt a multi-task training approach to train the model to generate word results in the TE, NDE, and TIE conditions. We calculate the word-level cross-entropy loss function using the following formula:

$$L_{TIE}(\theta) = -\sum_{t=1}^{T} log(p_\theta(w_t \mid v, v^*, w_{t-1})) \tag{13}$$

$$L_{NDE}(\theta) = -\sum_{t=1}^{T} log(p_\theta(w_t \mid v^*, w_{t-1})) \tag{14}$$

$$L_{TE}(\theta) = -\sum_{t=1}^{T} log(p_\theta(w_t \mid v, w_{t-1})) \tag{15}$$

$$L_{XE} = L_{TIE} + L_{NDE} + L_{TE} \tag{16}$$

where θ is a learnable parameter. Through joint multi-task training, we aim to train the model to generate words in all three conditions: TE, NDE, and TIE. Additionally, inspired by causal inference theory, to ensure that the feature distribution is similar in both the "treatment" and "control" conditions, we use KL divergence to measure the distance between the distributions in these two situations.

$$L_{KL} = \frac{1}{|V|} \sum_{V=v} -\theta(x_v) log(\theta(x_v^*)) \tag{17}$$

The final total loss function is a combination of L_{XE} and L_{KL}, expressed as:

$$L = L_{XE} + \alpha \cdot L_{KL} \tag{18}$$

In inference phrase, we use TIE to predict the output probability of each word at every time step.

$$\begin{aligned} TIE = TE - \alpha \cdot NDE &= Z_{v,w_{t-1},x} - \alpha \cdot Z_{v^*,w_{t-1},x} \\ &= h(Z_v, Z_{w_{t-1}}, Z_x) - \alpha \cdot h(Z_v^*, Z_{w_{t-1}}, Z_x) \end{aligned} \tag{19}$$

4   Experiments

4.1   Experimental Setup

Dataset: In our experiments, we validate the effectiveness of the proposed method using the MSCOCO dataset. This benchmark dataset consists of 123,287 images, each accompanied by five manually annotated sentences. For consistency with the comparison method experiments, we adopt the commonly used Karpathy split dataset for image captioning.

Evaluation Metrics: To evaluate the performance of different image captioning methods, we utilize standard evaluation metrics, including BLEU [12], METEOR [4], ROUGE [7], CIDEr [19], and SPICE [1]. Additionally, we use two measures, $CHAIR_s$ and $CHAIR_i$ [16], to quantify the degree of object bias in the generated descriptions.

Implementation Details: We primarily build upon the CIIC model, so the main implementation details are similar to the CIIC model. In image feature extraction, we use 1024-dimensional IOD features and 2048-dimensional bottom-up features to project onto a 512-dimensional vector and fed into the UFT encoder. For word representation, we use pre-trained GloVe word embeddings [14] in our experiments. Following the same settings as [18], we convert all sentences to lowercase, remove punctuation, and tokenize each caption. We build a new vocabulary by selecting words that appear more than five times. Additionally, we employ 8 attention heads in both the encoder and decoder. The latent dimension in each head is set as dh = d/h = 64, where d is the latent dimension of 512. We train our model on 2 Nvidia 2080ti GPUs with a batch size of 24 images and a total of 220K iterations. During training, we use the Adam optimizer [6] with 20,000 warm-up steps. Our model is trained for 30 epochs based on the XE loss, with a learning rate of 5×10^-6. During the inference phase, we also employ beam search [17] with a beam size of 3.

4.2 Ablation Studies

We conducted experiments to investigate the impact of each module on the performance of image caption generation. We compared the following models: (1) **Baseline**: The CIIC model serves as the baseline for comparison. It eliminates the visual and language confounders in image caption generation using the backdoor criterion. To further compare the generation of false descriptions, we incorporate the modules designed in this paper into the CIIC network. Therefore, we use the CIIC model as the baseline for comparison. (2) **Base+CF**: Based on the base model, we have incorporated the counterfactual reference framework for training. In addition to conducting TE training, this framework also involves NDE and TIE training. The Base+CF model eliminates the influence of language priors on word generation at each time step. (3) **Base+DCF**: We have introduced a dynamic adjustment mechanism based on the Base+CF model. This mechanism dynamically eliminates the language priors at each time step during the generation process. (4) **Base+DCF+discrepancy loss(dl)**: Based on the Base+DCF model, we incorporate the discrepancy loss between the fusion features of TE and NDE during training.

Results and Analysis . The experimental results are shown in Table 1. Compared to the baseline model(base), training with the counterfactual inference framework(base+CF) effectively reduces the occurrence of "false" objects in generated sentences, with CHs and CHi reduced to 4.9 and 3.5, respectively. However, incorporating the counterfactual reasoning framework leads to a decrease in

Table 1. Ablation experiments. All the models are trained with the XE loss. B@1, B@4, M, R, C, S, CHs and CHi are short for BLEU-1, BLEU-4, METEOR, ROUGE-L, CIDEr, SPICE CHAIRs and CHAIRi scores. "↑" and "↓" denote the lower the better and the higher the better, respectively.

model	B@1 ↑	B@2↑	B@3↑	B@4↑	M ↑	R ↑	C ↑	S ↑	CHs ↓	CHi ↓
Baeeline(CIIC)	76.54	60.49	46.74	35.97	28.03	56.75	125.7	21.31	6.3	4.3
Base+CF	75.45	59.00	45.35	34.67	27.67	55.73	121.4	21.14	4.9	3.5
Base+DCF	76.32	60.15	46.25	35.49	**28.31**	56.78	124.8	21.45	4.9	3.3
Base+DCF+dl	**77.23**	**61.20**	**47.36**	**36.43**	28.21	**56.99**	**126.6**	**21.51**	**4.7**	**3.2**

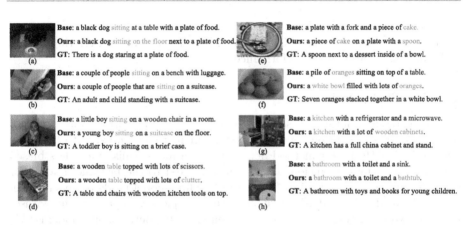

Fig. 5. Some generated captions by DCF-IC and the Transformer baseline in the case of object biases. The green contexts denote the language confounders which may induce biases. The correct and incorrect words are colored by blue and red, respectively.

various metrics for image captioning. We believe that the counterfactual framework eliminates some favorable language priors, resulting in a decrease across all metrics for image caption. Based on the Base+CF framework, Base+DCF introduces a dynamic adjustment mechanism to dynamically eliminate language priors. This mechanism controls the use of counterfactual inference when visual features appear abnormal, and reduces the weight of counterfactuals when visual features are normal. Based on the results in Table 1, Base+DCF shows further reductions in the CHs and Chi metrics compared to Base+CF. On the other hand, Base+DCF exhibits improvements in various evaluation metrics for image captioning compared to Base+CF. This indicates that the Base+DCF model can effectively utilize counterfactual inference dynamically. However, when compared to the baseline model, Base+DCF's performance is slightly inferior across various metrics. Based on the Base+BCF model, we introduced the discrepancy loss to reduce the differences between the "treatment group" and the "control group" during the training process, aiming to control other influencing factors. The results show that the Base+BCF+dl framework further improves performance on the CHs and Chi metrics and outperforms all the compared models in various evaluation metrics for image caption generation. This indicates that

Table 2. The bias analysis of different models on MSCOCO Karpathy split.

model	B@4↑	M ↑	R ↑	C ↑	CHs ↓	CHi ↓
Up-Down [2]	36.3	27.7	56.9	120.1	13.7	8.9
Transformer	36.3	27.7	56.9	120.1	13.7	8.9
UD-DICv1.0 [23]	39	28.8	58.8	128.8	10.1	6.5
Transformer+CATT [24]	39.4	29.3	58.9	131.7	9.7	6.5
CIIC [8]	40.2	29.5	59.4	133.1	7.7	4.5
DCF-IC (ours)	35.6	27.5	56.8	131.4	10.6	6.5

the Base+BCF+dl framework is capable of better controlling interfering factors and enhancing the model's performance.

4.3   Result Analysis

We conducted a qualitative assessment of our algorithm's performance. Figure 5 shows examples of caption generation using our method compared to the baseline method (CIIC). Our method demonstrates a more realistic and less biased performance in image caption generation compared to the baseline model. For example, in (a), (b), and (c) of Fig. 5, the baseline model tends to generate co-occurring words like "table" or "bench" that frequently appear in the dataset when the word "sitting" is present in the sentence. In contrast, our model is able to accurately describe the objects of the "sitting" action, such as "floor" and "suitcase". Similarly, in (e), "cake" and "fork", (h) "bathroom" and "sink", and (g) "kitchen" and "refrigerator" are all co-occurring word pairs that are either very common in the dataset or intuitively common. The baseline model tends to generate biased words during the generation process, whereas our model, through dynamic counterfactual inference, is able to generate accurate words during the word generation process. For example, it generates "cake" and "spoon" in (e), "bathroom" and "bathtub" in (h), and "kitchen" and "wooden cabinet" in (g). These examples demonstrate that our algorithm can effectively eliminate language confounders and further validate the effectiveness of our approach.

We conducted a quantitative assessment of our algorithm's performance. Table 1 and Table 2 respectively show the performance comparison results of our proposed model under cross-entropy and reinforcement learning training. Under cross-entropy training, according to the results in Table 1, our approach outperformed the SOTA model (CIIC) in various image description evaluation metrics, while achieving better results in the false object evaluation, with CHs and CHi reduced to 4.7 and 3.2 respectively. However, according to the results in Table 2, our method performs less well than other comparative models in terms of the BLEU4, Meteor, and ROUGE evaluation metrics. Although our model outperforms the Up-down, Transformer, and UD-DICv1.0 models in CIDEr scores, it still lags behind the Transformer+CATT and CIIC models. In fake object evaluation, our model outperforms the Up-down and Transformer model, is consistent with the results of UD-DICv1.0, but falls short of the Transformer+CATT and CIIC models. It is evident that our model, when trained using reinforcement learning strategies, did not exhibit a relative trend compared to the cross-entropy training method. This is most likely due to the fact that the current version of DCF-IC's loss function is not suitable for policy gradient computation. Therefore, in future work, we need to further explore how to adjust the DCF-IC model to adapt to reinforcement learning training.

5 Conclusion

This paper proposes a method based on a dynamic counterfactual reference framework to eliminate the problem of generating "false" objects in image description generation. The framework utilizes noisy data to compute direct language effect and adjusts the total effect by dynamically reducing language biases when the visual feature representation is restricted. Experiments show that our proposed dynamic counterfactual inference framework achieves competitive performance in the image description generation task on the MSCOCO dataset, and further reduces the number of "false" objects in generated sentences.

References

1. Anderson, P., Fernando, B., Johnson, M., Gould, S.: SPICE: semantic propositional image caption evaluation. In: Leibe, B., Matas, J., Sebe, N., Welling, M. (eds.) ECCV 2016. LNCS, vol. 9909, pp. 382–398. Springer, Cham (2016). https://doi.org/10.1007/978-3-319-46454-1_24
2. Anderson, P., et al.: Bottom-up and top-down attention for image captioning and visual question answering. In: Proceedings of the IEEE Conference on Computer Vision and Pattern recognition, pp. 6077–6086 (2018)
3. Bahdanau, D., Cho, K., Bengio, Y.: Neural machine translation by jointly learning to align and translate. In: 3rd International Conference on Learning Representations, ICLR 2015, San Diego, CA, USA, 7–9 May 2015, Conference Track Proceedings (2015). https://dblp.org/db/conf/iclr/iclr2015
4. Banerjee, S., Lavie, A.: Meteor: An automatic metric for MT evaluation with improved correlation with human judgments. In: Proceedings of the ACL Workshop on Intrinsic and Extrinsic Evaluation Measures for Machine Translation and/or Summarization, pp. 65–72 (2005). https://doi.org/10.3115/1626355.1626389
5. Cornia, M., Stefanini, M., Baraldi, L., Cucchiara, R.: Meshed-memory transformer for image captioning. In: 2020 IEEE/CVF Conference on Computer Vision and Pattern Recognition (CVPR), pp. 10575–10584. IEEE Computer Society, Los Alamitos (2020). https://doi.org/10.1109/CVPR42600.2020.01059
6. Kingma, D.P., Ba, J.: Adam: a method for stochastic optimization. In: 3rd International Conference on Learning Representations, ICLR, pp. 1–15 (2015)
7. Lin, C.Y.: Rouge: a package for automatic evaluation of summaries. In: Proceedings of the 42nd Association for Computational Linguistics, pp. 74–81 (2004)
8. Liu, B., et al.: Show, deconfound and tell: image captioning with causal inference. In: 2022 IEEE/CVF Conference on Computer Vision and Pattern Recognition (CVPR), vol. 44, pp. 18020–18029 (2022). https://doi.org/10.1109/CVPR52688.2022.01751

9. Lopez-Paz, D., Nishihara, R., Chintala, S., Scholkopf, B., Bottou, L.: Discovering causal signals in images. In: 2017 IEEE Conference on Computer Vision and Pattern Recognition (CVPR), pp. 58–66. IEEE Computer Society, Los Alamitos (2017)

10. Lu, J., Xiong, C., Parikh, D., Socher, R.: Knowing when to look: adaptive attention via a visual sentinel for image captioning. In: Proceedings of the IEEE Conference on Computer Vision and Pattern Recognition, pp. 375–383 (2017)

11. Niu, Y., Tang, K., Zhang, H., Lu, Z., Hua, X.S., Wen, J.R.: Counterfactual VQA: a cause-effect look at language bias. In: Proceedings of the IEEE/CVF Conference on Computer Vision and Pattern Recognition, pp. 12700–12710 (2021)

12. Papineni, K., Roukos, S., Ward, T., Zhu, W.J.: Bleu: a method for automatic evaluation of machine translation. In: Proceedings of the 40th Annual Meeting of the Association for Computational Linguistics, pp. 311–318 (2002)

13. Pearl, J., Glymour, M., Jewell, N.P.: Causal Inference in Statistics: A Primer. John Wiley & Sons, Hoboken (2016)

14. Pennington, J., Socher, R., Manning, C.: Glove: global vectors for word representation, vol. 14, pp. 1532–1543 (2014). https://doi.org/10.3115/v1/D14-1162

15. Qi, J., Niu, Y., Huang, J., Zhang, H.: Two causal principles for improving visual dialog. In: 2020 IEEE/CVF Conference on Computer Vision and Pattern Recognition (CVPR), pp. 10857–10866 (2020). https://doi.org/10.1109/CVPR42600.2020.01087

16. Rohrbach, A., Hendricks, L.A., Burns, K., Darrell, T., Saenko, K.: Object hallucination in image captioning. In: Conference on Empirical Methods in Natural Language Processing (2018). https://api.semanticscholar.org/CorpusID:52176506

17. Sutskever, I., Vinyals, O., Le, Q.V.: Sequence to sequence learning with neural networks. In: Ghahramani, Z., Welling, M., Cortes, C., Lawrence, N., Weinberger, K. (eds.) Advances in Neural Information Processing Systems, vol. 27. Curran Associates, Inc. (2014)

18. Vaswani, A., et al.: Attention is all you need. In: Advances in Neural Information Processing Systems, pp. 6000–6010 (2017).https://doi.org/10.5555/3295222.3295349

19. Vedantam, R., Lawrence Zitnick, C., Parikh, D.: Cider: consensus-based image description evaluation. In: Proceedings of the IEEE Conference on Computer Vision and Pattern Recognition, pp. 4566–4575 (2015)

20. Vinyals, O., Toshev, A., Bengio, S., Erhan, D.: Show and tell: a neural image caption generator. In: Proceedings of the IEEE Conference on Computer Vision and Pattern Recognition, pp. 3156–3164 (2015)

21. Wang, T., Huang, J., Zhang, H., Sun, Q.: Visual commonsense r-cnn. In: 2020 IEEE/CVF Conference on Computer Vision and Pattern Recognition (CVPR), pp. 10757–10767 (2020). https://doi.org/10.1109/CVPR42600.2020.01077

22. Xu, K., et al.: Show, attend and tell: neural image caption generation with visual attention. In: International Conference on Machine Learning, vol. 37, pp. 2048–2057. PMLR (2015)

23. Yang, X., Zhang, H., Cai, J.: Deconfounded image captioning: a causal retrospect. IEEE Trans. Pattern Anal. Mach. Intell. **45**(11), 12996–13010 (2023)

24. Yang, X., Zhang, H., Qi, G., Cai, J.: Causal attention for vision-language tasks. In: 2021 IEEE/CVF Conference on Computer Vision and Pattern Recognition (CVPR), pp. 9842–9852 (2021)

Modeling and Analysis of Rumor Propagation Dynamics in Social Media

Shan Liu[✉] and Hanfei Zhao

Department of Intelligent Science, Communication University of China,
Beijing 100024, People's Republic of China
liushan@cuc.edu.cn

Abstract. Exploring the nature of rumor propagation in social media is of great importance to mitigate the adverse effects of rumors and prevent rumor dissemination. To accurately model the complexity of rumor propagation dynamics in real social media and effectively ameliorate the effects of rumors on society, a new rumor propagation model named V-SEIR is proposed in this paper. The proposed V-SEIR model considers the node heterogeneity, individual behaviors, and network topologies, which can affect the node influence, prediction accuracy, and model generality, respectively. The rumor-free equilibrium point and the basic reproduction number R_0 are calculated to assess the model stability. The nodes are divided into important and ordinary parts based on their degree, to characterize node heterogeneity. Three non-linear metrics are defined and estimated: influence, bandwagon effect, and forgetting mechanism, to capture the individual behaviors. The empirical analysis reveals the dynamic behavior and complexity of rumor propagation. The V-SEIR model is evaluated in different network topologies and the impact of each metric parameter is verified. By comparing the V-SEIR model with the classic propagation model and validating it with actual rumor datasets from Weibo, the results demonstrate that the V-SEIR model has higher prediction accuracy, especially in the early and late stages of rumor propagation. This research can enhance our understanding of rumor propagation, making it possible to forecast and manage online public opinion in social media.

Keywords: Social media · Rumor propagation · Influence · Bandwagon effect · Forgetting mechanism

1 Introduction

Rumor propagation in social media has triggered cascade reactions, having seriously endangered public credibility. Rumor cascades are deeper than reshare cascades [8]. Rumors threaten societal stability by causing panic, worry, and confusion. Thus, the rumor propagation process and its influencing factors should be studied. Capturing the rumor dynamics and modeling individual behaviors are crucial to understanding and preventing rumors.

G. Zhai et al. (Eds.): IFTC 2023, CCIS 2066, pp. 153–167, 2024.
https://doi.org/10.1007/978-981-97-3623-2_12

The research of rumor propagation dynamics was initially introduced by Daley and Kendall in the 1960s, leading to the development of the DK model [5]. Maki [14] later modified and proposed the MK model based on this work. Zanette [22] was the first to apply the theory of complex networks to the research of rumor propagation, establishing a rumor propagation model on small-world networks. Moreno et al. [15] further developed a rumor propagation model on scale-free networks.

Due to the similarity between rumor propagation and disease transmission, where the population's states during rumor propagation can be analogously compared to infectious disease spread, most researchers choose to apply infectious disease transmission models to study rumor propagation. Most of the research methods incorporate ways of transmission, population states and social factors. Wang et al. [18] studied rumor propagation in multilingual environments. Yang et al. [21] added the lurker state to the SIR model. Chen et al. [2] constructed an SEIR model with a saturation infection rate and proposed effective strategies to suppress rumors. Chen et al. [4] considered scientific knowledge levels and social reinforcement in the model. Chen et al. [3] proposed the ISWR model and incorporated the wise man and social reinforcement. Ke et al. [10] modeled the role of government and media refutation in rumor propagation.

The previous researches mainly focus on factors at the global [2–4,10,18,21]. However, some researchers have started to investigate the dynamics of rumor propagation from a local perspective, considering psychological factors or individual behaviors. This helps in understanding and capturing the essence of information dissemination.

For example, Wang et al. [19] divide individuals into positive and negative categories, which will affect their transmission rate of information. Ma et al. [13] presented a rumor propagation model considering individual subjective judgment and diverse features. Li et al. [12] constructed a rumor propagation model incorporating individual behavior and refutation mechanism, where the involvement of refuters effectively reduced the number of infected individuals and suppressed rumors. Tong et al. [16] studied the impact of individual behaviors on rumor propagation in homogeneous networks. Yan et al. [20] paid attention to the endogenous psychological motivation of users, explored the psychological changes of users after exposure to rumors, and integrated rumor propagation with personal emotions.

Based on the above discussion, the research of this paper mainly focuses on the modeling of rumor propagation and exploring the propagation dynamics of rumors in social media. The major contributions in the paper are made as follows:

1. A new model named V-SEIR is proposed which can help us reveal the nature of rumor propagation. Nodes are categorized by degree to portray node heterogeneity. Degree affects the behavior, function, and importance of nodes. The analysis results reveal that the high-degree nodes spread information faster, while low-degree nodes are less influential. This feature can be used to

improve node heterogeneity and thus capture the individual behaviors accurately.

2. The portrayal of individual behavior helps to improve the predictive accuracy of the model. Thus, the V-SEIR model uses influence, bandwagon effect, and forgetting mechanism as metrics that capture individual characteristics. It helps us understand rumor dynamics and make predictions more realistic and accurate.

3. The proposed rumor propagation model is verified on various network topologies to validate the model generality. The empirical analysis reveals that the network topology is crucial for rumor propagation, especially the node degree distribution. The simulation results demonstrate that the V-SEIR model can adapt to different network topologies and perform better than other classic propagation models.

The rest of this article is arranged as follows. Some related works are reviewed in Sect. 2. In Sect. 3, we propose the V-SEIR rumor propagation model, outlining its propagation mechanism and providing the mean-field equations. In Sect. 4, simulations are performed in WS small-world networks, BA scale-free networks, ER random networks, and regular networks, multiple sets of comparison experiments are conducted. The model's accuracy has been confirmed through the Weibo datasets. Finally, Sect. 5 gives a brief summary to conclude this paper.

2 Related Work

Rumors in social media have caused negative impacts. Researchers model rumor propagation carefully. Most models are based on infectious disease models. For example, the SEIR model [1] has four states: Susceptible (S), Exposed (E), Infected (I), and Removed (R).

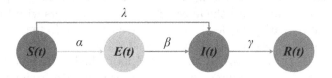

Fig. 1. Infectious disease SEIR model.

In this model, a portion of susceptible individuals is influenced by the rumor with a probability λ and becomes infected, while another portion is influenced with a probability α and becomes exposed. Exposed individuals, in turn, become infected with a probability β, and infected individuals lose interest and become removed with a probability γ. The classic SEIR (Susceptible-Exposed-Infected-Removed) model is illustrated in Fig. 1.

The SEIR model studies information propagation in social media. But it uses linear functions for transfer probability and ignores individual behavior changes due to network topology and information transfer components. This could cause inconsistency between the model and reality [11].

The mean-field equations of the SEIR model are defined as follows:

$$
\begin{cases}
\frac{dS(t)}{dt} = -\alpha S(t) E(t) - \lambda S(t) I(t) \\
\frac{dE(t)}{dt} = \alpha S(t) E(t) - \beta E(t) \\
\frac{dI(t)}{dt} = \beta E(t) + \lambda S(t) I(t) - \gamma I(t) \\
\frac{dR(t)}{dt} = \gamma I(t).
\end{cases}
\tag{1}
$$

2.1 Individual Behavior Metrics

Rumor propagation depends on the influence of each person. People are more likely to believe and spread rumors from influential sources. Moreover, the bandwagon effect influences the exposed and infected individuals based on the number of infected or removed individuals around them. Lastly, rumors can fade away if they are not propagated continuously. The probability of forgetting a rumor increases with time.

Influence. In social media, nodes are heterogeneous and they vary in importance. And the importance of a node is often measured by its degree, whereas a higher degree implies greater influence. As the key to rumor propagation lies in the propagation power of infected individuals, nodes with higher degree possess stronger propagation abilities. This is a quantifiable metric that must be considered.

Given the subsequent definition, where the average degree of the network is denoted as $\bar{k}$ and the degree of node i is denoted as k_i. If k_i is greater than $\bar{k}$, then node i is designated as an important node with a greater influence; otherwise, it is an ordinary node with a lesser influence. Suppose, at a particular time step, node i serves as the infected individual and node j represents the susceptible individual. When the infected individual interacts with the susceptible, the transition path of node j (to become exposed or infected) is determined by the relationship between its degree k_j and the network's average degree $\bar{k}$. If $k_j > \bar{k}$, node j transitions to an exposed individual with a probability α_2, and α_1 is set to 0, thereby interrupting the transition path from susceptible to infected. Similarly, if $k_j \leq \bar{k}$, node i transitions to an infected individual with a probability α_1, and α_2 is set to 0, effectively cutting off the transition path from susceptible to exposed.

The transition probability metric when an infected individual i interacts with a susceptible individual j is defined as:

$$
\alpha_1(i,j) = \alpha_2(i,j) = a \left(1 - \frac{k_j}{\sum_{r \in \omega(i)} k_r} \right).
\tag{2}
$$

where a is a constant, and $\omega(i)$ represents the set of neighboring nodes of node i.

It can be observed that, when considering an infected individual i, the sum of the degree of its neighboring nodes remains constant. The transition probability rises as the degree of susceptible individual j falls, indicating a stronger influence of i as compared to j. The aforementioned definition considers the effect of node influence on the transition path of susceptible individuals. Due to the heterogeneity of nodes, ordinary nodes may not be converted into infected individuals immediately when rumors are disseminated by ordinary nodes; instead, they may become exposed individuals. Important nodes can spread rumors, converting susceptible individuals into infected individuals instantly.

Bandwagon Effect. Social effects, such as the bandwagon effect, can influence individual opinions and behaviors [11]. It suggests that susceptible individuals may change their behavior due to peer pressure or popular beliefs, increasing the likelihood of being exposed to infected or removed individuals.

Wan et al. [17] defined the bandwagon effect as:

$$\beta(\beta_0, I(t)) = \beta_0 \cdot e^{-\ln(\beta_0) \cdot I(t)}. \tag{3}$$

where β_0 represents the initial transition probability of the rumor, influenced by factors related to the rumor itself, such as credibility, complexity, propagation platform, and timeliness.

However, it's important to note that the above expression for the bandwagon effect is determined by the global proportion of infected individuals, whereas this research's characterization of the bandwagon effect takes into account the influence of individual behaviors. Therefore, the probability function for the transition from exposed to infected is defined as:

$$\beta(\beta_0, i) = \beta_0 \cdot e^{-\ln(\beta_0) \cdot \left(\sum_{r \in \phi(i)} k_r\right)/k_i}. \tag{4}$$

where $\phi(i)$ represents the set of neighboring nodes connected to node i that are infected.

The exposed individual will transition with the initial transition probability β_0 when there are no infected individuals nearby, as can be observed. As the number of infected individuals around the exposed individual rises, the transition probability β also rises. In order to be more consistent with actual propagation mechanisms, this equation only considers infected individuals around node i.

Similarly, the probability function for the transition from exposed to removed is defined as:

$$\lambda_1(\lambda_{10}, i) = \lambda_{10} \cdot e^{-\ln(\lambda_{10}) \cdot \left(\sum_{r \in \sigma(i)} k_r\right)/k_i}. \tag{5}$$

And the probability function for the transition from infected to removed is defined as:

$$\gamma_1(\gamma_{10}, i) = \gamma_{10} \cdot e^{-\ln(\gamma_{10}) \cdot \left(\sum_{r \in \sigma(i)} k_r\right)/k_i}. \tag{6}$$

where $\sigma(i)$ represents the set of neighboring nodes connected to node i that are removed.

Forgetting Mechanism. Based on studies of short-term memory, German psychologist Ebbinghaus [7] created the Ebbinghaus forgetting curve, which simulates the deterioration of memory. For rumor propagation, most individuals only come into contact with a rumor once, forming a short-term memory. Thus, the Ebbinghaus forgetting curve is applicable for simulating the forgetting mechanism in rumor propagation. The amount of memory diminishes, and the likelihood of forgetting the rumor rises as the period of time since exposure to the rumor grows [23]. Gu et al. [9] studied the forgetting mechanism and found that the forgetting probability follows an exponential pattern. Although each person's forgetting rate and memory capacity vary, the statistical trend is constant. Therefore, the forgetting probability function is defined as:

$$f(\tau) = \begin{cases} 0, & b - e^{-\frac{\tau}{s}} < 0 \\ b - e^{-\frac{\tau}{s}}, & 0 \le b - e^{-\frac{\tau}{s}} \le 1 \\ 1, & b - e^{-\frac{\tau}{s}} > 1. \end{cases} \tag{7}$$

where τ represents the time since becoming exposed or infected. In this research, time is discretized into integers. b is the initial forgetting probability related to the importance of the rumor. s indicates the forgetting time constant, where $s > 0$, and $\frac{1}{s}$ represents the forgetting rate.

Additionally, it's important to note that the size of the rumor information content also affects memory retention. Greater information results in less forgetting. Therefore, we introduce the final forgetting probability function with self-information to measure the size of the rumor information content. The expression for self-information is defined as:

$$I(x) = -\ln P(x). \tag{8}$$

where $P(x)$ represents the probability of the rumor occurring. The resulting forget probability function is defined as:

$$P_f(\tau, x) = \frac{f(\tau)}{1 + I(x)}. \tag{9}$$

$$\lambda_2 = \gamma_2 = P_f(\tau, x). \tag{10}$$

where τ is set to 0 when an individual is exposed or infected. At this point, they forget the rumor and transition to a removed individual using the initial forgetting probability $\frac{b-1}{1+I(x)}$. Rumors can be seen to be less important and more quickly forgotten as b grows, increasing the initial forgetting probability. The likelihood of forgetting the rumor diminishes as s rises because the forgetting rate declines. The likelihood of forgetting likewise rises with an increase in $P(x)$. Given b, s, and $P(x)$, the likelihood of forgetting the rumor increases as τ increases.

Representation of State Transition Probabilities. The transition probabilities of states depend on many factors that affect individual behaviors. The transition probability is the weighted product of these factors. Exposed and infected individuals are influenced by the bandwagon effect and the forgetting mechanism when they become removed individuals. These two factors affect their transition probabilities. The expressions are as follows:

$$\lambda = \prod_{i=1}^{2}(\lambda_i \cdot w_i).$$
(11)

$$\gamma = \prod_{i=1}^{2}(\gamma_i \cdot w_i).$$
(12)

where w_i represents the weight corresponding to the metric.

3   The V-SEIR Rumor Propagation Model

To better simulate the rumor propagation process in social media, this research proposes the V-SEIR rumor propagation model, which takes into account individual behaviors. The four states from the classic SEIR model—Susceptible (S), Exposed (E), Infected (I), and Removed (R)—remain in the new model. Additionally, we introduce the concepts of influence, bandwagon effect, and forgetting mechanism, and add a transition path from exposed individuals to removed individuals, as shown in Fig. 2.

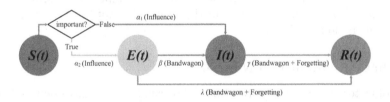

Fig. 2. V-SEIR rumor propagation model.

The specific rumor propagation process is as follows:

1. When an infected individual encounters a susceptible individual, the susceptible individual becomes an infected individual with a probability α_1 or an exposed individual with a probability α_2.
2. Exposed individuals are influenced by the surrounding infected individuals and become infected with a probability β. Simultaneously, exposed individuals are influenced by the surrounding removed individuals and become removed with a probability λ.
3. Infected individuals are influenced by the surrounding removed individuals and become removed with a probability γ.
4. Removed individuals remain unaffected and maintain their state throughout the propagation process.

The mean-field equations of the V-SEIR model are defined as follows:

$$\begin{cases} \frac{dS(t)}{dt} = -\alpha_1 S(t) I(t) - \alpha_2 S(t) I(t) \\ \frac{dE(t)}{dt} = \alpha_2 S(t) I(t) - \beta E(t) - \lambda E(t) \\ \frac{dI(t)}{dt} = \beta E(t) + \alpha_1 S(t) I(t) - \gamma I(t) \\ \frac{dR(t)}{dt} = \gamma I(t) + \lambda E(t). \end{cases} \tag{13}$$

where $S(t)$, $E(t)$, $I(t)$, and $R(t)$ represent the proportions of the four states in the rumor propagation process at time t. Therefore, each variable should satisfy the normalization condition:

$$S(t) + E(t) + I(t) + R(t) = 1. \tag{14}$$

3.1 Rumor-Free Equilibrium Point

When the time-dependent ratios of $S(t)$, $E(t)$, $I(t)$, and $R(t)$ become constant, the system reaches the equilibrium state which can be describe as,

$$\begin{cases} -\alpha_1 S(t) I(t) - \alpha_2 S(t) I(t) = 0 \\ \alpha_2 S(t) I(t) - \beta E(t) - \lambda E(t) = 0 \\ \beta E(t) + \alpha_1 S(t) I(t) - \gamma I(t) = 0 \\ \gamma I(t) + \lambda E(t) = 0. \end{cases} \tag{15}$$

From (15), we can obtain the rumor-free equilibrium(RFE) is denoted as $P_0 = (S^*, 0, 0, R^*)$ where $S^* + R^* = N$. At the rumor-free equilibrium point P_0, rumor propagation is stable, and the proportions of the four categories of individuals no longer change.

3.2 Basic Reproduction Number

According to the next-generation matrix method [6], we have determined the basic reproduction number R_0 of the V-SEIR model. Let $X = (S, E, I, R)^T$, then, (13) can be written as $\frac{dX}{dt} = \mathscr{F}(X) - \mathscr{V}(X)$, where

$$\mathscr{F}(X) = \begin{bmatrix} 0 \\ \alpha_2 SI \\ \alpha_1 SI \\ 0 \end{bmatrix}, \mathscr{V}(X) = \begin{bmatrix} \alpha_1 SI + \alpha_2 SI \\ \beta E + \lambda E \\ -\beta E + \gamma I \\ -\gamma I - \lambda E \end{bmatrix}. \tag{16}$$

Since the V-SEIR model has two compartments, $E(t)$ and $I(t)$, the Jacobian matrices of $\mathscr{F}(X)$ and $\mathscr{V}(X)$ at the rumor-free equilibrium point P_0 are

$$F(X) = \begin{bmatrix} 0 & \alpha_1 S^* \\ 0 & \alpha_2 S^* \end{bmatrix}, V(X) = \begin{bmatrix} \beta + \lambda & 0 \\ -\beta & \gamma \end{bmatrix}, \tag{17}$$

then

$$F(X)V^{-1}(X) = \begin{bmatrix} 0 & \alpha_1 S^* \\ 0 & \alpha_2 S^* \end{bmatrix} \begin{bmatrix} \frac{1}{\beta+\lambda} & 0 \\ \frac{\beta}{\gamma(\beta+\lambda)} & \frac{1}{\gamma} \end{bmatrix} = \begin{bmatrix} \frac{\alpha_1 S^* \beta}{\gamma(\beta+\lambda)} & \frac{\alpha_1 S^*}{\gamma} \\ \frac{\alpha_2 S^* \beta}{\gamma(\beta+\lambda)} & \frac{\alpha_2 S^*}{\gamma} \end{bmatrix}. \tag{18}$$

In the end, we obtain the basic reproduction number.

$$R_0 = \rho(FV^{-1}) = \frac{S^*}{\gamma}\left(\frac{\alpha_1\beta}{\beta+\lambda} + \alpha_2\right). \tag{19}$$

When the system stabilizes, the rumor will eventually disappear if $R_0 <$ 1, whereas the rumor will persist and continue to spread if $R_0 > 1$. $R_0 = 1$ represents a critical condition for rumor propagation.

4   Experimental Results and Analysis

The nature of social media is a complex network, which has some properties of complex networks, such as the small-world phenomenon as well as the scale-free phenomenon. Therefore, in this section, we simulate rumor propagation in several classical complex networks to reflect the network properties of social media. These networks include WS small-world networks, BA scale-free networks, ER random networks, and regular networks. Subsequently, we conduct several sets of experiments, including parameter analysis, ablation experiments, and model comparisons.

The basic information of each network is shown in Table 1, which includes the number of nodes N, average degree $\bar{k}$ and average clustering coefficient.

Table 1. Networks Information

Network	N	$\bar{k}$	Average clustering coefficient
WS small-world	1000	12.00	0.0945
BA scale-free	1000	13.90	0.0468
ER random	1000	20.34	0.0205
Regular	1000	12.00	0.0109

4.1   Model Simulation in Various Network Topologies

We simulate the V-SEIR model on four types of complex networks (WS, BA, ER, and regular) with $N = 1000$ nodes each, which can help us evaluate the model adaptability in different types of social media. We use random integer sequences to represent the node iteration order, making the simulation realistic. At $t = 0$, one node is randomly infected and the rest are susceptible. We repeat the experiments 100 times and compute the average values of $S(t), E(t), I(t)$, and $R(t)$.

From Fig. 3, it can be observed that the number of susceptible individuals gradually decreases, while the number of removed individuals increases, and the number of infected individuals initially rises and then declines. With the exception of the regular network, where there are no exposed individuals, the other

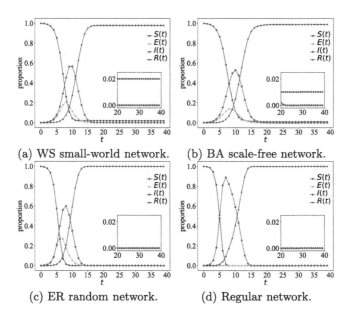

Fig. 3. V-SEIR model simulations in different network topologies. $a = 0.6$, $\beta_0 = \lambda_{10} = \gamma_{10} = 0.1$, $b = 1.1$, $s = 50$, $w_1 = 2$, $w_2 = 3$.

three networks exhibit a pattern of increasing and then decreasing exposed individuals. This trend is due to the absence of important nodes in the regular network, where all nodes have the same degree, thus leading to the absence of exposed individuals during rumor propagation. It is also noteworthy that the peak of exposed individuals occurs earlier than the peak of infected individuals, and this peak is concentrated in the early stages of rumor propagation. This can be attributed to the fact that nodes with higher degree, which are important nodes, are more likely to be exposed to the rumor early and become exposed. It is evident that both changes in network topology and variations in node degree significantly impact the dynamics of rumor propagation. They also lead to significant differences in the effectiveness of the individual behavior metrics.

4.2 Comparison of Individual Behavior Metrics on Rumor Propagation

To better understand the effects of network topology, influence, bandwagon effect, and forgetting mechanism on the rumor propagation process, this research conducted eight comparison experiments in WS an BA networks.

In SEIR model, the parameters were set as follows: $\lambda = \alpha = 0.8$, $\beta = 0.3$, $\gamma = 0.5$. In the influence metric, $a = 0.8$; in the bandwagon effect metric, $\beta_0 = \lambda_{10} = 0.3$, $\gamma_{10} = 0.5$; in the forgetting probability function, $b = 1.1$, $s = 50$, $P(x) = 0.8$; and the weights for the influencing factors were set as $w_1 = 2$, $w_2 = 3$.

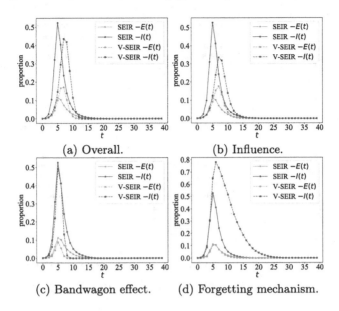

(a) Overall.

(b) Influence.

(c) Bandwagon effect.

(d) Forgetting mechanism.

Fig. 4. Comparison of individual behavior metrics in the WS small-world network.

From Figs. 4, it can be observed that in the WS small-world network:

1. The combined effect leads to a decrease in the peak of infected individuals and an increase in the peak of exposed individuals, and both peaks are shifted later. The duration of the rumor remains relatively unchanged. The overall impact on the entire rumor propagation process is significant.
2. Influence leads to a decrease in the peak of infected individuals and an increase in the peak of exposed individuals, and both peaks are shifted later. The duration of the rumor propagation process increases. The impact on the entire rumor propagation process is significant.
3. Bandwagon effect leads to a decrease in the peaks of infected and exposed individuals. The duration of the rumor propagation process decreases. The impact is significant in the later stages of rumor propagation.
4. Forgetting mechanism leads to an increase in the peak of infected individuals, delayed peak, with less significant impact on exposed individuals. The duration of the rumor propagation process increases. The impact is significant in the later stages of rumor propagation.

From Figs. 5, it can be observed that in the BA scale-free network:

1. The combined effect leads to a decrease in the peak of infected individuals, with less significant impact on exposed individuals, and both peaks are shifted later. The duration of the rumor remains relatively unchanged. The overall impact on the entire rumor propagation process is significant.
2. Influence leads to a decrease in the peaks of infected and exposed individuals, and both peaks are shifted later. The impact of the rumor decreases, and the

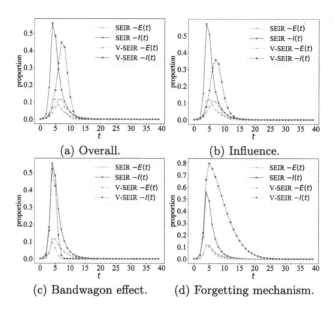

(a) Overall.   (b) Influence.

(c) Bandwagon effect.   (d) Forgetting mechanism.

Fig. 5. Comparison of individual behavior metrics in the BA scale-free network.

duration of the rumor propagation process increases. The impact on the entire rumor propagation process is significant.

3. Bandwagon effect leads to a decrease in the peaks of infected and exposed individuals. The duration of the rumor propagation process decreases. The impact is significant in the later stages of rumor propagation.

4. Forgetting mechanism leads to an increase in the peak of infected individuals, delayed peak, with less significant impact on exposed individuals. The duration of the rumor propagation process increases. The impact is significant in the later stages of rumor propagation.

The bottom line is that various individual behavior metrics have diverse effects on rumor propagation. It is vital to take into account the combined effects of various factors in order to generate simulation results that more accurately reflect real-world rumor propagation. Additionally, despite the fact that different metrics generally have a similar effect on rumor propagation in the WS small-world and the BA scale-free network, major variations can occur as a result of variations in the degree-based metrics.

4.3   Model Comparison Between V-SEIR and SEIR

As a famous type of social media, we select Weibo, the platform with the largest number of users, to validate our model. We use the rumor that *consuming monosodium glutamate causes cancer* as an example, and obtain information from a total of 432 users addressing this topic. Subsequently, we calculate and obtain the specific time points during the rumor propagation period at which these users debunked the rumor and became categorized as removed individuals. We use this as a dataset for model performance evaluation. Finally, we compare and analyze the simulation results of the V-SEIR and SEIR models, as depicted in Fig. 6, within the context of social media rumor propagation.

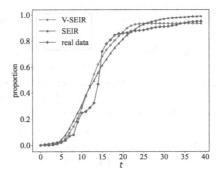

Fig. 6. Comparison of the model with Weibo datasets. In SEIR model, the parameters were set as follows: $\lambda = 0.2$, $\alpha = 0.4$, $\beta = 0.25$, $\gamma = 0.2$. In the influence metric, $a = 0.8$; in the bandwagon effect metric, $\beta_0 = 0.1$, $\lambda_{10} = \gamma_{10} = 0.2$; in the forgetting probability function, $b = 1.1$, $s = 50$, $P(x) = 0.8$; and the weights for the influencing factors were set as $w_1 = 2$, $w_2 = 3$.

We calculate the mean squared error(MSE), root mean squared error(RMSE), and mean absolute error(MAE) for both models, as detailed in Table 2. It can be observed that the V-SEIR model outperforms the SEIR model in all dimensions, confirming that the V-SEIR model can better simulate rumor propagation with higher prediction accuracy. The V-SEIR model showed excellent performance in predicting both the early and late stages of rumors. The simulation process identified a small number of individuals who had not been exposed to the rumor even after rumor propagation stabilized, but the SEIR model categorized all individuals as removed individuals. Furthermore, there is potential for enhancement in both models to better capture the variations and align with the actual data.

Table 2. Comparison of Model Performance

Model	MSE	RMSE	MAE
V-SEIR	0.0031	0.0558	0.0368
SEIR	0.0046	0.0681	0.0550

5   Conclusion

This paper proposed a new rumor propagation model called V-SEIR which can help us analyze the complexity of rumor propagation in the context of social media. By employing the V-SEIR model, we could look for insight into the essence of rumor dissemination and individual behaviors. The model's stability was contingent upon the basic reproduction number, denoted as R_0, serving as a critical determinant for the persistence or attenuation of rumors within the social media environment. Additionally, the model took into account node heterogeneity, the impact of influential nodes, the bandwagon effect, and the dynamics of forgetting. Extensive experiments on a variety of network topologies, as well as validation using datasets from Weibo, demonstrated that the V-SEIR model excels in forecasting the dynamics of rumor propagation in social media.

The highlight of this study was to provide insight into the relationship between individual behaviors and network topologies and analyze the impact of both on rumor propagation. This helped researchers understand how information flows through social media. It also allowed researchers to gain a deeper understanding of the complexity of information dissemination and thus develop more effective models and methods for rumor management.

Acknowledgements. The work of this paper was supported by the National Key Research and Development Program of China (Grant No. 2022YFC3302100), the National Natural Science Foundation of China (Grant No. 61901421), the National Social Science Fund of China (Grant No. 19ZDA272), and the Fundamental Research Funds for the Central Universities.

Disclosure of Interests. The authors have no competing interests to declare that are relevant to the content of this article.

References

1. Anderson, R.M., May, R.M.: Infectious Diseases of Humans: Dynamics and Control. Oxford University Press, Oxford (1991)
2. Chen, S., Jiang, H., Li, L., Li, J.: Dynamical behaviors and optimal control of rumor propagation model with saturation incidence on heterogeneous networks. Chaos Solit. Fractals **140**, 110206 (2020)
3. Chen, S., Zhao, L., et al.: Dynamic analysis of the rumor propagation model with consideration of the wise man and social reinforcement. Phys. A **571**, 125828 (2021)
4. Chen, S., et al.: Rumor propagation model with consideration of scientific knowledge level and social reinforcement in heterogeneous network. Phys. A **559**, 125063 (2020)
5. Daley, D.J., Kendall, D.G.: Epidemics and rumours. Nature **204**(4963), 1118 (1964)
6. Van den Driessche, P., Watmough, J.: Reproduction numbers and sub-threshold endemic equilibria for compartmental models of disease transmission. Math. Biosci. **180**(1–2), 29–48 (2002)
7. Ebbinghaus, H.: Memory: a contribution to experimental psychology. Ann. Neurosci. **20**(4), 155 (2013)

8. Friggeri, A., Adamic, L., Eckles, D., Cheng, J.: Rumor cascades. In: Proceedings of the International AAAI Conference on Web and Social Media, vol. 8, pp. 101–110 (2014)
9. Gu, J., Li, W., Cai, X.: The effect of the forget-remember mechanism on spreading. Eur. Phys. J. B **62**, 247–255 (2008)
10. Ke, Y., Zhu, L., Wu, P., Shi, L.: Dynamics of a reaction-diffusion rumor propagation model with non-smooth control. Appl. Math. Comput. **435**, 127478 (2022)
11. Latané, B.: The psychology of social impact. Am. Psychol. **36**(4), 343 (1981)
12. Li, R., Li, Y., Meng, Z., Song, Y., Jiang, G.: Rumor spreading model considering individual activity and refutation mechanism simultaneously. IEEE Access **8**, 63065–63076 (2020)
13. Ma, J., Zhu, H.: Rumor diffusion in heterogeneous networks by considering the individuals' subjective judgment and diverse characteristics. Phys. A **499**, 276–287 (2018)
14. Maki, D.P.: Mathematical models and applications: with emphasis on the social, life, and management sciences (1973)
15. Moreno, Y., Nekovee, M., Pacheco, A.F.: Dynamics of rumor spreading in complex networks. Phys. Rev. E **69**(6), 066130 (2004)
16. Tong, X., Jiang, H., Chen, X., Yu, S., Li, J.: Dynamic analysis and optimal control of rumor spreading model with recurrence and individual behaviors in heterogeneous networks. Entropy **24**(4), 464 (2022)
17. Wan, Y., Wang, X.: Rumor spreading model with conformity effect. J. Comput. Appl. **36**(9), 2381 (2016)
18. Wang, J., Jiang, H., Ma, T., Hu, C.: Global dynamics of the multi-lingual sir rumor spreading model with cross-transmitted mechanism. Chaos Solit. Fractals **126**, 148–157 (2019)
19. Wang, Y., Yuan, G., Fan, C., Hu, Y., Yang, Y.: Disease spreading model considering the activity of individuals on complex networks. Phys. A **530**, 121393 (2019)
20. Yan, Y., Wang, Y., Zheng, P.: Rumor detection on social networks focusing on endogenous psychological motivation. Neurocomputing **552**, 126548 (2023)
21. Yang, A., Huang, X., Cai, X., Zhu, X., Lu, L.: ILSR rumor spreading model with degree in complex network. Phys. A **531**, 121807 (2019)
22. Zanette, D.H.: Dynamics of rumor propagation on small-world networks. Phys. Rev. E **65**(4), 041908 (2002)
23. Zhao, L., Xie, W., Gao, H.O., Qiu, X., Wang, X., Zhang, S.: A rumor spreading model with variable forgetting rate. Phys. A **392**(23), 6146–6154 (2013)

Bridging Recommendations Across Domains: An Overview of Cross-Domain Recommendation

Xiaopeng Gu[1], Peili Xi[2], Lei Yan[2], Xiaocheng Hu[1], Bing Yang[1], Lele Sun[3], Litao Shang[3], and Jing Liu[3(⊠)]

[1] China Academy of Electronics and Information Technology, Beijing, China
[2] Shanghai Institute of Satellite Engineering, Shanghai, China
[3] School of Electrical and Information Engineering, Tianjin University, Tianjin, China
jliu_tju@tju.edu.cn

Abstract. As the Internet has become increasingly ubiquitous and information has experienced explosive growth, recommendation systems have evolved to become an indispensable component across various fields. Traditional recommendation systems typically rely on either user historical preferences or item similarity for generating suggestions. However, cross-domain recommendation systems transcend these traditional boundaries by harnessing not only user historical preferences but also their behavioral data across different domains, significantly enhancing recommendation precision and personalization. This paper aims to provide a comprehensive exploration of cross-domain recommendation systems, including their core concepts, diverse application scenarios, underlying algorithm models, and the evaluation metrics used to gauge their effectiveness. Additionally, we'll offer insights into potential future research directions. In an age where demand for more accurate and personalized recommendations continues to surge in our data-driven world, cross-domain recommendation systems are poised to play a pivotal role in shaping the future of information and content consumption.

Keywords: Recommender System · Cross-Domain Recommendation · Survey

1 Introduction

Recommendation systems are a vital application in the realm of the internet. They analyze users' historical behaviors and preferences to suggest items or services that users may find interesting. Traditional recommendation systems often rely on user history [1,2] or item similarity [3,4] within a single platform or domain. These systems have found widespread applications in e-commerce [5–7], social networks [8–10], news recommendations [11–13], and have demonstrated considerable effectiveness. However, they often only consider data within one domain, leading to data sparsity issues. Additionally, new users or those with minimal interactions on a platform pose challenges for recommendations (the cold start problem).

This is where cross-domain recommendation systems come into play. Cross-domain recommendation systems utilize user behavioral data across various domains, allowing them to merge user or item features from multiple domains for personalized recommendations. This approach enhances recommendation accuracy, personalization, and broadens the scope of recommendation systems.

2 Application of Cross-Domain Recommendation

Cross-domain recommendation systems can be applied to a variety of fields, and a few typical application scenarios are listed here.

2.1 e-Commerce Recommendation

In the e-commerce sector [14], cross-domain recommendation systems can assist users in discovering products of potential interest. For example, when a user is purchasing clothing, the system can utilize the user's activities in other areas, such as bags, home furnishings, and more, to gain insights into the user's preferred style, like minimalism. Subsequently, the system can recommend clothing items that align with this style [5,6]. This cross-domain recommendation enhances the user's shopping experience and can also boost the sales revenue of the e-commerce platform (Fig. 1).

(a) E-Commerce Recommendation   (b) Social Recommendation

Fig. 1. The application of cross-domain recommendation in e-commerce and social.

2.2   Social Recommendation

In social networks [15,16], cross-domain recommendation systems can assist users in discovering potential friends or communities that they might find interesting [8,9]. For example, the system can leverage user behavioral information across various social networks to discern their preferences, styles, or areas of interest. With this insight, it can recommend friends who share similar interests on different platforms. Alternatively, the system can make recommendations for similar products in one domain (e.g., books) based on the user's interests in another domain (e.g., movies). This cross-domain recommendation approach can enhance user engagement in social networks and improve overall user satisfaction.

2.3   News Recommendation

In the field of news recommendation, cross-domain recommendation systems can assist users in discovering news articles that they might find interesting [11, 12]. For example, the system can analyze a user's browsing history on various news websites and recommend news articles that are related to topics they have shown interest in. This cross-domain recommendation approach can enhance user engagement with news and improve their reading experience (Fig. 2).

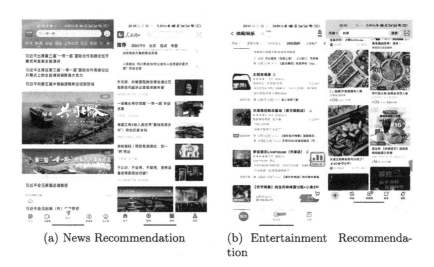

(a) News Recommendation   (b) Entertainment Recommendation

Fig. 2. The application of cross-domain recommendation in news and entertainment.

2.4   Entertainment Recommendation

In the realm of leisure and entertainment, a cross-domain recommendation system can comprehensively consider a user's interests across various domains to provide more accurate service recommendations [17]. For instance, if a user has a strong preference for dining in a specific region based on their dining history, the system can identify their areas of interest and recommend suitable travel itineraries and dining establishments, enhancing the user's overall leisure experience.

3   Models of Cross-Domain Recommendation

In different classification methods, cross-domain recommendations can be categorized into the following situations:

3.1   Classified by the Number of Domains

Dual-Domain Recommendation. In dual-domain recommendations, there are only two domains: the source domain and the target domain. These domains can be of different data types, such as music and movies, or they can be the same data type, such as products from different e-commerce websites. In dual-domain recommendations, it is necessary to transform user and item information from the source domain to the target domain in order to achieve cross-domain recommendations. Such as, CoNet [18] establishes a cross-connections network between two domains to achieve knowledge transfer for dual domains. DTCDR [19] (DTCDR: A Framework for Dual-Target Cross-Domain Recommendation) shares features learned from the same user in two different domains (e.g., books and movies) to enrich user feature representations, where both domains serve as the target domain for each other or as the source domain, improving recommendation performance. GA-DTCDR [20] (Graphical and Attentional framework for Dual-Target Cross-Domain Recommendation) enhances the above by incorporating textual information about users and items, expanding information by constructing a graphical structure. PPGN [21] (Cross-domain recommendation via preference propagation graphnet) enhances information using multiple stacked GNN layers for robust representations, while BITGCF [22] (Cross domain recommendation via bi-directional transfer graph collaborative filtering network) designs a feature fusion module during GNNs [23,24] for better knowledge transfer. EMCDR [25] (Cross-Domain Recommendation: An Embedding and Mapping Approach) acquires target domain user features by learning a behavior mapping from the source domain to the target domain for recommendation. TMCDR [26] (Transfer-Meta Framework for Cross-domain Recommendation to Cold-Start Users), based on EMCDR, jointly learns user and item embeddings in both source and target domains, incorporating meta-learning methods and task labels to optimize the meta-network. NATR [27] (Cross-domain Recommendation Without Sharing User-relevant Data) focuses on protecting user privacy and considers two domains with the same items, transferring features of items to be recommended from the source domain to the target domain.

In order to avoid negative transfer [28,29], many recent approaches disentangle user representations into domain-specific representations and domain-invariant representations. User domain-specific representations help to learn the collective relationship between users and items only within the domain, and user domain-invariant representations can perform cross-domain transfer for cross-domain information enhancement. ATLRec [30] (Atlrec: An attentional adversarial transfer learning network for cross-domain recommendation) utilizes two independent fully-connected networks to extract domain-specific representations and domain-invariant representations respectively. To align the domain-invariant representations of two domains, the GRL-based domain discriminator [31] are employed. MADD [32] (Multi-level attention-based domain disentanglement for bcdr) imposes orthogonal constraints based on ATLRec with respect to domain-specific representations and domain-invariant representations within the domain to distance them from each other. DisenCDR [33] introduces variational inference [34] into cross-domain recommendation and uses Kullback-Leibler (KL) [35] divergence to distance domain-specific representations and domain-invariant representations. DCCDR [36] (Disentangled contrastive learning for cross-domain recommendation), as the latest cdr methods, utilize contrastive learning [37,38] to achieve effective disentanglement.

Multi-domain Recommendation. In multi-domain recommendations, there are more than just two domains. Typically, there are multiple domains, each with its own set of users and items. These domains can also be of different data types, such as music and movies, or they can be of the same data type, like products from different e-commerce websites. In multi-domain recommendations, one or more domains, often referred to as the "target domains," are the domains for which recommendation performance needs improvement. The other domains are considered "auxiliary domains." The goal is to transfer user or item information from one or more auxiliary domains to one or more target domains.

For example, CAT-ART [39] (One for All, All for One: Learning and Transferring User Embeddings for Cross-Domain Recommendation) addresses the issue of negative transfer, learning global representations from multiple domains and enhancing performance by combining the original embeddings of the target domain with transfer information from other domains. AFT [40] (Adversarial Feature Translation for Multi-domain Recommendation) employs GAN networks to learn feature relationships across different domains, thereby improving the recommendation performance across all domains. HeroGRAPH [41] (Hero-GRAPH: A Heterogeneous Graph Framework for Multi-Target Cross-Domain Recommendation) collects user and item information from multiple domains and constructs a shared graph, aggregating user information from multiple domains. DRMTCDR [42] (Disentangled Representations Learning for Multi-target Cross-domain Recommendation) utilizes contrastive learning to disentangle multi-domain user representations.

3.2   Classified by Data Type

Data Content Lacks Consistency. In the context of recommendation systems, "data inconsistency" typically refers to the difference in data types between various domains, such as music and movies or products from different e-commerce websites. The aforementioned DTCDR [19] (DTCDR: A Framework for Dual-Target Cross-Domain Recommendation), GA-DTCDR [20] (Graphical and Attentional framework for Dual-Target Cross-Domain Recommendation), and others are all based on heterogeneous data for recommendations. DDTCDR [43] (Deep Dual Transfer Cross Domain Recommendation) uses deep bidirectional transfer learning to perform feature transformation in two domains effectively and can calculate inverse mapping through implicit orthogonal mapping. ETL-CDR [44] (Towards Equivalent Transformation of User Preferences in Cross Domain Recommendation) learns a transformer that captures joint distribution of user preferences in different domains. RL-ISN [45] (Reinforcement Learning-enhanced Shared-account Cross-domain Sequential Recommendation) uses reinforcement learning, treating cross-domain tasks as reinforcement learning tasks, and utilizes Markov chains to perform cross-domain reinforcement recommendation.

Data Content Exhibits Consistency. In the context of data content consistency, it refers to shared user and item information between different domains. For instance, if a user exhibits multiple behaviors (adding to cart, favoriting, purchasing, etc.) on a shopping platform, their user and item information remains consistent. Domain divisions are primarily based on users' different behaviors. MBGNN [46] (Graph Meta Network for Multi-Behavior Recommendation) effectively captures user behavior information by low-rank decomposition of multiple behaviors. HMG-CR [47] (Hyper Meta-Path Contrastive Learning for Multi-Behavior Recommendation) introduces the concept of hyper-meta paths to construct hyper-meta paths or hyper-graphs, which explicitly illustrate the dependencies between different user behaviors. Different hyper-graphs reflect varying user behavior patterns towards different products, and contrastive learning is applied between constructed hyper-graphs. S-MBRec [48] (Self-supervised Graph Neural Networks for Multi-behavior Recommendation) aims to capture commonalities between different behaviors and reduces differences between pairwise behaviors through contrastive learning. HGCL [49] (Heterogeneous Graph Contrastive Learning for Recommendation) simultaneously utilizes user-item collaborative interaction relationships, user-user social relationships, item-item similarity relationships, and leverages graph convolution and contrastive learning techniques to achieve efficient representation learning. KHGT [50] (Knowledge-Enhanced Hierarchical Graph Transformer Network for Multi-Behavior Recommendation) constructs user-item and item-item graph structures, embeds time features, and utilizes graph convolution to obtain features for the target behavior and recommended items.

4 Evaluation Metrics for Cross-Domain Recommendation

The evaluation metrics for cross-domain recommendation systems mainly include precision, recall, coverage, and diversity. Commonly used evaluation metrics in typical recommendation algorithms are as follows:

4.1 Normalized Cumulative Discounted Gain

Normalized Cumulative Discounted Gain (NDCG) emphasizes the order of recommendations and primarily considers the ranking of the top K recommended items by the recommendation system. The goal is to have items with higher relevance ranked closer to the top. Its formula is described as follows:

$$NDCG@K = \frac{1}{N} \sum_{i=1}^{N} \frac{1}{log_2(p_i + 1)} \tag{1}$$

where N denotes the number of test users and p_i denotes the position of the real access value of the i−th user in the recommendation list, if the value does not exist in the recommendation list, then $p \to \infty$.

4.2 Hit Rate

Hit Rate (HR) emphasizes the accuracy of recommendations, primarily focusing on the accuracy of the top K recommended items by the recommendation system. It aims to emphasize whether these items appear. Its formula is described as follows:

$$HR@K = \frac{1}{N} \sum_{i=1}^{N} hits(i) \tag{2}$$

where $hits(i)$ represents whether the value accessed by the i−th user is in the recommended list, 1 if yes, 0 otherwise.

4.3 Precision

Precision is the proportion of correctly predicted items among all the recommended items:

$$Precision = \frac{TP}{TP + FP} \tag{3}$$

where TP (True Positives) is the number of true instances and FP (False Positives) is the number of false positive instances. TP denotes the number of items that the model has successfully recommended out of the items that the user has actually preferred and FP denotes the number of items that the model has incorrectly recommended.

4.4 Recall

Recall emphasizes the proportion of correctly predicted items in the final recommendation list,

$$Precision = \frac{TP}{TP + FN} \tag{4}$$

where FN (False Negatives) is the number of false negative instances. FN denotes the number of items actually liked by the user that the model did not successfully recommend.

4.5   Mean Reciprocal Rank

Mean Reciprocal Rank (MRR) emphasizes the order of recommendations, focusing on the comparison between the predicted recommendation order and the actual recommendation order. Its formula is described as:

$$MRR = \frac{1}{N} \sum_{i=1}^{N} \frac{1}{rank_i} \tag{5}$$

where $rank_i$ is the rank of user i's first successful referral.

5   Future Directions for Cross-Domain Recommendation

Cross-domain recommendation systems represent a challenging research area. Future research directions mainly include the following aspects:

5.1   Explainability

To discuss cross-domain recommendation with a clearer logical structure and make it more persuasive, the interpretability of cross-domain recommendation systems has been a continual research focus. Future research can explore how to leverage interpretable machine learning models to construct cross-domain recommendation systems, thereby enhancing the interpretability of recommendation systems.

5.2   Real-Time

The real-time capability of cross-domain recommendation systems is a highly significant issue. Existing cross-domain recommendation systems often involve complex computations and data processing, resulting in recommendations that cannot be generated within a short timeframe. Future research can explore how to enhance the real-time performance of cross-domain recommendation systems by utilizing reinforcement learning methods.

5.3   Privacy-Preserving

Cross-domain recommendation systems involve user behavior information across different domains, making privacy protection a highly important issue. Future research can explore approaches to enhance the security and user trust in cross-domain recommendation systems from the perspective of user privacy protection.

6   Conclusion

Cross-domain recommendation systems are a method that leverages user behavior information across different domains to address recommendation challenges in a single domain and provide personalized recommendations through data processing. This article introduces the concept of cross-domain recommendation systems, their application scenarios, algorithm models, and evaluation metrics, and provides an outlook on future research directions. We are also exploring challenging areas such as privacy protection and would welcome the opportunity to engage in further discussions with the community.

Acknowledgement. This work is supported in part by the National Natural Science Foundation of China (U22B2037, 62371333).

References

1. Koren, Y.: Factorization meets the neighborhood: a multifaceted collaborative filtering model, in: Proceedings of the 14th ACM SIGKDD International Conference on Knowledge Discovery and Data Mining, pp. 426–434 (2008)
2. He, X., Zhang, H., Kan, M.-Y., Chua, T.-S.: Fast matrix factorization for online recommendation with implicit feedback. In: Proceedings of the 39th International ACM SIGIR Conference on Research and Development in Information Retrieval, pp. 549–558 (2016)
3. Zhang, H., Shen, F., Liu, W., He, X., Luan, H., Chua, T.-S.: Discrete collaborative filtering. In: Proceedings of the 39th International ACM SIGIR Conference on Research and Development in Information Retrieval, pp. 325–334 (2016)
4. Sarwar, B., Karypis, G., Konstan, J., Riedl, J.: Item-based collaborative filtering recommendation algorithms. In: Proceedings of the 10th International Conference on World Wide Web, pp. 285–295 (2001)
5. Sarwar, B., Karypis, G., Konstan, J., Riedl, J.: Analysis of recommendation algorithms for e-commerce. In: Proceedings of the 2nd ACM Conference on Electronic Commerce, pp. 158–167 (2000)
6. Schafer, J.B., Konstan, J.A., Riedl, J.: E-commerce recommendation applications. Data Min. Knowl. Disc. **5**, 115–153 (2001)
7. Chen, Q., Zhao, H., Li, W., Huang, P., Ou, W.: Behavior sequence transformer for e-commerce recommendation in alibaba. In: Proceedings of the 1st International Workshop on Deep Learning Practice for High-Dimensional Sparse Data, pp. 1–4 (2019)
8. Tang, J., Hu, X., Liu, H.: Social recommendation: a review. Soc. Netw. Anal. Min. **3**, 1113–1133 (2013)
9. Fan, W., et al.: Graph neural networks for social recommendation. In: The World Wide Web Conference, pp. 417–426 (2019)
10. Wu, L., Sun, P., Hong, R., Ge, Y., Wang, M.: Collaborative neural social recommendation. IEEE Trans. Syst. Man Cybern. Syst. **51**(1), 464–476 (2018)
11. Okura, S., Tagami, Y., Ono, S., Tajima, A.: Embedding-based news recommendation for millions of users. In: Proceedings of the 23rd ACM SIGKDD International Conference on Knowledge Discovery and Data Mining, pp. 1933–1942 (2017)

12. Zheng, G., et al.: DRN: a deep reinforcement learning framework for news recommendation. In: Proceedings of the 2018 World Wide Web Conference, pp. 167–176 (2018)
13. Li, L., Chu, W., Langford, J., Schapire, R.E.: A contextual-bandit approach to personalized news article recommendation. In: Proceedings of the 19th International Conference on World Wide Web, pp. 661–670 (2010)
14. Kim, T., Lee, J., Suh, J.: L-shape advertising for mobile video streaming services: less intrusive while still effective. Displays **78**, 102436 (2023)
15. Ottakath, N., et al.: ViDMASK dataset for face mask detection with social distance measurement. Displays **73**, 102235 (2022)
16. Yang, Y., et al.: Effects of social interaction on virtual reality cybersickness. Displays **80**, 102512 (2023)
17. Christensen, I.A., Schiaffino, S.: Entertainment recommender systems for group of users. Expert Syst. Appl. **38**(11), 14127–14135 (2011)
18. Hu, G., Zhang, Y., Yang, Q.: Conet: collaborative cross networks for cross-domain recommendation. In: Proceedings of the 27th ACM International Conference on Information and Knowledge Management, pp. 667–676 (2018)
19. Zhu, F., Chen, C., Wang, Y., Liu, G., Zheng, X.: DTCDR: a framework for dual-target cross-domain recommendation. In: Proceedings of the 28th ACM International Conference on Information and Knowledge Management, pp. 1533–1542 (2019)
20. Zhu, F., Wang, Y., Chen, C., Liu, G., Zheng, X.: A graphical and attentional framework for dual-target cross-domain recommendation. In: Proceedings of the Twenty-Ninth International Joint Conference on Artificial Intelligence, pp. 3001–3008 (2020)
21. Zhao, C., Li, C., Fu, C.: Cross-domain recommendation via preference propagation graphnet. In: Proceedings of the 28th ACM International Conference on Information and Knowledge Management, pp. 2165–2168 (2019)
22. Liu, M., Li, J., Li, G., Pan, P.: Cross domain recommendation via bi-directional transfer graph collaborative filtering networks. In: Proceedings of the 29th ACM International Conference on Information and Knowledge Management, pp. 885–894 (2020)
23. Wang, X., He, X., Wang, M., Feng, F., Chua, T.-S.: Neural graph collaborative filtering. In: Proceedings of the 42nd International ACM SIGIR Conference on Research and Development in Information Retrieval, pp. 165–174 (2019)
24. He, X., Deng, K., Wang, X., Li, Y., Zhang, Y., Wang, M.: Lightgcn: simplifying and powering graph convolution network for recommendation. In: Proceedings of the 43rd International ACM SIGIR Conference on Research and Development in Information Retrieval, pp. 639–648 (2020)
25. Man, T., Shen, H., Jin, X., Cheng, X.: Cross-domain recommendation: an embedding and mapping approach. In: Proceedings of the 26th International Joint Conference on Artificial Intelligence, pp. 2464–2470 (2017)
26. Zhu, Y., et al.: Transfer-meta framework for cross-domain recommendation to cold-start users. In: Proceedings of the 44th International ACM SIGIR Conference on Research and Development in Information Retrieval, pp. 1813–1817 (2021)
27. Gao, C., et al.: Cross-domain recommendation without sharing user-relevant data. In: The World Wide Web Conference, pp. 491–502 (2019)
28. Zhu, F., Wang, Y., Zhou, J., Chen, C., Li, L., Liu, G.: A unified framework for cross-domain and cross-system recommendations. IEEE Trans. Knowl. Data Eng. **35**(2), 1171–1184 (2023)

29. Pan, S.J., Yang, Q.: A survey on transfer learning. IEEE Trans. Knowl. Data Eng. **22**(10), 1345–1359 (2010)
30. Li, Y., Xu, J., Zhao, P., Fang, J., Chen, W., Zhao, L.: ATLREC: an attentional adversarial transfer learning network for cross-domain recommendation. J. Comput. Sci. Technol. **35**(4), 794–808 (2020)
31. Ganin, Y., Lempitsky, V.: Unsupervised domain adaptation by backpropagation. In: International Conference on Machine Learning, pp. 1180–1189 (2015)
32. Zhang, X., Li, J., Su, H., Zhu, L., Shen, H.T.: Multi-level attention-based domain disentanglement for bcdr. ACM Trans. Inf. Syst. **41**(4), 1–24 (2023)
33. Cao, J., Lin, X., Cong, X., Ya, J., Liu, T., Wang, B.: Disencdr: learning disentangled representations for cross-domain recommendation. In: Proceedings of the 45th International ACM SIGIR Conference on Research and Development in Information Retrieval, pp. 267–277 (2022)
34. Kingma, D.P., Welling, M.: Auto-encoding variational bayes. In: International Conference on Learning Representations, pp. 1–14 (2013)
35. Li, X., She, J.: Collaborative variational autoencoder for recommender systems. In: Proceedings of the 23rd ACM SIGKDD International Conference on Knowledge Discovery and Data Mining, pp. 305–314 (2017)
36. Zhang, R., Zang, T., Zhu, Y., Wang, C., Wang, K., Yu, J.: Disentangled contrastive learning for cross-domain recommendation. In: The 28th International Conference on Database Systems for Advanced Applications, pp. 163–178 (2023)
37. Gutmann, M.U., Hyvärinen, A.: Noise-contrastive estimation: a new estimation principle for unnormalized statistical models. In: International Conference on Artificial Intelligence and Statistics (2010)
38. Wu, J., et al.: Self-supervised graph learning for recommendation. In: Proceedings of the 44th International ACM SIGIR Conference on Research and Development in Information Retrieval, pp. 726–735 (2021)
39. Li, C., et al.: One for all, all for one: learning and transferring user embeddings for cross-domain recommendation. In: Proceedings of the Sixteenth ACM International Conference on Web Search and Data Mining, pp. 366–374 (2023)
40. Hao, X., et al.: Adversarial feature translation for multi-domain recommendation. In: Proceedings of the 27th ACM SIGKDD Conference on Knowledge Discovery & Data Mining, pp. 2964–2973 (2021)
41. Cui, Q., Wei, T., Zhang, Y., Zhang, Q.: HeroGRAPH: a heterogeneous graph framework for multi-target cross-domain recommendation. In: RecSys (2020)
42. Guo, X., et al.: Disentangled representations learning for multi-target cross-domain recommendation. ACM Trans. Inf. Syst. **41**(4) (2023)
43. Li, P., Tuzhilin, A.: DDTCDR: deep dual transfer cross domain recommendation. In: Proceedings of the 13th International Conference on Web Search and Data Mining, pp. 331–339 (2020)
44. Chen, X., Zhang, Y., Tsang, I.W., Pan, Y., Su, J.: Toward equivalent transformation of user preferences in cross domain recommendation. ACM Trans. Inf. Syst. **41**(1), 1–31 (2023)
45. Guo, L., Zhang, J., Chen, T., Wang, X., Yin, H.: Reinforcement learning-enhanced shared-account cross-domain sequential recommendation. IEEE Trans. Knowl. Data Eng. **35**(7), 7397–7411 (2023)
46. Xia, L., Xu, Y., Huang, C., Dai, P., Bo, L.: Graph meta network for multi-behavior recommendation. In: Proceedings of the 44th International ACM SIGIR Conference on Research and Development in Information Retrieval, pp. 757–766 (2021)

47. Yang, H., Chen, H., Li, L., Yu, P.S., Xu, G.: Hyper meta-path contrastive learning for multi-behavior recommendation. In: 2021 IEEE International Conference on Data Mining, pp. 787–796 (2021)
48. Gu, S., Wang, X., Shi, C., Xiao, D.: Self-supervised graph neural networks for multi-behavior recommendation. In: Proceedings of the Thirty-First International Joint Conference on Artificial Intelligence, pp. 2052–2058 (2022)
49. Chen, M., Huang, C., Xia, L., Wei, W., Xu, Y., Luo, R.: Heterogeneous graph contrastive learning for recommendation, in: Proceedings of the Sixteenth ACM International Conference on Web Search and Data Mining, pp. 544–552 (2023)
50. Xia, L., et al.: Knowledge-enhanced hierarchical graph transformer network for multi-behavior recommendation. In: Proceedings of the 35th AAAI Conference on Artificial Intelligence (2021)

Sequence Modeling Based Data Augmentation for Micro-expression Recognition

Xin Lin[1], Shaojie Ai[1], Junying Gao[1], Jing He[1], Lei Yan[1], Jiaqi Zhang[2], and Jing Liu[2(✉)]

[1] Shanghai Institute of Satellite Engineering, Shanghai, China
[2] School of Electrical and Information Engineering, Tianjin University, Tianjin, China
jliu_tju@tju.edu.cn

Abstract. Micro-expressions (MEs) can reveal people's true emotions and expose deceitful behaviors. With the introduction of deep learning, the accuracy of micro-expression recognition (MER) has been greatly improved. However, limited by insufficient and unbalanced ME samples, deep models are likely to suffer from overfitting and are easy to lean towards majority classes, resulting in unsatisfactory recognition performance. In this paper, we propose a novel sequence modeling based data augmentation (SM-DA) method to enrich the limited training samples. Specifically, we model ME sequences for a static face by remapping the motion information of an original ME sequence to it, thus synthesize new ME sequence. With current manually-annotated MEs and a large amount of publicly available static faces, the scale and diversity of ME samples could be greatly increased. Besides, to overcome the shortcoming of class-imbalance, we propose a balanced loss function, in which the loss of each category is weighted by a factor determined by both the actual sample size and effective sample size of this category. Experimental results on three benchmark ME databases demonstrate the superiority of our approach over other state-of-the-art methods.

Keywords: Micro-Expression Recognition · Data Augmentation · Balanced Loss · Shallow Network

1 Introduction

Facial expressions are the most commonly used nonverbal emotional communication approach for humans. As a special form of facial expression, micro-expressions (MEs) are instinctive and uncontrollable facial movements, which remain even if a person suppresses the experiencing emotion to conceal his (her) inner thoughts and intentions, especially in a high-stake environment. MEs are very brief (1/25 to 1/5 of a second), subtle and involuntary facial movements, occurring when people try to conceal their true feelings [1]. Owing to their powerful ability of exposing deceitful behaviors and potential applications in various fields [2,3], automatic micro-expression recognition (MER) has become an

© The Author(s), under exclusive license to Springer Nature Singapore Pte Ltd. 2024
G. Zhai et al. (Eds.): IFTC 2023, CCIS 2066, pp. 180–192, 2024.
https://doi.org/10.1007/978-981-97-3623-2_14

increasingly active research topic. However, as a result of these characteristics, ME analysis is challenging and difficult.

Traditional methods focused on designing features that can effectively model the subtle changes of MEs. Pfister et al. [4] first used LBP-TOP to describe the local spatio-temporal texture variation of MEs and successfully recognized spontaneous MEs. Subsequently, several variants (e.g., LBP-SIP [5], STLBP-IP [6], STCLQP [7] and ELBPTOP [8]) were proposed to improve the robustness of LBP-TOP. Besides, optical flow based features (e.g., MDMO [9], FDM [10], Bi-WOOF [11] and FHOFO [12]) were also widely investigated to capture the temporal dynamics of MEs. However, although handcrafted features have strong interpretability and low dependence on the size of dataset, it is difficult and cumbersome to adjust the parameters to establish an effective MER model.

Deep learning obviates manual feature design and allows to automatically connect a specific task to the features themselves. Several recent researches attempted to develop deep models for MER. Patel et al. [13] carried out evolutionary feature selection to search an optimal set of deep features. To extract spatio-temporal feature representation, Kim et al. [14] used CNN to encode MEs and performed expression-state constrained spatial feature learning, and then transferred the spatial features to LSTM to learn temporal features of MEs. Similarly, Khor et al. [15] also adopted this CNN+LSTM framework, while optical flow and optical strain was used to enrich the input data. In addition, some recent works [16,17] applied 3D-CNN to encode subtle facial changes jointly in spatial domain and temporal domain.

In general, deep MER models are shown to surpass traditional MER methods. However, they are still limited by insufficient and unbalanced ME samples [2,18]. First, due to the intrinsic characteristics (short-duration, low-intensity and local-motion) of MEs, it is difficult to induce, collect and label ME data, leading to a small amount of publicly available ME samples. For example, three most widely used spontaneous ME databases, i.e., SMIC [19], CASME II [20] and SAMM [21], have only 164, 255 and 159 samples, respectively. With limited training data, deep models tend to suffer from overfitting, resulting in poor recognition performance on unseen samples. Second, existing ME databases are heavily unbalanced, because some types of MEs are hardly triggered (e.g., fear, sadness and anger). Training with unbalanced data, the MER models are easily biased toward majority classes with low accuracy for minority classes.

Currently, there are mainly three strategies to solve the problem of applying deep models on small-scale ME databases.

1) Data augmentation (DA), which increases the amount of training data and improves the robustness of deep models. In [13], traditional DA techniques including flipping, rotation, translation and scaling were performed during training. Cai et al. [22] introduced a 3D facial images dataset that addresses the scarcity of facial images by generating landmark points through the rotate-and-render technique. This innovative approach compensates for the limited availability of facial images in the dataset. Takalkar et al. [23] converted each ME video into multiple frames to perform image-based MER. However, these

methods provide only a small increase in effective information and cannot increase the diversity of training data, resulting in limited performance improvement.

2) Transfer learning, which exploits the underlying rules learned in other fields to reduce the demand for data in current task. For example, in [24], the authors enhanced their model architecture by incorporating other similar high-quality datasets, which improved the robustness of feature processing and validated the feasibility of knowledge transfer. As expected, transfer learning has been applied to micro expression detection for a long time. In [25], ResNet10 pre-trained on ImageNet was first fine-tuned on large-scale macro-expression databases and then fine-tuned on ME databases. Wang et al. [26] used two steps of transfer learning, i.e., transferring from macro-expression data and transferring from single frame of ME video clips, to pre-train their deep model. Jia et al. [27] explored the connection between macro-expression and micro-expression features and proposed a macro-to-micro transformation model implemented by singular value decomposition. However, macro- and micro-expressions are obviously different in terms of duration, intensity, motion areas and even data distribution. Consequently, the knowledge transferred from macro-expression domain has a small improvement in the performance of MER.

3) Shallow network, which contains few convolutional layers for fewer parameters. Recently, several works (e.g., DSSN [28], STSTNet [29]) tried to exploit lightweight shallow networks to make the model easier to optimize and less likely to overfit. [30] makes use of a global attention module with shallow features in order to enrich the shallow information of network. However, shallow networks lack sufficient capability to extract discriminative features and details of MEs. Although class-imbalance has been explored a lot in visual recognition fields [31,32], only a few ME researches involved it. Li et al. [33] first performed micro-expression AU detection and used focal loss [34] to prevent the vast number of negatives from overwhelming the AU detector. Xia et al. [35] extended the binary balanced loss into a multi-class balanced loss, and re-weighted it by inverse class frequency for facilitating the unbalanced training.

In this paper, to tackle the problem of insufficient ME data, we propose a novel sequence modeling based data augmentation (SM-DA) method to enrich limited training samples. Specifically, a set of static facial images are involved and several of them with the most similar facial structure to original ME are used to synthesize new ME sequences. As optical flow can effectively capture the dynamic changes of MEs, we remap the dense optical flow fields between ME frames to the selected static facial images. Finally, several ME samples with the same expression label but different face identities as the original ME are synthesized and used as training samples. Additionally, we design a lightweight shallow CNN network as the backbone for our MER model. With optical flow features as input, discriminative spatio-temporal features can be effectively learned. We also propose a balanced loss to deal with the issue of class-imbalance. Leveraging the weighting factors determined by both actual sample size and effective sample size per class, some MEs that are rarely to be collected and difficult to be classified receive more attention and the biased prediction can be alleviated.

2   The Proposed Algorithm

2.1   Sequence Modeling Based Data Augmentation (SM-DA)

Considering the important role of motion information in reflecting the minor changes of MEs and the availability of massive static facial images, we propose a novel sequence modeling based data augmentation (SM-DA) method, to synthesize diverse ME training samples. The architecture of our proposed SM-DA method is illustrated in Fig. 1. It mainly contains three main procedures: face comparison, face cropping & alignment, motion extraction & remapping.

Face Comparison. To guarantee the quality of synthetic ME sequences, only similar faces to the face of original ME are selected for subsequent motion remapping. Specifically, given a static facial image set S, for each ME sequence $I = [I_1, I_2, \cdots, I_L]$, where L is the number of frames in this sequence, we extract a neural expression frame (onset frame) and compare it with the candidate static facial images in S using Baidu's face comparison API [36]. According to their similarity score, the N most similar static facial images are then selected out, denoted as $\{S^1, S^2, \cdots, S^N\}$.

Face Cropping and Alignment. To avoid the influence of useless background areas, each frame of the original ME sequence and the selected static facial images are cropped to have merely facial regions. Then face alignment is performed for all these cropped frames to remove the interference of head rotation. Next, to ensure that the deformation between ME frames comes from ME-related facial movements instead of unrelated head movements, we align each frame of the ME sequence with the first frame of it, following [37]. After that, each selected static facial image is also aligned with the first frame of original ME through affine transformation [38]. Dlib [39] and OpenCV [40] libraries are used to implement the above operations, including face detection, facial landmark detection and face alignment.

Define the facial landmarks of the ME onset frame as A_{dst}, and facial landmarks of the static facial image as A_{src}, then A_{src} is to be transformed to the same position as A_{dst}. The transformation formula can be expressed as:

$$A_{src} * C^T = A_{dst}, \tag{1}$$

where C^T represents the transformation matrix, parameters of which can be estimated using least square method. Finally, the estimated transformation matrix is used to align two frames.

Motion Extraction and Remapping. Optical flow reflects the displacements of each pixel from a frame to another and captures the motive information. Thus, we extract the optical flows between frames of original ME and remap them to the selected static faces. Denote the synthetic ME sequence obtained from I and the n-th selected static facial image S^n as $A^n = [A_1^n, A_2^n, \cdots, A_L^n]$, A_l^n can be generated as follows. First, Farneback [41] is used to calculate the dense optical flow field between I_1 and I_l, represented as $\boldsymbol{F}_l = [\boldsymbol{u}_l = d\boldsymbol{x}/dt, \boldsymbol{v}_l = d\boldsymbol{y}/dt]$, where $d\boldsymbol{x}$ and $d\boldsymbol{y}$ are the pixel displacement in horizontal and vertical direction, respectively. Second, S^n is treated as the first frame of A^n, i.e., $A_1^n = S^n$. Third, a warp operation is used to remap $\boldsymbol{F}_l$ to A_1^n, which can be formulated as:

$$A_l^n \left(x + \boldsymbol{u}_l \left(x, y \right), y + \boldsymbol{v}_l \left(x, y \right) \right) = A_1^n \left(x, y \right). \tag{2}$$

In this way, the synthesized N ME samples maintain the expression-related facial movements of original ME, while the face identity is replaced by one of the newly selected static faces. Figure 2 illustrates one of the synthetic ME sequences. The entire database is expanded to $N + 1$ times of the original size. Our proposed SM-DA method is generic and can transform an ME sequence into a new sequence with arbitrarily similar face. Taking into account the explosive growth of facial images online in recent years, this solution can greatly enrich current

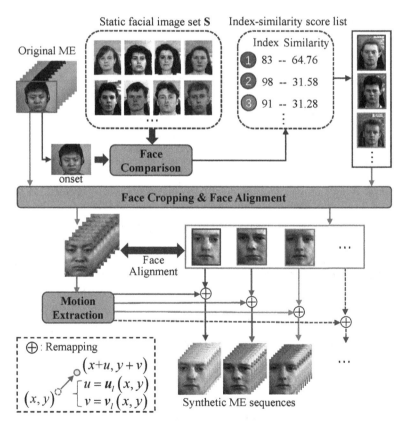

Fig. 1. Architecture of the proposed motion remapping based data augmentation (SM-DA) method

ME databases and increase the diversity of ME samples, thereby promoting the research of deep learning based MER.

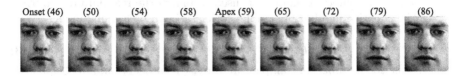

Onset (46)   (50)   (54)   (58)   Apex (59)   (65)   (72)   (79)   (86)

Fig. 2. Example of synthetic ME sequence. Numbers in brackets are frame indexes

2.2   Micro-expression Recognition Network

To reduce learnable parameters and prevent the network from overfitting, we design a shallow MER network containing the first two convolutional blocks of AlexNet [42] and a fully connected layer, as shown in Fig. 3. Although CNN has shown its powerful ability in learning spatial features, it is less efficient in capturing temporal dynamics between ME frames. Therefore, following previous works [28], we use optical flow as input to integrate spatio-temporal features and enhance the model's ability of characterizing MEs. In addition, optical flow emphasizes on meaningful motion and suppresses irrelevant information from non-motion areas. We use TV-L1 [43] to approximate the optical flow between the onset and apex frame of ME sequence. Then horizontal optical flow u, vertical optical flow v and flow amplitude $m = \sqrt{u^2 + v^2}$ are stacked in channel and used as the input data of our network.

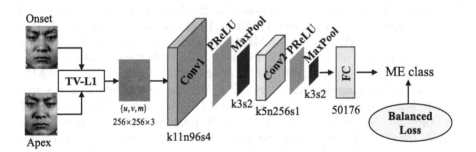

Fig. 3. Shallow MER network

Due to the extremely small size of ME databases, the commonly used class re-balancing strategies (e.g., under-sampling and over-sampling) cannot yield satisfactory performance on MER task. In addition to re-sampling, cost-sensitive re-weighting is widely adopted for CNN training on unbalanced datasets. Typically, a simple method is to re-weight the loss function by inverse class frequency

$1/N_i$. However, due to the intrinsic similarities among real-world data, it is highly possible that a sample is a near-duplicate of some other samples [44]. Considering the information overlap among input data, effective number of samples instead of actual number of samples is used to match the real data distribution in [44]. The effective number of samples for class i can be calculated as:

$$E_i = \left(1 - \beta^{N_i}\right) / (1 - \beta), \tag{3}$$

where N_i is the number of samples in the i-th category and $\beta \in [0, 1)$ is a hyperparameter. In this paper, we introduce a new weighting factor which integrates inverse class frequency and inverse effective number of samples, i.e., $\alpha_i = 1 / (E_i * N_i)$, to further balance the loss of different classes, whose effectiveness will be validated in Sect. 3.2.

Focal loss [45] was first proposed to handle the problem of foreground-background class-imbalance encountered in object detection task and was extended to other fields [46,47] subsequently. Inspired by focal loss, we also introduce a modulating factor γ ($\gamma = 2$ as [45]) to down-weight easy examples and thus focus on hard samples during training. Combining these strategies for addressing class-imbalance problem, we design a novel balanced loss defined as:

$$L = - \sum_{i=1}^{C} \frac{1 - \beta}{(1 - \beta^{N_i}) * N_i} \sum_{j=1}^{N_i} \left(1 - p_i^j\right)^\gamma log\left(p_i^j\right) \tag{4}$$

where C is the number of categories, p_i^j represents the probability that the j-th sample in the i-th category is correctly classified.

3   Experimental Results

3.1   Experimental Setup

Datasets. We evaluate our proposed method on three spontaneous ME databases: SMIC (164, 3 classes), CASME II (243, 5 classes) and SAMM (136, 5 classes). CASME II contains 255 ME samples from 26 subjects. We select five categories from this database, including happiness (32), disgust (61), repression (27), surprise (25) and others (98), which results in a total of 243 samples. SAMM contains 159 ME samples from 32 subjects. We also select five categories from this database. They are anger (57), contempt (12), happiness (26), surprise (15) and other (26), which results in a total of 136 samples. SMIC contains 164 ME samples from 16 subjects. All these samples are used, categorized as negative (70), happiness (51) and surprise (43). For ME samples in SMIC, their apex frames are located using D&C-RoIs [48] algorithm. Since MEs are subtle and easily disturbed by irrelevant factors (e.g., pose, illumination), currently existing spontaneous ME databases are all collected in controlled lab environments with frontal view, neural expression and normal light conditions. Therefore, the static facial images are expected to meet the similar requirements for ensuring effective remapping. In this paper, Nottingham scans [49] which contains 100 facial images from 50 males and 50 females is adopted as the static facial image set **S**.

Implementation Details. For all experiments, Leave One Subject Out Cross Validation (LOSOCV) is used to avoid person-dependent issue in the classification process. Weighted Average Recall (WAR), Unweighted Average Recall (UAR) and F1-Score are adopted as the evaluation metrics. WAR is the normal recognition accuracy, while UAR averages the accuracy of each individual class without considering class size. By comparing WAR and UAR indicators, the performance of a method can be fully revealed. F1-score provides a balanced metric when considering highly imbalanced data. Our MER model is implemented based on PyTorch framework. All layers of the network are randomly initialized. We use Adam optimizer with $\beta_1 = 0.9$ and batch size of 32 to train our model, and set the total number of epochs to 100. The initial learning rate is set to 0.0005 and decayed by factor 0.95 every epoch. Empirically, $\beta = 0.97$, $\gamma = 2$.

3.2   Ablation Study

Loss Ablation. To explore the impact of different loss re-weighting strategies, we train the MER network on CASME II with different forms of objective functions. L_{FL} is the original focal loss. L_{1/N_i} and L_{1/E_i} respectively uses inverse class frequency and inverse probability of effective number of samples as the weighting factor. $L_{balanced}$ is the proposed balanced loss in (4). Here, only original ME samples are used for training. As Table 1 shows, L_{FL} performs the worst. L_{1/E_i} provides a certain improvement than L_{1/N_i}. It is because that effective sample size fits the real data distribution better. By combining the above two weighting factors, our model achieves the best performance. It indicates that the proposed balanced loss provides a significant boost for MER model training with unbalanced data.

Table 1. Ablation studies with different loss re-weighting strategies

Loss	WAR	UAR	F1-Score
L_{FL}	0.6296	0.6117	0.6497
L_{1/N_i}	0.6379	0.6171	0.6529
L_{1/E_i}	0.6420	0.6162	0.6535
$L_{balanced}$	**0.6502**	**0.6352**	**0.6633**

Data Ablation. To validate the superiority of our proposed SM-DA method, we train the MER network on CASME II with data generated by different data augmentation techniques: flip-DA (horizontal flip), noise-DA (gaussian noise, $\mu = 0$, $\sigma = \sqrt{0.001}$) and SM-DA (for fair comparison, $N = 1$). Here, cross entropy loss is used for network optimization. Experimental results are shown in Table 2. Compared with traditional flip and noise augmentation, our SM-DA performs better because the diversity of samples is greatly improved. When SM-DA is combined with traditional DA techniques, the performance of MER model can be further improved (WAR: 0.6749, UAR: 0.7011, F1: 0.7036 for MR+flip-DA).

Table 2. Ablation studies with different training sample settings

Training samples	WAR	UAR	F1
w/o DA	0.6255	0.6013	0.6399
flip-DA	0.6420	0.6501	0.6626
noise-DA	0.6420	0.6470	0.6612
SM-DA	0.6543	0.6546	0.6691
Balanced SM-DA	**0.6667**	**0.6884**	**0.6889**

Considering that if generating more training samples for those small classes, the problem of class-imbalance could also be alleviated effectively, we perform different multiples of SM-DA for different classes in CASME II (happiness: 32×3, surprise: 25×4, disgust: 61×2, repression: 27×4, others: 98×1), so that the samples in five classes are relatively balanced. As shown in Table 2, Balanced SM-DA achieves better performance than SM-DA, which proves that the proposed SM-DA method can also solve the class-imbalance problem in MER task. In addition, when both Balanced SM-DA and balanced loss are used, all the three metrics are further improved (WAR: 0.6914, UAR: 0.7133, F1: 0.7122).

In order to investigate the generalization ability of SM-DA, apart from our shallow MER network, ELRCN [15] and MicroExp-STCNN [17] are also used as the baseline model. As observed from Table 3, the performance of both ELRCN and our shallow network on CASME II are improved when adopting the proposed data augmentation method. As for MicroExp-STCNN, we follow its setting to split SMIC dataset into 80% for training and 20% for testing. When combined with SM-DA, MicroExp-STCNN obtains an accuracy gain from 0.6563 to 0.7188. So we conclude that SM-DA is model-independent and can be generalized to more MER models.

Table 3. Ablation studies with different backbone

Backbone	Training samples	WAR	UAR	F1-Score
ELRCN	w/o DA	0.5267	0.4365	0.4720
ELRCN	SM-DA	**0.5556**	**0.4893**	**0.5145**
Ours	w/o DA	0.6502	0.6352	0.6633
Ours	SM-DA	**0.6749**	**0.6803**	**0.6945**

Network Ablation. We compare the proposed shallow network with two deeper models to verify its effectiveness. Deep-Conv adds a convolution block (the third convolution block of AlexNet) after the original two convolution blocks. Deep-FC adds a fully connected layer, whose input dimension is 4096 and output dimension is 5. As shown in Table 4, the recognition performance of deeper models on CASME II drops significantly because additional Conv layer or FC layer brings large amount of network parameters, making it more difficult for model optimization. By combining SM-DA and shallow network, our model achieves the best performance. It indicates that the hybridization of data augmentation and shallow network provides a significant boost to the MER task.

Table 4. Ablation studies with different network architectures

Network	WAR	UAR	F1-Score
Deep-Conv	0.6584	0.6694	0.6708
Deep-FC	0.6543	0.6634	0.6742
Shallow Network	**0.6749**	**0.6803**	**0.6945**

3.3 Comparison with State-of-the-Art Methods

As shown in Table 5, the proposed method achieves the best recognition performance on CASME II and SAMM. By introducing the novel data augmentation method SM-DA, both the sample size and data diversity are increased, which promotes the model training. In addition, the newly designed loss function balances the loss of each category and pays more attention to minority samples

Table 5. Comparison of recognition performance between the proposed method and state-of-the-art methods

Methods	SMIC		CASME II		SAMM	
	Acc	F1	Acc	F1	Acc	F1
LBP-TOP	0.4338	0.3421	0.3968	0.3589	0.3968	0.3589
LBP-SIP	0.4451	0.4492	0.4656	0.4480	–	–
STCLQP	**0.6402**	**0.6381**	0.5839	0.5835	–	–
MDMO	0.5897	0.5845	0.5169	0.4966	–	–
FDM	0.5244	0.5372	0.4593	0.4053	–	–
Bi-WOOF	0.6220	0.6200	0.5885	0.6100	–	–
CNN-LSTM	–	–	0.6098	–	–	–
ELRCN	–	–	0.5267	0.4720	–	–
3DFCNN	0.5549	–	0.5911	–	–	–
Ours	0.6159	0.6203	**0.6749**	**0.6945**	**0.5882**	**0.4793**

that are difficult to classify. For SMIC, the proposed method is less satisfactory than traditional spatio-temporal descriptors. We ascribe it to the absence of apex frame index in SMIC and the less accurate spotting algorithm. The experiments are also repeated multiple times to validate the performance stability of our proposed model with relative small standard deviation (<0.01).

4 Conclusion

In this paper, we propose a novel motion remapping based data augmentation (SM-DA) method to expand the limited ME samples and facilitate the training of deep MER models. First, several static faces with similar face structure to the original ME are carefully selected. Then the dense optical flow between ME frames which can model the dynamic changes of ME sequence is extracted and remapped to the selected static facial images. Taking advantage of massive available static faces, a large number of ME samples with diverse face identities could be synthesized. Furthermore, we design a balanced loss to pay more attention to those samples in minority and tough class, thus reducing the prediction bias caused by class-imbalance. Finally, we conduct experiments using three benchmark ME databases, and the results verify the effectiveness of our proposed approach compared to the state-of-the-art methods.

Acknowledgments. This work is supported in part by Shanghai Rising Star Project under grant 23QA1408800, in part by 166 Project under grant 211-CXCY-M115-00-01-01.

References

1. Ekman, P., Friesen, W.V.: Nonverbal leakage and clues to deception. Psychiatry **32**(1), 88–106 (1969)
2. Oh, Y.H., See, J., Le Ngo, A.C., Phan, R.C.W., Baskaran, V.M.: A survey of automatic facial micro-expression analysis: databases, methods and challenges. Front. Psychol. **9**, 1128 (2018)
3. Rathour, N., Singh, R., Gehlot, A., Akram, S.V., Thakur, A.K., Kumar, A.: The decadal perspective of facial emotion processing and recognition: a survey. Displays **75**, 102330 (2022)
4. Pfister, T., Li, X., Zhao, G., Pietikäinen, M.: Recognising spontaneous facial micro-expressions. In: International Conference on Computer Vision, pp. 1449–1456 (2011)
5. Wang, Y., See, J., Phan, R.C.W., Oh, Y.H.: Efficient spatio-temporal local binary patterns for spontaneous facial micro-expression recognition. PLoS ONE **10**(5), e0124674 (2015)
6. Huang, X., Wang, S., Zhao, G., Pietikäinen, M.: Facial micro-expression recognition using spatiotemporal local binary pattern with integral projection. In: International Conference on Computer Vision Workshop, pp. 1–9 (2015)
7. Huang, X., Zhao, G., Hong, X., Zheng, W., Pietikäinen, M.: Spontaneous facial micro-expression analysis using spatiotemporal completed local quantized patterns. Neurocomputing **175**, 564–578 (2016)

8. Guo, C., Liang, J., Zhan, G., Liu, Z., Pietikäinen, M., Liu, L.: Extended local binary patterns for efficient and robust spontaneous facial micro-expression recognition. IEEE Access **7**, 174517–174530 (2019)
9. Liu, Y., Zhang, J., Yan, W., Wang, S., Zhao, G., Fu, X.: A main directional mean optical flow feature for spontaneous micro-expression recognition. IEEE Trans. Affect. Comput. **7**(4), 299–310 (2016)
10. Xu, F., Zhang, J., Wang, J.Z.: Microexpression identification and categorization using a facial dynamics map. IEEE Trans. Affect. Comput. **8**(2), 254–267 (2017)
11. Liong, S., See, J., Wong, K., Phan, R.C.W.: Less is more: micro-expression recognition from video using apex frame. Signal Process. Image Commun. **62**, 82–92 (2018)
12. Happy, S.L., Routray, A.: Fuzzy histogram of optical flow orientations for micro-expression recognition. IEEE Trans. Affect. Comput. **10**(3), 394–406 (2019)
13. Patel, D., Hong, X., Zhao, G.: Selective deep features for micro-expression recognition. In: International Conference on Pattern Recognition, pp. 2258–2263 (2016)
14. Kim, D.H., Baddar, W.J., Ro, Y.M.: Micro-expression recognition with expression-state constrained spatio-temporal feature representations. In: ACM Conference on Multimedia, pp. 382–386 (2016)
15. Khor, H., See, J., Phan, R.C.W., Lin, W.: Enriched long-term recurrent convolutional network for facial micro-expression recognition. In: IEEE International Conference on Automation Face & Gesture Recognition, pp. 667–674 (2018)
16. Zhi, R., Xu, H., Wan, M., Li, T.: Combining 3D convolutional neural networks with transfer learning by supervised pre-training for facial micro-expression recognition. IEICE Trans. Inf. Syst. **102-D**(5), 1054–1064 (2019)
17. Reddy, S.P.T., Karri, S.T., Dubey, S.R., Mukherjee, S.: Spontaneous facial micro-expression recognition using 3D spatiotemporal convolutional neural networks. In: International Joint Conference on Neural Networks, pp. 1–8 (2019)
18. Goh, K.M., Ng, C.H., Lim, L.L., Sheikh, U.U.: Micro-expression recognition: an updated review of current trends, challenges and solutions. Vis. Comput. **36**(3), 445–468 (2020)
19. Li, X., Pfister, T., Huang, X., Zhao, G., Pietikäinen, M.: A spontaneous micro-expression database: inducement, collection and baseline. In: IEEE International Conference on Automation Face & Gesture Recognition, pp. 1–6 (2013)
20. Yan, W., et al.: CASME II: an improved spontaneous micro-expression database and the baseline evaluation. PLoS ONE **9**(1), e86041 (2014)
21. Davison, A.K., Lansley, C., Costen, N., Tan, K., Yap, M.H.: SAMM: a spontaneous micro-facial movement dataset. IEEE Trans. Affect. Comput. **9**(1), 116–129 (2018)
22. Cai, M., Zhang, S., Xiao, G., Fan, S.: 3D face reconstruction and dense alignment with a new generated dataset. Displays **70**, 102094 (2021)
23. Takalkar, M.A., Xu, M.: Image based facial micro-expression recognition using deep learning on small datasets. In: International Conference on Digital Image Computing: Techniques and Application, pp. 1–7 (2017)
24. Xue, W., Liu, J., Yan, S., Zhou, Y., Yuan, T., Guo, Q.: Alleviating data insufficiency for Chinese sign language recognition. Visual Intell. **1**(1), 26 (2023)
25. Peng, M., Wu, Z., Zhang, Z., Chen, T.: From macro to micro expression recognition: deep learning on small datasets using transfer learning. In: IEEE International Conference on Automation Face & Gesture Recognition, pp. 657–661 (2018)
26. Wang, S., et al.: Micro-expression recognition with small sample size by transferring long-term convolutional neural network. Neurocomputing **312**, 251–262 (2018)
27. Jia, X., Ben, X., Yuan, H., Kpalma, K., Meng, W.: Macro-to-micro transformation model for micro-expression recognition. J. Comput. Sci. **25**, 289–297 (2018)

28. Khor, H., See, J., Liong, S., Phan, R.C.W., Lin, W.: Dual-stream shallow networks for facial micro-expression recognition. In: IEEE International Conference on Image Processing, pp. 36–40 (2019)
29. Liong, S., Gan, Y.S., See, J., Khor, H., Huang, Y.: Shallow triple stream three-dimensional CNN (STSTNet) for micro-expression recognition. In: IEEE International Conference Automation Face & Gesture Recognition, pp. 1–5 (2019)
30. Wu, P., Jiang, L., Hua, Z., Li, J.: Multi-focus image fusion: transformer and shallow feature attention matters. Displays **76**, 102353 (2023)
31. Mishra, D., Jayendran, A., Prathosh, A.P.: Effect of the latent structure on clustering with GANs. IEEE Signal Process. Lett. **27**, 900–904 (2020)
32. Mirza, B., Haroon, D., Khan, B., Padhani, A., Syed, T.Q.: Deep generative models to counter class imbalance: a model-metric mapping with proportion calibration methodology. IEEE Access **9**, 55879–55897 (2021)
33. Li, Y., Huang, X., Zhao, G.: Micro-expression action unit detection with spatio-temporal adaptive pooling. arXiv Preprint arxiv:1907:05023 (2019)
34. Lin, T., Goyal, P., Girshick, R.B., He, K., Dollár, P.: Focal loss for dense object detection. IEEE Trans. Pattern Anal. Mach. Intell. **42**(2), 318–327 (2020)
35. Xia, Z., Hong, X., Gao, X., Feng, X., Zhao, G.: Spatiotemporal recurrent convolutional networks for recognizing spontaneous micro-expressions. IEEE Trans. Multimedia **22**(3), 626–640 (2020)
36. Baidu: Face comparison (2021). https://ai.baidu.com/tech/face/compare
37. Sun, B., Cao, S., Li, D., He, J., Yu, L.: Dynamic micro-expression recognition using knowledge distillation. IEEE Trans. Affect. Comput. **13**, 1037–1043 (2020)
38. Li, X., Xu, Y., Lv, Q., Dou, Y.: Affine-transformation parameters regression for face alignment. IEEE Signal Process. Lett. **23**(1), 55–59 (2016)
39. King, D.E.: DLIB-ML: a machine learning toolkit. J. Mach. Learn. Res. **10**, 1755–1758 (2009)
40. Bradski, G.: The opencv library. Dr. Dobb's J. Softw. Tools (2000)
41. Farnebäck, G.: Two-frame motion estimation based on polynomial expansion. In: Scandinavian Conference on Image Analysis, vol. 2749, pp. 363–370 (2003)
42. Krizhevsky, A., Sutskever, I., Hinton, G.E.: Imagenet classification with deep convolutional neural networks. In: Annual Conference on Neural Information Processing System, pp. 1106–1114 (2012)
43. Zach, C., Pock, T., Bischof, H.: A duality based approach for realtime TV-L^1 optical flow. In: Pattern Recognition, vol. 4713, pp. 214–223 (2007)
44. Cui, Y., Jia, M., Lin, T., Song, Y., Belongie, S.J.: Class-balanced loss based on effective number of samples. In: IEEE Conference on Computer Vision Pattern Recognition, pp. 9268–9277 (2019)
45. Lin, T., Goyal, P., Girshick, R.B., He, K., Dollár, P.: Focal loss for dense object detection. In: IEEE International Conference on Computer Vision, pp. 2999–3007 (2017)
46. Zhou, Q., et al.: Fine-grained spatial alignment model for person re-identification with focal triplet loss. IEEE Trans. Image Process. **29**, 7578–7589 (2020)
47. De, R., Chakraborty, A., Sarkar, R.: Document image binarization using dual discriminator generative adversarial networks. IEEE Signal Process. Lett. **27**, 1090–1094 (2020)
48. Liong, S., et al.: Automatic apex frame spotting in micro-expression database. In: Asian Conference on Pattern Recognition, pp. 665–669 (2015)
49. Hancock, P.: Psychological image collection at stirling (pics) (2008). http://pics.psych.stir.ac.uk/2D_face_sets.htm

Dual Transformer with Gated-Attention Fusion for News Disaster Image Captioning

Yinghua Li[1(✉)], Yaping Zhu[2], Yana Zhang[1], and Cheng Yang[1]

[1] State Key Laboratory of Media Convergence and Communication,
Communication University of China, Beijing, China
{Ymedia21,zynjenny,chy}@cuc.edu.cn
[2] Queensland University of Technology Online, Brisbane, Australia
yaping.zhu@qut.edu.au

Abstract. The disaster news image captioning is designed to automatically analyze and comprehend the content of disaster news images, generating precise image description, aiming to alleviate the workload of news editors and expedite the dissemination of disaster information. Current image caption algorithms rely on objects and their relationships, while objects within the disaster news image class are extremely similar and easy to confuse. To address the above issues, we propose a Dual Transformer with Gated-attention Fusion (DTGF). On the encoder side, we propose Gated-attention to effectively interact with region features and grid features, and adaptively filter out semantic noise during the interaction. On the decoder side, we introduced two cross-attention designs, Concat and Parallel, aiming to integrate enhanced visual representation and further improve model performance. Experiments on the DNICC19k dataset show that our model has achieved state-of-the-art performance. It is capable of extracting refined visual information and generating more accurate and specific descriptions of disaster news images without relying on additional prior knowledge.

Keywords: Image captioning · Gated-attention Fusion · Concat and Parallel Cross-attention · Dual Transformer

1 Introduction

With the advent of the new media era, the presentation of news has become increasingly diverse. Compared to textual reporting, visual reporting through images can provide readers with a more intuitive way of conveying relevant information. Major news media outlets have also seized this characteristic of the era by increasing the prominence of news images in their news dissemination, truly ushering in the "visual era". However, the significant increase in the volume of news image annotation tasks has added a considerable workload for news editors.

The disaster news image caption algorithm aims to generate sudden disaster news manuscripts that can concisely describe image content, in order to reduce the workload of news editors and journalists, improve news reporting efficiency and help people better

G. Zhai et al. (Eds.): IFTC 2023, CCIS 2066, pp. 193–207, 2024.
https://doi.org/10.1007/978-981-97-3623-2_15

understand and perceive sudden disaster events. Sudden disaster news is characterized by its high unpredictability, adverse reporting conditions, and a high demand for real-time reporting. Compared to other domains, image captioning for sudden disasters is more challenging.

Inspired by neural machine translation [1], mainstream approaches for this task involve encoding the image, extracting its visual features, and then inputting these features into an encoder-decoder framework to generate image descriptions [2].

Currently, region features and grid features are the primary methods used in the encoder for processing visual features. Region features directly extract object-level information from images by introducing object detectors, such as Faster R-CNN [3], to embed visual semantic representations. While this approach has achieved significant success, it still has certain limitations, such as a lack of contextual information and the risk of inaccurate detection. For disaster news images, images from the same disaster scene often feature significantly similar objects. The limitations of regional features in describing object details and contextual information make it difficult to distinguish visually similar samples. In such cases, the model is inclined to provide a broader description, overlooking the specific image details.

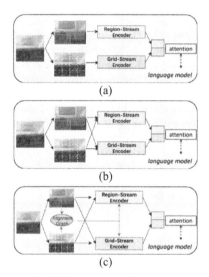

Fig. 1. (a) Integrates regions and grid features through concatenation. (b) Integrates regions and grid features through cross attention. (c) Introduces geometric alignment maps in cross attention to eliminate geometrically unrelated regions between two features.

In contrast, grid features cover all the content of a given image in a more fragmented form and can better represent contextual information. Due to the complementary strengths of both, a natural consideration is to integrate regional and grid features. However, recent research indicates that simple integration methods, such as concatenation or self-attention modules, as shown in Fig. 1(a) and Fig. 1(b), do not yield the desired results. The former overlooks interactions between regional and grid features, while the latter neglects the fact that not all regional and grid features are relevant, leading to some irrelevant interactions introducing semantic noise and redundancy. In addition, [4] introduced feature geometric alignment in the encoder to eliminate geometrically unrelated regions between the two features in the caption, as shown in Fig. 1(c). However, the fusion process requires external guidance, which reduces the model flexibility.

To address the above issues, we propose a Dual Transformer with Gated-attention Fusion (DTGF). Specifically, on the encoder side, we use a Dual-Way Self Attention module to independently process region features and grid features, modeling inter-layer relationships for both regions and grids. In addition, we also propose Gated-attention to effectively interact with region features and grid features, and adaptively filter out semantic noise during the interaction. On the decoder side, we consider two cross-attention designs to explore effective ways of integrating dual visual representations, resulting in more accurate image description sentences. We conducted extensive experiments on the Disaster News Image Chinese Caption Dataset (DNICC19k) [5], and the DTGF model achieved state-of-the-art performance.

The contributions of this paper are summarized as follows:

(1) On the encoder side, we propose Gated-attention to fuse dual visual features and adaptively filter out semantic noise generated during the fusion process. This simultaneously enhances both visual features, enriching visual information.
(2) On the decoder side, we propose two cross-attention designs, Concat and Parallel, to explore effective approaches for integrating dual visual representations, aiming to generate more precise image captions.
(3) We apply Gated-attention and Parallel Cross-attention to a Transformer framework to construct a novel Dual Transformer with Gated-attention Fusion (DTGF). When tested on DNICC19k, the model has achieved state-of-the-art results.

2 Related Work

2.1 News Image Captioning

The news image captioning aims to generate textual descriptions for news images based on their visual content and related news articles. Early news captioning algorithms primarily focused on learning the representativeness of news articles and their connection to images. Biten et al. [6] proposed a two-stage template-based caption generation approach that specifically modeled named entities. Recent research has integrated Transformer architectures [7]. Tran et al. [8] introduced an end-to-end Tell model that connects words in news articles with faces and objects in images within a transformer decoder to generate information about named entities. Liu et al. [9] adopted a multi-head attention-attention model and visual selective gate to better learn entity representations. Zhou et al. [10] demonstrated that entity-aware retrieval methods can further improve performance. Zhang et al. [11] designed a contextual entity suggestion module that uses Bi-LSTM to learn the most important content from the article, which is further employed using learned attention parameters after threshold selection.

Overall, most news captioning algorithms generate specific news description sentences by combining entity words from news articles. However, this approach has significant limitations in practical applications: (1) Not suitable for real-time reporting, it lowers the speed of news dissemination; (2) Reliance on prior knowledge, low model flexibility.

To address the limitations of traditional news image captioning, our laboratory has created a benchmark dataset in the news domain called the Disaster News Image Captioning Dataset (DNICC19k) [5]. Different from other news image caption datasets, DNICC19k provides only input images and their corresponding annotations. This design aims to train news captioning models to possess the capabilities of general captioning models, namely, generating descriptive sentences related to the image without relying on additional prior knowledge or background information.

2.2 Visual Representations for Image Captioning

Existing image captioning typically adopt an encoder-decoder architecture. Specifically, visual features are first extracted from the input image and then used to generate image descriptions. Therefore, it is crucial for accurately extracting visual features.

Early research [12] employed Convolutional Neural Networks (CNNs) to extract holistic image features, which were used as representations for the entire image. Although this method is simple and compact, it suffers from information loss and insufficient granularity. Subsequently, Anderson et al. [3] proposed using object detectors to extract region features. This approach directly encodes the detected object regions, contributing to more accurate image descriptions. However, region features have their limitations, including the inability to convey context information between objects, the risk of erroneous object detection, and high computational costs. In contrast to region features, grid features [12, 13] are extracted from the entire image, typically from high-level feature maps of backbone networks. While they do not explicitly capture object-level granularity, they are capable of representing contextual information, such as relationships between objects, and do not carry the risk of erroneous object detection. Therefore, grid features and regional features complement each other. Some studies consider integrating them together, but how to effectively fuse dual visual features still remains a challenge.

To address this issue, Wu et al. [14] proposed the NADGCN, which uses a dual-stream architecture to separately process region and grid features and obtains the final visual representation through concatenation. However, they overlooked the interaction between regions and grids. Xian et al. [15] proposed the Dual Global Enhancement Transformer (DGET) to combine region and grid features. It overlooks that not all region features and grid features are relevant, and performing irrelevant interactions introduces semantic noise and redundant information. Luo et al. [16] proposed the Dual-Level Cooperative Transformer (DLCT) network. They constructed a geometric alignment graph for precise alignment of these two features. However, this approach requires external guidance in the fusion process, reducing the flexibility of the model. Wu et al. [4] proposed using a two-step interaction strategy to fuse region features and grid features, thereby extracting more comprehensive image representations. Van-Quang et al. [17] introduced GRIT, a Transformer-based neural architecture that uses a special cross-attention caption generator to compute attention between region and grid dual features. This approach significantly improves performance and achieves state-of-the-art results at the time.

3   Dual Transformer with Gated-Attention Fusion

This section describes the architecture of Dual Transformer with Gated-attention Fusion (DTGF). As shown in Fig. 2, the network consists of two parts: The encoder is used to extract and interact dual visual features of input images (Sect. 3.1); The decoder is used to generate descriptive sentences based on enhanced dual visual representation (Sect. 3.2).

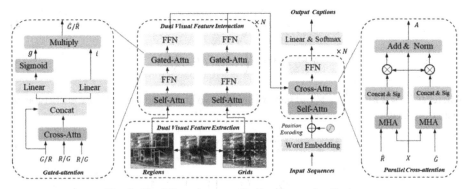

Fig. 2. Dual Transformer with Gated-attention Fusion.

3.1   Dual Vision Fusion Encoder

Given a disaster news image, we first extract the region features $V_R = \{v_i\}^{N_R}$ and grid features $V_G = \{v_i\}^{N_G}$ from the input image, where N_R and N_G correspond to the number of features. The encoder consists of two sub-modules: bidirectional self-attention and gated attention fusion.

Dual-Way Self Attention: Visual features are extracted through locally connected convolutions, making them isolated and relationship-agnostic. It is believed that the Transformer encoder significantly contributes to the performance of image captioning, as it can model relationships between inputs through self-attention, enriching visual features.

To better model the relationships of dual visual features, after obtaining the visual representations V_R and V_G, we first project these two visual features into three different compression matrices, namely query Q, key K, and value V. Then, we use a Dual-Way Self Attention [23], consisting of two separate self-attention modules, to explore the internal relationships of region features and grid features separately. The self-attention formula is as follows [11].

$$Attn(Q, K, V) = softmax\left(\frac{QK^T}{\sqrt{d_k}}\right)V \tag{1}$$

The multi-head self-attention formula is as follows [11]:

$$MHA(Q, K, V) = Concat(head_1, \ldots, head_h)W^O \tag{2}$$

$$head_i = Attn\left(QW_i^Q, KW_i^K, VW_i^V\right) \tag{3}$$

where d_k is the dimensionality of the keys, $head_i$ is the attention head index, and W^O, W_i^Q, W_i^K, W_i^V are learned matrices for results, queries, keys, and values, respectively.

Specifically, the hidden states of regions $H_r^{(l)}$ and grids $H_g^{(l)}$ are fed into the $(l+1)$-th DWSA to learn relation-aware representation. The formula is as follows:

$$V_r^{(l)} = MHA\left(H_r^{(l)}, H_r^{(l)}, H_r^{(l)}\right) \tag{4}$$

$$V_g^{(l)} = MHA\left(H_g^{(l)}, H_g^{(l)}, H_g^{(l)}\right) \tag{5}$$

where $H_r^{(0)} = V_R$, $H_g^{(0)} = V_G$. Then we adopt two independent FFN for each type of visual features:

$$V_R^{(l)} = FFN_r\left(V_r^{(l)}\right) \tag{6}$$

$$V_G^{(l)} = FFN_g\left(V_g^{(l)}\right) \tag{7}$$

Gated-attention Fusion: Traditional methods of fusing dual visual representations may introduce semantic noise that interferes with model predictions. To address this issue, we propose a novel Gated-attention Fusion mechanism, as shown in Fig. 3. It employs a two-stage fusion approach to simultaneously enhance both region features and grid features.

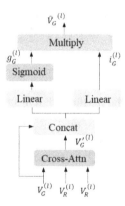

Fig. 3. Gated-attention (taking the aggregation of region feature information to enhance grid features as an example).

In the first stage, we use cross-attention to aggregate information from all grid (region) features to enhance region (grid) features. This involves alternately using grid features and region features as the source and target fields for the attention mechanism, achieving their initial fusion.

$$V_G'^{(l)} = Cross_{MHA}\left(V_G^{(l)}, V_R^{(l)}, V_R^{(l)}\right) \tag{8}$$

$$V_R'^{(l)} = Cross_{MHA}\left(V_R^{(l)}, V_G^{(l)}, V_G^{(l)}\right) \tag{9}$$

After that, grid features attend to regions to obtain high-level object information, while regions focus on grids to improve their understanding of global information and their ability to grasp inter-object relationships, thereby supplementing detailed textual information.

In the second stage, inspired by AoA [18], we introduce a gate control to further filter out irrelevant attention results during the fusion of region features and grid features, retaining only the effective feature interactions between them, thereby enhancing model performance.

Specifically, first, two independent linear transformations are applied to the enhanced grid features $V_G'^{(l)}$ and region features $V_R^{(l)}$, generating the "information vector" i and the "attention gate" g. Then, by performing element-wise multiplication between the attention gate and the information vector, it achieves gated constraints on the information vector to filter out ineffective attention, retaining only the functionality of valid interactions. Similarly, the region features undergo the same operation.

$$g_G^{(l)} = \sigma\left(W_g\left[V_G'^{(l)}; V_G^{(l)}\right]\right) \tag{10}$$

$$i_G^{(l)} = W_a\left[V_G'^{(l)}; V_G^{(l)}\right] \tag{11}$$

$$\widehat{V}_G^{(l)} = g_G^{(l)} \otimes i_G^{(l)} \tag{12}$$

$$g_R^{(l)} = \sigma\left(W_g\left[V_R'^{(l)}; V_R^{(l)}\right]\right) \tag{13}$$

$$i_R^{(l)} = W_a\left[V_R'^{(l)}; V_R^{(l)}\right] \tag{14}$$

$$\widehat{V}_R^{(l)} = g_R^{(l)} \otimes i_R^{(l)} \tag{15}$$

Among them, σ represents the sigmoid function, W_a, W_g are learnable parameter matrices, and $\otimes$ represents the dot product operation. After that, we use two independent position feedforward networks FFN to process the above dual visual features, as follows:

$$\widehat{V}_G^{(l)} = FFN_r\left(\widehat{V}_G^{(l)}\right) \tag{16}$$

$$\widehat{V}_R^{(l)} = FFN_r\left(\widehat{V}_R^{(l)}\right) \tag{17}$$

After N layers of stacked dual visual interaction layers, the final outputs of the model encoder are denoted as $\widehat{V}_G^{(l)}$ and $\widehat{V}_R^{(l)}$.

3.2 Dual Vision Fusion Decoder

Our decoder receives the encoded enhanced dual visual representation as input and adopts a basic design based on the Transformer decoder to generate image description sentences in an autoregressive manner.

Caption Generator: The caption generator consists of N layers of stacked Transformer decoder blocks. Each layer consists of three parts: masked self-attention, cross-attention, and position feedforward networks. Specifically, the caption input is first transformed into a word embedding matrix and positional encoding is added to obtain the sequence $X = \{x_i^{l-1}\}_{i=0}^t$, which is then fed into the bottom layer of the decoder as input. On the decoder side, the masked self-attention sub-layer receives the input sequence X at time step t, computes and applies self-attention on the input sequence, and uses a mask matrix to update the attention results to prevent interactions from future words during training.

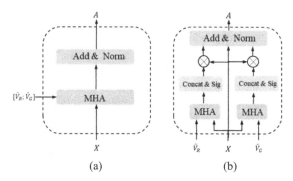

Fig. 4. Two Different Cross Attention Mechanisms

The cross-attention sub-layer is located after the masked self-attention sub-layer, and it fuses the output of the masked self-attention with the enhanced dual visual features to generate the feature representation A. In this paper, we consider two designs for cross-attention, as shown in Fig. 4.

The Concat Cross-attention mechanism, as shown in Fig. 4 (a), concatenates two visual features from the encoder and uses the concatenated result as the keys and values for the original multi-head attention sub-layer. The input words are used as queries.

The Parallel Cross-Attention mechanism, as shown in Fig. 4 (b), performs multi-head attention computations in parallel for two visual features. Specifically, the word features x_i' from the masked attention sub-layer output are used as queries for the multi-head attention, while the region features serve as keys and values for the computation. This generates attention features a_i^r for region features, and similarly, attention features a_i^g for grid features.

Next, we concatenate them as $[a_i^r; x_i']$ and $[a_i^g; x_i']$ separately. We apply linear transformations to map them to the d-dimensional space. Afterwards, we normalize them into probabilities using a sigmoid function, resulting in c_i^r and c_i^g. The computations for this process are as follows:

$$c_i^g = \sigma\left(W^g\left[a_i^g; x_i'\right] + b^g\right) \tag{18}$$

$$c_i^r = \sigma\left(W^r\left[a_i^r; x_i'\right] + b^r\right) \tag{19}$$

We then multiply them with a_i^r and a_i^g, add the resultant vectors to x_i', and finally feed to layer normalization, obtaining $A = \left\{a_i^{(l)}\right\}$ as follows:

$$a_i^{(l)} = LN\left(c_i^g \otimes a_i^g + c_i^r \otimes a_i^r + x_i'\right) \tag{20}$$

After the cross-attention processing, we use two independent position-wise feed-forward networks (FFNs) to process the feature A separately. The decoder layer is stacked N times to handle the processed features. Then, the output from the last layer is fed into a linear layer whose output dimension equals the vocabulary size for predicting the next word. Finally, the output is passed through the Softmax function to convert it into probabilities representing the likelihood of each word being the next word in the generated caption.

3.3 Objectives

Following a standard practice of image captioning studies, we pre-train our model with a cross-entropy loss (XE) and finetune it using the CIDEr-D optimization with self-critical sequence training strategy [19].

Specifically, the model is first trained to predict the next word y_t^* at $t = 1..T$, given the ground-truth sentence $y_{1:T}^*$. This is equal to minimize the following XE loss with respect to the model's parameter θ:

$$L_{XE}(\theta) = -\sum_{t=1}^{T} log\left(p_\theta\left(y_t^* \mid y_{0:t-1}^*\right)\right) \tag{21}$$

Then we continually optimize the non-differentiable CIDER-D score by Self-Critical Sequence Training (SCST) following:

$$\nabla_\theta L_{RL}(\theta) = -\frac{1}{k}\sum_{i=1}^{k}\left(r\left(y_{1:T}^i\right) - b\right)\nabla_\theta \, log \, p_\theta\left(y_{i:T}^i\right) \tag{22}$$

where k is the beam size, r is the CIDEr-D score function, and $b = \left(\Sigma_i r\left(y_{1:T}^i\right)\right)/k$ is the baseline.

4 Experiment

4.1 Dataset

To evaluate the performance of our text-to-image disaster news captioning model, we conducted experiments on the Disaster News Image Captioning Dataset (DNICC19k). This dataset is a cumulative result of our previous work and was initially introduced in the paper [5]. The DNICC19k dataset comprises 19,341 images categorized into 15 types of disaster events. During the experiments, we split the dataset into training, validation, and testing sets in a ratio of 7:1.5:1.5. Each image annotation in the dataset includes object bounding boxes, disaster types, and two Chinese descriptive sentences in different news language styles.

4.2 Experimental Settings

For the region features, each news entity is represented by a 1024-d feature vector extracted by Faster R-CNN [3]. The maximum number of regional features per image, n, is set to 50. For the grid features, we utilize the output of the layer 4 convolution of the Swin Transformer model [20], representing feature vectors of [49,768] dimensions, and transform them into 7x7 grids through dimension conversion.

In our model, we set the dimension d of each layer to 512, the number of heads to 8. The number of layers for both the encoder and decoder is set to 2, and the maximum length for each token is set to 25 characters. In the XE pre-training stage, we set the training cycle to 20 and batch size to 64. We warmed up the model for 5 epochs, with the learning rate initially increased to 1×10^{-4}. Then, we set the learning rate to 1×10^{-4} between epochs 5 and 11, to 1×10^{-5} between epochs 11 and 13, and then to 1×10^{-7} thereafter. After that, we began optimizing our model using the CIDEr reward, with a learning rate of 1×10^{-6} and a batch size of 20.

4.3 Performance Comparison

Ablation Study: In order to evaluate the impact of different visual representations on model performance, we conducted ablation experiments using the standard Transformer [7] as our baseline model.

Table 1. The impact of different visual representations on model performance.

Models	BLEU-1	BLEU-2	BLEU-3	BLEU-4	Meteor	Rouge_l	Cider
Region	49.00	32.52	22.93	16.43	23.74	44.56	56.64
Grid	49.54	32.92	23.17	16.55	23.90	44.78	56.59
G+R (Concat)	48.75	32.48	22.95	16.52	23.72	44.57	57.38
G+R (Cross-ATT)	49.48	33.10	23.46	16.84	23.89	44.90	57.45
G+R (Gated-ATT)	**50.38**	**34.08**	**24.40**	**17.71**	**24.31**	**45.64**	**60.97**

As shown in Table 1 (1) "Region" indicates that only the region features are used as visual input; (2) "Grid" indicates that only the grid features are used as visual input; (3) "G+R(Concat)" represents concatenating the dual visual representations, which have undergone Dual-Way Self Attention processing, as input to the decoder; (4) "G+R (Cross-ATT)" represents the fusion of dual visual representations through cross atten-tion as input to the decoder; (5) "G+R (Gated-ATT)" means fusion of dual visual representations through gated attention as input to the decoder.

On most evaluation indicators, the performance of (3) is lower than (1) and (2), indicating that direct splicing ignores the interaction between grid features and regional features, and even prevents them from exerting their individual advantages. The perfor-mance of (4) is slightly higher than (3), indicating that the interaction of dual visual representations can be enhanced and the visual representation refined through cross-attention. However, the scores on BLEU-1 and Meteor, (4) are slightly lower than (2), indicating that not all regional features and grid features are relevant, and performing some irrelevant interactions will introduce semantic noise and redundant information. On the contrary, it will reduce model performance. The performance of (5) is better than (1) and (2), which fully verifies the superiority of the gated attention mechanism used in this paper to fuse dual visual features. In addition, the performance of (5) is higher than (4), indicating that adding gating constraints can indeed adaptively filter out irrelevant attention results in the fusion process of regional features and grid features, thereby retaining only regions and networks.

Table 2. The impact of different Cross-attention on model performance.

Feature	Models	BLEU-1	BLEU-2	BLEU-3	BLEU-4	Meteor	Rouge_l	Cider
G+R	Gated-ATT +Concat	49.00	32.52	22.93	16.43	23.74	44.56	56.54
	Gated-ATT +Para-ATT	**49.54**	**32.92**	**23.17**	**16.55**	**23.90**	**44.78**	**56.59**

In order to evaluate the impact of different cross-attention mechanisms on subtitle generation, we conducted ablation experiments on the DTGF framework. As shown in Table 2, the Parallel Cross-attention outperforms Concat Cross-attention on all evaluation metrics. Among them, the Cider score reached 62.09, which is nearly a 2% improvement compared to the Concat Cross-attention. This experiment fully demonstrates that Parallel Cross-attention effectively leverages enhanced visual representations to generate more comprehensive image captions.

Quantitative results: To quantitatively evaluate our model, we report how our model compares with existing work including NIC [12], Show Attend [2], Bottom-up [3], AoANet [18], Transformer [7] and STCNet [5]) compared to performance. Since DNICC19k does not provide any news articles, it is difficult to compare the performance of current news picture captioning algorithms with this paper's algorithm. Therefore, we use the classic LSTM-based model and the Transformer-based model for comparison in experiments. As shown in Table 3, in the cross-entropy stage, the DTGF model achieves state-of-the-art performance on all evaluation metrics. It shows that the two-layer Transformer model based on gated fusion attention can effectively integrate regional features and grid features, obtain more comprehensive visual information, and thereby improve the performance of image caption.

The results obtained from the reinforcement learning stage are shown in Table 4. We observe that the BUTD achieves the best results in BLEU-1, BLEU-2, and Meteor, which indicates that the sentences generated by the BUTD have higher word accuracy. Therefore, the predictive ability of DTGF for word accuracy needs to be improved. For BLEU-3 and BLEU-4, the DTGF achieved the best results with scores of 24.63 and 17.81 respectively. This shows that the sentences generated by our model are smoother and more readable. Regarding the Cider metric, DTGF obtains the best score when the Cider score is used as the optimization gradient.

Table 3. Results obtained from cross entropy stage.

Models	BLEU-1	BLEU-2	BLEU-3	BLEU-4	Meteor	Rouge_l	Cider
NIC [12]	47.05	30.31	20.94	14.91	22.36	42.28	43.24
Show attend [2]	48.97	32.02	22.19	15.77	23.36	44.13	50.78
BUTD [3]	47.92	31.24	21.65	15.40	22.80	44.27	47.69
AoANet [18]	42.31	26.95	18.61	13.25	20.60	44.27	41.13
Transformer [7]	49.06	32.66	23.16	16.79	23.75	44.64	55.69
STCNet [5]	50.14	33.33	23.30	16.61	23.84	44.79	53.73
DTGF	**50.47**	**33.75**	**24.03**	**17.49**	**24.25**	**45.20**	**58.53**
Relative improvement	**0.7%**	**1.3%**	**3.1%**	**4.2%**	**1.7%**	**0.9%**	**5.1%**

Table 4. Results obtained from reinforcement learning stage.

Models	BLEU-1	BLEU-2	BLEU-3	BLEU-4	Meteor	Rouge_l	Cider
NIC [12]	48.99	31.46	21.55	15.03	22.68	43.50	49.93
Show attend [2]	51.88	34.19	23.51	16.43	24.21	45.25	57.90
BUTD [3]	**52.96**	**34.97**	23.99	16.73	**24.48**	45.67	59.35
AoANet [18]	50.97	33.78	23.54	16.69	24.16	45.25	59.20
Transformer [7]	49.00	32.52	22.93	16.43	23.74	44.56	56.64
STCNet [5]	52.56	34.88	23.97	16.79	24.26	45.76	58.54
DTGF	51.03	34.52	**24.63**	**17.81**	24.29	**45.97**	**62.09**

Qualitative analysis: We conduct a qualitative evaluation on sentences generated by STCNet [5], Transformer [7] and our model on the DNICC19k dataset. For news images, the evaluation criteria focus on the quality of the information generated describing the news event and its progression and consequences. Next, we analyze the quality of the generated sentences based on (1) the accuracy of predicting the disaster category for news events, (2) the consistency between the semantics of the generated sentences and the image details, and (3) the clarity and correctness of the sentences. This analysis is performed on the examples (a)–(d) shown in Fig. 5.

Figure 5 (a) shows the scene of a burned vehicle after the explosion. The STCNet incorrectly identified disaster types, resulting in false alarms of news events. Although the Transformer predicts correctly, the description sentences it generates are rough. When faced with confusing categories, our model can accurately identify details in the image, such as the explosion of a car and the presence of multiple workers, and predict the correct type of disaster. Figure 5 (b) is a scene of a building fire. All models can correctly identify disaster types, but only the DTGF generates more vivid words (such as "swallow", "thick smoke rising into the sky") and has high accuracy. Figure 5 (c) is a traffic accident scene.

Fig. 5. Comparisons of sentence generation on various models for different test instances.

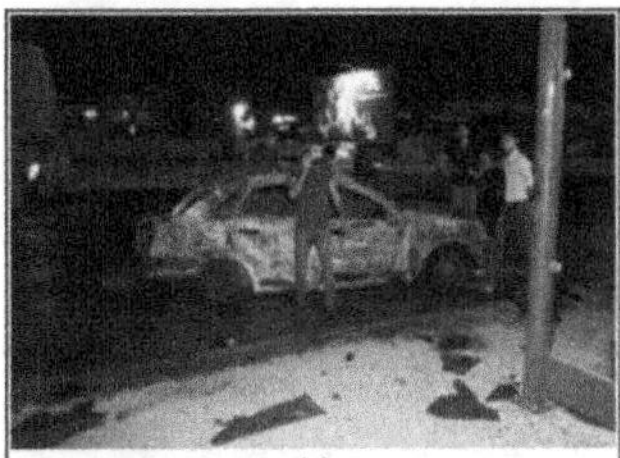

Compared with other models, the sentences generated by this model have consistency between semantics and image details. This model can simultaneously correctly identify emergency disaster categories ("traffic accidents"), news events ("a white car collided") and event consequences ("the front of the car is seriously deformed", "parts are scattered on the ground"), and form smooth image caption. Figure 5 (d) is the plane crash site after the air crash. The description sentences generated by the STCNet and Transformer only include descriptions of news events and ignore the description of the degree of damage, while our model generates a detailed description of "the fuselage was seriously damaged".

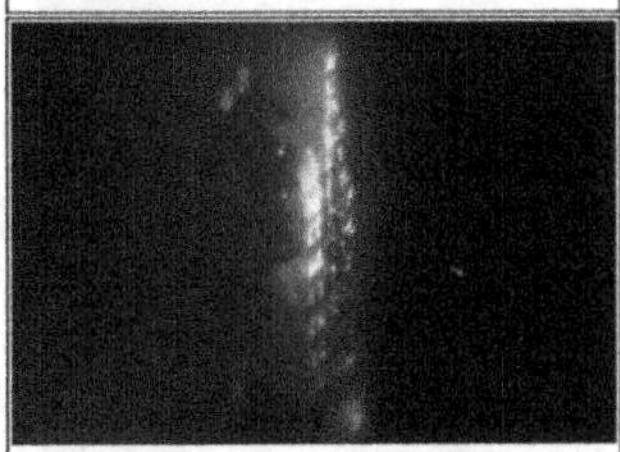

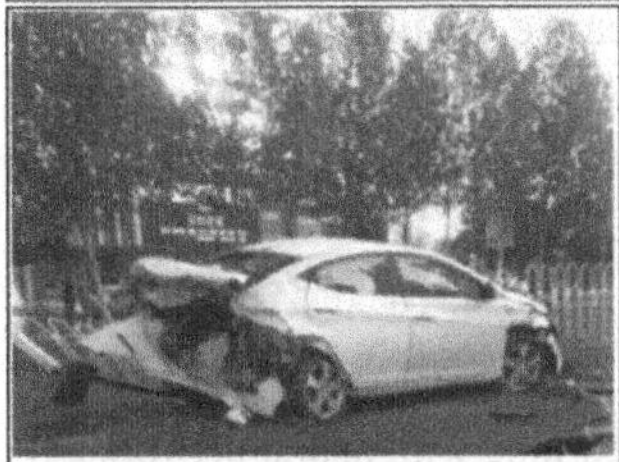

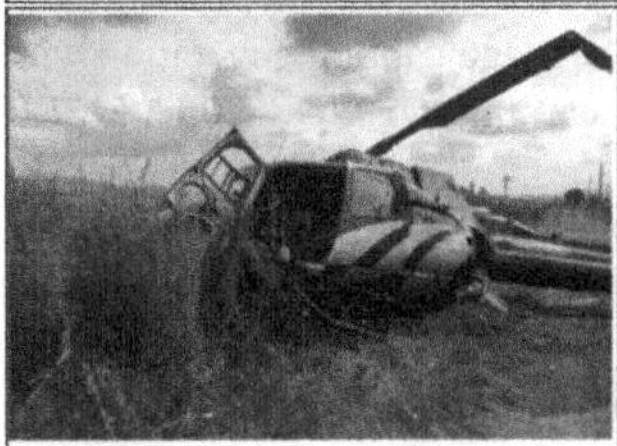

Observing the above examples, we find that the descriptions generated by the STCNet and Transformer models are relatively vague. Our model uses dual visual features based on gated attention, which effectively integrates the advantages of regional features and grid features, making the model significantly superior in capturing on-site details and ensuring the accuracy and completeness of generated sentences.

5 Conclusion

In this paper, we propose a news image caption algorithm called Dual-layer Transformer with Gated-attention Fusion (DTGF) for the domain of disasters. The algorithm maximizes the complementary advantages of region features and grid features to improve the accuracy of image captioning. On the encoder side, we introduce "Gated-attention" to fuse and filter the dual-level visual features effectively. On the decoder side, we consider two cross-attention designs, Concat and Parallel, to integrate enhanced visual representations. Extensive experiments on the DNICC19k dataset validate the superiority of our algorithm. We believe that this research is of great significance for improving the application of image captioning in disaster news reporting and will provide strong support for related research and practices in this field.

References

1. Sutskever, I., Vinyals, O., Le, Q.V.: Sequence to sequence learning with neural networks. In: Advances in Neural Information Processing Systems 27 (2014)
2. Xu, K., Ba, J., Kiros, R., et al.: Show, attend and tell: neural image caption generation with visual attention. In: International Conference on Machine Learning, pp. 2048–2057. PMLR (2015)
3. Anderson, P., He, X., Buehler, C., et al.: Bottom-up and top-down attention for image captioning and visual question answering. In: Proceedings of the IEEE Conference on Computer Vision and Pattern Recognition, pp. 6077–6086 (2018)
4. Wu, D., Li, H., Gu, C., et al.: Improving fusion of region features and grid features via two-step interaction for image-text retrieval. In: Proceedings of the 30th ACM International Conference on Multimedia, pp. 5055–5064 (2022)
5. Zhou, J., Zhu, Y., Zhang, Y., et al.: Spatial-aware topic-driven-based image Chinese caption for disaster news. Neural Comput. Appl. **35**(13), 9481–9500 (2023)
6. Biten, A.F., Gomez, L., Rusinol, M., et al.: Good news, everyone! context driven entity-aware captioning for news images. In: Proceedings of the IEEE/CVF Conference on Computer Vision and Pattern Recognition, pp. 12466–12475 (2019)
7. Vaswani, A., Shazeer, N., Parmar, N., et al.: Attention is all you need. In: Advances in Neural Information Processing Systems 30 (2017)
8. Tran, A., Mathews, A., Xie, L.: Transform and tell: entity-aware news image captioning. In: Proceedings of the IEEE/CVF Conference on Computer Vision and Pattern Recognition, pp. 13035–13045 (2020)
9. Liu, F., Wang, Y., Wang, T., et al.: Visual news: benchmark and challenges in news image captioning. arXiv preprint arXiv:2010.03743 (2021)
10. Zhou, M., Luo, G., Rohrbach, A., et al.: Focus! relevant and sufficient context selection for news image captioning. arXiv preprint arXiv:2212.00843 (2022)

11. Zhang, J., Fang, S., Mao, Z., et al.: Fine-tuning with multi-modal entity prompts for news image captioning. In: Proceedings of the 30th ACM International Conference on Multimedia, pp. 4365–4373 (2022)

12. Vinyals, O., Toshev, A., Bengio, S., et al.: Show and tell: a neural image caption generator. In: Proceedings of the IEEE Conference on Computer Vision and Pattern Recognition, pp. 3156–3164 (2015)

13. Lu, J., Xiong, C., Parikh, D., et al.: Knowing when to look: adaptive attention via a visual sentinel for image captioning. In: Proceedings of the IEEE Conference on Computer Vision and Pattern Recognition, pp. 375–383 (2017)

14. Wu, L., Xu, M., Sang, L., et al.: Noise augmented double-stream graph convolutional networks for image captioning. IEEE Trans. Circuits Syst. Video Technol. **31**(8), 3118–3127 (2020)

15. Xian, T., Li, Z., Zhang, C., et al.: Dual global enhanced transformer for image captioning. Neural Netw. **148**, 129–141 (2022)

16. Luo, Y., Ji, J., Sun, X., et al.: Dual-level collaborative transformer for image captioning. In: Proceedings of the AAAI Conference on Artificial Intelligence, vol. 35, no. 3, pp. 2286–2293 (2021)

17. Nguyen, V.Q., Suganuma, M., Okatani, T.: GRIT: faster and better image captioning transformer using dual visual features. In: Avidan, S., Brostow, G., Cissé, M., Farinella, G.M., Hassner, T. (eds.) ECCV 2022. LNCS, vol. 13696, pp. 167–184. Springer, Cham (2022). https://doi.org/10.1007/978-3-031-20059-5_10

18. Huang, L., Wang, W., Chen, J., et al.: Attention on attention for image captioning. In: Proceedings of the IEEE/CVF International Conference on Computer Vision, pp. 4634–4643 (2019)

19. Rennie, S.J., Marcheret, E., Mroueh, Y., et al.: Self-critical sequence training for image captioning. In: Proceedings of the IEEE Conference on Computer Vision and Pattern Recognition, pp. 7008–7024 (2017)

20. Liu, Z., Lin, Y., Cao, Y., et al.: Swin transformer: hierarchical vision transformer using shifted windows. In: Proceedings of the IEEE/CVF International Conference on Computer Vision, pp. 10012–10022 (2021)

Constructing Personal Knowledge Graph from Conversation via Deep Reinforcement Learning

Fei Cai[✉] and Xiao Guo

Communication University of China, Beijing 100024, China
{xhh,xguo}@cuc.edu.cn

Abstract. Due to the rise of intelligent assistants, a massive amount of user QA(question-and-answer) data has emerged on the Internet. This data contains valuable information about user concerns and preferences in specific domains. However, there has been limited research exploring the user-related information contained in such conversational data for constructing individual user knowledge graphs. We propose a method for learning to construct a personal knowledge graph from multi-turn QA data between agents and users. We build a reinforcement learning-based knowledge graph path reasoning model. This model maps user utterances to an action space composed of paths between entity nodes, enabling path reasoning on the graph and facilitating traversal to the next entity node. The approach utilizes emotional and intent information inferred from subsequent user responses as a reward signal for training the reinforcement learning policy network. We conduct experiments on the ConvRef dataset, consisting of 11k naturally occurring dialogues, and compare our method with state-of-the-art baselines. The results demonstrate that our approach effectively generates more accurate inference paths from user-agent dialogue interactions and constructs high-quality personal knowledge graphs.

Keywords: Natural Language Processing · Knowledge Graph · Reinforcement Learning · Deep learning · Emotion Recognition

1 Introduction

A knowledge graph is a structured representation of knowledge that captures associations between entities, relationships, and attributes [1], any knowledge graph overview. Due to its advanced capabilities in retrieval and inference, knowledge graphs find widespread applications in fields such as natural language processing, question-answering systems, and semantic search.

Mainstream categorizations of knowledge graphs include general-purpose knowledge graphs and domain-specific knowledge graphs. While both these

G. Zhai et al. (Eds.): IFTC 2023, CCIS 2066, pp. 208–219, 2024.
https://doi.org/10.1007/978-981-97-3623-2_16

mainstream knowledge graph types hold significant practical and academic significance, they often place excessive emphasis on universally applicable knowledge, potentially overlooking individual preferences. Knowledge points of interest to individuals in their daily lives, which may lack prominence or universality, might not be incorporated into mainstream knowledge graphs.

In light of this, Google researchers introduced the concept of Personal Knowledge Graphs (PKG) in 2019 [2]. PKGs encompass knowledge about entities that are of interest to individual users and inherently possess user-specificity. They hold paramount significance in realizing personalized artificial intelligence applications.

Currently, there is a vast amount of conversational data available on the internet, which reflects unique information about individuals' areas of interest, preferences, values, and behavioral characteristics. This wealth of data aligns with the essential requirements for constructing individual knowledge graphs. However, the current research on building knowledge graphs based on conversational data faces several challenges. Firstly, the sources of knowledge for constructing knowledge graphs across various domains are relatively limited, primarily relying on domain-specific books, patents, and similar resources [3], literature on knowledge graph construction. These mainstream approaches tend to overlook unstructured dialogues and interaction data containing rich individual-specific information. Consequently, there is a lack of available solutions to construct knowledge graphs from such data.

Secondly, most efforts that combine dialogue and graphs focus on generating dialogues from pre-constructed extensive knowledge graphs. Researchers leverage existing knowledge graphs to incorporate various knowledge into tasks such as sentiment analysis, intent mining, and dialogue generation [4–7]. Only a small fraction of work attempts to extract structured knowledge from dialogues [8–11], and this approach comes with significant limitations. These endeavors highly depend on automated extraction tools, where researchers use these tools to extract sets of entities and relationships from dialogue corpora, primarily relying on entity co-occurrence and mutual information. They often disregard the overall semantic context of dialogues and user feedback. This oversight, particularly ignoring emotional information and implicit feedback in user responses and follow-up questions, can lead to misinterpretation of semantic information, resulting in the construction of coarse and incomplete knowledge graphs.

Given the advantages and potential of reinforcement learning in tasks involving continuous decision-making and real-time environment awareness, it has found widespread applications in multi-hop reasoning on knowledge graphs and knowledge graph-based query tasks in recent years [12–17]. Reinforcement learning, as a machine learning method that autonomously learns from interactions with the environment through trial and error, enables reasoning and learning on knowledge graphs through agent interactions and exploration. Inspired by these works, we employ reinforcement learning to learn traversing and reasoning on knowledge graphs from interactions between users and agents, ultimately constructing individual knowledge graphs.

We propose a reinforcement learning inference method called KG-agent, which can extract and create a set of reliable entities from user context queries. Multiple agents embark on their journey from these entities, making stepwise decisions regarding their directions on the extensive knowledge graph, with the ultimate goal of reaching a designated entity. The policy network takes as input the context queries, relevant entities, and all possible next-step transition paths (i.e., relationships or properties between entities). This policy network is trained by detecting emotional and intent information extracted from subsequent user utterances, which serve as rewards. The path from the initial entity set to the final entity set represents the candidate user information request path for the current dialogue round, and the aggregation of final entity sets forms the candidate answers to user information needs. The optimal path represents the user's most relevant individual knowledge graph. Finally, we conduct experiments on the ConvRef dataset, demonstrating the feasibility, effectiveness, and superiority of our proposed reinforcement learning method, KG-agent, compared to baseline experiments. The main contributions of this paper are as follows:

1. We introduce a method for graph path inference based on agent-user interaction feedback, even in the absence of explicit information queries for $\langle entity - relation \rangle$.
2. Our model can generate reward scores for path credibility based on the emotional tendencies (satisfaction, neutrality, dissatisfaction) and information needs (new intent or old intent) of user follow-up utterances, even without explicit end-entity guidance.
3. Our experimental results on the ConvRef dataset, containing 11,000 natural dialogues, demonstrate that our model outperforms baseline models in path inference ability and constructs high-quality individual knowledge graphs.

2 The Proposed Method

In this section, we will provide a detailed explanation of the KG-agent approach for reasoning and constructing personal knowledge graphs from user-agent interactions in dialogues. We will begin by introducing the overall reinforcement learning system and key concepts involved in this task. Next, we will delve into the reinforcement learning modeling of this task, which constitutes the main components of KG-agent (environment, agent, actions, rewards). The overall system framework of KG-agent is illustrated in Fig. 2, where we formulate the reasoning process within the knowledge graph as a Markov decision process. Users make inquiries, the agent selects actions, the environment provides rewards, and the agent transitions to new states. This section will provide a detailed discussion of policy networks and the reward mechanism. Towards the end of this section, we will present an overview of the overall training process for this approach.

2.1 Framework Overview

The KG-agent model we propose is based on the reinforcement learning framework, aiming to learn the most relevant path to the user's information needs through user queries and follow-up utterances, there by constructing a personalized user knowledge graph. Reinforcement learning is intended to enhance the acquisition of an optimal behavioral strategy through the dynamic interaction between an intelligent agent and its environment [18], as depicted in Fig. 1. This process involves a decision-making procedure where the agent takes actions in various states and receives rewards as feedback. Reinforcement learning can be formalized as a Markov Decision Process (MDP) [19], with the key components of MDP including the state space S, action space A, state transition probability function P, and reward function R. This process can be summarized by the following formula, denoted as (1):

$$MDP = (S, A, P, R) \tag{1}$$

In Formula 1, the ultimate goal of reinforcement learning is to enable the agent to accumulate long-term rewards to the maximum extent through the process of learning and strategy optimization. The overall workflow of our system is depicted in Fig. 2: Initially, the user issues a query to satisfy a specific information need. The model utilizes named Entity Recognition and Entity Disambiguation techniques to identify and disambiguate entities relevant to the query. These identified entities form a set representing the initial knowledge graph starting point. Next, we filter all relationships or attributes related to the starting-entities as the set of actions that the agent can take, also known as the path collection. Subsequently, multiple reinforcement learning agents make decisions regarding their path by considering the current query, the current entity, and contextual entities. These agents navigate along these directions to reach the target entity, ultimately generating a response. Upon receiving the response, the user simulator provides a follow-up utterance.

Next, we input the user's follow-up utterance into an emotion recognition algorithm, obtaining normalized probabilities for three emotions: satisfaction, dissatisfaction, and neutrality. If the probability associated with the "satisfaction" label is the highest, the agent receives a positive reward. Conversely, a negative reward is assigned when other emotions predominate. If the "neutral-

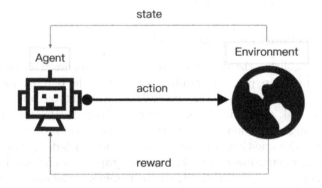

Fig. 1. Reinforcement Learning Schematic

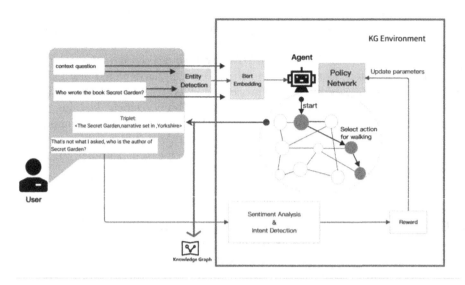

Fig. 2. The work flow of the proposed KG-agent method

ity" emotion has the highest probability, the user's follow-up utterance undergoes intent detection to determine whether it signifies a new intent or repeats an old one. If the probability suggests a new intent, it is assumed that the user is satisfied with the system's response, and the agent is rewarded positively; otherwise, a negative reward is applied. Based on the reward score, the reinforcement learning agent updates the parameters of the policy network while making new decisions in response to the user's subsequent queries. Upon concluding a conversation on a particular topic, the context entity set (the agent's starting point set) is cleaned and reset. With ongoing interaction and dialogue between the user and agent, the parameters of the policy network continuously update, allowing the reinforcement learning agent to increasingly infer the desired triplets for the user with higher accuracy. In the end, we build the knowledge graph by incorporating the highly confident graph inference paths.

2.2   Reinforcement Learning Modeling

This module establishes the reinforcement learning framework for task definition in this paper. In this paper, the training objective of the reinforcement learning agent is to deduce the answers that users desire from interactions in dialogues. We model this task as a finite Markov Decision Process(MDP) on a knowledge graph, comprising several key elements: states, actions, rewards, policy and transition function. The knowledge graph, in conjunction with dialogues, constitutes the overarching environment. The knowledge graph is represented as a set of triples$\{(e_1, r, e_2) \mid e_1, e_2 \in V, r \in R\}$, where V denotes the entity set, and represents the relation set. Entities and relations correspond to nodes and edges, respectively. The reinforcement learning agent navigates the graph using entities as starting or ending points and relations as paths. The agent selects actions based on the current observed environmental state, guided by a policy. The environment computes reward signals and provides them to the reinforcement learning algorithm. Through interaction with the reinforcement learning algorithm, the agent iteratively refines its policy based on observations and reward signals, aiming to maximize cumulative rewards. The following sections provide detailed definitions of each element:

- State: A state $s \in S$, represents the environmental condition observed by the agent at a specific moment, containing sufficient information for the agent to make decisions. In this task, the current round of utterance q_t and entity e_t, previous utterances q_{cxt} and entities e_{cxt} collectively constitute the current state.

$$s = q_t + q_{cxt} + e_t + e_{cxt} \tag{2}$$

- Action: An action $a \in A^s$, represents the actions that the agent can choose to take in the state s. The agent induces a state transition by executing actions. In this task, actions refer to the set of actions that can be chosen under the current utterance and context entities. The e^* below represents the entity node that the agent is currently traversing

$$\{A^s = relations|e^*\} \tag{3}$$

- Reward: Reward r signifies the immediate feedback that the agent receives for executing a specific action in a particular state. In our model, we employ sentiment analysis and intent detection results as reward scores. After the agent takes an action, the user responds with the next sentence, and we use sentiment classification algorithms to identify the sentiment tendency of this sentence. Negative sentiment results in a negative reward, while positive sentiment results in a positive reward. Additionally, we utilize intent detection algorithms to determine whether the current utterance repeats the intent of previous utterances. If repetition is detected, there is a high probability that the user is dissatisfied with the entity currently explored, leading to a negative reward.
- Policy: Due to the vastness of the state space, learning direct transition probabilities between states is highly costly. Therefore, we employ a parameterized policy network to learn the inference of knowledge graph paths from dialogues. The policy $\pi(a \mid s)$ represents the probability distribution of taking action a in state s.

2.3   Policy Network

We utilizes reinforcement learning based on policy networks, using neural networks to construct the policy network as a key component of the reinforcement learning process. In this approach, the policy network is responsible for directly mapping states to actions. It takes the current state of the environment as input and generates a probability distribution over possible actions. The structure of our policy network is depicted in Fig. 3. Our knowledge graph agent can be represented as a triplet $\langle s, A_s, \pi_\theta \rangle$. In essence, it needs to perform the mapping from state to action $\pi_\theta \to P(A_s)$. The policy network takes inputs consisting of the current question q_t, previous questions q_{cxt}, and the set of permissible transition relations A^s that can be selected at the current entity node e^* of the agent. Due to Bert's strong feature extraction and language representation capabilities, we opt to utilize Bert [20] for generating word embeddings from input text. In our approach, we employ Long Short-Term Memory networks (LSTM) and feedforward neural networks to further extract features from the questions [21]. Between the LSTM layer and the feedforward layer, we incorporate dropout techniques to mitigate the risk of overfitting. Prior to the element-wise multiplication with action vectors, we generate the final question embedding denoted as h_t.

$$q_t^{bert} = [BERT(q_{cxt}); BERT(q_t)] \tag{4}$$

$$A_s^{bert} = stack(BERT(A^s)) \tag{5}$$

$$q_t^{bert} \in R^d, a \in R^d, a \in A_s^{bert} \tag{6}$$

$$h_t = W * Dropout(LSTM(q_t^{bert})) \tag{7}$$

During the training phase, the policy network is updated through a process called policy optimization to improve its performance. Typically, optimization algorithms like gradient descent are used to adjust the network's parameters based on the observed rewards and taken actions in the environment. One commonly used technique in policy network-based reinforcement learning is the policy gradient method. This method leverages the gradient of the expected cumulative reward with respect to the policy parameters to update the network, encouraging actions that lead to higher rewards. The gradient is estimated using samples

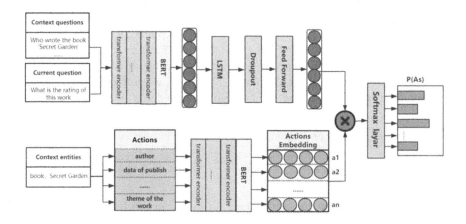

Fig. 3. Reinforcement of Learning Strategy Network Structure

collected from interactions with the environment. By iteratively updating the policy network based on observed rewards and actions, the network gradually learns to improve its decision-making capabilities and converges towards an optimal policy that maximizes long-term cumulative rewards. The policy network's ultimate output is represented by a softmax-normalized action probability distribution $P(A_s)$, as demonstrated in Formula (8). Thereafter, the agent selects and performs an action through sampling from this distribution, as exemplified in Formula (9). The anticipated reward is denoted by $J_R(\theta)$. As evidenced in Formulas (10) and (11), we set the maximization of $J_R(\theta)$ as the objective for updating the policy network's parameters.

$$P(A_s) = Softmax(A_s^{bert} \times h_t) \tag{8}$$

$$a \sim P(A_s) \tag{9}$$

$$J_R(\theta) = E_{s \in S} E_{a \in \pi_\theta}[R(s,a)] \tag{10}$$

$$\nabla J_R(\theta) = E_\pi[\alpha \cdot R^* \cdot \frac{\nabla \pi(a \mid s, \theta)}{\pi(a \mid s, \theta)} + \beta \cdot H_\pi(\cdot, s)] \tag{11}$$

3   Experiment

3.1   Evaluation Index

To measure the accuracy and effectiveness of our system in inferring graph paths during multi-turn dialog interactions, we used P@1, HIT@5, and MRR as the evaluation metrics for our experiments.

- Precision at 1 (P@1): P@1 is a metric that measures whether the system's top-ranked inference result is correct.
- Hit at 5 (HIT@5): HIT@5 is a metric that measures whether the top 5 ranked inference results contain the correct information.
- Mean Reciprocal Rank (MRR): MRR is a metric that measures the average effectiveness of the system in finding the correct path.

3.2   Dataset and Baseline Methods

Our experiments were conducted on the ConvRef dataset. This dataset comprises approximately 11,000 natural dialogues, as detailed in Table 1. Each conversation contains five distinct information intents, and each intent has four different expressions, including various emotional tones. To better capture the authentic user voice, we enhanced the emotional context of the dialogues. We chose the Wikimedia Knowledge Graph as the reinforcement learning environment. This graph is constructed from a Wikidata NTriples dump and contains approximately 2 billion triples, with a graph data size of 4.3 GB. We select the Conquer [22] and Convex [23] as the SOTA baseline methods.

Table 1. The ConvRef dataset

Dataset	Train	Validation	Test
Conversations	6720	2240	2240
Intents	5	5	5
Reformulations	4	4	4
Total Conversations	11200		

3.3 Experimental Setup

We conducted our experiments on Linux, using Python 3 as the programming language and TensorFlow 2.2.0 as the deep learning framework. We trained the reinforcement learning agents on a GPU platform with 32GB of video memory (VRAM). The hyperparameter settings are shown in Table 2, and the specific environment setup for the experiments is provided in Table 3.

Table 2. Hyperparameter

Hyperparameters	Value
seed	12345
Learning rate	0.001
Dropout	0.2
Episodes num	50
Rollouts num	20
Epochs	30

Table 3. Experimental environment setup

Library	Version
Tensorflow	2.2.0
Numpy	1.20.1
Tensorflow Probability	0.10.1
Transformers	3.5.1
TF-agents	0.5.0
Neo4j	1.7.2

3.4 Experimental Analysis

Tables 4 and 5 present the main results of our comparative experiments. The "simple" version of KG-agent is a model variation in which we employ a straightforward fully connected layer as the policy network. Comparative analysis in

Table 4 demonstrates that our model surpasses previous state-of-the-art models, Convex and Conquer, in the metrics P@1, HIT@5, and MRR. Compared to the best prior results, our model exhibits an improvement of 2.65% in P@1, 4.00% in HIT@5, and 3.5% in MRR. This signifies that our model can learn more accurate knowledge graph reasoning paths during interactions between the agent and the user. It can also obtain effective reward signals from the user's follow-up utterances, guiding the agent to update its policy network parameters for better decision-making. Table 5 records the number of responses satisfying the user in the first five attempts using different methods. From this table, it is evident that our model achieves the highest number of user-satisfying responses in the first response and also in the first five attempts. We present some visualization results in Fig. 4.

Table 4. The comparison results of P@1, HIT@5, and MRR metrics

Model	PRECISION@1	HITS@5	MRR
Convex	22.5	25.7	24.1
Conquer	33.9	42.1	37.5
KG-agent(Ours-Simple)	31.4	39.9	35
KG-agent(Ours)	**34.8**	**43.8**	**38.8**

Table 5. Record the number of statisfactory responses achieved on the n-th attempt

Model	1st	2nd	3rd	4th	5th	total
Convex	1980	278	**200**	24	35	2517
Conquer	3172	**356**	184	32	48	3792
KG-agent(Ours-Simple)	3012	228	102	**80**	100	3522
KG-agent(Ours)	**3202**	354	160	48	**134**	**3898**

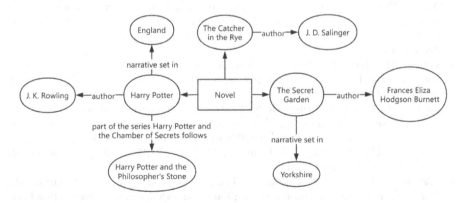

Fig. 4. Graphical Results Example

4   Conclusions

In this paper, we introduce KG-agent, a reinforcement learning-based approach for knowledge graph reasoning and construction. KG-agent leverages multi-turn dialog interactions between users and intelligent agents to learn reward scores derived from users' emotional tendencies and intent information in their follow-up responses. These scores guide the training of the policy network, enabling KG-agent to reason with higher confidence along various user utterances and extract individualized knowledge graphs. Experimental results demonstrate the superiority of our approach over state-of-the-art baselines, Convex and Conquer, achieving higher scores across multiple evaluation metrics with strong accuracy and effectiveness.

References

1. Ji, S., Pan, S., Cambria, E., Marttinen, P., Philip, S.Y.: A survey on knowledge graphs: representation, acquisition, and applications. IEEE Trans. Neural Netw. Learn. Syst. **33**(2), 494–514 (2021)
2. Balog, K., Kenter, T.: Personal knowledge graphs: a research agenda. In: Proceedings of the 2019 ACM SIGIR International Conference on Theory of Information Retrieval, Santa Clara, CA, USA, pp. 217–220. ACM (2019). https://doi.org/10.1145/3341981.3344241
3. Hao, X., et al.: Construction and application of a knowledge graph. Remote Sens. **13**(13), 2511 (2021)
4. Xiao, X.: Knowledge graph technology based on natural language processing and reinforcement learning e-commerce customer service. In: 2022 IEEE Conference on Telecommunications, Optics and Computer Science (TOCS), Dalian, China, pp. 495–500. IEEE (2022). https://doi.org/10.1109/TOCS56154.2022.10015978
5. Ji, H., Ke, P., Huang, S., Wei, F., Zhu, X., Huang, M.: Language generation with multi-hop reasoning on commonsense knowledge graph, arXiv preprint arXiv:2009.11692 (2020)
6. Xu, J., Wang, H., Niu, Z.-Y., Wu, H., Che, W., Liu, T.: Conversational graph grounded policy learning for open-domain conversation generation. In: Proceedings of the 58th Annual Meeting of the Association for Computational Linguistics, pp. 1835–1845 (2020)
7. Ghosal, D., Hong, P., Shen, S., Majumder, N., Mihalcea, R., Poria, S.: CIDER: commonsense inference for dialogue explanation and reasoning, arXiv preprint arXiv:2106.00510 (2021)
8. Ahmad, Z., Ekbal, A., Sengupta, S., Maitra, A., Ramnani, R., Bhattacharyya, P.: Unsupervised approach for knowledge-graph creation from conversation: the use of intent supervision for slot filling. In: 2021 International Joint Conference on Neural Networks (IJCNN), Shenzhen, China, pp. 1–8. IEEE (2021). https://doi.org/10.1109/IJCNN52387.2021.9534398
9. Ahmad, Z., Ekbal, A., Sengupta, S., Mitra, A., Rammani, R., Bhattacharyya, P.: Active learning based relation classification for knowledge graph construction from conversation data. In: Yang, H., Pasupa, K., Leung, A.C.-S., Kwok, J.T., Chan, J.H., King, I. (eds.) ICONIP 2020. CCIS, vol. 1332, pp. 617–625. Springer, Cham (2020). https://doi.org/10.1007/978-3-030-63820-7_70

10. Xie, Y., Li, J., Pu, P.: AFEC: A Knowledge Graph Capturing Social Intelligence in Casual Conversations. arXiv, 22 May 2022. http://arxiv.org/abs/2205.10850. Accessed 07 Nov 2023

11. Fu, X., et al.: A speech-to-knowledge-graph construction system. In: Proceedings of the Twenty-Ninth International Joint Conference on Artificial Intelligence, Yokohama, Japan: International Joint Conferences on Artificial Intelligence Organization, pp. 5303–5305, July 2020. https://doi.org/10.24963/ijcai.2020/777

12. Xiong, W., Hoang, T., Wang, W.Y.: Deeppath: a reinforcement learning method for knowledge graph reasoning, arXiv preprint arXiv:1707.06690 (2017)

13. Li, Z., Jin, X., Guan, S., Wang, Y., Cheng, X.: Path reasoning over knowledge graph: a multi-agent and reinforcement learning based method. In: 2018 IEEE International Conference on Data Mining Workshops (ICDMW), Singapore, Singapore, pp. 929–936. IEEE (2018). https://doi.org/10.1109/ICDMW.2018.00135

14. Das, R., et al.: Go for a walk and arrive at the answer: reasoning over paths in knowledge bases using reinforcement learning, arXiv preprint arXiv:1711.05851 (2017)

15. Godin, F., Kumar, A., Mittal, A.: Learning when not to answer: a ternary reward structure for reinforcement learning based question answering, arXiv preprint arXiv:1902.10236 (2019)

16. Wan, G., Pan, S., Gong, C., Zhou, C., Haffari, G.: Reasoning like human: hierarchical reinforcement learning for knowledge graph reasoning. In: Proceedings of the Twenty-Ninth International Joint Conference on Artificial Intelligence, Yokohama, Japan: International Joint Conferences on Artificial Intelligence Organization, pp. 1926–1932, July 2020. https://doi.org/10.24963/ijcai.2020/267

17. Wang, Q., Hao, Y., Cao, J.: ADRL: an attention-based deep reinforcement learning framework for knowledge graph reasoning. Knowl.-Based Syst. **197**, 105910 (2020). https://doi.org/10.1016/j.knosys.2020.105910

18. Kaelbling, L.P., Littman, M.L., Moore, A.W.: Reinforcement learning: a survey. J. Artif. Intell. Res. **4**, 237–285 (1996)

19. Garcia, F., Rachelson, E.: Markov decision processes. In: Markov Decision Processes in Artificial Intelligence, pp. 1–38 (2013)

20. Devlin, J., Chang, M.-W., Lee, K., Toutanova, K.: BERT, pre-training of deep bidirectional transformers for language understanding. In: NAACL-HLT (2019)

21. Yu, Y., et al.: A review of recurrent neural networks: LSTM cells and network architectures. Neural Comput. **31**(7), 1235–1270 (2019)

22. Kaiser, M., Saha Roy, R., Weikum, G.: Reinforcement learning from reformulations in conversational question answering over knowledge graphs. In: Proceedings of the 44th International ACM SIGIR Conference on Research and Development in Information Retrieval, Virtual Event Canada, pp. 459–469. ACM (2021). https://doi.org/10.1145/3404835.3462859

23. Christmann, P., Roy, R.S., Abujabal, A., Singh, J., Weikum, G.: Look before you hop: conversational question answering over knowledge graphs using judicious context expansion. In: Proceedings of the 28th ACM International Conference on Information and Knowledge Management, pp. 729–738 (2019). https://doi.org/10.1145/3357384.3358016

Exploring the Efficacy of Interactive Digital Humans in Cultural Communication

Simin Chen[1], Di Zhang[2], Wenshan Shi[1], Xinyue Ding[3], and Le Chang[4(✉)]

[1] School of Data Science and Intelligent Media, Communication University of China, Ministry of Education, Beijing 100024, China
[2] Key Laboratory of Media Audio and Video, Communication University of China, Ministry of Education, Beijing 100024, China
dizhang@cuc.edu.cn
[3] School of Information and Communication Engineering, Communication University of China, Ministry of Education, Beijing 100024, China
[4] SoundAI Technology Co., Ltd., Beijing 100024, China
changle@soundai.com

Abstract. In recent years, digital human technology has seen widespread application across various fields, and its emphasis on interactivity holds the promise of addressing the stereotypical and monotonous aspects of traditional cultural communication. It reveals that the dissemination of history and culture still primarily relies on a single communication channel, lacks interaction, and struggles to meet the growing demand for enriched emotional content and intelligent interaction from the audience. This paper focuses on leveraging virtual digital human technology to enhance historical and cultural communication efficacy. It delves into the impact of digital humans on the effectiveness of cultural communication and audience engagement. Experimental results demonstrate that digital humans with enhanced interactivity play a positive role in disseminating history and culture, with diversified interaction fostering greater public absorption of historical and cultural content, thus expanding the potential applications of digital humans. In conclusion, digital human technology is poised to offer a novel and efficient technological means for cultural communication, injecting new possibilities into the realm of cultural communication experiences.

Keyword: virtual digital human · human-computer interaction · education · historical and cultural communication

1 Introduction

With the development of digital human technologies such as the Unreal Engine MetaHuman, the combination of artificial intelligence and computer graphics has made it possible to create highly realistic virtual characters. This has a revolutionary impact on the entertainment industry and inspires new thinking and exploration in cultural communication. With the continuous development of media and communication technology, people have more diverse and efficient channels to obtain information. Most communication methods used to disseminate historical and cultural information have not been updated promptly, resulting in the public's inability to absorb and accept historical and cultural knowledge better [1]. Therefore, we use digital human technology to design an interactive explanatory system for cultural communication, aiming to explore new forms of cultural dissemination by incorporating innovative interactive features. The current channels of historical and cultural dissemination include educational and research institutions, book publishing, literary materials, documentaries, and films.

The current channels of historical and cultural dissemination include educational and research institutions, book publishing, literary materials, documentaries, and films [2].

However, there are problems such as audience limitation, insufficient interactivity, and accessibility. Traditional paper publications make it challenging to achieve interaction with readers. The traditionalism and rigidity of primary education in educational research institutions make it difficult to attract younger audiences; documentaries and films are limited by their length, making it challenging to show historical events fully, and their dissemination effectiveness and depth are insufficient [3–6]. However, using digital humans to promote history and culture can better solve these problems. With the development of digital human modeling technology, the appearance of digital humans has become more realistic [7]. Physical simulation algorithms have promoted more realistic clothing displays, rendering engines, and GPU computing power, improving the accuracy and real-time performance of digital human images [8]. The development of facial recognition technology has also made digital human facial expressions more subtle and automated, which can significantly enhance the interactivity of digital humans. Digital humans use rich gestures and expressions to more accurately mimic human language and behavior, making it easier for people to resonate and connect emotionally, promoting faster information transfer and deeper understanding, and ultimately improving cognitive efficiency. When conveying information through vivid gestures and expressions, digital humans can also simulate different tones and speech rhythms to present information [9]. Emotional communication increases the affinity for information, making the audience more likely to accept and digest the content delivered by digital humans, making the information more vivid and persuasive [10].

The virtual digital human technology we apply includes selecting photos of historical figures during their lifetime or restoration and continuously adjusting and optimizing the interactive advantages of digital humans, including gestures, expressions, and intonation, through 3D facial modeling [11], modeling refinement, capturing and generating character movements and expressions, and synthesizing audio and video for display and interaction [12]; enabling digital humans to attract audience attention [13] better, promote emotional resonance, make information easier to understand and remember, and achieve the best effect of disseminating historical and cultural information [14]. To this end, we conducted preliminary experiments by constructing digital humans that can be applied in cultural communication, building interactive digital human systems, designing experiments, and using questionnaire surveys to study in depth the effects of digital human interaction systems in cultural communication [14], in order to better improve the design and application direction of digital humans. In addition, the experiment further explores the audience's preference, acceptance, and learning effect of the digital human interaction system and studies the differences in the performance of the learning effect of the digital human interaction system under different communication scenarios so as to design a digital human image, interaction methods, and cultural communication scenarios that are more in line with the audience's needs, and improve the effect and influence of the digital human interaction system in cultural communication. The application of digital human technology not only provides new media and expressions but also can change the pattern of the traditional cultural communication industry. Through the use of digital human technology, the public can partake in more personalized and immersive cultural content, thus facilitating the spreading of historical and cultural knowledge. This paves the way for new possibilities in the development of cultural content dissemination.

2 Method

To better apply the digital person in cultural communication, we constructed a digital person that can be used in cultural communication. This digital human needs to have good interactivity and emotional expression ability, have a real and natural dialogue with the user and disseminate cultural content in multiple ways. We built an experimental system for producing the videos needed for the experiment and designed an experiment to verify the effectiveness of digital humans in historical and cultural communication.

In the experiment, we selected and produced three videos with representative cultural content that communicated different cultural contents and three forms. Then, we gave these videos to the subjects to watch and recorded the accuracy of the subjects' access to the information and their personal experiences and feelings in different forms.

2.1 Experimental System Design

2.1.1 Overall Design

This system mainly uses Unreal Engine, including MetaHuman, blueprint editing, level sequence editing, other operations, Avatar SDK, and Microsoft Azure build function modules. The overall design of the experimental system includes two modules; the first is the digital human image design, and then the system function module design.

2.1.2 Digital Human Identity Design

With the help of Avatar SDK, we used the frontal photo of a single person to generate a basic bald model, then imported the basic bald model into Unreal Engine and used the Metahuman plugin to perform a series of operations, such as tracking the active frames, ontology solving, mesh body binding, and so on, on this model. Then, in Quixel Bridge's Metahuman Creator, the model generated in the previous step was adjusted, including adding hair, modifying skin color, fine-tuning bones, and other operations, which made the generated digital human closer to the original image of the real person (Figs. 1 and 2).

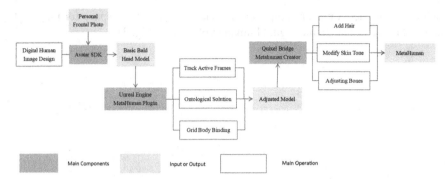

Fig. 1. Framework diagram for the design of the digital person

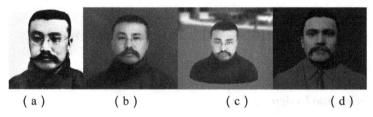

(a)   (b)   (c)   (d)

Fig. 2. (a) the front photo imported into Avatar SDK; (b) the basic model processed by Avatar SDK; (c) the model processed by Unreal Engine MetaHuman plugin; (d) the final model processed by Quixel Bridge MetaHuman Creator.

2.1.3 System Function Module Design

The system of this experiment mainly contains two functional modules: text-to-speech and lip-sync animation generation and video and animation playback.

In the text-to-speech and lip-sync animation generation module, we designed a user interface control in the Unreal Engine. The user can input text through the text box in the interface, which is processed by the control in the blueprint of the level, and accesses the voice service of Microsoft Azure. The blueprint control transmits the text entered by the user in the text box to Microsoft Azure, gets the corresponding speech audio assets generated according to the text content, and delivers them to the Unreal Engine to generate the corresponding digital human lip-sync animation with the help of the relevant blueprint control of the MetaHuman SDK, and realizes letting the digital human speak.

In the video and animation playback function module, the digital human action animation design is carried out first, and then the animation is created through the level sequence. We imported some action assets to create a digital human action animation. Through the IK redirection of Unreal Engine, these actions used for Mannequins, a third-person character of Unreal Engine, were redirected and processed to generate action assets that can be used for MetaHuman. After that, a level sequence is created, and the actor blueprint of MetaHuman in the level is added to the level sequence. The motion animation played by the digital human is designed based on the video content.

In addition, the media player component is placed in the virtual space for playing the video and audio to realize the digital human explanation (Fig. 3).

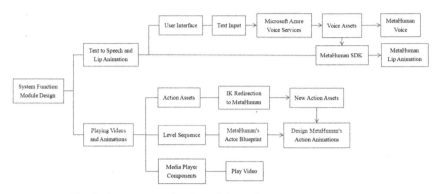

Fig. 3. System Functional Module Design Framework Diagram

2.2 Experimental Design

This experiment centers on the theme of historical and cultural communication of digital people and creates a digital human interpreter who chooses representative content in Chinese history to explain.

Considering that historical and cultural content contains multiple types, we chose three types of video subjects: historical figures, historical events, and historical buildings. For every kind of video subject matter, three different forms of videos were produced: traditional audio-visual, half-body digital human oral explanation video, and full-body digital human body language explanation video.

In addition, for the role and effect played by digital people in historical and cultural communication studied in this experiment, we used questionnaires and analysis to analyze the volunteers' objective performance and subjective feelings. Therefore, we designed two questionnaires: a multiple-choice questionnaire for the content of the video and a questionnaire for the individual's subjective evaluation of different forms of video.

Through the questionnaire survey and analysis, we compare the vividness, effectiveness, and interestingness of different forms of videos for historical and cultural communication and study the role played by digital people in historical and cultural communication. At the same time, we compare the effectiveness of digital human explanations in different topics. It explores the application scenarios in which digital people are more effective in communicating history and culture.

2.2.1 Video Theme

- **Historical Figures**

The historical figure chosen to be introduced in this experiment is Chen Duxiu, which is mainly about the content of Chen Duxiu's life. Chen Duxiu was one of the principal founders of the Communist Party of China. He founded the Youth Magazine, later known as New Youth, in September 1915 in Shanghai and advocated socialist ideology in the magazine, which had a far-reaching influence on the history of Chinese thought.

- **Historical Events**

The historical event chosen to be introduced in this experiment is the New Culture Movement, an ideological liberation movement against feudalism initiated by some advanced intellectuals in China at the beginning of the 20th century, advocating democracy and science. It is an unprecedented ideological liberation movement in China's modern history.

- **Historical Locations**

The historical location chosen to be introduced in this experiment is the Forbidden City, a royal palace in China during the Ming and Qing dynasties, which contains profound history and culture and is one of the largest and most well-preserved groups of ancient wooden structures in the world.

2.2.2 Video Format

- **Traditional Audiovisual Presentation**

Traditional audio-visual explanation refers to the video material shot by the shooting, voice-over explanation, and background music after editing and processing the video. Nowadays, it is a widely used form of video, applied to current affairs news, cultural communication, and other fields (Fig. 4).

Fig. 4. Experimental use of traditional audiovisuals in the category of historical figures

- **Half-Body Digital Dictation Explained**

The half-body digital human oral explanation is processed based on the traditional video and audio explanation. We utilized the text-to-speech function module of the system to input the text from the video to generate the audio of the digital human's speech and the mouth animation. Then, we used Ultimate Vocal Remover 5 to separate the human voice from the background dubbing of the original video audio, and superimposed the digital human's speech audio with the original video background dubbing, and combined it with the original video with the audio removed to generate a new video. Compared to the original video, the new video replaced only the narrator's voice audio, controlling for the audio variable in the narrated video viewed by volunteers. We created a half-body digital narrator video in which a digital person appeared in the video frame and described the content of the video with the same textual content as in the original video (Fig. 5).

(a)   (b)

Fig. 5. (a) Text-to-speech and lip-sync animation generation built for the experiment, (b) Experimentally used historical event-based half-body digital talking heads explainer video.

- **Full Body Digitizer Body Language Explained**

The full-body digital human body language explanation is based on the digital human oral explanation with the addition of digital human movements. We built a virtual space in the Unreal Engine and set up a widget in the area for playing the video. At the same time, we processed the video, again utilizing Ultimate Vocal Remover 5 to separate the human voice from the background voiceover of the video audio, removing the lecture voice audio of the original video and adding the lecture voice audio of the digital person. In addition, we imported action assets. It used IK redirection to generate action assets applicable to the digital person, which were used to enrich the body movements of the digital person during the explanation and increase the vividness and interestingness of the digital person. We establish level sequences and design the digital person's explanation actions through the level sequences to realize that the digital person explains on the side when the video is playing and simultaneously has specific actions (Fig. 6).

2.2.3 Questionnaire Design

We designed a questionnaire for each of the three video content topics, and each video topic was created with five single-choice questions from the explanatory videos. Each questionnaire question was designed with four options, and each question had only one correct answer. Through this questionnaire, we can obtain the degree of mastery of the video content as reflected by the objective performance of the volunteers after watching the explanatory videos, thus analyzing, to a certain extent, the effectiveness of the different video formats for disseminating history and culture.

We designed a questionnaire for individual subjective evaluation of different forms of video, with three parts, including volunteers' assessment of the video's vividness,

Fig. 6. Experimentally used full-body digital human body language explanation video for historical figures class

effectiveness, and interestingness. The questionnaire is divided into five levels with a total score of five, and the response options are from "1" (totally disagree) to "5" (totally agree), with the higher score representing the better the individual thinks the video's vividness, effectiveness, and interestingness are. Through this questionnaire, we can get the volunteers' subjective feelings about each type of video.

2.3   Experimental Procedure

The volunteers in this experiment were all current college students, totaling 30, aged between 18 and 25.

This experiment is divided into two stages; each stage is divided into two steps: watching the video and filling out the questionnaire.

The volunteers will be divided into groups A, B, and C in the first phase. Each group of subjects will watch the same video on three topics: group A will watch the traditional audio-visual explanation, group B will watch the half-body digital human oral explanation, and group C will watch the full-body digital human body language explanation. Each group of volunteers was required to watch three types of videos: historical figures, historical events, and historical places, and each volunteer was needed to fill out a questionnaire related to the content of the video after watching one type of video, with a total of three questionnaires to be filled out.

In the second stage, the volunteers were divided into three groups: historical figures, historical events, and historical locations. Each experimenter should watch the three forms of explanatory videos in their group and fill out a questionnaire about the level of personal interest in different video forms. Volunteers were required to rate the vividness, effectiveness, and interest of the three forms of video based on their subjective evaluations (Fig. 7).

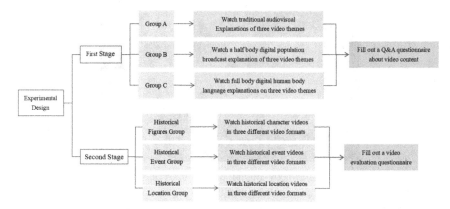

Fig. 7. Experimental process framework diagram

3   Results and Discussion

The questionnaire designed for this experiment was divided into two parts; the first part was some tests about the content of the video, and the second part was about the subjects' personal feelings about watching different video forms.

3.1   Objective Performance Analysis

We obtained and analyzed three groups of score samples, A, B, and C, to test the subjects' mastery of the knowledge in the video, to study the differences in the effect of knowledge dissemination of different forms of explanation video on the viewers, and also to compare the effect of information dissemination of the three video topics explained by digital people.

3.1.1   Definition and Description of Indicators

In this study, the three objective questionnaires answered by the subjects after watching the three kinds of historical material explanation videos were quantified according to the number of correct answers into three indicators reflecting the effectiveness of the video explanations, i.e., the efficacy of the explanation in the character category, the effectiveness of the explanation in the event category, and the effectiveness of the explanation in the location category.

3.1.2   Normality Test

As seen from the above figure, the three indicators summarized in the objective tests do not conform to normality (significance less than 0.05), so next, we will use a non-parametric test form to analyze the effect of the three groups of video lectures (Table 1).

Table 1. Normality Test

	Group	Kolmogorov Smirnov (V)[a]			Shapiro Wilke		
		Statisticians	Degrees of Freedom	Significance	Statisticians	Degrees of Freedom	Significance
Character	A	.396	9	**.000**	.684	9	**.001**
	B	.305	10	**.009**	.781	10	**.008**
	C	.232	11	.100	.822	11	**.018**
Event	A	.269	9	.059	.808	9	**.025**
	B	.286	10	**.020**	.885	10	.149
	C	.310	11	**.004**	.866	11	.069
Location	A	.244	9	.130	.864	9	.106
	B	.300	10	**.011**	.815	10	**.022**
	C	.332	11	**.001**	.756	11	**.002**

[a]**Ricci's Significance Correction.**

3.1.3 Nonparametric Test

For the grouping variable "group," the values 1, 2, and 3 represent the video type groups a, b, and c, respectively (Tables 2 and 3).

Table 2. Score Ranking

	Group	Number of Cases	Ordinal Mean
Character	1	9	7.56
	2	10	15.50
	3	11	22.00
	Total	30	
Event	1	9	9.50
	2	10	15.75
	3	11	20.18
	Total	30	
Location	1	9	10.78
	2	10	14.70
	3	11	20.09
	Total	30	

Table 3. Test Statistics, b

	Character	Event	Location
Kruskal Wallis H(K)	14.521	8.031	6.809
Degrees of Freedom	2	2	2
Asymptotic Significance	**.001**	**.018**	**.033**

[a]Kruskal-Wallis Test.
[b]Grouping Variables: Group.

From the asymptotic significance and the rank mean, it can be seen that there is a significant difference in the effectiveness of the three types of explanatory videos in terms of the three indicators of "character," "event," and "location". There is a significant difference in the effectiveness of the three types of explanation videos: in general, the effectiveness of Group C (full-body digital human body language explanation) is better than that of Group B (half-body digital human oral explanation) and better than that of Group A (traditional audio-video explanation).

On this basis, the video subject matter is categorized, and the video incorporating the intelligent digital human explanation form has the best performance in conveying the information and data about the life of the relevant historical figures; the explanation of the relevant historical events has the second best effect, and the explanation of the monuments and attractions that have no apparent connection with the image of the digital human has a slightly poorer effect.

3.1.4 Descriptive Statistics

Descriptive statistics regarding the number of objective questions answered correctly for the three categories of subjects are shown in the table below (Figs. 8, 9, 10 and Table 4).

Table 4. Descriptive Statistics

	N	Minimum Value	Maximum Value	Average Value	Standard Deviation
Character	30	2	5	3.40	1.003
Event	30	1	5	2.80	.997
Location	30	0	5	3.03	.928
The Effective Number of Cases (in columns)	30				

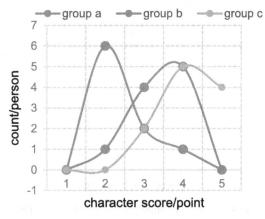

Fig. 8. Number of correct objective questions in three different forms of explanation videos in the category of historical figures (1 to 5)

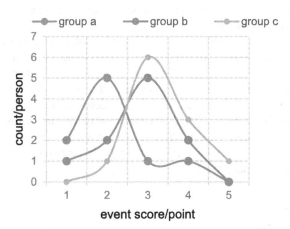

Fig. 9. Number of correct objective questions of three different forms of explanation videos in the category of historical events (1– 5)

3.2 Subjective Perception Analysis

We analyzed the three sets of subjective evaluation questionnaires obtained in the categories of historical figures, historical events, and historical places to study the subjective feelings of each group of subjects towards the three video forms: traditional audio-visual video, half-body digital person oral explanation video, and full-body digital person body language explanation video.

3.2.1 Definition and Description of Indicators

In addition to measuring the degree of effective explanation of each video form with the indicator of the correct rate of objective questions, this study also defines three indicators

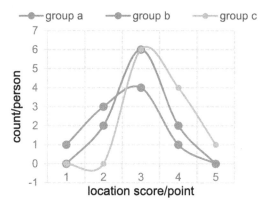

Fig. 10. Number of correct objective questions (1–5) for three different forms of explanation videos in the historical locations category

of vividness, effectiveness, and interest from the perspective of subjects' viewpoints to collect subjects' subjective opinions.

Vividness, i.e., whether the video explains the content of historical materials in a specific way; effectiveness, i.e., whether the video conveys the information points efficiently and leaves a deep impression; and interest, i.e., whether the subjects feel interested and willing to learn more in the process of watching the video.

In this study, each index was quantified as a subjective score (1–5), with A1, B1, and C1 representing the subjective scores of the vividness of the three forms of explanation; A2, B2, and C2 representing the subjective scores of the effectiveness of the three forms of explanation; and A3, B3, and C3 representing the subjective scores of the interest of the three forms of explanation.

3.2.2 Vividness

● Nonparametric Test

Table 5. Vividness Ranking

	Ordinal Mean
A1	1.08
B1	2.07
C1	2.85

From the asymptotic significance and rank mean, it can be seen that there is a significant difference in the subjective perception brought by different forms of explanation videos to the subjects in terms of the vividness index (Fig. 11 and Tables 5, 6).

Table 6. Test Statistics

Number of Cases	30
Chi-Square	51.761
Degrees of Freedom	2
Asymptotic Significance	**.000**

[a]Freedman's Test.

- Descriptive Statistics

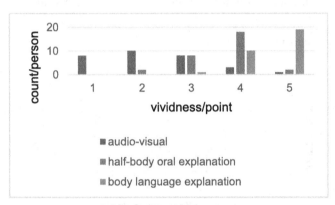

Fig. 11. Clustered bar graphs of subjects' subjective scores for the three types of explanation videos on the metric of vividness (for explanation types 1, 2, and 3 represent video type groups A, B, and C, respectively)

3.2.3 Effectiveness

- Nonparametric Test

Table 7. Effectiveness Ranking

	Ordinal Mean
A2	1.40
B2	2.15
C2	2.45

Table 8. Test Statistics

Number of Cases	30
Chi-Square	22.891
Degrees of Freedom	2
Asymptotic Significance	**.000**

[a]Freedman's Test.

From the asymptotic significance and the rank mean, it can be seen that there is a significant difference in the subjective perception brought by different forms of explanation videos to the subjects in terms of the effectiveness index (Fig. 12 and Tables 7, 8).

- Descriptive Statistics

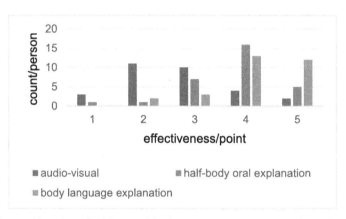

Fig. 12. Clustered bar chart of subjects' subjective scores on the indicator of validity for the three forms of explanation videos

3.2.4 Interest

- Nonparametric Test

From the asymptotic significance and rank mean, it can be seen that there is a significant difference in the subjective perception brought by different forms of explanation videos to the subjects in terms of the interest index (Fig. 13 and Tables 9, 10).

- Descriptive Statistics

Table 9. Interest Ranking

	Ordinal Mean
A3	1.13
B3	2.17
C3	2.70

Table 10. Test Statistics

Number of Cases	30
Chi-Square	43.923
Degrees of Freedom	2
Asymptotic Significance	**.000**

[a]Freedman's Test.

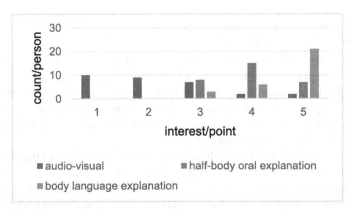

Fig. 13. Clustered bar chart of subjects' subjective scores on the indicator of validity for the three forms of explanation videos

3.3 Discussion

3.3.1 Objective Performance

Research has shown that digital human interpretation has advantages over traditional forms of cultural communication regarding the effect of objective information. One of the reasons for this may be those traditional forms of cultural communication, such as books, lectures, videos, etc., are usually one-way information transfer, making it difficult for learners to interact with them and get timely personalized feedback. In contrast, digital human explanations realize two-way communication with learners through intelligent technology. They can be personalized according to the actual situation of learners and focus on the key to better meet the needs of learners. This point has also been proved in the previous research: the digital human "virtual teacher" can not only realize the essential anthropomorphic teaching function, but at the same time, it has the corresponding anthropomorphic appearance, anthropomorphic expression, human performance ability, personalized voice, and other characteristics. In the teaching process, students can fully experience the personalized features of the digital human "virtual teacher" through communication and interaction with the digital human "virtual teacher" [17].

In addition, the digital human explanation can be combined with a variety of media forms, such as text, pictures, audio, video, etc., to present a more vivid, intuitive teaching content, simulating the experience of face-to-face communication with real people, which is conducive to improving the learners' understanding of the information and memory. The traditional form of cultural communication is often limited to a particular form of media, unable to achieve the integration of multimedia presentation, and lacks flexible learning mechanisms.

Therefore, compared to traditional forms of cultural communication, digital human interpretation has more substantial interactivity, multimedia integration, and vividness in the objective information communication effect, which can better meet the learners' individualized learning needs and improve the impact of information and cultural communication.

3.3.2 Subjective Perception

Subjects generally agreed that there is a significant difference in the perception of the three types of explanation videos: Group C (full-body digital human body language explanation) is better than Group B (half-body digital human oral explanation) and better than Group A (traditional audio-video explanation), especially in the comparison of vividness and interest, the video with the addition of the digital human form of explanation has achieved an absolute advantage.

From the above findings, it is not difficult to find that the majority of the experimental subjects were more favorable to the explanations with the addition of digital people, which is most likely related to the human perception of the self in the gaze of the projected image. Some studies have shown that the digital human image breaks through the relationship between the original and the facsimile in traditional images, breaks the separation between visual experience and image reproduction, and promotes the coherence of vision and appearance. The natural person and the digital person view and interact with each other, the image presentation and the viewer's psychological mapping are intertwined, and the self-reference of the digital person's image is transformed into an interpretive field open to the real world in mixed media. The digital human image intervenes in real life through the rapid development of digital technology, and the visual appearance of digital humans becomes one of the ways of knowledge production and transmission, emotional construction, and communication in the mutual gaze with natural people [18].

This means that the digital human explanation using artificial intelligence technology can not only realize the interactive communication with the viewer, making the learning process more participatory and interactive and based on its homogeneity with the viewer's image, to a certain extent, it can also more effectively stimulate the viewer's interest and motivation in learning.

3.3.3 Summary

Digital human application is a new technical tool that can utilize various intelligent technologies to present digitized characters in the real world. The emergence of digital people applications brings new possibilities for cultural communication, which can visualize cultural elements to users by replicating historical figures, traditional cultural symbols, or artistic images, thus promoting the inheritance and dissemination of culture.

First, digital people applications can make users feel the cultural elements more intuitively through lifelike digital character images. For example, the digital person application can reproduce significant figures in history, the scenes of traditional festivals, the characters in literary works, etc., so that the user can immerse in the charm of culture, which is of great significance for the dissemination of cultural knowledge and enhancement of cultural identity.

Secondly, the digital person application can also enhance the user's sense of participation and experience of culture through interactive experience. Users can have dialogues and interactions with virtual characters through digital people applications and even participate in virtual cultural scenes. This kind of participatory experience helps stimulate users' interest in culture and promotes the dissemination and exchange of culture.

In addition, the application of digital humans can also provide a cultural experience that meets the user's needs through personalized customization. Users can customize their favorite cultural experiences according to their interests and conditions, such as customizing the image of their digital historical figures and participating in virtual cultural activities, etc. This personalized customization helps to make cultural communication closer to users' lives and needs.

4 Conclusion

The experimental design and implementation in this study can provide some evidence for the positive impact of digital people on cultural communication. The addition of digital humans can stimulate the audience's interest in learning cultural knowledge and enhance the efficiency and effectiveness of cultural communication to a certain extent. On top of that, the vivid body language and very realistic facial simulation of the digital human can further promote interaction with the audience and obtain positive feedback compared with simple digital oral teaching.

In summary, as a new cultural communication tool, the digital human application is essential in promoting. It can stimulate the inheritance and dissemination of culture through intuitive display, interactive experience, and personalized customization and inject new vitality into the development of the cultural industry. However, there are still some problems and challenges in applying digital human interactive systems in cultural communication. In the process of application, whether the cultural image shown by the digital human application is accurate and real, and whether it respects the facts for the dissemination of culture, the degree of realism of the digital human, the ability of emotional expression, etc. The cost of the interactive system is higher, and more investment and technical support are needed, which are all issues that need further research and exploration.

References

1. Song, Y., Zhang, W., Chen, Z., Jiang, Y.: A survey on talking head generation. J. Comput. Aided Des. Comput. Graph.
2. Wang, K., et al.: MEAD: a large-scale audio-visual dataset for emotional talking-face generation. In: Vedaldi, A., Bischof, H., Brox, T., Frahm, J.M. (eds.) ECCV 2020. LNCS, vol. 12366, pp. 700–717. Springer, Cham (2020). https://doi.org/10.1007/978-3-030-58589-1_42
3. Korban, M., Li, X.: A survey on applications of digital human avatars toward virtual co-presence. arXiv preprint arXiv:2201.04168 (2022)
4. Chen, L., Maddox, R.K., Duan, Z., et al.: Hierarchical cross-modal talking face generation with dynamic pixel-wise loss. In: Proceedings of the IEEE/CVF Conference on Computer Vision and Pattern Recognition (2019)
5. Prajwal, K.R., Mukhopadhyay, R., Namboodiri, V.P., et al.: A lip sync expert is all you need for speech to lip generation in the wild. In: Proceedings of the 28th ACM International Conference on Multimedia, pp. 484–492 (2020)
6. Lahiri, A., Kwatra, V., Frueh, C., et al.: LipSync3D: data efficient learning of personalized 3D talking faces from video using pose and lighting normalization. In: Proceedings of the IEEE/CVF Conference on Computer Vision and Pattern Recognition, pp. 2755–2764 (2021)
7. Min, D., Song, M., Hwang, S.J.: Style Talker: One-shot Style-based Audio-driven Talking Head Video Generation. arXiv preprint arXiv:2208.10922 (2022)
8. Huynh-Thu, Q., Ghanbari, M.: Scope of validity of PSNR in image/video quality assessment. Electron. Lett. **44**(13), 800–801 (2008)
9. Shen, S., Li, W., Zhu, Z., Duan, Y., Zhou, J., Lu, J.: Learning dynamic facial radiance fields for few-shot talking head synthesis. In: Avidan, S., Brostow, G., Cissé, M., Farinella, G.M., Hassner, T. (eds.) ECCV 2022. LNCS, Part XII, vol. 13672, pp. 666–682. Springer, Cham (2022). https://doi.org/10.1007/978-3-031-19775-8_39
10. Zhu, X., Lei, Z., Liu, X., et al.: Face alignment across large poses: a 3D solution. In: Proceedings of the IEEE Conference on Computer Vision and Pattern Recognition, pp. 146–155 (2016)
11. Isola, P., Zhu, J.Y., Zhou, T., et al.: Image-to-image translation with conditional adversarial networks. In: Proceedings of the IEEE Conference on Computer Vision and Pattern Recognition, pp. 1125–1134 (2017)
12. Tzaban, R., Mokady, R., Gal, R., et al.: Stitch it in time: GAN-based facial editing of real videos. In: SIGGRAPH Asia 2022 Conference Papers, pp. 1–9 (2022)
13. Chen, L., Cui, G., Kou, Z., et al.: What comprises an excellent talking-head video generation? In: IEEE/CVF Conference on Computer Vision and Pattern Recognition Workshops (2020)
14. Cooke, M., Barker, J., Cunningham, S., et al.: An audio-visual corpus for speech perception and automatic speech recognition. J. Acoust. Soc. Am. **120**(5), 2421–2424 (2006)
15. Lahiri, A., Kwatra, V., Frueh, C., et al.: LipSync3D: data-efficient learning of personalized 3D talking faces from video using pose and lighting normalization. In: Proceedings of the IEEE/CVF Conference on Computer Vision and Pattern Recognition, pp. 2755–2764 (2021)
16. Devi, B., Preetha, M.M.S.J.: A descriptive survey on face emotion recognition techniques. Int. J. Image Graph., 2350008 (2021)
17. Lu, Q.: Application and practice of digital human technology in professional teaching. J. Yichun Coll. **45**(05), 121–125 (2023)
18. Wang, Y., Liang, X.: Virtual subjectivity and virtual materiality: on the image of digital people. J. Fujian Norm. Univ. (Philos. Soc. Sci. Ed.) (05), 49–58+170 (2022)
19. Yu, G., Wang, W., Feng, F., Xiu, L.: A review of the dissemination effect of synthesized speech news - EEG evidence on the effect of speech rate. Int. Journal. **43**(02), 6–26 (2021). https://doi.org/10.13495/j.cnki.cjjc.2021.02.001

20. Zhao, G., Tian, L.: The game of technology and art: reconfiguring the function of the host in the context of artificial intelligence. Contemp. Telev. (10), 93–96 (2019)
21. Jing, Z.: AI synthesized anchor: "crisis" and "opportunity" in broadcast hosting industry. Audiov. World (04), 111–113 (2021). https://doi.org/10.13994/j.cnki.stj.2021.04.030
22. Li, Y.: Discussion on the development trend of integration of AI virtual anchor and traditional broadcast hosting in the era of artificial intelligence. Southeast Commun. (10), 144–146 (2023). https://doi.org/10.13556/j.cnki.dncb.cn35-1274/j.2023.10.031
23. Yu, G., Han, T.: Measurement of users' memory effects in communication cognition: a research framework and technical route. Publ. Distrib. Res. (02), 56–61 (2019). https://doi.org/10.19393/j.cnki.cn11-1537/g2.2019.02.013
24. Tian, Y., Qi, G., Huang, X., Xiang, H., Wang, Y.: Cognitive neural mechanisms of social cues for online learning. Res. Electrochem. Educ. **42**(02), 63–69 (2021). https://doi.org/10.13811/j.cnki.eer.2021.02.009

Metaverse and Virtual Reality

EHA3D: Expressive Head Avatar via Disentangled Latent Code

Jiayu Zhou and Xiaoqiang Zhu[✉]

School of Communication and Information Engineering, Shanghai University,
Shanghai 200444, China
xqzhu@shu.edu.cn

Abstract. Current NeRF-based head avatars typically use either explicit mesh representations based on head templates or implicit expressive coefficients derived from head templates as driving signals. Although these approaches have achieved promising results, they often depend on robust tracking systems, complex head template representations, long optimization times, and suffer from limited generalization abilities. In this work, we propose a novel method for driving expressive neural head avatar using disentangled latent code to address these issues. Our approach involves two key steps. We perform an EG3D inversion, where we disentangle the expression code from the base latent code, utilizing a supervised method based on contrastive learning and optical flow field supervision. To address differences in latent encoding distributions across different identity domains, we introduce the residual emotional enhancement in the subsequent stage to enhance similarity between driving and target frame expressions. With these designs, we successfully overcome tracking and complex head template issues. Moreover, the encoder-decoder structure of our pipeline demonstrates strong generalization performance, allowing for real-time and expressive reenactment across individuals of differing identities after training. Our method has achieved favorable visual results in qualitative experiments and demonstrates performance comparable to other state-of-the-art methods in quantitative metrics.

Keywords: GAN Inversion · Neural Avatars · Volume Rendering

1 Introduction

The digitization of human faces is a crucial aspect of visual communication, and its 3D modeling has numerous applications in media production, virtual and augmented reality, as well as visual effects. For a long time, the development of high-quality, controllable 3D digital avatars has been a challenging research problem. In recent years, various solutions have made significant progress in this field. Early work focused on creating static textured facial models with monocular RGB cameras. With the emergence of neural radiance fields, methods based

© The Author(s), under exclusive license to Springer Nature Singapore Pte Ltd. 2024
G. Zhai et al. (Eds.): IFTC 2023, CCIS 2066, pp. 243–257, 2024.
https://doi.org/10.1007/978-981-97-3623-2_18

on volumetric rendering techniques have also made significant advancements, more recent work have learned highly realistic models that can be rendered from any angle (Fig. 1).

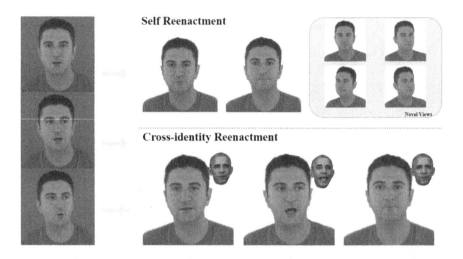

Fig. 1. Some results of our work. Given a monocular video input, our method excels in synthesizing expressive, high-fidelity, and view-consistent head avatars. Moreover, it can achieve effective facial expression reenactment.

Methods for generating human head avatars can generally be classified into two categories. The first utilizes explicit facial template meshes [7,10], while the second relies on neural implicit representations that are conditioned on various inputs [11,22]. Mesh-based approaches tend to be faster than those based on implicit coefficients, but their expressive capacity is limited by the number of vertices in the linear expressive skeleton. Some attempts have been made to enhance their expressive capacity by increasing the number of vertices, but this poses challenges when trying to achieve harmony between blend shape coefficients and the expanded skeleton, ultimately leading to suboptimal results. Moreover, the optimization process for these added vertices introduces significant computational cost. On the other hand, neural implicit representations deviate from the explicit mesh representation and, with the emergence of newer approaches such as NeRF [12], produce avatars with better multi-view continuity. These methods utilize facial key information, such as expressions, identity, and pose, as conditioning inputs for their multilayer perceptron, which generates a view-consistent 3D-aware avatar through a volume renderer. However, these methods encounter four key challenges: 1) heavy reliance on accurate tracking, as misalignment can result in inferior results 2) limited decoupling of input conditioning, which makes it challenging to fully leverage the network's design and control aspects such as identity and expressions during the final reenactment 3) long training periods and poor generalization, often requiring extensive training for a specific identity and still not ensuring generalization to other identities and 4) incompatibility with mainstream graphics processing pipelines, making it challenging to integrate these methods into specific industrial applications. These limitations hinder the application of both methods in various relevant domains.

Considering the issues mentioned above, we introduce EHA3D, a 3D-aware avatar with realistic emotional expression capability. The key idea in our approach is to thoroughly explore the latent space of EG3D and separate crucial expression latent codes as driving signals. Specifically, we initiate the disentangled face inversion process. Here, we creatively isolate the expression latent code from the global latent code. To ensure the independence of these two latent codes, we employ a contrastive learning method guided by optical flow field. By this step, we obtain the expression encoding corresponding to the input face image and the base encoding containing the rest of the facial information. Furthermore, to make the high-frequency details of facial expressions more realistic, we utilize a residual expression network to enhance the output tri-plane features, ensuring the precision of avatar expression portrayal.

Compared to prior work, our approach overcomes several limitations, including high computational costs, template dependency, limited expressive capacity, and poor disentanglement. We have also made significant improvements in terms of generalization. The first step is fundamentally based on an encoder-decoder structure, which, after training with a sufficient amount of data, ensures good generalization. This step keeps the weights frozen after training. The second step involves enhancing tri-plane features based on expressions from two different identity domains. While this part might not guarantee excellent generalization on its own, subsequent experiments have shown that only a few rounds of fine-tuning are needed to achieve good results. As a result, our method can rapidly generate avatars with distinct identities and expressions in a short amount of time. In summary, our contributions can be summarized as follows:

- We introduce EHA3D, a 3D-aware avatar driven by disentangled expression latent codes. To ensure effective decoupling of expression encodings, we propose an efficient contrastive learning approach.
- We creatively design a residual tri-plane feature enhancement network based on expression differences, which bridges the gap between different identity-expression domains, resulting in more realistic driving results.
- By following our training approach, better generalization performance and faster training speed can be achieved.

2   Related Work

In this section, we present a comprehensive review of the works relevant to this paper, with a particular emphasis on clarifying their interrelations and differentiations. This section reviews prior work on gan inversion and photorealistic human head avatar generation.

2.1   GAN Inversion

GAN inversion refers to the process of reversing image generation by projecting it back to its corresponding latent code. This technique facilitates precise reconstruction and simplifies semantic editing of latent codes, streamlining image editing. In the realm of 2D GAN, three distinct categories of GAN inversion exist. The challenges involved in 3D GAN inversion pose significant challenges, as direct use of 2D technique cannot guarantee 3D consistency. Optimization-based methodologies, such as HFGI3D [19], have been proposed to employ mesh guidance to yield more plausible outcomes. Encoder-based techniques leverage robust priors from the FLAME facial model and semantic segmentation to improve inversion quality and allow for enhanced control over facial features. Additionally, techniques like EG3DE [20] utilize an encoder to produce detailed textures. In conclusion, the inherent complexities of GAN inversion necessitate the use of specialized techniques. Although different methodologies have been developed to enhance efficiency, achieving satisfactory results remains a challenging pursuit.

2.2   Head Avatar

The task of reconstructing 3D head avatars from monocular videos is a challenging one that has received widespread attention in recent years. The conventional method involves constructing mesh-based head avatars using morphable face templates that have been tracked in training portrait videos, as demonstrated in publications such as [2,5]. However, these approaches face limitations in dealing with highly non-rigid content, such as hair, gaze, and teeth.

Researchers have therefore turned to more flexible representations, including neural implicit fields as proposed by [13] to overcome these limitations. IMavatar [22] is one such model that learns head avatars with implicit geometry and texture models, which eliminates the limitations associated with mesh templates' topology. With the emergence of neural radiance fields [12], several recent studies have explored leveraging their rendering power for neural head modeling.

Nonetheless, the majority of the aforementioned solutions depend on tracked facial models, utilizing the expression coefficients of such models as a driver for avatar animation. Nevertheless, there remains a necessity for techniques that can effectively handle significantly non-rigid content in head avatar reconstruction while additionally elevating the quality of texture.

3   Method

3.1   Preliminary

To establish a solid foundational understanding for this article, we commence with an introductory overview of the workflow involved in EG3D. Following this, we will explore the latent space of 3DGAN in greater depth.

EG3D. The EG3D technique [3] utilizes a tri-plane representation approach to transform 2D images into 3D geometric perception representations. This methodology enhances the latent code mapping strategy of StyleGAN [8] by integrating a random Gaussian noise vector z with a pose-conditioning vector p. These vectors are then fed into the mapping network to generate a latent code W, as denoted by the following equation:

$$W = \mathrm{MappingNetwork}(z, p) \qquad (1)$$

The latent code W, obtained from the input, is then fed into the StyleGAN2 generator [9]. This produces a feature map of dimensions $H \times W \times 96$. The 96-channel feature map is segmented into three $H \times W \times 32$ feature maps, each representing the three orthogonal planes (F_{xy}, F_{xz}, F_{yz}) of the object being generated. EG3D employs bilinear interpolation to obtain feature vectors along each view direction, guided by the aforementioned orthogonal planes. These feature vectors are then decoded using a volume renderer [12], which generates multi-view images with consistent geometry. Finally, the generated images undergo refinement through a super-resolution module to improve their quality.

Latent Space of 3DGAN. The latent space of 3DGAN exhibits similarities with that of 2D StyleGAN, featuring transformations across multiple latent spaces. Initially, the primary latent space Z follows a normal distribution. Subsequently, a random noise vector z is transformed through a series of fully connected layers into the subsequent latent space W, as described in StyleGAN [8]. Affine transformations denoted as $A(\cdot)$ project the W space into another latent space named as StyleSpace [14]. Notably, while the affine transformations differ in each layer, the latent code w remains consistent across the layers. A few studies [1,16,17] have demonstrated that utilizing distinct W encodings for each layer can enhance the quality of generated images. This approach leads to a new space, $W+$, which improves generation quality while preserving editability [21].

3.2 Disentangled Face Inversion

In this section, we provide a brief overview of the hybrid 3DGAN inversion framework and elaborate on our design principles. As illustrated in Fig. 2, our architecture adopts an encoder-decoder paradigm, with a pre-trained EG3D generator G as the decoder. The encoder consists of two principal branches, namely, the base encoding E_{base} and the facial expression encoder E_{expr}. The input image undergoes an encoding process via these two encoders, producing two distinct encodings: W_{base}, SS_{expr}. Respectively, these encodings represent the fundamental identity features and expression featureas demonstrated by the following equations:

$$I = G(W_{base} + SS_{expr}) \qquad (2)$$

The 18-dimensional feature representation of W_{base} effectively captures the fundamental facial characteristics, which is a firmly established observation in

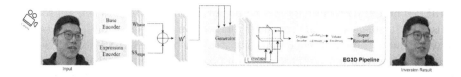

Fig. 2. Overview of disentangled face inversion. Given a portrait video, we first encode the single frame to the latent code W_{base} and SS_{expr}, which results in an RGB image.

the current literature [16, 18]. We examine these features in the $W+$ space, which has a proven track record in precisely capturing low-frequency facial attributes, including identity. Our encoding architecture has a structure identical to the DECA [5] structure, which comprises a ResNet-50 [6] model within E_{base}.

To creative a expressive neural head avatars, the depiction of facial expressions stands as a critical aspect. Hence, extracting latent codes of expressions holds significant importance. We use SS_{expr} to represent an individual's unique facial expression features, which are analyzed in the StyleSpace. This space allows for clearer separation of expressions, while avoiding potential jittering artifacts that may arise during high-resolution feature layer editing. For W_{expr}, a PSP encoder is employed, refining the pyramid structure to distribute features proportionately in a 5:3:2 ratio.

3.3   Contrastive Supervise

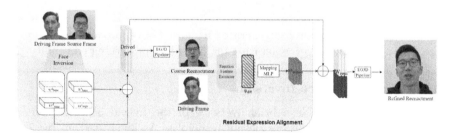

Fig. 3. Illustration of residual expression alignment module. In this module, the SS_{expr} of driving frame combined with the W_{base} is fed into the EG3D pipeline and firstly get the coarse reenactment result. To eliminate the emotion difference between the coarse result and the driving frame, mapping MLP is used to generate $SS_{aligned}$ to bridge difference. The SS_{expr}, W_{base} and $SS_{aligned}$ are concatenated together and fed into the EG3D pipeline to generate the final prediction.

To ensure the disentanglement of the two latent code components, we implemented a contrastive learning approach for supervision. Our training methodology is designed to guarantee that changes in the generated images are solely attributed to modifications made in each respective latent code component. As an illustration, during the training process of SS_{expr}, we utilize two distinct latent codes, SS_{expr1} and SS_{expr2}, while keeping W_{base} constant. Disparities unrelated to facial expressions between $X1$ and $X2$ are penalized (Fig. 3).

Supervision is necessary to ensure the accuracy and disentanglement of facial attributes in the context of SS_{expr}. The primary objective is to capture facial expressions that closely align with the intended ones, which is achieved through a rigorous evaluation system for identifying inaccuracies and discrepancies. Another critical aspect is disentangling the various facial attributes within SS_{expr}, with a specific focus on ensuring that any disparities observed between $X1$ and $X2$ predominantly reflect variations in facial expressions. Minimizing discrepancies related to other facial characteristics is crucial to ensure that SS_{expr} achieves its intended outcome as hypothesized.

In the first stage, we drew inspiration from EMOCA [4] and opted to incorporate an expression discriminator to guarantee coherence between the provided input and the generated facial expressions. To accomplish this, we utilized a pretrained expression encoder sourced from EMOCA. This encoder is equipped with a ResNet-50 architecture, and we made use of the weight parameters provided. The emotion feature, denoted by $\psi \in \mathbf{R}^{|\psi|}$, is extracted from the final layer of the network. Throughout the training process, we ensured that the generated output and the input were feature-consistent. This was done by minimizing the divergence between the characteristic features extracted from the input and the generated image as derived via the expression encoder. The mathematical expression for the expression consistency loss is as follows:

$$L_{\text{expr}} = \|\pi_{\text{expr}}(X_{\text{input}}) - \pi_{\text{expr}}(G(W_{\text{base}} + SS_{\text{expr}}))\|_2 \tag{3}$$

In the equation presented above, $\pi_{\text{expr}}(\cdot)$ refers to the expression discriminator, X_{input} represents the input image with its corresponding expression, and $G(\cdot)$ indicates the generator network that utilizes latent codes W_{base} and SS_{expr} as input to produce a synthesized image. The expression consistency loss is employed to ensure that the generated image accurately reflects the expression features of the input image, thereby ensuring precise representation of expression.

To address the secondary aspect of our investigation, we have developed a comparative methodology focused on achieving a clear delineation between the experimental subset of facial expressions denoted as SS_{expr} and the baseline subset denoted as W_{base}. In pursuit of this goal, we employ a warp operation leveraging optical flow to facilitate comparison of the neutral expression between unmodified and modified images. It is important to emphasize that preserving a high degree of expression fidelity in removal remains a significant challenge and continues to be the subject of ongoing investigation in the field of GAN-based facial image manipulation.

To overcome this challenge, we utilize a 3D Morphable Model (3DMM) of the human face to create a guidance flow field that is relevant to image warping. As shown in Fig. 4, given a particular iteration of the expression coefficient, denoted

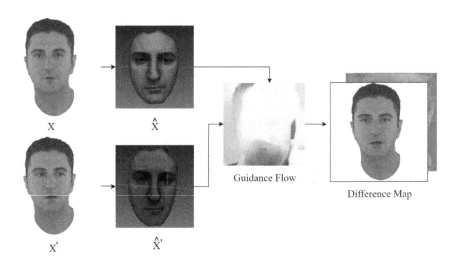

X $\hat{X}$

Guidance Flow

Difference Map

X' $\hat{X}'$

Fig. 4. Illustration of contrastive supervise.

as SS_{expr}, and its perturbed counterpart, denoted as SS_{expr}, we derive a pair of resulting outputs, denoted as X' and X. Next, we adjust the expression coefficient to generate a new 3DMM face with a neutral expression. Then, we render these two faces and use RAFT [15] to compute guiding optical flows, represented as $Flow$ and $Flow'$, respectively. Furthermore, we produce facial semantic segmentation maps, denoted as M and M', through image parsing. Facial expression warping is guided by optical flow fields and facial semantic segmentation maps, resulting in two outputs, θ_1 and θ_2. We enforce a constraint to ensure alignment between the two outputs. The specific supervision is elaborated below:

$$L_{\text{warp}} = \|\theta_1 - \theta_2\|_1 \qquad (4)$$

Furthermore, we employ a perceptual loss based on extracted feature representations. This loss function, denoted as $L_{perceptual}$, offers comprehensive guidance for facial semantic editing as a whole. As a result, the overall inversion loss function is defined as follows:

$$L_{\text{inv}} = \lambda_{\text{expr}}L_{\text{expr}} + \lambda_{\text{warp}}L_{\text{warp}} + \lambda_{\text{perceptual}}L_{\text{perceptual}} \qquad (5)$$

3.4   Residual Expression Alignment

After the aforementioned disentangled face inversion and contrastive supervise steps, we have achieved a sufficient disentanglement of SS_{expr} and W_{base}. At this stage, we can already obtain a highly realistic avatar. However, directly swapping the expression latent codes of the driving frame and the input frame often leads to suboptimal results, specifically in terms of less accurate expression portrayal. This is primarily because the spectrum of emotion distributions for the two individuals is not aligned in the latent space of the 3DGAN. Therefore, we propose the Residual Expression Alignment module to address this issue.

Network Architecture. As illustrated in the figure, we first perform face inversion on the driving frame and the input frame to obtain their respective SS_{expr} and W_{base}. Next, we replace the SS_{expr} of the input frame with that of the driving frame to obtain a coarse reenactment result, denoted as I_{coarse}. We calculate the offset ΔE by taking the difference between the expression features ψ_{coarse} corresponding to I_{coarse} and the expression features ψ_{drive} of the driving frame. In the subsequent branch, we utilize a residual mapping MLP to bridge the expression domains of the two identities. Specifically, we feed ΔE into the MLP, reshape the output of the residual mapping MLP to match the dimensionality of SS_{expr}, and then perform a channel-wise concatenation to obtain the aligned expression latent code. This aligned expression latent code, along with the base latent code of the input frame, is input into the volume renderer, resulting in the final outcome $I_{aligned}$:

$$I_{aligned} = G(W_{base} + SS_{expr} + SS_{align}) \qquad (6)$$

Loss Function. In total, we optimize:

$$L_{mlp} = \lambda_{emo}L_{emo} + \lambda_{gaze}L_{gaze} + \lambda_{eye}L_{eye} + \lambda_{mth}L_{mth} \qquad (7)$$

with emotion consistency loss L_{emo}, gaze direction loss L_{gaze}, eye closure loss L_{eye} and mouth closure loss L_{mth},each weight by a factor.

The emotion consistency loss constrains the facial expression features of the generated image $\theta_{gen} = \pi_{expr}(G)$ to align with the driving frame $\theta_{dri} = \pi_{expr}(D)$, computed as:

$$L_{emo} = \|\theta_{gen} - \theta_{dri}\|_2 \qquad (8)$$

The gaze direction loss computes the difference between the gaze direction of the generated image ψ_{gen} and the driving frame ψ_{dri}, computed as:

$$L_{gaze} = \|\psi_{gen} - \psi_{dri}\|_2 \qquad (9)$$

The eye closure loss computes the relative keypoints loss between upper and lower eyelid keypoint pairs. Due to slight discrepancies between image landmarks and projected 3D landmarks, employing conventional landmark reprojection losses may yield inaccurate results. However, implementing translation-invariant relative keypoints losses for eye closure, mouth closure, proves to be less vulnerable to misalignments and produces more reliable results. Thus, for the mouth closure loss, we compute the relative keypoints loss between upper and lower lip, just as same as the eye closure loss.

4   Experiments

4.1   Datasets

The dataset used for our training is divided into two parts. The first part consists of static images used to train the inversion branch, where we randomly selected 5,000 pairs of data from the FFHQ dataset. Due to the limitations of the FFHQ dataset, it primarily contains front-facing images, which somewhat limits our method's ability to generalize to extreme viewing angles. To address this, we utilized a pre-trained EG3D model to generate an additional 5,000 sets of data from left 45° to right 45° viewpoints as a supplement. For the validation set, we selected 1,500 pairs of images from CelebHQ and extracted 500 frames with varying angles from the MEAD dataset. To ensure optimal improvement of these datasets, we applied the data preprocessing techniques recommended in the official EG3D guidelines.

The second part of our dataset is used for evaluation and validation. Specifically, we sourced videos from several public datasets, including two from the MEAD dataset, one from Nerface, and one from Imavatar. For each video segment, we split the data into training and validation sets in a 9:1 ratio, resized them to 512×512 resolution, and extracted crucial data such as 68 facial keypoints, gaze direction, and iris information through prediction.

4.2   Implementation Details

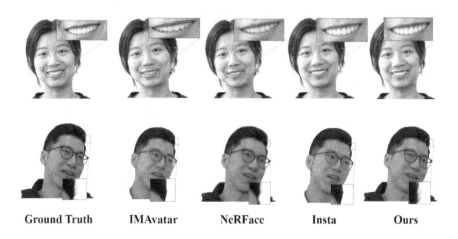

Ground Truth   **IMAvatar**   **NeRFace**   **Insta**   **Ours**

Fig. 5. Qualitative results of self-reenactment.

For the disentangled face inversion, we use an Adam optimizer. The learning rate is 1×10^{-4} for all learnable parameters. In the initial stage, E_{base} are fixed with random initial parameter, isolating the training of E_{expr} with the designated weights of 0.7 for λ_{expr} and 0.3 for λ_{warp}, while nullifying the $L_{perceptual}$. Subsequently, a comprehensive training of two encoders is performed with the assigned weights being 1 for λ_{expr}, 0.5 for λ_{warp} and 4 for $\lambda_{perceptual}$. The aforementioned hyperparameter configurations were established through a rigorous cycle of experimentation to assure optimal results and model robustness. Such configuration ensures not only satisfactory outcomes on the experimental datasets but also exemplary performance when confronted with in-the-wild images. This optimization time of the step is around 12 h with two NVIDIA 3090 for 10000 iterations.

For the residual expression alignment module, we divid the training process into two stages. The first stage involves training on the static dataset, primarily to enable the mapping MLP to have some level of generalization. In this stage, we set the learning rate for Adam to 1×10^{-4} with the weights of 0.5 for λ_{emo}, 0.2 for λ_{gaze}, 0.3 for λ_{eye} and 0.8 for λ_{mth}. The second stage, referred to as specificity training, aimed to fine-tune the weights for better adaptation when it comes to face reenactment task. We keep the hyperparametes and set the learning rate for Adam to 1×10^{-5}. This optimization time is around 8 h for the first stage. The duration of the second stage depends on the specific number of video frames and typically takes around 0.3 s per frame. All the stages are conducted on two NVIDIA 3090 s.

4.3   Comparison to Existing Methods

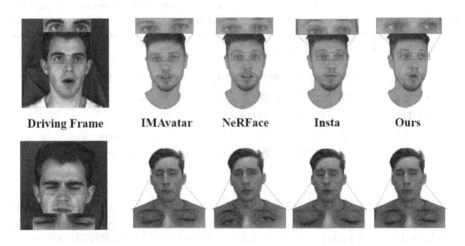

Fig. 6. Qualitative comparison of cross-identity reenactment.

We compared our method with IMAvatar, NeRFace, and INSTA. IMAvatar is based on an implicit representation method using FLAME, NeRFace combines 3DMM coefficients with NeRF representation, and INSTA integrates FLAME and INSTANT-NGP. Our comparison consists of two parts. First part is self reenactment. We evaluated this aspect using metrics such as Mean Square Error (MSE), Peak Signal-to-Noise Ratio (PSNR), Learned Perceptual Image Patch Similarity (LPIPS), tructure Similarity Index (SSIM) and time cost. These metrics were measured on four different datasets, and the average values were calculated as the final output. The second part is cross-identity reenactment. The evaluation metric for this part is the Average Expression Distance (AED). This metric is obtained using DECA to calculate the difference in expression coefficients for each pair of corresponding frames, and the average value is taken as the final result.

The Fig. 5 and Fig. 6 presented here provide a qualitative comparison of different methods in two aspects. It can be observed that IMAvatar produces relatively suboptimal results. This is primarily due to the fact that, compared to other methods, IMAvatar's expressive capabilities rely on the FLAME model and tracking algorithms. The expressive capacity of the FLAME model is limited, and it often struggles to accurately capture complex and rapidly changing facial expressions. NeRFace's results lack detail, such as gaze direction, and exhibit blurriness between frames. INSTA shares similar issues with the previous two methods, particularly in areas with fine details like teeth. In comparison to these three methods, our approach, thanks to its unique representation path and well-decoupled pipeline design, achieves better results and addresses many of the issues that other works of the same type commonly face.

Table 1. Comparison of our method's inversion quality with the current state-of-the-art approaches. The top-ranking indicator in each category is displayed in bold, and the second-ranking indicator is displayed with an underline. The most effective indicators were identified and highlighted in bold font. Our methodology achieved exceptional ranking across all evaluation metrics.

Methods	MSE?	PSNR?	SSIM?	LPIPS?	AED?	TIME?(1000frames)
IMavatar	0.0071	21.57	0.879	0.210	0.29	~17.5 h
NeRFace	0.0035	25.73	0.902	0.134	0.32	~23 h
INSTA	0.0032	26.25	0.917	0.132	0.24	~37 min
Ours	**0.0028**	**27.31**	**0.918**	**0.059**	**0.17**	**~23 min**

Table 1 provides quantitative comparisons of the different methods. In the self-reenactment scenario, our method achieves the best results in terms of MSE, SSIM, and LPIPS metrics, slightly falling behind INSTA in PSNR. It's worth noting that our method excels in terms of training time, thanks to our encoder-based disentangled inversion and efficient mapping MLP design. In the cross-identity reenactment scenario, our method demonstrates strong performance with the smallest AED, highlighting the effectiveness of disentangled representation and expression alignment (Fig. 7).

w/o L_{mou} Ours   Driving Frame

Fig. 7. Ablation study on mouth closure loss.

4.4 Ablation Study

We compared our training pipeline with a method that lacks the warp loss. From the fig, it's evident that without this loss as supervision, the expression code and base code do not disentangle as intended, resulting in less realistic expression representation.

5 Conclusion

In this work, we proposed EHA3D, a novel method for generating expressive 3D-aware neural head avatars. Our method takes a monocular RGB video as input and optimizes dynamic neural head avatar via disentangled latent code and expression alignment. Through qualitative and quantitative experiments, we have demonstrated the superiority of our method in terms of both quality and efficiency. We aim for our work to drive advancements in the field of telepresence applications.

References

1. Alaluf, Y., et al.: Third time's the charm? Image and video editing with stylegan3. In: Karlinsky, L., Michaeli, T., Nishino, K. (eds.) ECCV 2022. LNCS, vol. 13802, pp. 204–220. Springer, Cham (2022). https://doi.org/10.1007/978-3-031-25063-7_13
2. Cao, C., Bradley, D., Zhou, K., Beeler, T.: Real-time high-fidelity facial performance capture. ACM Trans. Graph. (ToG) **34**(4), 1–9 (2015)
3. Chan, E.R., et al.: Efficient geometry-aware 3D generative adversarial networks. In: Proceedings of the IEEE/CVF Conference on Computer Vision and Pattern Recognition, pp. 16123–16133 (2022)
4. Daněček, R., Black, M.J., Bolkart, T.: Emoca: emotion driven monocular face capture and animation. In: Proceedings of the IEEE/CVF Conference on Computer Vision and Pattern Recognition, pp. 20311–20322 (2022)
5. Feng, Y., Feng, H., Black, M.J., Bolkart, T.: Learning an animatable detailed 3D face model from in-the-wild images. ACM Trans. Graph. (ToG) **40**(4), 1–13 (2021)

6. He, K., Zhang, X., Ren, S., Sun, J.: Deep residual learning for image recognition. In: Proceedings of the IEEE Conference on Computer Vision and Pattern Recognition, pp. 770–778 (2016)
7. Hu, L., et al.: Avatar digitization from a single image for real-time rendering. ACM Trans. Graph. 1–14 (2017). https://doi.org/10.1145/3130800.31310887
8. Karras, T., Laine, S., Aila, T.: A style-based generator architecture for generative adversarial networks. In: Proceedings of the IEEE/CVF Conference on Computer Vision and Pattern Recognition, pp. 4401–4410 (2019)
9. Karras, T., Laine, S., Aittala, M., Hellsten, J., Lehtinen, J., Aila, T.: Analyzing and improving the image quality of stylegan. In: Proceedings of the IEEE/CVF Conference on Computer Vision and Pattern Recognition, pp. 8110–8119 (2020)
10. Khakhulin, T., Sklyarova, V., Lempitsky, V., Zakharov, E.: Realistic one-shot mesh-based head avatars. In: Avidan, S., Brostow, G., Cissé, M., Farinella, G.M., Hassner, T. (eds.) ECCV 2022. LNCS, vol. 13662, pp. 345–362. Springer, Cham (2022). https://doi.org/10.1007/978-3-031-20086-1_20
11. Lombardi, S., Simon, T., Schwartz, G., Zollhoefer, M., Sheikh, Y., Saragih, J.: Mixture of volumetric primitives for efficient neural rendering. ACM Trans. Graph. (ToG) **40**(4), 1–13 (2021)
12. Mildenhall, B., Srinivasan, P.P., Tancik, M., Barron, J.T., Ramamoorthi, R., Ng, R.: NeRF: representing scenes as neural radiance fields for view synthesis. Commun. ACM **65**(1), 99–106 (2021)
13. Park, J.J., Florence, P., Straub, J., Newcombe, R., Lovegrove, S.: Deepsdf: learning continuous signed distance functions for shape representation. In: Proceedings of the IEEE/CVF Conference on Computer Vision and Pattern Recognition, pp. 165–174 (2019)
14. Richardson, E., et al.: Encoding in style: a stylegan encoder for image-to-image translation. In: 2021 IEEE/CVF Conference on Computer Vision and Pattern Recognition (CVPR) (2021). https://doi.org/10.1109/cvpr46437.2021.00232
15. Teed, Z., Deng, J.: RAFT: recurrent all-pairs field transforms for optical flow. In: Vedaldi, A., Bischof, H., Brox, T., Frahm, J.-M. (eds.) ECCV 2020. LNCS, vol. 12347, pp. 402–419. Springer, Cham (2020). https://doi.org/10.1007/978-3-030-58536-5_24
16. Tov, O., Alaluf, Y., Nitzan, Y., Patashnik, O., Cohen-Or, D.: Designing an encoder for stylegan image manipulation. ACM Trans. Graph. 1–14 (2021). https://doi.org/10.1145/3450626.3459838
17. Tzaban, R., Mokady, R., Gal, R., Bermano, A., Cohen-Or, D.: Stitch it in time: Gan-based facial editing of real videos. In: SIGGRAPH Asia 2022 Conference Papers, pp. 1–9 (2022)
18. Wu, Z., Lischinski, D., Shechtman, E.: Stylespace analysis: disentangled controls for stylegan image generation. In: Proceedings of the IEEE/CVF Conference on Computer Vision and Pattern Recognition, pp. 12863–12872 (2021)
19. Xie, J., Ouyang, H., Piao, J., Lei, C., Chen, Q.: High-fidelity 3D GAN inversion by pseudo-multi-view optimization. In: Proceedings of the IEEE/CVF Conference on Computer Vision and Pattern Recognition, pp. 321–331 (2023)
20. Yang, S., Wang, W., Peng, B., Dong, J.: Designing a 3D-aware stylenerf encoder for face editing. In: ICASSP 2023-2023 IEEE International Conference on Acoustics, Speech and Signal Processing (ICASSP), pp. 1–5. IEEE (2023)

21. Yüksel, O.K., Simsar, E., Er, E.G., Yanardag, P.: Latentclr: a contrastive learning approach for unsupervised discovery of interpretable directions. In: Proceedings of the IEEE/CVF International Conference on Computer Vision, pp. 14263–14272 (2021)
22. Zheng, Y., Abrevaya, V.F., Bühler, M.C., Chen, X., Black, M.J., Hilliges, O.: Im avatar: implicit morphable head avatars from videos. In: Proceedings of the IEEE/CVF Conference on Computer Vision and Pattern Recognition, pp. 13545–13555 (2022)

Motion-Aware Topology Learning
for Skeleton-Based Action Recognition

Yanjun Chen[1], Hao Zhou[2], Yan Luo[1], Chongyang Zhang[1(✉)] (iD),
and Chuanping Hu[1,3]

[1] School of Electronic Information and Electrical Engineering,
Shanghai Jiao Tong University, Shanghai 200240, China
{luoyan_bb,sunny_zhang}@sjtu.edu.cn, cphu@zzu.edu.cn
[2] Alibaba Group, Hangzhou 311121, China
baishu.zh@alibaba-inc.com
[3] School of Cyber Science and Engineering, Zhengzhou University,
Zhengzhou 450001, China

Abstract. Graph convolutional networks have achieved great success
in skeleton-based action recognition area, in which topology learning is
the key component for extracting representative features. In this paper,
we propose a novel module called Motion-Aware Topology Graph Convolution (MAT-GC) that can boost the graph modeling ability with
motion-aware features and time-wise feature aggregation for skeleton-
based action recognition. In particular, feature-level temporal differences of joints from adjacent frames are sampled and combined to form
enhanced motion representations for a given frame. Moreover, a two-
pathway structure is adopted to model pairwise correlations at each time
step taking both short-term and long-term temporal motion variations
into account. Eventually, joint features are aggregated following the time-
wise topologies. Combined with temporal modeling modules, the overall
graph convolutional network MAT-GCN is constructed. Experimental
results on three popular skeleton-based action recognition datasets verify the effectiveness of the proposed method.

Keywords: Motion-aware · Time-wise · Topology learning ·
Skeleton-based action recognition

1 Introduction

Graph Convolutional Networks (GCNs) have witnessed great progress for
skeleton-based action recognition [1,2]. In GCNs, graph topology plays an important role in extracting representative features since it defines the rules for feature
aggregation.

The pioneering work ST-GCN [3] firstly implements GCN into skeleton-based
action recognition field. It proposes to build a spatio-temporal skeleton graph
based on natural connections of human joints for spatio-temporal feature extraction. Although this manually defined topology is simple and effective for improving action recognition accuracy, the static graph structure limits the capability of

© The Author(s), under exclusive license to Springer Nature Singapore Pte Ltd. 2024
G. Zhai et al. (Eds.): IFTC 2023, CCIS 2066, pp. 258–270, 2024.
https://doi.org/10.1007/978-981-97-3623-2_19

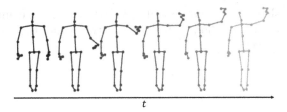

Fig. 1. Skeleton sequence for action *Taking a selfie*.

graph in modeling relationships between unnaturally connected joints. In order to further improve the performance of GCNs, 2 s-AGCN [4] proposes an adaptive graph convolutional network to model the relationship between disjoint nodes in a data-driven way. Inspired by this, many researches aiming to improve the diversity of graph topology have emerged [5–14]. However, these methods mainly focus on the modeling of topology along channel dimension by pooling joint features along the time dimension, which hinders the modeling of action variations. Figure 1 presents a skeleton sequence where the topology differs at different time steps.

This paper propose Motion-Aware Topology Graph Convolution (MAT-GC) module aiming at constructing a time-wise graph topology based on motion-aware features considering both short-term and long-term motion patterns. Specifically, feature-level displacement of joints in consecutive frames is calculated as the naive motion feature. These motion features are then sampled and combined in a duration of time to form enhanced motion feature, which can capture the informative motion patterns for each time step. Short-term and long-term motion dynamics are extracted by varying the effective motion range at a given time step, which can be complementary in characterizing the action variations. Finally, the motion-aware features are utilized to produce the time-wise topologies, which are then used for joint feature aggregation. Combining the proposed MAT-GC with temporal module, we propose a powerful graph convolutional network named MAT-GCN for skeleton-based action recognition. We perform experiments on three popular skeleton-based action recognition datasets to verify the effectiveness of the proposed method. The main contributions of this paper are three-fold:

- We propose a motion-aware time-wise topology learning method for graph convolution, which can dynamically compute the intrinsic topologies in different time steps based on enhanced motion features.
- We further propose to extract the motion-aware features from different scales to better characterize graph topologies from both short-term and long-term perspectives.

– Experiments show that the proposed MAT-GCN achieves comparable results with state-of-the-art methods, which demonstrates that the proposed method is efficient and feasible.

2   Related Work

2.1   General Action Recognition

With the rise of deep learning methods, there are numerous attempts to develop these methods from 2D image domain to fit into 3D video domain with an emphasis on temporal modeling [15–18].

Two-stream network [15] proposes to fuse results from spatial sub-net that capturing object appearance from a single RGB frame and temporal sub-net that capturing short-term motions from a stack of externally computed Optical Flow [19] frames. The recognition accuracy is promising while requires high computation consumption for Optical Flow calculation. TEA [17] proposes to use feature-level differences as an approximation of motion features to excite the motion-sensitive channels of the features. TDN [18] applies a temporal difference operator to a stack of frames to capture short-term and long-term motion information over the entire video.

Since the skeleton joints are explicitly aligned in different frames, the motion features can be simply calculated by the feature displacements in adjacent frames. In this paper, we propose to use temporal differences as motion feature to model the time-wise topology. Moreover, we sample and stack the motion features in short-short and long-term temporal ranges to better capture the motion variations.

2.2   Skeleton-Based Action Recognition

Early deep-learning-based algorithms for skeleton-based action recognition treat human skeleton sequence as vector sequences [20–23] or pseudo-images [24–29], which are then dealt by RNN and CNNs for classification. However, these methods represent skeleton as sequence or image while neglecting the inherent structure of joints. Since the human skeleton can be naturally represented by graph with joints as nodes and physical connections as edges, graph convolutional networks have been widely applied and achieved remarkable success in this field.

ST-GCN [3] firstly proposes to build spatial-temporal skeleton graph based on natural connections of human joints. However, the manually defined topology limits the flexibility in relation modeling for non-adjacent joints. MS-G3D [9] proposes the disentangled k-hop connection for each joints, aiming to build long-term relationships by gradually incorporating with the distant joints. Recent researches focus on the topology modeling in terms of attention or other mechanisms [5–14]. 2 s-AGCN [4] proposes an adaptive graph convolutional network where the topologies are learned in a data-driven way. It also introduces the second-order motion stream to combine with the joint stream in order to improve

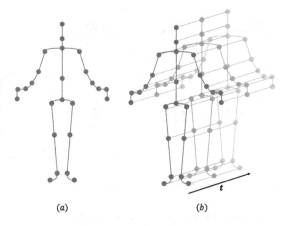

Fig. 2. (a) Illustration of the skeleton graph in a single frame. (b) Illustration of the spatio-temporal skeleton graph.

the performance. DC-GCN+ADG [8] proposes to divide the feature channel into several groups and assign different parameterized topologies for each group for representative feature learning.

These methods focus on increasing the diversity of topology along channel dimension while neglecting the variations along the time dimension. In this paper, we propose to model topologies at each time step based on motion-aware features to better depict the action statistics.

3 Approach

3.1 Preliminaries

The human skeleton can naturally be represented as graph with joints as nodes and physical connections of human body as spatial edges, as shown in Fig. 2(a). The spatio-temporal graph can be constructed with the corresponding joints between consecutive frames connected by temporal edges (green lines) as shown in Fig. 2(b). Each node is characterized by the coordinate vector of the corresponding joint.

Following the analysis in [3], the graph convolution for skeleton-based action recognition can be formulated as:

$$X^{out} = \widetilde{D}^{-\frac{1}{2}} \widetilde{A} \widetilde{D}^{-\frac{1}{2}} X^{in} W \tag{1}$$

where $X^{in} \in \mathbb{R}^{N \times C \times T \times V}$ is the input feature containing N samples of skeleton sequence. Each sequence has T frames, each frame contains V nodes and each node has C dimension feature. $\widetilde{A} = A + I_N$ with $A \in \mathbb{R}^{V \times V}$ is the adjacency matrix indicating the human body topology and I_N is the identity matrix showing the self-loop connection. $\widetilde{D}$ is the node degree matrix of $\widetilde{A}$ used for normalization. $W \in \mathbb{R}^{C \times C'}$ is the trainable weight matrix for graph convolution layer where C and C' is the input and output feature dimension respectively.

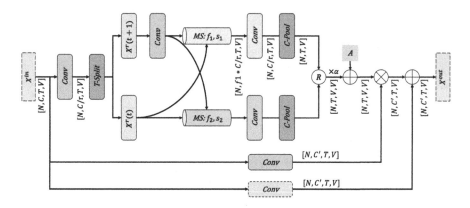

Fig. 3. The implementation of the Motion-Aware Topology Graph Convolution Layer.

3.2 Motion-Aware Topology Graph Convolutional Layer

The implementation of the Motion-Aware Topology Graph Convolutional (MAT-GC) layer is shown in Fig. 3. The input feature is firstly transformed into high-level representation. Then the motion-aware time-wise topologies that dynamically capture the correlations between nodes based on short-term and long-term motion patterns are constructed. Finally, the transformed input feature is aggregated according to the motion-aware topologies in a time-wise manner.

Feature Transformation. A simple 1×1 2D convolution layer is adopted as the feature transformation function written as:

$$X^{med} = conv(X^{in}) \tag{2}$$

where $X^{med} \in \mathbb{R}^{N \times C' \times T \times V}$ is the transformed feature with C' channels.

Motion-Aware Topology Modeling. The input spatio-temporal feature X^{in} firstly goes through a channel-wise convolution layer to reduce the channel dimension. The channel-reduced feature X^r is obtained by:

$$X^r = conv_{reduc}(X^{in}) \tag{3}$$

where r is the channel reduction ratio.

Then the naive motion feature can be calculated by the displacements in adjacent frames since the skeleton joints are explicitly aligned across frames. Instead of subtracting the original feature directly, a convolution layer is applied to transform the feature first. Hence, the naive motion feature at time step t can be formulated as:

$$M(t) = conv_{trans}(X^r(t+1)) - X^r(t), 1 \leq t \leq T-1 \tag{4}$$

The motion feature at the end of time steps is set to 0, $i.e.$, $M(T) = 0$. This motion feature formulation only calculated the displacements in consecutive frames, which limits the representative capability of motion dynamics. In order to include more motion dynamics to enhance the expressive power of motion feature, a sequence of motion feature is adopted. Specifically, the motion features contained in a time range specified by frame number f and stride s are concatenated to form the enhanced motion feature at time step t, denoted by:

$$MS(t) = [M(t-(f-1)s/2)||...||M(t-s)||M(t)||M(t+s)||...||M(t+(f-1)s/2)] \tag{5}$$

The time window defined by f, s is $(f-1)s+1$. Different configurations of frame number f and stride s indicate different temporal receptive fields. If the time window goes beyond skeleton sequence boundary, $M(t)$ is adopted for padding. This formulation can yield an efficient local motion representation for each frame.

The motion-aware topology can then be obtained by modeling the time-wise correlations between nodes based on the enhanced motion features. Given a pair of nodes (v_i, v_j) and their corresponding motion sequence features $MS(v_i), MS(v_j)$, a simple way for topology learning can be conducted by the time-wise subtractions, formulated as:

$$R(MS(v_i), MS(v_j)) = \sigma(\phi(MS(v_i)) - \varphi(MS(v_j))) \tag{6}$$

where $\sigma(\cdot)$ is activation function. Specifically, the function $\phi(\cdot)$ and $\varphi(\cdot)$ is implemented by a convolution layer followed by a pooling layer along the channel dimension to produce an output with shape $[N, T, V]$. In practice, we propose to apply different f, s in two pathways to capture relationships between pairwise nodes from short-term and long-term perspectives.

Eventually, the motion-aware adjacency matrix can be obtained based on the original static adjacency matrix A and the motion-aware time-specific correlations $R \in \mathbb{R}^{N \times T \times V \times V}$ as:

$$A^{mat} = A + \alpha \cdot R \tag{7}$$

The addition is implemented in a broadcast way where A is add to each time dimension. It is worth to note that A^{mat} differs across samples, times and layers. The overall adjacency matrix A^{mat} is learned through back-propagation and can largely increase the flexibility of topology modeling.

Time-Wise Aggregation. Given the motion-aware time-wise topologies A^{mat} and transformed high-level feature X^{med}, MAT-GC aggregates the feature in a time-wise manner. Specifically, the topology $A^{mat}_{:,t,:,:} \in \mathbb{R}^{N \times V \times V}$ at time t is matched to the corresponding transformed feature $X^{med}_{:,:,t,:} \in \mathbb{R}^{N \times C' \times V}$ and the final output $X^{out} \in \mathbb{R}^{N \times C' \times T \times V}$ is the concatenation results of features in the entire skeleton sequence, which can be formulated as:

$$X^{out} = [X^{med}_{:,:,0,:} * A^{mat}_{:,0,:,:}||X^{med}_{:,:,1,:} * A^{mat}_{:,1,:,:}||...||X^{med}_{:,:,T-1,:} * A^{mat}_{:,T-1,:,:}] \tag{8}$$

where $||$ is the concatenation operator and $*$ is the matrix multiplication. A residual branch is utilized to guarantee the training stability.

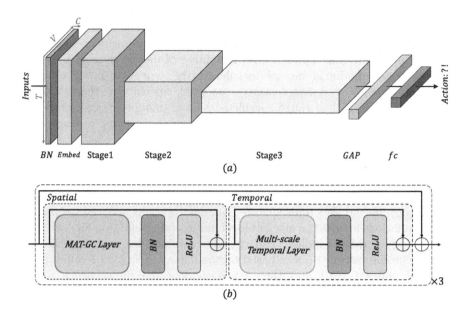

Fig. 4. (a) The overall framework of the proposed MAT-GCN. (b) The configuration of each stage for spatio-temporal feature extraction.

The proposed MAT-GC layer can adaptively learn the correspondence between nodes based on enhanced motion features from short-term and long-term perspectives for each frame, leading to flexible and effective topology modeling.

3.3   Multi-scale Temporal Layer

Following [9], a similar multi-scale temporal graph convolution layer is used for temporal modeling. For simplicity, only four branches are used, all starts with a 1×1 convolution layer for channel reduction. Three of the branches have an additional convolution layer with different dilations for multi-scale temporal feature extraction. The rest one branch utilizes a Maxpooling layer. Results from these four branches are concatenated to produce the temporal output.

3.4   Motion-Aware Topology Graph Convolutional Network

The overall framework of the proposed MAT-GCN is shown in Fig. 4. The input skeleton sequences first go through a BN layer and a feature embedding layer. Then 3 stages that each contains three consecutive MAT-GC layer and temporal multi-scale temporal layer are utilized for spatio-temopral feature extraction. At the end of each stage, the time dimension is halved and channel dimension is doubled. A Global Average Pooling layer is adopted at the end of the model to average the feature of all joints. Finally, the global representation is fed into a fc layer with sigmoid classifier to generate prediction scores used for action recognition.

4   Experiments

4.1   Datasets

NW-UCLA [30] contains 1494 video clips that are captured from three different views at the same time. The actions from the first two cameras are used as training data while the actions from the third camera are used as testing data.

NTU RGB+D [31] is a widely used dataset for skeleton-based action recognition task. Each skeleton sequence has no more than 300 frames of 25 3D coordinates of joints. The configuration of joints is shown in Fig 2. It is usually evaluated with two protocols: (1) Cross-Subject (X-sub): actions performed by 20 subjects are used as training data and actions performed by the other 20 subjects are used as testing data and (2) Cross-View (X-view): actions from camera views 2 and 3 are used as training data and actions from camera view 1 are used as testing data.

NTU RGB+D 120 [32] is an extension of NTU RGB+D [31] dataset with action classes increased from 60 to 120. It is usually evaluated with two protocols: (1) Cross-Subject (X-sub): actions performed by 53 subjects are used as training data and actions performed by the other 53 subjects are used as testing data and (2) Cross-Setup (X-set): actions from even setup IDs are used as training data and actions from odd setup IDs are used as testing data.

4.2   Experimental Settings

For NW-UCLA dataset, we follow the data pre-processing as in [7], the batchsize is set to 16. For NTU RGB+D 60 and NTU-RGB+D 120 datasets, we follow the data pre-processing as in [7], the window size is sampled to 64 frames, batchsize is set to 64 and prediction scores from four streams (joint, bone, joint motion and bone motion) are ensembled for final action recognition. Top1 accuracy is adopted to report the results.

All experiments are conducted with the PyTorch deep learning framework on one RTX 3090 Ti GPU. As shown in Fig. 4, the input data is first normalized and mapped from 3 to 64 channels. Then, temporal dimension is halved from 64 while channel dimension is doubled from 64 each time at the end of each stage. The parameters for enhanced motion feature in two pathways are set to $f_1 = 3, s_1 = 1$ and $f_2 = 3, s_2 = 2$. The model is trained by stochastic gradient descent (SGD) with Nesterov momentum (0.9) and weight decay is set to 0.0004. Cross-entropy loss is adopted as the loss function. The initial learning rate is set to 0.1 and divided by 10 at $35th$ and $55th$ epoch. A warm-up strategy is used in the beginning 5 epochs for stable training and the training process stops at $65th$ epoch.

4.3   Ablation Studies

Table 1. Comparisons of different configurations on the NTU RGB+D 120 dataset with X-Sub protocol.

Methods	f_1	s_1	f_2	s_2	Top1(%)
Baseline	–				83.4
A	3	1	3	1	83.9
B	3	2	3	2	84.1
C	5	1	5	1	84.2
D	3	1	3	2	84.6
E	3	1	5	1	84.5

In this section, we explore different configurations of MAT-GC, including frame f and stride s of motion-aware features on two pathways in topology modeling. The ST-GCN [3] with multi-scale temporal modeling is adopted as the baseline for a fair comparison. Experiments are carried out on NTU RGB+D 120 dataset under X-Sub protocol with joint stream. As shown in Table 1, models under all configurations show better results than baseline method, which proves the efficiency of the proposed MAT-GC. Model A, B and C adopt same settings on both pathways, where B and C has same but larger temporal receptive fields than A. It can be found that, with longer range of motion involved, the performance gradually increased. This indicates that the long-term motion information is beneficial in topology modeling. However, Model C is slightly better than B while having more channels in motion-aware feature representation. Hence, it is more efficient to enlarge the receptive field by increasing stride s. Model D and E show the results for different settings on two pathways. It can be found that different settings on two pathways can provide complementary information, resulting in the improved accuracy. Considering performance and efficiency, we choose model D as the final model.

4.4   Comparisons with SOTA Methods

We compare the proposed MAT-GCN with the state-of-the-art methods on NW-UCLA, NTU RGB+D and NTU RGB+D 120 datasets, as shown in Table 2 and Table 3. Since many state-of-the-art methods report results on a multi-stream fusion network, we also ensemble results from four modalities (joint, bone, joint motion and bone motion) to make the final prediction. On NW-UCLA dataset, the proposed MAT-GCN outperforms Ta-CNN [11] by 0.2%. On NTU RGB+D and NTU RGB+D 120 datasets, the proposed MAT-GCN reaches comparable results with existing methods under three evaluation protocols. The results verify the effectiveness of the motion-aware time-wise topology modeling, which is beneficial for skeleton-based action recognition.

Table 2. Classification accuracy comparison against SOTA methods on the NW-UCLA dataset.

Methods	Year	NW-UCLA
AGC-LSTM [28]	2019	93.3
Shift-GCN [7]	2020	94.6
DC-GCN+ADG [8]	2020	95.3
Graph2Net [10]	2022	95.3
Ta-CNN [11]	2022	96.1
MAT-GCN	–	96.3

Table 3. Classification accuracy comparison against SOTA methods on the NTU RGB+D and NTU RGB+D 120 dataset.

Methods	Year	NTU RGB+D		NTU RGB+D120	
		X-Sub	X-View	X-Sub	X-Set
ST-GCN [3]	2018	81.5	88.3	–	–
AS-GCN [5]	2019	86.8	94.2	–	–
2s-AGCN [4]	2019	88.5	95.1	83.7	85.8
Semantic GCN [6]	2020	89.0	94.5	79.2	81.5
Shift GCN [7]	2020	90.7	<u>96.5</u>	85.9	87.6
DC-GCN+ADG [8]	2020	90.8	**96.6**	86.5	88.1
MS-G3D [9]	2020	<u>91.5</u>	96.2	86.9	88.4
Graph2Net [10]	2022	90.1	96.0	86.0	87.6
Ta-CNN [11]	2022	90.4	94.8	85.4	86.8
ASE-GCN [12]	2023	89.4	96.2	–	–
MS&TA-HGCN-FC [13]	2023	90.8	96.4	87.0	88.4
EfficientGCN-B4 [14]	2023	**91.7**	95.7	**88.3**	**89.1**
MAT-GCN	–	<u>91.5</u>	96.4	<u>87.6</u>	**89.1**

5   Conclusion

In this paper, we propose a novel motion-aware time-wise topology graph convolution (MAT-GC) for skeleton-based action recognition. MAT-GC learns time-wise topologies based on motion-aware features from short-term and long-term motion patterns which shows its powerful capability in correlation modeling. Experimental results on three popular skeleton-based action recognition datasets achieve state-of-the-art accuracy and verify the effectiveness of the proposed method.

References

1. Ahmad, T., Jin, L., Zhang, X., Lai, S., Tang, G., Lin, L.: Graph convolutional neural network for human action recognition: a comprehensive survey. IEEE Trans. Artif. Intell. **2**(2), 128–145 (2021). https://doi.org/10.1109/TAI.2021.3076974
2. Sun, Z., Ke, Q., Rahmani, H., Bennamoun, M., Wang, G., Liu, J.: Human action recognition from various data modalities: a review. IEEE Trans. Pattern Anal. Mach. Intell. **45**(3), 3200–3225 (2023). https://doi.org/10.1109/TPAMI.2022.3183112
3. Yan, S., Xiong, Y., Lin, D.: Spatial temporal graph convolutional networks for skeleton-based action recognition. In: Thirty-Second AAAI Conference on Artificial Intelligence (2018)
4. Shi, L., Zhang, Y., Cheng, J., Lu, H.: Two-stream adaptive graph convolutional networks for skeleton-based action recognition. In: Proceedings of the IEEE Conference on Computer Vision and Pattern Recognition, pp. 12026–12035 (2019)
5. Li, M., Siheng, C., Xu, C., Ya, Z., Yanfeng, W., Qi, T.: Actional-structural graph convolutional networks for skeleton-based action recognition. In: Proceedings of the IEEE Conference on Computer Vision and Pattern Recognition, pp. 3595–3603 (2019)
6. Zhang, P., Lan, C., Zeng, W., Xing, J., Xue, J., Zheng, N.: Semantics-guided neural networks for efficient skeleton-based human action recognition. In: 2020 IEEE/CVF Conference on Computer Vision and Pattern Recognition (CVPR), pp. 1109–1118 (2020). https://doi.org/10.1109/CVPR42600.2020.00119
7. Cheng, K., Zhang, Y., He, X., Chen, W., Cheng, J., Lu, H.: Skeleton-based action recognition with shift graph convolutional network. In: Proceedings of the IEEE Conference on Computer Vision and Pattern Recognition (CVPR) (2020)
8. Cheng, K., Zhang, Y., Cao, C., Shi, L., Cheng, J., Lu, H.: Decoupling gcn with dropgraph module for skeleton-based action recognition. In: European Conference on Computer Vision (2020)
9. Liu, Z., Zhang, H., Chen, Z., Wang, Z., Ouyang, W.: Disentangling and unifying graph convolutions for skeleton-based action recognition. In: Proceedings of the IEEE/CVF Conference on Computer Vision and Pattern Recognition (CVPR) (2020)
10. Wu, C., Wu, X.J., Kittler, J.: Graph2net: perceptually-enriched graph learning for skeleton-based action recognition. IEEE Trans. Circuits Syst. Video Technol. **32**(4), 2120–2132 (2022). https://doi.org/10.1109/TCSVT.2021.3085959
11. Xu, K., Ye, F., Zhong, Q., Xie, D.: Topology-aware convolutional neural network for efficient skeleton-based action recognition. ArXiv arxiv:2112.04178 (2021). https://api.semanticscholar.org/CorpusID:244954773
12. Xiong, X., Min, W., Wang, Q., Zha, C.: Human skeleton feature optimizer and adaptive structure enhancement graph convolution network for action recognition. IEEE Trans. Circuits Syst. Video Technol. **33**(1), 342–353 (2023). https://doi.org/10.1109/TCSVT.2022.3201186
13. Huang, Z., Qin, Y., Lin, X., Liu, T., Feng, Z., Liu, Y.: Motion-driven spatial and temporal adaptive high-resolution graph convolutional networks for skeleton-based action recognition. IEEE Trans. Circuits Syst. Video Technol. **33**(4), 1868–1883 (2023). https://doi.org/10.1109/TCSVT.2022.3217763
14. Song, Y.F., Zhang, Z., Shan, C., Wang, L.: Constructing stronger and faster baselines for skeleton-based action recognition. IEEE Trans. Pattern Anal. Mach. Intell. **45**(2), 1474–1488 (2023). https://doi.org/10.1109/TPAMI.2022.3157033

15. Simonyan, K., Zisserman, A.: Two-stream convolutional networks for action recognition in videos. In: Advances in Neural Information Processing Systems, pp. 568–576 (2014)
16. Carreira, J., Zisserman, A.: Quo vadis, action recognition? a new model and the kinetics dataset. In: Proceedings of the IEEE Conference on Computer Vision and Pattern Recognition, pp. 6299–6308 (2017)
17. Li, Y., Ji, B., Shi, X., Zhang, J., Kang, B., Wang, L.: Tea: temporal excitation and aggregation for action recognition. In: 2020 IEEE/CVF Conference on Computer Vision and Pattern Recognition (CVPR), pp. 906–915 (2020). https://doi.org/10.1109/CVPR42600.2020.00099
18. Wang, L., Tong, Z., Ji, B., Wu, G.: TDN: temporal difference networks for efficient action recognition. In: Computer Vision and Pattern Recognition (2021)
19. Brox, T., Malik, J.: Large displacement optical flow: descriptor matching in variational motion estimation. IEEE Trans. Pattern Anal. Mach. Intell. **33**(3), 500–513 (2011)
20. Du, Y., Wang, W., Wang, L.: Hierarchical recurrent neural network for skeleton based action recognition. In: Proceedings of the IEEE Conference on Computer Vision and Pattern Recognition, pp. 1110–1118 (2015)
21. Liu, J., Shahroudy, A., Xu, D., Wang, G.: Spatio-temporal LSTM with trust gates for 3D human action recognition. In: Leibe, B., Matas, J., Sebe, N., Welling, M. (eds.) ECCV 2016. LNCS, vol. 9907, pp. 816–833. Springer, Cham (2016). https://doi.org/10.1007/978-3-319-46487-9_50
22. Zhang, P., Lan, C., Xing, J., Zeng, W., Xue, J., Zheng, N.: View adaptive recurrent neural networks for high performance human action recognition from skeleton data. In: Proceedings of the IEEE International Conference on Computer Vision, pp. 2117–2126 (2017)
23. Li, S., Li, W., Cook, C., Zhu, C., Gao, Y.: Independently recurrent neural network (indrnn): building a longer and deeper rnn. In: Proceedings of the IEEE Conference on Computer Vision and Pattern Recognition, pp. 5457–5466 (2018)
24. Kim, T.S., Reiter, A.: Interpretable 3D human action analysis with temporal convolutional networks. In: 2017 IEEE Conference on Computer Vision and Pattern Recognition Workshops (CVPRW), pp. 1623–1631. IEEE (2017)
25. Ke, Q., Bennamoun, M., An, S., Sohel, F., Boussaid, F.: A new representation of skeleton sequences for 3D action recognition. In: Proceedings of the IEEE Conference on Computer Vision and Pattern Recognition, pp. 3288–3297 (2017)
26. Liu, M., Liu, H., Chen, C.: Enhanced skeleton visualization for view invariant human action recognition. Pattern Recogn. **68**, 346–362 (2017)
27. Liu, M., Yuan, J.: Recognizing human actions as the evolution of pose estimation maps. In: Computer Vision and Pattern Recognition (2018)
28. Si, C., Chen, W., Wang, W., Wang, L., Tan, T.: An attention enhanced graph convolutional LSTM network for skeleton-based action recognition. In: Computer Vision and Pattern Recognition (2019)
29. Duan, H., Zhao, Y., Chen, K., Shao, D., Lin, D., Dai, B.: Revisiting skeleton-based action recognition. ArXiv Computer Vision and Pattern Recognition (2021)
30. Wang, J., Nie, X., Xia, Y., Wu, Y., Zhu, S.C.: Cross-view action modeling, learning, and recognition. In: 2014 IEEE Conference on Computer Vision and Pattern Recognition, pp. 2649–2656 (2014). https://api.semanticscholar.org/CorpusID:2239612

31. Shahroudy, A., Liu, J., Ng, T.T., Wang, G.: Ntu rgb+ d: a large scale dataset for 3D human activity analysis. In: Proceedings of the IEEE Conference on Computer Vision and Pattern Recognition, pp. 1010–1019 (2016)
32. Liu, J., Shahroudy, A., Perez, M., Wang, G., Duan, L.Y., Kot, A.C.: Ntu rgb+ d 120: a large-scale benchmark for 3d human activity understanding. IEEE Trans. Pattern Anal. Mach. Intell. **42**(10), 2684–2701 (2019)

MFNCA: Multi-level Fusion Network Based on Cross Attention for 3D Point Cloud Object Detection

Shuo Zhu[1], Yongfang Wang[1(✉)], Wei Chen[1], and Zhijun Fang[2]

[1] School of Communication and Information Engineering, Shanghai University, Shanghai 200444, China
yfw@shu.edu.cn

[2] School of Computer Science and Technology, Donghua University, Shanghai 201620, China

Abstract. 3D object detection methods based on point cloud have made significant progress due to providing rich depth information. However, the disability to obtain the complete shape by point cloud because of occlusion and signal loss leads to unsatisfactory detection performance. In the paper, a new multi-level fusion network based on cross attention (MFNCA) for 3D object detection is proposed to achieve impressive detection accuracy, which extracts not only voxel geometry features at multiple layer-level but also shape occupancy features including the missing parts of objects. Specifically, we introduce a sparse skip connection module to aggregate features from different levels and design a channel-wise pooling layer to enhance the global perspective of the model. Furthermore, RoI (Region of Interest) cross attention module is proposed to generate more accurate 3D bounding boxes by fusing multiple critical features. Extensive experiments on the challenging KITTI 3D dataset show that our method achieves promising performance compared with state-of-the-art methods.

Keywords: 3D object detection · point cloud · voxel · cross attention · multi-level features

1 Introduction

Compared with 2D images, Lidar point cloud which is a type of 3D data can provide rich geometric, shape and scale information [1, 2]. Lidar point cloud is important for 3D object detection, which has wide application in environment perception [3], autonomous driving and robot assistants [4].

Since point cloud is sparse and irregular, some methods [5–7] first converted point cloud into voxels, which were uniformly distributed in 3D Space. Then 3D sparse convolution networks were utilized for encoding the voxels to generate proposals later. Inspired by [8], we observed that the voxel features directly extracted from 3D feature volumes can get enough 3D information, and we propose a model that only utilizes voxels as input, which can balance accuracy and speed.

G. Zhai et al. (Eds.): IFTC 2023, CCIS 2066, pp. 271–283, 2024.
https://doi.org/10.1007/978-981-97-3623-2_20

(a)   (b)

Fig. 1. Whether it is occlusion or signal loss, the lack of complete shape of the objects makes detection difficult. (a) the Lidar point cloud of a road scene; (b) the corresponding RGB image.

However, point cloud do not provide the full shapes of objects because of the signal loss and occlusion. As shown in Fig. 1, a lot of points of the car are lost, making it more difficult to identify, leading to a decline in accuracy. Therefore, BtcDet [9] proposed to approximate the complete object shape by recovering lost points. Nevertheless, it incorporated point and voxel features, which causes it to run more slowly. We propose a voxel-based approach to meet the real-time requirements developed on it. We add it as an auxiliary task to recover the lost points and predict shape occupancy probability which is considered as occ features. Combining with the occ features, we enhance the voxel features extracted by 3D sparse convolution network.

In our model, we conduct spherical voxelization and then the shape occupancy network (SON) is used to obtain the occ features. After that, we introduce Multi-level Fusion Network (MFN) to efficiently fuse occ features with the voxel features. [10] introduces the concept of multi-level, but only at the context level, which limits its ability to extract effective features. To alleviate this issue, we design a new structure in the network module that can effectively fuse multi-level features. Besides, to better learn the features of approximate shapes, we also find an effective way to utilize occ features in the refinement stage. We assume the features generated by occ features with RoI pooling as RoI occ features, and we design a specific attention module to fuse RoI occ features into RoI features. Unlike most approaches that utilize attention mechanisms, e.g., [11] stacks 6 layers of attention module. Considering the computational resources and speed, we do not stack a large number of layers and apply just one attention layer.

In this paper, we propose a new voxel-based 3D object detection network named MFNCA. The experimental results show that the importance of introducing approximate shape information and validate the effectiveness of introducing multi-level concept in MFN network, as well as the effectiveness of the designed RoI cross attention module. At the same time, it can achieve the desired detection performance while maintaining significant speed. Our main contributions can be summarized as follows.

- We design a Multi-level Fusion Network (MFN) that extracts features from two branches containing voxel geometry features and shape occupancy probabilities. Specifically, we developed a sparse skip connection module to aggregate features from different levels. And we also design a global channel-wise pooling layer that adds global information for extracting features at different levels.

- We propose an RoI cross attention module (RCAM) to fuse multiple features and drive the model to focus on the critical information, which can provide rich features for final prediction.
- We propose MFNCA for 3D detection, it achieves significant performance in KITTI [12] dataset while meeting the need for real-time detection.

2 Related Works

In contrast with images where pixels are regularly distributed on the image plane [13], the Lidar point cloud is sparse and has highly variable point density. Therefore, how to process point cloud data has become one of the most critical challenges in 3D object detection.

To process the point cloud efficiently, some methods [5–9] converted point cloud into regular grids like voxels which can be processed by the convolution networks. VoxelNet [6] utilized voxel feature encoding (VFE) layer to encode point features inside voxel cells instead of manual algorithms, and 3D convolutional network was applied to extract features. SECOND [7] utilized sparse convolution to mitigate the numerous computation cost of normal 3D convolution. Voxel R-CNN [8] contained a refinement stage to get more fined 3D bounding boxes. BtcDet [9] considered the signal miss and occlusion of point cloud, and it proposed a shape occupancy network to predict the shape probability of the voxel grids.

Moreover, some methods [14–16] directly handled the point cloud without any transformation, which can avoid quantization loss. PointNet++ [14] proposed Set Abstraction (SA) layers to automatically learn features from raw points, which can obtain global and local information. PointRCNN [15] used Farthest Point Sampling (FPS) to down sample point cloud progressively and directly generated 3D boxes from the sampled points. Point-GNN [16] adopted the paradigm of PointRCNN and utilized voxel-based sampling to down sample the point cloud. These methods introduced diverse novel networks to handle raw points and achieve good performance.

3 MFNCA for 3D Object Detection

In this section, we will present the framework of MFNCA. As shown in Fig. 2, MFNCA includes (a) Shape Occupancy Network (SON) predicts the probability that each voxel whether contains objects, (b)Multi-level Fusion Network (MFN) extracts multi-level geometric voxel feature and fuse the occ features by SON, (c) Region Proposal Network (RPN) generates proposals, (d) RoI Cross Attention Module (RCAM) extracts RoI features and detect head for final prediction.

3.1 Shape Occupancy Estimation

Since the occlusion and signal miss, point cloud don't have the complete shape of objects. Therefore, we are going to approximate the shape and predict the shape of the missing part of the objects.

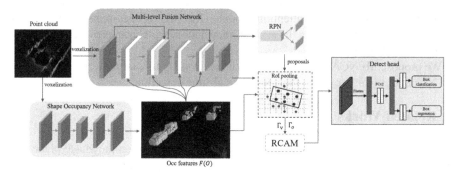

Fig. 2. The overall architecture of the proposed MFNCA. The input point cloud is first voxelized as spherical voxels and sent to Shape Occupancy Network to obtain occ features $F(O)$. MFN concatenates $F(O)$ to extract 3D voxel features, and RPN network generates 3D proposals. After that, features Γ_v and Γ_o are obtained by RoI pooling. Finally, MFNCA utilizes the RoI cross attention module (RCAM) to aggregate RoI features for detect head to predict the final bounding box.

We first identify the region of occlusion and signal miss, and we will generate training targets about these regions [9]. We then apply spherical voxelization to generate input voxels with the coordinates (r, φ, θ). SON consists of two down-sampling convolution layers and two up-sampling inverse convolution layers. The spherical voxels will be sent to SON to get the probability of shape occupancy $F(O)$, which can be fused in MFN and detect head to capture more information that represents the missing parts of objects.

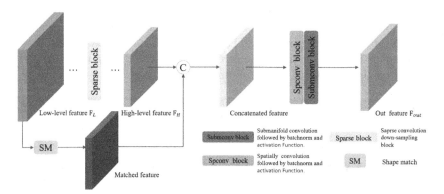

Fig. 3. Illustration of sparse skip connection module.

3.2 MFN for Feature Fusion

We propose a network named MFN to extract high-level semantic and geometric features. At the beginning of the model, we conduct both spherical voxelization and Cartesian voxelization. We can get two voxels set, one is for estimating $F(O)$, and the other is for multi-level voxel feature extraction and fusion.

Sparse Skip Connection. As shown in Fig. 3, because the feature map has different sizes in different level layers, we use SM block to unify the shape of the feature map. Considering few voxel volumes are non-empty, we choose the max pooling layer to down-sampling low-level feature map to retain the most critical information.

Specifically, for low-level feature map F_L and high-level feature map F_H, they are all dense tensors translated by corresponding sparse features so that we can utilize concatenation operations to aggregate them. If we regard these algorithms above as Φ, the sparse skip connection module can be described as follows:

$$F_{out} = \Phi\{Max(F_L); F_H\} \tag{1}$$

where Max represents the max pooling operation.

By adding the sparse skip connection module, the proposed network can accelerate model convergence and make it easier to learn deep features.

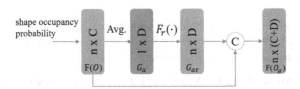

Fig. 4. Illustration of global channel-wise pooling. Avg. (Average pooling).

Multi-level Sparse Feature Fusion. The occ features $F(O)$ generated by SON only contain the local shape features of each voxel but lack global information. Therefore, we design a simple but effective module (see Fig. 4) with a global receptive field on the feature map. Besides, this module is also plug-and-play. We first get the global features G_a by average pooling. Then we will make it have the same channels as the original feature by F_r function. Specifically, in the network's second and fourth layers, we apply this module to enhance the 3D voxel features extracted by MFN.

3.3 Proposal Refinement

After translating the sparse features into dese features in the detect head, we propose to design an effective and low consumption RoI cross attention module to better fuse MFN and SON's features in the refinement stage (Fig. 5).

Local Gird Feature. We exploit the local gird features around the proposals to obtain accurate final bounding boxes. Each proposal starts by dividing into $GxGxG$ regular grids, and the center point is taken as the grid point of the corresponding grids. Specifically, given a grid point g_i, we first group a set of neighboring voxel $\chi_i = \{v_i^1, v_i^2, ..., v_i^K\}$ in the i_{th} level feature map. Later we aggregate all the voxels in X_i by a PointNet module Ψ:

$$\Gamma_i = \max_{k=1,2,...,K}\{\Psi([v_i^k - g_i; \gamma_k])\} \tag{2}$$

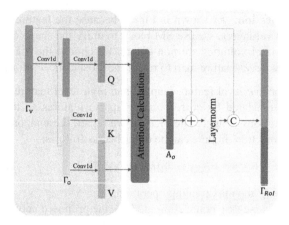

Fig. 5. Illustration of RoI cross attention module.

where the $v_i^k - g_i$ represents the relative coordinates, γ_k is the voxel features of k_{ih} neighboring voxel. We will apply this operation in the 3D voxels feature map and the occ feature map to get Γ_v and Γ_o respectively.

RoI Cross Attention Module. We utilize 1D convolution instead of full connection layer to generate Query tensor Q, Key tensor K, and Value tensor V. Since Γ_o carries the probability of voxel volumes containing objects, we want our network to focus on the high-probability regions and we set the Γ_v as Query. We get Q_v, K_o and V_o as follows:

$$Q_v = Conv1d(\Gamma_v);$$
$$X_o = Conv1d(\Gamma_o), X_o \in K_o, V_o \tag{3}$$

where X_o stands for K_o and V_o, and Conv1d means 1D convolution.

Specifically, Γ_v and Γ_o will be conducted downsampling in the attention map generation stage. When performing matrix multiplication, it can save a lot of computation and find the focus of the high-level features. Then we perform attention calculation using a generic approach to obtain attention map A_o:

$$A_o = softmax\left(\frac{Q_v K_o^T}{\sqrt{d_k}}\right) V_o \tag{4}$$

where d_k is a scale variable and K_o^T is the transpose of K_o.

Later, we utilize element-wise addition to aggregate Γ_o and A_o, and a Layernorm is followed for the aggregated features. Finally, the above feature normalized by Layernorm is concatenated with Γ_v to generate attention RoI features Γ_{RoI}, which will be used for classification and regression.

3.4 Experimental Setup

We conduct experiments on the popular autonomous driving datasets: KITTI [12]. There are 7481 LiDAR frames for training and 7518 LiDAR frames for testing in the KITTI

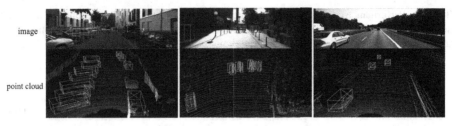

Fig. 6. Visualization results of our method on the test set. The objects are marked with green 3D boxes on the point cloud and images. (Color figure online)

Fig. 7. Visualization results of our method on the val set. The red boxes represent the ground truths and the green boxes are the predicted results. (Color figure online)

dataset covering three categories: car, pedestrian, and cyclist. We divided the train data into training set with 3712 frames and validation (val) set with 3769 frames according to the common protocol. When we use the train set for training, we evaluate on the val set.

Since the KITTI dataset only contains annotations of objects in the Field of View, we choose to clip the range of point cloud into $[-3, 1] \times [-40, 40] \times [0, 70.4]$ along z axis, x axis, y axis respectively. In the SON the coordinates of point cloud are converted from (x, y, z) to (r, Φ, θ), and we set a spherical voxel size (0.32 m, 0.52°, 0.45°) as input. Following SECOND [7], the MFN's input voxel size is set as (0.05 m, 0.05 m, 0.1 m).

3.5   Training and Inference Details

Training. Our network is end-to-end optimized with Adam optimizer. The learning rate is initialized as 0.003 and 0.01 for SON and others respectively, and updated by cosine annealing strategy. The network is trained on RTX 3060ti GPU for 80 epochs with batch size 2.

Inference. Firstly, we apply non-maximum suppression (NMS) with a threshold of 0.7 in the RPN to filter the top 100 proposals for the detect head. In the refinement stage, NMS is used again with a threshold of 0.1 to remove redundant boxes.

Table 1. Performance comparison in 3D detection AP (%) with 40 recall positions on KITTI test set. Moderate (Mod). No information (–). The best performance value is in bold, second-best is underlined.

Method	Modality	Car (3D Detection)			Pedestrian (3D Detection)			Cyclist (3D Detection)		
		Easy	Mod	Hard	Easy	Mod	Hard	Easy	Mod	Hard
VoxelNet [6]	LiDAR	77.47	65.11	57.73	39.48	33.69	31.51	61.22	48.36	44.37
SECOND [7]	LiDAR	83.34	72.55	65.82	–	–	–	71.33	52.08	45.83
PointPilar [5]	LiDAR	82.58	74.31	68.99	**51.45**	**41.92**	**38.89**	77.10	58.65	51.92
PointRCNN [15]	LiDAR	86.96	75.64	70.70	47.98	39.37	36.01	74.96	58.82	52.53
Voxel R-CNN [8]	LiDAR	**90.90**	81.62	77.06	–	–	–	–	–	–
CT3D [17]	LiDAR	87.83	81.77	77.16	–	–	–	–	–	–
CIA-SSD [18]	LiDAR	89.59	80.28	72.87	–	–	–	–	–	–
DVFENet [19]	LiDAR	86.20	79.18	74.58	43.55	37.50	35.33	78.73	62.00	55.18
JPV-Net [20]	LiDAR	88.66	81.73	76.94	-	-	-	**80.66**	**65.41**	**59.26**
ours	LiDAR	90.50	**81.93**	**77.35**	48.36	41.07	38.29	80.43	64.40	57.89

3.6 Comparison with the State-of-the-Arts

Evaluation on KITTI Test Set. We compare our method with state-of-the-art detectors on the KITTI official test server in recent years. Our models are trained on the training and val sets, testing on the test set with average precision (AP) calculated by 40 positions. The relevant results are shown in Table 1 and Table 2. We compare the performance of 3D detection and BEV tasks. Our method obtains significant results, especially in the car and cyclist categories, but the results are more general in the pedestrian category, which we assume the reason may be that the pedestrian is so tiny that voxels cannot obtain its fine shape.

The visualization results are shown in Fig. 6, our method is capable of recognizing objects not only in complex scenes but also at a distance.

Evaluation on KITTI Val Set. We evaluate our MFNCA on the KITTI val set with average precision (AP) calculated by 11 positions with the 0.8 score threshold. Since many state-of-the-art methods do not publish the validation results in val set of the pedestrian and cyclist categories, we only compared the validation results of the car category. As shown in Table 3, Our method performs best in all three splits.

Table 2. Performance comparison in BEV AP (%) with 40 recall positions on KITTI test set. Moderate (Mod). No information (–). The best performance value is in bold, second-best is underlined.

Method	Modality	Car (BEV)			Pedestrian (BEV)			Cyclist (BEV)		
		Easy	Mod	Hard	Easy	Mod	Hard	Easy	Mod	Hard
VoxelNet [6]	LiDAR	89.35	79.26	77.39	46.13	40.74	38.11	66.70	54.76	50.55
SECOND [7]	LiDAR	89.39	83.77	78.59	–	–	–	76.50	56.05	49.45
PointPilar [5]	LiDAR	90.07	86.56	82.81	**57.60**	**48.64**	**45.78**	79.90	62.73	55.58
PointRCNN [15]	LiDAR	92.13	87.39	82.72	<u>54.77</u>	46.13	42.84	<u>82.56</u>	67.24	60.28
Voxel R-CNN [8]	LiDAR	**94.85**	88.83	86.13	–	–	–	–	–	–
CT3D [17]	LiDAR	92.36	88.83	84.07	–	–	–	–	–	–
CIA-SSD [18]	LiDAR	93.74	89.84	82.39	–	–	–	–	–	–
DVFENet [19]	LiDAR	90.93	87.68	<u>84.60</u>	50.98	44.12	41.62	82.29	<u>67.40</u>	<u>60.71</u>
ours	LiDAR	<u>94.35</u>	**90.28**	**86.43**	53.64	<u>46.36</u>	<u>43.47</u>	**83.44**	**67.73**	**60.91**

The visualization results of our method are shown in Fig. 7. Our method can identify not only the objects in annotations but also those that are ignored to be annotated. For distant and occluded objects, our method is also able to identify them accurately.

3.7 Ablation Studies

We study the impact of the modules of the proposed MFNCA network in this section. All ablation experiments are trained on the train split which includes 3712 samples and evaluated on the val split with 40 recalls.

RoI Cross Attention. We will analyze the contribution of the our RoI cross attention module which is applied in the detect head. Moreover, we compare our method with the typical attention module (att). The results are shown in Table 4.

We can see the accuracy decline in all data splits with direct concatenation compared to the cross-attention based, especially for the moderate split. We can get the global receptive field through the attention mechanism, and our proposed structure can make the model focus on the critical information which brings 0.58 AP increase.

Multi-level Fusion. The 3D sparse convolution network MFN extracts 3D voxel features. After that, the sparse voxel features will be compressed into 2D dense features. Our proposed model both fuses $F(O_g)$ in MFN, RPN and the detect head.

Table 3. Performance comparison in 3D detection AP (%) with 11 recall positions on KITTI val set for the car class. Moderate (Mod)

Method	Car (3D Detection)		
	Easy	Mod	Hard
VoxelNet [6]	81.97	65.46	62.85
SECOND [7]	88.61	78.62	77.22
PointPilar [5]	86.62	76.06	68.91
DVFENet [19]	89.81	79.52	78.35
CT3D [17]	89.54	86.06	78.99
Voxel R-CNN [8]	89.41	84.52	78.93
JPV-Net [20]	89.71	84.61	79.09
ours	**90.02**	**86.31**	**79.21**

Table 4. Performance comparison of different integration methods. Moderate (Mod). concatenation (cat). attentio (att). attention with Batchnorm (att-B). attention with Layernorm (att-L).

Method	Car (3D Detection)		
	Easy	Mod	Hard
cat	92.99	85.58	83.39
att	92.78	85.66	83.44
att-B	92.37	85.35	83.06
att-L	**93.28**	**86.16**	**83.67**

Table 5. Performance comparison of networks with different fusion methods. Moderate (Mod). detect head (head).

Method	MFN	RPN	Head	Mod
(a)				84.71
(b)	√			85.44
(c)		√	√	86.08
(d)	√		√	85.71
(e)	√	√	√	**86.16**

We explore the impact of each of the three integration strategies on performance. The results are shown in Table 5. We examine the effects of each module through different combinations of fusion. Model (a) does not fuse $F(O_g)$ as a control group, model (b) only fuses $F(O_g)$ in MFN, model(c) fuses $F(O_g)$ both in RPN and detect head, model (d) comments out the fusion module in RPN, and model (e) retains all three fusion modules in the network.

As we can see, the 3D detection AP has increased by about 1.5% on the moderate split by our proposed methods. Models (b) and (c) show that fuse $F(O_g)$ in the middle and late stages can provide sufficient information for final detection.

Table 6. Runtime analysis. Moderate (Mod). Frames Per Second (FPS).

Method	Mod	FPS (Hz)
Voxel R-CNN [8]	84.52	35.71
BtcDet [9]	86.57	**6.52**
ours	**86.31**	17.15

3.8 Runtime Analysis

In this section, we analyze the performance and speeds between our methods and some state of the arts. Since our method is built on top of Voxel R-CNN and BtcDet, we choose to compare it with them. From Table 6, we can see that compared with Voxel R-CNN, our method has a reduced FPS due to the addition of the module for predicting the shape occlusion probability, but the performance is significantly improved based our proposed fusion methods. Also, since our method is a pure voxel-based approach that does not involve point features, compared to BtcDet we are almost three times faster, but the performance is almost close.

4 Conclusion

In this paper, we propose MFNCA, a voxel-based 3D object detection network that can achieve desirable detection performance while maintaining appreciable speed. We find a large number of missing shapes in the point cloud, which causes difficulties in detection, especially for distant and small objects. We explore to complete the point cloud. Specifically, we obtain the shape occlusion probability and fuse it with the features generated by the multi-level fusion network to enrich the object information. We use both spherical voxelization and Cartesian voxelization and extract features using the multi-level fusion network. The sparse feature fusion and global information pooling layer are used within the network to fuse the shape occlusion probabilities efficiently, and we increase the model's convergence by using the sparse skip connection module. In the refinement stage, we propose an RoI cross-attention module to fuse multiple features and drive the model to focus on the critical information. Our approach achieves good performance on KITTI and maintains a high detecting speed. In future research, in addition to innovations about the model structure, we hope there will be methods to alleviate the defects of point clouds. Such as alleviating the uneven distribution of point clouds due to distance to make point cloud-based 3D object detection more effective and reliable.

Acknowledgments. This work was supported by National Natural Science Foundation of China under Grant No. 61671283, U2033218, 62275148. Jiangsu Province's Industry Outlook and Key Core Technologies – Key Projects (BE2022055-4).

References

1. Guo, Y., Bennamoun, M., Sohel, F., Lu, M., Wan, J.: 3D object recognition in cluttered scenes with local surface features: a survey. IEEE Trans. Pattern Anal. Mach. Intell. **36**, 2270–2287 (2014)
2. Guo, Y., Sohel, F., Bennamoun, M., Lu, M., Wan, J.: Rotational projection statistics for 3D local surface description and object recognition. Int. J. Comput. Vis. **105**, 63–86 (2013)
3. Zhu, H., Yuen, K.-V., Mihaylova, L., Leung, H.: Overview of environment perception for intelligent vehicles. IEEE Trans. Intell. Transp. Syst. **18**, 2584–2601 (2017)
4. Friederich, J., Zschech, P.: Review and systematization of solutions for 3D object detection. Wirtschaftsinformatik, 1699–1711 (2020)
5. Lang, A.H., Vora, S., Caesar, H., Zhou, L., Yang, J., Beijbom, O.: PointPillars: fast encoders for object detection from point clouds. In: 2019 IEEE/CVF Conference on Computer Vision and Pattern Recognition (CVPR), pp. 12689–12697 (2019)
6. Zhou, Y., Tuzel, O.: VoxelNet: end-to-end learning for point cloud based 3D object detection. In: Proceedings of the IEEE Conference on Computer Vision and Pattern Recognition, pp. 4490–4499 (2018)
7. Peter, S., Kirschbaum, E., Both, M., et al.: Sparse convolutional coding for neuronal assembly detection. In: Advances in Neural Information Processing Systems, pp. 3678–3688 (2017)
8. Deng, J., Shi, S., Li, P., Zhou, W., Zhang, Y., Li, H.: Voxel R-CNN: towards high performance voxel-based 3D object detection. In: Proceedings of the AAAI Conference on Artificial Intelligence, vol. 35, pp. 1201–1209 (2021)
9. Xu, Q., Zhong, Y., Neumann, U.: Behind the curtain: learning occluded shapes for 3D object detection. In: Proceedings of the AAAI Conference on Artificial Intelligence, vol. 36, pp. 2893–2901 (2022)
10. Xie, Q., et al.: MLCVNet: multi-level context VoteNet for 3D object detection. In: Proceedings of the IEEE/CVF Conference on Computer Vision and Pattern Recognition (CVPR), pp. 10447–10456 (2020)
11. Liu, Z., Zhang, Z., Cao, Y., Hu, H., Tong, X.: Group-free 3D object detection via transformers. In: Proceedings of the IEEE/CVF International Conference on Computer Vision (ICCV), pp. 2949–2958 (2021)
12. Geiger, A., Lenz, P., Urtasun, R.: Are we ready for autonomous driving? The KITTI vision benchmark suite. In: 2012 IEEE Conference on Computer Vision and Pattern Recognition, pp. 3354–3361 (2012)
13. Mao, J., Shi, S., Wang, X., et al.: 3D object detection for autonomous driving: A comprehensive survey. Int. J. Comput. Vis., 1–55 (2023)
14. Qi, C.R., Yi, L., Su, H., Guibas, L.J.: PointNet++: deep hierarchical feature learning on point sets in a metric space. In: Proceedings of the 31st International Conference on Neural Information Processing Systems, pp. 5105–5114 (2017)
15. Shi, S., Wang, X., Li, H.: PointRCNN: 3D object proposal generation and detection from point cloud. In: Proceedings of the IEEE/CVF Conference on Computer Vision and Pattern Recognition, pp. 770–779 (2019)

16. Shi, W., Rajkumar, R.: Point-GNN: graph neural network for 3D object detection in a point cloud. In: Proceedings of the IEEE/CVF Conference on Computer Vision and Pattern Recognition, pp. 1711–1719 (2020)
17. Shenga, H., et al.: Improving 3D object detection with channel-wise transformer. In: 2021 IEEE/CVF International Conference on Computer Vision (ICCV), pp. 2723–2732 (2021)
18. Zheng, W., Tang, W., Chen, S., Jiang, L., Fu, C.-W.: CIA-SSD: confident IoU-aware single-stage object detector from point cloud. In: Proceedings of the AAAI Conference on Artificial Intelligence, vol. 35, pp. 3555–3562 (2021)
19. He, Y., et al.: DVFENet: dual-branch voxel feature extraction network for 3D object detection. Neurocomputing **459**, 201–211 (2021)
20. Song, N., Jiang, T., Yao, J.: JPY-Net: joint point-voxel representations for accurate 3D object detection. In: Proceedings of the AAAI Conference on Artificial Intelligence, vol. 36, pp. 2271–2279 (2022)

ART-InvRec: Acquiring Rotation Invariance of 3D Object Reconstruction via Adversarial Rotation

Rui Yang[1], Fei Hu[2(✉)], Zhiye Chen[3], and George Wang[3]

[1] Key Laboratory of Media Audio and Video, Ministry of Education,
Communication University of China, Beijing, China
[2] State Key Laboratory of Media Convergence and Communication,
Communication University of China, Beijing, China
hufei@cuc.edu.cn
[3] Guangdong South New Media Inc., Guangzhou, China

Abstract. 3D surface reconstruction from point clouds has shown promising advancements in the 3D computer vision community. However, most proposed approaches only pursue the reconstruction precision of objects in an aligned pose without considering the rotated inputs, thus failing to reconstruct stable results for rotated point clouds. This study introduces a novel perspective by demonstrating, for the first time, that achieving rotation invariance in 3D object reconstruction is feasible through adversarial training. Our proposed framework, termed ART-InvRec, treats point cloud rotation as an adversarial attack and attains rotation invariance by training the reconstruction network on inputs subjected to Adversarial RoTations. Specifically, we employ the axis-wise angles attack method to efficiently identify the most aggressive rotations and train the target reconstruction model with the rotation pool mechanism. Experiments demonstrate that ART-InvRec gets outstanding results, both qualitatively and quantitatively, for the challenging task of rotation-invariant object reconstruction. Notably, ART-InvRec performs better than state-of-the-art techniques on rotation-invariant reconstruction.

Keywords: 3D Reconstruction · Rotation Invariance · Adversarial Training

1 Introduction

There are numerous applications for creating a surface description from 3D points sampled at an object's surface, such as virtual reality and the processing of digital twins. Learning-based 3D object reconstruction from point clouds has been widely discussed in the computer vision community. In recent years, several implicit representation methods [1–4] have achieved remarkable successes in 3D reconstruction task. However, this success is limited to reconstructing 3D objects only in an aligned position. Once the input point clouds have been rotated, the reconstruction accuracy of these methods decreases significantly.

© The Author(s), under exclusive license to Springer Nature Singapore Pte Ltd. 2024
G. Zhai et al. (Eds.): IFTC 2023, CCIS 2066, pp. 284–296, 2024.
https://doi.org/10.1007/978-981-97-3623-2_21

Most existing methods pursue the reconstruction precision of objects in an aligned pose without considering the rotated inputs, thus failing to reconstruct stable results for rotated point clouds. In practical applications like indoor navigation, self-driving vehicles, and robotics, sensor-collected point cloud data is often in an unknown pose, not necessarily aligned. To get the aligned reconstruction results for all arbitrary rotated posed inputs, the simplest method is aligning all input point clouds, which is a resource-intensive process. To this end, how to acquire the rotation invariance of 3D object reconstruction from point clouds to arbitrary rotations becomes a research topic with practical significance.

We take inspiration from classical rotation-invariant tasks, such as point cloud classification. Expecting the network to produce stable predictions on inputs experiencing rigid changes like rotation is a fundamental prerequisite for point cloud classification. In this way, the existing practice of improving the rotation robustness of point cloud classifiers is of great reference significance to acquiring the rotation invariance of 3D object reconstruction. Most proposed solutions fall into three categories to make the network resistant to arbitrarily rotating inputs:

1. **Rotation Augmentation Methods** propose to augment the training data using rotations. Unfortunately, because of the mass of rotated data, data augmentation is rarely used to boost robustness against arbitrarily rotated data [5].
2. **Rotation Invariance Methods** propose the conversion of the input point clouds into rotation-invariant geometric descriptors. Existing typical invariant descriptors include the distance and angles between local point pairs [6–9], point norms [5, 10] and principal directions [8]. However, these methods only perform partially on aligned datasets since they necessitate time-consuming input pre-processing.
3. **Adversarial Training Methods** propose to augment training data with adversarial samples in each training loop, in order to ensure that adversarial trained models behave more normally when faced with adversarial data than standardly trained models. [11, 12] leverage adversarial training to defend against point cloud perturbations. [13] proposes an approach to boost the rotation robustness for point cloud classification by retraining networks on adversarial rotated inputs. However, using adversarial training to acquire the rotation-invariance of 3D object reconstruction has rarely been studied.

In this paper, we aim to explore an effective route for the rotation-invariance problem of 3D object reconstruction. Inspiring by the ART-Point framework [13] for point cloud classifiers, we develop the ART-InvRec framework to acquire the rotation invariance of 3D object reconstruction by training networks on inputs with **A**dversarial **R**o**T**ations. Similar to the typical framework of adversarial training, ART-InvRec formulates a min-max problem, with the max step identifying the most offensive rotations and the min step optimizing the parameters to minimize the loss. Referring to the technical route of ART-Point, we find the most offensive rotating samples for the max step by applying the axis-wise rotation attack technique. Retraining the network on the adversarial samples for the minimum step by inheriting to the original 3D reconstruction model's training scheme. We prepare three basic reconstruction models for attack and build a rotation pool that utilizes the adversarial rotations' transferability to broaden the variety of training data. Employing the one-step optimization method proposed in ART-Point, we efficiently attain the final rotation-invariant 3D object reconstruction model.

In summary, our contributions are as follows:

- For the first time, we successfully acquired the rotation invariance of 3D object reconstruction from the viewpoint of model attack and defense.
- We prepare three basic reconstruction models and use the axis-wise rotation attack technique to effectively obtain the most aggressively rotated examples on them to build the rotation pool.
- We confirm through experimentation that our ART-InvRec framework can effectively acquire the rotation invariance of 3D object reconstruction and demonstrate that the rotation invariance of it is beyond the state-of-the-art.

2   Related Works

2.1   Learning-Based 3D Reconstruction Methods

Aiming to obtain high-precision 3D reconstruction results, many researchers are exploring the ideal representation of 3D geometry. The output representations that learning-based 3D reconstruction techniques employed can be divided into four categories: voxels, points, meshes, and implicit representations. However, the first three representations are no longer commonly used because of their respective disadvantages. Specifically, voxels are limited in terms of resolution due to their cubic memory consumption. Points discard topological relations, so further post-processing procedures are required. Meshes are prone to producing either shapes with only simple topology or self-intersecting meshes.

In recent years, several implicit representation methods [1–4] have achieved remarkable successes in 3D reconstruction task. They can model shapes in a continuous way. The implicit description yields better detail preservation and more complex shape topologies. Unfortunately, these methods rarely consider the robustness of reconstruction. Most of them only consider the noise of the point cloud without consideration of the robustness to rotation. As a consequence, once the input point clouds have been rotated, the reconstruction accuracy of these methods decreases significantly. Hence, they still only pursue the reconstruction precision of objects in an aligned pose and they cannot handle rotation-invariant reconstruction.

Due to the lack of rotation invariance studies for 3D object reconstruction task, in the following, we briefly review the robust methods of rotation in typical invariant tasks like point cloud classification to draw inspiration from them. Existing works on improving the rotation robustness for point cloud classification can be broadly categorized into rotation augmentation, rotation invariance, and adversarial training.

2.2   Rotation Augmentation Methods

Augmenting the training set through rotations has been extensively employed in existing works. The classic point cloud classifiers, such as PointNet [14], PointNet++ [15] and DGCNN [16] implement rotation augmentation during training to boost rotation robustness. However, rotation augmentation is limited to creating models robust within a small scope of angles, and its application for improving robustness to arbitrary rotations is hindered by the vast number of rotated data instances.

2.3 Rotation Invariance Methods

Recently, in order to obtain models robust to arbitrary rotation angles, rotation invariance methods have been developed to extract invariant descriptors from point clouds as inputs. [6, 7, 9] introduce cleverly designed operations to construct distances and angles from local point pairs. [5, 8, 10] add global invariant contexts to local invariant descriptor as extensions. Furthermore, [17–19] design invariant convolutions to automatically learn various descriptors. However, these specific descriptors may reduce the classification performance on the aligned datasets due to alterations in the input space. Moreover, these methods all need a pre-processing procedure for inputs, which will take extra time and compute costs.

2.4 Adversarial Training Methods

The concentration effect seen in several adversarial samples found by [20], suggests that robustness against all other concentrated adversaries is produced through training on the most offensive adversary. Adversarial training aims to improve the robustness of models intrinsically [21], which has been proven to be the most effective approach against adversarial attacks [22–24] and has been widely used in various fields. In point cloud classification, Liu et al. [11] uses adversarial training to enhance the robustness of point shifting perturbations. Sun et al. [12] contributes an analysis of the behavior of adversarial training in point cloud classification. Zhao et al. [25] proposes a rotation attack strategy for point cloud classifiers but does not offer specific defensing tactics. ART-Point [13] designs a more effective attack algorithm and builds an adversarial training framework to boost the rotation robustness for point cloud classification.

Compared with rotation augmentation, adversarial training can increase the robustness of arbitrary rotations by determining the optimal solution to the worst-case. Compared with the rotation-invariant methods, adversarial training only needs to optimize network parameters without any geometric descriptor extractions or extra pre-processing.

Following the recent successful practice of improving the rotation robustness for point cloud classification via adversarial training and taking inspiration from ART-Point, we build a new framework to acquire the rotation invariance of 3D object reconstruction from the viewpoint of model attack and defense.

3 Methods

We begin this section with an introduction to the overall framework based on the formulation of the adversarial training objective under rotation attacks (Sect. 3.1). Then, we respectively describe how we achieve the objective through attack (Sect. 3.2) and defense (Sect. 3.3) processes.

3.1 Problem Formulation

The aim of rotation-invariant 3D object reconstruction is to obtain the aligned reconstruction results for all arbitrary rotated inputs. Our goal is to acquire the rotation invariance of 3D object reconstruction via adversarial training.

Adversarial training is a saddle point issue, which combines an inner maximizing problem and an outer minimizing problem. The inner maximizing needs to identify the worst-case samples for the given model, whereas the outer minimizing needs to train a model on these adversarial data. Based on the general saddle point problem, we specifically formulate our framework as follows:

$$\min_{\theta} \rho(\theta), where \ \rho(\theta) = E_{(p,x,o) \ D}[\max_{R \in SO(3)} L(\theta, Rp, x, o)], \tag{1}$$

where $\rho \in R^{n \times 3}$ refers to an input point cloud of size n, x is the observation proposed in the Occupancy Network [1] to be used with p as the input pair, and $o \in [0, 1]$ is the corresponding outputs, which is a real number representing the probability of occupancy. θ is the parameters of 3D object reconstruction models. Rp refers to the adversarial examples generated by using matrix R to rotate the input p and $SO(3)$ is the collection of all rotations around the R^3 Euclidean space origin, thus we ensure the goal is to make the model invariant to any rotations. $L(\theta, Rp, x, o)$ is the loss function for which we follow the setting of [1].

To obtain a robust solution to Eq. (1), we use the most aggressive rotation samples to train the models (Fig. 1).

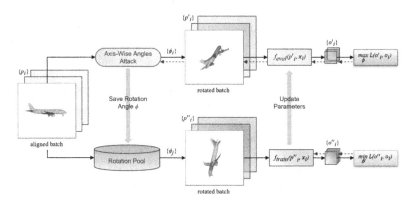

Fig. 1. The general pipeline of the ART-InvRec framework.

By maximizing the loss of the attacked basic model, the network shown in the upper branch determines the most offensive attack angles given an initial aligned batch of inputs. The rotation pool stores the attack angles according to category (total of 13 categories). To create adversarial samples for retraining the target model and ultimately develop the rotation-invariant reconstruction model, the target model shown in the lower branch samples angles from the rotation pool. The routes of the backward gradient are shown by the dashed lines. In implementations, we build the rotation pool by attacking PN-occ, PN2-occ, and DGCNN-occ, and we set PN-occ as our target model for defense.

3.2 Attack: Inner Maximization

For the inner maximizing, an efficient rotation attack technique is required to find the most offensive examples inducing high reconstruction loss. Meanwhile, we must ensure that the attack is pure rotation.

Attacked Basic Models. We prepare three basic 3D object reconstruction models to be attacked. Occupancy networks [1] descript the surface as the continuous decision boundary of a deep neural network classifier in an implicit manner, which provides inspiration for 3D reconstruction studies and has developed into a valuable tool for a wide variety of learning-based 3D applications. The architecture of occupancy networks consists of an encoder and a decoder. We use the occupancy networks in their original settings, which the encoder is based on PointNet [14], a pioneer network processing points individually, and the decoder is a fully-connected neural network with 5 ResNet blocks [26] with conditional batch normalization [27, 28]. Moreover, we exploit different encoder architectures to construct two new networks, whose encoders are based on PointNet++ [15], a hierarchical feature extraction network, and DGCNN [16], a graph-based feature extraction network, respectively. We pretrain the above three networks, respectively named PN-occ, PN2-occ, and DGCNN-occ, serving for the next attack process.

Axis-Wise Angles Attack. We optimize the attack via gradient descent on rotating angles rather than on coordinates to guarantee that the attack is pure rotation. Referring to the method proposed in [13], the final rotation matrix is computed from optimized angles as $R = R_{\varphi_z} R_{\varphi_y} R_{\varphi_x}$, where R_{φ_x} corresponds to the rotation matrix that rotates φ_x degrees around the x axis. Thus, we subdivide one rotation in SO(3) into three rotations around the x/y/z axes for optimization. Detailed derivations about the gradient calculation and matrix computation can be retrieved in [13]. Each time, we select the axis that is most influenced on final losses, as the target axis. Then we rotate one step in the opposite direction of gradient descent to finish an attack step.

Implementation Details. In real implementations, we initialize each input point cloud with a random rotation angle, then we start the axis-wise angles attack step. As with the method in [13], we use the Projected Gradient Descent [20] to constrain the optimized angles into certain scopes. We set the projected scope as $[-\pi/4, \pi/4]$, set the step size as 0.01 (radian system), and set the descent steps as 10.

3.3 Defense: Outer Minimization

For the outer minimization problem, we use Stochastic Gradient Descent [29] to re-train the model on the adversarial examples to reach the objective and obtain the final rotation-invariant model.

Rotation Pool. [13] noted that there is a strong transferability of the adversarial rotation observed on one sample to other samples in the same category. Although [13] aims to perform a point cloud classification task, the dataset we used for our reconstruction task also has category information for each point cloud, so we can refer to the technique of

[13]. We save the rotation angles produced through the above attack process by category to build a rotation pool:

$$R = [\{\phi_{i,1}\}_{i=1}^{n_1}, \{\phi_{i,2}\}_{i=1}^{n_2}, \ldots, \{\phi_{i,13}\}_{i=1}^{n_{13}}], \tag{2}$$

where $\phi_{i,1}$ refers to the rotation obtained on example i of the first category and there are 13 categories in the dataset we adopt. We save the rotations corresponding to all samples and go through all 13 categories to build the final rotation pool R. During the defense process, to convert the input into adversarial samples, we just need to sample rotations randomly from the pool based on the category.

Implementation Details. We not only attack the target reconstruction model PN-occ but also attack more models to build the rotation pool, including PN2-occ and DGCNN-occ. Attacking three models results in three times more aggressive rotations than the naive iterative optimization does. Hence, following the principle introduced in Ensemble Adversarial Training [30], we can finish the minimizing process in one step.

4 Experiments

4.1 Experiment Setup

Dataset. For all of our experiments, we use 13 classes of the ShapeNet [31] subset, following the train/validation/test split like Choy et al. [32]. Similar to [1], we sample 300 points from each watertight mesh and apply a Gaussian noise with zero mean and standard deviation 0.05.

Models. We pretrain PN-occ and construct two new 3D reconstruction models, PN2-occ and DGCNN-occ. These models all lack rotation invariance. We select PN-occ as the target reconstruction model, and attack PN-occ, PN2-occ, DGCNN-occ to construct the rotation pool.

Metric. Volumetric Intersection over Union (IoU) is defined as the ratio of the volume of the intersection to the union of the two meshes. In line with ONet [1], we derive unbiased estimates of the volume of the intersection and the union by randomly sampling 100,000 points from the bounding volume. The determination of whether these points lie inside or outside the ground truth/predicted mesh is used to calculate the IoU.

4.2 Comparison with Rotation Augmentation

We initially assess the effectiveness of our ART-InvRec in comparison to rotation augmentation (RA).

For reconstruction models using rotation augmentation, we train them with randomly rotated point clouds. Table 1 presents the comparison results. We show results on several train/test settings: aligned data without any rotation (I) – the standard evaluation setup for prior reconstruction models, and arbitrary rotations SO(3). ART refers to the adversarial training we proposed.

Table 1. Comparing three basic reconstruction models and corresponding ART-InvRec models under the metric of IoU (%).

Models	I/I	I/SO(3)	SO(3)/SO(3)	Models (ours)	ART/SO(3)
PN-occ	75	12.1	53	ART-PN-occ	**58.3**
PN2-occ	74	13.1	48.6	ART-PN2-occ	**54.1**
DGCNN-occ	74.7	12.3	52.6	ART-DGCNN-occ	**57.8**

Several observations can be obtained based on the table. Firstly, when three basic reconstruction models PN-occ, PN2-occ, and DGCNN-occ are trained on aligned data, they can only reach acceptable performance when test data is also aligned. Once testing them on the SO(3) rotated data, the performance declines significantly. It proves that the original models lack rotation invariance. Secondly, under the SO(3) rotated test set, models trained using our ART-InvRec outperform those trained with RA (corresponding to SO(3)/SO(3) in the table), exhibiting a maximum increase of 5.5%. The results suggest that ART-InvRec is a more effective technique to acquire the rotation invariance of 3D object reconstruction than augmentation method.

4.3   Comparison with Advanced 3D Reconstruction Models

We further compare our ART-InvRec models with advanced 3D reconstruction models, including POCO (state-of-the-art model) [4], DP-ConvONet [3] and ConvONet [2]. For fair comparisons, it should be noted that we retrain the three original advanced models with the same settings as [1], subsampling 300 points from the surface of each model in ShapeNet rather than 3k points as [2–4].

Table 2. Comparing three advanced reconstruction models and ART-InvRec models under the metric of IoU (%).

Models	I/I	I/SO(3)	ART/SO(3) (ours)
POCO	81.3	13.9	–
DP-ConvONet	79.6	13.1	–
ConvONet	78.6	13	–
ART-PN-occ	–	–	**58.3**
ART-PN2-occ	–	–	**54.1**
ART-DGCNN-occ	–	–	**57.8**

In Table 2, we show results on extreme train/test settings. Firstly, when three advanced reconstruction models POCO, DP-ConvONet, and ConvONet are trained and tested on aligned data (I/I), they achieve good performance. However, once testing them on the SO(3) rotated data, the performance declines significantly. That proves that the advanced reconstruction models are unable to handle the rotation invariant problem. Secondly, under the SO(3) rotated test set, the results of our models are significantly higher than those of advanced models, validating that our ART-InvRec framework is able to effectively acquire the rotation invariance of 3D object reconstruction and beyond the advanced models.

Furthermore, we present visualization results to qualitatively compare the rotation invariance of POCO (the state-of-the-art model) and our best model ART-PN-occ. Meshes are extracted using the Multi-resolution IsoSurface Extraction (MISE) method, as utilized in ONet [1]. It can be observed that POCO can only reconstruct the delicate details in the I/I case. In the I/SO(3) case, POCO totally fails, and the reconstruction results are blurry, indistinguishable, and seem to be in certain rotation poses. However, when arbitrary SO(3) rotations are applied to test our best model, ART-PN-occ can get stable reconstruction results no matter how the inputs rotate. That demonstrates the powerful rotation invariance of our model.

4.4 Ablation Study

In this part, we perform ablation studies to illustrate the impact of the attack process and the rotation pool we built. It is vital to notice that the target minimization model in all ablation experiments is PN-occ.

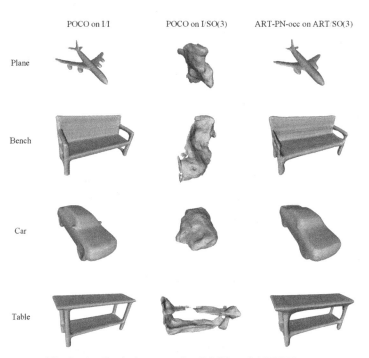

Fig. 2. Qualitatively comparing POCO and ART-PN-occ.

Effect of Axis-Wise Angles Attack. We employ multiple strategies to produce adversarial examples that yield distinct loss values, including the stochastic SO(3) rotation and our axis-wise angles attacks with different steps (Fig. 2).

Table 3. The average loss of adversarial examples produced by various attack techniques and the IoU (%) of the related ART-InvRec training on PN-occ.

Methods	Loss	IoU
SO(3)	788.1	53
ART (step = 1)	1093.3	56.1
ART (step = 5)	1256.8	57.4
ART (step = 10)	1375	**58.3**

In Table 3, we show the average loss of examples generated by various attacks and the results of our ART-InvRec technique using corresponding samples. It can be observed that the axis-wise angles attack with 10 steps gradient descent causes the highest loss. Defensing on these most aggressive attacks, our ART-PN-occ reaches the highest IoU for rotation-invariant reconstruction.

Effect of Rotation Pool. We demonstrate the effectiveness of building the rotation pool. We compare the results of adversarial training without and with different rotation pools, investigating the effect of constructing pools from different attacked basic models.

Table 4. The average loss of adversarial examples produced by various rotation pools and the IoU (%) of the related ART-InvRec training on PN-occ.

Methods	Loss	IoU
w/o RP	1217.1	43.8
RP (PN-occ)	1023.5	56.2
RP (PN-occ, PN2-occ)	1167.4	57.4
RP (PN-occ, DGCNN-occ)	1231.6	57.7
RP (PN-occ, PN2-occ, DGCNN-occ)	1375	**58.3**

In Table 4, we show the average loss of examples generated by various rotation pools and the results of our ART-InvRec technique using corresponding samples. RP(.) refers to the rotation pool constructed by attacking the pretrained basic reconstruction models in brackets. As shown in the first row of Table 4, although adversarial training without a rotation pool can also generate samples causing high loss, the final IoU is lower than training with a rotation pool, which is because of overfitting [33]. It can be observed that the rotation pool, which attacks PN-occ, PN2-occ, and DGCNN-occ, induces the highest loss. Defensing on this rotation pool, our ART-PN-occ reaches the highest IoU for rotation invariant reconstruction.

5 Conclusion

In this paper, we propose ART-InvRec to acquire the rotation invariance of 3D object reconstruction via adversarial training. ART-InvRec comprises an attack process that employs the axis-wise angles attack method to effectively identify the most aggressive rotated examples and a defense process incorporating the rotation pool mechanism. Our experiments showcase exceptional results in addressing the demanding task of rotation-invariant object reconstruction. Moreover, the rotation invariance of our best model ART-PN-occ outperforms existing advanced reconstruction models.

Since the experiments with our models mainly focus on the performance tested on rotated data, we plan to explore the results on aligned test data in our future work. Although the rotation-invariant task principally aims to deal with the rotated input, an ideal model is expected to maintain the original performance even if the aligned data is inputted. To this end, our next goal is to refine the model that achieves excellent rotation-invariant reconstruction on both rotated and aligned data, which can be applied to more comprehensive scientific scenarios straightforwardly, such as scene understanding [34].

Acknowledgements. This work is supported by National Key R&D Program of China under Grant No. 2021YFF0900504, the National Natural Science Foundation of China under Grant No. 61971383 and No. 62001432, the Fundamental Research Funds for the Central Universities under Grant No. CUC210C013, No. CUC21GZ007 and No. CUC18LG024, and the Horizontal Research Project under Grant No. HG23002.

References

1. Mescheder, L.M., Oechsle, M., Niemeyer, M., Nowozin, S., Geiger, A.: Occupancy networks: learning 3D reconstruction in function space. In: 2019 IEEE/CVF Conference on Computer Vision and Pattern Recognition (CVPR), pp. 4455–4465 (2018)
2. Peng, S., Niemeyer, M., Mescheder, L.M., Pollefeys, M., Geiger, A.: Convolutional occupancy networks. arXiv abs/2003.04618 (2020)
3. Lionar, S., Emtsev, D., Svilarkovic, D., Peng, S.: Dynamic plane convolutional occupancy networks. In: 2021 IEEE Winter Conference on Applications of Computer Vision (WACV), pp. 1828–1837 (2020)
4. Boulch, A., Marlet, R.: POCO: point convolution for surface reconstruction. In: 2022 IEEE/CVF Conference on Computer Vision and Pattern Recognition (CVPR), pp. 6292–6304 (2022)
5. Zhao, C., Yang, J., Xiong, X., Zhu, A., CAO, Z., Li, X.: Rotation invariant point cloud classification: where local geometry meets global topology. arXiv abs/1911.00195 (2019)
6. Chen, C., Li, G., Xu, R., Chen, T., Wang, M., Lin, L.: ClusterNet: deep hierarchical cluster network with rigorously rotation-invariant representation for point cloud analysis. In: 2019 IEEE/CVF Conference on Computer Vision and Pattern Recognition (CVPR), pp. 4989–4997 (2019)

7. Deng, H., Birdal, T., Ilic, S.: PPF-FoldNet: unsupervised learning of rotation invariant 3D local descriptors. arXiv abs/1808.10322 (2018)
8. Zhang, Z., Hua, B., Chen, W., Tian, Y., Yeung, S.: Global context aware convolutions for 3D point cloud understanding. In: 2020 International Conference on 3D Vision (3DV), pp. 210–219 (2020)
9. Zhang, Z., Hua, B., Rosen, D.W., Yeung, S.: Rotation invariant convolutions for 3D point clouds deep learning. In: 2019 International Conference on 3D Vision (3DV), pp. 204–213 (2019)
10. Li, X., Li, R., Chen, G., Fu, C., Cohen-Or, D., Heng, P.: A rotation-invariant framework for deep point cloud analysis. IEEE Trans. Vis. Comput. Graph. **28**, 4503–4514 (2020)
11. Liu, D., Yu, R., Su, H.: Extending adversarial attacks and defenses to deep 3D point cloud classifiers. In: 2019 IEEE International Conference on Image Processing (ICIP), pp. 2279–2283 (2019)
12. Sun, J., Koenig, K., Cao, Y., Chen, Q.A., Mao, Z.M.: On the adversarial robustness of 3D point cloud classification. arXiv abs/2011.11922 (2020)
13. Wang, R., Yang, Y., Tao, D.: ART-point: improving rotation robustness of point cloud classifiers via adversarial rotation. In: 2022 IEEE/CVF Conference on Computer Vision and Pattern Recognition (CVPR), pp. 14351–14360 (2022)
14. Qi, C., Su, H., Mo, K., Guibas, L.J.: PointNet: deep learning on point sets for 3D classification and segmentation. In: 2017 IEEE Conference on Computer Vision and Pattern Recognition (CVPR), pp. 77–85 (2016)
15. Qi, C., Yi, L., Su, H., Guibas, L.J.: PointNet++: deep hierarchical feature learning on point sets in a metric space. Neural Inf. Process. Syst. (2017)
16. Wang, Y., Sun, Y., Liu, Z., Sarma, S.E., Bronstein, M.M., Solomon, J.M.: Dynamic graph CNN for learning on point clouds. ACM Trans. Graph. (TOG) **38**, 1–12 (2018)
17. Poulenard, A., Rakotosaona, M., Ponty, Y., Ovsjanikov, M.: Effective rotation-invariant point CNN with spherical harmonics kernels. In: 2019 International Conference on 3D Vision (3DV), pp. 47–56 (2019)
18. Liu, M., Yao, F., Choi, C., Sinha, A., Ramani, K.: Deep learning 3D shapes using alt-az anisotropic 2-sphere convolution. In: International Conference on Learning Representations (2018)
19. Rao, Y., Lu, J., Zhou, J.: Spherical fractal convolutional neural networks for point cloud recognition. In: 2019 IEEE/CVF Conference on Computer Vision and Pattern Recognition (CVPR), pp. 452–460 (2019)
20. Madry, A., Makelov, A., Schmidt, L., Tsipras, D., Vladu, A.: Towards deep learning models resistant to adversarial attacks. arXiv abs/1706.06083 (2017)
21. Bai, T., Luo, J., Zhao, J., Wen, B., Wang, Q.: Recent advances in adversarial training for adversarial robustness. In: International Joint Conference on Artificial Intelligence (2021)
22. Maini, P., Wong, E., Kolter, J.Z.: Adversarial robustness against the union of multiple perturbation models. arXiv abs/1909.04068 (2019)
23. Pang, T., Yang, X., Dong, Y., Su, H., Zhu, J.: Bag of tricks for adversarial training. arXiv abs/2010.00467 (2020)
24. Schott, L., Rauber, J., Bethge, M., Brendel, W.: Towards the first adversarially robust neural network model on MNIST. arXiv: Computer Vision and Pattern Recognition (2018)
25. Zhao, Y., Wu, Y., Chen, C., Lim, A.: On isometry robustness of deep 3D point cloud models under adversarial attacks. In: 2020 IEEE/CVF Conference on Computer Vision and Pattern Recognition (CVPR), pp. 1198–1207 (2020)
26. He, K., Zhang, X., Ren, S., Sun, J.: Deep residual learning for image recognition. In: 2016 IEEE Conference on Computer Vision and Pattern Recognition (CVPR), pp. 770–778 (2015)
27. Vries, H.D., Strub, F., Mary, J., Larochelle, H., Pietquin, O., Courville, A.C.: Modulating early visual processing by language. Neural Inf. Process. Syst. (2017)

28. Dumoulin, V., et al.: Adversarially learned inference. arXiv abs/1606.00704 (2016)
29. Bottou, L.: Large-scale machine learning with stochastic gradient descent. In: International Conference on Computational Statistics (2010)
30. Tramèr, F., Kurakin, A., Papernot, N., Boneh, D., Mcdaniel, P.: Ensemble adversarial training: attacks and defenses. arXiv abs/1705.07204 (2017)
31. Chang, A.X., et al.: ShapeNet: an information-rich 3D model repository. arXiv abs/1512.03012 (2015)
32. Choy, C.B., Xu, D., Gwak, J., Chen, K., Savarese, S.: 3D-R2N2: a unified approach for single and multi-view 3D object reconstruction. arXiv abs/1604.00449 (2016)
33. Kurakin, A., Goodfellow, I.J., Bengio, S.: Adversarial machine learning at scale. arXiv abs/1611.01236 (2016)
34. Fan, D., Ji, G., Xu, P., Cheng, M., Sakaridis, C., Gool, L.V.: Advances in deep concealed scene understanding. Vis. Intell. 1, 1–24 (2023)

Multi-view Object Recognition Based on Deep Models

Xin Li[1], Shaojie Ai[2], and Jing Liu[1($\boxtimes$)]

[1] School of Electrical and Information Engineering, Tianjin University,
92 Weijin Road, Tianjin, China
{lixinge,jliu_tju}@tju.edu.cn
[2] Shanghai Institute of Satellite Engineering, Shanghai, China
asj1224@163.com

Abstract. Object classification and retrieval play important roles in many computer vision tasks. To achieve a good performance on RGB images, we propose a deep learning based multi-view method for both classification and retrieval. Different information of a static object is represented in multiple views, which makes the features extracted more stable against view variance and complex environment. To take advantage of both excellent performance of CNN architectures and rich information in multiple views, our approach is based on the Inception with Batch Normalization network for feature extraction and a post-fusion method is adopted. To reduce the effect of noise and improve computation efficiency, a denoising technology is explored to simulate infinite times corruption on the features for robust representation. The proposed method is capable of achieving high performance with a handful of training views, even better than some algorithms based on both RGB and depth modalities. The performance of the method is proved to be stable with different numbers of views as testing, and is comparable even with one testing view. Besides, the method is evaluated across datasets together with a popular Multi-view deep learning algorithms (MVCNN) and shows favourably influence can be brought by datasets transfer. This method is implemented on two kinds of benchmarks which are distinct in sizes to verify the efficiency and robustness of our method.

Keywords: Deep Learning · Multiple Views · Object Retrieval

1 Introduction

3D object classification and retrieval have attained a large amount of attention in computer vision, due to many applications in digital entertainment, computer-aided design, bioinformatics, robot navigation and so on [26]. Existing 3D object retrieval algorithms can be concluded into content-based retrieval [8] and text-based retrieval. Content-based retrieval arises much attention due to the popularization of 3D model compared to text-based retrieval where key words of the target object annotated by human are given for retrieval. Content-based retrieval

G. Zhai et al. (Eds.): IFTC 2023, CCIS 2066, pp. 297–313, 2024.
https://doi.org/10.1007/978-981-97-3623-2_22

aims to retrieve the objects that have the most relevant visual contents from the database. Our focus of content-based retrieval should be departed from instance-retrieval where the retrieving images contain the same object. We concentrate on class retrieval, where a query image or image set including a particular object may be given, and the aim is to retrieve a image or image set of the same class. On class level, 3D object retrieval is similar to 3D object classification. 3D retrieval requires both feature extracting and appropriate similarity measurement while 3D classification requires salient feature extracting and fine classifiers. Thus, feature extracting process is important for both classification and retrieval. When the features are discriminant and effective enough, simple classifiers and plain distance measurement can also achieve high performance on classification and retrieval.

According to different types of input, 3D object classification and retrieval methods can be divided into two typical categories, shape based [25,36] and 2D view based [22,39] ones. Shape based methods take spatial relations into considerations, such as surface distribution, geometric moment and voxels. They are intuitive for comprehension but more difficult to design. Researchers typically developed algorithms from 2D view images, where each 3D object is represented by a collection of images. Due to the outstanding capability of deep learning networks on extracting features of 2D view images, 2D view based algorithms become more popular in 3D object classification and retrieval.

According to different feature extraction ways, traditional hand-craft representation and promising deep feature are two major research topics. Traditionally, researchers made effort to analyze the properties of descriptors and design characteristic representations for a special task. Deep learning networks are popular nowadays and can outperform most hand-craft representations in both classification [11,36,37] and retrieval [4,24]. It's capable of recognizing objects in spite of scale inconsistency, background perturbations, occlusion, noise as well as extracting correlated information from different views.

In this paper, we propose a deep learning based multi-view classification and retrieval method. For feature description, we adopt the Inception with Batch Normalization network [10] as our base model since it's quick to converge and at the same time keeps high performance on classification tasks. We add a merge unit on our base model to fuse 2D visual features into a object-level feature. This arrangement helps extract the common information from different views despite the dynamic background. To reduce the influence of noise, a denoising method is also adopted to make the model more stable.

Our main contributions are summarized as follow. (i) We present a multi-view based 3D object classification architecture and a 3D object retrieval architecture. (ii) We put forward a robust multi-view feature extraction scheme. Instead of using one feature for each view, the feature extraction scheme generates one compact feature for each object, which reduces the computation complexity. (iii) The proposed method can achieve high performance by using a small number of training views, and the performance is stable even under a single test view. In addition, the method is evaluated on multiple datasets, and shows that dataset transfer is helpful to improve performance.

The remainder of the paper is organized as follows. Section 2 discusses the related works. Section 3 is an overview of the proposed method, followed by a detailed description of how to train the model and implement on the object classification and retrieval. We report experimental evaluation in Sect. 4 and the proposed method is concluded in Sect. 5.

2   Related Work

Multi-view based methods are popular in 3D object classification and retrieval due to its high flexibility. Cai et al. [2] proposed a novel voxel-based three-view hybrid parallel network for 3D shape classification, which obtains the depth projection views of the three-dimension model from the front view, the top view and the side view, so as to preserve the spatial information of the three-dimensional model to the greatest extent. For multi-view based methods, the content and the number of views will directly affect the final classification and retrieval performance. Therefore, traditional multi-view methods rely on the process of selecting representative views or specific camera arrays [4], which reduces its flexibility and generalization ability. Recently, various effective methods have been put forward to break the restriction of view changes. For instance, Liu *et al.* [17] jointly learned visual and spatial contexts for 3D object modeling to avoid the difficulty of representative view extraction.

Several deep learning classification methods are proposed based on 2D views. Lots of researchers prefer to explore depth images as complement for classification. Though the depth information provides models with color invariance and lighting invariance, the RGB data contains the major and rich visual information for classification tasks. It's still an open problem on how to make full use of RGB images information for classification. Muhammad Sohail et al. [30] developed a multiscale spectral-spatial feature learning network specifically designed for Hyperspectral images (HSI). Multi-view convolutional neural network [31] (MVCNN) method is a classical view-based method for 3D object classification, which maps points set into gray images to extract features. It achieved comparable performance on SHREC'2017 [27]. Lu *et al.* [20] proposed a post-fusion method where a RGB deep feature is combined with a depth deep feature at the last full-connection layers to enhance the performance. Different from the above two algorithms where the AlexNet is adopted as their base model, Nair *et al.* [21] used deep belief net instead to make use of good capability provided by deep models. Wang *et al.* [35] relied on ResNet-50 networks [9] to build their multi-modal networks, where common and special parts are learned from RGB and depth modalities. Some approaches leverage pose estimation to benefit classification accuracy. In RotationNet [11] method, a model derived from AlexNet jointly estimates view position and classifies objects. It achieved the best performances on both ModelNet10 and ModelNet40 hitherto. However, this kind of methods requires a model seen all directions of an object to infer the pose of a querying object.

In general, feature representation and similarity measurement are two crucial fundamentals in 3D object retrieval. With the excellent representations of deep networks, an distance metric is enough for 3D object retrieval in lots of algorithms instead of a complex matching algorithm for similarity computation. Therefore, lots of retrieval methods devote themselves to deep models for better feature representation. Gao *et al.* [7] developed a Group Pair Convolutional Neural Network for 3D object retrieval, which is trained from the similarity of each sample pair. Li *et al.* [15] added a View-wised Discriminative Ranking (VDR) scheme to base deep convolutional network, and then used the ranking information to retrain the base model. Nie *et al.* [23] trained the basic deep model on representative views rendered from 3D objects. Liu *et al.* [18] leveraged the similarity of different domains, for example, RGB image domain and 3D shape domain, to train deep model.

3   Overview

Different from previous 3D model classification and retrieval algorithms relying on traditional graph matching or other visual technologies, we focus on developing an efficient feature extracting method for multiple views based 3D object classification and retrieval in this paper. The architecture of the proposed method is shown on Fig. 1. The whole framework can be summarized in four steps: A set of multiple RGB views are chosen from each object. Views are then separately fed into the branches of BN-Inception for feature maps, where a multi-view consensus layer is employed to aggregate feature maps from different views. Thirdly, the aggregated descriptor will be sent into a multi-layers auto-encoder to learn a robust representation by simulating multiple times corruption. Finally, the representation for each object is used for similarity measure through a simple distance metric, e.g. Euclidean Distance.

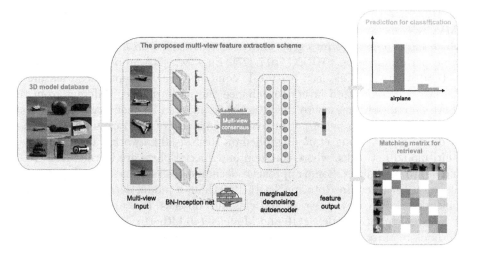

Fig. 1. Diagram of the proposed multi-view feature extraction algorithm for 3D object classification and retrieval architectures.

In this section, we first introduce the basic architecture of deep network and study the good practice in an aggregated descriptor combining information from multiple views. Then, the corruption denoising autoencoder is described to learn a robust representation of the objects.

3.1   Multi-view Deep Model

It is well known that deep networks would suffice to learn a discriminant representation under enormous amount of training data. Tens of thousands of parameters in the networks will over-fit with insufficient training data. This can be alleviated by pre-training on other huge dataset (eq. ImageNet [5]) and then updating and getting convergence on the target dataset with a little effort. Thus, the brilliant representation ability of deep networks can be employed in our framework with pretraining and data augmentation strategies to receive discriminant features.

Each view of an object will make a preliminary prediction of the object class. Then a consensus strategy over all input views will produce an object-level prediction. The loss value will be predicted at the object-level, rather than the view-level. We denote input views as $\{V_k\}_{k=1}^{S}$ of an object, where S is the number of input views of each object. The object-level prediction can be derived as follows:

$$p = g(f(V_1; W), f(V_2; W), ..., f(V_S; W)), \tag{1}$$

where $f(\cdot)$ represents the basic deep convolutional model to produce object-level predictions according to [33], and W is the parameters of the model. We aggregate every prediction of views by function $g(\cdot)$, and here a simple averaging strategy is adopted. The widely used Softmax function is chosen to predict probability of each object,

$$q_i = \frac{e^{p_i}}{\sum_{j=1}^{C} e^{p_j}}. \tag{2}$$

Combined with standard categorical cross-entropy loss, the final loss function is formed as:

$$Loss = -\sum_{i=1}^{C} y_i log(q_i), \tag{3}$$

where C is the number of object classes and y_i denotes the i-th class label. Since the function $g(\cdot)$ is an averaging function, Eq. 3 is differentiable and standard back-propagation algorithms can be applied for optimization. The gradients of model parameters W can be derived as follows:

$$\frac{\partial Loss}{\partial W} = \frac{\partial Loss}{\partial g} \sum_{k=1}^{S} \frac{\partial g}{\partial f(V_k; W)} \frac{\partial f(V_k; W)}{\partial W}. \tag{4}$$

In our work, we well adapt the BN-Inception model from beginning to the last fully connected layer as our base model, since it has proved its ability in faster convergence and at the same time obtaining an excellent performance. Our models are pre-trained on a large labelled dataset, ImageNet. This will offer a good initialization for fine-tuning on the target object dataset. Besides, too many Batch Normalization layers may rise an over-fitting problem, since the training dataset is limited. Thus we only preserve the first BN layer in the basic model when training like [33]. The training process utilizes standard back propagation and stochastic gradient descent (SGD). Data augmentation is adopted to elevate the performance. And we render their horizontal flips, totally 2 images from one view.

3.2   Marginalized Denoising Auto-encoder

Though deep networks behave brilliantly on most tasks, lacking of views may have severe influence on obtaining discriminant features. We propose an approach to increase the diversity of views latently and on the other hand mitigate the over-fitting problem. A marginalized denoising auto-encoder [3] is fitted for this purpose by simulating infinite times data corruption, which will gain a powerful generalization ability.

The auto-encoder has two layers. The features extracted by the previous procedure are taken as the input data x, which is then mapped by $f_1(\cdot)$ into hidden units h in the encoder layer. In the decoder layer, the hidden units will be decoded through $f_2(\cdot)$ to produce output o. The auto-encoder aims at decrease the reconstruction loss between the inputs and the outputs: $\|o - f_2(f_1(x))\|^2$.

The marginalized denoising auto-encoder performs a corruption procedure in reconstruction of the input data. We denote the input data as $X \in R^{d \times N}$, where N represents the number of the input samples, and d is the dimension of a sample. Then each element of the sample is randomly set to 0 with a probability no less than 0. We formulate the target squared reconstruction loss as $\left\| X - D\tilde{X} \right\|_F^2$, where $\tilde{X} \in R^{d \times N}$ denotes the input data after corruption, and the mapping matrix D denotes the process from encoding to decoding procedures. To lower the variance, m times different repetitions are performed over the training samples. Hence, the loss function will be re-written as:

$$\left\| \bar{X} - D\tilde{\bar{X}} \right\|_F^2 , \tag{5}$$

where $\bar{X} = [X, .., X] \in R^{d \times mN}$ and $\tilde{\bar{X}} \in R^{d \times mN}$ express m times different corruption of X. Equation 5 can be solved in closed-form with ordinary least squares. The mapping D can be derived from Eq. 5:

$$D = \bar{X}\tilde{\bar{X}}^T (\tilde{\bar{X}}\tilde{\bar{X}}^T)^{-1} . \tag{6}$$

Equation 6 can be computed by the weak law of large numbers, when m is treated as a very big number. $\bar{X}\tilde{\bar{X}}^T$ and $\tilde{\bar{X}}\tilde{\bar{X}}^T$ can be expressed by their expectations $E_p(\bar{X}\tilde{\bar{X}}^T)$ and $E_p(\tilde{\bar{X}}\tilde{\bar{X}}^T)$ with the corruption probability p, respectively, as studied in [3].

The input data is then be mapped into the same feature space with the learned mapping D and a non-linear squashing function. Several squashing functions are available, like sigmoid, hyperbolic tangent, rectifier function and so on. We choose the hyperbolic tangent $tanh(\cdot)$ in this work.

4   Experiments

4.1   Dataset

Three classic benchmarks including different amounts of data and distinct data sources are chosen for evaluation, seen from Fig. 2. We implement our models under two cases: *case1* pretrained on ImageNet dataset and fine-tuned on its own training set, *case2* pre-trained on ImageNet as well as any other 3D object dataset that different from its own but not fine-tuned on its own. Here, we choose either RGB-D or MV-RED-73 dataset in *case2* because of their rich categories. The three classic benchmarks and their experiment settings are introduced as follows:

ETH-80 dataset [14] contains 80 objects from 8 carefully chosen categories, 256×256 pixels RGB images. It is employed as an attempt on small scale dataset. The dataset is shown in Fig. 2, which is subdivided amidst small areas from fruits to vehicles. Objects from these areas are shoot from different facets, and each object is inclusive of 41 views spaced equally over the upper viewing hemisphere. Compared to existing epic benchmarks, this dataset seems to span small in inner class, which benefits the classification and retrieval a lot. According to [34], five instances of the same class are randomly selected as training data and the rest five are treated as testing data. 10 times random trials are carried out.

RGB-D dataset [13] is a much larger dataset in scale, numbers of categories and subcategories, varieties in resolutions and viewpoints than ETH dataset. The RGB-D object Dataset contains video sequences of 300 common everyday objects and 51 categories from multiple view angles totally 250,000 RGB-D images. Both color and depth images at 640×480 resolution are recorded by the cameras mounted at three different heights relative to the turntable, at approximately 30, 45 and 60° above the horizon.

RGB-D dataset provides two levels of classification: category level and instance level. Category level classification involves classifying previously unseen objects as belonging in the same category. Instance level classification identifies whether an object is physically the same object that has previously been seen under different viewpoints. The dataset is still challengeable, though several methods achieving saturating performance on their own evaluation criteria. For category classification, we randomly leave one object out from each category for testing and train the classifiers on the rest objects so as to check the performance on unseen objects. We average accuracies across 10 trials for category recognition. For instance classification, we train on the video sequences of each object where the camera is mounted 30° and 60° above the horizon and evaluate on the 45 degrees video sequence in order to perform a cross-view verification.

Fig. 2. Samples from ETH-80 dataset, RGB-D object dataset, MV-RED-73 dataset. (Color figure online)

MV-RED-73 dataset [16] is collected for retrieval with multi-modal views. It consists of 505 objects, divided into 61 categories. The complete version of MV-RED dataset captures from 721 views for each 3D object. A compact version of MV-RED, referred as MV-RED-73, renders 73 views from the complete version. 56 objects of different categories randomly selected are respected as testing set as the other five categories only contain one object, and the remains are utilized as training set. Meanwhile, image cropping is adopted for a better performance. After cutting, the object is in the middle of the picture and occupies most of the picture space. We implement 10 trials on MV-RED-73 dataset as well.

4.2 Implementation Details

For classification, we train a linear multi-class Support Vector Machine (SVM) model with object-level features. In our classification task, the accuracy is computed as follows:

$$Accuracy = \frac{tp + tn}{tp + tn + fp + fn}, \tag{7}$$

where tp, tn, fp, and fn denote true positive, true negative, false positive and false negative, respectively.

For retrieval, features are normalized to compute distances and various evaluation criteria are adopted. Since the extracted features are vectors in thousands of dimensions, it is too large for distance-wise retrieval methods. Supposed that two features are linearly correlated with large constant difference for each element, their distance will be large despite of their high similarity. Thus, before retrieval, a normalization on both training and testing set is necessary. We borrow ideas from [31], namely low-rank mahalanobis metric, which boosts the results a lot. Euclidean distances between object-level features are computed and sorted. The following measurements are employed for retrieval.

- *Nearest Neighbor (NN)*: It returns the second retrieval result, since the first returned one must be the query itself in our experiment;
- *First-Tier(FT)*: It denotes the recall of top τ relevant results in the whole dataset for the query, where τ is the number of objects in the ground truth class;
- *Second-Tier(ST)*: It denotes the recall of top 2τ relevant results;
- *F-measure (F)*: It jointly evaluates the precision and recall of first ι relevant results, where $\iota = 20$ in our experiment;
- *Discounted cumulative gain (DCG)*: It assigns higher weights to first correct results while lower on last results;
- *Average Normalized Modified Retrieval Rank (ANMRR)*: It considers the ranking order so that a lower ANMRR value represents a better result.
- *Mean Average Precision(mAP)*: It is the mean of the average precision scores for each query.

4.3 Experimental Results

Feature Space Visualization Analysis. The top figure of Fig. 3 is a feature map for ETH-80 dataset using T-SNE [32] tools. Feature vectors of eight objects are drawn on the map, from which we can see that feature vectors of the same class cluster closely while features in different object classes distributes far away from each other. It's indicated that the features learned by our framework is discriminant and easy to classify as well as retrieving. It can be observed that the testing object is very close to the training objects in the same class, which verifies the efficiency of our framework. The same conclusion can be derived from Fig. 3 on RGB-D dataset and MV-RED-73 dataset.

Table 1. Classification results on ETH-80 dataset, * denotes *case1*.

methods	Accuracy(%)
[12]	91.7±9
[29]	94.8±4.3
[34]	96.8±1.5
ours*	96.5±3.2
ours	**97.8 ± 3.2**

Table 2. Classification results on RGB-D object dataset using RGB modality only, * denotes *case1*.

methods	Category Accuracy (%)	Instance Accuracy (%)
[13]	83.8±3.5	74.8
[1]	82.4±3.1	92.1
[28]	83.1±2.0	92.0
[40]	89.0±2.1	–
[19]	89.6±2.0	–
ours*	92.6±2.6	**100.0**
ours	**93.3 ± 2.8**	**100.0**

Multi-view Classification. Table 1 offers a comparison with state-of-the-art methods on ETH-80 dataset. It's reported that our framework is comparable with the state-of-the-art methods in object classification. The performance of our model in *case1* follows that in *case2* closely by 1.3 percent on average value. The main restriction for our model in *case1* is the shortage in object views of ETH-80 dataset. Only 41 views are captured and in the meanwhile not all viewpoints of a same object can be captured. Thus, the redundancy of the views brings less views useful, which is not compatible with a network processing epic parameters. However, less views are as efficient as entire view set through our framework, which can be seen from Fig. 4 and will be discussed later. On the other hand, our model pre-trained on both ImageNet and RGB-D dataset in *case2* boosts the performance a lot instead of model in *case1*. The RGB-D dataset consists of similar categories in ETH-80 dataset, which does a favour on improving performance.

For category classification together with instance classification on RGB-D dataset, the proposed method outperforms other existing methods listed on the Table 2 in terms of RGB modality. For instance classification, our framework performs as high as 100 percent for the reason that the model has seen the object before. For category classification, the experimental results are better than those of the other methods providing with RGB information merely. Since 2011, the performance with RGB modality has been fluctuated under 90%, so recently people turn to pay more attention on the depth image. Our method breaks through the obstacle provided with RGB image by merely relying on the deep model and denoising autoencoder. Further, the results are even higher than those of the methods combining both RGB and depth modalities. For instance, Zia *et al.* [40] achieved 91.84% by making use of RGB and depth images. It means our models are capable of recognizing objects from limited modalities.

In Table 3 and Table 4, the popular MVCNN [31] method is employed to compare on recognition and retrieval. In Table 3, we fix the training and testing views at 15, respectively. Meanwhile, we implement the MVCNN method under two cases same as those on our models. From Table 3, the MVCNN method fails on both cases for classification tasks, obviously. Compared with two cases

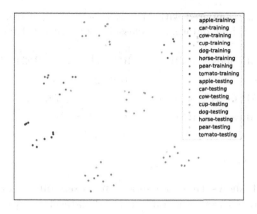

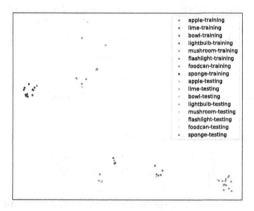

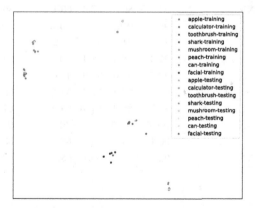

Fig. 3. From top to bottom are feature vectors of ETH-80 dataset, RGB-D dataset, MV-RED-73 dateset mapped using T-SNE tools respectively. The testing samples are marked with lighter colors. The testing and training samples in each class are tightly clustered and the clusters are far away from each other. (Color figure online)

Table 3. The results compared with MVCNN method when training and testing 15 views respectively on three datasets for classification tasks, * denotes *case1*.

Methods	ETH	RGB-D	MV-RED-73
ours*	95.5±3.3	92.6±2.9	**88.4 ± 3.4**
MVCNN*	88.5±6.0	76.4±4.5	77.0±3.6
ours	**97.8 ± 3.2**	**93.3 ± 2.8**	87.1±3.7
MVCNN	86.8±5.9	76.9±4.7	73.0±3.9

on our models, it shows that the model in *case2* outperforms the model in *case1* on first two datasets and on the third dataset the performances of two cases are approaching. It's illuminated that pre-trained on large dataset like ImageNet prevent the models from over-fitting and at the same time pre-trained on different object dataset will offer more information for object related tasks. For MVRED datasets, the number of categories in RGB-D datasets used for training is less than that in MVRED testing set, which may indirectly leads to the decline of the performance in *case2*. Similar phenomena appears in Fig. 6.

Table 4. Comparison with state-of-art methods on three datasets for retrieval tasks, * denotes *case1*.

Datasets	Similarity Evaluation	NN	FT	ST	F-measure	DCG	ANMRR	mAP
ETH	FusionOptimal [38]	87.5	69.2	89.9	61.6	91.3	25.3	–
	CNN-VDR [15]	96.3	70.4	82.3	62.4	83.1	17.2	–
	CNN-WBGM [6]	93.9	70.9	81.6	61.6	83.7	16.7	–
	ours*	**100.0**	**94.5**	**98.9**	66.0	**96.2**	**4.2**	**98.0**
	MVCNN*	95.0	86.4	96.5	64.7	86.6	12.5	90.6
	ours	**100.0**	93.3	**98.9**	**66.1**	95.4	5.2	97.6
	MVCNN	93.8	86.3	97.0	65.1	86.8	12.6	90.9
RGB-D	**ours***	**96.0**	**90.5**	**98.6**	**50.5**	**90.0**	**9.0**	**95.2**
	MVCNN*	87.3	71.6	82.3	44.2	70.2	26.6	79.0
	ours	95.3	88.5	98.4	**50.5**	88.1	10.8	94.3
	MVCNN	92.7	87.0	94.9	49.6	86.0	12.2	92.1
MV-RED-73	DeepEm [8]	92.9	57.4	72.2	58.1	69.3	34.0	–
	ours*	92.7	88.2	**97.6**	69.9	87.5	11.1	**93.0**
	MVCNN*	**94.7**	**92.5**	97.1	**70.3**	**91.4**	**6.9**	92.3
	ours	90.1	84.0	96.6	68.4	83.0	15.2	89.8
	MVCNN	92.7	87.4	95.7	68.1	86.6	11.8	91.4

Multi-view Retrieval. Table 4 shows the retrieval results on three datasets with different evaluation criteria, *NN, FT, ST, F-measure, DCG, ANMRR* and *mAP* as mentioned in Subsect. 4.2. The proposed algorithm is compared with hand-craft feature based method [38], deep learning based methods [8,15] and various matching methods [6,8,15]. The results in *case2* are not compared to those in *case1* for retrieval tasks, which is on the contrary in classification tasks. It is caused by distance metric in retrieval tasks. The model in *case2* learns discriminant features for classification but the features are more close to samples in other object dataset. The best results are still derived from our method except on MV-RED-73. On MV-RED-73, the MVCNN model in *case1* is comparable with ours. Our models are higher in ST and mAP evaluation criteria but fails on others. It is inferred that though the retrieval results are not the nearest but most of correct results are distributed at the top. This phenomenon indicates that our model learned on both ImageNet and MV-RED-73 training sets fails on distance measure though the features learned are discriminative for classification. In ETH-80 dataset and RGB-D dataset, our model in *case1* outperforms not only MVCNN under two cases but also other methods listed, even the model in *case2* can achieve the similar high results. It is attributed to the efficiency of features extracted by our models. Although the results of MVCNN are comparable under two cases to ours, the MVCNN method can not balance its recognition and retrieval performances, seen from Table 3. Therefore, our models are capable and effective for both classification and retrieval tasks and even with a handful views.

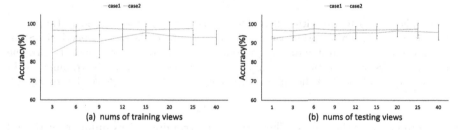

Fig. 4. The results tested with different numbers of training views and testing views respectively on ETH-80 dataset by randomly partitioning 10 objects into two sets of five objects for training and testing. Standard deviation on the test data in ten trials is expressed by error bars. In (a), the number of views of the testing set keeps in accordance with that of the training set. In (b), the number of views of the training set remains unchanged.

Analysis on Views Number Selection for Classification. *ETH-80*: Fig. 4 shows the average accuracy and standard derivation of 10-folds experiments in line. The performance of the model in *case2* outperforms that of the model in *case1* with a small derivation. It shows stable performance approaching 100 percent. For the model in *case1*, there is a palpable fluctuation in results with variant numbers of views along with a little larger derivation when 3 views are used for extracting training and testing features. It can be observed that the performances fall a little after rising at 15 views, which can be construed by

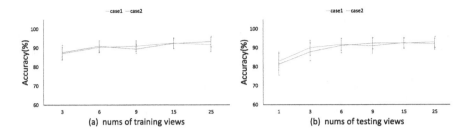

Fig. 5. The results tested with different numbers of training views and testing views under the leave-one-object principal on RGB-D object dataset, respectively. Standard deviation on the test data in ten trials is expressed by error bars. In (a), the number of views of the testing set keeps in accordance with that of the training set. In (b), the number of views of the training set remains unchanged.

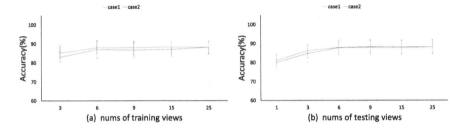

Fig. 6. The results tested with different numbers of training views and testing views under the leave-one-object principal on MV-RED-73 object dataset, respectively. Standard deviation on the test data in ten trials is expressed by error bars. In (a), the number of views of the testing set keeps in accordance with that of the training set. In (b), the number of views of the training set remains unchanged. (Color figure online)

the redundancy of the views. Then we fix the training views number as 15 and observe the impact of changes in the number of test views. The same setting holds for the following two datasets. From Fig. 4(b), the performance with only one view for extracting testing features rivals that with 40 views. It proves that less views are as efficient as entire view set through our framework. The performance is plateauing at 15 testing views, which means 15 views are enough for object classification on ETH-80 dataset.

RGB-D: In the Fig. 5(a), the performance rises and then slightly falls when the number of training views reaches 15 with the model in *case1*. For the model in *case2*, it achieves the highest performance at 25 views. MV-RED-73 dataset is in high receptive field but with small recognition area, it is difficult to transfer its knowledge to RGB-D environments. Thus more views provided with RGB-D dataset can benefit the results in spite of its fluctuation in results. It's illustrated that our method is robust to the variation in the numbers of training views. Even 6 views of an object can measure up to 90.79%. From Fig. 5(b), the performances become stable when more than 3 views are used for testing and the highest performance is obtained with more than 15 testing views. It's shown that our model is as strong as 85.3%±2.7 against even one view compare with 85.1% in [31]. Compared with the results in Fig. 4, the accuracy drops a little as the RGB-D dataset is more complex in object categories, views and amounts. However, it can still reach high performance with no more than 15 views, which illustrates our models are generalized to the diversities in the size or views of the dataset.

MV-RED-73: Figure 6 reports the results on MVRED dataset with different amounts of views for training and testing. The model in *case2* performs slightly worse than the model in *case1*. As mentioned earlier, it probably attributes to the smaller number of categories in the RGBD training set. And the two models achieve the same performance at about 25 views. The performance of the model in *case1* arrives at its climax at 15 views, and becomes converging at about 6 views. However, the general performance falls behind that on RGB-D dataset due to its small recognition area and complexities of categories. In addition, the standard deviations of different views are not very different, and remain small when the number of perspectives is less than three, which shows the stability of the extracted features for the change of views.

5   Conclusion

In this paper, we propose a multi-view based 3D object classification architecture and a 3D object retrieval architecture as well as a robust multi-view feature extraction scheme for extracting efficient features for both architectures. Different from other multi-view methods, our method utilizes deep Batch Normalization network for fast convergence as well as excellent performance. Our method enhances the robustness of the representations via a marginalized denoising autoencoder. Extensive experiments on three different 3D object datasets show the superiority of our approach from performance and show profitable influence can be brought by datasets transfer. In future work, we will focus on how to excavate the latent sematic structure information across views and extend our method for other more complex datasets.

Acknowledgment. This work is supported in part by National Natural Science Foundation of China under grant 62371333, in part by Shanghai Rising Star Project under grant 23QA1408800, and in part by 166 Project under grant 211-CXCY-M115-00–01-01.

References

1. Bo, L.F., Ren, X.F., Fox, D.: Unsupervised feature learning for RGB-D based object recognition. In: Experimental Robotics, pp. 387–402 (2013)
2. Cai, W., Liu, D., Ning, X., Wang, C., Xie, G.: Voxel-based three-view hybrid parallel network for 3d object classification. Displays **69**, 102076 (2021)

3. Chen, M., Xu, Z., Weinberger, K.Q., Sha, F.: Marginalized denoising autoencoders for domain adaptation. In: International Conference on Machine Learning, pp. 1627–1634 (2012)

4. Daras, P., Axenopoulos, A.: A 3D shape retrieval framework supporting multimodal queries. Int. J. Comput. Vision **89**(2–3), 229–247 (2010)

5. Deng, J., Dong, W., Socher, R., Li, L., Li, K., Li, F.: Imagenet: a large-scale hierarchical image database. In: IEEE Conference on Computer Vision and Pattern Recognition, pp. 248–255 (2009)

6. Gao, Y., Dai, Q.H., Wang, M., Zhang, N.Y.: 3D model retrieval using weighted bipartite graph matching. Signal Process. Image Commun. **26**(1), 39–47 (2011)

7. Gao, Z., Wang, D.Y., He, X.N., Zhang, H.: Group-pair convolutional neural networks for multi-view based 3D object retrieval. In: AAAI Conference on Artificial Intelligence, pp. 2223–2231 (2018)

8. Guo, H.Y., Wang, J.Q., Gao, Y., Li, J.Q., Lu, H.Q.: Multi-view 3D object retrieval with deep embedding network. IEEE Trans. Image Process. **25**(12), 5526–5537 (2016)

9. He, K.M., Zhang, X.Y., Ren, S.Q., Sun, J.: Deep residual learning for image recognition. In: IEEE Conference on Computer Vision and Pattern Recognition, pp. 770–778 (2016)

10. Ioffe, S., Szegedy, C.: Batch normalization: accelerating deep network training by reducing internal covariate shift. In: International Conference on Machine Learning, pp. 448–456 (2015)

11. Kanezaki, A., Matsushita, Y., Nishida, Y.: Rotationnet: joint object categorization and pose estimation using multiviews from unsupervised viewpoints. In: IEEE Conference on Computer Vision and Pattern Recognition, pp. 5010–5019 (2018)

12. Kim, T.K., Kittler, J., Cipolla, R.: Discriminative learning and recognition of image set classes using canonical correlations. IEEE Trans. Pattern Anal. Mach. Intell. **29**(6), 1005–1018 (2007)

13. Lai, K., Bo, L.F., Ren, X.F., Fox, D.: A large-scale hierarchical multi-view RGB-D object dataset. In: IEEE International Conference on Robotics and Automation, pp. 1817–1824 (2011)

14. Leibe, B., Schiele, B.: Analyzing appearance and contour based methods for object categorization. In: IEEE Conference on Computer Vision and Pattern Recognition, pp. 409–415 (2003)

15. Li, W.H., An, Y.: View-wised discriminative ranking for 3D object retrieval. Multimedia Tools Appl. **77**(17), 22035–22049 (2018)

16. Liu, A.A., Nie, W.Z., Gao, Y., Su, Y.T.: View-based 3D model retrieval: a benchmark. IEEE Trans. Cybern. **48**(3), 916–928 (2018)

17. Liu, A.A., Nie, W.Z., Su, Y.T.: 3D object retrieval based on multi-view latent variable model. IEEE Trans. Circuits Syst. Video Technol. **29**, 868–880 (2018)

18. Liu, A.A., Xiang, S., Li, W.H., Nie, W.Z., Su, Y.: Cross-domain 3D model retrieval via visual domain adaptation. In: International Joint Conference on Artificial Intelligence, pp. 828–834 (2018)

19. Loghmani, M.R., Planamente, M., Caputo, B., Vincze, M.: Recurrent convolutional fusion for RGB-D object recognition. arXiv preprint arXiv:1806.01673 (2018)

20. Lu, M.Q., Wei, L., Ning, Y.G.: 3D object classification based on multi convolutional neural networks. DEStech Trans. Eng. Technol. Res. (AMMA) (2017)

21. Nair, V., Hinton, G.E.: 3D object recognition with deep belief nets. In: Conference on Neural Information Processing Systems, pp. 1339–1347 (2009)

22. Nie, W.Z., Liu, A.A., Gao, Z., Su, Y.T.: Clique-graph matching by preserving global & local structure. In: IEEE Conference on Computer Vision and Pattern Recognition, pp. 4503–4510 (2015)
23. Nie, W.Z., Xiang, S., Liu, A.: Multi-scale cnns for 3D model retrieval. Multimedia Tools Appl. **77**(17), 22953–22963 (2018)
24. Papadakis, P., Pratikakis, I., Theoharis, T., Perantonis, S.: Panorama: a 3D shape descriptor based on panoramic views for unsupervised 3D object retrieval. Int. J. Comput. Vision **89**(2–3), 177–192 (2010)
25. Qi, C.R., Su, H., Mo, K., Guibas, L.J.: Pointnet: deep learning on point sets for 3D classification and segmentation. In: IEEE Conference on Computer Vision and Pattern Recognition, pp. 77–85 (2017)
26. Qi, S., Ning, X., Yang, G., Zhang, L., Long, P., Cai, W., Li, W.: Review of multi-view 3d object recognition methods based on deep learning. Displays **69**, 102053 (2021)
27. Savva, M., et al.: Large-scale 3D shape retrieval from ShapeNet Core55. In: Eurographics Workshop on 3D Object Retrieval (2017)
28. Schwarz, M., Schulz, H., Behnke, S.: RGB-D object recognition and pose estimation based on pre-trained convolutional neural network features. In: IEEE International Conference on Robotics and Automation, pp. 1329–1335 (2015)
29. Shah, S.A.A., Nadeem, U., Bennamoun, M., Sohel, F.A., Togneri, R.: Efficient image set classification using linear regression based image reconstruction. In: IEEE Conference on Computer Vision and Pattern Recognition, pp. 601–610 (2017)
30. Sohail, M., Chen, Z., Yang, B., Liu, G.: Multiscale spectral-spatial feature learning for hyperspectral image classification. Displays **74**, 102278 (2022)
31. Su, H., Maji, S., Kalogerakis, E., Learned-Miller, E.: Multi-view convolutional neural networks for 3D shape recognition. In: IEEE International Conference on Computer Vision, pp. 945–953 (2015)
32. Van Der Maaten, L.: Accelerating t-sne using tree-based algorithms. J. Mach. Learn. Res. **15**(1), 3221–3245 (2014)
33. Wang, L., et al.: Temporal segment networks: towards good practices for deep action recognition. In: European Conference Computer Vision, pp. 20–36 (2016)
34. Wang, R., Wu, X.J., Kittler, J.: A simple riemannian manifold network for image set classification. arXiv preprint arXiv:1805.10628 (2018)
35. Wang, Z.Y., Lu, J.W., Lin, R.G., Feng, J.J., et al.: Correlated and individual multi-modal deep learning for RGB-D object recognition. arXiv preprint arXiv:1604.01655 (2016)
36. Wu, Z., et al.: 3D shapenets: a deep representation for volumetric shapes. In: IEEE Conference on Computer Vision and Pattern Recognition, pp. 1912–1920 (2015)
37. Zhao, B., Feng, J.S., Wu, X., Yan, S.C.: A survey on deep learning-based fine-grained object classification and semantic segmentation. Int. J. Autom. Comput. **14**(2), 119–135 (2017)
38. Zhao, S., Yao, H., Zhang, Y., Wang, Y., Liu, S.: View-based 3D object retrieval via multi-modal graph learning. Signal Process. **112**, 110–118 (2015)
39. Zhu, Z.T., Wang, X.G., Bai, S., Yao, C., Bai, X.: Deep learning representation using autoencoder for 3D shape retrieval. Neurocomputing **204**, 41–50 (2016)
40. Zia, S., Yüksel, B., Yüret, D., Yemez, Y.: RGB-D object recognition using deep convolutional neural networks. In: IEEE Conference on Computer Vision and Pattern Recognition, pp. 896–903 (2017)

Combined Particle Filter and Its Application on Human Pose Estimation

Xinyang Liu[1], Long Ye[2,3(✉)], and Yinghao Yang[1]

[1] School of Information and Communication Engineering, Communication University of China, Beijing, China
{liuxinyang,yinghao_yang}@cuc.edu.cn
[2] State Key Laboratory of Media Convergence and Communication, Communication University of China, Beijing, China
yelong@cuc.edu.cn
[3] School of Data Science and Media Intelligence, Communication University of China, Beijing, China

Abstract. Time series analysis has a wide range of applications in various domains. When addressing this task, tracking and identification are usually solved as two separate problems. However, it introduces a lot of computational redundancy and makes it difficult to guarantee synchronization and real-time performance. We propose a joint problem combining recognition and tracking and use particle filtering to solve the state estimation problem. However, the general particle filter cannot accurately estimate the state of·the system in the time series state estimation task, because the system is time-varying and the prediction model of the particle filter is fixed. To address this issue, we assume that the system transition space is a set of finite prediction modes, and then propose a new Combined Particle Filter (CPF) framework that jointly achieves prediction mode recognition and state tracking. In the CPF, the prediction mode is regarded as a variable to be estimated, along with the system state variables. As a result, the resampled particle state set forms the global estimation of the system state, while the resampled mode variables indicate the optimal transition mode of the current frame. We construct an evaluation index system and conduct several evaluation tests to demonstrate the excellent performance of the CPF. Finally, we apply the CPF to the articulated human pose estimation task and obtain satisfactory results.

Keywords: Dynamic system · Particle filter · Human pose estimation · Timing analysis · Prediction model

1 Introduction

Tracking and recognition are two challenging problems in computer vision, with various applications such as autonomous driving, monitoring, robotics, virtual reality, etc. In previous works, tracking and recognition were often solved separately as two independent problems, without exploiting the mutual information

G. Zhai et al. (Eds.): IFTC 2023, CCIS 2066, pp. 314–329, 2024.
https://doi.org/10.1007/978-981-97-3623-2_23

between them. Therefore, we propose a joint problem of tracking and recognition, and develop a CPF algorithm that can effectively solve this problem.

Visual tracking faces many challenges, such as the interference from cluttered backgrounds and the changes of the environment (e.g., lighting). Visual object tracking methods can be generally categorized into two types: generative methods and discriminative methods. The generative methods extract target features from the target region in the first frame, and then search in each subsequent frame to find the region with the most similar features, and iteratively update the target model to achieve tracking. Typical generative methods include optical flow method [1], Kalman filter method [2], particle filter algorithm [3], mean shift algorithm [4], etc. These generative approaches track targets using a single model, which has significant limitations. When there are significant changes in environmental lighting, target rotation, or target motion, the tracking accuracy will degrade significantly. The discriminative methods consider both the target and the background information, and they detect the target from the current frame based on the difference between the target and the background. The methods based on deep learning are typical discriminative methods. Currently, CNN [5], SNN [6], RNN [7], GAN [8] and many advanced networks are used for visual object tracking tasks and have achieved good results. However, these tracking by detection methods ignore the temporal correlation. Moreover, as the end-to-end network will have a certain delay, the real-time tracking cannot be guaranteed.

In this work, we propose a CPF suitable for solving the tracking and recognition problems, which can effectively utilize the temporal information, maintain low latency, and also adapt to some changes in the system during the tracking process. For the two important processes that determine the performance of Particle Filter (PF), prediction and update, most of the existing methods optimize the particle sampling space for the update process in PF method, so as to improve the performance of PF. However, they ignore the prediction process which can provide a good resampling basis for the update stage. If an excellent prediction space can be given, PF can fit the system state with faster speed and higher accuracy in the update stage. In addition, tracking is a random variable estimation problem. Due to the probabilistic nature of this process, many problem formulations have a lot of uncertainty. A good tracking model and constraint assumptions can greatly improve the tracking effect. CPF focuses on the mode of the prediction process, and treats the mode as a variable that needs to be estimated as well. In the update stage, the modes of particles are also resampled, and the weighted statistics of the particle state after resampling are the transition mode of the current frame.

The contributions of our work can be summarized as follows.

1) We analyze the problems of existing tracking and recognition methods and define a joint problem of tracking and recognition.
2) We propose CPF to address the limitations of PF in tracking. Compared with general PF, CPF can obtain more accurate results in time series analysis problems. We compare CPF with other improved particle filters, and CPF achieves satisfactory results.

3) We verify the feasibility of our method in human pose tracking tasks. We build a gymnastics dataset to test our method and the human pose tracking results are satisfactory.

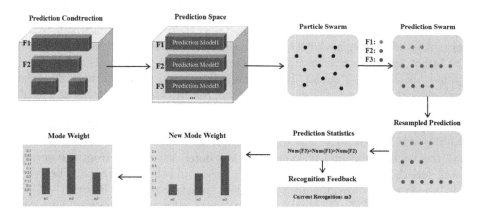

Fig. 1. Prediction resampling mechanism. This figure shows the prediction resampling and mode weight reconstruction of the algorithm framework in the event of transfer mode change.

2   Related Work

2.1   Visual Tracking

Various networks such as CNN, RNN, SNN, and GAN have been applied in visual tracking. WuYan et al. proposed a deep and shallow feature learning network, namely DSNet, which can learn multi-level same-resolution compressed (MSC) features by end-to-end CNNs [30]. Chen et al. formulated the visual tracking task as a parallel classification and regression problem and proposed a simple but effective visual tracking framework based on siamese neural network [31]. Yang et al. proposed a RNN-based visual tracking algorithm that can preserve the spatial structure of the target in the video [32]. Song et al. proposed using adversarial learning to solve the sample segmentation and classification problems in visual tracking [8]. The previous works treated tracking and recognition as two separate problems. They used the tracking results as the basis for recognition, which usually resulted in some computational redundancy.

2.2   Particle Filter

In PF method, multiple iterations will cause the weight of particles to converge to a few particles, which is the sample impoverishment problem [9]. To deal with this problem, Arulampalam et al. proposed the importance resampling PF algorithm (SIR-PF) [10], but long-term resampling will still reduce the sample diversity. Most of the studies focus on optimizing the sampling space for the update process and take the resampling process as the main object to improve PF. For example, Haque et al. proposed an Auxiliary Particle Filter (APF) [11] method, Van Der Merwe et al. proposed the unscented PF method (UPF) [12]. In view of the lack of samples caused by noise and resampling defects, regularized PF (RPF) [13], regularized auxiliary PF (RAPF) [14], and mixture PF (MPF) [15] are proposed to smooth the posterior probability density and resample based on continuous distribution.

The above methods focus on optimizing the update process while neglecting the importance of the prediction process. Several studies have proposed improvements to the problem of providing better prediction. Chu et al. proposed a multiprediction particle filter for efficient memory utilization [16], in which each basic particle generates a group of prediction particles, and a representative particle is reserved for each group of particles in the resampling stage. This method can effectively expand the prior of prediction, but it needs to spend redundant space to store redundant prediction particles in the implementation process. Fang et al. proposed a prediction method based on degradation characteristics [17], which is applied to lithium battery life prediction. This method determines the prediction model through the degradation characteristics of the historical series, which needs to spend additional computational cost to fit a good prediction model in each iteration. For the time series model with frequent and irregular changes, the excessive fitting of prior features cannot bring good prediction results. Based on the problem of the above prediction optimization, we propose CPF based on mode optimal prediction, so that PF method can adaptively adjust the prediction space and select the prediction model that best matches the current system state in each round of prediction. When the system has strong temporal regularity, the CPF of fusion mode will adjust the prediction space to a smaller and more specific threshold space. On the contrary, when the system has weak temporal regularity, CPF will predict in a more generalized space. This method can effectively improve the performance of the system temporal law, and also improve the adaptability of PF to system disorder to a certain extent.

3 Method

3.1 Overview of the PF and Problem Formulation

Particle Filter
Suppose in a time series scenario, the state transition model and the observation model are expressed as Eq. (1) and Eq. (2).

$$s_t = f_t\left(s_{t-1}, u_t\right) \tag{1}$$

$$o_t = h_t\left(s_t, v_t\right) \tag{2}$$

where s_t is the hidden state to be estimated, o_t is the observation on time series, u_t and v_t are the process and observation noises respectively. The transfer law f_t defines the evolution of the system state with time as a Markov process. The observation model h_t includes the noisy measurements to the hidden state [10,18–20].

Bayesian estimation works have two main steps: prediction and update. Prediction uses ChapmanKolmogorov (C-K) function to obtain target movement prior probability $p(s_t|o_{1:t-1})$, which can be shown as Eq. (3). In update stage, the likelihood in Bayes' theorem is used to modify the priori probability distribution function(PDF). Therefore posterior PDF can be approximated by Eq. (4).

$$p(s_t|o_{1:t-1}) = \int p(s_t|s_{t-1}, o_{1:t-1}) p(s_{t-1}|o_{1:t-1}) ds_{t-1} \tag{3}$$

$$p(s_t|o_{1:t}) = C_t p(o_t|s_t) p(s_t|o_{1:t-1}) \tag{4}$$

where C_t is the normalized constant, $p(s_t|s_{t-1}, o_{1:t-1})$ represents the process equation of the conditional transition of an observed state variable C_t and $p(s_t|o_{1:t})$ represents the observation conditioned on s_t, which is need to be estimated.

PF realizes the solution of recursive Bayesian function through Monte Carlo sampling [21,22], and estimates the hidden state of the system based on state transition model and observation model. In PF, the posterior PDF $p(s_t|o_{1:t})$ is represented by a set of random particles and their corresponding weights which are computed by the conditional likelihood of each particle, given the observation at that time moment [23,24]. The posterior density can be approximated as Eq. (5)

$$p(s_t|o_{1:t}) \approx \sum_{i=1}^{N} w_t^i \delta(s_t - s_t^i) \tag{5}$$

where δ is the Dirac function [25]. The weights of particle set w_t^i can be recursively updated using methods, such as the principle importance sampling with important density. The particle set is drawn from the prior PDF, which is often selected as the proposal distribution as shown by Eq. (6).

$$q(s_t|s_{t-1}, o_{1:t}) = p(s_t|s_{t-1}) \tag{6}$$

The weights of the particle set can be recursively estimated by Eq. (7)

$$w_t^i \propto w_{t-1}^i \frac{p(o_t|s_t^i) p(s_t^i|s_{t-1}^i)}{q(s_t^i|s_{t-1}^i, o_t)} \tag{7}$$

where $q(s_t^i|s_{t-1}^i, o_t)$ is the known importance sampling function and often be chosen as $p(s_t^i|s_{t-1}^i)$, then Eq. (8) becomes:

$$w_t^i \propto w_{t-1}^i p(o_t|s_t^i) \tag{8}$$

A simple way to improve the sample effectiveness is particle resampling which is designed for eliminating the effect that particle degeneration brings out. Generally, a resampling step is added in each time interval that replaces low probability particles with high probability particles, keeping the number of particles constant.

Problem Formulation

Considering that the actual pattern space is infinite and it is difficult to achieve pattern recognition in an infinite pattern space, we limit the problem to a finite pattern space for solution. The problem of tracking and identification is defined as follows. Assuming that the patterns in the pattern space are finite, the pattern space can be represented as Eq. (9)

$$S = \{F_1, F_2, ..., F_M\} \tag{9}$$

where, M is the number of modes in modes domain, F_i ($i \in \{1, 2, ..., M\}$) represents a mode in the modes domain. Based on prior knowledge, each pattern can correspond to a tracking prediction model.

Equation (10) is equivalent to expectation of the finite weighted prediction

$$\tilde{F} = E\{F_1, F_2, ..., F_M\} = \sum_{i=1}^{M} w_i F_i \tag{10}$$

where w_i ($i \in \{1, 2, ..., M\}$) represents the weight of F_i. If higher weight is assigned to excellent predictions and lower weight is assigned to inferior predictions, an excellent overall prediction can be obtained.

3.2   CPF Algorithm

Prediction Resamping

Based on the theory of SIR-PF, resampling of particles means that the particles closer to the real state will be given higher weight, so that they will be more likely to be sampled. Finally, the number of particles is taken as the PDF of the state. Similarly, in the proposed algorithm, the resampling of particles is also the resampling of the prediction models. A better prediction model will be sampled more frequently. Based on the large cardinality of particle swarm optimization, the number statistics of prediction models can also be used as the PDF of the prediction model in the current transition state, that is, the PDF of mode sequences. The probability distribution can be reassigned to each mode sequence as a weight, so that each particle can select a better prediction model in the current state for prediction in the next prediction frame, which shortens the time of iterative optimization. It is worth emphasizing that this process is completely done by the system adaptively, even if the system deals with the time-varying transition model, it can also fit the optimal mode in a short time. The resampling mechanism of prediction is the basis of mode recognition. When the system maintains the same transition mode for a period of time, the resampling

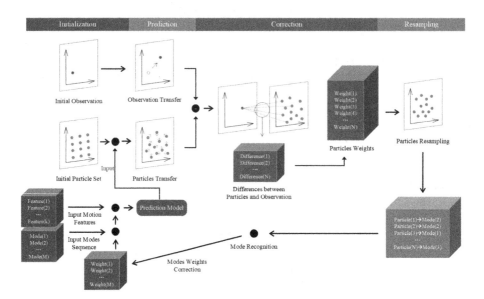

Fig. 2. The schematic diagram of the CPF algorithm operation. The modes are chosen from M modes according to a certain probability, and the chosen mode determines which properties in the state transition will be preserved to predict the initial randomly distributed particles. Then the differences between the particles and the observation are computed and these values decide the correction of the particles' weights. The new weights of the particle set guide the resampling process, such that better individuals and better modes are more likely to be resampled. After the resampling of the modes, the weights of the modes are also corrected, and then the modes will be chosen according to the modified weights in the next prediction. The particle set will gradually approach the real state in the loop.

mechanism will make the transition mode maintain a larger weight in this period of time, so as to ensure a higher recognition accuracy. When the transition mode changes, the resampling mechanism will transfer the weight from one mode to another, which will change the recognition result. The prediction resampling mechanism is shown in Fig. 1.

Weight Refreshing

Since the particle confidence can indicate the effectiveness of the prediction applied on the particle, the weights of modes can be assigned according to the confidence of the particle set. However, if the system keeps a transition law for a period of time, the weights of modes may degenerate as the system always assigns more weight to a certain mode. This causes the weights of some modes to decay [26,27] to zero, which means these modes will no longer be selected when the transition law changes, and the weight mechanism is paralyzed.

The resampling method is usually used to deal with the degeneration problems, but its limitation lies in the need for a large sample space. For the mode space with a small number of modes, the resampling method does not work for the degeneration phenomenon. To address this problem, we propose a weight refresh mechanism that the probability distribution of weights will be refreshed to be a discrete uniform distribution [28] when the transition law is maintained for a period and the weights of some modes decay to a small value.

The weight refresh mechanism will not affect the recognition because the recognition is accomplished in the update stage instead of the prediction stage. The particles using a better prediction model will always be resampled, which means even if each prediction model in the prediction space is used on the same number of particles, the recognition result still depends on the optimal individuals of particles. This relationship decides that although the weights of modes are refreshed to be a discrete uniform distribution, the recognition of the transition law will not be changed. The whole framework of CPF is illustrated in Fig. 2.

Table 1. Pose estimation result on our dataset. We report the PCKh@0.5 of our CPF and other algorithms.

Method	Head	Shoulder	Elbow	Wrist	Hip	Knee	Ankle	PCKh@0.5
ViTPose-H	99.99	99.99	99.89	97.94	99.99	99.99	99.99	99.69
ViTPose-B	99.99	99.67	99.44	94.08	99.61	99.55	99.78	98.88
AlphaPose	99.99	99.16	98.38	94.08	99.11	99.11	97.49	98.19
HRNet-W48	99.99	99.99	99.78	97.71	99.99	99.99	99.99	99.64
SIR-PF	43.75	28.18	14.51	12.95	39.40	44.31	31.81	30.29
CPF(Ours)	99.99	99.99	99.44	93.42	88.50	99.83	99.50	97.24

4   Evaluation and CPF Based Human Pose Estimation

4.1   Tracking Evaluation

In this part, we evaluate the performance of CPF from the perspective of state tracking. We use Root Mean Square Error (RMSE) to measure the tracking accuracy, standard deviation (SD) to measure the tracking robustness, and delay to measure the real-time performance. We compare the tracking performance of CPF with several improved PF algorithms, including the classical SIR-PF, Mixture Particle Filter (MPF) and Auxiliary Particle Filter (APF).

MPF [15] and APF [11] are widely used particle filter models. They are improved particle filter methods based on classical SIR-PF. In this section, we compare the performance of SIR-PF, MPF, APF and our proposed CPF by tracking the same system state. First, we briefly introduce the MPF and APF methods involved in the evaluation:

(1) MPF: MPF is an extension of standard SIR-PF. It is suitable for dealing with the multi-modal distribution of particle swarm in global localization. MPF clusters particle sets through clustering algorithms such as mean shift algorithm

[29]. Each cluster component is assigned a weight and resampled by divide and conquer. Finally, the state estimation is calculated based on the particle weight and cluster weight. The problem of MPF is that it has to spend a lot of computational cost on clustering particle sets, which will greatly reduce the efficiency of state tracking. On the other hand, there may be a case where the poor particle in the good cluster is better than the better particle in the bad cluster. This situation will have a negative impact on the state estimation.

(2) **APF:** APF is a variant of the standard SIR-PF. Before the prediction and update process, it generates hypothetical observations based on the particle swarm state of the $t - 1$ time node, and resamples the particle swarm based on the current observations. It is essentially an attempt to introduce future observations for resampling. Then it completes the routine prediction and update process. APF has to increase the computational cost of resampling process in each iteration round. Compared with the standard SIR-PF, the tracking delay increases significantly.

Compared with MPF and APF algorithms, our CPF algorithm does not add any other processes besides the standard prediction and update processes, and the iteration cycle does not change. CPF only increases the prediction paths that can be used by the particle set, and generates more effective predictions through these weighted paths. In the subsequent resampling stage, the particle set only needs to resample normally and make quantitative statistics on the prediction without additional computation.

To demonstrate the effectiveness of CPF method, we use the control variable method to track the same system state transition by SIR-PF, MPF, APF and CPF methods respectively. We set the particle swarm size as 300, and the process noise and observation noise as 5. We select the trajectory path of one random experiment as an example, and present the RMSE, prediction standard deviation and tracking delay of 100 random experiments, as shown in Fig. 3. The statistics of the average value of evaluation are shown in Table 2.

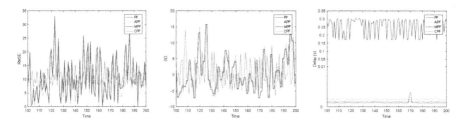

Fig. 3. Comparison between SIR-PF, MPF, APF and CPF. The left image shows the RMSE at different time steps, showing tracking accuracy. The middle image shows the SD at different time steps, showing tracking robustness. The right image shows the delay at different time steps, showing real-time tracking performance.

Table 2. Statistics of the average value of evaluation indexes of 100 random experiments.

Method	RMSE	SD	Delay
SIR-PF	10.6968	4.5051	0.0005
MPF	10.7223	4.5149	0.2574
APF	8.9236	3.9620	0.0009
CPF(Ours)	10.4750	3.7527	0.0006

4.2 CPF Based Human Pose Estimation

Overview of the Approach

In this work, we formulate the human pose tracking as a recognize-and-track problem. Considering our approach still has some limitations, we focus on human pose tracking of gymnastics task. Since the Combined Particle Filter can only perform periodic mode conversion, and the movement mode conversion of broadcast gymnastics is relatively regular, we choose to build a dataset for broadcast gymnastics to verify our method. We try to integrate the tracking, recognition and mode conversion in a multi-stage particle filter algorithm as shown in the chart presented in Fig. 4.

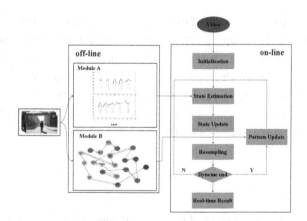

Fig. 4. System Diagram Two stages are shown in the diagram. In off-line stage there are two modules (A for generating motion templates and B for calculate transition probabilities). The on-line stage adopts a CPF framework for human pose tracking.

Our human pose tracking framework consists of two stages. In the off-line stage, there are two main modules. In Module A, we divide the motion space of broadcast gymnastics by defining 20 dynemes that can distinguish left and right movements. Through these dynemes, the broadcast gymnastics sequences can be clearly described. The inputs of Module A are the videos in the dataset, which have different backgrounds and characters. The output is a set of generated dyneme templates, which record the statistical average of the trajectories of 14 key points of the human body. The output dyneme templates will be used in the prediction model in particle filter. In Module B, we generate a state transition matrix, which stores the probability distribution of transitioning from each dyneme to the other 19 dynemes. The inputs of Module B are the videos in the dataset. We calculate the state transitions in those videos to get the output results. The transition matrix will be used in particle filter after the update of particles.

In the on-line stage, we use the framework of CPF to realize real-time human pose tracking. We use the joint motion trajectory generated in Module A as the prediction model in CPF. When the particles are in different motion modes, the corresponding motion trajectory is used to estimate the state of each particle. After the resampling, we determine whether the current dyneme is over. If it is not over, the algorithm will continue to repeat the particle filter operation. Otherwise, it will determine the type of the current dyneme according to the particle state, and then update the motion mode and predict the probability distribution of the next dyneme according to the state transition matrix generated by Module B.

Table 3. The PCKh@0.5 results on self-occlusion segments.

Methods	Head	Shoulder	Elbow	Wrist	Hip	Knee	Ankle	PCKh@0.5
ViTPose-H	99.11	99.99	95.76	93.08	90.85	99.99	99.99	96.94
ViTPose-B	98.21	96.43	93.30	92.41	83.48	90.40	93.97	92.60
AlphaPose	95.52	99.10	91.03	87.67	91.03	85.43	85.43	90.78
HRNet-W48	85.71	91.74	87.72	85.71	82.81	93.08	99.11	89.60
SIR-PF	41.85	28.11	13.43	13.23	35.90	45.71	33.12	30.19
CPF(Ours)	99.99	99.99	99.41	93.51	89.10	98.91	99.72	97.23

Dyneme Model

In this work, we use the concept of motion dynemes [25] for the division of motion space. We selected broadcast gymnastics to verify our method. It is known that the movements of human beings in broadcast gymnastics are limited, so we divided the movement space of broadcast gymnastics according to the idea of movement dynemes, and generated an alphabet containing 20 kinds of dynemes. There are many kinds of motion sequences that can be generated by using these permutations and combinations of motion dynemes, but some of these sequences are far more likely to occur than others. Therefore, we can use Hidden Markov Model and transition matrix to describe the probability distribution of the next motion dyneme after the end of current dyneme.

We divide 20 kinds of motion dynemes that can distinguish left and right movements, which are: preparatory, stretch, chest-expanding, kick, lateral exercise, twist, back exercise, jump, cooling down and ending for left and right side. We generate corresponding templates for each motion dyneme. The way we generate the motion templates is to record the motion trajectories by different characters in the dataset. And then we statistically average all the motion trajectories to get 14 average trajectories (14 key points). Finally we fit the corresponding trajectory curves according to the recorded trajectory points.

Dataset

In this paper, we build a single person pose sequential dataset covering various clothing styles and diverse complex scenes. The dataset is built in a virtual environment considering the requirement for human pose estimation in virtual scenes and the convenience of collecting data in the unreal engine. We capture the 3D motion data of the broadcast gymnastics and use the motion capture data to drive different avatars in the unreal engine to get the corresponding animation blueprints. To ensure the diversity of the dataset, we select several different character models with diverse appearance and let these avatars perform the motions in different scenes. We record 14 avatars doing broadcast gymnastics in different scenes, and the dataset contains a total of 42 sequences.

Data Annotation. We provide annotation of 14 keypoints for each human instance collected. Considering the large number of instances in the dataset, we first use HRNet-W32 [28] to roughly detect the keypoints, and then manually pick out the frames with detection errors. For frames that are detected incorrectly, we manually annotate the keypoints to ensure the quality of our annotation.

Evaluation Metrics. Considering that we constructed a 2D single-person dataset, we used the "PCKh" metric mentioned in [29] to evaluate the accuracy of joint detection. The keypoint is considered as a successful detection if the distance between the detected joint position and the ground truth is less than 50% of the head segment length. We also compare our method with the human pose tracking method using the classical SIR-PF by PCKh and RMSE.

Results on Dataset

Performance Evaluation. We compare the performance of our method with others by PCKh, which is commonly used in human pose estimation. Since the COCO dataset [24] is very rich and diverse, we still choose to train other models using the COCO dataset and then test them on our broadcast gymnastics dataset. We also compare the performance of our CPF based pose tracking method with the method using traditional SIR-PF, and we select the root mean square error (RMSE) as a metric to evaluate the tracking accuracy.

We report the results of our method with other state-of-the-art methods and classic SIR-PF method in Table 1. Compared to other high performance algorithms, our method achieves a slightly lower PCKh@0.5 score. There is a significant decrease in accuracy in detecting both wrist and hip compared to ViTPose-H and HRNet-W48, and a decrease in accuracy in detecting hip compared to ViTPose-B and AlphaPose. Because of the high similarity of color features throughout the waist segment, our method does not have an advantage in detecting hip segment. Compared to classical SIR-PF method, our method has a significant improvement in PCKh@0.5 score. The RMSE of our method is reduced to one ninth of that of the SIR-PF method. Due to the fixed prediction equation required by SIR-PF, it is difficult to adapt to tracking problems such as human pose estimation with pattern changes. On the other hand, CPF can effectively handle tracking problems with pattern transitions, while other particle filters may fail during pattern transitions.

Fig. 5. Human pose estimation results on self-occlusion segments.

Self-occlusion. Self-occlusion is a significant challenge in human pose estimation tasks. Due to the fixed position of a monocular camera, different parts of the human body may intersect or occlude each other during the movement of human entities, making it difficult for algorithms to detect the position and posture of the occluded parts. Both AlphaPose and HRNet have paid attention to the temporal features, but their temporal features are mainly used for human instance tracking in multi person scenarios and do not learn the temporal information of keypoints between adjacent frames. We extracted multiple segments with severe self occlusion, including turning and bending, and tested our CPF method, existing superior deep learning algorithms, and traditional particle filter algorithms on these segments. Even the most advanced ViTPose did not perform as well in detecting these heavily occluded segments as CPF. The comparison results are shown in the Table 3. The human pose estimation results on self-occlusion segments are shown in Fig. 5.

5   Conclusion

This paper proposes a new combined particle filter (CPF) that integrates state estimation and mode prediction for the state estimation problem of time-varying transition models. CPF uses the prior information of the prediction model to constrain the prediction space of the system state to a small domain, so that more effective predictions can be generated in each iteration. On the one hand, more effective predictions can provide a better sampling space for the resampling stage, and better particle sets can be obtained even by using general resampling methods. On the other hand, CPF only uses more prediction paths for the particle set, without adding additional auxiliary processes or changing the pre-optimization of the particle set itself, which will not incur a lot of additional computational costs. Experiments show that CPF can ensure real-time performance and high state tracking accuracy. Especially in dealing with the system state tracking problem with changeable and irregular changes of state transition model, CPF can greatly exhibit its advantages of high-granularity prediction and improve the effectiveness of prediction to the greatest extent. The effectiveness of CPF has also been successfully verified in practical applications such as human pose estimation.

References

1. Decarlo, D., Metaxas, D.: Optical flow constraints on deformable models with applications to face tracking. Int. J. Comput. Vision **38**(2), 99–127 (2000)
2. Arroyo-Marioli, F., Bullano, F., Kucinskas, S., et al.: Tracking R of COVID-19: a new real-time estimation using the Kalman filter. PLoS ONE **16**(1), e0244474 (2021)
3. Deng, X., Mousavian, A., Xiang, Y., et al.: PoseRBPF: a rao-blackwellized particle filter for 6-D object pose tracking. IEEE Trans. Rob. **37**(5), 1328–1342 (2021)
4. Zhao, M., Jha, A., Liu, Q., et al.: Faster mean-shift: GPU-accelerated clustering for cosine embedding-based cell segmentation and tracking. Med. Image Anal. **71**, 102048 (2021)
5. Nam, H., Han, B.: Learning multi-domain convolutional neural networks for visual tracking. In: Proceedings of the IEEE Conference on Computer Vision and Pattern Recognition, pp. 4293–4302 (2016)
6. Dong, X., Shen, J.: Triplet loss in siamese network for object tracking. In: Proceedings of the European Conference on Computer Vision (ECCV), pp. 459–474 (2018)
7. Milan, A., Rezatofighi, S.H., Dick, A., et al.: Online multi-target tracking using recurrent neural networks. In: Proceedings of the AAAI Conference on Artificial Intelligence, vol. 31, no. 1 (2017)
8. Song, Y., Ma, C., Wu, X., et al.: Vital: visual tracking via adversarial learning. In: Proceedings of the IEEE Conference on Computer Vision and Pattern Recognition, pp. 8990–8999 (2018)
9. Li, T., Sun, S., Sattar, T.P., et al.: Fight sample degeneracy and impoverishment in particle filters: a review of intelligent approaches. Expert Syst. Appl. **41**(8), 3944–3954 (2014)
10. Arulampalam, M.S., Maskell, S., Gordon, N., et al.: A tutorial on particle filters for online nonlinear/non-Gaussian Bayesian tracking. IEEE Trans. Signal Process. **50**(2), 174–188 (2002)
11. Haque, M.S., Choi, S., Baek, J.: Auxiliary particle filtering-based estimation of remaining useful life of IGBT. IEEE Trans. Industr. Electron. **65**(3), 2693–2703 (2017)

12. Van Der Merwe, R., Doucet, A., De Freitas, N., et al.: The unscented particle filter. In: Advances in Neural Information Processing Systems, vol. 13 (2000)
13. Oudjane, N., Musso, C.: Progressive correction for regularized particle filters. In: Proceedings of the Third International Conference on Information Fusion, vol. 2, pp. THB2/10–THB2/17. IEEE (2000)
14. Liu, J., Wang, W., Ma, F.: A regularized auxiliary particle filtering approach for system state estimation and battery life prediction. Smart Mater. Struct. **20**(7), 075021 (2011)
15. Murangira, A., Musso, C., Dahia, K.: A mixture regularized rao-blackwellized particle filter for terrain positioning. IEEE Trans. Aerosp. Electron. Syst. **52**(4), 1967–1985 (2016)
16. Chu, C.Y., Chao, C.H., Chao, M.A., et al.: Multi-prediction particle filter for efficient memory utilization. In: 2010 IEEE Workshop on Signal Processing Systems, pp. 295–298. IEEE (2010)
17. Fang, H., Fan, H., Ma, H., et al.: Lithium-ion batteries life prediction method basedon degenerative characters and improved particle filter. In: 2015 IEEE Conference on Prognostics and Health Management (PHM), pp. 1–10. IEEE (2015)
18. Rabiner, L., Juang, B.: An introduction to hidden Markov models. IEEE ASSP Mag. **3**(1), 4–16 (1986)
19. Eddy, S.R.: Profile hidden Markov models. Bioinformatics **14**(9), 755–763 (1998)
20. Jouin, M., Gouriveau, R., Hissel, D., et al.: Particle filter-based prognostics: review, discussion and perspectives. Mech. Syst. Signal Process. **72**, 2–31 (2016)
21. Metropolis, N., Ulam, S.: The Monte Carlo method. J. Am. Stat. Assoc. **44**(247), 335–341 (1949)
22. Seila, A.F.: Simulation and the Monte Carlo method. Technometrics **24**(2), 167–168 (2007)
23. Jouin, M., Gouriveau, R., Hissel, D., Péra, M.-C., Zerhouni, N.: Particle filter-based prognostics: review, discussion and perspectives. Mech. Syst. Signal Process. **72**, 2–31 (2016)
24. Simon, D.: Optimal State Estimation: Kalman, H Infinity, and Nonlinear Approaches. Wiley, Hoboken (2006)
25. Balakrishnan, V.: All about the dirac delta function (?). Resonance **8**(8), 48–58 (2003)
26. Park, S., Hwang, J.P., Kim, E., Kang, H.-J.: A new evolutionary particle filter for the prevention of sample impoverishment. IEEE Trans. Evol. Comput. **13**(4), 801–809 (2009)
27. Li, T., Sattar, T.P., Sun, S.: Deterministic resampling: unbiased sampling to avoid sample impoverishment in particle filters. Signal Process. **92**(7), 1637–1645 (2012)
28. Sandhya, E., Prasanth, C.: Marshall-olkin discrete uniform distribution. J. Probab. **2014** (2014)
29. Comaniciu, D., Meer, P.: Mean shift analysis and applications. In: Proceedings of the Seventh IEEE International Conference on Computer Vision, vol. 2, pp. 1197–1203. IEEE (1999)
30. Wu, Q., Yan, Y., Liang, Y., Liu, Y., Wang, H.: DSNet: deep and shallow feature learning for efficient visual tracking. In: Jawahar, C.V., Li, H., Mori, G., Schindler, K. (eds.) ACCV 2018. LNCS, vol. 11365, pp. 119–134. Springer, Cham (2019). https://doi.org/10.1007/978-3-030-20873-8_8

31. Chen, Z., Zhong, B., Li, G., et al.: Siamese box adaptive network for visual tracking. In: Proceedings of the IEEE/CVF Conference on Computer Vision and Pattern Recognition, pp. 6668–6677 (2020)
32. Yang, T., Chan, A.B.: Recurrent filter learning for visual tracking. In: Proceedings of the IEEE International Conference on Computer Vision Workshops, pp. 2010–2019 (2017)

A Human Posture Estimation Method for Image Interaction System Based on ECA

Shuqi Wang[1], Da Pan[1], Yangrui Zhao[1], Kai Jia[2], Yichun Zhang[3(✉)], and Tianyu Liang[3]

[1] School of Communication and Information Engineering, Communication University of China, Beijing, China
sqwang@cuc.edu.cn
[2] China Electronics Standardization Institute, Beijing, China
jiakai@cesi.cn
[3] China Institute of Arts Science and Technology, Beijing, China
zhangyichun@casti.org.cn

Abstract. Nowadays, human posture estimation intelligent algorithm is widely used in image interaction system for better interaction and accuracy. In the paper we proposed an effective human posture estimation method based on multi-scale feature extraction and Efficient Channel Attention (ECA) mechanism. In our proposed method, we first extract muti-scale feature through attention-driven convolutional neural network. Besides, we use a combination of bottom-up and top-down approaches to aggregate the feature maps from different levels through multiple paths for cross-scale feature representations. Finally, the feature is regressed and classified to predict the position and confidence of the human bounding boxes, as well as the coordinates of the 17 human posture keypoints within each bounding box. Based on the human posture estimation module, we designed an image interaction system to achieve interaction between the human and the screen with action recognition and virtual scene construction. Experimental results showed that the human posture estimation method has high accuracy and real-time performance and the image interactive system has good interactivity and creativity.

Keywords: Human Posture Estimation · Image Interaction System · Attention Mechanism

1 Introduction

Image interaction system has come into the public with the rapid development of technology. In recent years, some experts have done meaningful researches on human posture estimation, as a novel interactive artificial intelligence. Human posture estimation methods based on deep learning can be divided into three categories: coordinate regression-based approach, heat map detection-based approach and hybrid approach [1].

The coordinate regression-based approach is to learn the mapping from input images to predefined kinematic joints through an end-to-end network and regressing keypoints coordinates directly. Toshev et al. [2] proposed a multi-stage cascade network Deep Pose to progressively optimize the pose estimation results of the initial coordinate network. Carreira et al. [3] proposed an iterative error feedback based human posture estimation model, IEF, which cascades the heat map as a feature map with the original image containing texture information. Li et al. [4] proposed a transformer-based cascade network for regressing human keypoints. The self-attention mechanism captures the spatial correlation of joints and appearance. Li et al. [5] introduced a normalizing flow model called RLE (Log-likelihood Estimation) to capture the distribution of joint location. The model aims to find optimized parameters by residual log-likelihood estimation, which is different from previous methods.

However, it is difficult to obtain accurate coordinates of keypoints by solely relying on the regression algorithm due to the neglect of the structural information between the joints of the human body.

The heat map detection-based approach is to represent the coordinates of the joints through a probability map. Tompson et al. [6] conducted joint training of CNN and GCN, and integrated local details and global information of keypoints feature. In order to simplify the network structure and training scale, Wei et al. [7] proposed the classical convolutional posture machine CPM to construct a multi-stage cascade deep network. Newell et al. [8] proposed Hourglass, a stacked hourglass network, to learn the local positional feature of the keypoints with multi-resolution heat maps, and to obtain the structural feature among the joints by learning through a multi-scale sensory field mechanism. Cai Y et al. [9] designed a stacked hourglass-like network, which aggregates features with the same spatial size to produce a subtle local description. To mitigate constraints to estimating the human poses in general scenarios, Liu et. al [10] presented an efficient human pose estimation model with joint direction cues and Gaussian coordinate encoding, which is the first time that the skeleton direction cues is introduced to the heatmap encoding in HPE task.

In recent years, research priority heat map has been transferred from physical structure Modeling Network to keypoints detection network in the hybrid approach. Sun K et al. [11] proposed Deep High-Resolution Attitude Estimation Network (DeepHR-Net) to aggregat the characterization information from the high-resolution convolution. Bazarevsky et al. [12] proposed BlazePose and combined a gating mechanism and a feature-attention module for selecting and fusing discriminative and attentional-perceptual features. Due to the similarity between human posture estimation and object detection, in recent years researchers have designed lots of human posture estimation models based on object detection models. Jiarui X. et al. [13] proposed YOLOv3-Human-Pose to achieve real-time multi-person posture estimation. Kumar et al. [14] designed a model named pose-SSD with null-space pyramid pooling to improve the accuracy and speed. Li et al. [15] proposed a model named Cascade YOLO to optimize by a cascade approach, which enables high accuracy and real-time. Debapriya et al. [16] proposed an end-to-end training model named YOLO-Pose, which jointly detects multiple individual bounding boxes and corresponding 2D postures in a single forward pass and groups the detected keypoints into a skeleton. Papaioannidis et al. [17] presented a novel neural module for enhancing existing fast and lightweight 2D human pose estimation CNNs, which is tasked to encode global spatial and semantic information and provide it to the stem network during inference. Wang et al. [18] designed LitePose, an efficient single-branch architecture for pose estimation, and introduced two simple approaches to enhance the capacity of LitePose, including fusion deconv head and large kernel conv.

In recent years, digital interaction systems based on human posture estimation have been widely used in digital artworks. Creative Technology Ltd [19] released Creative Senz3D, a creative tool software based on human posture estimation, which captures the users' body posture information in real time and allows the users to use body movements and gestures to perform drawing, editing, creation and other operations. Ishan C. et al. [20] designed a large-screen interactive installation artwork, Gaze+Gesture, based on human posture estimation, allowing users control the graphics and images on the screen through gestures and body movements. Futuristic Folktales [21], an interactive dance work was presented, in which a digital interactive system based on the human posture estimation provides real-time visual feedback to the dancers. Fang et al. [22] proposed several new techniques: Symmetric Integral Keypoint Regression (SIKR) for fast and fine localization, Parametric Pose Non-Maximum-Suppression (P-NMS) for eliminating redundant human detections and Pose Aware Identity Embedding for jointly posture real-time estimation and tracking in an interactive system. However, the current image interaction works based on human posture estimation have some shortcomings such as low accuracy, low real-time, and insufficient sense of interaction, which need to be solved urgently.

In this paper, an image interaction system based on human posture estimation is proposed. In general, the main contributions of the proposed model can be divided into the following three folds:

1. A human posture estimation method based on ECA is proposed. The model uses ECA to achieve enhance the model's focus on important features and designs joint top-down and bottom-up feature fusion to enhance the receptive field and semantic information.
2. An image interaction system is constructed. The system implements an action recognition module for action recognition and action category information transfer and a virtual scene module for 3D modelling and interaction system.
3. Experimental results showed that our human posture estimation method has high accuracy and good real-time performance and the image interactive system has good interactivity and creativity.

2   Proposed Human Posture Estimation Methods

Human posture estimation method is based on YOLOv5 [23] and ECA [24] mechanism in this paper. The method consists of three parts: multi-scale feature extraction module, cross-scale feature fusion module and human posture keypoints prediction module, as shown in Fig. 1. In the multi-scale feature extraction module, Efficient Channel Attention (ECA) is improved for extracting feature information from the input image, better focusing on the features required for human posture estimation. Afterwards, in the cross-scale feature fusion module, multi-scale features are extracted and fused. Finally, the prediction module applies the features to the convolution layer and predicts coordinate positions and confidence of human posture keypoints.

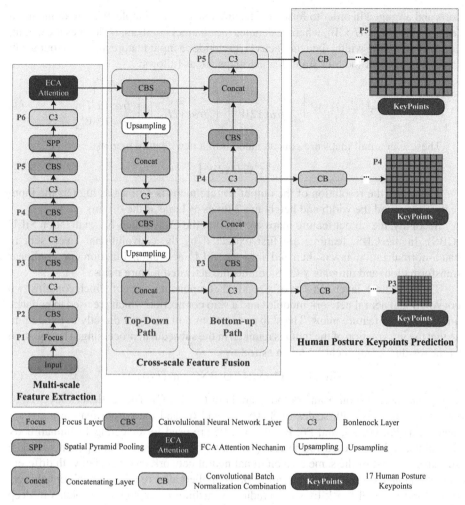

Fig. 1. The framework of the proposed model.

2.1 Multi-scale Feature Extraction Module

The multi-scale feature extraction module adopts CSPNet [25] as the backbone model and merges different levels of feature maps into final feature map and allows the network to automatically learn which feature are more important during the feature extraction by ECA, as shown in the left part of Fig. 1.

Firstly, the focus layer downsizes the channel numbers of the input low-resolution feature maps and compress the spatial dimensions according to a specified step size to obtain high-resolution feature maps. The specific process is to use 1×1 convolution and pixel rearrangement on the input feature maps to reduce the height and width dimensions to half of the origin and amplify the channel numbers to four times of the origin, so as to obtain high-resolution feature maps. Then, the input feature map is divided into four parts and arranged in order to form new feature maps. For example, the size of the input feature map is $C \times H \times W$, where C denotes the channel numbers, H denotes the height, and W denotes the width, then the focus layer divides a input feature map into four small maps. The sizes of the four small feature maps are as follows:

$$\left[\frac{C \times \frac{1}{4} \times W}{4H} \backslash H \backslash W \right], \left[\begin{matrix} C \times \frac{1}{4} \backslash H \\ frac12W \end{matrix} \right], \left[\begin{matrix} C \times \frac{1}{4} \backslash W \\ frac12H \end{matrix} \right], \left[\begin{matrix} C \times \frac{1}{4} \\ frac12H \\ frac12W \end{matrix} \right] \quad (1)$$

These four small maps are concatenated into a new feature map as:

$$\left[C \backslash 2H \backslash 2W \right] \quad (2)$$

Therefore, the resolution of the output feature maps is 4 times as high as the input feature map, and the width and height are 2 times as large as the origin.

Secondly, the output feature maps are fed into the Conv Batch-Normalization SiLU (CBS). In the CBS, features are first extracted by the convolutional layer, sent to batch-normalization layer, then fed into the SiLU activation function for nonlinear transformation, and ultimately CBS outputs the activated feature maps.

The bottleneck layer consists of x residual components, each of which contains two convolutional neural network modules and a skip connection which are used to enhance and enlarge the feature maps. The skip connections add the input directly to the output, so that the information of the input is retained in the subsequent processing. The equation of the residual component is shown as follows:

$$y = \text{SiLU}(\text{BN}(\text{Conv}(\text{SiLU}(\text{BN}(\text{Conv}(x)))))) + x \quad (3)$$

where the sizes of input x and output y are both (H, W, C). The bottleneck layer comprises 4 sub-layers with scales of 8, 16, 32, and 64 and the output feature maps are denoted as P3, P4, P5, and P6. P3, P4, and P5 are used for detecting 17 human body keypoints, and P6 is used for detecting human posture. Residual components in each sub-layer consist of the same convolutional neural network modules, but with different output channel number. A skip connection is applied after the first convolutional layer of the first residual block to avoid gradient vanishing or exploding problems in deep networks.

Furthermore, in the spatial pyramid pooling layer, the first process is to use 1×1 convolution and then three pooling operations of different sizes ($5 \times 5, 9 \times 9$ and 13×13) and are performed, and the outputs of each pooling layer are concatenated together. The pooling operation aims to extract features from the input at different scales, enabling the network to better recognize objects of various sizes.

Finally, the feature maps are fed into the ECA mechanism module after the bottleneck layer. The ECA mechanism module is used to enhances the features, which can learn the weights of each feature channel adaptively, enabling network to focus more on the features that are beneficial for classification. The structure of the ECA mechanism module is illustrated in Fig. 2.

The ECA computes the channel importance by applying global average pooling on each channel, as follows:

$$z = \frac{1}{H \times W} \sum_{i=1}^{H} \sum_{j=1}^{W} x_{cij}, \forall c \quad (4)$$

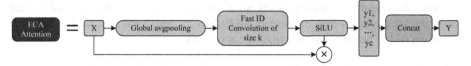

Fig. 2. ECA module structure.

where z is the global average pooling output of channel c. Then the channel weights are scaled and shifted to enhance the representation capabilities of models. Finally, all the channels are concatenated.

2.2 Cross-scale Feature Fusion Module

In the cross-scale feature fusion module, multi-scale feature extraction and cross-scale feature fusion are performed to enhance the receptive field and semantic information of model. The core idea is path aggregation, that is, to aggregate the feature maps from different levels through multiple paths, to generate cross-scale feature representations. The cross-scale feature fusion module, shown in Fig. 3, uses a combination of bottom-up and top-down approaches to extract feature maps.

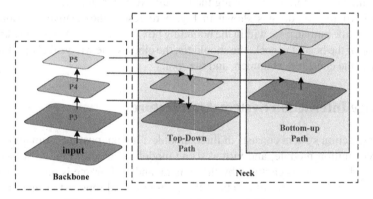

Fig. 3. Cross-scale feature fusion module structure

For the top-down path, high-level feature maps are upsampled level by level to obtain feature maps of the same size as the low-level feature maps, then added to the low-level feature maps to obtain the fused feature maps. In this way, the high semantic information in the high-level feature maps can be passed to the low-level feature maps, enhancing the semantic expression ability of the low-level feature maps.

For the bottom-up path, starting from the bottom-level feature maps, feature maps are convolved and downsampled to obtain the feature maps of the previous level, and so on, until the highest-level feature maps are obtained.

After the bottom-up and top-down paths are both calculated, the obtained feature maps are fused by regarding the bottom-up path as the backbone path, with combining top-down path. The path fusion formula is as follows:

$$F_{pan} = W_3 \times F_3 + W_2 \times U(D(W_3 \times F_3)) + W_1 \times U(D(W_2 \times U(D(W_3 \times F_3)))) \tag{5}$$

where F_{pan} is the final feature map, W_i is the weight, D denotes the downsampling operation and U denotes the upsampling operation.

2.3 Human Posture Keypoints Prediction Module

Human posture keypoints prediction module regresses and classifies the feature maps and predict the position and confidence of the human bounding boxes, as well as the coordinates of the 17 human posture keypoints within each bounding box.

Specifically, the input of the prediction module is P3, P4, and P5 feature maps, which correspond to different scales of feature information for good prediction ability at different scales. Each branch of the prediction module, which correspond to each feature map, has multiple Conv Batch-Normalization (CB) layer to extract features, shown in the right part of Fig. 5. The superposition of multiple CB layer increases the depth and width of the model, further improving the feature extraction ability.

The keypoint coordinates shown in Fig. 5 represent the relative positions of 17 keypoints in the human pose within the bounding box. These 17 human posture keypoints are the top of the head, the neck, the shoulders, the elbows, the wrists, the hips, the knees, the ankles, the chest, the abdomen, and the root.

3   Image Interaction System Architecture

Image interaction system consists of three modules: human posture estimation module, action recognition module, and virtual scene module, shown in Fig. 4. In the system, first, the video stream is captured by the camera, and each frame is processed, so as to capture and analyze the posture data of the visitors in real time. After that, the human posture estimation model in Sect. 2 is used to obtain the coordinates of the human posture keypoints, which provide the basic data for the action recognition. Next, the action recognition module performs based on the pre-trained model, and when the visitor makes a specific action, the module send an action category number to the virtual scene module through socket communication. Finally, the virtual scene module generates different three-dimensional transformation effects according to the action category number and this module is made on TouchDesigner. TouchDesigner is a visual programming software used for creative programming and interactive media art production. It adopts a node-based programming architecture, which is centered around a group of visual nodes representing different functions and operations such as input, output, processing and control. By connecting the nodes, a complete program can be constructed. TouchDesigner is chosen mainly for three prominent features: multi-platform compatibility, real-time 3D rendering and high-resolution synthesis capability.

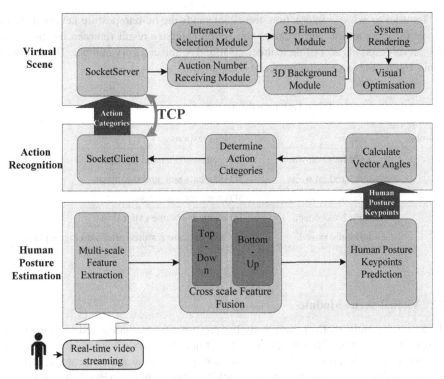

Fig. 4. Image interactive system structure.

3.1 Action Recognition Module

The action recognition module sets up five basic interactive actions, namely including right hand on waist, left hand on waist, both hands on waist, right hand raised, and left hand raised. The recognition of the five actions is mainly determined by the vector angles formed by six human key points among the 17 human key points, which are left shoulder, right shoulder, left elbow, right elbow, left wrist and right wrist. The action definition is shown in Fig. 5. Action category can be determined by calculating the angle between the left and right arms and the horizontal direction, and the angle of the left and right elbows.

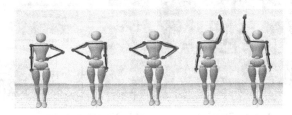

Fig. 5. Interactive action.

In order to achieve interaction, the client sends the human posture keypoints to the server for recognition, and receives the action category result returned by the server. The server responds according to the transmitted action category number. The following Table 1 gives the interaction response comparison.

Table 1. Interactive response comparison table.

Number	Action	System response
1	right hand on waist	3D elements float and disappear
2	left hand on waist	3D elements sink and disappear
3	both hands on waist	3D elements move faster
4	right hand raised	3D element volume expansion
5	left hand raised	3D elements are restored after shaking in place

3.2 Virtual Scene Module

Based on the multi-platform interactivity, real-time 3D rendering and high-resolution compositing features of TouchDesigner, the virtual scene module is actually a secondary creation of the 3D model of C4D in TouchDesigner. The graphical program structure diagram of the virtual scene module in TouchDesigner is shown in Fig. 6, which includes the action number receiving module, the interaction selection module, the material control module, the three-dimensional element module, the system rendering module, the three-dimensional background module, and the visual effect optimization module.

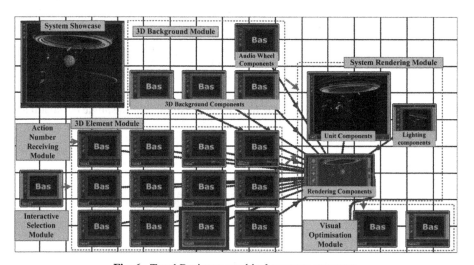

Fig. 6. TouchDesigner graphical program structure.

4 Experiment

4.1 Human Posture Estimation Dataset

We use COCO 2017 as the human posture keypoints dataset, which contains more than 250,000 images of people in different poses and corresponding human posture keypoints, making it a good choice for training pose estimation models.

4.2 Implementation Details

Our experiments are coded using the Pytorch framework, using the windows 11 operating system with a GPU of 1650ti. Optimization is performed using Adam, with initial weight set to 0.01, model momentum parameter set to 0.937, IoU threshold set to 0.5 and batchsize set to 16. For each training, we randomly select 80% of the images as the training set and 20% as the test set. In the testing process of the model, we use CLOU as human bounding box loss function and its definition is as follows:

$$L(s, i, j, k) = \left(1 - CIoU\left(Box_{gt}^{s,i,j,k}, Box_{pred}^{s,i,j,k}\right)\right) \tag{6}$$

where $Box_{gt}^{s,i,j,k}$ is a predicting bounding box, whose location is (i, j), scale is s and number is k.

Besides, we use OKS as human posture keypoints loss function and its definition is as follows:

$$L_{kpts}(s, i, j, k) = 1 - \sum_{n=1}^{N_{kpts}} OKS = 1 - \frac{\sum_{n=1}^{N_{kpts}} \exp\left(\frac{d_n^2}{2s^2 k_n^2}\right)\delta(v_n > 0)}{\sum_{n=1}^{N_{kpts}} \delta(v_n > 0)} \tag{7}$$

where d_n is the Euclidean distance between the predicted and true keypoints, k_n is the keypoints weight, and $\delta(v_n)$ is the visibility flag of each keypoint. Corresponding to each keypoint, confidence is learned to show whether human has keypoint or not and confidence loss function is as follows:

$$L_{kpts\_conf}(s, i, j, k) = 1 - \sum_{n=1}^{N_{kpts}} BCE\left(\delta(v_n > 0), p_{kpts}^n\right) \tag{8}$$

where p_{kpts}^n is the confidence of the keypoints. Finally, the total loss consists of the losses for all scales, all anchors, and all positions, as shown as follows:

$$L_{total} = \sum_{s,i,j,k} \left(\lambda_{cls} L_{cls} + \lambda_{box} L_{box} + \lambda_{kpts} L_{kpts} + \lambda_{kpts\_conf} L_{kpts\_conf}\right) \tag{9}$$

where $\lambda_{cls} = 0.5$, $\lambda_{box} = 0.05$, $\lambda_{kpts} = 0.1$, $\lambda_{kpts\_conf} = 0.5$.

In our experiments, we adopted average precision (AP), AP50, AP70 and AP$_L$ as metrics to evaluate human posture estimation model performance.

4.3 Experimental Results on Human Posture Estimation

Ablation Experiment. In order to verify the effectiveness of the ECA attention mechanism, we carry out ablation experiments. The ECA-based method improves significantly than YOLO-pose in AP metrics and AP_L metrics which expresses the effectiveness of the ECA, as shown in Table 2. In addition, the accuracy of method with ECA is lower than YOLO-pose on the APL metric, suggesting that incorporating attentional mechanisms is not dominant in predicting at a long term.

Table 2. ECA ablation table.

Method	AP	AP50	AP75	APL
YOLO-pose [22]	62.9	87.7	69.4	**71.8**
YOLO-Pose+SE	66.7	**88.6**	71.6	70.9
YOLO-Pose+CBAM	66.8	88.4	72.2	70.7
YOLO-Pose+ECA	**66.9**	88.5	**72.3**	71.0

Accuracy Comparison. In this section, three methods of OpenPose, Hourglass and HRNet are selected to compare with the YOLO-Pose+ECA method in this paper. The comparison results are shown in Table 3. The YOLO-pose+ECA predicts human posture much better than the other three methods in AP metrics and AP50 metrics, and slightly lower than HRNet in AP75 and APL metrics. Overall, our method performs better in the four evaluation metrics.

Table 3. Performance comparison of different models.

Method	Backbone	AP	AP50	AP75	APL
OpenPose [13]	–	61.8	84.9	67.5	68.2
Hourglass [8]	Hourglass	56.6	81.8	61.8	67.0
HRNet [26]	HRNet-W32	66.5	88.0	**72.6**	**72.3**
YOLO-Pose+ECA	Darknet_csp-d53-m	**66.9**	**88.5**	72.3	71.0

Real-Time Performance Comparison. In the experiment, we test the model real-time performance of three 3D human posture estimation methods proposed in recent years to compare with the YOLO-Pose+ECA method in this paper. The results of the real-time evaluation of the methods are shown in Table 4. Our method has better real-time performance compared with other methods and it can be tried to extend it to the application of real-time scenarios.

Table 4. Real-time performance comparison of different models.

Method	Backbone	FPS
OpenPose [13]	–	24
Hourglass [8]	Hourglass	18
HRNet [26]	HRNet-W32	23
YOLO-Pose+ECA	Darknet_csp-d53-m	29

Visual Analysis. In this experiment, the keypoints predicted by the human posture estimation network are marked in the figure with different colors of points and line, as shown in the Fig. 7. It can be seen that the proposed method can distinguish keypoints and background for gray images or images where the human and the background have similar tones, indicating that the network is robust to illumination and background interference. Besides, for images where some body parts are occluded, the model can output posture estimation results consistent with human cognitive intuition, indicating that the model implicitly learns the structure of the human body.

Fig. 7. Visualization results for human posture estimation

4.4 Experimental Results on Image Interactive System

Function Testing. This system involves five interactive actions corresponding to five 3D element variations as shown in the Table 1, respectively, the system response to these five actions was tested with a frame rate of 60, and the example figures are as Fig. 8. The system interacts with 5 actions according to the setting at a frame rate of 60 and runs without lag.

Subjective Testing. The subjective testing is in the form of a questionnaire, according to the evaluation standards of the International Design Center Berlin (IDZ), where 20 subjects are invited to fill in the questionnaire after experiencing different themes of the image interaction system. The questionnaire has a score of 30 points, a total of 6 questions, and each question is worth 5 points, and after calculating the mean value of

Frame 101 (float)   Frame 201 (float)   Frame 301 (float)

Fig. 8. Right hand on the waist - 3D elements float and disappear

the questionnaire scores, we can make a quantitative evaluation of the interaction design of this system. The quantitative evaluation result is as shown as Table 5. Overall, this image interaction system based on human posture estimation has a good experience among most subjects, but further improvement and exploration are needed in some aspects.

Table 5. Subjective testing performance comparison of our system.

Questions	Emotional experience	Cognitive load reduction	Facilitating interaction
Average value	3.75	3.70	4.55
Questions	Values Transmission	Appearances	Creativity
Average value	4.45	4.40	4.20

Objective Testing. In this experiment, RT, MSE, stability and usability are calculated by adjusting the frame rate, as shown in Table 6. It can be seen that when the frame rate is greater than 60 fps, RT tends to be stable, and the image quality, stability and usability are relatively reduced. Therefore, the system sets the frame rate to 60 fps in TouchDesigner to make the system the best state.

Table 6. Objective testing performance comparison of our system.

FPS	RT (ms)	MSE	Stability	Usability
15	174.94	0.298	1	0.88
30	162.34	0.313	1	0.88
45	159.43	0.326	0.92	0.88
60	138.82	0.345	1	0.88
75	135.78	0.389	0.34	0.80
90	136.32	0.391	1	0.78
105	139.87	0.429	0.26	0.88

5 Conclusion

In this paper, a human posture estimation intelligent algorithm based on attention mechanism is presented and an image interaction system is constructed. The human posture estimation method designs ECA attention mechanisms to enhance the model's focus on important features in the multi-scale feature extraction module. In the cross-scale feature fusion module, joint top-down and bottom-up feature fusion are performed to enhance the receptive field and semantic information. In the human posture keypoints prediction module, the feature map is regressed and classified and the location and confidence of the bounding boxes are predicted, as well as the coordinates of the key points within each bounding box. The image interaction system implements an action recognition module for action recognition and action category information transfer and a virtual scene module for 3D modelling and interaction system. Experimental results showed that our human posture estimation method has high accuracy and good real-time performance. Besides, the image interactive system has good interactivity and creativity.

References

1. Zheng, C., et al.: Deep learning-based human pose estimation: a survey. ACM Comput. Surv. **56**, 1–37 (2023)
2. Toshev, A., Szegedy, C.: DeepPose: human pose estimation via deep neural networks. In: Proceedings of the IEEE Conference on Computer Vision and Pattern Recognition, pp. 1653–1660 (2014)
3. Carreira, J., Agrawal, P., Fragkiadaki, K., Malik, J.: Human pose estimation with iterative error feedback. In: Proceedings of the IEEE Conference on Computer Vision and Pattern Recognition, pp. 4733–4742 (2016)
4. Li, K., Wang, S., Zhang, X., Xu, Y., Xu, W., Tu, Z.: Pose recognition with cascade transformers. In: Proceedings of the IEEE Conference on Computer Vision and Pattern Recognition (2021)
5. Li, J., et al.: Human pose regression with residual log-likelihood estimation. In: Proceedings of the IEEE International Conference on Computer Vision, pp. 11025–11034 (2021)
6. Tompson, J.J., Jain, A., Lecun, Y., Bregler, C.: Joint training of a convolutional network and a graphical model for human pose estimation 27 (2014)
7. Wei, S.-E., Ramakrishna, V., Kanade, T., Sheikh, Y.: Convolutional pose machines. In: Proceedings of the IEEE Conference on Computer Vision and Pattern Recognition, pp. 4724–4732 (2016)
8. Newell, A., Yang, K., Deng, J.: Stacked hourglass networks for human pose estimation. In: Proceeding of the IEEE European Conference Computer Vision, pp. 483–499 (2016)
9. Cai, Y., et al.: Learning delicate local representations for multi-person pose estimation. In: Proceeding of the IEEE European Conference Computer Vision, pp. 455–472 (2020)
10. Liu, H., Liu, T., Chen, Y., Zhang, Z., Li, Y.-F.: EHPE: skeleton cues-based gaussian coordinate encoding for efficient human pose estimation. IEEE Trans. Multimedia (2022)
11. Sun, K., Xiao, B., Liu, D., Wang, J.: Deep high-resolution representation learning for human pose estimation. In: Proceedings of the IEEE Conference on Computer Vision and Pattern Recognition, pp. 5693–5703 (2019)
12. Bazarevsky, V., Grishchenko, I., Raveendran, K.J.A.: BlazePose: on-device real-time body pose tracking 2020 (2006). 10.48550
13. Cao, Z., Simon, T., Wei, S.-E., Sheikh, Y.: Realtime multi-person 2D pose estimation using part affinity fields. In: Proceedings of the IEEE Conference on Computer Vision and Pattern Recognition, pp. 7291–7299 (2017)

14. Kumar, C., et al.: VRU pose-SSD: multiperson pose estimation for automated driving. In: Proceedings of the AAAI Conference on Artificial Intelligence, pp. 15331–15338 (2021)
15. Li, X., He, M., Liu, Y., Luo, H., Ju, M.: SPCS: a spatial pyramid convolutional shuffle module for YOLO to detect occluded object. Complex Intell. Syst. **9**, 301–315 (2023)
16. Maji, D., Nagori, S., Mathew, M., Poddar, D.: YOLO-pose: enhancing yolo for multi person pose estimation using object keypoint similarity loss. In: Proceedings of the IEEE Conference on Computer Vision and Pattern Recognition, pp. 2637–2646 (2022)
17. Papaioannidis, C., Mademlis, I., Pitas, I.: Fast single-person 2D human pose estimation using multi-task convolutional neural networks. In: IEEE International Conference Speech and Signal Processing, pp. 1–5 (2023)
18. Wang, Y., Li, M., Cai, H., Chen, W.-M., Han, S.: Lite pose: efficient architecture design for 2D human pose estimation. In: Proceedings of the IEEE Conference on Computer Vision and Pattern Recognition, pp. 13126–13136 (2022)
19. Senz3d, C.C. https://cn.creative.com/. Accessed June 2021
20. Chatterjee, I., Xiao, R., Harrison, C.: Gaze+ gesture: expressive, precise and targeted free-space interactions. In: Proceedings of the ACM on International Conference on Multimodal Interaction, pp. 131–138 (2015)
21. Isabell, Folktales, F.: https://www.whatsoninedinburgh.co.uk/event/115313-futuristic-folkta les/. Accessed 16 Feb 2023
22. Fang, H.-S., et al.: AlphaPose: whole-body regional multi-person pose estimation and tracking in real-time. IEEE Trans. Pattern Anal. Mach. Intell. (2022)
23. Bochkovskiy, A., Wang, C.-Y., Liao, H.-Y.M.: Yolov4: optimal speed and accuracy of object detection. arXiv preprint arXiv:10934 (2020)
24. Wang, Q., Wu, B., Zhu, P., Li, P., Zuo, W., Hu, Q.: ECA-Net: efficient channel attention for deep convolutional neural networks. In: Proceedings of the IEEE Conference on Computer Vision and Pattern Recognition, pp. 11534–11542 (2020)
25. Wang, C.Y., et al.: CSPNet: a new backbone that can enhance learning capability of CNN. In: Proceedings of the IEEE Conference on Computer Vision and Pattern Recognition Workshops, pp. 390–391 (2020)
26. Redmon, J., Farhadi, A.: YOLOv3: an incremental improvement (2018)

PU-SSIM: A Perceptual Constraint for Point Cloud Up-Sampling

Tiangang Huang, Xiaochuan Wang[✉], Ruijun Liu, and Haisheng Li

Beijing Technology and Business University, Beijing, China
wangxc@btbu.edu.cn

Abstract. Point cloud data acquired through scanning typically exhibits sparse, non-uniform distribution, and a certain level of noise. Therefore, it is necessary to generate a dense and high-quality point cloud via up-sampling. In recent years, point cloud up-sampling techniques gain significant advantages due to the development of deep learning. In particular, most of current end-to-end up-sampling networks adopt point-wise constraints, e.g., Chamfer distance to train the up-sampling model. However, these point-wise constraints are inadequate to reduce residual noise, meanwhile would induce structural distortions. To further improve the capability of up-sampling networks, we propose a perception-wise constraints, namely PU-SSIM. Specifically, we adopt the typical full-reference point cloud quality metric to measure the structural similarity between the generated high-resolution point cloud and the ground truth. We managed to embed it into the up-sampling network, providing a plug-in capability. The experimental results indicate that the PU-SSIM can maintain the structural details, meanwhile reduce the residual noises. The proposed perception constraint is compatible to most mainstream methods, which would benefit the community to some extend.

Keywords: point cloud up-sampling · point cloud quality assessment · perceptual constraint · deep geometric learning

1 Introduction

The point cloud data obtained by laser scanning has a wide range of applications, but the point cloud obtained by scanning is often uneven and sparse. Therefore, up-sampling on the point cloud has become an indispensable step.

The up-sampling process for point clouds aims to augment the point density while preserving critical geometric properties in the input data. The current research achieves point cloud surface reconstruction through various techniques such as meshing, voxelization [15], MLS smoothing [12], and Poisson reconstruction [9]. Because of the rapid advancements in deep learning, many researchers have begun to leverage this technology for tasks like point cloud classification [21,22], segmentation [5,7,8,20], up-sampling [6,13,22–24,29,30], and other operations.

In the context of point-based up-sampling, PointNet++ [22] employs interpolation to increase the number of points, while Yu et al. [30] introduce a well-known up-sampling framework called PU-Net which expand the point count through MLP. However, due to the non-uniform distribution of the input point cloud, interpolation methods struggle to determine the interpolation point locations. Conversely, duplication methods fail to provide information about point location variations, potentially causing overlaps or proximity to the original points. To solve the overlap issue of PU-Net, MPU [29] introduces a random assignment of one-dimensional codes within the up-sampling module. This approach ensures that the up-sampled points exhibit varying position variations. Point clouds, given their irregular and disorderly nature, pose challenges for existing point-based up-sampling methods. During training, this approach requires extracting point cloud patches from previous training steps, which can be intricate and time-consuming, especially when dealing with substantial up-sampling rates.

Apart from the point-based up-sampling approach, contemporary researchers also opt for two-dimensionalizing and up-sampling point clouds. PU-GAN [13] initially regulates the point cloud by employing a grid structure in the FoldingNet, followed by the addition of a vector to duplicated feature. This process introduces subtle differences in the duplicated point features. However, PU-GAN does not effectively analyze the ability to preserve geometric structure. Results indicate that the improvement is attributed to the utilization of the discriminator. The overarching architecture of PUCRN [4] comprises three distinct stages, each characterized by a consistent network architecture designed for varying degrees of offset prediction and refinement, ultimately achieving point cloud up-sampling. Most of methods employ non-Euclidean distance constraints during the training process for point cloud up-sampling.

In this paper, we use the point quality assessment method to constrain the training process of up-sampling, so as to reduce the distortion of the up-sampling results and pay more attention to the geometric properties. Specifically, depend on point cloud attributes, we extract some futures based on distributions's dispersion. These features encompass information such as the geometry, normal, and curvature of point clouds. And calculate the structural similarity score based on the relative differences in feature values to constraining the generation of point clouds. Through testing and evaluation of the up-sampling results obtained using this constraint method, we observe a significant improvement in accuracy compared to classical and existing methods, demonstrating the superiority of PU-SSIM. The main contributions of our work are as follows:

- We design a novel perceptual constraint, namely PU-SSIM, for the point cloud up-sampling task. The proposed constraint is inspired by point cloud quality assessment, with the aim to improve the perception quality of generated high-resolution point clouds.
- We embed the proposed PU-SSIM into point cloud up-sampling network, training the models with adopted PCQA scores. In particular, the proposed PU-SSIM provides a plug-in capability.

– We conducted testing and evaluation on networks incorporating PU-SSIM, and the results indicate that PU-SSIM contributes to performance enhancement in the networks, demonstrating superior accuracy compared to numerous existing technologies.

– Experimental results demonstrate that the proposed PU-SSIM can alleviate noises and structural distortions in the generated dense point clouds, indicating its practical utility to a certain extent.

2   Related Work

2.1   Point Cloud Up-Sampling

Currently, point cloud up-sampling methods can mainly be categorized into two folds, i.e., optimization-based and learning-based methods.

Optimization-based up-sampling methods aim to improve the resolution of high point clouds by optimizing certain criteria. Traditional algorithms based on point interpolation initially insert additional points into the original point cloud. These new points are subsequently optimized through iterative algorithms, thus preserving local geometrical structures. Alexa et al. [1] utilizes point sets to represent shapes, evaluate locally based on image resolution and inserts points to vertices. Lipman et al. [14] divides the up-sampling task into two sub-goals and proposes a task decomposition based on the multi-objective characteristics. Wu et al. [27] later suggest a method for point-set consolidation by combine surface points into deep points located on the shape. However, optimization-based approaches might be unsuccessful if the initial assumptions aren't met.

Deep learning-based methods have become predominant and lead the latest advancements. Notably, PU-Net [30] introduced a foundational learning-driven up-sampling structure comprised of three key elements: feature extraction, feature expansion and coordinate reconstruction. Subsequent studies have been inspired by this foundational structure, aiming to refine various facets like up-sampling scheme, training supervision. For example, Li et al. [13] applies GAN architecture to point clouds and introduces PU-GAN. The emphasis is on improving the quantitative performance of up-sampled point clouds through a self-attention unit and the incorporation of a compound loss. Hou et al. [24] proposes utilizing linear transformations to convert PUGeo-NET from two dimensions to three dimensions, and Qian et al. [23]'s PU-GCN incorporates NodeShuffle in the up-sampling stage to enhance the accuracy of the results.

2.2   Point Cloud Quality Assessment

Point cloud quality assessment is another important branch of point clouds, which aims to evaluate the perception quality of point clouds with respect to human subjective ratings. The criteria for evaluating point cloud quality typically revolve around resolution, density, noise level, and completeness.

PCQA methods often involve geometric-based approaches, where the focus is on measuring deviations from a reference model or surface. To calculate geometric distortion, the PC-MSDM [18] measures the curvature similarities between the original and distorted point clouds. However, due to the high susceptibility of point cloud normal to various normal retrieval techniques, the normal utilized in the aforementioned measures [2,16,17,25] can result in inconsistent outcomes. Yang et al. [28] suggest employing graph signal processing to extract color gradients from the point cloud as a means of estimating the quality. The generalized Hausdorff distance measure [10] uses multiple rankings to determine the highest-quality model based on its correlation with subjective quality assessments, thus addressing the issue of the traditional Hausdorff distance's excessive sensitivity to outlier data. Wang et al. [11] introduces a point-to-distribution quality evaluation framework that leverages the relationship between a single point and a cluster of points within a localized area. Similarity measure [26], previously validated for their effectiveness in assessing the quality of general images, are now being adapted for PCQA, with researchers beginning to use spatial structural characteristics as an index of quality. In [3], features based on geometry, color, normal, and curvature are extracted from point clouds. Following this, similarities in geometry and color features are assessed and integrated to compute overall objective scores akin to SSIM [26].

3   Perceptual Constraint for Point Cloud Up-Sampling

Up-sampling results with CD loss alone still have surface distortion. We borrow the idea from PCQA to assess a series of statistical dispersion measurements and compare the corresponding feature values. The quality of point cloud up-sampling is improved by aggregating individual quality scores as constraints obtained from each region through error pooling.

Thus, we have formulated a loss function based on PointSSIM [26] in the field of PCQA to strengthen perceptual constraints, aiming to improve the network's up-sampling ability and structure retention ability. The overall computational workflow is delineated in the lower portion of Fig. 1.

As illustrated in Fig. 1, We calculate the neighborhood of each point and thereby find local properties. Certain data is computed based on the attributes of the point cloud and its neighborhood, which are either intrinsic, such as geometric properties, or estimable in the absence of explicit information, for instance, normal vectors. Due to the exclusion of color information in the point cloud utilized for up-sampling, we have employed three distinct categories of attributes in this context: structural relationship, normal vector information and curvature values.

Calculations of structural relationship rely on the Euclidean distances from a central point to every point within its surrounding vicinity, serving to assess the coherence of local geometric structures. Similarly, measures pertaining to normal vectors are derived by calculating angular similarities between the normal vectors of a specific point and its neighboring points, aimed at evaluating the

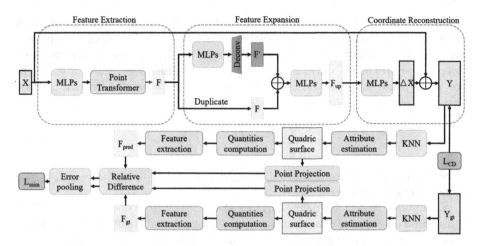

Fig. 1. Schematic diagram of the overall network architecture, The upper half is the baseline and the lower half is the calculation method of PU-SSIM.

uniformity of local surface shapes. And curvature values are employed for the same purpose. To estimate the scale parameters of the three attributes, compute some numerical values, such as the mean absolute deviation. Then features are extracted based on the calculation results.

Subsequently, based on the similarity between the features derived from ground truth data and the upsampled point cloud, each neighborhood of γ^{Pred} is associated with the corresponding neighborhood of γ^{GT} by identifying, for each point p in γ^{Pred}, its nearest point q in γ^{GT}. Then calculate the relative difference between the tow corresponding feature values, as follow:

$$S_{\gamma^{Pred}(p)} = \frac{|F_{\gamma^{GT}(q)} - F_{\gamma^{Pred}(p)}|}{\max\{|F_{\gamma^{GT}(q)}|, |F_{\gamma^{Pred}(p)}|\}} \tag{1}$$

The method for selecting corresponding eigenvalues to calculate similarity refers to [19], where it is necessary to establish a relationship between γ^{Pred} and γ^{GT} For each point p in γ^{Pred}, its projection point $\hat{p}$ in γ^{GT} is calculated by fitting a local least squares quadratic surface, as shown in Fig. 2.

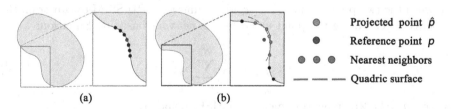

Fig. 2. Illustration of the method for computing quadratic surfaces, where (a) represents the ground truth point cloud, and (b) represents the predicted point cloud.

As depicted in Fig. 2, we initially identify the k-nearest neighbors for each point. Then we approximate a tangent plane through Principal Component Analysis, establishing an orthonormal frame (u_x, u_y, u_z) where u_z is oriented along an approximate normal to the surface. In this local frame, the neighbor p_i of p has coordinates (x_i, y_i, z_i). We thus look for the quadric surface $Q(x, y) = ax^2 + by^2 + cxy + dx + ey + f$, minimizing:

$$\sum_i ||z_i - Q(x_i, y_i)||_2^2 \tag{2}$$

Once the quadric surface Q is fitted, $\hat{p}$ is given as $(0, 0, Q(0, 0))$ in the (u_x, u_y, u_z) frame mentioned above.

Simultaneously, high-quality surfaces also contribute to obtaining better features based on curvature and normal. The average curvature at the central point is determined using the coefficients from the quadric surface that has been approximated. Then, based on p and $\hat{p}$, two curvature values are calculated, denoted as ρ_p and $\rho_{\hat{p}}$. After that, three types of features are computed:

$$f_1^p = \frac{||\mu_p^\rho - \mu_{\hat{p}}^\rho||}{max(\mu_p^\rho, \mu_{\hat{p}}^\rho) + k_1} \tag{3}$$

$$f_2^p = \frac{||\sigma_p^\rho - \sigma_{\hat{p}}^\rho||}{max(\sigma_p^\rho, \sigma_{\hat{p}}^\rho) + k_2} \tag{4}$$

$$f_3^p = \frac{||\sigma_p^\rho \sigma_{\hat{p}}^\rho - \sigma_{p\hat{p}}^\rho||}{\sigma_p^\rho \sigma_{\hat{p}}^\rho + k_3} \tag{5}$$

where k_i are constants to avoid instability when denominators are close to zero. μ_p^ρ and $\mu_{\hat{p}}^\rho$ are Gaussian-weighted averages of curvature over the 3D points belonging to each neighborhoods. Similarly $\sigma_p^\rho, \sigma_{\hat{p}}^\rho$ and $\sigma_{p\hat{p}}^\rho$ are standard deviations and covariance of curvature over these neighborhoods. The normal vectors for each point in the new coordinate are determined by computing the gradient of the quadratic surface.

Finally, we aggregate the relative differences of all points Np in the point cloud as an assessment of the point cloud's similarity score. Perform the same operation on both the predicted point cloud and the ground truth, obtaining two sets of scores. Compare two scores and select the minimum as the symmetric error between the two points, and use it as a loss function LPU-SSIM to constrain the process of generating the point cloud by the network based on Equation:

$$L_{PU-SSIM} = \frac{1}{N_p} \sum_{p=1}^{N_p} S_{\gamma^{Pred}(p)^m} \tag{6}$$

where $m = \{1, 2\}$, indicating mean and MSE, respectively.

4 Vanilla Network

We select PUCRN [4] as the baseline, which is an up-sampling network through effective cascaded refinement. The overview of the baseline is shown in the upper half of Fig. 1.

4.1 Network Architecture

The vanilla network is composed of three modules, i.e., feature extraction, feature expansion and coordinate reconstruction.

Feature Extraction: In the feature extraction, the features $F = \{f_i\}_{i=1}^{N}$ of $N \times C$ are extracted from high-resolution point cloud X. Using the point cloud sampling module based on Point-Transformer, we can obtain relatively accurate local and global features. Following the approach in PointNet [22], a low-resolution point cloud is inputted, and point features are extracted through a series of multi layer perceptrons. Subsequently, global features are obtained through the max pooling operation. We then duplicate the global features and concatenate them with the original features to obtain the output point features. After that, we input these features into a point transformer layer to obtain features that can reflect local information. The self-attention operation is shown as follows:

$$f_i = x_i \oplus \sum_{j \in N(i)} softmax(\gamma(\varphi(x_i) - \psi(x_j) + \delta)) \odot (\alpha(x_j) + \delta) \tag{7}$$

where f_i is the feature. ϕ, ψ, and α are point features. δ is a position code. In this way, we can aiming the local points and the whole point cloud and encode the point features.

Feature Expansion: The feature expansion unit aims to expand the number of features in the feature space to obtain r times up-sampled point features.

Firstly, we duplicate the input features $F = \{f_i\}_{i=1}^{N}$ by r times. Then we use a transposed convolution branch to obtain features. Finally, we input point features into MLPs, resulting in the expanded features, denoting as $F_{up} = \{f_i\}_{i=1}^{rN}$.

Coordinate Reconstruction: We adopt residual learning scheme for coordinate reconstruction, aiming to generate a new point set $S = \{s_i\}_{i=1}^{rN}$ from the expanded feature $F_{up} = \{f_i\}_{i=1}^{rN}$. In particular, we predict the offset of each point via MLPs to adjust the initial position, which can be formulated as

$$P_{output} = MLP(F_{up}) + Dup(P_{input}, r) \tag{8}$$

where r is the up-sampling rate and P_{input} is the initial point cloud.

4.2   Constraints

We now present the compound losses designed for training in an end-to-end fashion.

CD Loss: Given that point cloud up-sampling constitutes a low-level task necessitating a focused examination of local geometric structures, during the end-to-end training of PU-SSIM, our initial choice for the loss function is the Chamfer Distance. This metric is employed to quantify the point-wise disparity between the predicted point cloud and the ground truth.

$$L_{CD} = \frac{1}{|\gamma^{\mathrm{Pred}}|} \sum_{p \in \gamma^{\mathrm{Pred}}} \min_{q \in \gamma^{GT}} ||p - q||_2^2 + \frac{1}{|\gamma^{GT}|} \sum_{q \in \gamma^{GT}} \min_{p \in \gamma^{\mathrm{Pred}}} ||p - q||_2^2 \tag{9}$$

where γ^{Pred} is the predicted point cloud, γ^{GT} is the ground truth, p and q are points from each point cloud.

Total Loss: We learn to encourage the uniformity of the generated point cloud and improving the visual quality by minimizing the loss function below:

$$L_{\mathrm{total}} = \alpha L_{CD} + \beta L_{PU-SSIM} \tag{10}$$

where α and β are balance weights to make each term contribute equally.

5   Experiment

In this section, we perform several experiments aimed at conducting quantitative and qualitative comparisons of our approach against state-of-the-art point up-sampling methods, as well as assessing various aspects of our model.

5.1   Experiment Settings

Datasets: We utilized two datasets, PU1K [23] and PU-GAN [13], for experimentation. The PU-GAN dataset have 24000 training patches. PU1K dataset offers a more diverse collection of point clouds and boasts many point cloud models. There are 1147 3D models, split into 1020 training samples, and 127 test point clouds. Overall, PU1K encompasses a wide range of 3D objects, including both simple and complex shapes.

Training: We employ Poisson disk sampling on the original meshes to create pairs of point clouds for training. Our models undergo training for a total of 100 epochs. Set the batch size to 32. The initial learning rate is 0.001. We randomly sub-sample 256 points from the ground truth as the training input. End-to-end training is conducted using the ground truth containing 1024 points.

Testing and Evaluation: In line with conventional practices for quantitative evaluation, we employ the Chamfer distance (CD), Hausdorff distance (HD), and point-to-surface distance (P2F) to quantify the deviation between the output points and the ground truth meshes. A lower value for these metrics signifies superior performance.

5.2   Results

PU1K Dataset: We perform experiments on point clouds with different input point numbers and then proceed to compare outcomes. Table 1 illustrates the degree of improvement achieved by our method in contrast to the previous up-sampling network. By examining the information presented in the table, it is evident that there has been an enhancement in the impact of evaluation indices.

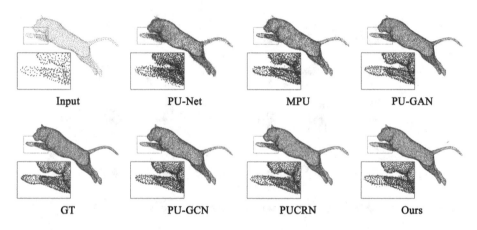

Fig. 3. Up-sampling visualization results of a point cloud. We show the up-sampled results when processed input point clouds by different up-sampling networks. Our method keeps the boundary information of objects well.

We compare the effect of our method with PU-Net, MPU, PU-GAN, PU-GCN and PUCRN. Analyzing the information provided in the table reveals that as the quantity of inputs rises, the influence of the upsampling network progressively intensifies. CD improved by 0.022×10^{-3}, HD improved by 0.73×10^{-3} and P2F improved by 0.019×10^{-3} compared to PUCRN. Our method consistently shown significant enhancements over existing methods, thereby validating its robustness across different input sizes. Moreover, for the purpose of visualization, we render the point cloud model after up-sampling task. With 2048 input numbers. The visualization also illustrate that, with the PU-SSIM, the point cloud exhibits the ability to produce a surface that is more uniform, featuring enhanced details and reduced presence of outliers. As shown in Figs. 3 and 4, we use color to indicate the distance between the predicted point and the GT point cloud, and blue represents the point with small distance.

Table 1. Comparison of results with four times up-sampling on the PU1K dataset. After using the PU-SSIM loss, our method outperforms the comparison methods in almost all metrics. The values of CD, HD, and P2F are multiplied by 10^3. A Bold denotes the best performance.

Method	512 input			1024 input			2048 input		
	CD	HD	P2D	CD	HD	P2F	CD	HD	P2F
PU-Net [30]	3.014	35.597	11.88	1.891	24.065	7.501	1.121	15.31	4.963
MPU [29]	2.858	31.236	8.228	1.695	20.783	5.444	0.904	12.943	3.571
PU-GAN [13]	2.807	23.568	6.921	1.181	15.374	4.931	0.686	10.052	3.194
PU-GCN [23]	2.067	23.529	6.543	1.123	14.626	4.151	0.645	9.768	2.617
PUCRN [4]	1.657	**18.991**	5.222	0.873	**11.95**	3.319	0.509	8.368	2.097
Ours	**1.596**	19.101	**4.87**	**0.824**	12.017	**3.048**	**0.487**	**7.638**	**1.907**

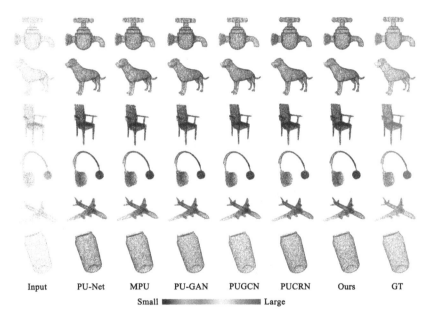

Fig. 4. Results on PU1K dataset. The point clouds are colored based on point to surface distance between the original meshes and the output of each method, with the blue representing the point that is closer to the surface. (Color figure online)

Upsampling Point Sets of Varying Sizes: Figure 5 displays the outcomes of up-sampling point sets of varying sizes; our approach remains consistent, even when the input consists of as few as 256 points.

PU-GAN Dataset: Refer to the setting of PU-GAN [13], we replicate experiments utilizing an input size of 1,024 on the PU-GAN dataset. The quantitative results for ×4 up-sampling rates are presented in Table 2. In general, our app-

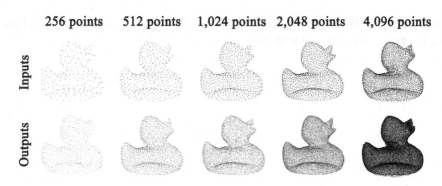

Fig. 5. Upsampling point sets of varying sizes.(There is no data of 4096 points and corresponding ground truth in the PU1K dataset, 1024 points are input for two times of ×4 upsampling).

roach demonstrates superior performance across various metrics, emerging as the most effective method.

Table 2. Comparison on PU-GAN [13] dataset. The input size of point cloud is 1,024. The values are multiplied by 10^3.

Methods	1024 input		
	CD	HD	P2F
PU-Net [30]	0.896	7.072	7.093
MPU [29]	0.621	5.757	4.579
PU-GAN [13]	0.597	5.917	4.619
PU-GCN [23]	0.602	4.963	4.159
PUCRN [4]	**0.556**	5.791	3.461
Ours	0.557	**5.687**	**13.286**

5.3   Ablation Study

To compare the effects of the PU-SSIM, we performed ablation experiments to quantitatively evaluate the contribution. e maintain the uniformity of other parameter selections across all experiments to guarantee the precision of the outcomes. The dataset for training and evaluating is PU1K. We compared the impact of PU-SSIM based on different weights on the network. The input point number is 2048. The quantitative results are shown in Fig. 6. A weight of 0 indicates that this constraint is not being used. It can be observed that all networks using the PU-SSIM show better performance. The up-sampled results of the PUCRN network using PU-SSIM with a weight of 4 exhibit the smallest

CD, HD, and P2F distances, which indicates its capacity to drive up-sampling points approaching the underlying surface.

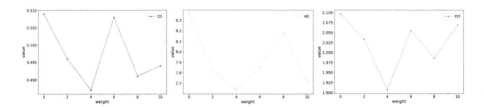

Fig. 6. The results with the use of different weightings of PU-SSIM on PU1K dataset. The values of CD, HD, and P2F are multiplied by 10^3. A Bold denotes the best performance.

6   Conclusion

In this paper, we integrate the typical full-reference point cloud quality metric PointSSIM into an up-sampling network, thereby establishing a methodology for constraining the up-sampled results, denoted as PU-SSIM. Leveraging disparities in information pertaining to point cloud attributes such as geometry, normal vectors, and curvature, we compute similarity scores to serve as perceptual constraints for enhancing the training of the network. Our results indicate that, in the two datasets tested, our method achieved excellent performance in the upsampling network. Both quantitative and qualitative results have proved that our method surpasses advanced methods. Future work will focus on optimizing the training speed and scalability of the loss function, and extending the work to point clouds that include color information.

Acknowledgments. This work was supported by the Beijing Natural Science Foundation (No. 4232020) and the National Natural Science Foundation of China (No. 62201017, No. 62201018).

References

1. Alexa, M., Behr, J., Cohen-Or, D., Fleishman, S., Levin, D., Silva, C.T.: Computing and rendering point set surfaces. IEEE Trans. Visual Comput. Graphics **9**(1), 3–15 (2003)
2. Alexiou, E., Ebrahimi, T.: Point cloud quality assessment metric based on angular similarity. In: 2018 IEEE International Conference on Multimedia and Expo (ICME), pp. 1–6. IEEE (2018)
3. Alexiou, E., Ebrahimi, T.: Towards a point cloud structural similarity metric. In: 2020 IEEE International Conference on Multimedia & Expo Workshops (ICMEW), pp. 1–6. IEEE (2020)

4. Du, H., Yan, X., Wang, J., Xie, D., Pu, S.: Point cloud upsampling via cascaded refinement network. In: Proceedings of the Asian Conference on Computer Vision, pp. 586–601 (2022)

5. Fan, S., Dong, Q., Zhu, F., Lv, Y., Ye, P., Wang, F.Y.: SCF-net: learning spatial contextual features for large-scale point cloud segmentation. In: Proceedings of the IEEE/CVF Conference on Computer Vision and Pattern Recognition, pp. 14504–14513 (2021)

6. Feng, W., Li, J., Cai, H., Luo, X., Zhang, J.: Neural points: point cloud representation with neural fields for arbitrary upsampling. In: Proceedings of the IEEE/CVF Conference on Computer Vision and Pattern Recognition, pp. 18633–18642 (2022)

7. He, T., et al.: Geonet: deep geodesic networks for point cloud analysis. In: Proceedings of the IEEE/CVF Conference on Computer Vision and Pattern Recognition, pp. 6888–6897 (2019)

8. Hu, Q., et al.: Randla-net: efficient semantic segmentation of large-scale point clouds. In: Proceedings of the IEEE/CVF Conference on Computer Vision and Pattern Recognition, pp. 11108–11117 (2020)

9. Huang, K., Tang, Y., Zou, X., Chen, M., Fang, Y., Lei, Z.: Poisson surface reconstruction algorithm based on improved normal orientation. Laser Optoelectron. Prog. **56**(14), 141005 (2019)

10. Javaheri, A., Brites, C., Pereira, F., Ascenso, J.: A generalized hausdorff distance based quality metric for point cloud geometry. In: 2020 Twelfth International Conference on Quality of Multimedia Experience (QoMEX), pp. 1–6. IEEE (2020)

11. Javaheri, A., Brites, C., Pereira, F., Ascenso, J.: Mahalanobis based point to distribution metric for point cloud geometry quality evaluation. IEEE Signal Process. Lett. **27**, 1350–1354 (2020)

12. Jian, W.: A lidar point cloud encryption algorithm based on mobile least squares. Urban Geotechnical Investigation & Surveying (2019)

13. Li, R., Li, X., Fu, C.W., Cohen-Or, D., Heng, P.A.: PU-GAN: a point cloud upsampling adversarial network. In: Proceedings of the IEEE/CVF International Conference on Computer Vision, pp. 7203–7212 (2019)

14. Lipman, Y., Cohen-Or, D., Levin, D., Tal-Ezer, H.: Parameterization-free projection for geometry reconstruction. ACM Trans. Graph. (TOG) **26**(3), 22-es (2007)

15. Lv, C., Lin, W., Zhao, B.: Voxel structure-based mesh reconstruction from a 3D point cloud. IEEE Trans. Multimedia **24**, 1815–1829 (2021)

16. Mekuria, R., Li, Z., Tulvan, C., Chou, P.: Evaluation criteria for PCC (point cloud compression) (2016)

17. Mekuria, R., Blom, K., Cesar, P.: Design, implementation, and evaluation of a point cloud codec for tele-immersive video. IEEE Trans. Circuits Syst. Video Technol. **27**(4), 828–842 (2016)

18. Meynet, G., Digne, J., Lavoué, G.: PC-MSDM: a quality metric for 3D point clouds. In: 2019 Eleventh International Conference on Quality of Multimedia Experience (QoMEX), pp. 1–3. IEEE (2019)

19. Meynet, G., Nehmé, Y., Digne, J., Lavoué, G.: PCQM: a full-reference quality metric for colored 3D point clouds. In: 2020 Twelfth International Conference on Quality of Multimedia Experience (QoMEX), pp. 1–6. IEEE (2020)

20. Nie, Y., Hou, J., Han, X., Nießner, M.: RFD-net: point scene understanding by semantic instance reconstruction. In: Proceedings of the IEEE/CVF Conference on Computer Vision and Pattern Recognition, pp. 4608–4618 (2021)

21. Qi, C.R., Su, H., Mo, K., Guibas, L.J.: Pointnet: deep learning on point sets for 3D classification and segmentation. In: Proceedings of the IEEE Conference on Computer Vision and Pattern Recognition, pp. 652–660 (2017)

22. Qi, C.R., Yi, L., Su, H., Guibas, L.J.: Pointnet++: deep hierarchical feature learning on point sets in a metric space. In: Advances in Neural Information Processing Systems, vol. 30 (2017)
23. Qian, G., Abualshour, A., Li, G., Thabet, A., Ghanem, B.: PU-GCN: point cloud upsampling using graph convolutional networks. In: Proceedings of the IEEE/CVF Conference on Computer Vision and Pattern Recognition, pp. 11683–11692 (2021)
24. Qian, Y., Hou, J., Kwong, S., He, Y.: PUGeo-Net: a geometry-centric network for 3D point cloud upsampling. In: Vedaldi, A., Bischof, H., Brox, T., Frahm, J.-M. (eds.) ECCV 2020. LNCS, vol. 12364, pp. 752–769. Springer, Cham (2020). https://doi.org/10.1007/978-3-030-58529-7_44
25. Tian, D., Ochimizu, H., Feng, C., Cohen, R., Vetro, A.: Geometric distortion metrics for point cloud compression. In: 2017 IEEE International Conference on Image Processing (ICIP), pp. 3460–3464. IEEE (2017)
26. Wang, Z., Bovik, A.C., Sheikh, H.R., Simoncelli, E.P.: Image quality assessment: from error visibility to structural similarity. IEEE Trans. Image Process. **13**(4), 600–612 (2004)
27. Wu, S., Huang, H., Gong, M., Zwicker, M., Cohen-Or, D.: Deep points consolidation. ACM Trans. Graph. (ToG) **34**(6), 1–13 (2015)
28. Yang, Q., Ma, Z., Xu, Y., Li, Z., Sun, J.: Inferring point cloud quality via graph similarity. IEEE Trans. Pattern Anal. Mach. Intell. **44**(6), 3015–3029 (2020)
29. Yifan, W., Wu, S., Huang, H., Cohen-Or, D., Sorkine-Hornung, O.: Patch-based progressive 3D point set upsampling. In: Proceedings of the IEEE/CVF Conference on Computer Vision and Pattern Recognition, pp. 5958–5967 (2019)
30. Yu, L., Li, X., Fu, C.W., Cohen-Or, D., Heng, P.A.: Pu-net: point cloud upsampling network. In: Proceedings of the IEEE Conference on Computer Vision and Pattern Recognition, pp. 2790–2799 (2018)

Quality Enhancement via Spatial-Angular Deformable Convolution for Compressed Light Field

Yongjie Lu, Xinpeng Huang, Chao Yang, and Ping An[✉]

Key Laboratory of Specialty Fiber Optics and Optical Access Networks, School of
Communication and Information Engineering, Shanghai University,
Shanghai 200444, China
anping@shu.edu.cn

Abstract. To address the complexity of data in high-dimensional light field (LF), LF compression has emerged as a prominent research focus in recent years. However, diverse compression methods inevitably entail the loss of scene information, leading to notable distortions. To rectify this issue and recover lost information during the LF compression process, this paper introduces an innovative algorithm for enhancing the quality of compressed LF images. The proposed method addresses LF quality enhancement in two stages for any given LF viewpoint. In the initial stage, we leverage both local and global viewpoints for shallow feature extraction. Local viewpoints integrate spatial-angular contextual information through deformable convolution networks, while global viewpoints serve as auxiliary features to preserve fine details in the LF. In the subsequent stage, a dense residual network is employed for fine quality enhancement, resulting in improved LF viewpoints. Numerous experiments affirm that our approach has attained state-of-the-art performance, significantly enhancing the quality of compressed LF images.

Keywords: Light Field (LF) · Compression Quality Enhancement · Deformable Convolution

1 Introduction

The high-dimensional characteristics of light field (LF) pose significant challenges to data storage, with LF compression emerging as an essential means for storing and transmitting such data under limited bandwidth conditions. However, current LF compression algorithms often introduce various artifacts as the bit rates decrease, leading to a substantial degradation in LF image quality and a decrease in Quality of Experience (QoE). The low quality and distortions in compressed LF may also impact the performance of subsequent visual tasks in

This work was supported in part by the National Natural Science Foundation of China under Grant 62020106011, Grant 62071287, Grant 62001279 and Grant 62371278.

low-bandwidth applications, such as super-resolution [1], depth estimation [2], refocusing [3,4], and 3D reconstruction [5]. Dedicating efforts to enhance the quality of compressed LF data is instrumental in expanding the applicability of LF in various domains. This endeavor aims to provide users with superior visual experiences and facilitate more efficient execution of subsequent tasks. By focusing on elevating the quality of compressed LF data, we contribute to the exploration of broader LF application areas, fostering advancements in digital visual technologies.

In prior research, there has been extensive investigation into the removal of artifacts and quality enhancement in two-dimensional compressed images [6,7]. Traditional methods involve optimizing transform coefficients according to specific standards, while more recent approaches leverage Convolutional Neural Networks to achieve efficient and nonlinear mappings [8,9]. In the realm of video quality enhancement, emphasis is placed on the utilization of temporal information through multi-frame schemes, addressing challenges related to motion by employing techniques such as optical flow estimation [10] and deformable convolution [11].

Applying conventional image and video quality enhancement methods directly to LF poses challenges due to the multidimensional nature of LF, which encompass additional directional information compared to conventional two-dimensional images. It is evident that there is currently a lack of standardized methods and tools for enhancing compressed LF quality.

Considering that the LF is a multidimensional dataset containing information from various directions of light rays, in LF with structural consistency, the spatial and angular relationships between neighboring viewpoints are similar. This consistency allows us to infer or reconstruct information obtained from one viewpoint to other viewpoints. Therefore, by leveraging the information from neighboring viewpoints, we can gain a better understanding of the scene in the LF. Additionally, we can correct or complement damaged or missing pixel regions in one viewpoint due to compression or other factors.

However, challenges in viewpoint alignment may arise when handling LF data, as the disparities between viewpoints in the LF result in positional variations of objects within the same scene observed from different viewpoints. To address this issue, this paper considers the use of deformable convolutions for implicit view alignment. This approach aims to adaptively adjust convolutional kernels, allowing them to better capture relevant information when dealing with misaligned LF data. This implicit view alignment technique is designed to enhance the effectiveness of quality enhancement by aligning viewpoints in a manner that accommodates the disparities present in the LF.

In particular, we propose a compression LF quality enhancement framework based on spatial-Angular deformable convolution. The aim is to eliminate artifacts caused by compression and improve the image quality of compressed LF. For a given LF viewpoint, our approach executes quality enhancement in two stages, progressing from coarse to fine. In the first stage, we perform shallow feature extraction using both local neighborhood viewpoints and global viewpoints.

The local neighborhood viewpoints introduce spatial-angular contextual information through the fusion of deformable convolutional networks. The global features provide additional specific information to overcome noise, enhance details, and a fusion process is applied to merge these two types of features. In the quality enhancement second stage, we utilize a dense residual network to extract refined hierarchical features from aligned feature maps. By introducing global residual learning, we simulate compression artifacts generated in the LF, resulting in an enhanced compressed LF image. By leveraging this proposed framework, we effectively address various distortions in compressed LF, achieving significant improvements in LF image quality.

In the second section of this paper, we present a comprehensive elucidation of the compressive LF quality enhancement model, which is based on spatial-angular deformable convolutions. The third section is dedicated to comparing our model with the state-of-the-art quality enhancement models currently available, with the aim of showcasing the superiority of our proposed model. In the last section, the paper concludes by encapsulating a comprehensive summary of the entire study, highlighting the key points and findings.

2   Proposed Method

2.1   Overview of Network Architecture

In this section, we discuss the spatial-angular deformable network proposed by use for mitigating compression artifacts in LF image compression. In Fig. 1, the entire workflow of the proposed method for enhancing LF image quality is illustrated. Our approach is designed to eliminate compression artifacts, thereby augmenting the LF image quality of compressed LF images.

Our methodology follows a two-stage process, wherein we independently apply a quality enhancement network to each viewpoint in the LF. For the target viewpoint in need of enhancement, we initiate by creating an auxiliary viewpoint set. This set comprises the eight nearest neighboring viewpoints, along with specific viewpoints along all four global directions (horizontal, vertical, and two diagonals). To meet the requirements of adjacent viewpoints in the auxiliary set, viewpoints at the edges are complemented by the current viewpoint.

In the first stage, we leverage a deformable convolutional network to merge spatial-angular contextual information from the local neighborhood viewpoint set. This aids in achieving implicit alignment of viewpoints and extracting local auxiliary features. However, this process may introduce noise interference from adjacent viewpoint positions at the current viewpoint position. To tackle this challenge, we introduce a global auxiliary feature network designed to ensure the structural consistency of compressed viewpoints. The primary objective of this network is to alleviate noise interference and uphold the overall quality enhancement process.

After integrating global and local auxiliary features, we leverage a dense residual network to extract layered features from aligned feature maps. Our approach incorporates both local and global residual learning, accompanied by a fusion strategy, to capture densely global features for the LF. The incorporation of global residual learning enables us to emulate the compression distortions inherent in LF generation, leading to enhanced LF images. The following section will provide a thorough elucidation of the architecture of our proposed Spatial Angular Deformation Network.

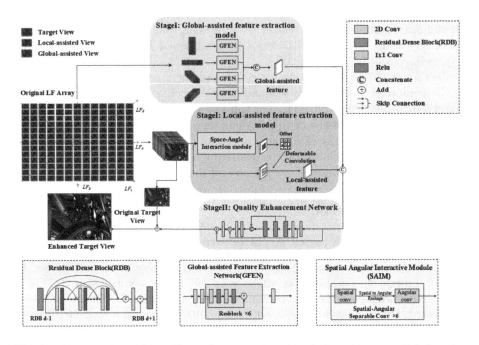

Fig. 1. An overview of quality enhancement network based on spatial-Angular deformable convolution for compressed LF.

2.2 Local-Assisted Feature Extraction Module

The Local Feature Enhancement Module (LFEM) is designed to extract complementary information from neighboring perspectives, facilitating the restoration of distorted pixel regions in the current viewpoint. Our LFEM incorporates the design of variable convolution v2 as implemented in [12]. Deformable Convolution v2 introduces adaptive non-linear deformation for enhanced feature alignment. The output feature map Y is computed by convolving the input feature map X with the adjusted convolutional kernel W'. The deformable offsets q are determined by the position in the output feature map p, control points k, and offset values Δ:

$$Y(p) = \sum X(q) * W'(p,q) \tag{1}$$

$$q = p + \sum G(k) * \Delta(p,k) \tag{2}$$

Modulation coefficients M are obtained through a modulation network, taking local information from the input feature map and position p as inputs:

$$M(p, q) = modulation\_network([X(q), p]) \tag{3}$$

These coefficients adjust the original convolutional kernel weights, yielding the adjusted kernel W':

$$W'(p, q) = W(p, q) * M(p, q) \tag{4}$$

This approach allows for precise modeling and alignment of targets, improving the quality and effectiveness of subsequent LF processing tasks compared to traditional alignment methods such as depth estimation.

To comprehensively exploit the interdependence among LF viewpoints, we design an Offset Prediction Network based on the Spatial-Angular Interaction Module (SAIM), aiming to capture extensive spatial-angular relationships for LF representation. The SAIM consists of six layers of spatial-angular separable convolutions. Given that the learned offsets may be fractional, we employ the method proposed by Dai et al. [13], utilizing differentiable bilinear interpolation for sub-pixel sampling. Following offset learning, the convolutional kernel can adapt its shape within the perceptual field, enabling flexible capture of nonlinear features in the input data. This flexibility endows deformable convolution with a pronounced advantage in handling complex scenarios involving irregular shapes, occlusions, and scale variations, facilitating a more accurate representation of structural consistency within the LF. Ultimately, aligned neighboring viewpoints are utilized as locally enhanced features for the current viewpoint.

2.3   Global-Assisted Feature Extraction Module

When engaging in local-assisted feature extraction, the introduction of interference, such as noise stemming from neighboring viewpoint positions, presents a notable challenge in maintaining consistency within the target viewpoint. In response to this issue, we propose the integration of a Global-assisted Feature Extraction Module (GFEM), specifically crafted to preserve the spatial structure of compressed viewpoints and guide the sustained coherence of LF throughout the network learning process.

Comprising four branches denoted as LF_a, LF_b, LF_c, and LF_d, each branch is associated with distinct viewpoint sequences. These sequences are thoughtfully selected and interconnected based on directional cues, as illustrated in Fig. 1. These branches play a pivotal role in capturing global features essential for ensuring coherence across diverse viewpoints.

The architecture of the Global-assisted Feature Extraction Network (GFEM) incorporates residual blocks with a depth of 6. These blocks adeptly capture and enhance features critical for global information extraction. The global features obtained from the four branches are then fused and harnessed as enriched information for the view reconstruction network. This augmented information proves instrumental in reconstructing input viewpoints, thereby alleviating the impact of interference and noise introduced during the local feature extraction process.

2.4   Quality Enhancement Module

To further restore the LF details lost during the compression process, we employ the Residual Dense Network (RDN) to globally extract hierarchical features of the LF. This network demonstrates significant advancements in the fields of image super-resolution [14] and restoration [15].

As depicted in Fig. 1, we employ Residual Dense Blocks (RDBs) to construct the Residual Dense Network (RDN). Each RDB comprises densely connected layers and incorporates local feature fusion with residual learning. The advantages of this design lie in the promotion of effective feature reuse through dense connections, facilitating superior information propagation, thereby enhancing the model's capability to capture intricate high-dimensional LF representations. Simultaneously, the local feature fusion enables the network to adeptly integrate information from different hierarchical levels, allowing the model to fully exploit both low-level and high-level features. This proves beneficial for extracting rich spatial-angular structural features inherent in the LF. The introduction of residual learning mechanisms facilitates the training process by directing the model's focus towards learning the residual information between input and output, as opposed to direct mapping, thereby further augmenting the network's performance.

2.5   Training Scheme

Employing an integrated end-to-end optimization methodology, we leverage the intrinsic differentiability of LFEM, GFEM, and QE modules, owing to their fully convolutional characteristics. The comprehensive loss function, denoted as L, sums the squared errors between the enhanced target view $\hat{I}_{t_0}^{HQ}$ and the original view $I_{t_0}^{HQ}$:

$$L = ||\hat{I}_{t_0}^{HQ} - I_{t_0}^{HQ}||_2^2 \tag{5}$$

It's essential to underscore that the training of the offset prediction network is inherently unsupervised, given the absence of ground truth for the deformation offset set. The training process exclusively relies on the overarching loss function L. Additionally, we introduce cosine annealing to dynamically modulate the learning rate. This adjustment ensures a seamless transition, contributing significantly to the stability of model convergence and, consequently, augmenting the model's generalization capability.

3   Experiments

3.1   Experimental Settings

In order to validate the efficacy of our proposed LF quality enhancement network and highlight the superiority of the designed architecture, we strictly adhere to the JPEG Pleno LF Common Test Conditions [16]. For the sake of convenience in application and to facilitate a meaningful comparison of our enhancement method in the compression domain, we make use of the publicly available EPFL dataset [17] for both training and testing.

In accordance with the guidelines specified in [18], we curate a test set consisting of 12 LF instances from the set of 118 LFs captured by Lytro cameras. The remaining instances are allocated for the training set. The original angular and spatial resolutions of the 4D LF are 15×15 and 434×625, respectively. To mitigate the inclusion of dark views associated with vignetting, only the central 13×13 views are utilized. Additionally, the spatial resolution of the LF is adjusted to 432×624 through cropping to meet the requirements of the encoder.

In consideration of the heightened sensitivity of the human visual system to luminance information and the increased significance of the Y-channel in compression encoding, our image enhancement process adopts a selective strategy, focusing exclusively on the luminance channel.

The proposed method is implemented using the PyTorch framework and is based on the Nvidia GTX 3090 GPU, along with the MMDetection toolbox [19], for training the deformable convolutional model. During the training process, the patch size is set to 64×64.

Throughout the training regimen, a batch size of 16 is implemented, employing the Adam optimizer [20] with meticulously chosen parameters: $\beta_1 = 0.9$, $\beta_2 = 0.999$, and $\varepsilon = 10^{-8}$ over an extensive span of 3×10^8 iterations. The initial learning rate is established at 1×10^{-4}, and to facilitate a gradual descent, a cosine annealing algorithm is strategically applied. This algorithm adeptly modulates the learning rate, orchestrating a smooth reduction to 0 throughout the entirety of the training duration.

To assess our quality enhancement method against various LF compression techniques, we focus on two methods and adjust compression parameters to create four distortion levels for each. Abbreviations are as follows:

HEVC. We employ a snake-like scanning order to construct a pseudo video sequence following the Common Test Conditions outlined in JPEG Pleno LF [16]. The H.265/HEVC software (HM16.20) is utilized to compress the sequence with quantization parameters (QP) set to $27, 32, 37, 42$, generating training data for four distortion levels. Four models are then trained to adapt to different distortion types.

JPEG PLENO. This method, as proposed in [21], leverages LF's 4D redundancy through a 4D transform and a sixteen-tree structure. The JPEG Pleno Reference Software is employed with adjustments made to the Lagrange multiplier (λ) set at $10^3, 10^4, 10^5, 10^6$. This results in training data for four distortion levels, where larger λ values intensify quantization and 4D blocks, leading to more severe distortion.

We assess three image quality enhancement methods (ARCNN [22], DnCNN [23], and RDN [15]), along with two video quality enhancement methods (DCAD [24] and STDF [12]), known for their outstanding performance in single-image/video quality enhancement.

As there are no specialized approaches for compressed LF quality enhancement, and recognizing the intrinsic correlation between removing compression artifacts and super-resolution, we conduct a comparative analysis. We exclude the upsampling module (PixelShuffle) from super-resolution networks for quality enhancement tasks. Two LF super-resolution methods, LFSSR [25] and LF-InterNet [26], are introduced for this comparative assessment. All these methodologies are evaluated for their effectiveness in enhancing the quality of compressed LF.

3.2   Experimental Results

Quantitative Results. As depicted in Table 1, our proposed method is compared against seven existing image/video/LF quality enhancement techniques using two key metrics: Delta Peak Signal-to-Noise Ratio (ΔPSNR-Y) and Delta Structural Similarity Index (ΔSSIM). The results demonstrate a significant advantage of our proposed approach. Notably, our method consistently outperforms all compared methods in the average ΔPSNR-Y/ΔSSIM across the eight tested LF instances.

Single-image enhancement methods and frame-based video quality enhancement methods (DCAD) exhibit limited enhancement effects from an objective standpoint. This limitation arises because they solely leverage spatial information from each viewpoint in LF, neglecting the structural consistency of the LF. On the other hand, the multi-frame video quality enhancement method, STDF, achieves superior quality enhancement by leveraging supplementary information from adjacent frames.

In contrast, two LF methods (LFSSR and LF_InterNet) that exploit both spatial and angular features of LF and execute information interaction demonstrate superior performance in image/video quality enhancement. However, our compressed LF quality enhancement model is specially designed and optimized for the structural characteristics of the LF. It addresses the alignment issues of neighboring viewpoints, enabling us to effectively utilize complementary information between views, resulting in higher objective metrics.

Table 1. Quantitative results for the testing LF under four distinct levels of two encoding distortions are presented in terms of ΔPSNR$\uparrow$ (dB)/ΔSSIM$\uparrow$ (10^{-2}). The best results are in **bold faces.**

Distortion Type	ARCNN	DnCNN	RDN	DCAD	STDF	LFSSR	LF_InterNet	Ours
HEVC(QP=32)	0.421/0.511	0.411/0.480	0.510/0.594	0.612/0.677	0.721/0.769	0.692/0.761	0.742/0.830	**1.121/1.074**
HEVC(QP=37)	0.432/0.542	0.392/0.498	0.582/0.657	0.721/0.768	0.719/0.848	0.913/1.032	1.072/1.180	**1.290/1.472**
HEVC(QP=42)	0.498/0.613	0.410/0.525	0.556/0.689	0.732/0.802	0.771/0.924	1.101/1.205	1.143/1.612	**1.222/1.847**
HEVC(QP=47)	0.342/0.701	0.322/0.667	0.592/0.898	0.642/1.238	0.730/1.302	0.719/1.421	0.903/1.721	**1.080/2.031**
Average	0.423/0.592	0.384/0.543	0.560/0.710	0.677/0.871	0.735/0.961	0.856/1.105	0.965/1.336	**1.178/1.606**
JPEG PLENO($\lambda = 10^3$)	0.392/0.296	0.408/0.341	0.459/0.376	0.603/0.445	0.659/0.575	0.832/0.632	0.891/0.698	**1.040/0.846**
JPEG PLENO($\lambda = 10^4$)	0.420/0.602	0.428/0.709	0.582/0.801	0.721/0.890	0.811/1.012	1.021/1.082	1.188/1.131	**1.396/1.539**
JPEG PLENO($\lambda = 10^5$)	0.421/0.702	0.412/0.842	0.632/0.979	0.782/1.230	0.812/1.591	1.159/1.721	1.272/2.035	**1.494/2.343**
JPEG PLENO($\lambda = 10^6$)	0.414/1.329	0.404/1.441	0.552/1.623	0.592/1.842	0.601/1.862	0.696/2.024	0.721/2.421	**0.972/2.941**
Average	0.412/0.732	0.413/0.833	0.556/0.945	0.675/1.102	0.721/1.260	0.927/1.365	1.018/1.571	**1.226/1.917**

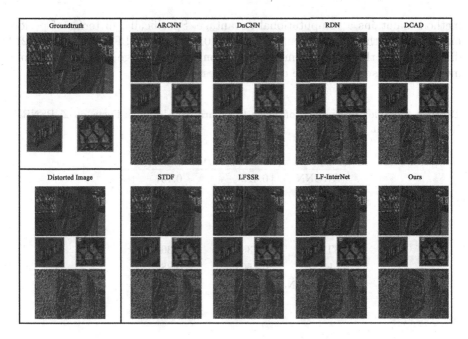

Fig. 2. Qualitative results of the central view of the test LF Danger_de_Mort under HEVC Compression artifact (QP = 42)

Qualitative Results. We conduct a subjective evaluation to assess the visual quality of the enhanced LF images. We compare our proposed compressed LF quality enhancement network with seven existing quality enhancement methods. Figure 2 depict qualitative results for the test LF Danger_de_Mort under HEVC Compression artifact (QP = 42), presenting their differences in the form of error maps and detailed zoomed-in images. It is evident that, due to various compression artifacts, the compressed central viewpoint experiences severe distortion. The LF views enhanced by our model exhibit closer proximity to the ground truth views, featuring smaller error values and richer texture details, as exemplified in Fig. 2 by the window details of the house behind the fence. In contrast, other methods manifest varying degrees of blurring and artifacts.

Complexity Analysis. Table 2 employs Δ PSNR-Y and parameter count (Param) to assess the quality and model complexity of each method. Taking HEVC-encoded distortion as an example, the parameter count is computed based on LF data with a 13×13 angular resolution and utilizing 64×64 image blocks.

From Table 2, it is evident that our proposed method excels in terms of Δ PSNR-Y, achieving a notable improvement of 1.178 dB. This signifies a significant enhancement in image quality. Despite a higher parameter count, our method maintains a computational advantage. Specifically, in terms of performance, our method outperforms LFSSR by 0.322 dB and LF-InterNet by 0.213 dB. Consequently, in the domain of LF-compressed image enhancement, our method demonstrates notable competitiveness.

Table 2. Complexity Analysis of Seven Comparative Methods: Focus on Δ PSNR-Y ↑(dB) and Param ↓(M).

Method	ΔPSNR-Y/dB	Param/M
ARCNN	0.423	0.107
DNCNN	0.384	0.556
RDN	0.560	2.232
DCAD	0.667	0.297
STDF	0.735	0.365
LFSSR	0.856	0.888
LF-InterNet	0.965	24.403
Ours	1.178	3.535

Ablation Study. The proposed method in this study utilizes a Spatial-Angular Variable Network to eliminate compression artifacts in LF image compression. An evaluation is conducted through multiple ablation experiments, and the results in Table 2 demonstrate the significant roles played by each component of the proposed method, including the LFEM, GFEM, and QEM, in enhancing the quality of compressed LF images. The removal of any module results in a certain degree of degradation in quality performance. Particularly noteworthy is the substantial degradation (0.414dB) observed when the QEM module is removed, indicating that the effectiveness of the dense residual mechanism in QEM for quality enhancement tasks, albeit accompanied by a substantial increase in parameter count (2.272M). When the SAIM within LFEM is replaced with a U-Net-based module [13], there is a decrease in quality enhancement performance accompanied by an increase in parameter count. This suggests that SAIM possesses unique advantages in extracting inter-view information and utilizing spatial-angular relationships. Overall, the ablation experiments affirm the effectiveness of each component of the proposed method in enhancing the quality of compressed LF images (Table 3).

Table 3. Evaluation of Module Effects on Δ PSNR-Y $\uparrow$ (dB) and Param $\downarrow$ (M).

LFEM	GFEM	QEM	ΔPSNR-Y	Param(M)
$\checkmark$	$\times$	$\checkmark$	1.001	2.894
$\times$	$\checkmark$	$\checkmark$	0.882	2.903
$\checkmark$	$\checkmark$	$\times$	0.767	1.263
U-net	$\checkmark$	$\checkmark$	1.031	3.651
$\checkmark$	$\checkmark$	$\checkmark$	1.181	3.535

4   Conclusions

In this paper, we propose an end-to-end compression LF image quality enhancement framework based on spatial-Angular deformable convolution. Our approach leverages complementary information from neighboring viewpoints, employing spatial-Angular deformable fusion, while utilizing global viewpoints as auxiliary features to preserve details in LF. The quality enhancement is performed in two stages, progressing from coarse to fine. Our method outperforms seven existing image/video/LF quality enhancement methods in terms of PSNR-Y and SSIM gains, consistently achieving the highest scores in the average scores of 12 test LF images. Additionally, we conduct a qualitative evaluation to assess the visual quality of the enhanced LF images. Our proposed method demonstrates the highest subjective performance across all evaluation metrics.

Furthermore, we conduct ablation experiments to validate the effectiveness of each component in our proposed method, including LFEM, GFEM, and QEM. The results indicate that each component plays a crucial role in improving the quality of compressed LF images. Despite the apparent performance advantages of our method, it suffers from the drawback of a relatively high parameter count. Future research directions may focus on lightweight model design, integration of human perception assessments, and practical applications.

References

1. Hu, Z., Chen, X., Yeung, H.W.F., et al.: Texture-enhanced light field super-resolution with spatio-angular decomposition kernels. IEEE Trans. Instrum. Meas. **71**, 1–16 (2022)
2. Liu, D., Huang, Y., Wu, Q., et al.: Multi-angular epipolar geometry based light field angular reconstruction network. IEEE Trans. Comput. Imaging **6**(12), 1507–1522 (2020)
3. Huang, X., Chen, Y., An, P., et al.: Prediction-oriented disparity rectification model for geometry-based light field compression. IEEE Trans. Broadcast. **69**(1), 62–74 (2023)
4. Huang, X., An, P., Chen, Y., et al.: Low bit rate light field compression with geometry and content consistency. IEEE Trans. Multimedia **24**, 152–165 (2020)
5. Hu, Z., Yeung, H.W.F., Chen, X., et al.: Efficient light field reconstruction via spatio-angular dense network. IEEE Trans. Instrum. Meas. **70**, 1–14 (2021)

6. Dong, W., Zhang, L., Shi, G., et al.: Nonlocally centralized sparse representation for image restoration. IEEE Trans. Image Process. **22**(4), 1620–1630 (2012)

7. Dong, W., Shi, G., Ma, Y., et al.: Image restoration via simultaneous sparse coding: where structured sparsity meets Gaussian scale mixture. Int. J. Comput. Vision **114**, 217–232 (2015)

8. Jin, Z., Iqbal, M.Z., Zou, W., et al.: Dual-stream multi-path recursive residual network for JPEG image compression artifacts reduction. IEEE Trans. Circuits Syst. Video Technol. **31**(2), 467–479 (2020)

9. Zheng, B., Chen, Y., Tian, X., et al.: Implicit dual-domain convolutional network for robust color image compression artifact reduction. IEEE Trans. Circuits Syst. Video Technol. **30**(11), 3982–3994 (2019)

10. Buades, A., Lisani, J.L.: Enhancement of noisy and compressed videos by optical flow and non-local denoising. IEEE Trans. Circuits Syst. Video Technol. **30**(7), 1960–1974 (2019)

11. Zhu, X., Hu, H., Lin, S., et al.: Deformable convnets V2: more deformable, better results. In: Proceedings of the IEEE/CVF Conference on Computer Vision and Pattern Recognition, pp. 9308–9316 (2019)

12. Deng, J., Wang, L., Pu, S., et al.: Spatio-temporal deformable convolution for compressed video quality enhancement. In: Proceedings of the AAAI Conference on Artificial Intelligence, pp. 10696–10703 (2020)

13. Dai, J., Qi, H., Xiong, Y., et al.: Deformable convolutional networks. In: Proceedings of the IEEE International Conference on Computer Vision, pp. 764–773 (2017)

14. Zhang, Y., Tian, Y., Kong, Y., et al.: Residual dense network for image super-resolution. In: Proceedings of the IEEE Conference on Computer Vision and Pattern Recognition, pp. 2472–2481 (2018)

15. Zhang, Y., Tian, Y., Kong, Y., et al.: Residual dense network for image restoration. IEEE Trans. Pattern Anal. Mach. Intell. **43**(7), 2480–2495 (2020)

16. ISO/IEC JTC 1/SC 29/WG 1, JPEG: JPEG PLENO LIGHT FIELD CODING COMMON TEST CONDITIONS V3.3. Doc. N804025, Brussels, Belgium, July (2019)

17. Rerabek, M., Ebrahimi, T.: New light field image dataset. In: 8th International Conference on Quality of Multimedia Experience (QoMEX) (2016)

18. Rerabek, M., Bruylants, T., Ebrahimi, T., et al.: ICME 2016 Grand Challenge: Light-field image compression. Call for Proposals and Evaluation Procedure (2016)

19. Chen, K., Wang, J., Pang, J., et al.: MMDetection: open mmlab detection toolbox and benchmark. arXiv preprint arXiv:1906.07155 (2019)

20. Kingma, D.P., Ba, J.: Adam: a method for stochastic optimization. arXiv preprint arXiv:1412.6980 (2014)

21. de Carvalho, M.B., Pereira, M.P., Alves, G., et al.: A 4D DCT-based lenslet light field codec. In: 2018 25th IEEE International Conference on Image Processing (ICIP), pp. 435–439 (2018)

22. Dong, C., Deng, Y., Loy, C.C., et al.: Compression artifacts reduction by a deep convolutional network. In: Proceedings of the IEEE International Conference on Computer Vision, pp. 576–584 (2015)

23. Zhang, K., Zuo, W., Chen, Y., et al.: Beyond a Gaussian denoiser: residual learning of deep CNN for image denoising. IEEE Trans. Image Process. **26**(7), 3142–3155 (2017)

24. Wang, T., Chen, M., Chao, H.: A novel deep learning-based method of improving coding efficiency from the decoder-end for HEVC. In: 2017 Data Compression Conference (DCC), pp. 410–419 (2017)

25. Yeung, H.W.F., Hou, J., Chen, X., et al.: Light field spatial super-resolution using deep efficient spatial-angular separable convolution. IEEE Trans. Image Process. **28**(5), 2319–2330 (2018)

26. Wang, Y., Wang, L., Yang, J., An, W., Yu, J., Guo, Y.: Spatial-angular interaction for light field image super-resolution. In: Vedaldi, A., Bischof, H., Brox, T., Frahm, J.-M. (eds.) ECCV 2020. LNCS, vol. 12368, pp. 290–308. Springer, Cham (2020). https://doi.org/10.1007/978-3-030-58592-1_18

Multimedia Communication

Link-Breakage Recovery Strategies for Tactical MANET Based on OLSR

Lianghui Ding[1(✉)], Hongyu Gao[1], Huan Lin[1], Chen Li[2], Yangyang Liu[2], and Feng Yang[3]

[1] Institute of Image Communication and Network Engineering,
Shanghai Jiao Tong University, Shanghai 200240, China
lhding@sjtu.edu.cn
[2] Shanghai Electro-Mechanical Engineering Institute, Shanghai 201109, China
[3] Institute of Wireless Communication Technologies, Shanghai Jiao Tong University,
Shanghai 200240, China

Abstract. Link breakages happen in Tactical MANET due to dynamic topology, leading to interruptions of the end-to-end path and loss of time-sensitive communication messages. The cut-edge problem and the loop issue are the main cause of poor performance of existing routing protocols. In this paper, we propose a Link Breakage Recovery mechanism to enhance the OLSR with LLN, called LBR-OLSR. Specifically, considering the cut-edge link can split the entire network, a connectivity protection mechanism is applied to judge a cut-edge link and maintain it in topology. We also present a loop suppression algorithm through *LB* messages and conflict node set, which reduces the time to determine a routing loop. Simulation in NS3 shows that LBR-OLSR can effectively handle the link-breakage problem and achieve significant performance gain in terms of packet delivery ratio and throughput.

Keywords: Tactical MANET · OLSR · Link Breakage Recovery · Topology Management

1 Introduction

Routing protocols provide paths for multi-hop end-to-end communication and play essential roles in MANET. However, for Tactical MANET applied in the battleground, link breakage happens frequently due to node movements, node faults, and environment interferences, which severely degrades the routing performance. Furthermore, [1] shows that the failure of routing protocols to recover the link interruptions in time leads to interrupted transmissions. It's challenging to design routing protocols for Tactical MANETs.

MANET routing protocols can be divided into proactive, reactive, and hybrid protocols, suggested by [2] and [9]. In proactive protocols, nodes store the global topology information through periodical routing discovery, thus the routing results are invariably available. In contrast, routing requests are generated on-demand in reactive protocols.

G. Zhai et al. (Eds.): IFTC 2023, CCIS 2066, pp. 375–389, 2024.
https://doi.org/10.1007/978-981-97-3623-2_27

When a transmission is required, the node broadcasts the routing requests and establishes the path with the response from the destination. Hybrid protocols combine the characteristics of proactive and reactive protocols, e.g., [7] segments the network into multiple zones, while applying proactive routing within one zone and reactive routing among zones. However, existing routing protocols achieve poor performance for Tactical MANETs typically.

Tactical communication networks require low routing delay in high dynamic scenes. Therefore, proactive protocols are preferred for their better latency performance compared with the other two types, shown in [3] and [11].

Optimized Link State Routing (OLSR), proposed in [4] and [8], is one of the most representative proactive routing protocols. In OLSR, each node calculates the routing table based on the global topology repository constructed by periodical neighbor detection and the topology dissemination, based on *HELLO* messages and Topology Control (*TC*) messages, respectively.

Moreover, [6] and [5] figure out the better scalability of OLSR because of its Multi-Point Relaying (MPR) mechanism, which can effectively reduce routing overhead, especially in a large-scale and high-density network.

OLSR updates link information periodically in the topology repository with *HELLO* or *TC* messages, aiming to form a robust network. However, this mechanism may result in a slow routing response. When a link fault happens, the broken link may be used in routing computation continuously. Then data packets are misrouted, causing the transmission interruption. In this situation, OLSR achieves unsatisfying performance in time-sensitive Tactical MANETs. The simplest way to alleviate the impact of link breakage on the network performance is to increase the frequency of topology updates, which accelerates the routing response but leads to heavy overhead simultaneously.

A smarter way is to detect the link interruption and then notify the other nodes to avoid the broken link. Link Layer Notification (LLN), defined in RFC3626 [4], is the most widely used link layer-based link interruption detection scheme. Ref. [10] then implemented the OLSR with Link Breakage Detection (LBD-OLSR), based on the LLN judging whether a link is broken by counting the re-transmission failures of the link layer. Afterwords, the topology repository removes the broken link and the routing table is re-calculated for recovery. However, the deletion of the only link connecting two isolated groups of nodes, known as the Cut Edge, may result in severe network splitting issues. Besides, LLN may cause loop issues for increasing confliction of routing results between different nodes that congests the related zone. In [13], loop issues in OLSR with LLN are resolved with two loop detection techniques: Mid-loop Detection (LD-Mid) and Post-loop Detection (LD-Post). LD-Mid compares the packet address of the next hop with the previous hop to determine whether the packet has been forwarded by itself. LD-Post records all forwarded packets and compares each new incoming packet with the records. Comparatively, LD-Mid detects loops in one hop with a simple calculation, yet LD-Post can detect all loops with large memory. Nevertheless, they both lack a re-forwarding scheme for the loop packets.

To establish a more robust network in Tactical MANET, we propose a novel **Link Breakage Recovery** mechanism based on LLN in OLSR, called LBR-OLSR. The main contributions of this paper consist of three aspects: **1. Connectivity Protection Mechanism (CPM) has been proposed to solve the cut-edge problem in LLN.** The cut-edge links that can disconnect the network topology are reserved even if judged as broken. **2. Loop Suppression Algorithm (LSA) has been proposed to solve the route loop issue caused by LLN.** The broken link information is broadcasted to neighboring nodes in given hop ranges to trigger updating of topology repositories and routing tables. **3. The LBR-OLSR achieves a 67% reduction on route recovery time and a 5% to 14% margin of packet delivery ratio outperforming the OLSR and LBD-OLSR,** simulated in NS3.

The remainder of the paper is organized as follows. Section 2 presents the approach of the proposed LBR-OLSR protocol. Section 3 focused on performance evaluation of LBR-OLSR algorithm through simulations in NS3, and conclusions are made in Sect. 4.

2 Approach of LBR-OLSR

Our approach aims to resolve the network splitting issues and loop issues in LLN, and specifically, it includes two parts: a **Connectivity Protection Mechanism** to protect the cut-edge links from deletion, and a **Loop Suppression Algorithm** to trigger topology repository updates while avoiding generate the loop route.

2.1 Problem Statement of LLN

Cut Edge Problem. A cut edge denotes a critical edge that when removed, splits the topology into two components. Although LLN can fasten the detection of link breakage, the temporary fluctuation of the link quality may cause the misjudgment. When there is more than one link for the end-to-end route path,

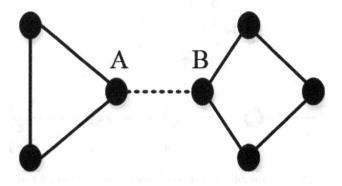

Fig. 1. An example of a cut edge.

the impact of misjudgments is limited. However, when the broken link is the cut edge of the network, the removal may result in serious disconnection of the network topology.

As the example shown in Fig. 1, the link $A - B$ is a cut edge of the network that the removal will result in disconnection of the network. Therefore, a Connectivity Protection Mechanism is proposed in Sect. 2.2 to enhance the robustness of link breakage detection.

Route Loop Problem. Typically, the process of route recovery is as follows: when link breakage happens on an end-to-end path from the source node S to the destination node D, the node that detects the breakage link will try to find a new path to forward packets from itself to the destination node D. For the example shown in Fig. 2, nodes $n1$ and $n5$ are the source and destination node, respectively, and the end-to-end path is $n1 - n2 - n3 - n4 - n5$. When the link $n3 - n4$ breaks down, node $n3$ will update its topology repository and routing table. Meanwhile, node $n3$ will find the intermediate path from node $n3$ to node $n5$, denoted as L. Then the end-to-end path from node S to node D becomes $n1 - n2 - n3 - L - n5$.

In some cases, the loop issue happens on the path L, since each node running OLSR takes the Shortest Path Algorithm to calculate routes based on the local routing table. If the topology known by two neighboring nodes are different, their routing results may conflict with each other and result in a routing loop. For example, as shown in Fig. 3, the recovered path for $n3$ is $n3 - n2 - L - n5$ with $n4$ determined as broken. In contrast, $n2$ may not update the topology promptly and point the packets back to $n3$, hence a loop happens between $n2$ and $n3$.

OLSR suppresses loops by broadcasting TC messages to reduce confliction. Therefore, the loop between $n3$ and $n2$ will last until $n2$ receives TC message from $n3$, which is one TC interval in the worst case. Therefore, a Loop

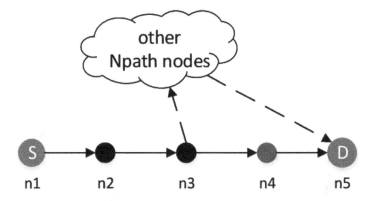

Fig. 2. An example of route recovery in the end-to-end path.

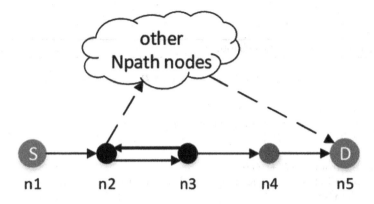

Fig. 3. An example of a routing loop

Suppression Algorithm is proposed in Sect. 2.3 to enhance the robustness of link breakage detection.

2.2   Connectivity Protection Mechanism

Inspired by [10], we use LLN to detect link breakage in our LBR-OLSR. The process is that each packet will count the re-transmission failures until reaching the threshold LLN_{TH}, then the link is considered as broken. Ref. [10] also shows that higher threshold leads to better performance in throughput. Therefore, we set LLN_{TH} as the maximum re-transmission number N_{rt}, e.g., between 4 and 7 in the well-known CSMA/CA. When the number of re-transmission failures reaches N_{rt}, the current packet will be copied to pass to the routing layer and discarded afterward. LLN obtains the IP addresses of both ends of the broken link and remove them from the topology. Then each node recalculates the routing table based on the updated topology repository.

However, the LLN may delete the important links, i.e., the Cut Edge, mistakenly. A **Connectivity Protection Mechanism** is proposed to avoid the network splitting. The CPM notifies cut edges and marks them in TC messages, then LLN will maintain these links even if they are detected as broken. The Cut Edge Decision algorithm is applied to judge whether a link is a cut edge in Algorithm 1. The algorithm is based on the topology repository of OLSR, including Neighbor Set, Two Hop Neighbor Set, and Topology Set. The basic idea is to apply Depth-First-Search (DFS) from one end of the input link and if the other end cannot be visited, the link is judged as a cut edge.

2.3   Loop Suppression Algorithm

To reduce the time to determine a loop issue, we propose a **Loop Suppression Algorithm** including four steps:

Algorithm 1. Cut Edge Decision.

Input:
    Neighbor Set NBs, Two Hop Neighbor Set $2NBs$, Topology Set TPs, Broken Link
    $e = \{a, b\}$
Output:
    TRUE/FALSE (Whether e is a cut edge.)
1: $G \leftarrow \{NBs, 2NBs, TPs\}$
2: Visited Node Set $Vis \leftarrow \{\}$
3: Remove e from G: $G_e \leftarrow G/e$
4: Do Depth-First-Search form a in G_e and record visited nodes in Vis
5: **if** $b \in Vis$ **then**
6:     **return** FALSE
7: **else**
8:     **return** TRUE
9: **end if**

Algorithm 2. Conflict Node Set Generation.

Input:
    Neighbor Set NBs, Two Hop Neighbor Set $2NBs$, Topology Set TPs, Broken Link
    $e = \{a, b\}$, Data Stream Destination Node $Dnode$, Current Node $Bnode$
Output:
    Conflict Node Set CNs
1: $G \leftarrow \{NBs, 2NBs, TPs\}$
2: $G' \leftarrow G$, $CNs \leftarrow \{\}$
3: Remove e from G: $G_e \leftarrow G/e$
4: Npath $Np \leftarrow Dijkstra(G_e, Bnode, Dnode)$
5: $N \leftarrow Length of Npath$
6: **for** $i \leftarrow 1 : N - 1$ **do**
7:     $Inode_i \leftarrow$ the ith node in Np
8:     **if** $i = 1$ **then**
9:         $Inode_{i-1} \leftarrow Bnode$
10:     **else**
11:         $Inode_{i-1} \leftarrow$ the $i - 1$th node in Np
12:     **end if**
13:     $p \leftarrow Dijkstra(G', Inode_i, Dnode)$
14:     $Nxt_i \leftarrow$ The next hop of $Inode_i$ in p
15:     **if** $Nxt_i = Inode_{i-1}$ **then**
16:         $CNs \leftarrow CNs \cup Inode_i$
17:     **end if**
18: **end for**
19: **return** CNs

Msg Type	TU_HOP	Message Size
Originator Address		
TTL	Hop Count	Message Sequence Number
ANSN		Reserved
Broken-link Address: FROM		
Broken-link Address: TO		

Fig. 4. Structure of *LB* message.

i. The network constructs and maintains a Conflict Node Set, which consists of nodes on path L that will turn back the data stream and cause loops, with the Conflict Node Set Generation (CNSG) algorithm shown in Algorithm 2 to calculate the set. Specifically, each current node calculates the routing results of other nodes on the path L of the data stream based on the local topology repository. If the route of one node points the data packet to the last hop node, the node is judged as a Conflict Node.

ii. LSA finds the maximum hop from nodes in the Conflict Node Set to the current node, denoted as H.

iii. A novel type of control messages, Link Breakage (LB) messages, is applied to broadcast the information of broken links. The current node broadcasts the LB messages to other nodes in the range of H to inform them of the broken link and trigger them to update routing tables.

iv. When upstream nodes of node B receive the message of the broken link, they change the route in advance so that the recovery process can be accelerated in a short time.

The format of LB messages is presented in Fig. 4, where the Message Type is defined as 5, and the TTL is set as H to limit the broadcast range. Additionally, LB messages contain IP addresses of both ends of the broken link, and the ANSN field is used to reflect whether the message represents the latest status of its sending node thus coordinating with the TC message.

3   Performance Evaluation

3.1   Experimental Setup

1) Simulation Platform: We use NS3 network simulator [12] as the platform based on Ubuntu 16.04 LTS, and compare the performance of our LBR-OLSR with original OLSR [4] and LBD-OLSR [8].

2) Inference: The basic parameters of our simulation are presented in Table 1. The performance is evaluated in terms of three metrics, i.e., packet delivery ratio, instantaneous throughput, and router recovery time.

Table 1. Basic Parameters of Simulation

Name	Value
Application Start Time	15 s
Payload Size	512 bytes
L4 Protocol	UDP
HELLO Interval	2 s
TC Interval	5 s
MAC Protocol	CSMS/CA
MAC Retransmission Up-limit	7
Enable RTS/CTS	no
Transmission Loss Model	Friis
PHY Standard	802.11b 11Mbps
Tx Power	30 dbm
Rx Energy Threshold	−76.684 dbm

The packet delivery ratio (PDR) is computed by

$$\text{PDR} = N_r/N_s \tag{1}$$

where N_r and N_s denote the number of received packets at the destination node and the number of sent packets from the source node, respectively. PDR represents the link breakage recovery capability of different protocols, and higher PDR leads to less impact of link breakage on routing.

The instantaneous throughput $R(t)$ is defined as the throughput from time $t - \Delta$ to the current time t, and the definition is given as

$$R(t) = \begin{cases} 0 & t < \Delta \\ \frac{N(t) - N(t-\Delta)}{\Delta} & t \geq \Delta \end{cases} \tag{2}$$

where Δ is the interval for throughput calculation, and $N(t)$ is the total number of bits received in the interval. Instantaneous throughput is used to evaluate the real-time transmission quality.

The route recovery time (RRT) for link breakage is defined as

$$\text{RRT}(lb) = t_e - t_s \tag{3}$$

where t_s denotes the time when the link breakage occurs in the network. t_e is the time when the network fixes the link breakage issue completely. RRT measures the sensitivity of the routing protocols to link breakage and the recovery rate after link interruption.

3.2   Results with Sparse Topology

Networks with several nodes and sparse topologies are sensitive to link breakages, thus we use two simple topologies to analyze the performances with the worst impact of link interruptions.

Triangle Topology. The triangle topology experiment is shown in Fig. 5, with a traffic flow from node A to node C transmitting continuously. The initial positions of nodes A, B and C are $[0\,m, 0\,m]$, $[800\,m, 0\,m]$ and $[500\,m, 800\,m]$, respectively. With node C moves towards right with a constant velocity, the link $A - C$ will disconnect and node A needs to change the path to maintain the communication with node C.

We compare the instantaneous throughput of LBR-OLSR, LBD-OLSR, and OLSR at a 500 kbps data rate in this scenario. As shown in Fig. 6, the real-time throughput of OLSR falls to zero when the link breaks and then lasts for 4.75 s, while LBD-OLSR and LBR-OLSR respond to the link breakage and recover the end-to-end communication in a short time. The results present that OLSR cannot recover the route quickly due to the requirement of 3 *HELLO* intervals to detect a link breakage. The LLN in LBD-OLSR and the *LB* message in our methods reduce the detect time efficiently.

Ring Topology. With a ring topology, we pour attention into the loop issue. As shown in Fig. 7, the source node S transmits data to the destination node D through the shortest path $S - n2 - n3 - n4 - D$. In case of breakage of link $n3 - n4$, node $n3$ will update its routing table once detecting the breakage and cause mismatch with routing tables of other nodes. For packets destined to node D, node $n2$ and $n3$ will specify each other as the next hop, causing the loop issue. The result of average route recovery time is listed in Table 2. It figures out that LLN in LBD-OLSR does little benefits on the loop issue compared with OLSR. By contrast, our LBR-OLSR outperforms LBD-OLSR with a 67% reduction on route recovery time with LSA.

Furthermore, congestion may happen more frequently with higher data rates, because LLN makes nodes aware of link breakage earlier than cache expiration

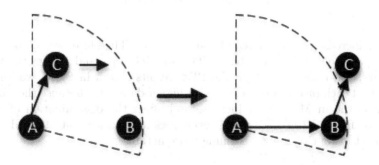

Fig. 5. Scene of triangle topology with node movement.

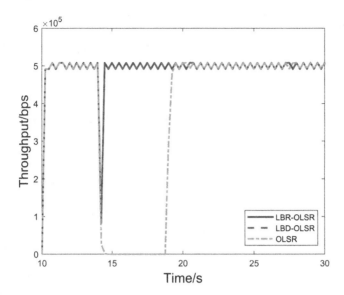

Fig. 6. Real-time throughput of different protocols versus data rate in triangle topology.

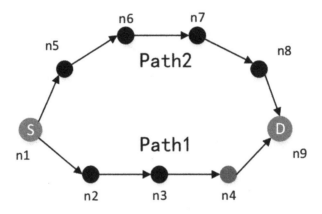

Fig. 7. Scene of ring topology.

and may increase the mismatch of routing tables. Therefore, we compare three routing protocols with data rates at 100 kbps, 500 kbps, and 1 Mbps to evaluate the congestion resistance. With the PDR results shown in Fig. 8, we find that the PDR of each protocol decreases with higher data rates because the collisions of packets the in MAC layer increase and affect the dissemination of control messages. The PDR of LBD-OLSR even goes lower than that of OLSR due to the impact of routing loops becoming more notable.

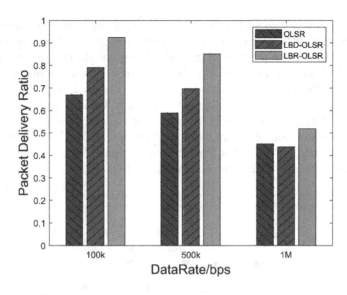

Fig. 8. PDR of different protocols versus data rate in ring topology.

3.3   Results with Complex Topology

To evaluate the performance of our LBR-OLSR in more realistic situations, we establish large-scale networks with complex topology, and apply random node movements as the typical MANET and random node destructions to access the resilience of each protocol. The data rate and the simulation time is 500 kbps and 60 s, respectively.

Table 2. Route Recovery Time of different protocols

Protocol	Route Recovery Time
OLSR	6.23594 s
LBD-OLSR	5.967535 s
LBR-OLSR	2.00924 s

Random Node Movement. A network consisting of 100 random-moving nodes within a $6000 \times 6000 \, \text{m}^2$ area is constructed in Fig. 9. The source and destination nodes are marked in blue while the other nodes in hollow dark move randomly with velocity in $[V_{min}, V_{max}]$ and direction in $[0, 2\pi]$. To adapt to different application scenarios, we consider 5 velocity ranges, i.e., $[0, 10]$, $[0, 30]$, $[0, 50]$, $[20, 50]$, $[40, 50]$ in m/s, and the corresponding average velocities are 5 m/s, 15 m/s, 25 m/s, 35 m/s and 45 m/s, respectively. The 5 m/s and 15 m/s fit the low-speed moving scenes such as individual combat and march in formation. The average velocity of 25 m/s corresponds to wide-range speed moving situations, e.g., battlefields with a mixture of individual soldiers, drones, and vehicles. The average velocities of 35 m/s and 45 m/s represent for high-dynamic moving scenarios, especially the UAV formation operations. Results in Fig. 10 illustrate the PDR of three protocols under different velocities. We can find that increasing velocities lead to decreases in PDR, and that's mainly because the topology changes faster and link breakage happens more frequently. For the comparative performance, our LBR-OLSR is less affected by dynamics and achieves a 5% to 9% PDR gain outperforming the advanced LBD-OLSR.

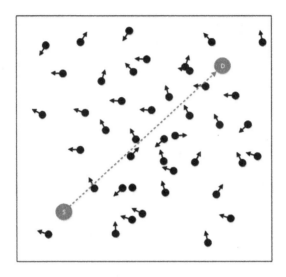

Fig. 9. Scene of large-scale network with random node movements.

Random Node Destruction. Node destruction is another common reason for link breakages on battlefields. Therefore, we construct a 10×10 grid topology with equal distances in both the vertical and horizontal directions, shown in Fig. 11. The source and destination nodes are marked in blue likewise, while the black nodes are kept as relay node and the red nodes are randomly destroyed during the communication period. We test the PDR with three damage rates, e.g., 0.1, 0.2, and 0.3, which denote the proportion of destructed nodes in the total nodes.

As shown in Fig. 12, the PDR decreases rapidly with increasing damage rates in each protocol, and LBR-OLSR has the best performance in all cases especially achieving a 14% gain compared with OLSR. That means our method is less sensitive to node destructions and has more efficient recovery abilities.

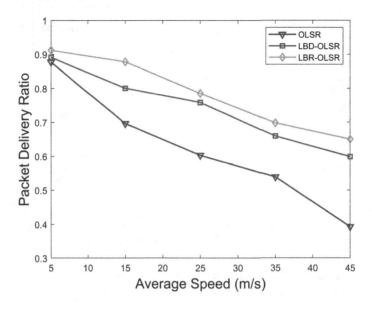

Fig. 10. PDR of different protocols versus average velocities.

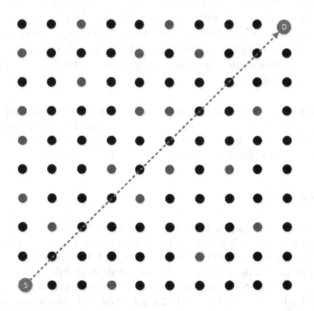

Fig. 11. Scene of large-scale network with random node destructions.

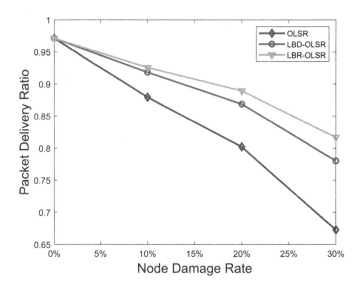

Fig. 12. PDR of different protocols vs. node damage rate.

4   Conclusion

In this paper, we proposed a novel link-breakage recovery enhanced optimized link state routing protocol (LBR-OLSR). LBR-OLSR enhances the routing performance through two auxiliary functions: Connectivity Protection and Loop Suppression, to solve the cut-edge problem and the loop issue in advanced protocols respectively. Simulation results verified that the proposed LBR-OLSR achieves better performance in dynamic networks with frequent link breakages than OLSR and LBD-OLSR.

Acknowledgment. This paper is supported in part by Shanghai Key Laboratory Funding (STCSM1-5DZ2270400), Joint Fund on Advanced Space Technology (USCAST 2020-26, USCAST 2021-17), and the Program for Professor of Special Appointment (Eastern Scholar) at Shanghai Institutions of Higher Learning.

References

1. Abujassar, R.S.: Mitigation fault of node mobility for the manet networks by constructing a backup path with loop free: enhance the recovery mechanism for proactive manet protocol. Wireless Netw. **22**(1), 119–133 (2016)
2. Bala, M., Kaur, H.: Review on routing protocols in mobile adhoc networks (2017)
3. Cheng, B.N., Moore, S.: A comparison of manet routing protocols on airborne tactical networks. In: MILCOM 2012-2012 IEEE Military Communications Conference, pp. 1–6. IEEE (2012)
4. Clausen, T., Jacquet, P.: Optimized link state routing protocol (OLSR). Technical report (2003)

5. Fotohi, R., Jamali, S., Sarkohaki, F.: Performance evaluation of AODV, LHC-AODV, OLSR, UL-OLSR, DSDV routing protocols. Int. J. Inf. Technol. Comput. Sci. (IJITCS) **5**, 21 (2013)
6. Gupta, N., Jain, A., Vaisla, K.S., Kumar, A., Kumar, R.: Performance analysis of DSDV and OLSR wireless sensor network routing protocols using FPGA hardware and machine learning. Multimedia Tools Appl. **80**, 22301–22319 (2021)
7. Haas, Z.J., Pearlman, M.R.: The zone routing protocol (ZRP) for ad hoc networks. Intemet draft (2002)
8. Jacquet, P., Muhlethaler, P., Clausen, T., Laouiti, A., Qayyum, A., Viennot, L.: Optimized link state routing protocol for ad hoc networks. In: Proceedings of IEEE International Multi Topic Conference, IEEE INMIC 2001. Technology for the 21st Century, pp. 62–68. IEEE (2001)
9. Macker, J.P., Corson, M.S.: Mobile ad hoc networks (MANETs): routing technology for dynamic wireless networking. Mob. Ad Hoc Netw. 255–273 (2004)
10. Owada, Y., Maeno, T., Imai, H., Mase, K.: OLSRv2 implementation and performance evaluation with link layer feedback. In: Proceedings of the 2007 International Conference on Wireless Communications and Mobile Computing, pp. 67–72 (2007)
11. Plesse, T., et al.: OLSR performance measurement in a military mobile ad hoc network. Ad Hoc Netw. **3**(5), 575–588 (2005)
12. Riley, G.F., Henderson, T.R.: The NS-3 network simulator. In: Modeling and Tools for Network Simulation, pp. 15–34 (2010)
13. Speakman, L., Owada, Y., Mase, K.: Looping in OLSRv2 in mobile ad-hoc networks, loop suppression and loop correction. IEICE Trans. Commun. **92**(4), 1210–1221 (2009)

Design of Distributed Synchronization Header for Short Burst Communication with Low Earth Orbit Satellites

Zehua Ding[1][(✉)], Tian Hao[1], Ni Zeng[1], Lingna Hu[2], Li Li[3], Lianghui Ding[4], and Feng Yang[1]

[1] Institute of Wireless Communication Technologies, Shanghai Jiao Tong University, Shanghai 200240, China
{Ze_hua,optimization,zengxiaoni,yangfeng}@sjtu.edu.cn
[2] Shanghai Institute of Satellite Engineering, Shanghai 200240, China
[3] Wuhan Maritime Communication Research Institute, Wuhan 430000, China
[4] Institute of Image Communication and Network Engineering, Shanghai Jiao Tong University, Shanghai 200240, China
lhding@sjtu.edu.cn

Abstract. With the rapid development of low Earth orbit satellite communication technology, achieving efficient communication in multi-user access scenarios has become a highly regarded challenge. The associated frame synchronization issues also require special attention. This paper proposes an innovative distributed synchronization header design scheme for frame synchronization. By jointly optimizing the phase factors and position factors, the synchronization header symbols are distributed in each frame in a specific pattern to improve the autocorrelation characteristics of the current synchronization header, thereby improving synchronization performance. Compared with previous distributed synchronization header design schemes, this scheme achieves an approximately 10% improvement in synchronization accuracy at lower signal-to-noise ratios.

Keywords: Frame synchronization · Distributed patterns · Joint optimization

1 Introduction

In recent times, with the vigorous development of communication technology, Low Earth Orbit (LEO) satellites have gained widespread attention as a core component of integrated aerial networks. Their unique orbital characteristics have positioned LEO satellites as a focal point in the research of 5th (B5G) and 6th generation (6G) mobile communication systems. As space communication technology matures, satellite communication has evolved from its initial narrowband voice services to encompass broadband multimedia services.

G. Zhai et al. (Eds.): IFTC 2023, CCIS 2066, pp. 390–400, 2024.
https://doi.org/10.1007/978-981-97-3623-2_28

However, due to the potential long propagation delays between a large number of Internet of Things (IoT) user terminals and LEO satellites, traditional handshake protocols exhibit inefficiency in coordinating uplink access channel resources. Grant free-random access (GF-RA), as a paradigm for large-scale access in IoT, allows user terminals to directly transmit their respective preamble codes and valid data to the base station without a prior handshake process. However, in this process, determining the frame boundaries for the transmitted signal, known as frame detection, becomes a critical prerequisite for ensuring communication stability [1].

Bursty communication is also a common scenario in satellite communication. To ensure data transmission within a limited time, bursty communication typically adopts a short-frame structure. Compared to the traditional long-frame structure, short-frame structures offer greater flexibility to meet sudden communication demands while also reduce error accumulation during transmission, thereby enhancing communication reliability.

However, in this dynamic and complex communication environment, frame detection technology faces a series of challenges. Firstly, the high-speed motion of satellites and multiple influencing factors lead to signal transmission instability, increasing the difficulty of frame detection. Secondly, the high-speed operation of the system and complex environment also imposes higher requirements on traditional frame detection methods.

The commonly used frame detection algorithms typically involve embedding a portion of the synchronization sequence at the beginning of a data sequence. This allows the receiver to recognize the presence of the signal, thereby determining the specific position of the data. A more common approach is to use the correlation between the received signal and the locally generated synchronization header signal to detect the presence and position of the synchronization sequence in the received signal [2].

To reduce the false alarm and miss detection probabilities of frame detection and improve the accuracy of frame start position estimation, the autocorrelation sidelobes of the synchronization sequence need to be small, and the main lobe should drop rapidly. Depending on whether the synchronization header is distributed in the frame structure, synchronization header design can be classified as distributed or centralized. Centralized synchronization header design is simple but has poor autocorrelation properties. Distributed synchronization header design is complex but performs better [3].

Current research on frame synchronization predominantly concentrates on algorithmic design to achieve enhanced performance [4–7], while studies regarding distributed synchronization headers remain relatively scarce. In reference [8], a novel approach to distributed synchronization is introduced, demonstrating notable advantages and presenting two distinct distributed sequences. Recognizing that the design of distributed synchronization headers in the cited literature solely considers the position of symbols within the frame, this paper introduces the influence of phase factors, enabling a more expansive exploration of synchronization header distribution. Moreover, the scheme proposed in reference [8] can be encompassed as a specific case within this proposed framework.

This paper presents a novel design scheme for distributed synchronization headers that jointly optimizes phase and position factors. Through analysis, demonstration, and simulation, it is shown that the synchronization accuracy of the proposed scheme is approximately 20% higher compared to centralized distributed header synchronization, and about 10% higher compared to traditional distributed synchronization sequences.

2   Distributed Synchronization Header Design Scheme

To enhance synchronization performance, it is necessary to gather all synchronization signals as much as possible under the assumption of H_1 (correct synchronization), while under the assumption of H_0 (incorrect synchronization), there should be only unknown information data and as few synchronization signals as possible. In other words, it is crucial to minimize the sidelobes of autocorrelation for a given sequence.

This introduces a function z_h, which is used to denote the placement of the synchronization header signal in the frame. It also incorporates the introduced phase information, i.e:

$$z_h(i) = \begin{cases} e^{j\theta_i}, ae^{j\theta_i} \text{ at } h \\ 0, \text{ data at } h \end{cases} \qquad (1)$$

where a represents a synchronization header symbol, h denotes the position in the frame, and $\theta = \{\theta_0, \theta_c h11, \ldots, \theta_{L_{pre}-1}\}$ represents the phase, where θ_i signifies the phase of the i-th synchronization header. z is a sequence of length L_F (frame length), consisting of $L_F - L_{pre}$ zeros and L_{pre} non-zeros, where L_{pre} denotes the length of the synchronization header. In this scheme, a phase offset is introduced for the synchronization header symbol, allowing z_h to contain both positional information and the influence of phase. The autocorrelation function of z is as follows:

$$R_z(n) = \sum_{h=0}^{L_F-n-1} z_h z_{h+n}^* \qquad (2)$$

$R_z(n)$ represents the correlation result of z with the presence of an offset of n positions. To reduce the false alarm probability at low signal-to-noise ratios, it is necessary to minimize the sidelobes of the autocorrelation function as much as possible. Therefore, the optimization objective can be formulated as follows:

$$\min_z \max_{n \neq 0} \left| \sum_{h=0}^{L_F-n-1} z_h z_{h+n}^* \right|^2$$

$$s.t. \quad \sum_{h=0}^{L_F-1} z_h z_h^* = L_{pre} \qquad (3)$$

$$\forall h \quad (|z_h| - 1)|z_h| = 0$$

Let $\eta = \min_{z} \max_{n \neq 0} \sum_{h=0}^{L_F - n - 1} z_h z_{h+n}^*$, where η represents the maximum value of sidelobes. In the case where $L_{pre} > 1$, let's assume that i and j are the positions of the first and last synchronization headers respectively, with phases θ_i and θ_j, where $j > i$. Then:

$$|R_z(j-i)|^2 = \left| \sum_{h=0}^{L_F - j + i - 1} z_h z_{h+j-i}^* \right|^2$$

$$= \left| \sum_{h=0}^{i-1} z_h z_{h+j-i}^* + z_i z_j^* + \sum_{h=i+1}^{L_F - j + i - 1} z_h z_{h+j-i}^* \right|^2 = \left| z_i z_j^* \right|^2 \tag{4}$$

$$= \left| e^{j\theta_i} e^{-j\theta_j} \right|^2 = \left| e^{j(\theta_i - \theta_j)} \right|^2 = 1$$

Hence, it can be concluded that $\eta \geq 1$. In ideal conditions, the value of η is 1. However, for traditional schemes, specifically those employing centralized synchronization headers, the value of η is $L_{pre} - 1$. Therefore, for traditional schemes, it is necessary to use special sequences or modulation methods to achieve good correlation.

To achieve the aforementioned objectives, the following heuristic algorithm can be employed to address the design of distributed synchronization headers, i.e., to find the positions h where each synchronization header should be placed, along with the phase offset information to be added to each synchronization header symbol:

Algorithm 1. Distributed Synchronization Header Design Algorithm

---

Input: Frame length L_F, synchronization header length L_{pre}, phase range $(-\theta_l, \theta_u]$, maximum iteration count N_{iter}

Output: Vector Z_{fin} containing synchronization header phase and position information, maximum value of sidelobes η

1: In the phase range, randomly generate L_{pre} phases θ_i. Randomly select L_{pre} different positions h_i in the range $[1, L_F]$. Generate the initial solution Z_0 according to Formula (1). Calculate $\max(|R_z(n)|) = S_0$ using Formula (2). Set the iteration count to $t = 0$

2: **for** $t < N_{iter}$ **do**

3:   $t = t + 1$

4:   Randomly generate a new set of solutions Z_1 and calculate $\max(|R_z(n)|) = S_1$

5:   **if** $S_1 < S_0$ **then**

6:     Update the current solution, $Z_0 = Z_1, S_0 = S_1$

7:   **else**

8:     Use the Metropolis criterion to calculate the probability of updating the current solution

9:   **end if**

10: **end for**

11: **return** the feasible solution : $Z_{fin} = Z_0, \eta = S_0$

Figure 1 illustrates the autocorrelation properties of the obtained distributed synchronization sequence. It is evident from the graph that the autocorrelation attains its maximum value only when aligned, and at other times, the autocorrelation results are relatively small. This indicates the attainment of an ideal synchronization sequence.

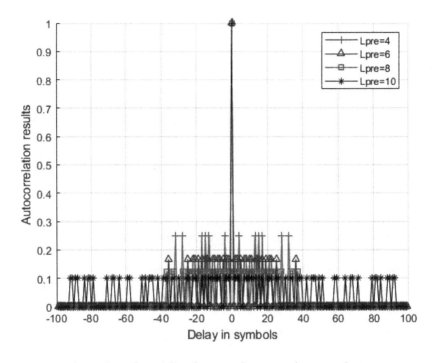

Fig. 1. Distributed Synchronous Sequence Autocorrelation

Figure 2 displays the ratio between sidelobes and the main peak of the distributed synchronization header compared to the centralized synchronization header. It can be observed that as the synchronization header length increases, the sidelobe-to-main ratio of the distributed synchronization header gradually decreases, while that of the centralized synchronization header gradually increases. Additionally, the sidelobe-to-main ratio of the distributed synchronization header is relatively small. A smaller sidelobe-to-main ratio implies better synchronization performance. Therefore, the synchronization performance of the distributed synchronization header sequence surpasses that of the centralized synchronization header.

At the same time, Fig. 3 illustrates the 3 dB main lobe width of distributed synchronization headers compared to centralized synchronization headers. It can be observed that with an increase in synchronization header length, the 3 dB main lobe width of centralized synchronization headers gradually expands, and

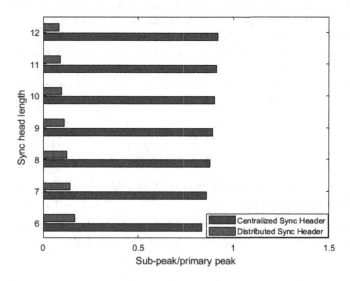

Fig. 2. Ratio of Centralized to Distributed Synchronization Peak-to-Secondary Peak

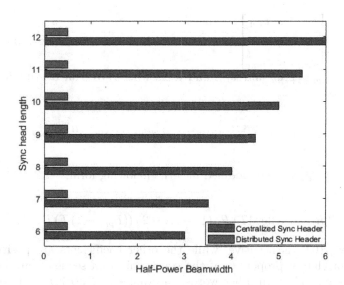

Fig. 3. Comparison of 3dB Bandwidth of Centralized and Distributed Synchronization Main Lobes

is significantly larger than that of distributed synchronization headers. This indicates that the main lobe of distributed synchronization headers decreases at a faster rate, resulting in superior synchronization performance.

Simultaneously, based on the following derivation, it can be observed that distributed synchronization headers also enhance the Cramér-Rao Lower Bound (CRLB) for both timing offset and frequency offset.

The CRLB for timing offset estimation, as computed in reference [9], is given by the following formula:

$$CRLB\left(\tau\right) = \frac{ch11}{2\left(\frac{E_s}{N_0}\right)Q_\tau} \tag{5}$$

where, $\frac{E_s}{N_0}$ represents the signal-to-noise ratio, $Q_\tau \triangleq a^H \ddot{G} a$, where a is the synchronization header signal, $[\ddot{G}]_{i,j} \triangleq -\ddot{g}[(i-j)T]$, T is the sampling time, $\ddot{g}(t) \triangleq \frac{\partial^2 g(t)}{\partial^2 t}, g(t) \triangleq w(t) * w(-t)$, where $w(t)$ is the pulse function of the transmitted signal. It can be observed that $\ddot{G}$ has the following property:

For any $x \in [0, L_{pre} - \max(i,j)]$, it holds that:

$$[\ddot{G}]_{i,j} = [\ddot{G}]_{i+x,j+x} \tag{6}$$

Therefore, $\ddot{G}$ can be expressed as the sum of multiple matrices:

$$\ddot{G} = -\ddot{g}(0T)X_1 - 2\ddot{g}(1T)X_2 - \ldots - 2\ddot{g}((L_{pre}-1)T)X_{L_{pre}} \tag{7}$$

where $X_n = \begin{bmatrix} x_{11} & \cdots & x_{1m} \\ \vdots & \ddots & \vdots \\ x_{m1} & \cdots & x_{mm} \end{bmatrix}$ is a matrix with all elements being 1 along the line connecting $x_{(m-n+1)m}$ and x_{1n}, and 0 elsewhere. We can rewrite R_z into the following form:

$$R_z(n) = \sum_{h=0}^{L_F-n-1} z_h z_{h+n}^* = z^H X_{n+1} z = a^H X_{n+1} a \tag{8}$$

Consequently, Q_τ can be modified into the following form:

$$\begin{aligned} Q_\tau &\triangleq a^H \ddot{G} a \\ &= -\ddot{g}(0T)R_z(0) - 2\ddot{g}(1T)R_z(1) - \ldots - 2\ddot{g}((L_{pre}-1)T)R_z(L_{pre}-1) \end{aligned} \tag{9}$$

Since only $\ddot{g}(0T)$ is negative, while the other coefficients are positive, when the autocorrelation properties of the synchronization sequence are better, the sidelobes are smaller. In other words, the values of $R_z(n), n > 0$ are smaller. Consequently, Q_τ becomes larger. Under the same signal-to-noise ratio, this leads to a smaller Cramér-Rao Lower Bound (CRLB) for timing offset estimation.

The reduction in CRLB for timing offset estimation implies an improvement in the optimal performance achievable by timing offset estimation. As a result, with the increase in accuracy of timing offset estimation, the accuracy of frequency offset estimation will also improve.

When a satellite is in a low Earth orbit, the Doppler effect becomes particularly pronounced because they orbit the Earth at a relatively high speed. This rapid motion causes a significant shift in frequency, leading to noticeable frequency offsets, which can pose a challenge to frequency offset estimation. Distributed synchronization headers can further enhance the performance of frequency offset estimation by reducing the Cramér-Rao lower bound (CRLB) on phase estimation.

3   Simulation Results and Performance Analysis

Consider a system with QPSK modulation, simulated under a Gaussian white noise channel. The simulation is conducted 1000 times per signal-to-noise ratio (SNR) value. Calculate the synchronization accuracy for different synchronization headers at various SNR levels, which is defined as the number of correct synchronizations divided by the total number of simulations.

Figure 4 compares the frame detection probabilities as a function of signal-to-noise ratio (SNR) for using the distributed synchronization headers proposed in this paper and traditional centralized synchronization headers. From the simulation results, it can be observed that the distributed synchronization sequence designed in this paper outperforms the centralized synchronization sequence in an AWGN channel. Additionally, as the synchronization header length increases, the synchronization performance improves.

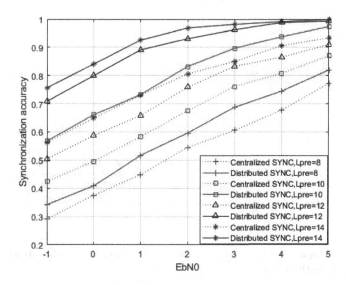

Fig. 4. Comparison of Synchronization Performance between Distributed and Centralized Synchronization Sequences with Frame Length of 100

In reference [7], the optimal distribution of synchronization sequence positions is provided for the case of optimal performance. However, in situations where the frame length is the same but the synchronization header length is longer, the literature is unable to specify the distribution positions. Yet, for this paper, with the additional consideration of phase factors, it is possible to find better feasible solutions with longer synchronization headers under the same frame length.

This paper still retains the variation of positions, so it's possible to simply fix the phase parameter to 0, obtaining data similar to that in previous literature. However, in comparison to the iterative algorithm used in previous literature, the algorithm in this paper is better at finding more optimal feasible solutions. For instance, after fixing the phase value, using the algorithm in this paper can still find an ideal solution in the case of a synchronization header length of 12 and a frame length of 100. This widens the application of distributed synchronization headers significantly.

Figures 5, 6 and Fig. 7 compare the synchronization probabilities with varying signal-to-noise ratio (SNR) for different frame lengths, using the distributed synchronization headers proposed in this paper and the ones designed in reference [7]. From the simulation results, it is evident that as the frame length remains constant while the synchronization header length increases, the performance of the synchronization sequences designed in this paper is significantly better. This aligns with the analysis presented earlier.

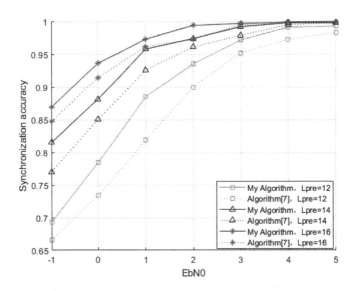

Fig. 5. Performance Comparison of Different Distributed Synchronization Headers with Frame Length of 100

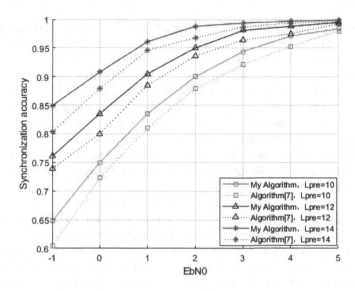

Fig. 6. Performance Comparison of Different Distributed Synchronization Headers with Frame Length of 50

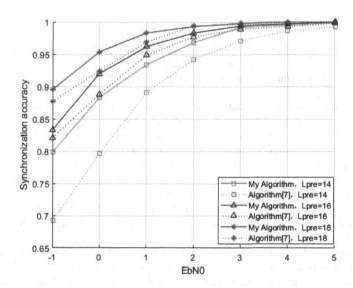

Fig. 7. Performance Comparison of Different Distributed Synchronization Headers with Frame Length of 150

4   Conclusion

The simulation results demonstrate a significant performance advantage of the synchronization sequences designed in this paper compared to the scheme proposed in reference [7]. Specifically, this advantage is evident when the frame length is 100 and the synchronization header length is 12 or more, as well as when the frame length is 50 and the synchronization header length is 10 or more. In general, the synchronization sequences designed in this study exhibit remarkable performance advantages when the frame length is fixed, but the synchronization header length is relatively long. Alternatively, it can be stated that, with a constant synchronization header length, the synchronization sequences designed in this paper exhibit a significant performance advantage when the frame length is relatively short.

This research has made significant strides in the field of low Earth orbit satellite communication technology. By introducing an innovative distributed synchronization header design, it successfully addresses the challenge of achieving frame synchronization in multi-user access scenarios. Through the joint optimization of phase and position factors, the side-lobe height of the sequence auto-correlation is effectively reduced, further enhancing the performance of the synchronization design. Additionally, the use of heuristic algorithms extends the distribution pattern of traditional distributed synchronization headers, enabling the attainment of better feasible solutions especially when the synchronization header length is long and the frame length is short.

References

1. Ying, K., Gao, Z., Chen, S., et al.: Quasi-synchronous random access for massive MIMO-based LEO satellite constellations. IEEE J. Sel. Areas Commun. (2023)
2. Massey, J.: Optimum frame synchronization. IEEE Trans. Commun. **20**(2), 115–119 (1972)
3. Van Wijngaarden, A.J.D.L., Willink, T.J.: Frame synchronization using distributed sequences. IEEE Trans. Commun. **48**(12), 2127–2138 (2000)
4. Choi, Z.Y., Lee, Y.H.: Frame synchronization in the presence of frequency offset. IEEE Trans. Commun. **50**(7), 1062–1065 (2002)
5. Corazza, G.E., Pedone, R., Villanti, M.: Frame acquisition for continuous and discontinuous transmission in the forward link of satellite systems. Int. J. Satell. Commun. Network **24**(2), 185–201 (2006)
6. Villanti, M., Salmi, P., Corazza, G.E.: Differential post detection integration techniques for robust code acquisition. IEEE Trans. Commun. **55**(11), 2172–2184 (2007)
7. Corazza, G.E., Pedone, R.: Generalized and average likelihood ratio testing for post detection integration. IEEE Trans. Commun. **55**(11), 2159–2171 (2007)
8. Villanti, M., Iubatti, M., Vanelli-Coralli, A., et al.: Design of distributed unique words for enhanced frame synchronization. IEEE Trans. Commun. **57**(8), 2430–2440 (2009)
9. Tavares, G.N., Tavares, L.M.: Sequence design for data-aided estimation of synchronization parameters. IEEE Trans. Commun. **55**(4), 670–677 (2007)

User Preferences Based Preloading and ABR Algorithm for Short Video Streaming

Lanju Zhang, Yuan Zhang$^{(\boxtimes)}$, and Jinyao Yan

Communication University of China, Beijing 100024, China
{flora_zhang,yuanzhang,jyan}@cuc.edu.cn

Abstract. Due to mobile networks and multimedia technology, short video streaming has become increasingly popular. However, traditional ABR algorithms are not suitable for short videos and waste bandwidth. To address this, a user preferences-based preloading and ABR algorithm called USP-ABR has been proposed. It analyzes QoE preferences and divides users into three categories, improving accuracy and saving bandwidth. Experimental findings show significant improvements compared to benchmark algorithms. According to the experimental findings, the three QoE models have improved accuracy by 21.43%, 26.75% and 16.39%, respectively, when compared to the standard user QoE model. Besides, by comparison with two benchmark algorithms, the USP-ABR algorithm can save up to 66.1%, 65.6% and 60.7% of bandwidth overhead and improve QoE by 15.1%, 13.5% and 9.6% under the three categories of QoE models.

Keywords: Short video streaming · QoE model · Preloading mechanism · ABR algorithm

1 Introduction

Compared to traditional long videos, short videos are more popular among the younger generation as they immediately capture the user's attention and consolidate information within a few seconds.

The primary distinction between short and long videos is that viewers tend to switch short videos more frequently if they are not interested, resulting in more bandwidth waste [1].

High-performance ABR algorithms for short video streams require a balance between quality of experience and efficient use of bandwidth resources. However, striving to save bandwidth overhead can conflict with the high quality of experience that users desire, making setting the short video stream preload mechanism and ABR algorithm a challenging issue.

Funded by the High-quality and Cutting-edge Disciplines Construction Project for Universities in Beijing (Internet Information, Communication University of China), the National Natural Science Foundation of China under Grant 61971382 and the Fundamental Research Funds for the Central Universities.

G. Zhai et al. (Eds.): IFTC 2023, CCIS 2066, pp. 401–412, 2024.
https://doi.org/10.1007/978-981-97-3623-2_29

In addition, when watching videos, there are multiple factors that can affect the quality of experience (QoE). These factors include the video bitrate, smoothness, and rebuffering - all of which are related to network conditions.

Hence, striking a balance between QoE-related factors and limited bandwidth resources, and designing QoE models based on user preferences, is also crucial.

So, this paper proposes a short video stream joint preloading and ABR algorithm based on user preference (USP-ABR). In the three QoE models, USP-ABR can guarantee the user's QoE while saving the bandwidth overhead. This paper has three main innovations:

- We conducted a QoE experiment with 87 participants, using H.264 to encode 7 original 4K videos. We created 35 videos of varying quality and identified three user QoE models based on their preferences.
- Our system analyzes network data and user retention to recommend preloading mechanisms and queue videos accordingly.
- We developed a new ABR algorithm for short videos using DRL. It considers different parameters to determine the next block's bitrate, resulting in a smoother viewing experience.

Next, we discuss the related work and their deficiencies in Sect. 2. The user preference oriented QoE model is described in Sect. 3. The USP-ABR algorithm is described in Sect. 4. The evaluation results are presented in Sect. 5. We summarize our work in Sect. 6.

2   Related Work

User experience quality refers to the comprehensive subjective perception of users on the quality and performance (including effectiveness and usability) of devices, networks, systems, applications, or businesses [2]. Due to various subjective and objective factors that affect the user experience quality of video, how to eliminate adverse factors and improve user experience quality has become one of the most concerned issues for mobile video platforms [3–5].

Since the viewing behavior of short video is different from that of traditional long video users, more and more download mechanisms are designed for short video [6–9].

ABR algorithm is an adaptive network video streaming technology. It can automatically adjust the video bitrate to improve QoE based on the user's real-time network situation. ABR algorithms fall into the following two categories. The first type is the traditional ABR algorithm, including rate based ABR algorithm (e.g., FESITIVE [10], PANDA [11]), buffer based ABR algorithm (e.g., BBA [12], BOLA [13]), rate and buffer based mixed ABR algorithm (e.g., FESITIVE [10], PANDA [11]). The second type is ABR algorithm based on reinforcement learning (e.g. [16–19]).

3   User Preference Oriented QoE Model

According to Ruyi [20], users have different preferences for various QoE factors. Limited bandwidth affects video quality, causing stuttering and visual distortions. Users have varying tolerance levels for these distortions, so it's essential to consider different preferences and develop mechanisms to improve user experience. A subjective QoE experiment can help establish a model based on user preference perception.

3.1   Subjective QoE Experiment

To improve the user experience when watching videos, each frame of the video needs to be visually appealing and have noticeable changes. In this experiment, we collected 7 high-quality 4K videos that cover a variety of topics, such as movies, animals, games, and sports. Each video was cut into shorter segments of 15–20 s and the audio was removed to ensure that it didn't affect the video quality. Then, in order to assess the user experience at various resolutions, we utilized an H.264 video encoder to convert the 7 initial 4K videos into 1080P and 360P, generating 21 reference videos. The 21 reference videos were grouped together to create 35 test videos, each with its own unique damage type. Each video of the 7 original video materials is edited separately in the following ways:

- 4K. The original 4K video is taken as the benchmark video with high definition and no lag in the playback process.
- 360+rebuf. The video encoded as 360P is randomly introduced into two 1-second lag times, with the lowest clarity and two lag times.
- 1080+rebuf. Randomly introduce 1080P video into two 1-second time-outs as a high-definition but stutter video.
- 360. Direct use of 360P video as playback process but low definition video.
- 360+1080. In order to measure users' preference for smoothness, the original 4K video was first selected, and 3 s 1080P and 360P videos were randomly inserted during playback to simulate the situation of resolution decline.

3.2   Subjects Data Analysis

In this experiment, 87 subjects participated in the data collection work. Each subject watched 35 videos and obtained 3045 (87*35) data on subjective QoE rating scores on perceived video preferences. We divide videos into five categories, each of which contains seven videos of different types and contents. Therefore, in order to calculate subjects' perception of video preference and exclude the impact of video content on QoE score, we calculated the average score of each subject on each type of video and carried out visualization processing on the results. Through preliminary data screening, 84 valid subjects' data were obtained.

All the scoring data of each video are displayed, as shown in Fig. 1a. Where the abscissa is the subject serial number, and the ordinate is the subject's score.

Figure 1b shows PCC between each pair of 84 subjects. The color of the small square at the intersection of row i and column j indicates the PCC between subject i and subject j. The higher the PCC, the darker the red color of the small square, the more similar the preferences between the subjects. As can be seen from Fig. 1b, 90% of subjects' scores had a positive correlation with varying degrees of strength. Therefore, we can conclude that subjects' preferences can be classified and different QoE models can be established according to different types.

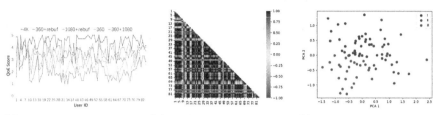

(a) Subjects subjective QoE(b) PCC for each pair of sub-(c) Kmeans clustering classi-
score.   jects.   fication.

Fig. 1. Subjective QoE scores.

In order to create and confirm the QoE model, the scoring dataset for all subjects who watched videos was split in this experiment. 70% of the data was used for training, while 30% was reserved for verification. Due to the correlation among users' subjective QoE scores, users were classified accordingly. The experiment employed the Kmeans clustering algorithm to classify QoE score data, which is multidimensional. The Kmeans algorithm was selected for its simplicity, ease of understanding, automatic clustering capability, and the fact that it doesn't require any parameter settings - only the number of clustering K needs to be specified. Since the clustering number K is unknown, we utilized the Elbow Method, which relies on the SSE (sum of squared errors) core index. Based on this experiment, K was set to 3, and the user QoE data was categorized into three groups.

To simplify the subjective QoE score data, this experiment utilizes Principle Component Analysis (PCA) which reduces the dimensions from five to two. PCA maps N-dimensional features to new orthogonal features, called principal components, and then reconstructs the original N-dimensional features into K-dimensional features. The classification results are visualized in Fig. 1c.

3.3 Establishment of QoE Model

QoE is a discrete additive model. In the n-th class QoE model, users' preference QoE for video i is shown in (1). Since this experiment is a QoE model oriented to users' preference, the weight of the three influencing factors of QoE is unknown.

We set the preference weights of w_{1n}, w_{2n}, w_{3n} for the n-th class QoE model according to the classification. In order to obtain the modular weight of QoE of each category, the QoE scores of five groups of videos of each category are averaged first, as shown in (2).

$$QoE_n^i = \sum_t (w_{1n} \cdot bitrate_t^i - w_{2n} \cdot rebuffer_t^i - w_{3n} \cdot smooth_t^i) \qquad (1)$$

$$\varphi_{mn} = \frac{\sum_{m=1}^M QoE_m}{M} \qquad (2)$$

We use linear regression method to derive the weight value of each index of QoE after classification. First, assume that a QoE weight value w_{1n}, w_{2n}, w_{3n} has been calculated for each category of QoE, then these weight values can be taken as the target variable (that is, the dependent variable in the regression problem). A linear regression model is established with video feature $bitrate_t^i$, $rebuffer_t^i$ and $smooth_t^i$ as independent variables. Therefore, the weights of different preference indicators of the three QoE models are: When $n = 1$, $w_{11} = 1.54, w_{21} = 1.16, w_{31} = 0.63$. When $n = 2$, $w_{12} = 1.16, w_{22} = 1.52, w_{32} = 0.32$. When $n = 3$, $w_{13} = 1.68, w_{23} = 1.28, w_{33} = 0.57$.

4 USP-ABR System Construction

4.1 Preloading Mechanism for Short Video Streaming

With the feature of short videos randomly switching, there is a risk of wasting high-quality video chunks that are preloaded by the player. To prevent this, it is essential to develop a good video player download strategy that takes into account the retention rate of users. The player should stop loading once enough video chunks have been downloaded to avoid unnecessary bandwidth overhead. In order to reduce platform bandwidth overhead, we propose a short video streaming preloading mechanism based on heuristics.

A buffer is a temporary storage space in memory used for storing input/output data. This section explains how to set the maximum sliding buffer. Let's consider video i in each recommended queue as an example, where $i = 0$ represents the current video being watched. The chunk t in video i has a bit rate of R_t^i, encoding size of $d_t^i(R_t^i)$, and an average download speed of C_t^i. L represents the duration of each video chunk, and ΔT_t^i represents the download time of chunk t in video i. When the player downloads the maximum allowable download size, all videos stop downloading. B_t^i represents the buffer occupancy rate when the video player downloads chunk t in video i, with a range of $0 \le B_t^i \le B_{max}^i(t)$. Here, $B_{max}^i(t)$ is the maximum buffer size of chunk t in video i. To dynamically set $B_{max}^i(t)$ based on the current chunk retention rate p_t^i and to reduce the waste of bandwidth resources, we have designed the following dynamic maximum buffer model:

$$B_1 = \exp\left(p_t^i\right) \times L + \frac{d_t^i\left(R_t^i\right)}{c_t^i} + rebuf_t^i - \Delta T_t^i \qquad (3)$$

$$B_2 = L + \frac{d_t^i\left(R_t^i\right)}{c_t^i} + \Delta T_t^i + rebuf_t^i \tag{4}$$

$$B_{\max}^i(t) = \max(B_1, B_2) \tag{5}$$

We take the retention rate of the video block when the retention rate drops sharply as the retention rate threshold. The retention rate in the real dataset is obtained by statistics of user viewing behavior, while the retention rate in the simulated dataset is generated by the software. Therefore, let p_t^i be the retention rate of chunk t in video i, where p_t^i reflects the attractiveness of the video to the user. Let d^i indicates the degree and trend of the drop in retention rate. When d^i reaches its maximum value, it means that the attractiveness of the current video block has dropped to its lowest compared to the previous video chunk. Therefore, the retention rate threshold P^i in (7) is set to be the retention rate of the previous video chunk p_{t-1}^i.

$$d^i = \frac{p_{t-1}^i - p_t^i}{p_{t-1}^i} \tag{6}$$

$$P^i = \underset{p_{t-1}^i}{\mathrm{argmax}} d^i \tag{7}$$

4.2   DRL-Based ABR Algorithm for Short Video Streaming

Different from long videos, short videos require smooth transitions between each video in the recommendation queue, making it difficult to ensure a good user experience. We have created a short video stream algorithm using DRL to address this issue.

There are three key parts, namely State, Action and Reward. Each is described as follows:

State: Set the sequence number of the current downloaded video as i and the download block id as t. The Agent of state space is $S_t^i = \left\{b_t^i, \tau_t^i, c_t^i, B_t^i, r_t^i\right\}$, where b_t^i represents the past block throughput, τ_t^i on behalf of each chunk of download time in the past, c_t^i representative at the end of the chunk size, B_t^i represents the current buffer size, and r_t^i represents the bit-rate size of the previous block.

Action: The action space of the Agent is $A_t^i = [0, 1, 2]$, where $[0, 1, 2]$ indicates the bit rate level of 750, 1200, and 1850 kbps.

Reward: The main purpose of deep reinforcement learning is to maximize the expectation of reward, so the setting of reward is a key part of whether the DRL algorithm can converge quickly. When the user watches a certain video, it needs to increase the bit rate, reduce the lag, and reduce the bit rate switch. Therefore, the traditional QoE formula is used to calculate the Reward in this chapter. Let $bitrate_t^i$ be the bitrate for block t in video i. $rebuffer_t^i$ be the rebuffering for block t in video i. $smooth_t^i$ be the smoothness for block t in video i. Where w_1, w_2 and w_3 can be adjusted freely in the training process in (8).

$$R^i = \Sigma_t(w_1 \cdot bitrate_t^i - w_2 \cdot rebuffer_t^i - w_3 \cdot smooth_t^i) \tag{8}$$

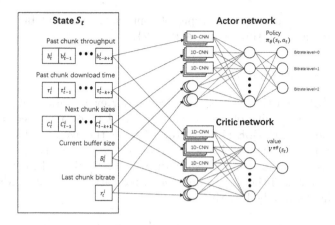

Fig. 2. Short video streaming ABR network structure based on DRL.

Figure 2 shows the network architecture diagram of this algorithm, with input, model processing and output from left to right. The input of the neural network is, after downloading each piece of video, the receiving state of Agent S_t^i. The output of Actor is a bit-rate-level decision. While the output of Critic is $V_\pi^\theta \left(s_t^i\right)$, that is, the rating of the action selected by the Actor. Since the first three variables b_t^i, τ_t^i, c_t^i all contain multiple historical values, the Actor network needs to use sliding window to extract features through the convolutional network of $1 * 4$. The last two variables, B_t^i and r_t^i, take only the current state values, and use the convolutional network of $1 * 1$. Through the constant update of network parameters of Actor and Critic, the Agent can adapt to network conditions and make the Reward greater.

5   Evaluation

UPS-ABR experiment divides video into several blocks. $V_i = \{1, 2, \cdots, K\}$. In the traditional long video, the test video is encoded into various bit rates (or resolutions) and divided into fixed lengths, usually 2–10 s [21]. However, in short video streaming, the length of each video chunk is set to 1 s in order to make more granular decisions about how to download the video. Therefore, the total length of the i short video is K seconds. The rate level needs to be determined by the rate at which the video is encoded.

Every 5 videos for a short video push stubble queue, equivalent to a sliding window. When users finish watching a video, they add a new video to the queue. When the current user finishes watching the video, the player stops downloading until the next user watches it. Data sets are used to randomly select the data needed for training and testing. These include different quality of video block size, network status, user retention, etc.

We used the MMGC competition official data set [22]. There were seven videos, each ranging in length from 7 to 125 s. Including life, study, entertainment, games and other different types of content. The output bit rate of video block R is divided into three levels $\in \{0, 1, 2\}$.

5.1   Experimental Settings

The UPS-ABR algorithm uses two indicators for evaluation, namely QoE and ratio. QoE is the quality of user experience, and there are three factors that determine the value of QoE (1). The total QoE is the average QoE of all video chunks. Ratio is the bandwidth waste rate. *ratio* is used as an indicator for evaluation, as shown in (9). *dowload* indicates the total bandwidth used by all downloaded chunks of the player, and *watch* indicates the total bandwidth used by all the chunks watched by the user.

$$ratio^i = \frac{dowload^i - watch^i}{dowload^i} \tag{9}$$

Since there are few ABR algorithms for short videos, we use two public algorithms as benchmarks to verify the performance of the USP-ABR algorithm [22]. The benchmark algorithms in this experiment include two short video streaming preload mechanisms, which are no-save and fixed-preload. The no-save algorithm first downloads the currently playing video. Periodically preload the videos in subsequent players after the current video download, each video is pre-loaded at 800 KB. The fixd-preload algorithm first downloads the video currently being watched. When the retention rate is less than 0.65, the next video in the queue will be downloaded. When all the videos in the queue are downloaded, the download will be paused. The RobustMPC model is used for bit-rate decisions of both algorithms. RobustMPC increases the use of errors to adjust throughput predicted by the MPC model compared to the MPC model.

5.2   QoE Model Accuracy

In order to verify the validity of the three QoE models, 30% subjective MOS score of users was used in this experiment to compare with the average QoE weight model of users. The average QoE weight models of users are $w_{1n} = 1.59$, $w_{2n} = 1.27$, $w_{3n} = 0.52$.

The performance of the three QoE models was compared with the average QoE model. PCC and RMSE were used to evaluate the accuracy. The RMSEs of three QoE models and average QoE models are 1.154, 1.127, 1.820, 2.476, respectively. The PCCs of three QoE models and average QoE models are 0.867, 0.905, 0.831, 0.714, respectively.

Compared with the average QoE model, the three QoE models can increase 21.43%, 26.75% and 16.39%, respectively. Are above the average QoE model. Therefore, the classification QoE model is more reliable and advantageous in this paper.

5.3   Bandwidth Waste Eatio Evaluation

Figure 3 shows the bandwidth waste rate of 20 users, represented by ratio. The lower the bandwidth waste rate, the better the algorithm performance of the short video stream preloading mechanism.

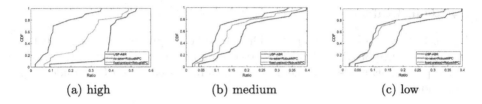

(a) high   (b) medium   (c) low

Fig. 3. CDF of ratio of 20 users at high, medium and low bandwidth

Table 1. Average Ratio of 20 Users of Different Models

QoE Model	Network	USP-ABR	No-save+RobustMPC	Fixed-preload+RobustMPC
I	high	0.136	0.399	0.267
	medium	0.131	0.204	0.162
	low	0.134	0.203	0.139
II	high	0.145	0.421	0.282
	medium	0.137	0.274	0.187
	low	0.140	0.177	0.146
III	high	0.132	0.389	0.298
	medium	0.128	0.216	0.174
	low	0.149	0.183	0.156
Average	high	0.148	0.403	0.311
	medium	0.141	0.225	0.179
	low	0.152	0.179	0.167

In order to detect the algorithm performance under different bandwidth conditions, comparative experiments were carried out in three groups of bandwidth: high, medium and low. Each group of bandwidth had 20 network tracks. The bandwidth waste rate of a user is the average value of the algorithm under 20 network paths.

According to the experimental results, the first type of QoE model has the most obvious savings on bandwidth overhead under high bandwidth.

Table 1 shows the average ratio of 20 users of the three algorithms in three types of QoE models. The average bandwidth wastage rates of 20 users of USP-ABR algorithm and two benchmark algorithms under various network conditions are shown respectively. According to the data, in the three types of QoE models, compared with the benchmark algorithm, USP-ABR can save up to 66.1%, 65.6% and 60.7% bandwidth overhead respectively. Compared with the average QoE model, USP-ABR saves 7.4%, 2.0%, 10.8% of bandwidth overhead under the three QoE models, respectively.

5.4   QoE Evaluation

Figure 4 shows QoE for 20 users. The higher the QoE represents the better the performance of ABR algorithm. According to the experimental results, the first type of QoE model has the most obvious improvement on QoE under high bandwidth.

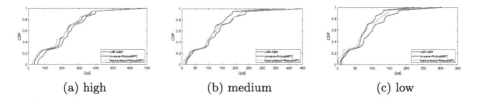

(a) high   (b) medium   (c) low

Fig. 4. CDF of QoE of 20 users at high, medium and low bandwidth

However, when the network condition is poor, the QoE of the USP-ABR algorithm is lower compared to the two benchmark algorithms. This is because there are tradeoffs between video QoE and bandwidth waste rates at low to medium bandwidths.

Table 2. Average QoE of 20 Users of Different Models

QoE Model	Network	USP-ABR	No-save+RobustMPC	Fixed-preload+RobustMPC
I	high	248.14	225.59	215.68
	medium	117.02	134.56	125.04
	low	77.98	97.01	78.85
II	high	241.92	221.81	213.08
	medium	119.76	132.15	123.81
	low	80.20	95.82	78.18
III	high	230.37	203.76	195.14
	medium	90.69	109.83	93.11
	low	68.71	77.97	49.65
Average	high	197.19	175.75	169.07
	medium	87.53	91.14	84.69
	low	54.24	59.13	51.77

The average QoE of 20 users of USP-ABR and the two benchmark algorithms under various network conditions is shown in Table 2. Compared with the benchmark algorithm, USP-ABR can respectively increase the QoE by up to 15.1%, 13.5% and 9.6%. Compared with the average QoE model, USP-ABR improved QoE by 28.4%, 25.2% and 19.2% under the three QoE models, respectively.

6   Conclusion

In order to meet the needs of short video users, this paper designs a user preferences based preloading and ABR algorithm for short video streaming (USP-ABR). USP-ABR can reduce bandwidth waste and improve user QoE for three types of user QoE models with different preferences under various network environments.

However, there is still room for improvement in the optimization of the USP-ABR algorithm. For instance, supporting more rate levels or leveraging various information can help more accurately select the appropriate bit rate level.

Acknowledgements. This work was supported by the National Natural Science Foundation of China under Grant 61971382 and in part by the Fundamental Research Funds for the Central Universities.

References

1. Gao, W., Zhang, L., Yang, H., et al.: DHP: a joint video download and dynamic bitrate adaptation algorithm for short video streaming. In: Dang-Nguyen, D.T., et al. (eds.) MMM 2023. LNCS, vol. 13834, pp. 587–598. Springer, Cham (2023). https://doi.org/10.1007/978-3-031-27818-1_48
2. Xiao, A., Huang, X., Wu, S., et al.: Traffic-aware rate adaptation for improving time-varying QoE factors in mobile video streaming. IEEE Trans. Netw. Sci. Eng. **7**(4), 2392–2405 (2020)
3. Robitza, W., Garcia, M.N., Raake, A.: A modular http adaptive streaming QoE model-candidate for ITU-TP.1203 ("P. NATS"). In: 2017 Ninth International Conference on Quality of Multimedia Experience (QoMEX), pp. 1–6. IEEE (2017)
4. Eswara, N., Ashique, S., Panchbhai, A., et al.: Streaming video QoE modeling and prediction: a long short-term memory approach. IEEE Trans. Circ. Syst. Video Technol. **30**(3), 661–673 (2019)
5. Xiao, A., Liu, J., Li, Y., et al.: Two-phase rate adaptation strategy for improving real-time video QoE in mobile networks. China Commun. **15**(10), 12–24 (2018)
6. Zhou, C., Ban, Y., Zhao, Y., et al.: PDAS: probability-driven adaptive streaming for short video. In: Proceedings of the 30th ACM International Conference on Multimedia, pp. 7021–7025 (2022)
7. Ran, D., Hong, H., Chen, Y., et al.: Preference-aware dynamic bitrate adaptation for mobile short-form video feed streaming. IEEE Access **8**, 220083–220094 (2020)
8. Li, Z., Xie, Y., Netravali, R., et al.: Dashlet: Taming Swipe Uncertainty for Robust Short Video Streaming. arXiv preprint arXiv:2204.12954 (2022)

9. Lu, L., Xiao, J., Ni, W., et al.: Deep-reinforcement-learning-based user-preference-aware rate adaptation for video streaming. In: 2022 IEEE 23rd International Symposium on a World of Wireless, Mobile and Multimedia Networks (WoWMoM), pp. 416–424. IEEE (2022)

10. Jiang, J., Sekar, V., Zhang, H.: Improving fairness, efficiency, and stability in http-based adaptive video streaming with festive. In: Proceedings of the 8th International Conference on Emerging Networking Experiments and Technologies, pp. 97–108 (2012)

11. Li, Z., Zhu, X., Gahm, J., et al.: Probe and adapt: rate adaptation for HTTP video streaming at scale. IEEE J. Sel. Areas Commun. **32**(4), 719–733 (2014)

12. Huang, T.Y., Johari, R., McKeown, N., et al.: A buffer-based approach to rate adaptation: evidence from a large video streaming service. In: Proceedings of the ACM Conference on SIGCOMM 2014, pp. 187–198 (2014)

13. Spiteri, K., Urgaonkar, R., Sitaraman, R.K.: BOLA: near-optimal bitrate adaptation for online videos. IEEE/ACM Trans. Networking **28**(4), 1698–1711 (2020). https://doi.org/10.1109/TNET.2020.2996964

14. Yin, X., Jindal, A., Sekar, V., et al.: A control-theoretic approach for dynamic adaptive video streaming over HTTP. In: Proceedings of the ACM Conference on Special Interest Group on Data Communication 2015, pp. 325–338 (2015)

15. De Cicco, L., Caldaralo, V., Palmisano, V., et al.: Elastic: a client-side controller for dynamic adaptive streaming over http (dash). In: 2013 20th International Packet Video Workshop, pp. 1–8. IEEE (2013)

16. Mao, H., Netravali, R., Alizadeh, M.: Neural adaptive video streaming with pensieve. In: Proceedings of the Conference of the ACM Special Interest Group on Data Communication, pp. 197–210 (2017)

17. Huang, T., Yao, X., Wu, C., et al.: Tiyuntsong: a self-play reinforcement learning approach for ABR video streaming. In: 2019 IEEE International Conference on Multimedia and Expo (ICME), pp. 1678–1683. IEEE (2019)

18. Huang, T., Zhang, R.X., Sun, L.: Self-play reinforcement learning for video transmission. In: Proceedings of the 30th ACM Workshop on Network and Operating Systems Support for Digital Audio and Video, pp. 7–13 (2020)

19. Huo, L., Wang, Z., Xu, M., et al.: A meta-learning framework for learning multi-user preferences in QoE optimization of DASH. IEEE Trans. Circuits Syst. Video Technol. **30**(9), 3210–3225 (2019)

20. Zuo, X., Yang, J., Wang, M., et al.: Adaptive bitrate with user-level QOE preference for video streaming. In: IEEE INFOCOM 2022-IEEE Conference on Computer Communications, pp. 1279–1288. IEEE (2022)

21. Yeo, H., Jung, Y., Kim, J., et al.: Neural adaptive content-aware internet video delivery. In: 13th USENIX Symposium on Operating Systems Design and Implementation (OSDI 2018), pp. 645–661 (2018)

22. Zuo, X., Li, Y., Xu, M., et al.: Bandwidth-efficient multi-video prefetching for short video streaming. arXiv preprint arXiv:2206.09839 (2022)

Author Index

G. Zhai et al. (Eds.): IFTC 2023, CCIS 2066, pp. 413–415, 2024.
https://doi.org/10.1007/978-981-97-3623-2

Printed in the United States
by Baker & Taylor Publisher Services